Ready-to-Use Examples

All the examples in this book and its CD-ROM demonstrate advanced Delphi programming features and techniques; many are also valuable tools you can use in your own projects—applications, components, and wizards. Here are some samples:

- VclHiera, a hierarchy viewer of the VCL classes, based on a tree view control (**Chapter 1**).

- StrComp, a DFM file editor that also creates the corresponding PAS file (**Chapter 3**).

- PasToWeb (**Chapter 3**), a tool that creates Pascal syntax-highlighted HTML files, also available as a wizard (**Chapter 14**).

- A collection of VCL components, including the Animated Button, the Semaphore (or traffic light), the Graph component (all in **Chapter 5**), the TabEdit component (**Chapter 7**), a Form Extender, an Application Extender, a Star component, (**Chapter 8**), and an OLE drag-and-drop component (**Chapter 11**).

- The SimpleWord application, an RTF editor with scripting (through OLE Automation), drag-and-drop, and shell context menu support (**Chapter 11**).

- The Name and Tag property editors, with support for multiple components (**Chapter 12**).

- A class template wizard that lets you create collections of classes based on the data types you work with, a grid form wizard, and several other wizards (**Chapter 14**).

- A simple version control system, which automatically writes the author name in each file when it is saved (**Chapter 15**).

- The My Delphi IDE extender (**Chapter 15**), which allows you to change the font of the Object Inspector and change the Components palette to a multi-line tab control.

- The Object Debugger, a run-time clone of Delphi's Object Inspector, which allows you to view and change properties of all the components and forms while the program is running (**Chapter 16**).

- A series of field-oriented and record-oriented data-aware controls, including a custom DBGrid that displays graphic fields and memo fields on multiple lines (**Chapter 17**).

- A database form wizard, which you can easily customize to streamline the creation database forms your own way (**Chapter 18**).

- An Object Data Set component, which you can use to save components in a file and load their properties into data-aware controls (**Chapter 19**)

Delphi Developer's Handbook

Delphi™ Developer's Handbook™

Marco Cantù
Tim Gooch
with John F. Lam

SYBEX®

San Francisco • Düsseldorf • Soest • Paris

Associate Publisher: Gary Masters
Acquisitions Manager: Kristine Plachy
Acquisitions & Developmental Editor: Peter Kuhns
Editor: James A. Compton
Technical Editors: Ralph Friedman, Juancarlo Añez
Book Designers: Patrick Dintino, Inbar Berman
Graphic Illustrator: Inbar Berman, Andrew Benzie
Desktop Publisher: Tony Jonick
Production Coordinator: Duncan J. A. Watson
Proofreaders: Katherine Cooley, Theresa Gonzalez, Charles
Mathews, Eryn Osterhaus, and Amy Eoff
Indexer: Nancy Guenther
Companion CD: Molly Sharp and John D. Wright
Cover Designer and Illustrator: DesignSite

Screen reproductions produced with Collage Plus.

Collage Plus is a trademark of Inner Media Inc.

SYBEX is a registered trademark of SYBEX Inc.

Developer's Handbook is a trademark of SYBEX Inc.

TRADEMARKS: SYBEX has attempted throughout this book to
distinguish proprietary trademarks from descriptive terms by following the capitalization style used by the manufacturer.

Library of Congress Card Number: 97-61715
ISBN: 0-7821-1987-5

Manufactured in the United States of America

10 9 8 7 6 5 4 3 2 1

To Lella, with love.
—MC

To Tyler and Spencer, who always ask why.
—TG

ACKNOWLEDGMENTS

First, we'd like to thank Borland and the various member of the Delphi team who've become our friends over the years. They've become more than professional contacts; they've become advisors for our research, and they've consistently gone the extra mile. In particular we would like to thank David Intersimone, the "last barbarian" at Borland, and Nan Borreson, our supportive book contact.

Another "thank you" is for the people at Sybex who made this book possible. In particular, Jim Compton and Peter Kuhns were instrumental in shepherding this book over a development cycle lasting more than a year. We tested their patience with numerous changes and revisions, all with the intent of making the book as up-to-date as possible and providing the best technical value. Gary Masters also provided insight and support along the way. Once the manuscript was finally in their hands, desktop publisher Tony Jonick and production coordinator Duncan Watson turned it into a book quickly and accurately.

The two tech reviewers, Ralph Friedman and Juancarlo Añez, helped us set the technical tone for the book and suggested many clarifications of complex examples.

The companion CD-ROM was also the work of many people. At Sybex, Dale Wright and Molly Sharp handled the technical side of putting it together, and Mary Reeg handled the paperwork of obtaining permission to include the third-party software. We are grateful to all of the contributors, particularly those who assembled material specifically for this project or made an extra effort to ensure that we had current software.

We are grateful to the Delphi programming community for developing a sense of collaboration and shared responsibility for the future of this product, and to the readers of our books and articles for their continuous feedback and support.

Marco wishes to thank the Italian Delphi community, and the people who work for and with Borland in Italy. He would also like to express heartfelt thanks to his wife Lella for putting up with the tight schedule of the book and the many weekends spent working on it (when not traveling abroad).

Tim wishes to thank Mike Stephens and Mark Crane of The Cobb Group and many other people within Ziff-Davis Publishing Inc. who made it possible for him to work on this book in addition to sometimes performing his regular duties. He would also like to express his sincere appreciation to his wife Leeann and his sons Tyler and Spencer for allowing him to be a grumpy and frequently absent husband and father.

CONTENTS AT A GLANCE

Part IV: **Delphi Database Programming**

TABLE OF CONTENTS

INTRODUCTION

Why another large Delphi programming book? With each new version of Delphi, the breadth of topics to cover has grown geometrically with the feature set. Marco's *Mastering Delphi 3* (Sybex, 1997) was an in-depth exploration of the basic and intermediate features of Delphi, but there were many advanced topics it did not address. *Delphi Developer's Handbook* follows the earlier book's hands-on, example-based approach, unearthing and exposing those features that *Mastering* couldn't cover. Among many other topics, you'll learn how to build DLL and DCU wizards to streamline application development, how to write data-aware components, and how to take advantage of Client/Server Delphi's support for three-tier database architecture. As its title suggests, this book is designed to meet the needs of working professionals, developing Delphi applications either for use within an organization or for commercial or shareware distribution.

Appropriately, we've focused this book on Delphi 3 techniques and features, even though much of the information will apply to previous versions and will almost certainly apply to subsequent ones.

You'll find no beginning-level material in this book. From the outset, we're assuming that you are familiar with basic topics covered in *Mastering Delphi* and other intermediate-level Delphi books. However, you'll be rewarded with solid information, and useful examples that will take your Delphi knowledge to a new level.

As you can see, this is a book with multiple authors, but we've taken a rather unusual approach in this collaboration. Marco set the general structure and technical tone for the book and was responsible for creating most of the examples, components, and add-in tools. Tim took Marco's notes and text and turned them into a more readable and approachable style. For expertise in the complex world of COM programming, we had an outstanding contribution from John Lam, which you'll find in Chapters 10 and 11.

How the Book Is Organized

We've divided the book into four major sections:

Part I: Delphi Foundations The first six chapters explore Object Pascal and VCL topics such as accessing protected properties and component ownership, as well as issues related to streaming and persistency, run-time type information (RTTI), building components, and using packages to distribute components.

Part II: Delphi and Windows Chapters 7–9 focus on Delphi's interaction with the Windows environment, including an extended discussion of the VCL and Windows, advanced window components, threads, and Windows and Delphi memory management. Chapters 10 and 11 offer an in-depth look at the theory of COM and the Windows and Delphi tools for implementing it.

Part III: Extending the Delphi Environment In Chapters 12–16 you'll learn valuable ways to customize the Delphi IDE to streamline and safeguard the development process. You'll build property editors, component editors, and wizards, explore version control systems, and finally walk through all the decisions we made in creating an object debugger.

Part IV: Delphi Database Programming Chapters 17–20 explore—and extend—Delphi's support for database applications. You'll build data-aware components, customize the DBGrid, and create a database form wizard. You'll also work in the three-tier database model, building remote data modules and thin clients; and you'll explore Delphi's tools for publishing a database on the Web.

In each section we've created as many examples and components as possible, to demonstrate the features and techniques discussed in the text. Although the purpose of the examples is primarily to teach effective Delphi programming techniques, some of them are also useful tools in their own right. We haven't padded the book with long source code listings, but have instead focused on presenting and explaining the core code. Finally, we decided not to duplicate the reference material already available to you in the online help and VCL source files; we'll direct you to those sources where appropriate.

The Companion CD

You'll find the source code and executable files for all the examples, components, and add-in tools described in the text on the companion CD. This way, you can choose whether to simply run a finished sample application and study its source code, or follow the whole process of building and compiling it. To simplify navigating the source code on the CD, we've included HTML-formatted versions of the source code files and linked them for your convenience. In addition, we've cross-referenced all the significant keywords and identifiers in the HTML files, to help you locate a particular file or code sample.

There too, you'll find various tools, documentation, and demonstration versions of some of today's most powerful companion products for Delphi. See the page facing the CD for a complete list of these third-party tools.

How to Contact the Authors

For the latest information and updates to the examples and the text, you can check Marco's Web site at

```
http://www.marcocantu.com
```

or the Sybex site at

```
http://www.sybex.com
```

If all else fails, you can contact Marco at `marco@marcocantu.com` or Tim at `tim_gooch@cobb.com`.

PART I

Delphi Foundations

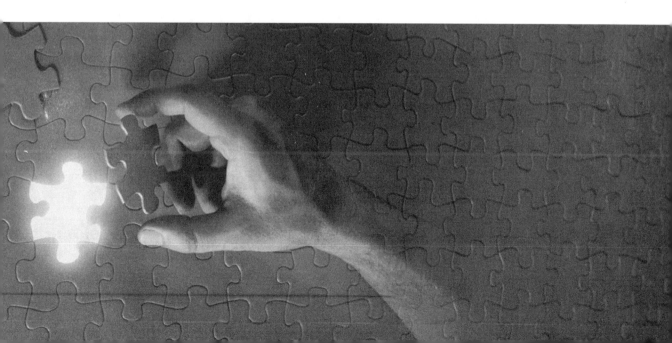

Object Pascal Secrets

- Delphi Long Strings

- Integer Bitwise Manipulations in Pascal

- Class References

- Delphi's Protection Anomaly

While Object Pascal is easier to learn than some other languages, there are still some areas that remain a mystery even to many experienced Delphi programmers. In this chapter, we'll review some of these less-known features. This won't be a tutorial as such, but an in-depth look at some key concepts that form the basis of much of the programming we will do throughout this book:

- How Delphi implements long strings

- Manipulating individual bits

- Using class references to identify class hierarchies and dynamically create objects by class name

- Hacking access to protected data

Developing a solid understanding of these topics will not only help you get the most out of later chapters but also make you a more capable Delphi programmer. In fact, each of them is essential to an in-depth understanding of Delphi.

NOTE
We will explore these topics using program examples that you'll find on the accompanying CD-ROM. As outlined in the Introduction, there are several ways to navigate the CD, but the directory structure is quite simple. The main DDHCODE folder contains all the book's examples, grouped into folders by chapter: 01, 02, and so on. Each chapter's folder then contains a subfolder for each program, with its EXE, PAS, and related files. Because the examples are designed to demonstrate particular Delphi features, we won't build each one from scratch or display entire listings; we'll just look at the code that's relevant to the point at hand.

Delphi Long Strings

First, let's examine one of the most visible features of Delphi since version 2: long strings. (In the on-line help, you'll see these described as AnsiString objects, but since their most distinguishing feature is that they can be longer than 255 bytes, most people call them "long strings.") The 32-bit versions of Delphi use long strings by default, although you can control their use with the $H compiler directive. You can continue to use the old-style strings by using the ShortString type, but this makes sense only in few circumstances, as when packing strings inside records or other data structures.

In Delphi 1 and earlier versions of Turbo and Borland Pascal, a `String` variable typically existed on the stack. In contrast, long strings are heap-based objects (just like objects of `TObject`-derived classes), but they're allocated and reallocated automatically. This is important, as it makes it possible for Delphi to optimize the use of a string that's used in more than one place (each instance is a pointer to the same location) using *reference counting*. For example, if you write:

```
var
  S1: String;
```

you create an automatically dereferenced pointer to a long string in memory. Initially, this pointer has a value of `nil`. As soon as you assign something to it:

```
S1 := 'Test';
```

Delphi allocates enough memory for the string, makes S1 point to the new string, and attempts to release the memory it originally addressed. (More on this in a moment.)

TIP

By the way, you can use the `SetLength` function to force Delphi to allocate a specific amount of memory for the long string.

One of the biggest advantages of using the *reference model* for long strings (automatically dereferencing heap-based strings) is that it makes reference counting possible. For each string (in memory), Delphi stores an associated integer indicating the string's size, and one indicating the number of references to the string.

Suppose you copy a long string by writing

```
S2 := S1;
```

Instead of duplicating the string S1 (and its storage), Delphi increases the reference count and alters the second string variable, S2, to address the same memory location as the first one. As a result, there's only one copy of the string in memory, but two variables that use it. If you later change one of the two strings, Delphi will copy the first string to a new memory location, since the change should affect only one of the strings, and not both of them. This technique is known as *copy-on-write*. When all the variables that reference a long string are no longer in scope, the reference count will drop to zero, and Delphi will release the string's memory.

Looking at String References

To help you better understand how Delphi implements long strings, we've written a small program, named LString, that displays string memory addresses and string references. (In fact, this program does something more, as we'll see in the next section.) To run the LString program and see its complete source code, go to the CD's DDHCODE\01\LSTRING folder.

Figure 1.1 shows the LString project's main form at startup. The list box in the middle shows information about the Test string: its current text, its length (computed in different ways), its memory address (that is, the value of the variable referencing the string), and its current reference count.

FIGURE 1.1:

The output of the LString program at start-up

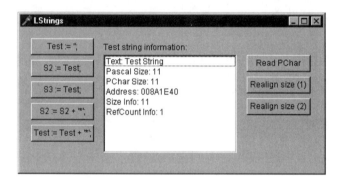

Here is the code of the UpdateInfo method, which we call first in the OnCreate event handler and then every time the program changes the string:

```
procedure TForm1.UpdateInfo;
begin
  with Listbox1.Items do
  begin
    Clear;
    Add ('Text: ' + Test);
    Add ('Pascal Size: ' + IntToStr (Length (Test)));
    Add ('PChar Size: ' + IntToStr (StrLen (PChar (Test))));
    Add (Format ('Address: %p', [Pointer (Test)]));
    Add ('Size Info: ' + IntToStr ( GetSize (Test)));
    Add ('RefCount Info: ' + IntToStr (GetRefCount (Test)));
  end;
end;
```

Notice that we compute both the traditional "Pascal size" and the "PChar size" (looking for the null terminator) of the string. As discussed in the following section, there are some cases when the two are not the same. To display the memory address of the string, we simply cast its variable as a pointer and then use the standard `Format` library function to convert it to text. The pointer itself refers to the first byte of the string, which simplifies converting a string to a `PChar` and vice versa. As a result, Delphi stores the length information and the reference count at a negative offset from the first byte of the string, as you can see in Figure 1.2.

FIGURE 1.2:

The memory layout of a long string

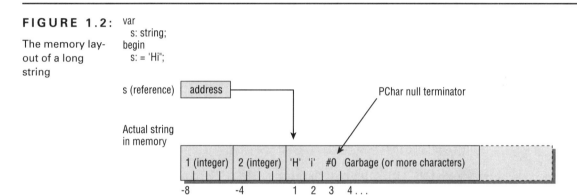

Unfortunately, Delphi provides no standard way to access the reference count and length byte. To solve this, we created two custom functions, `GetRefCount` and `GetSize`, to retrieve this information. Here is the code:

```
function GetRefCount (const s: string) : Integer;
var
  RefCountPointer: Pointer;
begin
  if Pointer(s) <> nil then
  begin
    RefCountPointer :=
      Pointer (Integer (Pointer (s)) - 8);
    Result := Integer (RefCountPointer^);
  end
  else
    Result := 0;
end;

function GetSize (const s: String) : Integer;
```

```
var
  SizePointer: Pointer;
begin
  if Pointer(s) <> nil then
  begin
    SizePointer := Pointer (
      Integer (Pointer (s)) - 4);
    Result := Integer (SizePointer^);
  end
  else
    Result := 0;
end;
```

In both of these functions, you'll notice a peculiar combination of casts. The first, casting the string as a `Pointer`:

```
Pointer(s)
```

yields the address of the variable. The second, casting the pointer as an `Integer`:

```
Integer(Pointer(s))
```

is necessary so we can perform some *pointer arithmetic* on the address (subtracting eight bytes for the reference count and four bytes to retrieve the size byte). The final cast, casting the string back to a `Pointer`:

```
Pointer(Integer(Pointer(s) - 8)
```

is necessary to initialize a temporary `Pointer` variable, which we then dereference and cast as an Integer.

You'll notice that we've declared the string parameters of these functions as `const` parameters. This is important, since passing the string as a non-`const` parameter would copy the string, and thus increment the reference count temporarily. Also, you'll notice that we test to see if the string is `nil`, which is the case for an empty string or for a new, uninitialized string.

Now, as you click any of the five buttons on the left side of the form, you can change the status of the string, and see the result in the list box. It is easy to understand what each button does, because we've copied its code into its caption. Here is an example:

```
procedure TForm1.Button3Click(Sender: TObject);
begin
  S2 := S2 + '*';
```

```
    UpdateInfo;
  end;
```

By clicking different buttons, you can:

- Reset the string's value to an empty string (the *Test := ''*; button). This releases the allocated memory and sets the address of the string to nil.

- Create more references to the string (*S2 := Test*; and *S2 := Test*;).

- Change the text of one of the other strings (*S2 := S2 + '*'*;); if S2 was previously assigned to Test, this reduces the reference count for the Test string.

- Change the text of the original Test string (*Test := Test + '*'*;). If you've created other references to the string, Delphi copies Test to a new memory location (as you can immediately see on the screen when you run the program).

Long Strings and PChar Problems

The buttons on the right side of the form demonstrate a complication that arises with long strings and PChar pointers. The event handler for the first button's OnClick event performs an apparently simple operation; it copies the caption of the form to the Test string by calling the GetWindowText Windows API function. To do so, we need to cast the string variable as a PChar:

```
procedure TForm1.Button6Click(Sender: TObject);
begin
  SetLength (Test, 100);
  GetWindowText (Handle, PChar (Test), 100);
  UpdateInfo;
end;
```

As a result of this operation, if there are other references to the string, Delphi will copy the string to a new memory location and update that copy. However, something strange happens, as you can see in Figure 1.3. The Pascal size of the string (retrieved from the internal string information and returned by using the Length function) doesn't match the actual size that's accurately returned by the StrLen function (which looks for the null terminator). Since Delphi has no way of knowing that you've modified the string by passing its address to the GetWindowText function, it can't automatically reset the size information for the string.

FIGURE 1.3:

The output of the LString program when the user clicks the *Read PChar* button

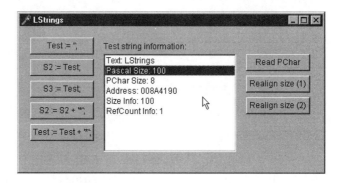

For example, if you click the *Read PChar* button and then add new text to the string by pressing the last button of the left column, Delphi will append the new characters to the end of the string. Unfortunately, this leaves the null terminator where it is and therefore does not affect the actual output of the string.

To resolve the situation, you can use one of several tricks. The LString program implements two alternatives. The first *Realign size* button fixes the string length problem by forcing a redundant cast. The code casts the data type back to a string (after forcing it to a PChar again):

```
Test := PChar (Test);
```

This is equivalent to writing

```
Test := String (PChar (Test));
```

since Delphi automatically converts PChar pointers to long strings.

The second *Realign size* button resets the length of the long string to the current length of the PChar string:

```
SetLength (Test, StrLen (PChar (Test)));
```

As you might guess, this operation actually reduces the size of the string in memory; and since it doesn't move the string, it should be faster than the first approach (which forces Delphi to copy the string, as you can see from its address). After a redundant cast or a size realignment, the string displays correctly as it did before.

Integer Bitwise Manipulations in Pascal

One aspect of Pascal that doesn't receive much coverage (it is more common in C/C++) is *bitwise manipulation* of integral values. Typically, a Delphi application uses sets to manipulate a group of binary values in a neat, readable, and type-safe manner, and you don't need to concern yourself with setting or clearing bits within a given byte. One example of Delphi using a set is the Style property for text. You can change the Style property by writing

```
Style := Style + [fsBold, fsItalic] - [fsUnderline];
```

This statement removes the Underline attribute and adds the Bold and Italic attributes to the Style property set.

However, when working with the Windows API, we'll need to use techniques borrowed from C/C++ to alter individual bits of a 16-bit or 32-bit value. Every time you pass a flag to a Windows API function, it is basically a collection of bits.

There are two approaches to manipulating bits in a Delphi application: using the Pascal bitwise operators, or using the TBits class.

Using Bitwise Operators

Pascal provides several Boolean operators and standard operations. For example, the shl and shr operators allow you to shift the bits of an integral value left or right, respectively. Similarly, the and, or, xor, and not operators make it possible to perform standard Boolean operations on either Boolean values or the bits in an integral value (in this second case these operators are known as *bitwise operators*). Below, we've provided some common functions for altering and testing specific bits within an Integer value:

```
function IsBitOn (Value: Integer; Bit: Byte): Boolean;
begin
  Result := (Value and (1 shl Bit)) <> 0;
end;

function TurnBitOn (Value: Integer; Bit: Byte): Integer;
begin
  Result := Value or (1 shl Bit);
end;
```

```
function TurnBitOff (Value: Integer; Bit: Byte): Integer;
begin
  Result := Value and not (1 shl Bit);
end;
```

To see these functions in action, take a look at the Bits1 example project. On the main form, you'll find an UpDown component, a read-only edit box (limited to values 0–31), and five check boxes in a group box (each box corresponds to a bit in the value that we'll adjust), as shown in Figure 1.4. To simplify the code that tests and sets the state of each check box, we've set each one's Tag property to the value of its bit position, which will help us identify them at run-time.

FIGURE 1.4:

The form displayed by the Bits1 program

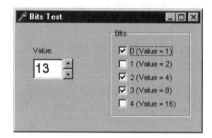

When you adjust the value of the edit box by clicking a spin arrow, we adjust the check boxes using the following event handler:

```
procedure TForm1.Edit1Change(Sender: TObject);
var
  I: Integer;
  CheckBox: TCheckBox;
begin
  for I := 1 to 5 do
  begin
    Checkbox := FindComponent (
      'Checkbox' + IntToStr (I)) as TCheckbox;
    CheckBox.Checked :=
      IsBitOn (UpDown1.Position, CheckBox.Tag);
  end;
end;
```

In this function, we simply append the bit position we're interested in to the text string "CheckBox," call the FindComponent method to return a reference to the appropriate check box, and then cast it to the appropriate type.

However, you can also modify the check boxes directly, so we respond to that type of event using this code:

```
procedure TForm1.CheckBoxClick(Sender: TObject);
var
  Val: Integer;
begin
  Val := UpDown1.Position;
  with Sender as TCheckBox do
    if Checked then
      Val := TurnBitOn (Val, Tag)
    else
      Val := TurnBitOff (Val, Tag);
  UpDown1.Position := Val;
end;
```

Here, you'll notice that we use the Tag property as the second parameter of the TurnBitOn and TurnBitOff function calls, which tells those functions which bit to modify. As you'll recall, we set each check box's Tag property according to the position it represents within the value. Now, we can use this value to determine which bit position should change.

The TBits Class

As an alternative to manipulating bits using the functions we just provided, Delphi gives you another option: the TBits class. If you're not familiar with this class, don't be surprised, since it's not documented very thoroughly. The TBits class simplifies manipulating bits within an integral value by providing an array interface to the individual bits, via the Bits property, which is declared as

```
property Bits[Index: Integer]: Boolean
  read GetBit write SetBit; default;
```

Internally, the TBits class stores the bits in one or more bytes, storing eight bits per byte. Fortunately, you don't have to worry about navigating the boundaries of the bytes if you need to manipulate more than eight bits; you just specify the appropriate bit position as an array index. Instead of discussing this further, let's examine how you can use the TBits class by examining the Bits2 example, a new version of the Bits1 program.

Running Bits2 and looking at its source code, you'll immediately notice that we removed the UpDown component as well as the code that allows you to enter a value into the Edit component directly. (We did this to simplify the example and highlight the behavior of the TBits class.) If you examine the form's declaration, you'll find that we've declared a TBits field and an UpdateEdit procedure in the private section.

The other property that the TBits class declares is Size, which sets or returns the amount of memory that the TBits object will use to store the bits. Before we can use the TBits object, we need to construct it, and then use the Size property to specify the number of bits it will contain. (By the way, if you try to access a bit that's not within the specified size boundary, the TBits class will raise an exception.) In the Bits2 example, we handle these tasks in the FormCreate method, and then destroy the object in the FormDestroy method:

```
procedure TForm1.FormCreate(Sender: TObject);
begin
  MyBits := TBits.Create;
  MyBits.Size := 5;
end;

procedure TForm1.FormDestroy(Sender: TObject);
begin
  MyBits.Free;
end;
```

When a user clicks on a check box, we once again use the corresponding component's Tag property to determine which bit to modify. Using the TBits class, we can use this value as an array index and perform a simple inversion:

```
procedure TForm1.CheckBoxClick(Sender: TObject);
begin
  MyBits.Bits [(Sender as TCheckBox).Tag] :=
    not MyBits.Bits [(Sender as TCheckBox).Tag];
  UpdateEdit;
end;
```

When a check box changes state, the UpdateEdit method iterates the array of bits, and builds the resulting integral value using the power of 2 relative to the bit position in the array:

```
procedure TForm1.UpdateEdit;
var
  I, Total: Integer;
begin
```

```
      Total := 0;
      for I := 0 to 4 do
        if MyBits.Bits [I] then
          Total := Total + Round (Power (2, I));
      Edit1.Text := IntToStr (Total);
    end;
```

As you might expect, the result of using the TBits class to manipulate the individual bits of an integer is no different from using the functions we provided earlier. However, the TBits class does provide two important advantages for performing general bit manipulation. First, since the member functions of the TBits class rely heavily on assembler, all the operations on the bits are very fast. In most cases the difference in speed probably won't be noticeable, but in some applications this could be an important benefit. Second, the maximum number of bits you can manipulate using a TBits object is 32,768. You can easily create an array of five, twenty, or 500 bits, and in each case you'll be able to use the same array notation for accessing the bit values.

On the downside, the TBits class doesn't provide any direct way of accessing the integral value that actually stores the bits. This is unfortunate, since there are many situations where you may want to manipulate the bits within a value that you've retrieved from an external data structure or that you need to pass to another application. Without some other means of initializing or retrieving those bytes directly, you'll need to resort to a technique such as the one we've used in the UpdateEdit method.

The one element of the TBits class we haven't mentioned is the OpenBit function. This function does exactly what its name implies: it returns the position value of the lowest bit that's not set.

Class References

It is important to underscore at the outset some key points we will frequently use in the rest of this book. Some of the topics discussed in this section are far from obvious, even to programmers fluent in Delphi.

A peculiar element of Object Pascal is support for class references. These are objects that store information about each class as a whole ("meta-classes" in Smalltalk or Borland C++Builder terminology) instead of storing information for a specific instance of a class. A class reference in Delphi has a specific data type, declared as:

```
type
  TMyCRef := class of TMyClass;
var
  MyCRef: TMyCRef;
```

In this example, the class reference data type TMyCRef can refer only to the TMyClass class and its subclasses. In other words, class references use the type compatibility rules relative to inheritance, just like other objects. If you examine the Delphi VCL source code closely, you'll notice that it defines several class references, such as TClass (which is a *class of* TObject), TComponentClass, TControlClass, and many more. As you might expect, you can assign any class to a TClass class reference (all classes are derived from TObject; all class references from TClass). However, it is quite common to work with component or control classes.

What can we use class references for? Primarily, we can use them to provide access to type information or to create objects of a given class. The second use is what the Delphi form designer does when you add a new component to a form.

TObject and Class Information

The first thing we'll do with class references is access information that pertains to the entire class. Naturally, for any TClass class reference you can apply any of the class methods of the TObject class, such as the ones listed below:

> ClassName: Returns a string with the name of the class.
>
> ClassNameIs: Checks the class name.
>
> ClassParent: Returns a class reference to the parent class.
>
> ClassInfo: Returns a pointer to the Run-Time Type Information (RTTI) of the class, which we'll discuss in Chapter 4.
>
> InheritsFrom: Tests whether the class inherits (directly or indirectly) from a given base class.
>
> InstanceSize: Returns the size of the objects.

However, some methods of the TObject class are not class methods, and therefore you can't apply them to a class reference. One example is the ClassType function, which returns the class type.

To demonstrate the use of these class references, we've written the ClassInfo program. The form displayed by this program contains a panel on the right to which you can drag one of the many components on the left. (Actually you must drop the components onto the shape we've placed on top of the panel.) When you drop a component on this shape, the ClassInfo example fills the Edit and ListBox components of the panel with the corresponding class information. The Edit component displays the name of the class and the size of the objects, and the list box displays the names of all the parent classes (as you can see in Figure 1.5).

FIGURE 1.5:

The form displayed by the ClassInfo program at run-time. Notice that the information about one of the components appears in the Edit and ListBox components of the right panel.

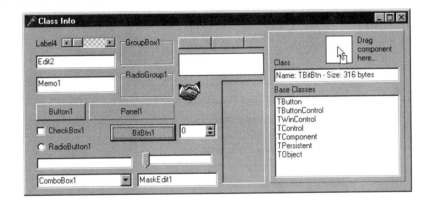

To make this form work, we've set the DragMode property of all the components on the left side to dmAutomatic, and we've set the Accept reference parameter of the OnDragOver event handler so that the shape component of the panel will accept dragging from every source:

```
procedure TForm1.Shape1DragOver(
  Sender, Source: TObject; X, Y: Integer;
  State: TDragState; var Accept: Boolean);
begin
  Accept := True;
end;
```

When you drop a component onto the shape (the OnDragDrop event), we simply copy the component's class information to the Edit and Listbox components of the panel:

```
procedure TForm1.Shape1DragDrop(
  Sender, Source: TObject; X, Y: Integer);
var
```

```
    MyClass: TClass;
begin
  Edit1.Text := Format ('Name: %s - Size: %d bytes',
    [Source.ClassName, Source.InstanceSize]);
  MyClass := Source.ClassType;
  with Listbox1.Items do
  begin
    Clear;
    while MyClass.ClassParent <> nil do
    begin
      MyClass := MyClass.ClassParent;
      Add (MyClass.ClassName);
    end;
  end;
end;
```

NOTE

When you examine this code, you may wonder why we chose to use the Format function instead of simply concatenating the strings. The answer is that the Format function is significantly faster than using the + operator. The price you pay for the improved performance is poorer type checking of the parameters than with the + operator.

You'll notice that we use a class reference at the heart of the while loop, where we test for a situation where the class has no parent class (this means the current class is TObject). Alternatively, we could have written the while statement as:

```
while not MyClass.ClassNameIs ('TObject') do...
```

or

```
while MyClass <> TObject do...
```

You can use ClassInfo to display information about other classes by adding different components to the left part of the form. However, we can't really use this program as a general-purpose tool since the form must contain at least one of the components we want to investigate. Our next example will overcome this limitation.

Registering and Finding Classes

To use a class's methods, we need an object or class reference. Obviously, the class must be one that's available in our program (that is, one for which we've included the appropriate units), and we need to find a general technique that we can use to access a class's methods. One way to do this is to use the FindClass or GetClass functions, which return a class reference from a given class name. (Although these two functions seem to do the same thing, FindClass raises an exception if it doesn't find the class name, whereas GetClass returns a nil pointer.)

At first glance, these functions appear to give us exactly what we need: a valid reference to a class, which we can then use to call various class methods. However, you'll have to register a class for either of these functions to find it. Why do we need to do this? Well, the Delphi type system needs to contain a complete description of how to build a given class's objects in various situations, including building objects from a description in a file stream. (Chapter 2 discusses the Delphi streaming system.) Accordingly, the RegisterClass function (which you'll use to tell the Delphi type system about a new class) accepts a TPersistentClass parameter, which means you can only register, and therefore stream, persistent objects.

Now let's examine the RegClasses example project to see how we can update the previous example. First, we replaced all those components on the left side of the form with a simple ComboBox (set the Style property to csSimple). Now, when a user enters a class name, we simply look up that class in the sorted list of registered classes. (We register all the classes before we load them into the ComboBox.) You can see the resulting user interface in Figure 1.6.

FIGURE 1.6:

The form displayed by the RegClasses program

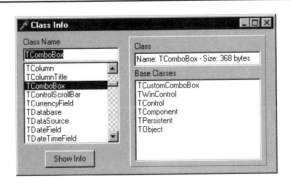

When the user presses the *Show Info* button, we display the information about that class (using code similar to that of the previous example):

```
procedure TForm1.ButtonShowClick(Sender: TObject);
var
  MyClass: TClass;
begin
  MyClass := GetClass (ComboBox1.Text);
  if MyClass = nil then
    Beep
  else
  begin
    Edit1.Text := Format ('Name: %s - Size: %d bytes',
      [MyClass.ClassName, MyClass.InstanceSize]);
    with Listbox1.Items do
    begin
      Clear;
      while MyClass.ClassParent <> nil do
      begin
        MyClass := MyClass.ClassParent;
        Add (MyClass.ClassName);
      end; // while
    end; // with
  end; // else
end;
```

This simple code is executed when the user double-clicks on the combo box:

```
procedure TForm1.ComboBox1DblClick(Sender: TObject);
begin
  ButtonShowClick (Sender);
end;
```

However, as mentioned before, the program needs to register each of the classes that it is going to add to the ComboBox component. Since the program needs the same information twice, we've built an array of persistent classes, declared as:

```
type
  TClassArray = array [1..140] of TPersistentClass;

const
  ClassArray: TClassArray = (
    TBitmap, TGraphic, TOutlineNode, TGraphicsObject,
    TBrush, THeaderSection, TParams, TCanvas, ...
```

and so on for 132 more elements. Now we can use this array to register the classes *and* fill the combo box:

```
procedure TForm1.FormCreate(Sender: TObject);
var
  I: Integer;
begin
  // register all of the classes
  RegisterClasses (ClassArray);
  // copy class names to the listbox
  for I := Low (ClassArray) to High (ClassArray) do
    ComboBox1.Items.Add (ClassArray [I].ClassName);
end;
```

We've written the code as generically as possible, because we haven't included every possible class in the array. When we need to add a new class, we can simply increase the size of the array in the type declaration and add the new element.

This example accomplishes what we set out to do in the beginning of this section: it allows us to display information about the persistent classes of the system. How can we display information about nonpersistent classes as well? Simply by skipping the FindClass/GetClass approach, circumventing the Delphi type system, and directly associating class information with the items of the ComboBox:

```
for I := Low (ClassArray) to High (ClassArray) do
  ComboBox1.Items.AddObject (
    ClassArray [I].ClassName, Pointer(ClassArray [I]));
```

We'll use a similar approach in the next example.

A Hierarchy of Classes

Instead of using a plain ComboBox as we did in the previous example, why not build a full-blown tree of classes using the class references and class information? Delphi includes a TreeView component, which encapsulates the corresponding Windows 95 control, so we only need to fill the tree with the classes. However, you typically fill a TreeView from the root towards the leaves, while we have currently discussed only leaf classes, and not any of the intermediate base classes (classes you don't—or can't—instantiate).

Before we can pursue this, we need to create a more complete array of classes, including the noncomponent classes, the exception classes, and all the appropriate base classes. In the ClassHiera program example, we've built such an array and declared it as follows:

```
type
  TClassArray = array [1..498] of TClass;

const
  ClassArray: TClassArray = (
    EAbort,
    EAccessViolation,
    EAssertionFailed,
    EBitsError,
    EClassNotFound,
    EComponentError,
    ...
```

WARNING We've tried to build a complete list of the classes available in Delphi 3 Client/Server. This means that, although you can run ClassHiera.EXE from the CD, the source code cannot be recompiled with a different version of Delphi. If you own a different version, you'll have to remove all the units and all the components not available in that version in order to rebuild the program.

Now ClassHiera needs to add each of these classes to the TreeView. To do so, we execute the following code when the user presses the *Build Tree* button:

```
procedure TForm1.Button1Click(Sender: TObject);
var
  I: Integer;
begin
  // don't restart this loop
  Button1.Enabled := False;
  // add the root class
  TreeView1.Items.AddObject (nil, 'TObject',
    Pointer (TObject));
  // add each class to the tree
  ProgressBar1.Min := Low (ClassArray);
  ProgressBar1.Max := High (ClassArray);
  for I := Low (ClassArray) to High (ClassArray) do
  begin
    AddClass (ClassArray [I]);
```

```
        ProgressBar1.Position := I;
    end;
    Beep;
    ShowMessage ('Tree Completed');
    Button2.Enabled := True;
    Button1.Enabled := False;
  end;
```

This function calls the AddObject method of the TTreeNodes class (the items of the tree view), to create a TObject root node. This is important, because TObject is the ultimate base class for any class, and we use this fact to determine when we've finished building a given branch of the tree. (We'll work our way back up the class hierarchy, adding classes along the way as necessary, and stop when we're about to add the TObject class.) When we call the TTreeView class's AddObject method, we use the text TObject as the root node, and then embed a pointer to the TObject class in the same node. By the way, TreeView, ListBox, ComboBox, and ListView components all allow you to store data along with an item's text. This data can be up to four bytes long, which is suitable for a long integer, a pointer, an object reference, or even a class reference.

After creating the root object, the Button1Click method adds each element from the array and updates a ProgressBar component appropriately. (You'll notice that we initialize the ProgressBar with the upper and lower bounds of the array.) When we finish adding new classes to the TreeView, we alert the user. Then we disable the *Build Tree* button and enable the *Sort Tree* button, which we'll use to sort the elements of the TreeView alphabetically. (We'll describe the sorting code later.)

For each of the array elements, you'll notice that we call the form's AddClass method. This method checks to see if we've already added a class to the TreeView, and if not, adds the class to the TreeView as a subnode of its immediate parent class:

```
function TForm1.AddClass (NewClass: TClass): TTreeNode;
var
  ParentNode: TTreeNode;
begin
```

```
// if the class is not there...
Result := GetNode (NewClass);
if Result = nil then
begin
  // look for the parent (eventually adding it)
  ParentNode := AddClass (NewClass.ClassParent);
  // add the new class
  Result := TreeView1.Items.AddChildObject (
    ParentNode,
    NewClass.ClassName,
    Pointer (NewClass));
  end;
end;
```

You'll notice that we call AddClass recursively to find the parent node instead of simply calling the GetNode method. We do this because the parent class might not exist yet either, and calling this method recursively ensures that we've added all of the parent classes back to the TObject class, which you'll recall we added at the very beginning. This works because the AddClass method returns a node corresponding to the class, even if the class is already in the TreeView. If the class isn't in the TreeView, the AddClass method adds the class and returns the node of the new class.

In contrast, the GetNode method simply searches for a node that corresponds to a class. If the class isn't in the TreeView, the GetNode method returns nil to indicate failure. Here is the code of the GetNode method:

```
function TForm1.GetNode (BaseClass: TClass): TTreeNode;
var
  Node1: TTreeNode;
begin
  Result := nil; // not found
  // find the node in the tree
  Node1 := TreeView1.Items.GetFirstNode;
  while Node1 <> nil do
  begin
    if Node1.Text = BaseClass.ClassName then
    begin
      Result := Node1;
      Exit;
    end;
    Node1 := Node1.GetNext;
```

```
    Application.ProcessMessages;
  end;
end;
```

The function starts with the root node of the tree (returned by the `GetFirstNode` method) and scans the full tree using the `GetNext` method, which returns each node in turn, regardless of its level in the nodes hierarchy. This code is not very fast, but the alternative code we could have used (listed below) was even slower:

```
// slower loop...
for I := 0 to TreeView1.Items.Count - 1 do
begin
  if TreeView1.Items [I].Text = BaseClass.ClassName then
  begin
    Result := TreeView1.Items [I];
    Exit;
  end;
  Application.ProcessMessages;
end;
```

The effect of this code appears to be the same, but the first version, based on the `GetNext` call, is actually faster. The reason is that the items are not physically stored as a list, but as a tree, so accessing the next item is faster than trying to determine the element in a given position. In fact, most of the TreeView methods are really slow. For example, consider the sorting algorithm: adding nodes to a TreeView that sorts the nodes on the fly takes much more time than adding the items without sorting them, and sorting the 500 entries afterwards (on a slow machine) might take two minutes or more. Here is the sorting code, connected with the *Sort Tree* button of the form:

```
procedure TForm1.Button2Click(Sender: TObject);
begin
  Screen.Cursor := crHourglass;
  TreeView1.SortType := stText;
  Screen.Cursor := crDefault;
  Button2.Enabled := False;
end;
```

Simply setting the `SortType` property sorts the nodes in the TreeView, but it takes a while. Since building the tree takes some time as well (because the program spends a lot of time scanning the tree to find existing classes), We've added a call to the `ProcessMessages` method of the global `Application` object, to let the user manipulate the tree view items while we build the rest of the tree.

NOTE   The global Application object manages the event loop and many other aspects of the application. For more information on the global Application object and on the `ProcessMessages` method, see Chapters 7 and 8.

You can see a partially built TreeView (notice the ProgressBar position) in Figure 1.7. While the application is building the TreeView, you can resize the form, which in turn resizes the TreeView (it's aligned to the form's client area), while the Panel always occupies the same area (it's aligned to the right).

FIGURE 1.7:

The ClassHiera program at run-time, with a partial tree of classes

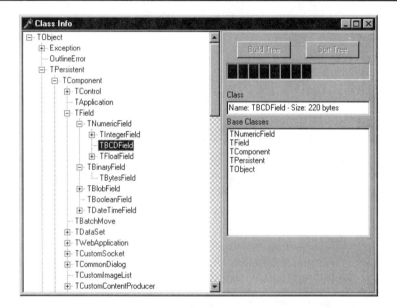

While we build the TreeView, you can select a class and then view the usual information in the *Base Classes* list box. The only unusual step we need to take to display this information is to extract a class reference from the TreeView node we've selected (remember that we embedded this data in the node along with the text of the class name), and cast it as a class reference. Once we've created this reference, we simply enter a loop that reassigns the `MyClass` reference with the class's parent class and then adds the name of that class to the ListBox. When the `MyClass` reference's `ClassParent` property is `nil`, we exit the loop.

```
procedure TForm1.TreeView1Change (
    Sender: TObject; Node: TTreeNode);
```

```
var
  MyClass: TClass;
begin
  MyClass := TClass (Node.Data);
  Edit1.Text := Format ('Name: %s - Size: %d bytes',
    [MyClass.ClassName, MyClass.InstanceSize]);
  with Listbox1.Items do
  begin
    Clear;
    while MyClass.ClassParent <> nil do
    begin
      MyClass := MyClass.ClassParent;
      Add (MyClass.ClassName);
    end; // while
  end; // with
end;
```

By the way, you'll notice that the OnChange event of the TreeView passes the selected node to this event handler. However, since the TTreeView class doesn't support multiple selections, you can simply use the Selected property to determine the current tree node if you want to do so in another part of the program.

The ClassHiera example is quite interesting for the data it displays (as well as the techniques used to build it). However, it is extremely slow to use. The structure of the tree must be re-created each time, and it takes a few minutes to build and sort it—even on a fast computer. To overcome this problem we've extended the example, splitting the construction of the tree and the visualization of the information in two different programs. Both programs have been saved in the 01/VCLHIERA directory.

The first program is called VclHCreate (which stands for VCL Hierarchy Create) and has capabilities very similar to the previous program, ClassHiera. The user interface is slightly different, though. To make the form more flexible we've placed in it two components (a TreeView and a Memo) separated by a Splitter component, as you can see in Figure 1.8.

The real difference is that this program has a button you can use to save the structure of the TreeView to a text file. Once you have created the tree and sorted its entries, you can press that button, save the data to a file, and then load the data in the VclHiera example.

FIGURE 1.8:

The output of the VclHCreate program, similar to the ClassHiera example

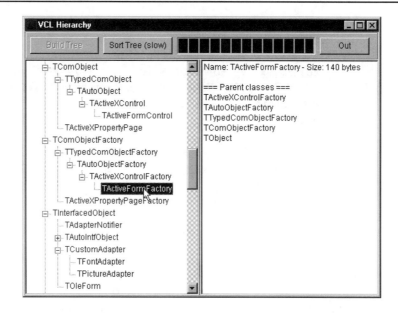

The VclHiera example, in fact, can only display the data. It has the same TreeView component as the VclHCreate program, but the initial data of the TreeView is simply loaded at design time from the text file created with the other program. This is simple to accomplish: Select the TreeView component, move to the Items property, activate the property editor, and in the TreeView Items Editor dialog box, simply press the *Load* button.

In this viewer program the class information is not available as part of the data of the TreeView, and we cannot access it using FindClass, because not all the classes inherit from TPersistent. The solution is to keep the array of classes used to create the tree in memory. This time we do not create the tree, but use the array for access to the class information. The program simply scans the array looking for a string matching the text of the TreeView item:

```
procedure TForm1.TreeView1Change (
  Sender: TObject; Node: TTreeNode);
var
  MyClass: TClass;
  I: Integer;
begin
  MyClass := nil;
```

```
    for I := Low (ClassArray) to High (ClassArray) do
      if ClassArray [I].ClassName = Node.Text then
        MyClass := ClassArray [I];
  Memo1.Lines.Clear;
  if MyClass = nil then
    Memo1.Lines.Add ('RTTI information not found')
  else
  begin
    Memo1.Lines.Add (Format ('Name: %s - Size: %d bytes',
      [MyClass.ClassName, MyClass.InstanceSize]));
    Memo1.Lines.Add ('');
    Memo1.Lines.Add ('=== Parent classes ===');
    while MyClass.ClassParent <> nil do
    begin
      MyClass := MyClass.ClassParent;
      Memo1.Lines.Add (MyClass.ClassName);
    end;
  end;
end;
```

This code is slower than the routine we used in the previous version, but it is fast enough to display the information in the right pane without any noticeable delay. The advantage, however, is that as you run the program, the class hierarchy is now immediately available. As you can see in Figure 1.9, the viewer program also has a couple of buttons to expand or collapse the entire TreeView.

Creating Objects and Components at Run-Time

As we mentioned before, another very important use of class references (besides retrieving class information) is to create objects dynamically. However, instead of creating specific instances of a given component, we can write some highly generic code that can create any kind of component. To accomplish this, we can extend the RegClasses example presented earlier, by displaying only the component classes in the ComboBox, placing the ComboBox in a toolbar, and creating a component of the selected kind whenever the user clicks on the form. In Figure 1.10 you can see the CreateComp example at run-time.

First let's review how to create a component at run-time:

```
procedure TForm1.Button1Click (Sender: TObject);
var
  NewButton: TButton;
```

FIGURE 1.9:

The VclHiera program, which displays a tree of the classes in the VCL but doesn't re-create it each time

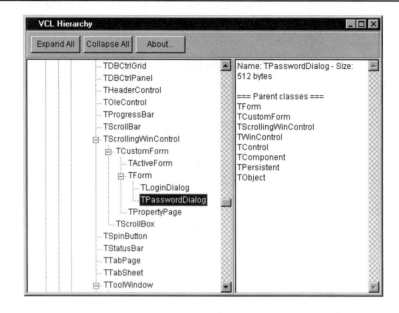

FIGURE 1.10:

The CreateComp program at run-time, after we've created some components

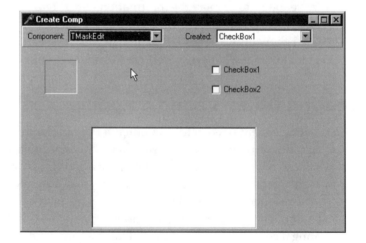

```
begin
  NewButton := TButton.Create (self);
  NewButton.Name := 'Button2';
  NewButton.Left := 100;
  NewButton.Top := 100;
  NewButton.Parent := self;
end;
```

This code creates a new button, gives it a name—the name of a component must be unique in a form—sets its position, and assigns its Parent property. Every control (not all of the components, only those derived from TControl) must have a parent; that is, the TWindow-derived component that contains it.

NOTE

The Parent and Owner properties are similar but distinct. The Parent property allows a TControl-derived component to associate properly with its window. In contrast, the Owner property is set during the call to the constructor—in this case, TButton.Create(self). The Owner property determines which component is responsible for destroying another component. In the code above, the form is the owner and parent of the Button component. Therefore, the form's window manages displaying the button, and the form will destroy the button when the application destroys the form.

To transform the code of the Button1Click above into something more generic, we only need to replace the NewButton variable with a generic component variable, and then replace the TButton data type in the Create statement with the class we retrieve from the ComboBox selection. Here is the code, which we've connected to the OnMouseDown event of the form to determine the initial position of the new component:

```
procedure TForm1.FormMouseDown(
  Sender: TObject; Button: TMouseButton;
  Shift: TShiftState; X, Y: Integer);
var
  MyClass: TComponentClass;
  MyComp: TComponent;
begin
  MyClass := TComponentClass (
    GetClass (ComboBox1.Text));
  if MyClass = nil then
    Beep
  else
  begin
    MyComp := MyClass.Create (self);
    MyComp.Name := GetNextName (MyClass);
    if MyClass.InheritsFrom (TControl) then
    begin
      TControl (MyComp).Left := X;
      TControl (MyComp).Top := Y;
```

```
        TControl (MyComp).Parent := self;
      end;
    end;
    UpdateList;
  end;
```

If you examine this code closely, you'll realize that casting GetClass to TComponentClass is risky; you must be sure all the classes in the global array are really component classes. To ensure this you can temporarily change the data type of the array to:

```
TClassArray = array [1..133] of TComponentClass;
```

However, you must then cast it back to the TPersistentClass data type to be able to pass it to the RegisterClasses function. The benefit of this change is that it lets us compile the code to confirm that all of the classes we've added to the array really descend from TComponent.

Later in this function, you'll notice that we've set the Name property of the component using the return value from the GetNextName method. This method searches the form's Components array, counts the number of components of a given type that already exist on the form, and then appends that number to the component's class name (less the initial T) to manufacture a unique name for the component within the form:

```
function TForm1.GetNextName (
  MyClass: TComponentClass): string;
var
  I, nTot: Integer;
begin
  nTot := 0;
  for I := 0 to ComponentCount - 1 do
    if Components [I].ClassType = MyClass then
      Inc (nTot);
  Result := Copy (MyClass.ClassName, 2,
    Length (MyClass.ClassName) - 1) + IntToStr (nTot);
end;
```

After setting the Name property, the FormMouseDown event handler determines the position and parent window of the component, but only if it is a visual component, a control. Notice the test:

```
if MyClass.InheritsFrom (TControl) then
```

It's necessary to perform the test this way because the is operator isn't valid for testing the type of a class reference. Of course, we could change the test to the following:

```
if MyComp is TControl then
```

and it would work just as well. At the end of the OnMouseDown handler there is a call to UpdateList. This custom method simply fills the second ComboBox with the names of the components on the form. We need to do this so that users will know which components we've created, since some of them won't be visible. Here is the code for the UpdateList method:

```
procedure TForm1.UpdateList;
var
  I: Integer;
begin
  Combobox2.Items.Clear;
  for I := 0 to ComponentCount - 1 do
    ComboBox2.Items.Add (Components [I].Name);
end;
```

You'll notice that we also call this method at the end of the OnCreate handler. Elsewhere in the OnCreate event-handler, we fill the first ComboBox with the names of the available component classes.

As you're no doubt aware, Delphi creates components in a manner similar to the one we've shown here. Accordingly, we don't expect you to build a Delphi clone, but in some situations (such as recreating objects from information in files or a database) you may want to create components dynamically using these techniques.

In the next chapter, we'll extend this example to save the forms we produce, producing the DFM file and a skeleton PAS file.

Cloning Objects

Besides creating new objects from a string with the name of a class, we can use class references to clone existing objects. We've created a simple example, called ObjClone, to demonstrate this technique.

This program has a button you can use to create a clone of the current form. Actually, the event handler creates a clone of the self object. Here is the code; you can see its effect in Figure 1.11:

```
procedure TForm1.Button1Click(Sender: TObject);
var
  AForm: TForm;
begin
  // clone the 'self' object
  Application.CreateForm (
    TFormClass(Self.ClassType), AForm);
  // move the form and show it
  AForm.Left := Left  + 50;
  AForm.Top := Top  + 50;
  AForm.Show;
end;
```

FIGURE 1.11:

The output of the ObjClone program after cloning the form a couple of times

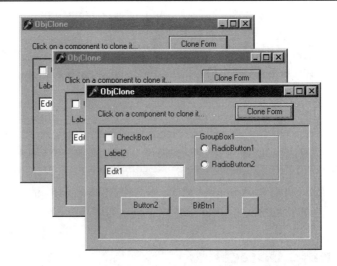

The program has another capability: you can click on any individual control inside the ScrollBox component to clone that control. The OnClick event of all of those controls is connected to a single method:

```
procedure TForm1.ClickComp(Sender: TObject);
var
  ControlText: string;
begin
```

```
with TControlClass (Sender.ClassType).Create (self) do
begin
  Parent := (Sender as TControl).Parent;
  Left := (Sender as TControl).Left + 10;
  Top := (Sender as TControl).Top + 10;
  SetLength (ControlText, 50);
  (Sender as TControl).GetTextBuf(
    PChar(ControlText), 50);
  ControlText := PChar(ControlText) + ' *';
  SetTextBuf (PChar (ControlText));
end;
end;
```

This method takes the class of the Sender object, the component clicked by the user, and calls the Create constructor. To call the Create constructor of the TControl class instead of calling that of the TObject class, however, the program has to cast the class reference to the proper type. When we cast to TControlClass and then call Create, the result is an object of class TControl. This object is used inside the with statement, and the program sets its Parent, Left, and Top properties, using information extracted from the Sender control.

At the end of the with statement, the program extracts the text of the Sender object, using a method available for every control, GetTextBuf. In fact, the Text and Caption properties aren't defined inside the TControl class (at least not as public fields, although later on in this chapter you'll see how to use a trick to overcome this problem). After adding an asterisk to the string, the program uses it as the new text of the control, again calling the SetTextBuf method of the class TControl.

You can see the effect of cloning some of the controls of the example in Figure 1.12.

Delphi's Protection Anomaly

Delphi implements object encapsulation and protection in an unusual way. In Delphi, the private and protected data of a class is accessible to any functions or methods that appear *in the same unit as the class*. This surprises many programmers, but it is actually quite logical from the perspective that most classes and methods you define within a given unit are typically related in some way. If you're familiar with the concept of a friend class in C++, the effect is roughly the same. However, this approach to object encapsulation has interesting ramifications.

The ObjClone program can be used to clone some of the controls included in the ScrollBox component.

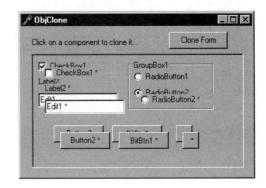

For example, consider this simple class (part of the Protection example):

```
type
  TTest = class
  protected
    ProtectedData: Integer;
  public
    PublicData: Integer;
    function GetValue: string;
  end;
```

The GetValue method simply returns a string with the two integer values:

```
function TTest.GetValue: string;
begin
  Result := Format ('Public: %d, Protected: %d',
    [PublicData, ProtectedData]);
end;
```

Once you place this class in its own unit, you won't be able to access its protected portion from other units directly. Accordingly, if you write the following:

```
procedure TForm1.Button1Click(Sender: TObject);
var
  Obj: TTest;
begin
  Obj := TTest.Create;
  Obj.PublicData := 10;
  Obj.ProtectedData := 20;  // won't compile
  ShowMessage (Obj.GetValue);
```

```
  Obj.Free;
end;
```

the compiler will issue an error message, *Undeclared identifier: "ProtectedData."* At this point, you might think there is no way to access the protected data of a class defined in a different unit. (In fact, that is what Delphi manuals and most Delphi books say.) However, there is a way around it. Consider what happens if you create an apparently useless derived class, such as:

```
type
  TFake = class (TTest):
```

Now, if you downcast the object to the new class before accessing the protected data:

```
procedure TForm1.Button2Click(Sender: TObject);
var
  Obj: TTest;
begin
  Obj := TTest.Create;
  Obj.PublicData := 10;
  TFake (Obj).ProtectedData := 20; // compiles!
  ShowMessage (Obj.GetValue);
  Obj.Free;
end;
```

you'll find that it not only compiles, it works as well. Figure 1.13 shows the sample output from the Protected example.

FIGURE 1.13:

When you press the *Hack* button (Button2) of the Protection program, the proper output is displayed.

How is it possible for this approach to work? Well, if you think about it, the TFake class automatically inherits in its interface the protected fields of the TTest base class, and since the TFake class is in the same unit as the code that tries to access the data in the inherited fields, the protected data is accessible. As you would expect, if you move the declaration of the TFake class to a secondary unit, the program won't compile.

Now that we've shown you how to do this, we must warn you that violating the class protection mechanism this way is very likely to induce errors in your program (from accessing data that you really shouldn't), and it runs counter to good object-oriented programming (OOP) technique. However, there are times when using this technique is the best solution, as we'll demonstrate in the two following examples.

Accessing Protected Properties: Text

One of the best-known protected properties is the Text property. This is declared in the TControl class and surfaced only in few subclasses (as TEdit or TMemo). Most of the other classes rename this property as Caption, and in few cases it is simply not available (as in a list box). The reason this property is implemented in TControl (and TWinControl) is that it basically relies on a feature of the system: Every window has a text string you can set using the wm_SetText message. This text is used in different ways, and at times it is not used at all (for example by list boxes). Delphi actually extends this feature to the TGraphicControl class, so that it applies to every control.

The problem, however, is that this property is not directly accessible. A workaround is to call the public methods GetText and SetText, which are based on PChar strings. We saw an example earlier in this chapter, in the ObjClone program's ClickComp method.

The alternative is to use the technique described in the last section, as we've done in the TextProp example:

```
type
  TControlHack = class (TControl);

procedure TForm1.Button1Click(Sender: TObject);
var
  I: Integer;
begin
  for I := 0 to ControlCount - 1 do
    TControlHack (Controls [I]).Text :=
      TControlHack (Controls [I]).Text + '*';
end;
```

The effect of executing this code is that an asterisk is appended to the text or caption of every control of the form (besides the list box), as you can see in Figure 1.14.

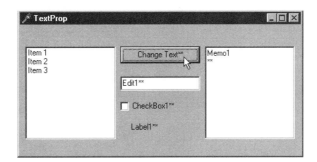

Accessing Protected Properties: DBGrid Row and Column

As a further example, consider the following scenario: You place a DBGrid component in a form, and when the user moves to a column (by clicking with the mouse or pressing the arrow keys) you'd like to display the numeric value of the selected column (or simply keep track of it for internal purposes). In fact, the TDBGrid class defines both Row and Column properties, but it declares them as protected properties. As a result, you may conclude that you can't access this important information. (By the way, we don't know why Borland chose to declare these properties as protected, since we've discovered no danger in exposing them to the rest of the program.)

To solve this problem, we can simply declare a fake subclass, as we've done in the DBGridCol example. There, we derive our fake class from the TDBGrid class using:

```
type
    TFake = class (TDBGrid);
```

Now, we can implement an OnColEnter event handler, which will display the number of the current column and row in a label:

```
procedure TForm1.DBGrid1ColEnter(Sender: TObject);
begin
    Label1.Caption := Format (
```

```
          'Column: %2d; Row: %2d',
          [TFake (DbGrid1).Col,
          TFake (DbGrid1).Row]);
    end;
```

Naturally, we'll want to execute the same code if the user moves to a new record. This action doesn't generate an event for the DBGrid, but it does generate an OnDataChange event for the DataSource component. Here is the handler for this event:

```
    procedure TForm1.DataSource1DataChange(
      Sender: TObject; Field: TField);
    begin
      DBGrid1ColEnter (sender);
    end;
```

You can see the effect of this code in Figure 1.15, or by running the example and testing it. By the way, you'll notice that when you move to a different column in the grid, the column numbers reflect the column position, not the order of the corresponding field of the table.

FIGURE 1.15:

The information about the current column and row of the DBGrid, displayed by the DBGridCol program

What's Next

In this chapter, we've examined several poorly understood and under-documented features of Delphi: the behavior of long strings, manipulating individual bits, the appropriate use of class methods and class references, and how you can bypass Delphi's protection model to gain access to the protected data in an externally declared class.

Using this information, we can now move on to a similar topic related to the VCL, and not to the language. We've actually started delving into VCL-related topics with the last two examples. It is now time to explore some VCL secrets. Only after doing that will we be fully capable of exploring component building.

CHAPTER
TWO

2

VCL Secrets

Moving on from the first chapter, where we explored Object Pascal topics, this chapter delves into topics more specific to the VCL than to the language. We'll start with an in-depth discussion of component ownership and problems relating to destroying objects. Then we'll focus on the Name property of components, and finish by describing how to use the TList class as a type-safe container.

Component Ownership

When you create a component object in a Delphi application (by placing the component on a form or by writing some code), you typically specify the new component's owner. The Create constructor of the TComponent class accepts the component's owner as its only parameter, and this constructor is overridden by all the other components.

The component you pass to the constructor is accessible via the Owner property of the component. On the other side, the owner component stores a list of the components it owns in the Components array property (the ComponentCount property indicates the number of "owned" components). In fact, the TComponent constructor calls the owner's InsertComponent method, as shown below:

```
constructor TComponent.Create (AOwner: TComponent);
begin
  FComponentStyle := [csInheritable];
  if AOwner <> nil then
    AOwner.InsertComponent (Self);
end;
```

This code demonstrates that there's no reason to insert a component in the owner's list after creating it, something we've seen in many Delphi applications. The above code also illustrates that it's legal to pass nil as the AOwner parameter. However, if the component has no owner, you'll need to destroy it manually. (By default, owner components destroy all the components they own, as we'll see in the section "Freeing an Object Twice" later in this chapter.)

Changing the Owner

Another common misconception is that you cannot change a component's owner. Of course, to move a component from the current form to another one (Form2), you cannot write

```
Button1.Owner := Form2;
```

simply because Owner is a read-only property. A simple workaround would be to call RemoveComponent for the first form and InsertComponent for the second one:

```
RemoveComponent (Button1);
Form2.InsertComponent (Button1);
```

Unfortunately, this won't work either. (If you try this code, it produces a memory access violation.)

The reason you can't move a component this way is quite complex, and depends on the fact that when you remove a component from a form, you actually end up disconnecting the component from the form field that corresponds to the component itself. (As you'll recall, the Delphi form designer adds a field to the form class declaration for every component you place on a form.) As you can see below, the RemoveComponent method calls the SetReference method:

```
procedure TComponent.RemoveComponent(AComponent: TComponent);
begin
  Notification(AComponent, opRemove);
  AComponent.SetReference(False);
  Remove(AComponent);
  AComponent.SetDesigning(False);
  ValidateRename(AComponent, AComponent.FName, '');
end;
```

Depending on the value of the Boolean parameter, the SetReference method either connects the component to a corresponding field in the class or sets the field to nil:

```
procedure TComponent.SetReference(Enable: Boolean);
var
  Field: ^TComponent;
begin
  if FOwner <> nil then
  begin
    Field := FOwner.FieldAddress(FName);
    if Field <> nil then
```

```
    if Enable then
       Field^ := Self
    else
       Field^ := nil;
  end;
end;
```

To make this connection, the SetReference method in turn calls the FieldAddress method of the owner. FieldAddress simply returns the memory address of a published field of the owner (usually a form) that has the same name as the Name property of the component. This is possible thanks to the use of RTTI information, something we will cover in-depth in Chapter 4. Delphi creates the connection between the form class's field and the component when you place the component (actually, when there is a call to the InsertComponent method).

In other words, the two lines of code we suggested earlier for changing the Owner correspond to the following:

```
RemoveComponent (Button1);
Button1 := nil;
Form2.InsertComponent (Button1);
```

Obviously, this code isn't correct, since the last statement passes a nil value for the new component to insert in Form2. Fortunately, this isn't a big problem. The solution is to store a reference to the original component in a temporary variable before removing it:

```
procedure TForm1.Button2Click(Sender: TObject);
var
  AComp: TComponent;
begin
  if Assigned (Button1) then
  begin
    // change parent
    Button1.Parent := Form2;
    // change owner
    AComp := Button1;
    RemoveComponent (AComp);
    Form2.InsertComponent (AComp);
  end;
end;
```

This method (extracted from the ChangeOwner example) changes the owner and parent of the Button1 component, moving it to the second form. You can see the effect of this code in Figure 2.1.

FIGURE 2.1:

Pressing the Change button of the ChangeOwner example moves the Button1 component to the second form.

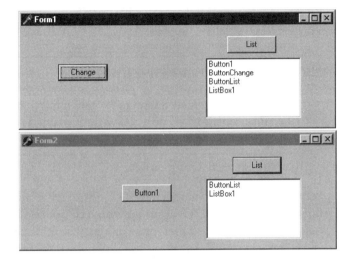

To demonstrate that the Owner of the Button1 component actually changes, we've added another feature to both forms. The *List* button fills the list box with the names of the components each form owns:

```
procedure TForm1.ButtonListClick(Sender: TObject);
var
  I: Integer;
begin
  ListBox1.Items.Clear;
  for I := 0 to ComponentCount - 1 do
    ListBox1.Items.Add (Components[I].Name);
end;
```

If you click the two buttons right after the program starts, you'll see the names of the components you placed on the forms at design-time. After changing the owner, however, the two lists will be different, as you can see in Figure 2.1.

There is a final feature of the ChangeOwner example to note. The Button1 component has a simple event handler, the Button1Click method of the TForm1 class:

```
procedure TForm1.Button1Click(Sender: TObject);
begin
```

```
ShowMessage ('My owner is ' +
  ((Sender as TButton).Owner as TForm).Caption);
end;
```

The resulting message indicates the owner of the button, and you can use it as a further test of the change. Notice that we had to convert the Sender parameter to the TButton class, and the button's Owner property to the TForm class.

> **NOTE**
>
> We cannot use the Name property of the Owner, simply because forms generally have no name (the name is set to an empty string). This causes confusion for many newcomers to Delphi; but it doesn't present a problem, because most of the code you write is inside form methods where you can reference the form object via the Self keyword.

What's important to realize is what happens when you change the Owner of the component. First, the value of the OnClick event of the Button1 component does not change. As a result, we end up with a component that is owned by the Form2 object, but has an event that refers to a method of the Form1 object. Destroying Form1 and clicking the button could generate a serious error. For our example, there's no problem, simply because destroying the main form of the program terminates the application.

To summarize, you can indeed change a component's owner, but you'll want to watch out for leftover references to other components or event handlers. Unfortunately, there's another problem that relates to the destruction of components: By changing the owner or removing it, you become responsible for destroying the object. To do this correctly, you should destroy objects only once.

Freeing an Object Twice

A frequent source of Delphi programming errors is freeing the same object twice. Of course, good programmers avoid memory leaks by freeing all objects they create. Unfortunately, some programmers become too aggressive in trying to avoid memory leaks, and free objects twice. This causes severe memory errors, and typically terminates the application instead of simply raising an exception. In some cases, freeing an object twice may even totally lock up the computer (particularly if you're running the program under the Delphi debugger).

To understand this problem, let's examine what happens when you call an object's Free method. In this method, Delphi calls the Destroy destructor unless the object reference is `nil`. For example, the following code produces an error, as you can see in Figure 2.2:

```
procedure TForm1.Button1Click(Sender: TObject);
var
  B: TButton;
begin
  B := TButton.Create (self);
  B.Free;
  B.Free;
end;
```

FIGURE 2.2:

The error message produced by the FreeTest program when you press the first button

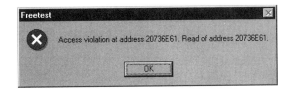

As we mentioned, when you're using the Delphi integrated debugger, the effect of pressing this button can really be dangerous. (Of course, you'd never intentionally call `Free` for an object twice in a row, but this might be the effect of executing multiple event handlers.) If you instead write:

```
  B.Free;
  B := nil;
  B.Free;
```

the program will run properly. To understand why, consider what happens when you call the `Free` method. First, it confirms that the object reference isn't `nil`. If it isn't, `Free` assumes the object still exists, uses the object reference to locate it, and then calls `Destroy` to release the memory for the object and clean up any relevant virtual method table information.

However, `Destroy` doesn't make any dramatic changes to the memory location where the object existed, so if you were to examine that memory after calling `Destroy`, it might still appear to be valid. This is the principal danger of freeing an object twice: some operations *might* still work on the destroyed object, but it's not predictable.

When you call `Free` twice for an object and don't set the object reference to `nil`, the object reference will still refer to the memory location where the object existed prior to destruction. While some operations might work (such as retrieving field values), calling a virtual method like Destroy will almost certainly fail, and with disastrous results. Setting the object reference to nil prevents the application from trying to reuse the memory of the destroyed object.

In addition to the simple event handler above, we've built the FreeTest program to demonstrate the double destruction problem that can occur when you free an object that has an owner. First, the right way:

```
procedure TForm1.Button2Click(Sender: TObject);
var
  B1, B2: TButton;
begin
  // correct code
  B1 := TButton.Create (self);
  B2 := TButton.Create (B1); // B1 is the owner
  B2.Free;
  B1.Free;
end;
```

The Button2Click method is correct: When you free an object that has an owner, the Destroy method calls the owner's RemoveComponent method to remove itself from the owner's list of components:

```
destructor TComponent.Destroy;
begin
  ...
  DestroyComponents;
  if FOwner <> nil then
    FOwner.RemoveComponent(Self);
  inherited Destroy;
end;
```

In the Button2Click method the call B2.Free removes the B2 object from the list of the objects owned by B1, so B1 won't try to free B2 during the B1.Destroy method. In contrast, the Button3Click method produces an error, even though it appears to do the same thing as Button2Click:

```
procedure TForm1.Button3Click(Sender: TObject);
var
  B1, B2: TButton;
begin
  // wrong code
  B1 := TButton.Create (self);
```

```
    B2 := TButton.Create (B1); // B1 is the owner
    B1.Free;
    B2.Free;
  end;
```

This time, we destroy the owner first. Calling B1.Destroy destroys the owned components:

```
procedure TComponent.DestroyComponents;
var
  Instance: TComponent;
begin
  while FComponents <> nil do
  begin
    Instance := FComponents.Last;
    Remove(Instance);
    Instance.Destroy;
  end;
end;
```

When the Button3Click method calls B1.Free, the B2 object is destroyed (but this doesn't set the B2 variable to nil). The following call to B2.Free produces an inevitable error, because B2 now contains the address of a destroyed object.

Avoiding this error is actually simple: You should almost never directly destroy an object that has an owner. However, there are at least two important exceptions to this rule: First, you can free an owned component before the owner is destroyed; second, you can free a component that appears in the published section of its owner's class declaration, as usually happens with forms. This second exception requires a more in-depth understanding of the ownership mechanism for forms, as you'll see shortly in the section "The Surprising Name Property."

For now, consider the following example. The FreeTest program destroys the components of its form while the form is being destroyed:

```
procedure TForm1.FormDestroy(Sender: TObject);
begin
  Button1.Free;
end;

destructor TForm1.Destroy;
begin
  Button2.Free;
  inherited Destroy;
```

```
    Button3.Free;
  end;
```

In the `FormDestroy` event handler (which executes before the VCL calls the form's `Destroy` method and before the destructor calls `inherited Destroy`), you can safely free the objects (according to the first exception to the rule, described above). At first glance, calling `Button3.Free` might seem to produce an error. However, this is not the case according to the second exception. When you free owned objects, if they correspond to `published` fields in the owner's class, these fields (which are object references) are automatically set to `nil`.

To demonstrate this, we've added an extra `private` field to the form class, called `Button4`; we've then created it in the `OnCreate` event handler and destroyed it in the destructor:

```
procedure TForm1.FormCreate(Sender: TObject);
begin
  Button4 := TButton.Create (self);
end;

destructor TForm1.Destroy;
begin
  Button2.Free; // OK
  inherited Destroy;
  Button3.Free; // OK
  Button4.Free; // Error!
end;
```

Although the call to `Button4.Free` seems to be similar to `Button3.Free`, one is correct while the other produces an error. The difference is that `Button3` is a published field of the class `TForm1`, while `Button4` is a private field.

The Surprising Name Property

We've already mentioned that the name of a component (the value of its `Name` property) has a special relationship with the name of the corresponding form class's field that references the component. This affects the `Name` property in some important ways.

We've built an example, called NameProp, to demonstrate various approaches to accessing an object other than just using the corresponding field in the owner form's class. Then we'll delve into the problem of changing the Name of a component at run-time, which is a questionable practice anyway.

The NameProp example's form contains a list box that the *Update* button's OnClick event handler uses to list all the names of a form's components, using the code we developed for the ChangeOwner example:

```
procedure TForm1.ButtonUpdateClick(Sender: TObject);
var
  I: Integer;
begin
  ListBox1.Items.Clear;
  for I := 0 to ComponentCount - 1 do
    ListBox1.Items.Add (Components [I].Name);
end;
```

You can see the result of the ButtonUpdateClick method in Figure 2.3.

FIGURE 2.3:

The output of the NameProp program after the Update button has been pressed

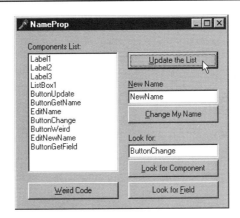

Using a form's Components property, you can always access each component of the form. However, if you need access to a specific component, you can use the owner form's FindComponent method instead of comparing the name of each component with the name of the component you are looking for. In fact, the TComponent class's FindComponent method compares a given name with the names of each component in the Components array, so it's not any faster than the code we might write:

```
function TComponent.FindComponent(
  const AName: string): TComponent;
var
```

```
    I: Integer;
begin
  if (AName <> '') and (FComponents <> nil) then
    for I := 0 to FComponents.Count - 1 do
    begin
      Result := FComponents[I];
      if CompareText(Result.FName, AName) = 0 then
        Exit;
    end;
  Result := nil;
end;
```

The Test button's OnClick event in the NameProp example shows how to use this method:

```
procedure TForm1.ButtonGetNameClick(Sender: TObject);
begin
  if FindComponent (EditName.Text) <> nil then
    ShowMessage (EditName.Text + ' component exists')
  else
    ShowMessage (EditName.Text +
      ' component doesn''t exist');
end;
```

If the form has a component with the name you enter in the edit box, you get a confirmation message; if not, you get an error message. In contrast, the *Change* button of the form does something very strange—it changes the Name property of a component:

```
procedure TForm1.ButtonChangeClick(Sender: TObject);
begin
  if Assigned (ButtonChange) then
    ButtonChange.Name := EditNewName.Text
  else
    Beep;
end;
```

While this code may appear quite innocent, assigning a new value for a component's Name property at run-time produces a *terrible side effect*: It will set the form field for that component to nil! The happens because the TComponent class's SetName method calls the SetReference method twice: It first disconnects the component from the form field, and then tries to reconnect the component to a field that corresponds with the component's new name.

```
procedure TComponent.SetName(const NewName: TComponentName);
begin
  if FName <> NewName then
  begin
    if (NewName <> '') and not IsValidIdent(NewName) then
      raise EComponentError.CreateFmt(
        SInvalidName, [NewName]);
    if FOwner <> nil then
      FOwner.ValidateRename(Self, FName, NewName)
    else
      ValidateRename(nil, FName, NewName);
    SetReference(False);
    ChangeName(NewName);
    SetReference(True);
  end;
end;
```

Calling the ChangeName method simply assigns a new value to the field that corresponds to the Name property. We've already discussed how the SetReference method works, but you might want to review it to make sure you understand what happens.

In our example, the effect is to set the ButtonChange object's field to nil. Naturally, if we try using the ButtonChange identifier later in the application, we'll undoubtedly see a memory protection error. This is why we placed the if Assigned statement at the beginning of the ButtonChangeClick method. If you run this program and click the Change button twice, on the second click you'll hear the beep. If you remove the if Assigned test, the second click will generate an exception.

After looking at the SetReference method's code, we realized that there are other ways to access a component. Instead of searching its owner's Components array (either directly or by calling FindComponent) you can look for the form field that corresponds to the component:

```
procedure TForm1.ButtonGetFieldClick(Sender: TObject);
var
  Field: ^TComponent;
begin
  Field := FieldAddress (EditName.Text);
  if Field <> nil then
  begin
    if Field^ = nil then
```

```
      ShowMessage (EditName.Text +
        ' field found, but not connected with a component')
    else
      ShowMessage (EditName.Text + ' field found');
  end;
end;
```

Consider for a moment that the field might not exist (in this case the Field-Address method returns nil). In other cases the field might exist but be set to nil, (that is, it may not refer to a component). This is exactly what happens if you change the name of the component by pressing the *Change* button. After doing this, look for a field called ButtonChange.

To sum up what we have seen in this section, the general rule for beginners is: Never change the value of the Name property of a component at run-time unless you have created that component at run-time. Expert Delphi programmers can change a component's Name property, although we haven't found any examples where this is particularly useful. For a nonsense example you can look at the handler of the OnClick event of the ButtonWeird component:

```
procedure TForm1.ButtonWeirdClick(Sender: TObject);
var
  Temp: TComponent;
begin
  // exchange the names
  Temp := ButtonUpdate;
  ButtonUpdate.Name := 'Temp999';
  ButtonWeird.Name := 'ButtonUpdate';
  Temp.Name := 'ButtonWeird';
  // which button is disabled/moved?
  ButtonUpdate.Enabled := False;
  ButtonWeird.Left := ButtonWeird.Left + 5;
end;
```

This method swaps the names of the two components. To accomplish this it uses a temporary name and a temporary component reference. Two components on the same form cannot have the same name, and when you assign the new name to ButtonWeird, the ButtonUpdate field is disconnected from the original component (however, you can still use the Temp reference).

In practice, this method's effect is to exchange the two fields of the form referring to the components. As a result, the last two statements of this method don't produce the effect you'd expect. When a user presses the button, the ButtonWeird component is disabled and the `ButtonUpdate` component is moved! Again, this is not a useful example, but it does demonstrate the power and extreme danger of these techniques.

Looking for a Component

We've already used several techniques to access components, but the basic one is the `FindComponent` function. If you browse the VCL source code, you may find a similar function with an interesting name, `FindGlobalComponent`. There's no online help for this function, so you might think it's a powerful, undocumented function you can use to find a component not in a specific form, but in any of the forms of the application.

Sadly, trying to use this function reveals it isn't that powerful; it simply finds a form or data module that has a given name. You can easily see this by looking at the function's source code:

```
function FindGlobalComponent(
  const Name: string): TComponent;
var
  I: Integer;
begin
  for I := 0 to Screen.FormCount - 1 do
  begin
    Result := Screen.Forms[I];
    if CompareText(Name, Result.Name) = 0 then
      Exit;
  end;
  for I := 0 to Screen.DataModuleCount - 1 do
  begin
    Result := Screen.DataModules[I];
    if CompareText(Name, Result.Name) = 0 then
      Exit;
  end;
  Result := nil;
end;
```

While this function isn't terribly useful, we can easily rewrite it to do what we want. In nearly every Delphi application, components are owned by either a form or a data module, so we can simply perform the search above, and then search inside each of the possible owners.

However, the problem is that component names aren't unique within an application. Two forms or data modules can both own a Button1 or Table1 component. To deal with this possibility, we could create a function that returns a TList reference and stores the found components in that list. Even better, we can return a TComponentList reference (the class definition is in the DsgnIntf unit). We'll discuss the TComponentList class in the next section, along with techniques to make a list type-safe. For the moment, simply think of a TComponentList as a list of TPersistent objects.

Here is the code of our revised FindGlobalComp function:

```
function FindGlobalComp (const Name: string;
  List: TComponentList): Boolean;
var
  I, J, InitCount: Integer;
  Form, Comp: TComponent;
begin
  InitCount := List.Count;
  for I := 0 to Screen.FormCount - 1 do
  begin
    Form := Screen.Forms[I];
    if CompareText(Name, Form.Name) = 0 then
      List.Add (Form);
    for J := 0 to Form.ComponentCount - 1 do
    begin
      Comp := Form.Components [J];
      if CompareText(Name, Comp.Name) = 0 then
        List.Add (Comp);
    end;
  end;
  for I := 0 to Screen.DataModuleCount - 1 do
  begin
    Form := Screen.DataModules[I];
    if CompareText(Name, Form.Name) = 0 then
      List.Add (Form);
    for J := 0 to Form.ComponentCount - 1 do
    begin
      Comp := Form.Components [J];
      if CompareText(Name, Comp.Name) = 0 then
```

```
        List.Add (Comp);
    end;
  end;
  // true if found
  Result := (List.Count - InitCount) > 0;
end;
```

NOTE   The original FindGlobalComponent function of the VCL returns an object that is created within the function. This is dangerous, as it may not be obvious to the user of the function that the object should be freed when it is no longer useful. An alternative approach is for the caller of the function to create the object and pass it as a parameter to the function. This is the approach we've used in our version of the function, which returns a Boolean value indicating whether any new object has been added to the list of components.

We use this function in the FindComp demo program. Its main form (see Figure 2.4) displays an edit box where a user can enter a component name, a button to perform the search, and a list box to show the results. Here is the code of the button's OnClick event handler:

```
procedure TForm1.Button1Click(Sender: TObject);
var
  I: Integer;
  Comp: TComponent;
  List: TComponentList;
begin
  ListBox1.Items.Clear;
  List := TComponentList.Create;
  try
    if not FindGlobalComp (Edit1.Text, List) then
      ListBox1.Items.Add ('No components found')
    else
      for I := 0 to List.Count - 1 do
      begin
        Comp := List.Items[I] as TComponent;
        ListBox1.Items.Add (Format (
          '%s (%s): %s (%s)',
          [Comp.Name, Comp.ClassName,
          Comp.Owner.Name, Comp.Owner.ClassName]));
      end;
```

```
        finally
            List.Free;
        end;
    end;
```

FIGURE 2.4:

The user interface
of the FindComp
program

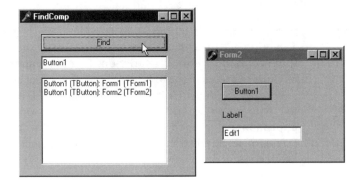

The Button1Click method above simply calls the FindGlobalComp function and then displays information for each of the found components, if any.

Type-Safe Lists

In the previous section, we used a custom list of objects, TComponentList. The reason for building custom list classes, instead of using TList, is that they are more *type-safe*. A TList object accepts any kind of data for its items. This is good for flexibility, but it means the compiler can't help you avoid adding the wrong type of object to a list that should contain only one type of data.

To ensure that the data in a list is homogenous, you can check the type of the data you extract before you use it. Similarly, you can check the type of the objects when you insert them in the list, which makes the list a little more type-safe. However, adding run-time type checking such as this is error-prone, slows down a program, and is risky—a programmer might fail to check the type in some of the data-access calls.

Building a List of a Specific Type

Instead, you can create specific list classes for given data types, and fashion the code from the existing TList class. There are two approaches to accomplish this:

- Derive a new class from TList and customize the Add method and the element access methods, which relate to the Items property.

- Create a brand-new class that contains a TList object, and map the methods of the new class to the internal list using proper type checking.

We've implemented both solutions (and a third one we'll describe later) in the DateList example, which defines a list of TDate objects. In the listing below you'll find the declaration of the two classes, the inheritance-based TDateListI class and the wrapper class TDateListW.

NOTE   A wrapper is a simple class that "wraps" around an existing record or data structure to simplify reading and writing the data with an OOP approach, or that "wraps" another class to provide a different or limited access to its functionalities. In this case TDateListW is a wrapper around the FList field of type TList and restricts the usage of the original class to a specific data type.

```
type
  // inheritance based
  TDateListI = class (TList)
  protected
    procedure Put(Index: Integer; Item: TDate);
    function Get (Index: Integer): TDate;
  public
    procedure Add (Obj: TDate);
    property Items[Index: Integer]: TDate
      read Get write Put; default;
  end;

  // wrapper based
  TDateListW = class(TObject)
  private
    FList: TList;
    function Get(Index: Integer): TDate;
    procedure Put(Index: Integer; Item: TDate);
```

```
      function GetCount: Integer;
    public
      constructor Create;
      destructor Destroy; override;
      function Add(Item: TDate): Integer;
      function Equals(List: TDateListW): Boolean;
      property Count: Integer
        read GetCount;
      property Items[Index: Integer]: TDate
        read Get; default;
    end;
```

Obviously, the first class is simpler to write—it has fewer methods—but it has some drawbacks, which we'll discuss in a moment. Here is the code for the TDateListI class's methods:

```
procedure TDateListI.Add (Obj: TDate);
begin
  inherited Add (Obj)
end;

procedure TDateListI.Put(Index: Integer; Item: TDate);
begin
  inherited Put (Index, Item)
end;

function TDateListI.Get (Index: Integer): TDate;
begin
  Result := inherited Get (Index);
end;
```

If you decide not to use inheritance, you end up writing a lot of code, because you need to reproduce each and every one of the original TList methods:

```
constructor TDateListW.Create;
begin
  inherited Create;
  FList := TList.Create;
end;

destructor TDateListW.Destroy;
begin
  FList.Free;
```

```
    inherited Destroy;
  end;

  function TDateListW.Get(Index: Integer): TDate;
  begin
    Result := FList[Index];
  end;

  procedure TDateListW.Put(Index: Integer; Item: TDate);
  begin
    FList[Index] := Item;
  end;

  function TDateListW.GetCount: Integer;
  begin
    Result := FList.Count;
  end;

  function TDateListW.Add(Item: TDate): Integer;
  begin
    Result := FList.Add(Item);
  end;

  function TDateListW.Equals(List: TDateListW): Boolean;
  var
    I: Integer;
  begin
    Result := False;
    if List.Count <> FList.Count then
      Exit;
    for I := 0 to List.Count - 1 do
      if List[I] <> FList[I] then
        Exit;
    Result := True;
  end;
```

Both of these approaches provide good type checking. After you've created an instance of one of these list classes, you can add only objects of the appropriate type, and the objects you extract will naturally be of the correct type. Everything seems to work fine, but the TDateListI class is subject to a risk: You can pass a TDateListI object to a routine that expects a TList, and that routine can then add other objects to the list as a result of the implicit conversion.

This is demonstrated by the DateList example. This program has a few buttons, a combo box to let a user choose which of the lists to show, and a list box to show the actual values of the list. At startup we create the two lists:

```
procedure TForm1.FormCreate(Sender: TObject);
begin
  ListI := TDateListI.Create;
  ListW := TDateListW.Create;
  ComboBox1.ItemIndex := 0;
end;
```

The first button adds ten items to each list, using random values, and then updates the output:

```
procedure TForm1.ButtonAddDatesClick(Sender: TObject);
var
  I: Integer;
  Date: TDate;
begin
  Randomize;
  for I := 1 to 10 do
  begin
    Date := TDate.Init (
      1 + Random (12),
      1 + Random (28), // required to be safe
      1900 + Random (200));
    ListI.Add (Date);
  end;
  // same code for ListW...
  UpdateList;
end;
```

The final call to the UpdateList method updates the content of the list box, which might also include an error message if the code raises any exceptions (as you can see in Figure 2.5):

```
procedure TForm1.UpdateList;
var
  I: Integer;
begin
  ListBox1.Clear;
  try
    if ComboBox1.ItemIndex = 0 then
      for I := 0 to ListI.Count - 1 do
```

The output of the DateList example when an error occurs: instead of displaying the exception information in a message box, the program adds the message of the exception to the list box.

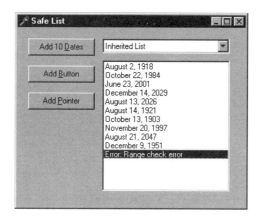

```
        Listbox1.Items.Add (ListI [I].GetText)
    else
      // same code for ListW...
    except
      on E:Exception do
        Listbox1.Items.Add ('Error: ' + E.MEssage);
    end;
  end;
```

Problems occur because the program adds a button and a pointer to the list of TDate objects. To add an object of a different type to the TDateListI list, we can simply convert the list to its base class, TList. This might accidentally happen if you pass the list as a parameter to a method that expects a base class object (and doesn't expect polymorphism).

In contrast, for the TDateListW list to fail we must explicitly cast the object to TDate before inserting it, something a programmer should never do:

```
procedure TForm1.ButtonAddButtonClick(Sender: TObject);
begin
  ListW.Add (TDate(Sender));
  TList(ListI).Add (Sender);
  UpdateList;
end;
```

Besides the error that appears when we update the list box, you'll get an error as you exit from the program when the OnDestroy event handler tries to free each of the objects of the list. It is much easier—and equally dangerous—to create problems using pointers, because a pointer is compatible with any type of object:

```
procedure TForm1.ButtonAddPointerClick(Sender: TObject);
var
  P: Pointer;
begin
  P := @Form1;
  ListW.Add (P);
  ListI.Add (P);
  UpdateList;
end;
```

Again, a wise programmer should never write the above code. Among the situations we've just described, the most dangerous is that of adding an object to a list derived from TList, after first casting the object to its base class. This should be a safe action, and it generally is!

Writing a wrapper list instead of one that's based on inheritance tends to be a little safer, although it requires more coding. Unfortunately, the Object Pascal language has no way to create generic types checked by the compiler, as templates allow you to do in the C++ language.

NOTE   Instead of rewriting wrapper-style list classes for different types, you can create a wizard that generates the code for a list that contains a given data type and then adds the new unit to the current project. This is not as powerful as a language mechanism, but it is quite handy. We'll show you how to build a list-template wizard in Chapter 14.

A Run-Time Safe List

Instead of creating a list for each kind of object, we can try to make the generic list a little safer by embedding type information into it. This technique relies on the use of class references, a topic we've covered in some detail in the previous chapter.

In contrast to a plain list, the safe list can have a constructor that requires a data type as a parameter. The Add and Put methods will then use this data type to confirm that the objects are of the proper type. This guarantees that all the objects in the list are compatible with a given type. To prevent someone from adding other data types after casting or converting the list to a base type, we'll declare the safe list in a separate class, which doesn't derive from TList.

Here is the declaration of the new class (available in the file SList.PAS of the SafeList example):

```
type
  TSafeList = class
  private
    LType: TClass;
    FList: TList;
    function Get (Index: Integer): TObject;
    procedure Put (Index: Integer; Item: TObject);
    function GetCount: Integer;
  public
    constructor Create (CType: TClass);
    destructor Destroy; override;
    function Add (Item: TObject): Integer;
    function Equals(List: TSafeList): Boolean;
    property Count: Integer
      read GetCount;
    property Items [Index: Integer]: TObject
      read Get write Put; default;
  end;
```

As you can see, the class redefines all of the methods of the original TList class, as we did for the TListDateW class of the previous section. The only new feature is the presence of a private field to store the class reference. We'll set this field in the constructor:

```
constructor TSafeList.Create (CType: TClass);
begin
  FList := TList.Create;
  LType := CType;
end;
```

Most of the methods contain the code you'd expect, with the exception of the Add and Put methods, which have to check the type of the object a program is trying to insert into the list. There are two checks the code has to make: the passed parameter must be an object, and it must be type-compatible with the class reference. By simply writing:

```
Item is LType;
```

you can perform both tests simultaneously. If Item is not an object, the test will raise an exception. If it *is* an object, the result of the is expression will indicate whether the object is compatible with the given type. Taking this into account, we can write the Add method in the following way:

```
function TSafeList.Add (Item: TObject): Integer;
var
  Test: Boolean;
begin
  try
    Test := Item is LType;
  except
    on Exception do
      raise EInvalidCast.Create (Format (
        'SafeList: Cannot add a non-object to ' +
        'a list of %s objects',
        [LType.ClassName]));
  end;
  if Test then
    Result := FList.Add (Item)
  else
    raise EInvalidCast.Create (Format (
      'SafeList: Cannot add a %s object to ' +
      'a list of %s objects',
      [Item.ClassName, LType.ClassName]));
end;
```

The try-except block at the beginning is necessary in case Obj isn't an object but a generic pointer or value. As we mentioned above, this case will raise an invalid memory access exception. Instead of letting the exception pass through (making it difficult to understand what went wrong), we can raise a new exception that explains the details (as you can see in Figure 2.6). The Put method has very similar code, so we haven't listed it in the text.

FIGURE 2.6:

The error message displayed by the SafeList example when the program tries to add a pointer to the list of dates

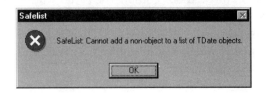

To test this class (which you can use in your own applications) we've built the SafeList example, which tests what happens when you try adding illegal data to the list. The form is similar to that of the last example, DateList. The form has a private data object of type TSafeList, called List. We initialize this object in the FormCreate method, and set the type we want to use:

```
procedure TForm1.FormCreate(Sender: TObject);
begin
  List := TSafeList.Create (TDate);
end;
```

The first button of the form adds a bunch of dates to the list, using random values, and then calls the custom UpdateList method, as in the previous example. However, if you click one of the other two *Add* buttons, the program displays an error message indicating that the data type isn't valid, as you saw in Figure 2.6 and you can see also in Figure 2.7:

```
procedure TForm1.ButtonAddButtonClick(Sender: TObject);
begin
  List.Add (Sender);
  UpdateList;
end;


procedure TForm1.ButtonAddPointerClick(Sender: TObject);
var
  P: Pointer;
begin
  P := @Form1;
  List.Add (P);
  UpdateList;
end;
```

Both of these methods produce errors, although they encounter different raise statements in the TSafeList class's Add method that we've shown before. The other three buttons of the form simply change the value of one of the existing objects, List[1], using either a TDate object, a button, or a pointer. You see similar behavior, but this time you are calling the Put method, instead of the Add method.

To summarize, there are three basic approaches to using lists. You can:

- Use plain lists and check the type of the items when you retrieve them from the list. This is what the VCL does most of the time, but if you forget to check the data type, you'll have problems.

FIGURE 2.7:

The main form of the SafeList program and the error message displayed when you add to the list an object of an incompatible data type

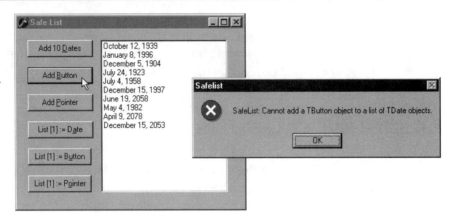

- Write a specific TList class for each type you want to handle, as we did in the previous section. This lets the compiler perform the type checking but it requires a lot of coding, unless you create a wizard, as we'll show you in Chapter 14.

- Use the TSafeList approach we've just discussed, and check the item types as you add them to the list. This is quite safe (and certainly better than using the plain TList class), but performs all the type checking at run-time instead of compile-time.

A completely different approach is to use the TCollection class. Collections, however, are more appropriate for properties of components, and aren't well suited to be general-purpose containers. Even so, they're a tool for component builders, and we'll discuss them in the next chapter.

What's Next

In this chapter we've covered many topics related to the use of components and unveiled many secrets of the basic classes of the VCL library. In the next chapter we'll focus on using VCL classes again, particularly the stream classes and the filer classes.

The next two chapters will complete our coverage of the foundations of the VCL library, and then we'll be able to move to a key topic: writing components. We'll explore other areas of the VCL in Chapter 7, which looks at the relationship between the VCL and the Windows API.

CHAPTER

THREE

3

Streaming and Persistency

Traditional Pascal programs manipulate files in several ways, such as using the Pascal file type or DOS and Windows file-handling routines. However, Delphi introduces a new concept—the *stream*—and uses it extensively. Since most Delphi books (including *Mastering Delphi 3*, by Marco Cantù) cover other forms of file handling, we've decided to provide an overview of Delphi's streaming capabilities instead.

Specifically, this chapter introduces the TStream class and its most common derivatives, the TReader and TWriter classes, the TPersistent class, and the TComponent class. Along the way, we'll examine how Delphi reads and writes form description files (files with a DFM extension), since these files are the most visible example of Delphi streams in action. While some of the examples in this chapter may seem trivial, they present important concepts that we'll build upon in later chapters.

Delphi Stream Classes

If you're not familiar with streams as a programming concept, the basic idea parallels streams in nature. Every stream has a definite beginning and end, and you can typically specify your position in terms relative to the beginning and end of the stream. In addition, just because you return to the same position in a stream, there's no guarantee that you're adjacent to the same water, plants, or fish.

Similarly, a stream in programming has a beginning and an end, and you can specify a position in that stream relative to those points. As with streams in nature, there's no guarantee that the same position in a given stream will yield the same data. With this in mind, you can probably think of many types of data whose behavior corresponds to a stream, such as blocks of memory, files on a disk, or even a series of bytes going to or from a serial or parallel port.

The Classes unit in the VCL defines an abstract class named TStream, and several direct descendant classes:

TFileStream defines a stream that manipulates a disk file (a file that exists on a local or network disk) represented by a filename. It inherits from THandleStream.

THandleStream defines a stream that manipulates a disk file represented by a Windows file handle.

TMemoryStream defines a stream that manipulates a sequence of bytes in memory. It inherits from TCustomMemoryStream.

TResourceStream defines a stream that manipulates a sequence of bytes in memory, and also provides resource conversion capabilities. It inherits from TCustomMemoryStream.

TBlobStream defines a stream that provides simple access to database BLOB fields.

TVirtualStream defines a sparsely documented class used by the Tool Services (or ToolsAPI) Delphi interfaces.

TOleStreamobject (introduced in Delphi 3) defines a stream for reading and writing information over the interface for streaming provided by an OLE .

TStringStream (introduced in Delphi 3) provides a simple way for streaming a long string.

TWinSocketStream (introduced in Delphi 3) provides streaming support for a socket connection.

NOTE The ToolsAPI (which we'll examine in Chapter 15) defines three more stream classes—TIStream, TIFileStream, and TIMemoryStream—which inherit not from TStream, but from a separate hierarchy.

The TStream class defines two properties, Size and Position, that are common to all of the stream classes. If you think of a stream as being similar to a piece of wire or string, you'll have a useful working analogy. Any given piece of wire, rope, or string has a definite size (length), and you typically work with the material at a specific position along that length. How you measure the position and size (inches, centimeters, or whatever) may be different from one material to another, but the concepts are the same.

Similarly, all stream objects have a specific size, and you must specify a position within the stream where you want to either read or write information. Reading and writing bytes in a THandleStream has a different result than reading and writing BLOB fields in a database, but in both cases you don't need to know much more than the size of the stream and your relative position in the stream to read or write data. In fact, that's one of the advantages of using streams. The basic interface remains the same whether you're manipulating a disk file, a BLOB field, or a long sequence of bytes in memory.

In addition to the Size and Position properties, the TStream class also defines several important methods, most of which are virtual and abstract. (In other words, the TStream class doesn't define what these methods do; therefore, derived classes are responsible for implementing them.) Some of these methods are important only in the context of reading or writing components within a stream (for instance, ReadComponent and WriteComponent), but some of these methods are useful in other contexts, too. Here is the declaration of the TStream class:

```
TStream = class(TObject)
public
  // read and write a buffer
  function Read(var Buffer; Count: Longint): Longint;
    virtual; abstract;
  function Write(const Buffer; Count: Longint): Longint;
    virtual; abstract;
  procedure ReadBuffer(var Buffer; Count: Longint);
  procedure WriteBuffer(const Buffer; Count: Longint);

  // move to a specific position
  function Seek(Offset: Longint; Origin: Word): Longint;
    virtual; abstract;

  // copy the stream
  function CopyFrom(Source: TStream; Count: Longint): Longint;

  // read or write a component
  function ReadComponent(Instance: TComponent): TComponent;
  function ReadComponentRes(Instance: TComponent): TComponent;
  procedure WriteComponent(Instance: TComponent);
  procedure WriteComponentRes(
    const ResName: string; Instance: TComponent);
  procedure WriteDescendent(Instance, Ancestor: TComponent);
  procedure WriteDescendentRes(
    const ResName: string; Instance, Ancestor: TComponent);
  procedure ReadResHeader;

  // properties
  property Position: Longint read GetPosition write SetPosition;
  property Size: Longint read GetSize;
end;
```

Obviously, it doesn't make sense to try to create a `TStream` object, since this class doesn't define how to read or write the data to the stream. Instead, the `TStream` class specifies a standard interface for all the stream classes. In fact, if you try to create a `TStream` object and access its methods, you'll probably generate an *Error 102* run-time error, which indicates that your program has called an `abstract` function but hasn't provided an implementation for the function.

Instead, you'll want to create instances of one of the derived classes, such as `TFileStream`. In fact, this class makes it very simple to manipulate the data in a disk file.

File Streams

As we mentioned earlier, the VCL defines two stream classes that you can use to manipulate files, `TFileStream` and `THandleStream`. If you know the name of the file you want to manipulate, but don't have a handle to the file already (a Windows file handle), you'll want to use `TFileStream`. For instance, if you prompt the user for a filename using one of the common dialog boxes, you'll determine the name of the file from the user's input. On the other hand, if you want to open and close a file using the Windows API functions, you'll want to use `THandleStream` to manipulate the file.

For either of these classes, you pass the appropriate file information in the `Create` constructor:

```
constructor TFileStream.Create(
   const FileName: string; Mode: Word);
constructor THandleStream.Create(AHandle: Integer);
```

Since the `TFileStream` constructor will attempt to open the file, you'll need to specify whether to share the contents of the file you are manipulating. The various modes (which appear in the online help) correlate with the `OF_XXX` mode values for the `OpenFile` function in the Windows API.

NOTE   Of the different modes, the most important are `fmShareDenyWrite`, which you'll use when you're simply reading data from a shared file, and `fmShareExclusive`, which you'll use when you're writing data to a shared file.

As you might expect, creating and using a file stream can be quite simple. In fact, most of the time you can simply create a stream and then call an appropriate component's method to read or write its data. For instance, the following classes define a `LoadFromStream` or `SaveToStream` method: `TBlobField`, `TGraphicField`, `TMemoField`, `TOutline`, `TStrings`, `TStringList`, `TMetafile`, `TIcon`, and `TBitmap`.

Interestingly, many of the VCL components (including some of the ones we've listed above) also provide methods you can use to load or save their data directly to a file. Obviously, if you know that your application will always be reading or writing component data using a file, it makes more sense to use these direct methods instead of creating a stream object and then passing that object to the component for reading and writing tasks. However, this approach doesn't save a great deal of code, and it does limit your options rather dramatically (it won't be easy to change the program so that it uses a region of memory instead of a file).

In contrast, copying a `TFileStream` or `THandleStream` is simply a matter of calling the `CopyFrom` method. This is much easier than setting up buffers yourself and performing explicit read and write operations on a file.

Streaming Methods in Action: the MemoStr Program

To see some of the methods mentioned in the last paragraph in action, let's take a look at the MemoStr program, shown in Figure 3.1. (Again, you can find the executable and source files on the CD in the DdhCode\03\MemoStr\ folder; the same DdhCode*chapter number**program name*\ structure is used for all of the examples.)

FIGURE 3.1:

The MemoStr example displays a Memo component and three buttons to load, save, and copy files.

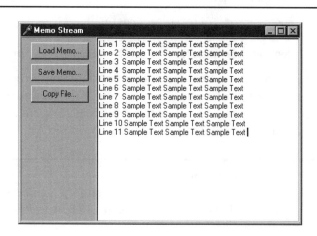

In this example, we use TFileStream objects to perform the following tasks:

- Load data into a Memo component from a file.
- Save a Memo component's data to a file.
- Copy a file.

To handle each task, we've provided a Button component and a corresponding event handler:

```
procedure TForm1.ButtonSaveMemoClick(Sender: TObject);
var
  MyStream: TFileStream;
begin
  if SaveDialog1.Execute then
  begin
    if FileExists (SaveDialog1.FileName) then
      MyStream := TFileStream.Create (
        SaveDialog1.FileName, fmOpenWrite)
    else
      MyStream := TFileStream.Create (
        SaveDialog1.FileName, fmOpenWrite or fmCreate);
    try
      Memo1.Lines.SaveToStream (MyStream);
    finally
      MyStream.Free;
    end;
  end;
end;


procedure TForm1.ButtonLoadMemoClick(Sender: TObject);
var
  MyStream: TFileStream;
begin
  if OpenDialog1.Execute then
  begin
    MyStream := TFileStream.Create (
      OpenDialog1.FileName, fmOpenRead);
    try
      Memo1.Lines.LoadFromStream (MyStream);
    finally
      MyStream.Free;
    end;
  end;
end;
```

```
procedure TForm1.ButtonCopyFileClick(Sender: TObject);
var
  Stream1, Stream2: TFileStream;
begin
  if OpenDialog1.Execute and SaveDialog1.Execute then
  begin
    Stream1 := TFileStream.Create (
      Open Dialog1.FileName, fmOpenRead);
    try
      Stream2 := TFileStream.Create (
        SaveDialog1.FileName, fmOpenWrite or fmCreate);
      try
        Stream2.CopyFrom (Stream1, Stream1.Size);
      finally
        Stream2.Free;
      end;
    finally
      Stream1.Free;
    end;
  end;
end;
```

Now that you've seen some basic examples of how file stream objects are used, we can move on to an example of the use of a memory stream object, and then proceed with more advanced topics.

Memory Streams

In the MemoStr example, we showed how you can copy a file using TFileStream objects. To do so, we didn't have to create an in-memory buffer, because the TFileStream classes automatically handle this for you.

However, there are some cases where you'll want to create an explicit region of memory so that you can perform operations on the data without the speed limitations of accessing a file. In this case, you'll want to create a TMemoryStream object, which operates just like any other stream (having both Size and Position properties), but operates on a region of memory instead of reading and writing data in a disk file.

Obviously, you need to import data into a memory region in the first place. To do that, the TMemoryStream class defines special methods to copy its contents to or from another stream, which may be a TFileStream, THandleStream, or other stream object. TMemoryStream objects are particularly useful when you need to create a temporary stream or simulate a temporary file in memory.

In addition to the Size and Position properties that it inherits from the TStream class, the TMemoryStream class inherits a Memory property from the TCustomMemoryStream class. This property simply returns a pointer to the block of memory that the TMemoryStream object manipulates. Once you have this pointer, you can perform operations on it; but you can't do so directly, because it's a read-only property. To associate the object with another block of memory (perhaps one that already contains data), you'll use the SetPointer method.

The MemoryS Program Example

As an example, let's examine the MemoryS program. In this program, we provide two buttons: one to load data from a file into a TMemoryStream, and the other to display this data using the Memory property we described above. Figure 3.2 shows the main form of the MemoryS example.

FIGURE 3.2:

The MemoryS example loads files into a Memo component using a TMemoryStream object.

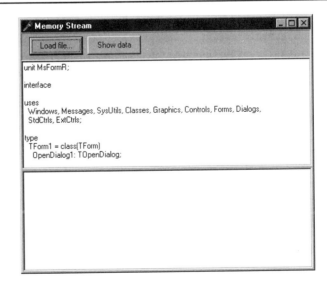

First, you'll notice that we've declared the memory stream as a private field of the form. We did this because we'll want to use the same TMemoryStream object across function or procedure calls. One of these calls is the ShowMemStr procedure, which we'll use to display the contents of the memory stream via the Memory property.

```
private
  MemStr1: TMemoryStream;
  procedure ShowMemStr;
```

As you would expect, we create the memory stream in the form's OnCreate event handler:

```
procedure TForm1.FormCreate(Sender: TObject);
begin
  MemStr1 := TMemoryStream.Create;
end;
```

Similarly, we delete it in the form's OnDestroy event handler:

```
procedure TForm1.FormDestroy(Sender: TObject);begin
  MemStr1.Free;
end;
```

When the user clicks the *Load File* button, we'll load the data into the TMemoryStream using a TFileStream:

```
procedure TForm1.Button1Click(Sender: TObject);
var
  Str1: TFileStream;
begin
  OpenDialog1.Filter :=
    'Any file (*.*)|*.*';
  OpenDialog1.DefaultExt := '*';
  if OpenDialog1.Execute then
  begin
    Str1 := TFileStream.Create (
      OpenDialog1.Filename, fmOpenRead);
    try
      MemStr1.LoadFromStream (Str1);
      ShowMemStr;
      Button2.Enabled := true;
    finally
      Str1.Free;
    end;
```

```
    end;
  end;
```

The only new code we're using here is a call to the LoadFromStream method, which simply copies the data from the file stream to the memory stream. In fact, since the TMemoryStream class provides a LoadFromFile method, we could have used that method in the following manner:

```
procedure TForm1.Button1Click(Sender: TObject);
begin
  OpenDialog1.Filter :=
    'Any file (*.*)|*.*';
  OpenDialog1.DefaultExt := '*';
  if OpenDialog1.Execute then
  begin
    MemStr1.LoadFromFile (OpenDialog1.Filename);
    ShowMemStr;
    end;
  end;
end;
```

Next, we simply copy the data from the memory stream into the Memo component using the TMemo class's LoadFromStream method.

Copying the memory stream to the Memo is straightforward:

```
procedure TForm1.ShowMemStr;
begin
  Memo1.Lines.LoadFromStream (MemStr1);
end;
```

Obviously, we could have simply loaded the file directly into the Memo component by changing the Load File event handler to

```
procedure TForm1.Button1Click(Sender: TObject);
begin
  OpenDialog1.Filter :=
    'Any file (*.*)|*.*';
  OpenDialog1.DefaultExt := '*';
  if OpenDialog1.Execute then
  begin
    Memo1.Lines.LoadFromFile (OpenDialog1.Filename);
    end;
  end;
end;
```

However, this approach wouldn't have initialized the memory stream with the data, as we want to do in this example.

Finally, we provide a button named *Show Data*. When the user clicks this button, we execute some rather complex code to display the data in the memory stream via the Memory property. In a first version of the example (not on the companion CD) we wrote the following code:

```
procedure TForm1.Button2Click(Sender: TObject);
var
  pch: PChar;
begin
  pch := MemStr1.Memory;
  while (pch <> nil) and (MessageDlg (
      'Character is ' + pch^ + #13#13 +
      'Do you want to see the following one?',
      mtConfirmation, [mbYes, mbNo], 0) = mrYes) do
    Inc(pch);
end;
```

This function begins by initializing a Char pointer, pch, to address the memory location at the beginning of the memory stream. Next, we enter a while loop that first checks to see if the pch pointer is nil, and then displays a dialog box and checks the user's response. In the process of displaying the dialog box, we build a string that contains the character that the Char pointer is addressing by simply dereferencing the pointer (pch^). If the user selects the *Yes* button in this dialog box, we then increment the pointer using Inc(pch).

To examine each successive character, we simply increment the pointer. You'll notice that we used the Inc procedure to do this instead of writing

```
pch := pch + 1;
```

We did this because even though Object Pascal supports pointer arithmetic for some data types (such as PChar), it doesn't support it as a general language feature. In fact, by declaring

```
var
  pch : ^Char;
```

we would have made it impossible to apply the standard arithmetic operations on the pointer.

In contrast, the Inc procedure manipulates pointers based on the size of the data the pointer is addressing. Since the type of the pointer specifies that it addresses individual bytes (characters), calling Inc with this type of pointer will simply move the pointer to address the next byte.

Why doesn't Object Pascal support pointer arithmetic, as C/C++ does? Because pointer arithmetic is a common source of errors. Instead, Object Pascal uses information about a pointer's data type to enable you to apply the Inc and Dec procedures to a pointer safely.

This approach is interesting, but the user has to click OK over and over. For this reason we decided to change the code, and show the initial characters of the text in the memory stream inside the list box in the lower portion of the screen. To accomplish this we actually use a trick: we write a null character in the memory stream to indicate the end of the portion of the string we want to display. After showing the data in the list box, we then restore the character.

The interesting aspect of this code is that it shows how to change the data in the memory stream, by accessing it directly with a pointer (although you'll need to pay attention to follow the pointer arithmetic in this method):

```
procedure TForm1.Button2Click(Sender: TObject);
const
  ndx: LongInt = 1;
var
  pch:  PChar;
  tmpC: Char;
begin
  pch := MemStr1.Memory;
  tmpC := pch[ndx];
  pch[ndx] := #0;
  ListBox1.Items.SetText(MemStr1.Memory);
  pch[ndx] := tmpC;

  if ndx < MemStr1.Size then
    Inc(ndx)
  else
    Button2.Enabled := False;
end;
```

This time we access a specific location inside the memory block by using a PChar and the square brackets to reference a specific byte of memory as the nth character of a string.

Notice also the usage of a local constant to keep a value in memory between different executions of this method, without adding a local field to the form. Figure 3.3 shows the result when you load a file into the Memo and then begin viewing the data from the memory stream, adding it to the list box below.

The dialog box displays individual characters from the memory stream.

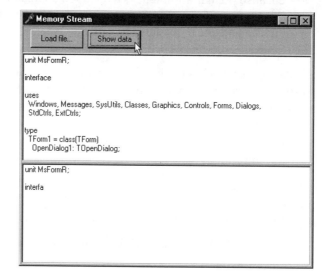

Writing a Custom Stream Class

Besides using the existing stream classes, Delphi programmers can write their own stream classes, and use them in place of the existing ones. To accomplish this, you need only specify how a generic block of row data is saved and loaded, and the VCL will be able to use your new class wherever you call for it. You may not need to create a brand-new stream class for working with a new type of media, but only need to customize an existing stream. In that case, all you have to do is write the proper read and write methods.

As an example, we decided to create a class to encode and decode a generic file stream. Although this example is limited by its use of a dumb encoding mechanism, it fully integrates with the VCL and works properly. The new stream class simply declares the two core reading and writing methods, and has a property that stores a key.

```
type
  TEncodedStream = class (TFileStream)
  private
    FKey: Char;
  public
    constructor Create(
      const FileName: string; Mode: Word);
    function Read(var Buffer; Count: Longint):
      Longint; override;
    function Write(const Buffer; Count: Longint):
      Longint; override;
    property Key: Char
      read FKey write FKey default 'A';
  end;
```

The value of the key is simply added to each of the bytes saved to a file, and subtracted when the data is read. Here is the complete code of the two methods:

```
constructor TEncodedStream.Create(
  const FileName: string; Mode: Word);
begin
  inherited Create (FileName, Mode);
  FKey := 'A';
end;

function TEncodedStream.Write(const Buffer;
  Count: Longint): Longint;
var
  pBuf, pEnc: PChar;
  I, EncVal: Integer;
begin
  // allocate memory for the encoded buffer
  GetMem (pEnc, Count);
  try
    // use the buffer as an array of characters
    pBuf := PChar (@Buffer);
    // for every character of the buffer
    for I := 0 to Count - 1 do
    begin
      // encode the value and store it
      EncVal := ( Ord (pBuf[I]) + Ord(Key) ) mod 256;
      pEnc [I] := Chr (EncVal);
    end;
```

```
        // write the encoded buffer to the file
        Result := inherited Write (pEnc^, Count);
      finally
        FreeMem (pEnc, Count);
      end;
  end;


  function TEncodedStream.Read(var Buffer;
    Count: Longint): Longint;
  var
    pBuf, pEnc: PChar;
    I, CountRead, EncVal: Integer;
  begin
    // allocate memory for the encoded buffer
    GetMem (pEnc, Count);
    try
      // read the encoded buffer from the file
      CountRead := inherited Read (pEnc^, Count);
      // use the output buffer as a string
      pBuf := PChar (@Buffer);
      // for every character actually read
      for I := 0 to CountRead - 1 do
      begin
        // decode the value and store it
        EncVal := ( Ord (pEnc[I]) - Ord(Key) ) mod 256;
        pBuf [I] := Chr (EncVal);
      end;
    finally
      FreeMem (pEnc, Count);
    end;
    // return the number of characters read
    Result := CountRead;
  end;
```

The comments in the code should help you understand the details. Now that we have a simple encoded stream, we can try to use it in a demo program, which is called EncDemo. The form of this program has two memo components and three buttons: The first button loads a plain text file in the first memo; the second button saves the text of this first memo in an encoded file; and the last button reloads the encoded file into the second memo, decoding it.

Figure 3.4 shows the form displayed by this program at run-time. In this figure, after encoding the file, we've loaded it again in the first memo as a plain text file, but of course it is not readable.

FIGURE 3.4:

An example of the EncDemo program. On the left you can see an encoded file (*Encoded.TXT*), and on the right the same file after it has been decoded.

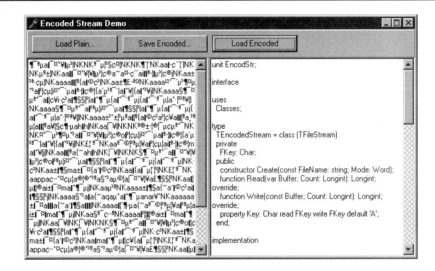

Since we have the encoded stream class available, the code of this program is very similar to that of any other program using streams. For example, here are the two methods used to load or save the encoded file (you can compare them to the methods based on streams shown earlier in this chapter):

```
procedure TFormEncode.BtnSaveEncodedClick(Sender: TObject);
var
  EncStr: TEncodedStream;
begin
  if SaveDialog1.Execute then
  begin
    EncStr := TEncodedStream.Create(
      SaveDialog1.Filename, fmCreate);
    try
      Memo1.Lines.SaveToStream (EncStr);
    finally
      EncStr.Free;
    end;
  end;
end;
```

```
procedure TFormEncode.BtnLoadEncodedClick(Sender: TObject);
var
  EncStr: TEncodedStream;
begin
  if OpenDialog1.Execute then
  begin
    EncStr := TEncodedStream.Create(
      OpenDialog1.FileName, fmOpenRead);
    try
      Memo2.Lines.LoadFromStream (EncStr);
    finally
      EncStr.Free;
    end;
  end;
end;
```

The TReader and TWriter Classes

By themselves, the stream classes of the VCL don't provide much support for reading or writing data. In fact, these classes don't implement much beyond simply reading and writing blocks of data. If you want to load or save specific data types in a stream (and don't want to perform a great deal of casting), you'll need to use the TReader and TWriter classes, which derive from the TFiler class.

Basically, the TReader and TWriter classes exist to simplify loading and saving stream data according to its type, and not just as a sequence of bytes. To do this, TWriter embeds special signatures into the stream which specify the type for each object's data. Conversely, the TReader class reads these signatures from the stream, creates the appropriate objects, and then initializes those objects using the subsequent data from the stream.

In addition to reading and writing simple objects in a stream, these classes also support loading and saving a series (or list) of elements. (Don't confuse the term *list* in this context with the TList VCL class. They're completely different.)

Here are the different writing methods of the TWriter class, demonstrating that you can use this class to write all of the standard data types:

```
procedure Write(const Buf; Count: Longint);
procedure WriteBoolean(Value: Boolean);
procedure WriteCollection(Value: TCollection);
```

```
procedure WriteComponent(Component: TComponent);
procedure WriteChar(Value: Char);
procedure WriteDescendent(
  Root: TComponent; AAncestor: TComponent);
procedure WriteFloat(Value: Extended);
procedure WriteIdent(const Ident: string);
procedure WriteInteger(Value: Longint);
procedure WriteListBegin;
procedure WriteListEnd;
procedure WriteRootComponent(Root: TComponent);
procedure WriteSignature;
procedure WriteStr(const Value: string);
procedure WriteString(const Value: string);
```

As you would expect, the TReader class defines corresponding reading methods for each of these types. Notice the WriteListBegin and WriteListEnd methods; WriteListBegin inserts into the stream a marker that identifies the beginning of a list, and WriteListEnd inserts a similar marker that identifies the end of a list. In between those two markers, every item that appears is part of the list.

When a TReader object reads the information back from a stream, it begins building the list of items when it reads the beginning marker, and finishes building the list when it encounters the ending marker. To test for the ending marker, you can call the TReader.EndOfList method.

The ReadWrite Program

Now let's look at an example that uses the TReader and TWriter classes, appropriately named ReadWrite. Figure 3.5 shows the main form of this example.

As you can see, we've based this example on a Memo component, just like the previous examples; and to load the text, we provide a *Read Text File* button. However, in this program, you can save the text of the Memo as a list of strings. To do so, we use a TWriter object:

```
procedure TForm1.ButtonWriteLinesClick(Sender: TObject);
var
  Str1: TFileStream;
  Writer1: TWriter;
  I: Integer;
begin
  SaveDialog1.Filter :=
```

FIGURE 3.5:

The ReadWrite program can reverse and scramble the lines from a text file.

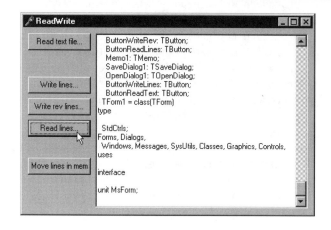

```
          'Read Write file (*.rwf)|*.rwf|Any file (*.*)|*.*';
   SaveDialog1.FilterIndex := 1;
   SaveDialog1.DefaultExt := 'rwf';
   if SaveDialog1.Execute then
   begin
     Str1 := TFileStream.Create (
       SaveDialog1.FileName, fmCreate or fmOpenWrite);
     Writer1 := TWriter.Create (Str1, 1024);
     try
       Writer1.WriteListBegin;
       for I := 0 to Memo1.Lines.Count - 1 do
         Writer1.WriteString (Memo1.Lines [I]);
       Writer1.WriteListEnd;
     finally
       Writer1.Free;
       Str1.Free;
     end;
   end;
end;
```

When the user clicks the *Write Lines* button, we use the SaveDialog1 component to retrieve the filename, and then create a TFileStream using the name the user provides. Next we create a TWriter object, and, in the Create constructor, associate it with the TFileStream and set the size of its buffer to 1024. Finally, we call WriteListBegin, call the WriteString method to output each of the lines of the Memo component, and then call the WriteListEnd method.

In the event handler above, notice that we're altering the `Filter` and `DefaultExt` properties of the `SaveDialog1` object. We've done this to force a new extension—specifically, RWF—for a file stream that comprises a list of lines. Similarly, we'll look for the same file extension when we're ready to read a list of lines in a file stream.

This is important, because embedding the beginning and ending markers for the list, along with markers to identify the type of each item within the list as a string, turns the file stream into something other than a simple text file. To confirm this, you can try using a text editor such as NotePad to open the RWF files that this example produces. Figure 3.6 shows the result of trying to view a RWF file in a text editor.

FIGURE 3.6:

You can see the effect of the TWriter type markers by opening an RWF file in a text editor.

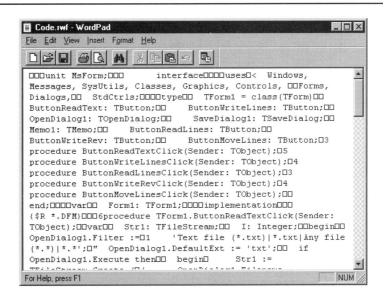

Now let's consider some other ways we can store the data from the Memo component. If the user clicks the *Write Rev Lines* button, we execute an event handler similar to the previous one, but we cycle through the lines of the Memo component in reverse order:

```
Writer1.WriteListBegin;
for I := Memo1.Lines.Count - 1 downto 0 do
  Writer1.WriteString (Memo1.Lines [I]);
Writer1.WriteListEnd;
```

Except for reversing the order of the lines, the format of the file is the same, including the beginning and ending markers for the list, and the type markers for each of the strings.

When the user clicks on the *Read Lines* button, we read the list of strings back in from the file stream:

```
procedure TForm1.ButtonReadLinesClick(Sender: TObject);
var
  Str1: TFileStream;
  Reader1: TReader;
  I: Integer;
begin
  OpenDialog1.Filter :=
    'Text File (*.txt)|*.txt|Pascal File (*.pas)|*.pas|' +
    'ReadWrite File (*.rwt)|*.rwt|Any file (*.*)|*.*';
  OpenDialog1.FilterIndex := 1;
  OpenDialog1.DefaultExt := 'rwt';
  if OpenDialog1.Execute then
  begin
    Str1 := TFileStream.Create (
      OpenDialog1.Filename, fmOpenRead);
    Reader1 := TReader.Create (Str1, 1024);
    try
      Reader1.ReadListBegin;
      Memo1.Lines.Clear;
      while not Reader1.EndOfList do
      begin
        Memo1.Lines.Add (Reader1.ReadString);
        Application.ProcessMessages;
      end;
      Reader1.ReadListEnd;
    finally
      Reader1.Free;
      Str1.Free;
    end;
    // enable all buttons
    for I := 0 to ControlCount - 1 do
      if Controls [I] is TButton then
        TButton (Controls [I]).Enabled := True;
  end;
end;
```

As we mentioned earlier, you can use the `TReader` class's `EndOfList` method to test for a stream's list-ending marker. In this event handler, we perform the test using:

```
while not Reader1.EndOfList do
```

We can now create a list of strings, even though we don't know in advance how big that list will be. Also, keep in mind that the only way to test for the presence of the list's ending marker is to read past the marker in the stream. This read operation also makes sure that subsequent read operations (to read objects that may be in the stream following the list of strings) don't encounter the list's ending marker.

You may have noticed that using the *Read Lines* button to load the Memo takes quite a while. This is because we haven't disabled the Memo component and are loading the lines one by one. (This is the effect we wanted, because it allows you to see the loading take place.) To make sure that the application still responds to user commands during this time, we call the `ProcessMessages` method of the `Application` global object. Unfortunately, since we haven't disabled the *Read Lines* button, it's possible to interrupt the loading process by reading in a new file, which produces some strange results.

At the end of this function, we enable the other button components that are disabled at design time. It doesn't make sense to enable them unless we've loaded a file into the Memo. You'll notice that this code isn't part of the `finally` block. As you'll recall, any code that you place in this section of a `try-finally` block will execute whether there's an exception or not. By placing the code to enable these buttons after the end of the `try-finally` block, we can ensure that the code won't execute if there's an exception. (The program will exit this procedure at the end of the `try-finally` block and skip the button-enabling code.)

In the event handler for the *Write Rev Lines* button, we saved the lines of the Memo component in reverse order. If you want to perform this operation on the Memo, you can do so by writing the lines to a memory stream. Simply create the memory stream, save the data in some other order using a `TWriter` object (as we've already done), read the data back in using a `TReader` object, and then destroy the memory stream. We do this in the example when the user clicks on the *Move Lines In Mem* button:

```
procedure TForm1.ButtonMoveLinesClick(Sender: TObject);
var
  MemStr1: TMemoryStream;
```

```
      Writer1: TWriter;
      Reader1: TReader;
      I: Integer;
    begin
      MemStr1 := TMemoryStream.Create;
      try
        Writer1 := TWriter.Create (MemStr1, 1024);
        try
          Writer1.WriteListBegin;
          Randomize;
          while Memo1.Lines.Count > 0 do
          begin
            I := Random (Memo1.Lines.Count);
            Writer1.WriteString (Memo1.Lines [I]);
            Memo1.Lines.Delete (I);
            Application.ProcessMessages;
          end;
          Writer1.WriteListEnd;
        finally
          Writer1.Free;
        end;
        // reset, rewind, move back
        // to the beginning of the stream
        MemStr1.Seek (0, soFromBeginning);
        Reader1 := TReader.Create (MemStr1, 1024);
        try
          Reader1.ReadListBegin;
          while not Reader1.EndOfList do
          begin
            Memo1.Lines.Add (Reader1.ReadString);
            Application.ProcessMessages;
          end;
          Reader1.ReadListEnd;
        finally
          Reader1.Free;
        end;
      finally
        memStr1.Free;
      end;
    end;
```

In this event handler, we take exactly the steps we just described, except that we use the Random function to reorder the lines in the Memo. If you load a Pascal source file and click the *Move Lines In Mem* button, you'll probably see some amusing results, as shown in Figure 3.7.

FIGURE 3.7:

You can use the ReadWrite program to reorder the lines of a Pascal source file.

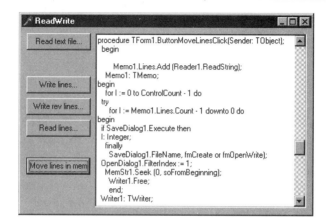

By the way, if you examine this event handler closely you'll notice that we call

```
MemStr1.Seek (0, soFromBeginning);
```

before we try to use another TFiler object with a stream. This call resets the Position property of the stream so that subsequent read or write operations will start at the beginning of the file. This is necessary because a TFiler object doesn't reset its associated stream when it reaches the end.

Writing and Reading Components

For the Delphi environment, streaming plays a crucial role in the IDE's ability to save and load the state and properties of components. In fact, most of the support that Delphi provides for streaming was necessary so that Delphi can provide the design-time environment that it has. When it comes to reading and writing something other than the simple types that TReader and TWriter can handle, the TPersistent class adds the necessary functionality. TPersistent is a low-level class, and most of the VCL classes derive from it.

The TPersistent Class

As its name implies, the TPersistent class specifies an interface for derived classes to use for saving and restoring an object's state or field information. If you examine the source code for this class, you may be surprised to see how simple the class is, and you might wonder how it could be so important to Delphi. Here's the entire class declaration:

```
TPersistent = class(TObject)
  private
    procedure AssignError(Source: TPersistent);
  protected
    procedure AssignTo(Dest: TPersistent); virtual;
    procedure DefineProperties(Filer: TFiler); virtual;
    function GetOwner: TPersistent; dynamic;
  public
    destructor Destroy; override;
    procedure Assign(Source: TPersistent); virtual;
    function GetNamePath: string; dynamic;
  end;
```

Let's examine the work done by these six methods.

AssignError is a private method that raises an exception if your program calls the base version of the AssignTo virtual method.

Assign is a public method that allows a component to copy its data to another component of the same class. The default implementation checks for a nil Source parameter and calls the virtual AssignTo method if the Source object is valid. Several classes override the Assign method to check for an exact class match prior to copying the object data. If the classes don't match, the version of Assign for that class typically calls the TPersistent version, which raises an exception.

AssignTo is a protected, virtual method that derived classes override to customize the copy operation when the Source class doesn't match the destination class. The default version of the AssignTo method is not a virtual abstract method; its code simply raises a conversion error. One reason for this behavior may be to avoid the error you see when your program calls a virtual abstract method that hasn't been implemented. This doesn't generate an exception—it terminates the program.

DefineProperties is a protected, virtual method that derived classes can use to create pseudoproperties (properties that don't map directly to a field) that the class will store and load along with the normal properties.

GetOwner returns the owner of the component. The default implementation simply returns nil. This method is used by the GetNamePath method.

GetNamePath is an internal method used by the Object Inspector to determine the name of a collection object and let the Object Inspector display it along with the other properties. (We'll see an example of this in Chapter 13.)

Now, even though this class is so simple, the TWriter class can use its WriteProperties method and the RTTI (Run-Time Type Information) of a class to save the published properties of a TPersistent-derived object. We'll examine this subject in more detail in Chapter 4. In the meantime, let's consider how we could go about storing and loading user-defined objects in a stream, and then we'll consider the streaming of components.

Writing and Reading a Simple Custom Object

To read or write an object's data in a stream, you can take either of two routes. The first approach is to create your own "read data" and "write data" methods, and then call those methods from within your own custom streaming framework. This is the simplest solution, and one that you've probably seen in various articles in Delphi magazines. The other technique involves learning to stream components the same way the VCL does, which is not particularly easy and is not well documented. This is the approach we'll pursue, because we want to learn how to use Delphi effectively, not how to build our own structure on top of the VCL.

As we mentioned above, the TWriter class's WriteProperties method is capable of saving the published properties of a class by taking advantage of its RTTI information. Unfortunately, WriteProperties is a private method, and therefore isn't accessible outside TWriter. However, a bit of research reveals that the TWriter class's WriteData and WriteCollection methods call this method, and both of these methods are public. Not coincidentally, these two methods are essential for reading and writing object data for anything other than the basic or simple types (Boolean, String, Float, Char, and so on).

Now let's consider a user-defined type that we might want to store and load in a stream:

```
type
  TDdhPoint = class (TPersistent)
```

```
private
  fX, fY: Integer;
public
  Text: string;
  procedure WriteText (Writer: TWriter);
  procedure ReadText (Reader: TReader);
  procedure DefineProperties (Filer: TFiler); override;
  procedure Paint (Canvas: TCanvas);
published
  property X: Integer
    read fX write fX;
  property Y: Integer
    read fY write fY;
end;
```

This class simply represents a point that can paint a circle (on an appropriate Canvas component) at its coordinate position, along with an identifying label. We've defined this in the Paint method:

```
procedure TDdhPoint.Paint (Canvas: TCanvas);
begin
  Canvas.Ellipse (fX - 3, fY - 3, fX + 3, fY + 3);
  Canvas.TextOut (fX + 5, fY + 5, Text);
end;
```

We publish two properties, X and Y, which represent the position of the point. However, we also want to store and load the Text field, which isn't a property, but simply a public field.

NOTE

Properties are an important element of Object Pascal, and much of Delphi's RTTI functionality is based on them. At the most basic level, properties are simply persistent fields. In this light, it's easy to see how properties, streams, and the Delphi design-time environment are interdependent. We'll examine properties more closely in Chapters 4 and 5.

We can solve this problem in either of two ways. The first is simply to publish the Text field as a property by renaming the field fText and then adding a property declaration, such as:

```
property Text: String read fText write fText;
```

The second way to store and load this data is to override the DefineProperties by creating a pseudoproperty (a property that doesn't map directly to a field) for the Text field. In fact, this is how nonvisual components store their position, and we'll look at this method in the next section. By default, a component derived from TComponent doesn't publish a Left or Top property. However, you'll notice that even the simplest nonvisual components retain their position, even if you close and reopen a form.

Streaming Object Properties

To store and retrieve position information, the TComponent class overrides the DefineProperties method, which calls the DefineProperty method to simulate the Left and Top properties. In turn, the DefineProperty method reads or writes the component's position values via calls to the ReadTop, ReadLeft, WriteTop, and WriteLeft methods. Since the TComponent class is rather complex, let's consider how we can achieve the same behavior in the TDdhPoint class, which is much simpler.

For our class, we want to store and load the Text field. However, since we don't publish this field as a property, the WriteProperties method won't be able to access the RTTI data for the property, and therefore won't store or load it in a stream. The TReader.ReadProperty and TWriter.WriteProperty methods call the DefineProperties method to give objects a chance to read or write this "hidden" data.

Accordingly, our TDdhPoint class overrides the DefineProperties method in the following manner:

```
procedure TDdhPoint.DefineProperties (Filer: TFiler);
begin
  Filer.DefineProperty (
    'Text', ReadText, WriteText, (Text <> ''));
end;
```

To understand what this method does, you need to understand how the Define-Property method works. The declaration for the TFiler class's DefineProperty method is

```
procedure DefineProperty(const Name: string;
                         ReadData: TReaderProc;
                         WriteData: TWriterProc;
                         HasData: Boolean);
```

The parameters for this method have the following meanings:

Name refers to the text description of the property.

ReadData is a method pointer for a procedure that accepts a TReader object as a parameter and reads the property from it.

WriteData is a method pointer for a procedure that accepts a TWriter object as a parameter and writes the property to it.

HasData is a Boolean value that determines whether the method should save the property or ignore it (in the event that a derived class publishes the property in the normal manner).

In our TDdhPoint.DefineProperties method, we pass "Text" as the name of the property, name the ReadText and WriteText methods as the procedures that read and write the property, and then specify that we only want to save this property if the Text field isn't an empty string. Here are the implementations of the ReadText and WriteText methods:

```
procedure TDdhPoint.ReadText (Reader: TReader);
begin
  Text := Reader.ReadString;
end;

procedure TDdhPoint.WriteText (Writer: TWriter);
begin
  Writer.WriteString (Text);
end;
```

Obviously, if we needed to store something other than a simple type for our pseudoproperty, these methods would need to be more complex. One exception to this approach is if you define a binary pseudoproperty. In that case, you can simply call the DefineBinaryProperty method in your DefineProperties method:

```
procedure TDummyClass.DefineProperties (Filer: TFiler);
begin
  Filer.DefineBinaryProperty (
    'BinProp', BinReadField, BinWriteField,
    (BinReadField <> True));
end;
```

This version defines a new property, named `BinProp`, and it specifies that the binary data to read and write is in a field named `BinField` and that we want to store and retrieve the data only if its value is `False`. For most cases, though, defining a pseudoproperty is fairly straightforward, as it is for the `TDdhPoint` class.

Streaming a Collection

Earlier, we mentioned that the `TPersistent` class was a key element of Delphi's stream framework. However, there's no easy way to store or load a `TPersistent`-derived object in a stream. Yes, the `TPersistent` class provides the `DefineProperties` method, which, as we've just seen, combines with the `TReader.ReadProperties` and `TWriter.WriteProperties` methods to provide a powerful way for classes to read and write published and unpublished properties and fields in a stream. However, this is all the `TPersistent` class does. To actually implement streaming of an object you must either derive your class from `TComponent` (which adds the necessary functionality) or be a bit clever. Since the former approach is rather obvious (and will be covered in Chapter 5), we'll take the latter route.

There are several reasons to look at streaming of `TPersistent`-derived objects, instead of components. First, the streaming mechanism is really built into the `TPersistent` class, and if it is not directly available there, it is only because of some methods declared as private. There is no apparent motive for this structure, although there is probably a good one; Borland might change the code of this class in the future and does not want to expose its internals. The second reason for examining the `TPersistent` class, and a sort of proof of what we've just stated, is that if you look at the VCL's class hierarchy, there are some relevant classes that are not components. Examples are `TStrings` and `TStringList`, `TCollection` and `TCollectionItem`, most of the graphic classes, and some classes of nodes/items. These classes mainly describe objects that are part of other components, but some of them can be used by themselves.

As you'll recall from the previous section, the `TWriter.WriteProperties` method is private (and therefore inaccessible), but the class's `WriteData` and `WriteCollection` methods are public. Unfortunately, the `TWriter.WriteData` method expects a `TComponent` parameter, so it's not useful to us unless we want to derive a class from `TComponent`. (Is this beginning to sound familiar?) This leaves us with the `TWriter.WriteCollection` method.

The solution to streaming a `TPersistent`-derived object (that doesn't derive from `TComponent`) is to embed the object in a collection, even if you want to read or write a single object. The `TWriter.WriteCollection` method expects a

TCollection object as its parameter, and passing a collection that contains a single object is a perfectly valid operation. The only remaining consideration is that the TCollection class's items must derive from the TCollectionItem class. Fortunately, the TCollectionItem class is a direct descendant of the TPersistent class, and adds only a single field, a reference to the TCollection object that owns the item. Here is the declaration of the TCollectionItem class:

```
type
  TCollectionItem = class(TPersistent)
  private
    FCollection: TCollection;
    FID: Integer;
    function GetIndex: Integer;
    procedure SetCollection(Value: TCollection);
  protected
    procedure Changed(AllItems: Boolean);
    function GetNamePath: string; override;
    function GetOwner: TPersistent; override;
    function GetDisplayName: string; virtual;
    procedure SetIndex(Value: Integer); virtual;
    procedure SetDisplayName(const Value: string); virtual;
  public
    constructor Create(Collection: TCollection); virtual;
    destructor Destroy; override;
    property Collection: TCollection
      read FCollection write SetCollection;
    property ID: Integer
      read FID;
    property Index: Integer
      read GetIndex write SetIndex;
    property DisplayName: string
      read GetDisplayName write SetDisplayName;
  end;
```

Since this class doesn't declare any virtual abstract methods, and since the implementations of its virtual methods provide safe defaults, we don't have to provide new versions of any of the TCollectionItem methods. However, we do need to override either the Assign or AssignTo methods of the TPersistent class (since the default versions raise a conversion exception). Here is the new version of the TDdhPoint class:

```
type
  TDdhPoint = class (TCollectionItem)
```

```
private
  fX, fY: Integer;
public
  Text: string;
  procedure WriteText (Writer: TWriter);
  procedure ReadText (Reader: TReader);
  procedure DefineProperties (Filer: TFiler); override;
  procedure Paint (Canvas: TCanvas);
  procedure Assign (Pt: TPersistent); override;
published
  property X: Integer
    read fX write fX;
  property Y: Integer
    read fY write fY;
end;
```

If you look closely, you'll see that we added only one method, the overridden version of Assign. Here's our implementation of that method:

```
procedure TDdhPoint.Assign (Pt: TPersistent);
begin
  if Pt is TDdhPoint then
  begin
    fx := TDdhPoint (Pt).fX;
    fY := TDdhPoint (Pt).fY;
    Text := TDdhPoint (Pt).Text;
  end
  else
    // raise an exception
    inherited Assign (pt);
end;
```

Since the point of the Assign method is to copy the data from one object to another object of the same class, we use

```
if Pt is TDdhPoint then
```

to test for this condition. If the object is of the same class, we then copy each of the fields. If the classes don't match, we call the version of Assign that the class inherits from TPersistent, which raises the conversion error exception.

The Persist Program Example

Earlier in this chapter, we set out to create a class that we could read and write directly to a stream. At this point, we've created a class that accomplishes this goal. In addition, since we use a TCollection object to handle reading and writing the objects to a stream, we can load and store a single object of this class, or multiple objects. To see the class in action, take a look at the Persist example program, whose main form appears in Figure 3.8.

FIGURE 3.8:

The Persist example demonstrates how you can load and store simple objects to a stream.

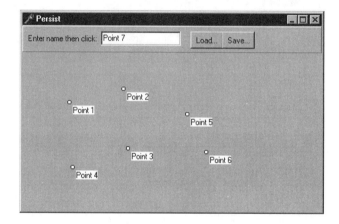

This program provides a simple interface to allow the user to create a collection of TDdhPoint objects that will appear on the main form. Then we provide a *Save* button to store the objects in a file (using a TFileStream) and a *Load* button to retrieve those objects from the file (again using a TFileStream).

First, we declared a TCollection object as a private field of the form. Naturally, we create this in the form's OnCreate event handler and free it in the OnDestroy event handler:

```
procedure TForm1.FormCreate(Sender: TObject);
begin
  PtList := TCollection.Create (TDdhPoint);
end;

procedure TForm1.FormDestroy(Sender: TObject);
begin
  // empty and destroy the list
  PtList.Clear;
```

```
    PtList.Free;
  end;
```

By the way, if you're not familiar with the TCollection class, you'll notice that we pass a class reference to its constructor instead of an object reference. This is important because a TCollection object is homogeneous (in sharp contrast with a TList object). That is, it can contain only objects of the type you pass to its constructor.

For instance, if you try to place any other type of object in the PtList collection, you'll generate a run-time exception. Another reason the collection needs a class reference in its constructor is that it defines an Add method that creates a new, uninitialized object in the collection. (The corresponding method in the TList class adds a reference to the object passed as a parameter to the method.)

NOTE   You'll typically use collections as component properties and not as general-purpose base classes. If you're using a collection to implement a property, you'll probably derive a new class from TCollection, declare a new data type for it to contain, and create a property editor for collections of those types of items. We'll see a complete example in the next chapter.

In the Persist example program, we can simply save the collection to a stream by using a TWriter object:

```
  Writer.WriteSignature;
  Writer.WriteCollection (PtList);
```

Similarly, you might expect that we could read the collection from the stream by calling the ReadCollection method of the TReader class. We can't, however, because the ReadCollection method is private. The VCL code calls the ReadCollection method only as a result of loading a component from a stream. (Once again, does this sound familiar? It should, because as we stated earlier, almost all of the stream support in the VCL was designed to support loading and storing components in the Delphi environment. Storing and loading noncomponent objects in streams was not a significant consideration.)

Because of this limitation, we need to do a bit more work. Since the ReadComponent method will call the ReadCollection method if a component contains a collection property, all we need to do is create a simple TComponent-derived wrapper class. This class will have a single property—the collection we want to stream. (At this point, it should be rather obvious why most of the magazine articles about streaming objects in Delphi have taken the other approach and created their own stream framework. It's not that much better than doing things the way the VCL does, but it is much easier to understand.)

Since we're going to have to use a wrapper component to manage reading the collection from the stream, we might as well use the same technique to write the collection. In both cases, we don't need to keep the wrapper component around for long. We can create it just before we read or write to the stream, and then free it as soon as we complete the stream operation. Here's the resulting code for our TWrapper class:

```
TWrapper = class (TComponent)
  private
    FColl: TCollection;
  published
    property MyColl: TCollection
      read FColl write FColl;
  public
    constructor Create (Owner: TComponent); override;
    destructor Destroy; override;
  end;

constructor TWrapper.Create (Owner: TComponent);
begin
  inherited Create (Owner);
  FColl := TCollection.Create (TDdhPoint);
end;

destructor TWrapper.Destroy;
begin
  FColl.Clear;
  FColl.Free;
  inherited Destroy;
end;
```

When the user clicks the *Save* speed button, we execute the following code:

```
procedure TForm1.SpeedButtonSaveClick(Sender: TObject);
var
  Str1: TFileStream;
  Wrap: TWrapper;
begin
  if SaveDialog1.Execute then
  begin
```

```
Str1 := TFileStream.Create (
  SaveDialog1.FileName,
  fmOpenWrite or fmCreate);
try
  Wrap := TWrapper.Create (self);
  try
    Wrap.MyColl.Assign (ptList);
    Str1.WriteComponent (Wrap);
  finally
    Wrap.Free;
  end;
finally
  Str1.Free;
end;
  end;
end;
```

While most of this code should seem familiar by now, you'll notice that we've added a local TWrapper variable, which we construct prior to using the stream, and destroy immediately afterwards. After constructing the wrapper component, we call the embedded TCollection object's Assign method to copy each of the TDdhPoint objects from the form's collection to the wrapper object's collection. Then we call the stream's WriteComponent method to write the data.

If you examine the source code for the TCollection.Assign method, you'll find that it first clears the collection, and then calls Add.Assign for each item in the source collection. As we mentioned previously, the Add method creates a new, uninitialized item in the collection. The call to the Assign method becomes a call to the Assign method of our TCollectionItem-derived class, TDdhPoint. This is why we had to define that method, even if we didn't need to copy objects of this type explicitly.

By now, you may be wondering how we're calling the WriteComponent method when we haven't even created a TWriter object. In fact, the TStream class defines an identical method, which simply creates a temporary TWriter object for you, and then calls its WriteComponent method. In turn, the TWriter.WriteComponent method begins writing out the data, beginning with the component's most basic ancestor class (TObject) and proceeding down to the component class itself. Along the way, this method calls the TWriter.WriteData method to handle storing the specific data for the fields of each class.

When the user clicks on the *Load* speed button, we execute the following event handler:

```
procedure TForm1.SpeedButtonLoadClick(Sender: TObject);
var
  Str1: TFileStream;
  Wrap: TWrapper;
begin
  if OpenDialog1.Execute then
  begin
    Str1 := TFileStream.Create (
      OpenDialog1.Filename, fmOpenRead);
    try
      Wrap := TWrapper.Create (self);
      try
        Wrap := Str1.ReadComponent (Wrap) as TWrapper;
        ptList.Assign (Wrap.MyColl);
      finally
        Wrap.Free;
      end;
    finally
      Str1.Free;
      Invalidate;
      Edit1.Text := 'Point ' + IntToStr (PtList.Count + 1);
    end;
  end;
end;
```

As before, most of this code should be familiar. However, in addition to implementing the opposite operations from the *Save* button event handler, we update the value in the Edit component. We do this to help ensure that we don't automatically assign to a new point the same description as that of a point we've loaded from the file stream.

Notice that we don't need to call the `RegisterClass` procedure for the `TWrapper` component, and we can still read objects of this class from a stream. This is possible because we create the objects and pass them to the `ReadComponent` method of the file stream ourselves. The class registration is required, instead, when you pass `nil` to the `ReadComponent` method, and want the method to create the objects while reading their data. This second approach is compulsory when you don't know the data type of the components you are reading. In this example, instead, we know we are reading only `TWrapper` components, so we can easily adopt the first approach.

Now let's take a look at the user interface code. When the user clicks on the form, we create a new TDdhPoint object, set its positional properties based on the location of the mouse click, and use the text from the Edit component to build a unique caption for the point:

```
procedure TForm1.FormMouseDown(
  Sender: TObject; Button: TMouseButton;
  Shift: TShiftState; X, Y: Integer);
var
  Pt: TDdhPoint;
begin
  Pt := PtList.Add as TDdhPoint;
  Pt.X := X;
  Pt.Y := Y;
  Pt.Text := Edit1.Text;
  Edit1.Text := 'Point ' +
    IntToStr (PtList.Count + 1);
  Invalidate;
end;
```

Here, you'll notice that we call the TCollection.Add method to create a new object in the collection. This time we use the Add method to create the new objects, and then we set the three fields based on the position of the mouse and the text in the Edit component. After setting the Text field of the new point, we change the text in the Edit component to represent the next point.

Finally, let's take a look at the OnPaint event handler. This method simply iterates the collection of points and calls the Paint method for each one:

```
procedure TForm1.FormPaint(Sender: TObject);
var
  I: Integer;
begin
  for I := 0 to PtList.Count - 1 do
    TDdhPoint (PtList.Items [I]).Paint (Canvas);
end;
```

This isn't particularly efficient, since it forces a repaint of each point whether we need to do so or not. However, it does ensure that we've painted all the points correctly, as shown in Figure 3.9, and it's reasonably fast, even for a large number of points.

Now that we've successfully read and written noncomponent objects to a stream, what have we learned? Well, first and foremost, we've learned that it is

FIGURE 3.9:

The Persist example will display a large number of points correctly.

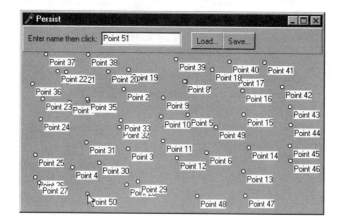

possible to stream noncomponent objects, but there is a fair amount of work no matter which approach you take. Second, because we'll have to create a wrapper component to stream a noncomponent object anyway, deriving the object from the TComponent class may be the best solution (unless you need to stream a collection of these objects).

Writing and Reading Components

In the last example, we saw that it was rather simple to save components to a stream. In fact, unless you want to create your own stream framework, it's the only way to save user-defined data types. For this reason, most Delphi programmers derive new classes from the TComponent class rather than from TPersistent. Obviously, then, we could rewrite the Persist example rather easily to derive the TDdhPoint class from TComponent, replace the TCollection of points with a TList, and then store and load each one from the stream. Better yet, we could create the point objects with another component as their owner, and then use the TStream-.WriteComponent method to save that component (and, via the TWriter-.WriteRootComponent method, save all the points).

Instead, let's consider what we'll need to do to extend the previous example into a more general program that will create different types of components dynamically, and then store and load those components in a stream. You might want to use this technique to build a program that can configure itself, letting the user customize the interface (such as building a toolbar or a menu dynamically). However, before we build such a program, let's take a look at the CRef example program from *Mastering Delphi 3*, and make some minor changes to its code. (On the CD, you'll find this example in the CRefNew directory.) The intent of this example was to create components at run-time, and to demonstrate how to store and load them from a file.

First, let's examine the SaveAs1Click method. Instead of using the techniques we've learned about in this chapter, this method simply iterates the components in the Controls array (these will be the TControl-derived components on the form), and writes each one to a TFileStream using its WriteComponent method:

```
procedure TForm1.SaveAs1Click(Sender: TObject);
var
  S: TFileStream;
  I: Integer;
begin
  if SaveDialog1.Execute then
  begin
    {open or create the stream file}
    S := TFileStream.Create (
      SaveDialog1.FileName,
      fmOpenWrite or fmCreate);
    try
      {save each component except the panel}
      for I := 0 to ControlCount - 1 do
        if Controls[I].ClassName <> 'TPanel' then
          S.WriteComponent (Controls[I]);
    finally
      S.Free;
    end;
  end;
end;
```

Similarly, the Open1Click method creates new components, initializes them from the stream (using the ReadComponent method), and then adds them to the form using the InsertControl method. When the stream's current position is equal to the size of the stream or greater, it means we have reached the end of the file, and we exit the loop. Interestingly, the CRef program took advantage of the fact that passing nil to the ReadComponent method forces it to create a new object (of the appropriate type) from the stream data. The Open1Click method appears below:

```
procedure TForm1.Open1Click(Sender: TObject);
var
  S: TFileStream;
```

```
      New: TComponent;
  begin
    if OpenDialog1.Execute then
    begin
      {open the stream}
      S := TFileStream.Create (
        OpenDialog1.FileName, fmOpenRead);
      try
        while S.Position < S.Size do
        begin
          {read a component and add it to the form}
          New := S.ReadComponent (nil);
          InsertControl (New as TControl);
          Inc (Counter);
        end;
      finally
        S.Free;
      end;
    end;
  end;
```

One of the side effects of this approach is that we needed to call the RegisterClasses procedure so that the program would have access to the RTTI information for the different types it would create from the stream. However (as we learned from a *Mastering Delphi* reader), you can't use this technique to stream all the different types of components. For instance, if you try to use this code to load a TMemo object from a stream, you'll generate a "Control has no Parent" exception. In this situation, the program is trying to insert the component into the form (which sets both its Owner and Parent properties) *after* the stream has initialized the component's properties. Unfortunately, some components require you to set the Parent property before you can initialize the rest of the object's fields.

In fact, you can do this by using a TReader object to read the components from the stream for you. The TReader object has its own Parent property (which is unusual for a class that doesn't derive from TControl) and an Owner property (even though the TReader class doesn't derive from TComponent). Instead of representing the parent or owner component for the TReader object, these properties specify the parent and owner components for the objects loaded from the stream.

WARNING Contrary to the description in the Delphi documentation, however, setting the Owner property of the TReader object doesn't affect the Owner property of the components read from the stream. Only the Parent property works as documented. The workaround to this problem is to give an owner to the components by calling the InsertComponent method of the owner itself (that is, the form). Only with this approach can you avoid causing a memory leak; components without an owner are not automatically destroyed.

Below, we've updated the Open1Click method to support setting the Parent property of the component we are loading using a TReader object, and we've used the InsertComponent method of the form to give components an owner, as described in the warning above:

```
procedure TForm1.Open1Click(Sender: TObject);
var
  S: TFileStream;
  New: TComponent;
  Reader1: TReader; // new line
begin
  if OpenDialog1.Execute then
  begin
    {remove existing controls}
    New1Click (self);

    {open the stream}
    S := TFileStream.Create (OpenDialog1.FileName,
      fmOpenRead);
    try
      while S.Position < S.Size do
      begin
        {read a component and add it to the form}
        // new code:
        Reader1 := TReader.Create (S, 4096);
        try
          Reader1.Parent := self;
          New := Reader1.ReadRootComponent (nil);
          InsertComponent (New);
        finally
          Reader1.Free;
        end;
```

```
        Inc (Counter);
    end;
finally
    S.Free;
end;
end;
end;
```

Reading and Writing Form Files

In the example above, from *Mastering Delphi 3*, we were doing something a bit strange. We were reading and writing components whose Owner property was the main form of the application. The strange part of this is that we weren't reading and writing the form's data, only that of most of the components. On the other hand, when reading the data in from a file, we weren't able to set the Owner property for each of the components, even if we set the TReader object's Owner property explicitly, just as we did for the Parent property.

Instead of reading and writing each component explicitly, you can simply read and write a single component, the form, and it will automatically read and write all of the components it owns. (As you'll recall, the TForm class derives from TComponent, so component operations apply to forms as well.) For instance, to store a form in a stream you can simply write:

```
MyStream.WriteComponent(self);
```

from any method of the form. Likewise, you can load a form from a stream by writing:

```
MyStream.ReadComponent(self);
```

By now, you've probably figured out that this is almost exactly what Delphi does to create the DFM files that store properties for a form and all of its components. Again, almost.

If you examine the structure of a DFM file carefully, you'll discover that it's really just a resource file that contains a custom format resource. Inside this resource, you'll find the component information for the form (Delphi creates a separate DFM file for each form) and for each of the components it owns. As you would expect, the stream classes provide two methods to read and write this custom resource data for components: WriteComponentRes to store the data, and

`ReadComponentRes` to load it. Now let's consider another example, StrComp, which is an extension of the CreateComp example from Chapter 1. Figure 3.10 shows the program in action.

The StrComp example uses its main form to manage the reading and writing of secondary forms.

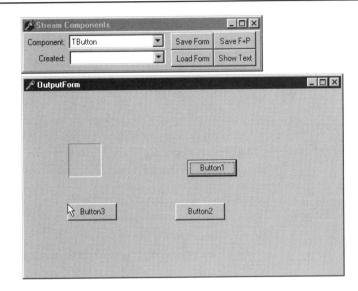

As you can see, the main form is now simply a toolbar. Instead of creating components on the main form, we create a secondary form where the user can add new components at run-time. By performing all of our work on a secondary form, we can store and load the entire form instead of just reading in groups of components. Making this change forced us to make several other changes, such as modifying the `UpdateList` method to refer to the components on the other form (which is now a bit simpler since we don't have to bypass the components of the original form that add and view the user's new components). Here's the code for the `UpdateList` method:

```
procedure TMainForm.UpdateList;
var
  I: Integer;
begin
  Combobox2.Items.Clear;
  with OutputForm do
    for I := 0 to ComponentCount - 1 do
      ComboBox2.Items.Add (Components [I].Name);
end;
```

The method is simple, and just adds the names of the components to the created ComboBox.

The code to create the new components hasn't changed, so we won't look at it again. However, the *Save Form* and *Load Form* buttons are new, and implement the form-writing and -reading capabilities we've just described:

```
procedure TMainForm.SpeedSaveFormClick(Sender: TObject);
var
  Str1 : TFileStream;
begin
  if SaveDialog1.Execute then
  begin
    Str1 := TFileStream.Create (
      SaveDialog1.FileName,
      fmOpenWrite or fmCreate);
    try
      // disable the event
      OutputForm.OnMouseDown := nil;
      Str1.WriteComponentRes (
        OutputForm.ClassName, OutputForm);
    finally
      Str1.Free;
      OutputForm.OnMouseDown :=
        OutputForm.FormMouseDown;
    end;
  end;
end;
```

In this method, the only code that we haven't discussed is the statement that disables the OutputForm object's OnMouseDown event by setting it to nil. We've done this to keep the WriteComponentRes method from saving the OnMouseDown event property, which we use to create the new components. After writing the form file, we reset this event property to once again use the FormMouseDown method.

Now, build and run the StrComp project, add a few components, and save the form to a new DFM file. When you do this, you can then reload the form using the *Load* button. The event handler for this task is approximately what you would expect:

```
procedure TMainForm.SpeedLoadFormClick(Sender: TObject);
var
  Str1: TFileStream;
```

```
    TempForm1: TOutputForm;
  begin
    if OpenDialog1.Execute then
    begin
      Str1 := TFileStream.Create (
        OpenDialog1.FileName, fmOpenRead);
      try
        TempForm1 := TOutputForm.Create (Application);
        Str1.ReadComponentRes (TempForm1);
        OutputForm.Free;
        OutputForm := TempForm1;
        OutputForm.Show;
        OutputForm.OnMouseDown :=
          OutputForm.FormMouseDown;
      finally
        Str1.Free;
      end;
    end;
  end;
```

Once again, you'll notice that we must explicitly set the OnMouseDown event for the form. Once we've done this, the user can continue adding components to the reloaded form. Now, you can return to Delphi and load the form you created with StrComp into Delphi itself, as shown in Figure 3.11.

FIGURE 3.11:

When Delphi loads a DFM file without a corresponding PAS file, it displays only the text description.

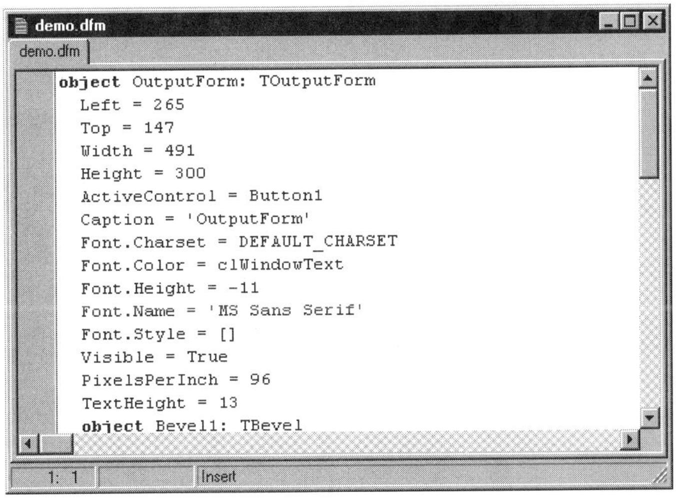

```
object OutputForm: TOutputForm
  Left = 265
  Top = 147
  Width = 491
  Height = 300
  ActiveControl = Button1
  Caption = 'OutputForm'
  Font.Charset = DEFAULT_CHARSET
  Font.Color = clWindowText
  Font.Height = -11
  Font.Name = 'MS Sans Serif'
  Font.Style = []
  Visible = True
  PixelsPerInch = 96
  TextHeight = 13
  object Bevel1: TBevel
```

When the form file appears, you'll see the text description of the form, and not the visual representation. However, the text description does match the format that you've probably seen for Delphi-created forms. If you want to view the form visually, you'll need to create a corresponding source file (PAS) to go with the form description file.

Saving a Complete Form (Including the Pascal File)

In Delphi, there's an important relationship between a DFM file and a PAS file that has the same name. The DFM file represents the form's data (properties), and the PAS file represents the form's behavior (methods). In addition, the PAS file provides an interface between a form and the rest of the program via the form's class declaration. Obviously, duplicating all of Delphi's design-time capabilities would represent a great deal of work. However, you can write out a simple PAS file that provides a class declaration for the form, containing fields that correspond to each of the form's components.

In our example, we provide just this capability via the *Write F+P* (Form plus Pascal) button. Here's its event handler:

```
procedure TMainForm.SpeedSavePasClick(Sender: TObject);
var
  File1 : TextFile;
  FileName: string;
  I: Integer;
begin
  // save the DFM file
  SpeedSaveFormClick (self);
  // change extension (using the proper VCL routine)
  FileName := SaveDialog1.FileName;
  FileName := ChangeFileExt (FileName, '.pas');
  AssignFile (File1, FileName);
  try
    // create the Pascal file...
    Rewrite (File1);
    FileName := ChangeFileExt (FileName, '');
    Writeln (File1, 'unit ' +
      ExtractFileName (FileName) + ';');
    Writeln (File1, '');
    Writeln (File1, 'interface');
    Writeln (File1, '');
```

```
      Writeln (File1, 'uses');
      Writeln (File1, '  Windows, Messages, SysUtils, ' +
        'Classes, Graphics, Controls, Forms,');
      Writeln (File1, '  StdCtrls, ExtCtrls, Buttons, ' +
        'Clipbrd, Comctrls, Db, Dbcgrids,');
      Writeln (File1, '  Dbctrls, Dbgrids, Dblookup, ' +
        'Dbtables, Ddeman, Dialogs,');
      Writeln (File1, '  Filectrl, Grids, Mask, Menus, ' +
        'Mplayer, Oleauto, Oleconst, Olectnrs,');
      Writeln (File1, '  Olectrls, Outline, Report, ' +
        'Tabnotbk, Tabs;');
      Writeln (File1, '');
      Writeln (File1, 'type');
      Writeln (File1, '  TOutputForm = class(TForm)');
      // add component declarations
      for I := 0 to OutputForm.ComponentCount - 1 do
      begin
        Writeln (File1, '    ' +
          OutputForm.Components[I].Name + ': ' +
          OutputForm.Components[I].ClassName + ';');
      end;
      Writeln (File1, '  private');
      Writeln (File1, '    { Private declarations }');
      Writeln (File1, '  public');
      Writeln (File1, '    { Public declarations }');
      Writeln (File1, '  end;');
      Writeln (File1, '');
      Writeln (File1, 'var');
      Writeln (File1, '  OutputForm: TOutputForm;');
      Writeln (File1, '');
      Writeln (File1, 'implementation');
      Writeln (File1, '');
      Writeln (File1, '{$R *.DFM}');
      Writeln (File1, '');
      Writeln (File1, 'end.');
    finally
      CloseFile (File1);
    end;
  end;
```

In the above method, you'll notice two important things. First, we don't try to determine which units should appear in the interface section's uses clause.

Instead, we always add all of the possible units. This is not a good approach to creating Pascal source files, but it does create a file that Delphi will be able to use.

> **NOTE**
>
> We will see how to determine which unit defines each component in Chapter 6. This information, in fact, is available in the RTTI data of components.

Second, we iterate the form's Components array, and create field declarations for those components, using the Name and ClassName properties of each one. If you use the *Write F+P* button to store a form, you'll be able to open that form in Delphi, *and* view the form visually, as shown in Figure 3.12.

FIGURE 3.12:

The form created by the StrComp example can be loaded in the Delphi environment.

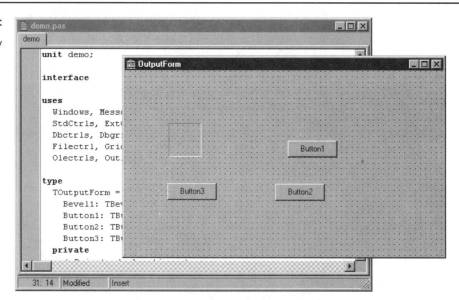

Converting Delphi Form Files

One of Delphi's more surprising capabilities is that it can display a text description of a form, listing its components and properties, as well as its visual representation. If you've examined Delphi's BIN directory, you may also have discovered the CONVERT.EXE program, which you can use to convert a DFM file into a TXT file outside the Delphi environment. (This program is useful for performing global changes to captions or other text in the DFM file, as well as for documenting the structure of your forms.) However, the VCL provides you with the same power, via two methods:

```
procedure ObjectResourceToText(Input, Output: TStream);
procedure ObjectTextToResource(Input, Output: TStream);
```

As you might guess, these functions make it rather simple to duplicate the CONVERT.EXE program's functionality. In the StrComp example, however, we used this ability to display descriptions of forms we've created dynamically. Below is the code for the *Show Text* button's event handler:

```
procedure TMainForm.SpeedTextClick(Sender: TObject);
var
  StrBin, StrTxt: TMemoryStream;
begin
  StrBin := TMemoryStream.Create;
  StrTxt := TMemoryStream.Create;
  try
    OutputForm.OnMouseDown := nil;
    // write the form to a memory stream
    StrBin.WriteComponentRes (
      OutputForm.ClassName, OutputForm);
    // go back to the beginning
    StrBin.Seek (0, soFromBeginning);
    // convert the form to text
    ObjectResourceToText (StrBin, StrTxt);
    // go back to the beginning
    StrTxt.Seek (0, soFromBeginning);
    // load the text
    FormMemo.Memo1.Lines.LoadFromStream (StrTxt);
    FormMemo.ShowModal;
  finally
    StrBin.Free;
    StrTxt.Free;
    OutputForm.OnMouseDown :=
      OutputForm.FormMouseDown;
  end;
end;
```

In this method, we start to see some of the flexibility of using streams—we can use the same approach to writing the form data to a memory stream that we've used to write to a file stream. At the beginning, we create two TMemoryStream objects. Next, we write the DFM data to the StrBin stream, seek back to the beginning of the stream, and then use the `ObjectResourceToText` procedure to write the text description to the other memory stream. As with the `StrBin` stream, we seek back to the beginning of the `StrTxt` stream, and then load the text from this stream into the `Memo` component of another form (defined in the MEMOF.PAS unit). To view the text, we display the form modally, as shown in Figure 3.13.

FIGURE 3.13:

If you click the *Show Text* button on the main form, you'll see the Form Textual Description form.

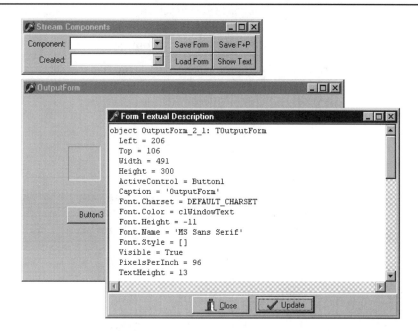

NOTE It's important to stress that after you've written data to a stream, you must explicitly seek back to the beginning before you can use the stream further, unless you want to append data to the stream, of course.

On the Form Textual Description form, you'll see two buttons: one to close the form and the other labeled *Update*. In the event handler for this button, you'll see that we attempt to convert the form text description back to a DFM file:

```
procedure TFormMemo.BitBtn2Click(Sender: TObject);
var
  StrBin, StrTxt: TMemoryStream;
  TempForm1: TOutputForm;
begin
```

```
StrBin := TMemoryStream.Create;
StrTxt := TMemoryStream.Create;
// copy the text of the memo
Memo1.Lines.SaveToStream (StrTxt);
// go back to the beginning
StrTxt.Seek (0, soFromBeginning);
try
  // convert to binary
  ObjectTextToResource (StrTxt, StrBin);
  // go back to the beginning
  StrBin.Seek (0, soFromBeginning);
  // loading code...
  TempForm1 := TOutputForm.Create (Application);
  StrBin.ReadComponentRes (TempForm1);
  OutputForm.Free;
  OutputForm := TempForm1;
  OutputForm.Show;
  // close the memo form
  ModalResult := mrOk;
except
  on E: Exception do
  begin
    E.Message :=
      'Error converting form'#13#13 +
      '(' + E.Message + ')';
    Application.ShowException (E);
  end;
end;
end;
```

In this method, we're hoping that the user has made changes to the form's text description. If the user makes changes that the `ObjectTextToResource` procedure can't convert, or if there's some other problem, the procedure will raise an exception. Otherwise, the program executes statements similar to those it uses to display the text, including seeking back to the beginning of the streams after saving the text from the Memo, and after converting the text. Of course, this time, it does the opposite conversion.

If the `ObjectTextToResource` procedure raises an exception, it will typically be because the user changed the text description to something inappropriate. In this case, the exceptions will come from `TParser` objects, which this procedure uses in the conversion process. We'll cover this class before the end of the chapter.

Extracting Form Files from Resources

Besides extracting the component information of a form from a DFM file, or from a form at run-time, you can also extract this information from a DFM file that's bound to the executable file of a Delphi program. This can be particularly useful if you don't have the source code for the program. The beauty of this approach is that we can extract the description of the form from the current application's executable file, using the TResourceStream class.

The FormRes example demonstrates this approach. When you press the form's button (*Show Text of Form*), the textual description of the form is added to a Memo component:

```
procedure TForm1.Button1Click(Sender: TObject);
var
  ResStr: TResourceStream;
  MemStr: TMemoryStream;
begin
  ResStr := TResourceStream.Create(
    hInstance, 'TFORM1', RT_RCDATA);
  try
    MemStr := TMemoryStream.Create;
    ResStr.Position := 0;
    ObjectBinaryToText (ResStr, MemStr);
    MemStr.Position := 0;
    Memo1.Lines.LoadFromStream (
      MemStr);
  finally
    ResStr.Free
  end;
end;
```

You can see the effect of this code in Figure 3.14.

NOTE   To get back to the beginning of a stream you can set the Position property to 0, or call the Seek method using the soFromBeginning flag. This second method, used in the example above, is more efficient.

FIGURE 3.14:

The FormRes exam-
ple with the textual
description of its
form loaded from its
resources

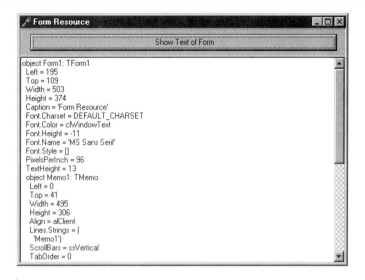

Using the TParser Class

As we've already mentioned, the VCL includes a class for parsing a textual description of a DFM file's form. Unfortunately, the TParser class is completely undocumented (and therefore subject to future changes), and isn't typically of much use to
Delphi programmers. However, since the TParser class uses an internal stream,
let's take a quick look at its use of streams to facilitate the conversion process. Then
we'll try to figure out if it's possible to take advantage of its capabilities.

The TParser class (defined in the Classes unit) is really nothing more than a
simple token or lexical scanner. Using the NextToken method, you can use a
TParser object to process a stream token-by-token, and identify the type and
value of each token in the file. The TParser class can identify the following types
of tokens:

toEOF: the end-of-file marker

toString: a text string

toInteger: an integral value

toFloat: a floating point value

toSymbol: anything else

The type of the token is indicated by the Token property of the class, which can assume one of the five values above or the value of an actual character (one of the language symbols and punctuation marks).

Besides the Token property, the TParser class has the following elements:

- a Create constructor, which accepts the source stream as a parameter

- a NextToken function, which you can use to move to the next token in the source file

- a function and a property that return the actual position in the file (SourcePos and SourceLine)

- some conversion functions, including TokenFloat, TokenInt, and TokenString

The basic approach in using this class is to write a while loop that scans the source code file, and a case statement within the while loop to analyze the various items. You can see the structure of this code in the following listing:

```
Parse := TParser.Create (SourceStream);
while Parse.Token <> toEOF do
begin
  case Parse.Token of
    // main tokens
    toSymbol: ... // identifier or keyword (or comment)
    toString: ... // string (including special characters)
    toInteger: .. // numeric constant
    toFloat: ... // floating-point constant
    // other tokens
    '{':
    '}':
    '/':
    ...
  end; // case
  // move to the next token
  Parse.NextToken;
end; // while
```

A Pascal-to-HTML Converter

The HTML format is becoming a standard for documentation, not just on the Web but also in CD-ROM products and on the Windows platform, where it will probably replace the HLP file format. For this book, and also for *Mastering Delphi 3*, we needed to convert the source code files to HTML to make them easier to browse on the CD.

For this reason, we've built a Pascal-to-HTML converter, called *PasToWeb*, which reproduces the standard color syntax highlighting of the Delphi code editor. This converter is basically a parser that can analyze the source code and recognize keywords and comments.

As you'll see, using the TParser class to build this application was probably not a wise design decision, but is seemed the most obvious as we started writing this code. This class was intended for a different purpose and isn't easily adaptable. (We decided to leave this example as it was developed, as it shows a typical real-world approach to programming on tight deadlines, which isn't always the best condition and approach.)

There are several problems with TParser, which you can see from the final listing of the previous section. First, this class doesn't distinguish between comments and keywords or symbols. Second, TParser skips all the "white spaces" (spaces, tabs, newline characters, and so on). Third, Pascal strings might include special characters (such as #13), but TParser merges the special characters inside strings. We need to extract them to retain the correct formatting.

The first step in building this complex program is to define an abstract TCodeParser class, which has absolutely no knowledge of HTML. This class will define a special constructor, a Convert procedure, a few local data fields for various methods, and a list of virtual methods. Below is the class declaration:

```
type
  TCodeParser = class (TNewParser)
  public
    constructor Create (SSource, SDest: TStream);
    procedure SetKeywordType (Kt: KeywordType);
    // conversion
    procedure Convert;
  protected
    // virtual methods (mostly virtual abstract)
    procedure BeforeString; virtual; abstract;
    procedure AfterString; virtual; abstract;
    procedure BeforeKeyword; virtual; abstract;
    procedure AfterKeyword; virtual; abstract;
    procedure BeforeComment; virtual; abstract;
    procedure AfterComment; virtual; abstract;
    procedure InitFile; virtual; abstract;
```

```
      procedure EndFile; virtual; abstract;
      function CheckSpecialToken (Ch1: char): string; virtual;
      function MakeStringLegal (S: String): string; virtual;
   protected
      Source, Dest: TStream;
      OutStr: string;
      FKeywords: TStrings;
      Line, Pos: Integer;
   end;
```

Why are there so many virtual abstract methods, and few non-abstract virtual methods? The idea is simple: We want this class to be a generic extension of the TParser class that we can later extend to produce HTML files, RTF files, or files of any other format we might want. We'll base all these versions on a single engine (the Convert method), which will in turn call the subclasses' virtual methods to provide the appropriate output. Here is an excerpt of the code we'll use when we find a keyword:

```
BeforeKeyword;
AppendStr (OutStr, TokenString);
AfterKeyword;
```

The first and last lines call two virtual methods, which we'll define so as to add specific elements to the output string (OutStr). In this case, we want to add the HTML <B> and </B> tags to display boldface code. Here is the code of the two methods for the THtmlParser subclass:

```
procedure THtmlParser.BeforeKeyword;
begin
   AppendStr (OutStr, '<B>');
end;

procedure THtmlParser.AfterKeyword;
begin
   AppendStr (OutStr, '</B>');
end;
```

When you create a TCodeParser object, the constructor stores the source and destination streams, defines an output string (which we'll later save to the destination stream), and specifies either Pascal or DFM as the type of keywords to process. You can modify this later using the SetKeywordType method:

```
constructor TCodeParser.Create (SSource, SDest: TStream);
begin
```

```
    inherited Create (SSource);
    Source := SSource;
    Dest := SDest;
    SetLength (OutStr, 10000);
    OutStr := '';
    FKeywords := PascalKeywords;
  end;

  procedure TCodeParser.SetKeywordType (Kt: KeywordType);
  begin
    case Kt of
      ktPascal: FKeywords := PascalKeywords;
      ktDfm: FKeywords := DfmKeywords;
    else
      raise Exception.Create ('Undefined keywords type');
    end;
  end;
```

As we mentioned earlier, the core of the TCodeParser class is the Convert method. The code of this method is actually quite long, but it is worth listing it to understand how the program works:

```
  procedure TCodeParser.Convert;
  begin
    InitFile; // virtual
    Line := 1;
    Pos := 0;
    // parse the entire source file
    while Token <> toEOF do
    begin
      // if the source code line has changed,
      // add the proper newline character
      while SourceLine > Line do
      begin
        AppendStr (OutStr, #13#10);
        Inc (Line);
        Pos := Pos + 2; // 2 characters, cr+lf
      end;
      // add proper white spaces (formatting)
      while SourcePos > Pos do
      begin
        AppendStr (OutStr, ' ');
        Inc (Pos);
```

```pascal
  end;
  // check the token
  case Token of
    toSymbol:
    begin
      // if the token is not a keyword
      if FKeywords.IndexOf (TokenString) < 0 then
        // add the plain token
        AppendStr (OutStr, TokenString)
      else
      begin
        BeforeKeyword; // virtual
        AppendStr (OutStr, TokenString);
        AfterKeyword; // virtual
      end;
    end;
    toString:
    begin
      BeforeString; // virtual
      if (Length (TokenString) = 1) and
        (Ord (TokenString [1]) < 32) then
        begin
          AppendStr (OutStr, '#' +
            IntToStr (Ord (TokenString [1])));
          if Ord (TokenString [1]) < 10 then
            Pos := Pos + 1
          else
            Pos := Pos + 2;
        end
      else
      begin
        AppendStr (OutStr, MakeStringLegal (TokenString));
        Pos := Pos + 2; // 2 x hyphen
      end;
      AfterString; // virtual
    end;
    toInteger:
      AppendStr (OutStr, TokenString);
    toFloat:
      AppendStr (OutStr, TokenString);
    toComment:
    begin
```

```
        BeforeComment; // virtual
        AppendStr (OutStr, MakeCommentLegal (TokenString));
        AfterComment; // virtual
      end;
      else
        // any other token
        AppendStr (OutStr, CheckSpecialToken (Token));
    end; // case Token of
    // increase the current position
    Pos := Pos + Length (TokenString);
    // move to the next token
    NextToken;
  end; // while Token <> toEOF do
  // add final code
  EndFile; // virtual
  // add the string to the stream
  Dest.WriteBuffer (Pointer(OutStr)^, Length (OutStr));
end;
```

The entire conversion code works on an output string (OutStr). When we finish converting the input data, we'll send this string to the output stream (Dest) by copying its actual data, as shown in the last line above.

To format code properly, we've added variables that store the current line and the current position of the output file: Line and Pos. By simply comparing these two values with the information from the input file (SourceLine and SourcePos) you can determine whether you need to add extra white spaces or new lines. For example, the code adds white spaces to the output string to synchronize it with the current position in the input file (which you can see in the while SourcePos > Pos loop in the listing above). Something similar happens at the end of a line.

Detecting Keywords, Strings, and Comments

Detecting keywords is actually one of the simplest things you can do with TParser-derived classes. I've prepared a couple of string lists with all the Pascal keywords and with the two keywords used in DFM files, *object* and *end*. When the program finds a symbol, it checks to see if the symbol is one of the keywords in the list, as you can see in the source code of the Convert method above.

If handling keywords is actually quite simple, handling strings is a nightmare. The problem is that the TParser class elaborates strings, performing operations you have to undo to make the code work properly. This is why you might want to eliminate this base class, and write the entire code from scratch.

In addition, a string can be a single character, possibly one of the constant characters whose ASCII value is below 32 (which you generally add using the # symbol, as in #13 for the newline character). These special characters can also be the first, last, or an intermediate character of a string, and we must recognize them.

For multicharacter strings this operation is performed by the MakeStringLegal virtual function:

```
const
  Quote = '''';

function TCodeParser.MakeStringLegal (S: String): string;
var
  I: Integer;
begin
  if Length (S) < 1 then
  begin
    Result := Quote + Quote;
    Exit;
  end;

  // if the first character is not special,
  // add the open quote
  if S[1] > #31 then
    Result := Quote
  else
    Result := '';

  // for each character of the string
  for I := 1 to Length (S) do
    case S [I] of
      // quotes must be doubled
      Quote: begin
        AppendStr (Result, Quote + Quote);
        Pos := Pos + 1;
      end;
      // special characters (characters below the value 32)
      #0..#31: begin
        Pos := Pos + Length (IntToStr (Ord (S[I])));
        // if preceding characters are plain ones,
```

```
    // close the string
    if (I > 1) and (S[I-1] > #31) then
      AppendStr (Result, Quote);
    // add the special character
    AppendStr (Result, '#' + IntToStr (Ord (S[I])));
    // if the following characters are plain ones,
    // open the string
    if (I < Length (S) - 1) and (S[I+1] > #31) then
      AppendStr (Result, Quote);
  end;
else
  AppendStr (Result, CheckSpecialToken(S[I]));
end;


// if the last character was not special,
// add closing quote
if (S[Length (S)] > #31) then
  AppendStr (Result, Quote);
end;
```

The details are quite complex, but the method above contains enough comments to help you understand what's going on. Keep in mind that we need to perform an extra check. Every character, whether inside or outside a string, must be checked for special cases. For example, you cannot use the < and > characters inside an HTML file. You must convert them to the corresponding sequences, using the CheckSpecialToken function of the THtmlParser class:

```
function THtmlParser.CheckSpecialToken (
  Ch1: char): string;
begin
  case Ch1 of
    '<': Result := '&lt;';
    '>': Result := '&gt;';
    '&': Result := '&amp;';
    '"': Result := '&quot;';
  else
    Result := Ch1;
  end;
end;
```

Handling comments is even more complex, because the TParser class ignores them. The program must identify comments of different kinds, and must, therefore examine multiple tokens (actually multiple characters) to determine if a slash or an open parenthesis represents the beginning of a comment or not. For example, when the program encounters a slash character, it should defer converting the next token until it determines whether it needs to call the `BeforeComment` virtual method before passing the characters on to the output.

It is possible to try customizing the conversion code to help it process strings correctly, but a comment may contain invalid strings. That is, comments may contain a single quote, as in *don't*. This is not legal in a Delphi string (you have to write *don''t*), and the parser will determine that it's encountered a string that doesn't terminate before the newline character, which results in a run-time error. To fix this, the only reasonable solution is to alter the `TParser` class to help it handle comments directly. As a result, we'll be able to use the `toComment` extra token, as you've already seen in the `Convert` method.

Changing the Code of the TParser Class

As a last resort, we decided to modify the `TParser` class so it will handle comments directly. This way, a comment becomes a single token, like a string, but represented by a new constant:

```
const
  toComment = Char(5);
```

After copying the `TParser` source code to the `NewParse` unit, we edited it a bit, renaming the class as `TNewParser` (this is the class `TCodeParser` inherits from, as you might have noticed in an earlier listing).

Other than the class name, the declaration and definition of the new class are the same as the original, as are most of its methods. The differences appear in the `NextToken` function, which extracts tokens from the source code. Here is the initial portion of this function (where P is the pointer to the current character, while `FSourcePtr` indicates the beginning of the current token):

```
function TNewParser.NextToken: Char;
var
  I: Integer;
  P, S: PChar;
begin
  SkipBlanks;
  P := FSourcePtr;
  FTokenPtr := P;
  case P^ of
```

```
'A'..'Z', 'a'..'z', '_':
  begin
    Inc(P);
    while P^ in ['A'..'Z', 'a'..'z', '0'..'9', '_'] do
      Inc(P);
    Result := toSymbol;
  end;
```

Here, we can simply add a new branch to the case statement to handle multi-line comments. With this change, the program will keep scanning the code until it finds a closing brace:

```
'{':
  begin
    // look for closing brace
    while P^ <> '}' do
      Inc(P);
    // move to the next
    Inc(P);
    Result := toComment;
  end;
else
  if (P^ = '/') and (P^ <> toEOF) and ((P+1)^ = '/') then
  begin
    // single line comment
    while P^ <> #13 do
      Inc(P);
    Result := toComment;
  end
  else
    // original code of the else branch
```

For single-line comments (those using the double slash, //), we must use a different approach: We must add the code to the else branch of the case statement, check to see that we are not at the end of the file, and then examine the next character using the expression (P+1)^. To make this program truly robust, you might want to add the ability to recognize the (* and *) comment tokens, something the current version of PasToWeb cannot handle.

The THtmlParser Class

From the basic class of the conversion framework, the PasToWeb program derives the THtmlParser class, which provides the code to generate the HTML:

```
type
  THtmlParser = class (TCodeParser)
  public
    FileName: string;
    Copyright: string;
    Alone: Boolean;
    procedure AddFileHeader (FileName: string);
    class function HtmlHead (Filename: string): string;
    class function HtmlTail (Copyright: string): string;
  protected
    procedure BeforeString; override;
    procedure AfterString; override;
    procedure BeforeKeyword; override;
    procedure AfterKeyword; override;
    procedure BeforeComment; override;
    procedure AfterComment; override;
    procedure InitFile; override;
    procedure EndFile; override;
    function CheckSpecialToken (Ch1: char): string; override;
  end;
```

We have already seen some of the method definitions for this class, which are generally very simple.

The two class methods (HtmlHead and HtmlTail) simply generate the initial and final portion of the HTML file, with a title and default background color at the beginning, and copyright information at the end:

```
class function THtmlParser.HtmlHead (
  Filename: string): string;
begin
  Result := '<HTML><HEAD>' + #13#10 +
    '<TITLE>File: ' +
    ExtractFileName(Filename) +
    '</TITLE>' + #13#10 +
    '<META NAME="GENERATOR" ' +
    'CONTENT="PasToWeb[Marco Cantù]">'#13#10 +
    '</HEAD>'#13#10 +
```

```
    '<BODY BGCOLOR="#FFFFFF">'#13#10;
  end;

  class function THtmlParser.HtmlTail (
    Copyright: string): string;
  begin
    Result := '<HR><CENTER<I>Generated by PasToWeb,' +
      ' a tool by Marco Cant&ugrave;.<P>' + #13#10 +
      Copyright + '</CENTER></I>'#13#10 +
      '</BODY> </HTML>';
  end;
```

You might also want to use these two methods in other cases, but we call them only in the InitFile and EndFile functions:

```
  procedure THtmlParser.InitFile;
  begin
    if Alone then
      AppendStr (OutStr, HtmlHead (Filename));
    AddFileHeader (Filename);
    AppendStr (OutStr, '<PRE>'#13#10);
  end;

  procedure THtmlParser.EndFile;
  begin
    AppendStr (OutStr, '</PRE>');
    if Alone then
      AppendStr (OutStr, HtmlTail (Copyright))
    else
      AppendStr (OutStr, #13#10'<HR>'#13#10#13#10); // separator
  end;
```

What's more interesting is the AddFileHeader method, which adds a header that contains the name of the translated file, and defines a bookmark inside the HTML file. This is a trick to support a version of the program that allows you to place multiple source files within a single HTML file, and provide local jumps (which we'll see in a while). The core of this method is a format statement with the NAME directive that defines the bookmark inside an HTML anchor:

```
  procedure THtmlParser.AddFileHeader (FileName: string);
  var
    FName: string;
  begin
```

```
    FName := Uppercase (ExtractFilename (FileName));
    AppendStr (OutStr, Format (
      '<A NAME=%s><H3>%s</H3></A>' + #13#10 + #13#10,
      [FName, FName]));
  end;
```

Using PasToWeb

All the code we've discussed up to now relates to the core of the PasToWeb program, which you'll find in the Convert.PAS unit. We've built a program around this unit and provided a very simple user interface. The main form (see Figure 3.15) allows a user to convert files in three steps.

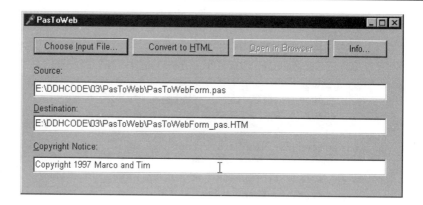

The first step is where you select the Pascal or DFM file, through an OpenDialog component. When the user selects a file, the program suggests a name for the resulting output file, such as *PasToWebForm_pas.HTM*, as shown in Figure 3.15. Naturally, the user can modify the suggested name inside the edit box.

The second step is to perform the actual file conversion. The program must prepare the proper streams, create a THtmlParser object, initialize it, and call its Convert method:

```
procedure TForm1.BtnHTMLClick(Sender: TObject);
var
  Source, BinSource, Dest: TStream;
  Parser: THtmlParser;
begin
```

```
// extract the target file name
if FileExists (EditDest.Text) then
  if MessageDlg ('Overwrite the existing file ' +
    EditDest.Text + '?',
    mtConfirmation, [mbYes, mbNo], 0) = idNo then
  Exit;
// create the two streams
Dest := TFileStream.Create (EditDest.Text,
  fmCreate or fmOpenWrite);
if ExtractFileExt(EditSource.Text) = '.dfm' then
begin
  // convert the DFM file to text
  BinSource := TFileStream.Create (
    EditSource.Text, fmOpenRead);
  Source := TMemoryStream.Create;
  ObjectResourceToText (BinSource, Source);
  Source.Position := 0;
end
else
begin
  Source := TFileStream.Create (EditSource.Text, fmOpenRead);
  BinSource := nil;
end;
// parse the source code
try
  Parser := THtmlParser.Create (Source, Dest);
  try
    Parser.Alone := True;
    Parser.Filename := EditSource.Text;
    Parser.Copyright := EditCopyr.Text;
    if ExtractFileExt(EditSource.Text) = '.dfm' then
      Parser.SetKeywordType (ktDfm);
    Parser.Convert;
  finally
    Parser.Free;
  end;
finally
  Dest.Free;
  Source.Free;
  BinSource.Free;
end;
// enable the third button
```

```
    BtnOpen.Enabled := True;
  end;
```

Notice, in particular, the code we use to convert the binary DFM file into the textual description. We call the `ObjectResourceToText` procedure, and use the next statement to reset the stream.

The third step is to load the newly generated HTML file in the user's default browser. The program accomplishes this by simply calling the `ShellExecute` API function and passing the filename and the *Open* command as parameters:

```
procedure TForm1.BtnOpenClick(Sender: TObject);
begin
  ShellExecute (Handle, 'open',
      PChar (EditDest.Text), '', '', sw_ShowNormal);
end;
```

You can see the effect of clicking the third button (and an example of the PasToWeb program source code converted to HTML) in Figure 3.16.

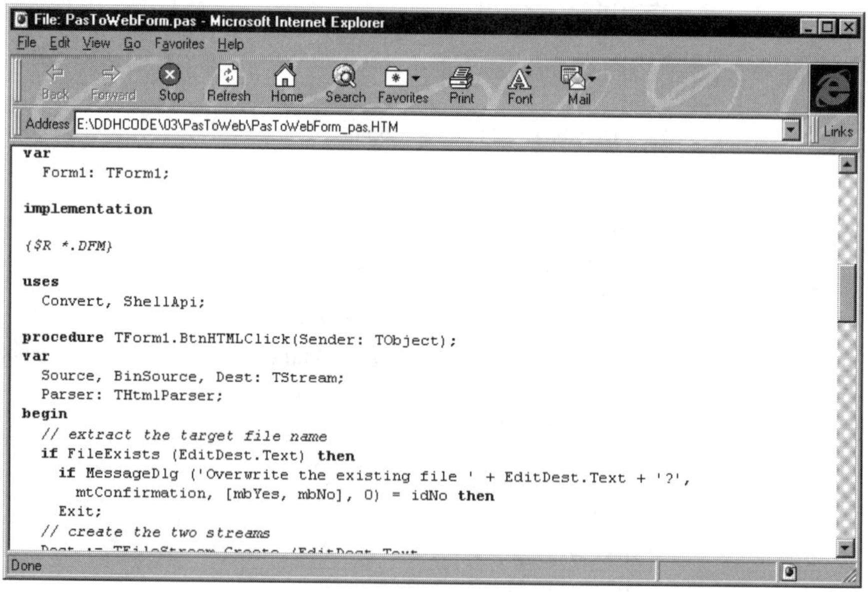

FIGURE 3.16:

The formatted source code of the program, viewed from Internet Explorer

```
var
  Form1: TForm1;

implementation

{$R *.DFM}

uses
  Convert, ShellApi;

procedure TForm1.BtnHTMLClick(Sender: TObject);
var
  Source, BinSource, Dest: TStream;
  Parser: THtmlParser;
begin
  // extract the target file name
  if FileExists (EditDest.Text) then
    if MessageDlg ('Overwrite the existing file ' + EditDest.Text + '?',
      mtConfirmation, [mbYes, mbNo], 0) = idNo then
      Exit;
  // create the two streams
```

What's Next

In this chapter, we've examined several ways you can use `TMemoryStream` and `TFileStream` classes. These classes are important, but not always easy to use. Their value becomes apparent as soon as you understand the role the `TReader` and `TWriter` classes play in loading and storing user-defined data, particularly components, in a stream. Once you've familiarized yourself with reading and writing components in a stream, Delphi's use of these classes in the design environment becomes much more obvious.

In future chapters, we'll revisit the notion of reading and writing DFM and PAS files (in the context of writing a wizard or expert). However, now that we've seen how components relate to the form that owns them (within the DFM files at least), and how you can access the properties of a streamed component, let's look at how Delphi manages RTTI information in memory. Then we'll be able to move to a central topic: creating new components.

Run-Time Type Information

- ■ Accessing Type Information

- ■ RTTI for Ordinal Types

- ■ RTTI for Method Pointers

- ■ RTTI for Classes

- ■ Accessing Property Values

You might have heard that Delphi uses Run-Time Type Information (RTTI) in many complex ways, but in the help file (and most of the available books) you'll find little or nothing on this subject. This is surprising, because RTTI is very important in the Delphi development environment.

Consider this common scenario: You write a new component that defines custom properties based on your own data types, and these properties appear automatically in the Object Inspector. How does the Object Inspector know about the code you've written? How can it list the values of an enumerated type or a set type you've defined? The magic behind this behavior is RTTI.

Wouldn't it be nice if your applications could access this information in a similar dynamic fashion? They can, and that's exactly what this chapter is about. We won't be able to tell you everything you want to know about this topic, simply because what we know is a result of research and experimentation. All Borland tells us about RTTI appears in the sparsely commented TypInfo.PAS file (in the SOURCE\VCL directory). This file includes no comments at all, in sharp contrast to most of the other VCL source code files.

Why isn't RTTI documented? The answer is probably that Borland wants to be free to change how RTTI works in future versions of Delphi. However, in looking at the first three versions of Delphi, we can say that this area seems to be quite stable. Even so, you must use caution when writing code that depends on the RTTI infrastructure, since it is completely unsupported by Borland (even though RTTI is frequently discussed in the Delphi forums on CompuServe, Usenet newsgroups, and mailing lists).

WARNING   Keep in mind that depending on compiled code and standard techniques is much faster than using RTTI! You should use RTTI only when you must, and not as a general approach to Delphi programming! Using RTTI is much too complex and produces very slow code!

Accessing Type Information

The basic idea behind RTTI is to access *information* about a given data *type* at *run-time*. The type can be a class or a simple Pascal data type (int, string, char and so on). As we'll see later on, you can also get the type information for a property.

Since the documentation on RTTI is nonexistent, we'll start exploring it by looking at the appropriate VCL source code files. If you look for the class TObject in the help or source files, you'll notice a couple of interesting methods that relate to RTTI, but they're barely documented:

```
type
  TObject = class

    ...
    class function ClassInfo: Pointer;
    class function MethodAddress(const Name: ShortString): Pointer;
    class function MethodName(Address: Pointer): ShortString;
    function FieldAddress(const Name: ShortString): Pointer;
  end;
```

The last three methods do approximately what you'd expect, and we'll use one of them later on. For the moment, we want to concentrate on the first one, which returns an untyped pointer. This pointer actually refers to an area in memory that holds the RTTI information for the class, which Delphi automatically generates when you compile the program. Notice that unlike the ClassType method of TObject (discussed in Chapter 1), this method doesn't return a class reference.

NOTE   The RTTI description of a class is a sort of metaclass, to borrow SmallTalk jargon. Actually, this class information is not part of a class itself, but only some internal and undocumented data used by Delphi at design and compile time. It's interesting to note that the C++Builder documentation uses the term *metaclass* to describe what we call a class reference in Delphi.

Looking at TypInfo.PAS

To understand the role of the ClassInfo pointer, we have to begin in the TypInfo.PAS file. It turns out that the ClassInfo pointer is actually of type PTypeInfo. The same pointer type is returned by another Delphi function, which allows you to access the type information of non-class data types:

```
function TypeInfo (TypeIdent): Pointer;
```

We've found several online references that suggest you can obtain RTTI information only for classes and properties. Although this is the most common use of RTTI, it's also possible to get similar information for plain data types and for classes with no published members.

The TTypeInfo Structure

Here is the definition of TTypeInfo, the data structure that PTypeInfo points to:

```
type
  PPTypeInfo = ^PTypeInfo; // a pointer to a pointer
  PTypeInfo = ^TTypeInfo; // a pointer to TTypeInfo
  TTypeInfo = record
    Kind: TTypeKind;
    Name: ShortString;
    {TypeData: TTypeData}
  end;
```

The Kind field holds an enumerated value, with the following definition:

```
type
  TTypeKind = (tkUnknown, tkInteger, tkChar, tkEnumeration,
    tkFloat, tkString, tkSet, tkClass, tkMethod, tkWChar,
    tkLString, tkLWString, tkVariant, tkArray, tkRecord,
    tkInterface);
```

Notice the support for long strings, wide (16-bit) characters, and long strings of wide characters. The last three types (array, record, and interface) have been introduced in Delphi 3. Some of these types have further specifications, listed in other enumerated types:

```
TOrdType = (otSByte, otUByte, otSWord, otUWord, otSLong);
TFloatType = (ftSingle, ftDouble, ftExtended, ftComp, ftCurr);
TMethodKind = (mkProcedure, mkFunction,
  mkSafeProcedure, mkSafeFunction);
TParamFlags = set of (pfVar, pfConst, pfArray, pfAddress,
  pfReference, pfOut);
TIntfFlags = set of (ifHasGuid, ifDispInterface, ifDispatch);
```

These further specifications are used by the TTypeData structure, as we'll see in the next section.

The TTypeData Structure

The TTypeData structure, in fact, is the type to which the *commented* TypeData member of the TTypeInfo record belongs. You can access it either by finding your way with pointer arithmetic (looking at the actual size of the string), or by following the official approach, using the GetTypeData function:

```
function GetTypeData(TypeInfo: PTypeInfo): PTypeData;
```

This function basically returns a pointer to the last field of the TTypeInfo structure. Which kind of type information do we get access to? This basically depends on the TTypeKind. The TTypeData structure, in fact, is a big variant record, with up to three levels of nested variant structures. Instead of showing you the original listing, we've tried to reformulate it in a more readable way, adding some comments as well:

```
type
  PTypeData = ^TTypeData; // a pointer to TTypeData
  TTypeData = packed record
    case TTypeKind of
      tkUnknown: ();  // no information
      tkLString: ();  // no information
      tkLWString: ();  // no information
      tkVariant: ();  // no information
      tkInteger: (
        OrdType: TOrdType;
        // otSByte, otUByte, otSWord, otUWord, otSLong;
        MinValue: Longint;
        MaxValue: Longint);
      tkChar, tkWChar: (
        OrdType: TOrdType;
        // otSByte, otUByte, otSWord, otUWord, otSLong;
        MinValue: Longint;
        MaxValue: Longint);
      tkEnumeration: (
        OrdType: TOrdType;
        // otSByte, otUByte, otSWord, otUWord, otSLong;
        MinValue: Longint;
        MaxValue: Longint;
        BaseType: PPTypeInfo;
        // the original type definition
        NameList: ShortString);
        // the enumeration names (see GetEnumName)
```

```
    tkSet: (
      OrdType: TOrdType;
      // otSByte, otUByte, otSWord, otUWord, otSLong;
      CompType: PPTypeInfo);
      // the enumerated type the set is built from
    tkFloat: (
      FloatType: TFloatType);
      // ftSingle, ftDouble, ftExtended, ftComp, ftCurr
    tkString: (
      MaxLength: Byte);
    tkClass: (
      ClassType: TClass;
      // the class reference
      ParentInfo: PPTypeInfo;
      // the parent type information
      PropCount: SmallInt;
      // the number of properties
      UnitName: ShortString
      // the unit defining the class type
      {PropData: TPropData});
      // the properties data: to access this information
      // call procedure GetPropInfos or function
      // GetPropList
  tkMethod: (
      MethodKind: TMethodKind;
      // mkProcedure, mkFunction,
      // mkSafeProcedure, mkSafeFunction
      ParamCount: Byte;
      // the number of parameters
      ParamList: array[0..1023] of Char
      // the parameters list, better described as:
      {ParamList: array[1..ParamCount] of
        record
          Flags: TParamFlags;
          // TParamFlags = set of (pfVar, pfConst, pfArray,
          //   pfAddress, pfReference, pfOut);
          ParamName: ShortString;
          TypeName: ShortString;
        end;
      ResultType: ShortString});
      // the return type
  tkInterface: (
```

```
      IntfParent : PPTypeInfo;
      // ancestor type
      IntfFlags : TIntfFlags;
      // set of (ifHasGuid, ifDispInterface, ifDispatch)
      GUID : TGUID;
      // the GUID of the interface
      IntfUnit : ShortString;
      // the unit defining the interface type
    {PropData: TPropData});
      // the properties data
  end;
```

Armed with this information, we can start writing some helper functions and test them in simple programs. We'll return to the TypInfo.PAS file later, to explore some further data structures and routines defined there.

TIP   In the directory for this chapter on the companion CD-ROM, you'll find a fully commented version of the TypInfo.PAS file, renamed CTypInfo.PAS. It can be a handy reference when using RTTI information in your programs.

RTTI for Ordinal Types

The simplest RTTI techniques relate to extracting information about ordinal types, including simple ones (integers and characters), enumerated types, and sets. Once you understand the TTypeData structure, learning to store your own RTTI information is fairly straightforward. We can now start writing some helper routines; then we'll build the program.

The first helper routine is the ShowOrdinal procedure, which adds RTTI information for enumerated data types to a list of strings (a TStrings object) that you pass as the second parameter. The first parameter is a PTypeInfo pointer.

```
procedure ShowOrdinal (pti: PTypeInfo; sList: TStrings);
var
  ptd: PTypeData;
begin
  // protect against misuse
  if not (pti^.Kind in [tkInteger, tkChar,
```

```
      tkEnumeration, tkSet, tkWChar]) then
    raise Exception.Create ('Invalid type information');

  // get a pointer to the TTypeData structure
  ptd := GetTypeData (pti);

  // access the TTypeInfo structure
  sList.Add ('Type Name: ' + pti^.Name);
  sList.Add ('Type Kind: ' + GetEnumName (
    TypeInfo (TTypeKind), Integer (pti^.Kind)));

  // access the TTypeData structure
  sList.Add ('Implement: ' + GetEnumName (
    TypeInfo (TOrdType), Integer (ptd^.OrdType)));

  // a set has no min and max
  if pti^.Kind <> tkSet then
  begin
    sList.Add ('Min Value: ' + IntToStr (ptd^.MinValue));
    sList.Add ('Max Value: ' + IntToStr (ptd^.MaxValue));
  end;

  // add the enumeration base type
  // and the list of the values
  if pti^.Kind = tkEnumeration then
  begin
    sList.Add ('Base Type: ' + (ptd^.BaseType)^.Name);
    sList.Add ('');
    sList.Add ('Values...');
    ListEnum (pti, sList);
  end;

  // show RRTI info about set base type
  if  pti^.Kind = tkSet then
  begin
    sList.Add ('');
    sList.Add ('Set base type information...');
    ShowOrdinal (ptd.CompType^, sList);
  end;
end;
```

In addition to the basic information about an enumerated type, this procedure lists the minimum and maximum values (if the data type is not a set), and lists specific values for enumerated and set types. Enumerated types have a base type (the type this enumeration was built from) and a list of values. The base type is usually just the type itself, but in some rare cases (for example, the TBorderStyle type) the base type is an enumeration with more values. Accordingly, the BaseType field is a TypeInfo pointer (PTypeInfo), so we can determine the base type name by dereferencing the pointer. To list the enumerated type's possible values, we use a second helper routine, ListEnum (described later on).

For a set, we just show the data of the base type by calling the ShowOrdinal procedure again. This is simple, because the CompType field stores the PTypeInfo pointer we need to pass to the procedure.

Listing the Values of an Enumerated Type

In the procedure above, you'll notice that we use the GetEnumName function a couple of times. We pass this function the appropriate type information (obtained by passing the enumerated data type to the TypeInfo function) and the enumeration value of the enumeration we're looking for. For example, we can write:

```
GetEnumName (TypeInfo (TFormStyle), 0)
```

to retrieve the fsNormal string from the TFormStyle enumeration. The code related to the TTypeKind and TOrdType enumerated types is only slightly more complex, in part because we have to cast the value of the enumerated type to an integer, as in:

```
GetEnumName (TypeInfo (TFormStyle), Integer (fsNormal))
```

This returns the string corresponding to the enumeration value we passed as the second parameter. We can perform the reverse operation as well, by calling the GetEnumValue function.

What's interesting is that if we know the minimum and maximum value of an enumerated type, we can easily list all of the names. This is what the procedure ListEnum does in few lines of code:

```
procedure ListEnum (pti: PTypeInfo; sList: TStrings);
var
  I: Integer;
begin
  with GetTypeData(pti)^ do
```

```
      for I := MinValue to MaxValue do
        sList.Add ('   ' + IntToStr (I) + '. ' +
          GetEnumName (pti, I));
  end;
```

The OrdType Example

Using the helper functions from the previous section, we can now build a simple example that displays ordinal type information. We need to provide a component that displays a list of strings (a list box or a memo will do), and an interface for selecting a data type.

A good solution would be to use a list box or a combo box to select a data type. However, if we add the names of the data types to this list, we'll have no way to retrieve the type information. You might remember we faced a similar problem in Chapter 1, but in that case we were listing classes, and using the GetClass function to display the type information of a *registered* class.

Here, we'll have to follow a different approach. One solution is to create a list that contains both the class names *and* the class information. This is easy to do because the TStrings and TStringList classes allow us to associate objects with the strings they contain. Since these object associations are simply 32-bit pointers, we can store any similar pointer by casting it as a TObject pointer:

```
ListBox1.Items.AddObject('Integer',
  TObject (TypeInfo (Integer)))
```

Since we'd like to add many data types to the list, we can wrap this statement inside a form method, which accepts a PTypeInfo parameter:

```
procedure TForm1.AddType (pti: PTypeInfo);
begin
  ListBox1.Items.AddObject(pti^.Name, TObject (pti))
end;
```

When the application creates the form, the OrdType program calls this AddType method about 200 times, passing both system and VCL types:

```
procedure TForm1.FormCreate(Sender: TObject);
begin
  AddType (TypeInfo (Boolean));
  AddType (TypeInfo (Char));
  AddType (TypeInfo (Integer));
  AddType (TypeInfo (TAlignment));
```

```
AddType (TypeInfo (TComponentState));
AddType (TypeInfo (TShiftState));
...
```

Of course, you can add more system types (provided they are ordinal types) and many more VCL types. We've picked just a few. Now when the user clicks on an item of the list box, the following procedure will retrieve the pointer to the type information and update the list:

```
procedure TForm1.Listbox1Click(Sender: TObject);
var
   pti: PTypeInfo;
begin
   pti := PTypeInfo (ListBox1.Items.Objects [
      Listbox1.ItemIndex]);
   ListBox2.Items.Clear;
   ShowOrdinal (pti, ListBox2.Items);
end;
```

The result of all of this work is the form shown in Figure 4.1. In this case, the program is displaying the RTTI information of an enumerated type, but you should try running it with plain ordinal values and sets, too. You'll see that sets sometimes show a very odd behavior, as illustrated in Figure 4.2.

FIGURE 4.1:

The list of possible values of an ordinal type as displayed by the OrdType program

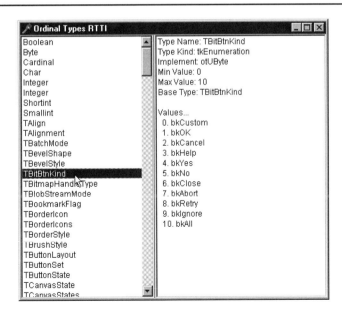

The OrdType program can show the RTTI information of a set, but in this case the base type number is actually a number.

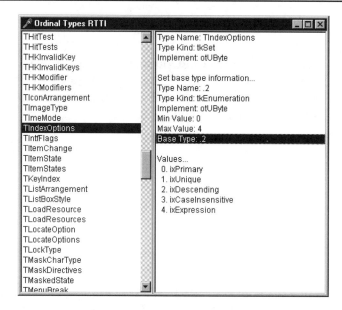

For this type, the list of the set's base type values is correct, but the name of this base type is a number. This may seem odd, but it's perfectly logical from the compiler's point of view. In fact, the Pascal compiler (internally) uses a number to refer to every *unnamed* data type. A data type is unnamed if you define it without giving it a name explicitly. Generally, you might let it go unnamed when you are within another declaration. For example, you can use an array as a record field or function parameter, without giving the array a formal type name (in a standard type declaration). In a similar fashion, you can define an enumerated type within the definition of a set, without giving it a name. The definition of the TComponentStyle type in the VCL source code is a good example:

```
type
   TComponentStyle = set of (
     csInheritable, csCheckPropAvail);
```

Special Functions for Cursors and Color

If you run the OrdType example and examine the TColor and TCursor data types, you'll notice that they appear as numeric values and not enumerated types, even though their behavior in the Object Inspector might seem to indicate that they are enumerated types. However, even though these are not enumerated types, our

program is able to display the cursor or color names anyway (see Figure 4.3).
How did we accomplish that?

The list of colors
displayed by the
OrdType pro-
gram. Notice that
TColor is not an
enumerated type,
so we have to use
a special function
to display the
information for its
values.

The answer is that Delphi provides special procedures that enable us to retrieve a
lot of information about these two particular data types. For instance, to see a list of
available cursors or colors, you can call the GetCursorValues and GetColorValues
procedures, respectively. These two procedures behave like *enumerated functions*:
They accept a method as parameter, and then call that method once for each value in
the type range. Here's the method we'll pass to these procedures:

```
procedure TForm1.AddToList (S: String);
begin
  ListBox2.Items.Add (S);
end;
```

And here is the updated version of the `ListBox1Click` method of the form:

```
procedure TForm1.Listbox1Click(Sender: TObject);
var
  pti: PTypeInfo;
begin
  pti := PTypeInfo (ListBox1.Items.Objects [
    Listbox1.ItemIndex]);
  ListBox2.Items.Clear;
  ShowOrdinal (pti, ListBox2.Items);

  // special case: TColor
  if ListBox1.Items [ListBox1.ItemIndex] = 'TColor' then
  begin
    ListBox2.Items.Add ('');
    ListBox2.Items.Add ('Values...');
    GetColorValues (AddToList);
  end;

  // special case: TCursor
  if ListBox1.Items [ListBox1.ItemIndex] = 'TCursor' then
  begin
    ListBox2.Items.Add ('');
    ListBox2.Items.Add ('Values...');
    GetCursorValues (AddToList);
  end;
end;
```

Delphi provides several other support functions for manipulating colors and cursors, such as ColorToString and CursorToString (to convert a numeric value into the corresponding color or cursor string), and StringToColor and StringToCursor (which convert a valid identifier string to the corresponding numeric value). There are actually more routines for manipulating these types, including ColorToIdent and IdentToColor, as well as IdentToCursor and CursorToIdent, which perform similar actions.

RTTI for Method Pointers

Accessing the RTTI data for ordinal types isn't too difficult once you understand the basic concepts. Acquiring the same information for method pointers is slightly more complex. The example we're going to build (MethType) is very similar to the OrdType example we've just seen.

Again, we display the information in two list boxes, one for the type names, and the other for the RTTI data we've retrieved. As before, we'll fill the first list box by calling the AddType method, which adds the type name to the list and type data to the corresponding item of the list's `Objects` array property. However, we're now passing method pointer types to the AddType method instead of data types:

```
procedure TForm1.FormCreate(Sender: TObject);
begin
  AddType (TypeInfo (TNotifyEvent));
  AddType (TypeInfo (TFindMethodEvent));
  AddType (TypeInfo (THelpEvent));
  AddType (TypeInfo (TSetNameEvent));
  ...
```

When the user selects a new item in this list box, the second box displays the appropriate type information by calling the ShowMethod helper routine:

```
procedure TForm1.Listbox1Click(Sender: TObject);
var
  pti: PTypeInfo;
begin
  pti := PTypeInfo (ListBox1.Items.Objects [
    Listbox1.ItemIndex]);
  ListBox2.Items.Clear;
  ShowMethod (pti, ListBox2.Items);
end;
```

All the important code for this example is in one procedure, called ShowMethod. This is a rather complex procedure, so we'll discuss it one section at a time. The first part of the procedure resembles the ShowOrdinal procedure of the last example:

```
procedure ShowMethod (pti: PTypeInfo; sList: TStrings);
var
  ptd: PTypeData;
begin
  // protect against misuse
  if pti^.Kind <> tkMethod then
    raise Exception.Create ('Invalid type information');

  // get a pointer to the TTypeData structure
  ptd := GetTypeData (pti);
```

```
// 1: access the TTypeInfo structure
sList.Add ('Type Name: ' + pti^.Name);
sList.Add ('Type Kind: ' + GetEnumName (
  TypeInfo (TTypeKind),
  Integer (pti^.Kind)));
```

Getting a Method's Parameters

Once we've displayed the basic type information, we can start looking at the specific method data:

```
// 2: access the TTypeData structure
sList.Add ('Method Kind: ' + GetEnumName (
  TypeInfo (TMethodKind),
  Integer (ptd^.MethodKind)));
sList.Add ('Number of parameters: ' +
  IntToStr (ptd^.ParamCount));
```

Here we determine the kind of method (either procedure or function) and the number of parameters it accepts. Displaying the parameter information is where things get a bit complicated. You may want to review the TTypeData record (shown in the first section) before proceeding. Since the actual structure of the parameters' data was commented out in the earlier listing, we've redefined it as:

```
type
  TParamData = record
    Flags: TParamFlags;
    ParamName: ShortString;
    TypeName: ShortString;
  end;
  PParamData = ^TParamData;
```

In practice, for each parameter there is the flag, followed by two strings. The problem is that the physical length of each string corresponds to the actual length of its data, so we have to examine the length bytes (these are traditional Pascal short strings) to see where the next string begins. In fact, we cannot use the TypeName field to access the second string, since the record definition suggests a fixed string length. Instead, once we have a pointer to the beginning of the structure, we can calculate a pointer to the beginning of the TypeName string using the following code:

```
var
  pParam: PParamData;
```

```
  pTypeString: ^ShortString;
...
  pTypeString := Pointer (Integer (pParam) +
    sizeof (TParamFlags) +
    Length (pParam^.ParamName) + 1);
```

After casting the pParam pointer as an integer (to perform some pointer arithmetic) and then casting it back as a generic pointer, this statement increments the pParam pointer by the size of the flags plus the length of the string (including its length byte). Similar pointer arithmetic moves the pointer to the data structure of the next parameter, or to a final string that holds the method's return type (if it's a function). The return type is available at the end of the parameter list.

Here's the last section of code (including the variables for that section); it's complex, so we've included plenty of comments:

```
var
  pParam: PParamData;
  nParam: Integer;
  Line: string;
  pTypeString, pReturnString: ^ShortString;
...
  // 3: access the ParamList
  // get the initial pointer and
  // reset the parameters counter
  pParam := PParamData (@(ptd^.ParamList));
  nParam := 1;
  // loop until all parameters are done
  while nParam <= ptd^.ParamCount do
  begin
    // read the information
    Line := 'Param ' + IntToStr (nParam) + ' > ';
    // add type of parameter
    if pfVar in pParam^.Flags then
      Line := Line + 'var ';
    if pfConst in pParam^.Flags then
      Line := Line + 'const ';
    if pfOut in pParam^.Flags then
      Line := Line + 'out ';
    // get the parameter name
    Line := Line + pParam^.ParamName + ': ';
    // one more type of parameter
    if pfArray in pParam^.Flags then
```

```
      Line := Line + ' array of ';
      // the type name string must be located...
      // moving a pointer past the params and
      // the string (including its size byte)
      pTypeString := Pointer (Integer (pParam) +
        sizeof (TParamFlags) +
        Length (pParam^.ParamName) + 1);
      // add the type name
      Line := Line + pTypeString^;
      // finally, output the string
      sList.Add (Line);
      // move the pointer to the next structure,
      // past the two strings (including size byte)
      pParam := PParamData (Integer (pParam) +
        sizeof (TParamFlags) +
        Length (pParam^.ParamName) + 1 +
        Length (pTypeString^) + 1);
      // increase the parameter counter
      Inc (nParam);
    end;
    // show the return type if a function
    if ptd^.MethodKind = mkFunction then
    begin
      // at the end, instead of param data,
      // there is the return string
      pReturnString := Pointer (pParam);
      sList.Add ('Returns > ' + pReturnString^);
    end;
  end;
```

You can see the output of this example in Figure 4.4. Most of the methods we've used here are procedures. Only the THelpEvent method type refers to a function. Of course, you can look for more method pointer types in the Delphi help files or the VCL source code, and add them to the list.

NOTE　　In Chapter 5, we'll see that Delphi is capable of creating a method from the parameters of a given user-defined event, and in Chapter 13 we'll see how this actually happens when you call the CreateMethod function of the TFormDesigner class. The RTTI information of a method pointer type includes everything Delphi needs to write the signature of a compatible method, including the names of the parameters.

FIGURE 4.4:

The output of the
MethType exam-
ple, showing RTTI
information for
method pointer
types

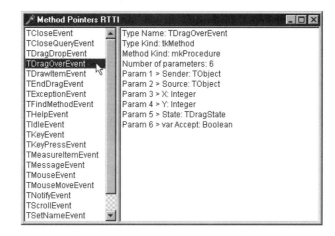

RTTI for Classes

After displaying RTTI data for ordinal types and method pointers, we are now
ready to tackle the more complex task of displaying RTTI for classes. Needless to
say, we'll build an example with a user interface similar to the last two, and write
a helper routine to add a class's RTTI data to a TStrings object.

As in the previous examples, we'll use one list box to display class names and
contain the pointers to the RTTI structures, and another to display the RTTI data.
For this example, we'll display RTTI data for more than 200 classes:

```
procedure TForm1.FormCreate(Sender: TObject);
begin
  AddType (TypeInfo (TApplication));
  AddType (TypeInfo (TAutoIncField));
  AddType (TypeInfo (TBatchMove));
  AddType (TypeInfo (TBCDField));
  AddType (TypeInfo (TBevel));
  AddType (TypeInfo (TBitBtn));
  ...
```

We'll use another helper routine, ShowClass, to add the RTTI data to the second
list when the user selects a class type. This procedure has the same structure as

the helper procedures we've seen in the two previous examples, so the first part should be familiar:

```
procedure ShowClass (pti: PTypeInfo; sList: TStrings);
var
  ptd: PTypeData;
begin
  // protect against misuse
  if pti^.Kind <> tkClass then
    raise Exception.Create ('Invalid type information');

  // get a pointer to the TTypeData structure
  ptd := GetTypeData (pti);

  // access the TTypeInfo structure
  sList.Add ('Type Name: ' + pti^.Name);
  sList.Add ('Type Kind: ' + GetEnumName (
    TypeInfo (TTypeKind),
    Integer (pti^.Kind)));

  // access the TTypeData structure
  {omitted: the same information of pti^.Name...
  sList.Add ('ClassType: ' + ptd^.ClassType.ClassName);}
  sList.Add ('Size: ' + IntToStr (
    ptd^.ClassType.InstanceSize) + ' bytes');
  sList.Add ('Defined in: ' + ptd^.UnitName + '.pas');
```

NOTE   In addition to the RTTI data you might expect, we can also access the name of the unit that defined a class data structure. This information is available only for classes (it's used by Delphi to add referenced units automatically when you place a component on a form).

In the above code we use the TTypeData record's ClassType member to display the instance size (the size of an object in memory) of that class. Of course, given this information we can show additional class data. What's probably most interesting is that we can list a class's parent classes, using code adapted from the ClassInfo example of Chapter 1:

```
var
  ParentClass: TClass;
...
  // add the list of parent classes (if any)
```

```
ParentClass := ptd^.ClassType.ClassParent;
if ParentClass <> nil then
begin
  sList.Add ('');
  sList.Add ('=== Parent classes ===');
  while ParentClass <> nil do
  begin
    sList.Add (ParentClass.ClassName);
    ParentClass := ParentClass.ClassParent;
  end;
end;
```

In Figure 4.5 you can see the RTTI data of a class and the names of its parent classes. In this example, you can click on one of the parent class names to view the RTTI data for that class. We accomplish this by determining whether the first list box contains a string that corresponds to the string a user has clicked in the second list box:

```
procedure TForm1.ListBox2Click(Sender: TObject);
var
  Text: string;
  Index: Integer;
  pti: PTypeInfo;
begin
  // get the current item
  Text := ListBox2.Items [ListBox2.ItemIndex];
  // search the first list box
  Index := ListBox1.Items.IndexOf (Text);
  // if found, it was a parent class: show RTTI
  if Index >= 0 then
  begin
    pti := PTypeInfo (ListBox1.Items.Objects [Index]);
    Caption := 'RTTI information for ' + Text;
    ListBox2.Items.Clear;
    ShowClass (pti, ListBox2.Items);
  end;
end;
```

Besides showing some interesting RTTI data for class types, the ClassTyp example also has an interesting user interface. Even so, there's more we want to add. In the next section, we'll extend this program to show information about properties, too.

FIGURE 4.5:

FIGURE 4.5:

The output of the ClassTyp program, showing some RTTI data and the list of parent classes. Clicking on one of the parent classes allows you to view that class's RTTI data.

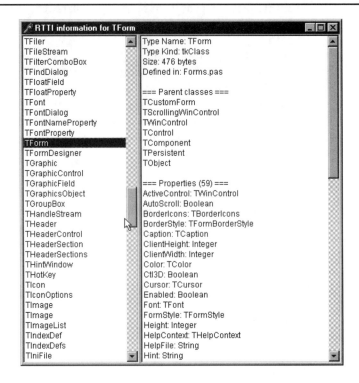

Getting the List of Properties

We began this chapter by discussing the data structures defined in the TypInfo.PAS file. Now it's time to complete that discussion. If you recall, the TTypeData record's tkClass section included the commented definition of the field PropData, which is a TPropData record instance. Here's the definition of this data type:

```
type
  TPropData = packed record
    PropCount: Word;
    PropList: record end;
    {PropList: array[1..PropCount] of TPropInfo}
  end;
```

As it turns out, the TPropData structure is seldom used. The reason is that it's easier to access this information using one of the following two routines (defined in TypInfo.PAS):

```
procedure GetPropInfos(TypeInfo: PTypeInfo; PropList: PPropList);
function GetPropList(TypeInfo: PTypeInfo; TypeKinds: TTypeKinds;
    PropList: PPropList): Integer;
```

These two routines fill the PropList list with pointers to each property's RTTI data. The GetPropInfos procedure retrieves all of the properties, while the GetPropList function allows you to specify a filter for the kind of properties you're interested in, and returns the properties that match the filter criteria.

WARNING   Remember that all the property information we're displaying is available only for published properties. Public properties generate no RTTI.

The PropList parameter used by these two routines is similar to the last parameter of the TPropData record above:

```
type
  PPropList = ^TPropList;
  TPropList = array[0..16379] of PPropInfo;
```

In practice, TPropList is a list of pointers to each property's RTTI data, and PPropList is a pointer to the list of pointers. You'll notice that these type definitions and the TPropData record all refer to another data type, TPropInfo. The GetPropInfo function also returns a pointer to this data type, and it extracts the PPropInfo pointer for a specific property passed by name:

```
function GetPropInfo(TypeInfo: PTypeInfo;
    const PropName: string): PPropInfo;
```

You can use this function to access specific properties by name, and we'll find it very useful in future examples. For the moment, though, we'll turn our attention to the TPropInfo data structure:

```
type
  PPropInfo = ^TPropInfo;
  TPropInfo = packed record
    PropType: PTypeInfo; // property type RTTI
    GetProc: Pointer; // read method
    SetProc: Pointer; // write method
    StoredProc: Pointer; // store method
```

```
      Index: Integer; // property index
      Default: Longint; // default value (odd type)
      NameIndex: SmallInt; // index of the name
      Name: ShortString; // name
    end;
```

This structure reveals a lot of information about a property: the property's name, the index of its name (probably referring to a list of names, possibly as an optimization to save memory), an index of the property, and a pointer to the property type's RTTI data.

In addition, there are three method pointers that specify (if the property defines them) how to read, write, and store the property's value. In fact, these pointers reference the methods from the read, write, and stored sections of the property definition. We can use the pointers to determine if the methods are defined, and if so, we can then retrieve a method's memory address. Unfortunately, we can't determine the method names, because it is very uncommon to use published methods (and only published methods have RTTI data) to implement property access.

The final element of this record is the default value of the property. The strange thing here is the data type of this field, LongInt. In fact, the actual meaning of this value is determined by the data type of the property, so it's possible to use the default value only after casting it to the proper type (although we are not going to use it in the example).

With this long introduction, we're now ready to examine the final part of the ShowClass procedure from the ClassTyp example of the last section. The code reads the number of properties from the TPropData structure, and if it finds any properties, it generates an initial line (to specify the start of the property information), and then displays a line describing each property. We retrieve the property information by calling the GetPropInfos function and passing a block of memory as the PPropInfo parameter, which we've allocated the proper size (which is equal to the size of the list pointers multiplied by the number of properties).

```
var
  ppi: PPropInfo;
  pProps: PPropList;
  nProps, I: Integer;
...
  // add the list of properties (if any)
  nProps := ptd^.PropCount;
  if nProps > 0 then
```

```
begin
  // format the initial output
  sList.Add ('');
  sList.Add ('=== Properties (' +
    IntToStr (nProps) + ') ===');
  // allocate the required memory
  GetMem (pProps, sizeof (PPropInfo) * nProps);
  // protect the memory allocation
  try
    // fill the TPropList structure
    // pointed to by pProps
    GetPropInfos(pti, pProps);
    // sort the properties
    SortPropList(pProps, nProps);
    // show name and data type of each property
    for I := 0 to nProps - 1 do
    begin
      ppi := pProps [I];
      sList.Add (ppi^.Name + ': ' +
        ppi^.PropType^.Name);
    end;
  finally
    // free the allocated memory
    FreeMem (pProps, sizeof (PPropInfo) * nProps);
  end;
end;
```

Inside the try-finally block (also used to free the memory in the case of an exception), we retrieve the property information, and display each property name and type inside a for loop. In between these statements, however, we call another procedure, SortPropList. As the name implies, this procedure sorts the properties alphabetically in the list.

NOTE   By default, property lists are sorted *in order of definition*: The first property in the list is the first defined in the source code of the higher-level parent class, followed by those defined by lower-level classes, and ending with the specific properties of the class. For this reason, sorting the properties alphabetically improves the output considerably.

We found the SortPropList procedure while looking at the implementation section of the TypInfo unit. Unfortunately, this procedure isn't exported. Well, that's not a big problem: We can simply *borrow* its code and copy it into the source code of our program. Now, don't even think about editing this code unless you are well versed in assembler! That's right, the code of this procedure is not written in Pascal but in inline assembler. In fact, about 70 percent of the source code for the routines in the TypInfo.PAS file is in assembler.

To give you an idea of what this code looks like, here's a fragment of the SortPropList procedure. As you can see, it is actually fully commented and quite understandable:

```
procedure SortPropList(PropList: PPropList;
  PropCount: Integer); assembler;
asm
  { ->     EAX Pointer to prop list      }
  {        EDX Property count            }
  { <-     nothing                       }
  PUSH    EBX
  PUSH    ESI
  PUSH    EDI
  MOV     ECX,EAX
  XOR     EAX,EAX
  DEC     EDX
  CALL    @@qsort
  ...
```

Now we've reviewed all the code of the ClassTyp program. You can see an example of its output, including a list of properties, in Figure 4.6. However, you should really try running the program to fully appreciate its behavior.

So far in this chapter we've delved into the TypInfo.PAS file (and introduced a few routines we'll see later on), and built simple programs that display RTTI data for ordinal types, method pointers, and classes. At this point, we could have put everything together in a comprehensive example that displays RTTI data for every class. However, considering the structure of these programs and the helper routines that add data to lists of strings, it should be pretty simple for you to build this type of application, if you want. We'll incorporate similar RTTI techniques in other, more advanced examples.

The initial part of
the list of the
properties of the
TButton class,
shown by the
ClassTyp program

Accessing Property Values

We've just seen that it's possible to retrieve the list of properties for a given class, but that capability isn't very useful for most programs. We've also seen that we can use the GetPropInfo function to determine the RTTI data for a property based on its name. Again, this is not terribly useful by itself. It would be nice to be able to access a given property's data, based on the property name.

Usually, the property access methods for a program are fully compiled, and the compiler replaces references to the property itself (such as Button1.Caption) with the corresponding methods indicated in the read and write definitions of the property. This is some of the work the Delphi compiler does to make our programs run fast.

Having said this, it is interesting to know there is a dynamic (or run-time) technique to access the value of *published* properties. It is important to emphasize that this applies only to published properties; only methods and fields that appear under this access specifier will generate the RTTI information we need. You cannot access public properties (also called *run-time* properties) using RTTI.

Once we have a pointer to property information (that is, a PPropInfo pointer), you may be wondering how we get the real values. The TypInfo.PAS file helps us again, by providing the following routines:

```
function GetOrdProp (Instance: TObject;
  PropInfo: PPropInfo): Longint;
procedure SetOrdProp (Instance: TObject;
  PropInfo: PPropInfo; Value: Longint);

function GetStrProp (Instance: TObject;
  PropInfo: PPropInfo): string;
procedure SetStrProp (Instance: TObject;
  PropInfo: PPropInfo; const Value: string);

function GetFloatProp (Instance: TObject;
  PropInfo: PPropInfo): Extended;
procedure SetFloatProp (Instance: TObject;
  PropInfo: PPropInfo; Value: Extended);

function GetVariantProp (Instance: TObject;
  PropInfo: PPropInfo): Variant;
procedure SetVariantProp (Instance: TObject;
  PropInfo: PPropInfo; const Value: Variant);

function GetMethodProp (Instance: TObject;
  PropInfo: PPropInfo): TMethod;
procedure SetMethodProp (Instance: TObject;
  PropInfo: PPropInfo; const Value: TMethod);
```

As you can see, there is a Set procedure and a Get function for each *kind* of data (as indicated by the TTypeKind enumeration). Each routine accepts an Instance parameter (the pointer to the object), and a PProfInfo parameter that specifies the property you want to access.

For the first time in this chapter we're now dealing with specific objects (instances), and not the type information for a class or other data type. This is because we're now looking for values, and the properties (as part of a data type) have no *value* until you create an instance of that type. Only objects can store a value for a property.

There's an exception to what we've just said: It's possible to create a property that you can access without a valid instance. However, to do so, you must use class methods for the *Get* and *Set* methods of the property. Then, you can reference that property by using an identifier for that class—even if you've never initialized the instance! This is a useful technique for simulating class fields, which store a value that's common among all the objects in a class.

Getting String Properties

The first example of dynamic property access is quite simple. We've placed a button on a form (inside a bevel to make it stand out) and added a few more components to interact with it. You can see the form at design-time in Figure 4.7, and the textual description of its key elements below (in particular, notice the component names, which we use in the source code):

```
object Form1: TForm1
  Caption = 'Property Access'
  object Label1: TLabel
    Caption = 'String Property:'
  end
  object Bevel1: TBevel...
  object Label2: TLabel
    Caption = 'Result:'
  end
  object LabelResult: TLabel...
    // will show the result of the get operation
  object Label3: TLabel
    Caption = 'New value:'
  end
  object ButtonGet: TButton
    Caption = 'Get Value'
    OnClick = ButtonGetClick
    // start the get-property-value operation
  end
  object EditProperty: TEdit
    Text = 'Caption'
    // the caption you want to get or set
  end
```

```
object ButtonTrial: TButton
  Hint = 'Hello!'
  Caption = 'Trial Button'
  ShowHint = True
  // the target of the get and set operations
end
object ButtonSet: TButton
  Caption = 'Set Value'
  OnClick = ButtonSetClick
  // start the set-property-value operation
end
object EditValue: TEdit
  Text = 'Button'
  // the new value of the property
end
end
```

FIGURE 4.7

The StrProp
program's form
at design time

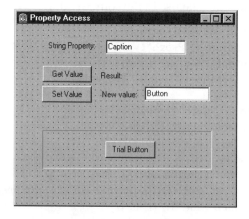

Now that you have an idea of what the various components do, you can probably figure out the following code, which retrieves the current value of the property specified in one of the edit boxes:

```
procedure TForm1.ButtonGetClick(Sender: TObject);
var
  PropInfo: PPropInfo;
begin
if not Assigned (ButtonTrial) then
    ShowMessage ('The button has been renamed')
```

```
else
begin
PropInfo := GetPropInfo (
  ButtonTrial.ClassInfo, EditProperty.Text);
if PropInfo <> nil then
  if PropInfo^.PropType^.Kind =
      tkLString then
    LabelResult.Caption :=
      GetStrProp (ButtonTrial, PropInfo)
  else
    ShowMessage ('Not a string property')
else
  ShowMessage ('Property doesn''t exist');
end;
end;
```

After acquiring the necessary property information (using GetPropInfo), this procedure performs two tests. First, it checks whether the return value from calling GetPropInfo was nil. If so, the property was not found (it doesn't exist for a TButton object). Next, this procedure checks whether the property kind is tkLString, and it displays an error message if not. Notice that we use two different if statements (instead of placing both conditions in a single one) to show more detailed error messages.

If both tests are successful, the program simply calls the GetStrProp function, and passes the object reference and a pointer to its property information as parameters for the function. The result is the current property value for the object.

By writing similar code for the SetStrProp procedure, we can dynamically store a new value for the property:

```
procedure TForm1.ButtonSetClick(Sender: TObject);
var
  PropInfo: PPropInfo;
begin
  PropInfo := GetPropInfo (
    ButtonTrial.ClassInfo, EditProperty.Text);
  if PropInfo <> nil then
    if PropInfo^.PropType^.Kind =
        tkLString then
      SetStrProp (ButtonTrial, PropInfo, EditValue.Text)
    else
      ShowMessage ('Not a string property')
```

```
  else
    ShowMessage ('Property doesn''t exist');
end;
```

If you specify a new value for the button's Caption, you'll see it immediately at run-time. The only other string property you'll want to change is the Hint property. You might change the component's Name, but this causes problems, as discussed in Chapter 2 (it resets the form field for the component to nil, which causes the program to crash if any code references the component). To avoid the problems related to dynamically changing the name of the ButtonTrial component, we've added this test to the beginning of the methods that set and retrieve the property value:

```
if Assigned (ButtonTrial) then ...
```

As a result of calling this function first, you may not change the button's property, but at least the program doesn't crash.

Enumerated Types at Run-Time

Just to reinforce the idea of dynamically accessing and altering properties, let's consider how you can do something similar with enumerated property types. In our next example, ListEnum, the user can select a property name from a combo box instead of typing one in an edit box, and see all the possible values in a list box. In addition to this (which you can do with *static* RTTI data), the user can select the current value of a property from a list of enumerated types, and then change the current value by selecting a different item of the list.

When the program launches, we begin by initializing the property selection combo box with all the enumerated properties of the TForm class:

```
procedure TForm1.FormCreate(Sender: TObject);
var
  pProps: PPropList;
  nTotProps, nProps, I: Integer;
begin
  // set the initial value
  SelPropName := '';

  // get the total number of properties
  nTotProps := GetTypeData(ClassInfo).PropCount;
  // allocate the required memory
```

```
GetMem (pProps, sizeof (PPropInfo) * nTotProps);
// protect the memory allocation
try
  // fill the pProps with a filtered list
  nProps := GetPropList (ClassInfo,
    [tkEnumeration], pProps);
  // fill the combo box
  for I := 0 to nProps - 1 do
    ComboBox1.Items.Add (pProps[I].Name);
finally
  // free the allocated memory
  FreeMem (pProps, sizeof (PPropInfo) * nTotProps);
end;
end;
```

This method sets the TForm1 class's SelPropName field, which we use to store the name of the selected property, to an empty string. Then it examines the RTTI data for the form class (calling ClassInfo without specifying a class effectively calls the method for the current object, self), allocates memory for the PPropList, and fills the list only with the enumerated properties, using the GetPropList function. At the end, we copy the names of the properties and then release the memory we allocated.

Once we've filled the combo box with the enumerated property names, selecting an item in the list displays the corresponding constants of the enumeration in the list box:

```
procedure TForm1.ComboBox1Change(Sender: TObject);
var
  PropInfo: PPropInfo;
  ptd: PTypeData;
  I: Integer;
  PropValue: Integer;
begin
  // set the name of the current property
  if ComboBox1.Text <> '' then
    SelPropName := ComboBox1.Text;
  // add to the listbox the values
  // of the enumerated type
  ListBox1.Items.Clear;
  PropInfo := GetPropInfo (
    ClassInfo, SelPropName);
```

```
    ptd := GetTypeData (PropInfo.PropType^);
    // list the values
    for I := ptd.MinValue to ptd.MaxValue do
      ListBox1.Items.Add (GetEnumName (
        PropInfo.PropType^, I));
    // select the current value
    PropValue := GetOrdProp (self, PropInfo);
    ListBox1.ItemIndex := ptd.MinValue + PropValue;
  end;
```

We've already seen code that lists the values of an enumeration, so the only really new code here is the last two lines. To set the current property's value, we simply alter the list box item that has the corresponding index. You can see the effect of this code in Figure 4.8.

FIGURE 4.8:

The output of the ListEnum program shows the possible values of an enumerated property, with the current value selected.

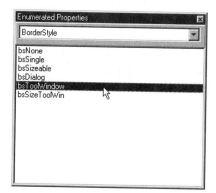

Now comes the interesting part. By clicking on the list box you can execute a similar piece of code to set a new value for the enumerated property:

```
procedure TForm1.ListBox1Click(Sender: TObject);
var
  itemIndex: integer;
  PropInfo: PPropInfo;
  ptd: PTypeData;
begin
  if SelPropName <> '' then
  begin
    PropInfo := GetPropInfo (
      ClassInfo, SelPropName);
    ptd := GetTypeData(PropInfo.PropType^);
```

```
// Save combo box index
itemIndex := ComboBox1.ItemIndex;

// Select the current value
SetOrdProp (self, PropInfo,
 ListBox1.ItemIndex - ptd.MinValue);

// Restore combo box index
ComboBox1.OnChange  := nil;
ComboBox1.ItemIndex := itemIndex;
ComboBox1.OnChange  := ComboBox1Change;

  end;
end;
```

Setting the Caption of Any Component

Many Delphi programmers have asked, "How do I set the caption of a component if I don't know its data type?" For example, you may want to set the caption of a button using the Sender parameter of an event-response method. To accomplish this, the most obvious technique is to cast the data type back to the original type, as in:

```
(Sender as TButton).Caption := 'New caption';
```

What if we want to allow our user to set the caption of a check box or radio button, or even an edit component (which uses Text as the name of the corresponding property)? There are two solutions to this problem.

First, we can use the SetTextBuf and GetTextBuf methods, which are available for every TControl-derived class:

```
procedure TForm1.AnyClick(Sender: TObject);
var
  pcCapt: array [0..100] of Char;
begin
  // get the current value
  (Sender as TControl).GetTextBuf (
    pcCapt, sizeof (pcCapt));
  // add a *
  StrCat (pcCapt, '*');
  // set the new value
```

```
  (Sender as TControl).SetTextBuf (pcCapt);
end;
```

The second solution is to use dynamic property access, as we demonstrated in the last few examples. This time, however, we can access either the Caption or the Text property of different components, but with the same piece of code:

```
procedure TForm1.AnyClick(Sender: TObject);
var
  PropInfo: PPropInfo;
  Capt: string;
begin
  // get property RTTI
  PropInfo := GetPropInfo (Sender.ClassInfo, 'Caption');
  // try again
  if PropInfo = nil then
    PropInfo := GetPropInfo (Sender.ClassInfo, 'Text');

  // if found, apply the new value
  if PropInfo <> nil then
  begin
    Capt := GetStrProp (Sender, PropInfo);
    Capt := Capt + '*';
    SetStrProp (Sender, PropInfo, Capt);
  end;
end;
```

This code is part of the SetTitle example, where it's part of the OnClick event-handler of many components: a button, an edit box, a group box, two radio buttons, a label, and even the form itself. You can see an example of the form (with the asterisk (*) added to the captions) in Figure 4.9.

As we mentioned before, in this case there was a good alternative to using RTTI data for properties, so it wasn't really the best approach. In other cases, however, there is no alternative solution, and you should use dynamic RTTI techniques. We'll see an example of this in Chapter 18.

FIGURE 4.9:

The output of the SetTitle example, which has a single method accessing different properties of different components

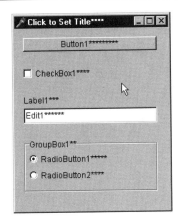

What's Next

In this chapter we've explored little-known information about RTTI and dynamic property access. As we've already emphasized, all of this information comes from a study of the VCL source code, plus a few hints in the Delphi help files. While this code *might* change completely in future versions of Delphi, we don't really think that will happen, since it changed only slightly from Delphi 1 to Delphi 3. This technology is at the foundation of the Delphi development environment, so it's probably here to stay.

Knowing how to access RTTI data should enable you to create some very advanced tools. We'll explore one tool of this kind in Chapter 16, where we'll build an add-on that you can use to explore all of the component properties of a program at run-time. In addition to these special cases, knowing the details of RTTI will help any Delphi programmer to better understand how Delphi works, and to apply that knowledge to many different programming situations.

CHAPTER

FIVE

5

Building Components

When you write Windows applications in Delphi, you typically use existing Delphi components. In fact, this is what people usually mean by the term *visual programming*: placing components on a visual form and writing some code to glue them together. Unlike most other visual programming tools, however, Delphi allows you to build your own components from *within the same environment*. In fact, it's extremely simple to do so.

For this reason, we've devoted this chapter to building components. As we'll discuss shortly, building components is something every Delphi programmer should know how to when the need arises. However, in this chapter we won't build powerful components—just a few simple ones. This chapter is merely an introduction to building components (albeit a fast-paced one), just like the other chapters in the first part of this book. We'll discuss more advanced components in other chapters, particularly when we discuss features that we can easily encapsulate in a component.

In any case, this chapter is *not a primer* on building components; it's simply a recap of the key concepts, with some examples that illustrate fundamental ideas. In addition, we'll use many of these examples as the basis for other projects, such as the property and component editor examples of Chapters 12 and 13. For a more step-by-step introduction to building components, see Marco Cantù's *Mastering Delphi 3 (Sybex, 1997)*.

Why and How to Build Components

It is hard to overstate the importance of components in Delphi. After all, components are the foundation of Delphi programming, and the `property` and `published` keywords are probably Delphi's most notable extensions to the Object Pascal language.

There are some fundamental reasons to build components in Delphi. Here is our short list of them:

Personal reusability: The goal here is to avoid writing the same code twice in a program or different programs. Although Delphi provides alternative techniques to attain reusability (including form inheritance), encapsulating code in components is one of the best. After all, reusing a component is generally easier than other forms of reuse, simply because it's a more visual operation. At the same time, reusing code through components is much more flexible than applying visual form inheritance. For example, you can add several custom components to a form, and thereby reuse code from two different sources in the same form. However, you cannot use visual form inheritance to inherit from two base forms simultaneously.

Group reusability: The goal here is to share components that you've written with your co-workers, and vice-versa. Again, there are alternatives, but being able to install fellow programmers' components right into the Visual Component Library can radically improve productivity. This is particularly true if the programmers in a group have different levels of expertise in implementing the code for specific tasks. Each programmer can write the components that he or she can implement most efficiently. The other programmers might not have been able to create such components, but they can easily learn how to use them.

Global reusability: The goal here is to publish or sell your components to any of the hundreds of thousands of other current Delphi programmers. You can find many simple components (although they may not be state-of-the-art) on the Internet, frequently with the complete source code for the component. Once you've spent a considerable amount of time researching and developing a complex component, you may be able to sell it as shareware or as a commercial package. The reason this form of reusability works (as it has with VBX components and OCX/ActiveX Controls) is that there are enough potential buyers to justify charging a low price for the components.

In each case, the goal is some form of reusability. For this same reason, programmers have traditionally collected function and class libraries, and then bought and sold those libraries. However, using functions or classes out of libraries usually requires a lot of hard work. On the other hand, using a component in a visual programming environment, with an intuitive set of properties and events, is far easier.

NOTE   While several programming tools have applied this concept of component-based visual programming (most notably Visual Basic), Delphi is the only tool that has fully integrated the object-oriented concept of classes with the concept of components. The result is a unique ability to extend existing components by deriving a new class.

General Guidelines

Now that we've considered why you would want to build your own components, let's look at some design and planning considerations behind component building. As before, we're assuming that this is not your first exposure to the topic.

A component should be complete. A single method or function that implements an algorithm isn't (by itself) a component, even though you can build a component around a function that performs some important or complex action. Also, consider that a partially implemented component can be very hard to use: Although you save time while you're creating the component, making it complete will save you much more time later on. Having said this, you should remember that, as in many software development processes, building a component often requires some iterations (or test versions) and a certain amount of trial and error.

A component should be focused. Each component should have a *single* purpose, and not several. In other words, avoid building a "Swiss Army knife" component to show a graphic on the screen, retrieve data from the Internet, and check your e-mail over the company network, all the while storing data in an InterBase server (perhaps preparing a cup of coffee at the same time). Instead, build a set of interrelated components, even if the components pertain to the same area. In fact, this is what many component vendors do by providing collections of data-aware components, Internet components, reporting components, and so on.

> **NOTE** The two points above may seem to contradict each other. When you're building components, you have to find a proper balance between completeness and focus, two goals that tend to drive your development efforts in different directions.

A component and its methods, properties, and events should be easy to understand. You need to make the purpose of the component clear, explain in a few words how the component fulfills its tasks, and alert the reader to the component's limits. You may want to document the component with its own help file.

A component should do something new. Before creating a component, see whether there is already a component that does exactly the same thing. In particular, check to see if Borland has written such a Delphi component, and if it's freely available. (It's astonishing to see how many IniFile and Registry components do exactly what Delphi's own `TIniFile` and `TRegistry` classes already do.) Of course, if you can improve on an existing component, go ahead and make a new component.

Debug your components before installing them. As we'll see in a moment, installing a component in the VCL requires just a small amount of time. However, a buggy component can crash Delphi and prevent it from loading!

NOTE

In Delphi 1 and Delphi 2, debugging components before installing them and making a backup of the VCL was particularly important because all the compiled code for the components was placed in a single component library file. In Delphi 3, Borland has introduced the *package* architecture. This allows you to place groups of components in separate component libraries (called packages), and then activate or deactivate them on a project-by-project basis. It's still important to debug your components thoroughly, because a buggy component can crash the development environment. However, with the new package architecture you can simply remove the package that's causing the errors, and fix the broken component inside it.

Consider using a third-party component development tool. Although in this book we teach you how to build components, remember that component writing is often tedious and time-consuming. It isn't a visual process, but a matter of editing source code. There are some commercial tools, however, that allow you to build components *visually*, which makes component building much easier and much faster—even for experienced Delphi programmers. Table 5.1 summarizes the tools we know of. However, we haven't used all these tools extensively and there might be later versions available, so we suggest you check the Web sites mentioned in the table to choose the best tool for your needs. (We're not recommending a specific product or trying to "plug" a particular vendor, although we do have our preferences.) In this book we focus on building components *by hand* simply because we want you to understand the rationale behind the behavior of the components and their interaction with Delphi. Even so, if you build components frequently, we strongly suggest that you consider one of these tools (we've even built our own simple Component Wizard, as you'll see in Chapter 14).

TABLE 5.1: Some Third-Party Tools for Building Delphi Components

Tool	Description
Component Create, by David A. Price of Potomac Document Software, Inc. `http://www.compcreate.com`	The first Delphi component writing tool. Features include creating components from form files, building complex data-aware components, generating skeletons of custom property editors, and many more.
Component Builder, by John C. Taylor `http://www.jt.w1.com/sharewar.htm`	A simple shareware tool that creates the Pascal source code of components, including properties, methods, and message handlers. It is not as feature-rich as some of the commercial tools, but the price is much lower.
TRANSFORM Component Expert, by Objective Software Technology `http://www.obsof.com`	A wizard that gives you access to the classes of the VCL and their properties, this tool allows you to create aggregate components by placing the subcomponents on a form. You build a form as usual, and the tool turns the form into a new VCL component, allowing you to select the properties you want to publish.
Component Development Kit (CDK), by Mark Miller from Eagle Software `http://www.eagle-software.com`	A full-featured component building tool, which even allows you to parse an existing component for further extension. With CDK you can create composite components, data-aware components, and professional business objects. This tool supports component and property editors, has an extensive help file with detailed information on component building, and allows you to build very complex components with little coding.

Key Ideas

Before we examine some of the technical aspects of building components, there are a few more things you should consider. First, learn everything you can about Object Pascal's object-oriented capabilities *before* you try to write your own components. We don't provide an overview of Object Pascal in this book, but instead cover a few of the language's features in depth. Therefore, if you don't know Object Pascal (such as what a virtual method is, or what the `abstract` and `protected` keywords mean), you should read another book first, such as *Mastering Delphi 3*.

Second, you should know how to use Delphi's Component Wizard. This is a very simple tool that comes with Delphi, but its value is limited, since it generates just a few lines of code. You can use it as a starting point if you want, but we won't use it in the book.

To create a brand-new component and install it, follow these simple steps:

1. From the main Delphi menu, select Component ➤ New Component.

2. Fill in the edit boxes of the Component Wizard (the New Component dialog box) with the ancestor class name, the new class name, and the new unit file name. Then click the Install button.

3. In the Install dialog box, select an existing package or move to the next page and type the name and the description of a new package. Then click the OK button.

4. The package editor will ask you to confirm the installation of the package and the included component. When you click the Yes button, the package editor will install the component and display it in Delphi's Component palette.

5. You can now use the package editor to open the source code of the component in the editor and change it, or to add further components to the package, including auxiliary units.

If you need to uninstall a component, remove it from the package that defined it. You can open packages for editing using Delphi's File ➤ Open command. If you need to remove a package from a project, you can do so using the Project ➤ Options command.

It's important to stress that package library files are simply DLLs that contain the code of installed (compiled) components. Delphi uses this code at design-time, but may also use it at run-time if you choose to use packages when you distribute your application. For reasons discussed in the next chapter, you may decide not to use the packages at run-time; in that case, Delphi will need the DCU files (which contain the compiled code for individual units) for linking the components to the executable file of your application.

Types of Components

In Delphi, there are basically three types of components. Although you are probably already aware of the key differences between the *families* of Delphi components, we've decided to review this topic anyway because it is so funda-mental. The three types are:

Nonvisual components: These are components that display an icon when you place them on a form at design-time, but don't appear at run-time.

Visual components: These are components that show up on a form and have a position and size. Visual components are usually called *controls*.

Windowed controls: These are components based on an actual window (that is, they encapsulate the handle to a window). They form the biggest group.

Graphical controls: These are visual components that aren't based on a window. These controls draw themselves on the window that hosts them, and therefore don't rely on many of the operating-system features (you cannot use Windows API functions with a graphical control). One ratio-nale behind graphical controls is to save Windows handles and resources, and to speed up the application a little bit. (Saving Windows resources is still an issue in Windows 95, although less so than in previous versions.)

Basically, the differences between these components are a result of their position in the VCL hierarchy (see Figure 5.1). The base class, TComponent, provides the common framework, while subclasses such as TGraphicControl and TWinControl are the basis of all the graphical and windowed controls (respectively). The same graphical capabilities available in the TGraphicControl class are missing for a generic TWinControl. The derived TCustomControl class, however, fills this gap.

FIGURE 5.1:

The fundamental component classes of the VCL library

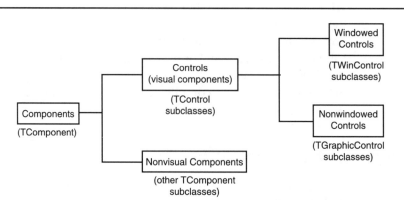

Compiling Components

When you use the Component Wizard to create the source file of a new component (or if you generate one from scratch), and you don't immediately install it in a package, you'll notice that Delphi disables the compilation commands in the Project menu. In Delphi, you compile and build *projects,* not *source files.*

Well, this is true unless you open the Pascal source file. If you save a source file and then click the Project Open toolbar button to reopen the PAS file, you'll be able to check your unit's syntax and compile it (with the component definition) to a DCU file. Of course, if you try to run this project you'll see an error message.

While this approach is generally quite helpful, it has two minor drawbacks. First, Delphi will parse the source file as if it were a project file, and format some of the source code accordingly. For example, Delphi will list all the units of your uses statements on different rows (so you have to scroll down to reach the actual code):

```
interface

uses
  SysUtils,
  WinTypes,
  WinProcs,
  Messages,
  Classes,
  Graphics,
  ...
```

The second problem is that Delphi creates a resource file for the file, as for any project, with the typical Delphi project icon. Fortunately, this is a file you can simply delete later on. In addition, Delphi creates the typical DOF and DSK files for the file/project, but these files might actually be useful.

Actually, this was an issue only in Delphi 1 and Delphi 2. With the advent of package technology in Delphi 3, you can simply install your component in a package, recompile the package to see if the code is correct, and install the component (perhaps after further revision). The main difference is that compiling a package is much faster than recompiling the entire VCL library, which you had to do in previous versions of Delphi.

Debugging Components

When you build a new component, you can install it immediately and build a simple project to test its features. By activating its published properties at design-time you can easily determine if they are correct, and update the user interface or other related properties according to the specs. This is probably a good approach for most components, but not all of them.

When you write a complex component, in fact, you should keep in mind that installing and using it might crash the Delphi environment (and you'll lose the component's code if you haven't saved it). If you anticipate problems, you can write a simple test program that creates the component dynamically (for example, in the FormCreate method) and allows you to edit and test the various properties with buttons, check boxes, edit boxes, and combo boxes. By writing some additional code, you can even test component events.

As you might expect, this testing process is a little boring, which is why most programmers immediately install the components in the VCL and use the Delphi environment itself to test the new components. They can then begin building a test program sooner and more easily.

However, it's not terribly difficult to generate a component-test program automatically, and some component-generation tools do just that. One variation of this approach is to create a run-time object inspector that uses the component's RTTI data (described in the last chapter) to manipulate the properties of the new component. In Chapter 16 we'll show you how to build such a tool.

Building Simple Components

Now that we've laid out some basic rules and strategies for building components, let's create some simple ones. Keep in mind that the code presented here is fairly simple (compared to other chapters in the book), but since writing components is something not all Delphi programmers have attempted to do, we'll start with some basic material to fill this gap. As a side benefit, building these components will give us a chance to provide an overview of many component writing topics. However, the examples will quickly move on to demonstrate some advanced tips and tricks, so even if you are already familiar with the basics of component writing, don't skip this chapter altogether.

You can install all the example components for this chapter at once by installing a single package file, DdhCh5.DPL, which has the description "DDH - Chapter 5 Components". This package file is stored in the 05\COMPS directory, which includes the source code for all the components. Other directories include sample programs you can use to test the components. Of course, you won't be able to open the sample programs in the Delphi environment unless you install the appropriate component package first.

Exposing Parent Properties: The Nothing Component

The first component we discuss is a "do nothing" component. You can write such a component with the following simple code:

```
type
  TDdhNothing = class(TGraphicControl)
  end;
```

Prefacing *Ddh* to the component name will become our standard for the book, and using mnemonic prefixes is also the approach of many component vendors. We've done this because you cannot install two Delphi components that have the same name. Using a prefix is a good way to make class names unique. If you follow the same convention (using your own prefix), you'll be doing a favor to the Delphi programming community.

Not much code! This is probably the simplest component you can create, and since it's a graphical (nonwindowed) control, it uses no Windows resources. However, this apparently useless component inherits several capabilities from its ancestors: TComponent, TControl, and TGraphicControl. These classes define positional and dimensional properties, hints, mouse events, and many other features. Some of the properties are published by their base classes. You can publish the others simply by redeclaring them in the published section of the class declaration:

```
type
  TDdhNothing = class(TGraphicControl)
  published
    property Align;
```

```
    property ShowHint;
    property Visible;
    property Enabled;
    property OnClick;
    property OnDblClick;
    property OnMouseDown;
    property OnMouseUp;
    property OnMouseMove;
    property OnDragDrop;
    property OnDragOver;
    property OnEndDrag;
    property OnStartDrag;
  end;
```

We could have named this component THintArea or TClickArea and pretended that it was a useful component. Despite the name we've given it, you can actually use this terribly simple component for the purposes mentioned above (for example, as a hint or click area that defines a "hotspot" in an image).

Of course, you'll need to install the TDdhNothing component in Delphi's VCL before you can use it. (Since we didn't write any code for this component, it's at least as bug-free as the TGraphicControl class from which we derived it. Therefore, we won't explore debugging this component.) During this process Delphi will add the component's code to the library, and will call the Register procedure for each component the unit defines. The Register procedure makes the component available to the Delphi design environment, and places it in a specific page of the palette:

```
procedure Register;
begin
  RegisterComponents('DDHB', [TDdhNothing]);
end;
```

By default, we'll place all of the components for this book on the Delphi Developer's Handbook (DDHB) page of the Component palette.

In addition to creating the class declaration and specifying the palette page, we've also provided a small icon that Delphi will use for this component. The icon should be a 24 × 24 pixel bitmap that has the same name as the component's class (but using uppercase letters, such as *TDDHNOTHING*). In Delphi 1 and 2, you had to save the icon in a resource file with the same name as the component's unit, but with a DCR extension (such as *DDHNOTH.DCR* for the *DDHNOTH.PAS* unit).

NOTE
The name of the source code file for the component is *DDHNOTH.PAS*. Like component class names, unit names must also be unique. As a result, two different packages (that you'll use in a given project) can't contain a unit with the same name. Again, we are using the DDH prefix for file names to avoid any collision with the unit names of other components you might have installed.

In Delphi 3, when you place a component in a package, the package editor checks if the DCR file is available, and if so, generates the corresponding $R directive (in the package source file) to include it. However, this doesn't always work. If it doesn't, you can try removing and inserting the component's unit in the package or edit the package source code manually (again, we'll cover this topic in the next chapter).

TIP
Even better, to install a component bitmap you can simply include a {$R *.DCR} directive in the component's unit. Since the resource file typically has the same name as the unit file (although this is not mandatory), this directive will work for any component you write. This is the approach we've followed in the book.

Once you've built the TDdhNothing component, you can try to use it. If you place this component on a form, you'll notice that its default height and width will be one pixel. By merely placing the component from within the Delphi environment, we've already found a problem. To fix the problem, we must override the constructor (which sets the dimensions of the component) and change the Height and Width property declarations:

```
type
  TDdhNothing = class(TGraphicControl)
  public
    constructor Create (Owner: TComponent); override;
  published
    property Width default 50;
    property Height default 50;
    property Align;
    . . .
```

NOTE   Remember to add the override keyword to the constructor declaration, or the VCL will never call your version of the constructor!

Here is the implementation of the TDdhNothing constructor:

```
constructor TDdhNothing.Create (Owner: TComponent);
begin
  // call parent class constructor first
  inherited Create (Owner);
  // set the size
  Width := 50;
  Height := 50;
end;
```

Since we are setting a default value for these properties in the constructor, we need to reflect these values in the property declaration (or redeclaration, in this case) by adding the default keyword and specifying the values we use in the constructor.

Delphi doesn't use the default value of a property to set its value automatically. In fact, Delphi uses this value only to save a property to a stream—not when it is read from a stream or created initially. As a result, if a property's current value is the same as its default value, the component won't save that property to the stream at all. (There's no reason to load these values if the constructor will set them correctly anyway.) The component constructor is generally responsible for setting default values properly.

To demonstrate the TDdhNothing component class, we've built an example that displays pop-up hints (but no other visual clue) on the empty regions of a form, a hint for an Image component, and a different hint for a specific region of the image. To accomplish this, we placed Nothing components on either side of the Image, and a Nothing component over part of the image to create a hotspot (an area that displays a different hint and then a specific message when you click on it). Figure 5.2 shows the main form and the hotspot hint.

FIGURE 5.2:

The output of the Nothing demo program

NOTE

You'll find this example in the 05\NOTHING subdirectory of the companion CD-ROM, while the source code of the component itself is in the 05\COMPS directory. This is where you'll find all the components and the package used to install them.

Here is an abbreviated form description, showing only the properties relevant for this example:

```
object Form1: TForm1
  BorderStyle = bsDialog
  Caption = 'Nothing component Demo'
  ClientHeight = 448
  ClientWidth = 632
  ShowHint = True
  object Image1: TImage
    Left = 89
    Top = 0
```

```
      Width = 423
      Height = 448
      Hint = 'Not a mouse'
      Align = alClient
      Picture.Data = {...}
      OnClick = Image1Click
    end
    object DdhNothing1: TDdhNothing
      Left = 0
      Top = 0
      Width = 89
      Height = 448
      Hint = 'Move right...'
      Align = alLeft
    end
    object DdhNothing2: TDdhNothing
      Left = 512
      Top = 0
      Width = 120
      Height = 448
      Hint = 'Move left...'
      Align = alRight
    end
    object DdhNothing3: TDdhNothing
      Left = 168
      Top = 280
      Width = 313
      Height = 169
      Hint = 'Mouse !!!'
      OnClick = DdhNothing3Click
    end
  end
```

A Graphical Component: The LED

To show you a more usable graphical component, we've built yet another LED component. (LED is an acronym for Light-Emitting Diode, a solid-state electronic light that's typically used for indicating binary conditions such as the send/receive status of a modem.) Instead of calling it *TYALC* (for Yet Another LED Component), we've called it TDdhLed, using the Ddh prefix convention we mentioned earlier.

Here is the declaration of this simple component class. As you can see, there are only two custom properties, Color and Status:

```
type
  TDdhLedStatus = (lsOn, lsOff);

  TDdhLed = class (TGraphicControl)
  private
    fStatus: TDdhLedStatus;
    fColor: TColor;
  protected
    procedure SetStatus (Value: TDdhLedStatus);
    procedure SetColor (Value: TColor);
  public
    constructor Create (Owner: TComponent); override;
    procedure Paint; override;
  published
    property Status: TDdhLedStatus
      read fStatus write SetStatus default lsOn;
    property Color: TColor
      read fColor write SetColor default clRed;
    property Width default 20;
    property Height default 20;
    property OnClick;
    property OnDblClick;
  end;
```

For the Status property, we've defined an enumerated data type (TDdhLedStatus), which is more understandable and flexible than a Boolean data type. By convention, you should use the initial letter of the component and property name (ls for LED Status) to build the names of the enumerated values (for example, lsOn).

If you examine the property declarations, you notice that we've applied the read and write directives to specify how to set or retrieve the property's current value. For these directives, you can specify either a local field of the class, a function (to retrieve the property), or a procedure that accepts a single parameter of the same type (to set the property). In the declaration above, we've supplied private variables for the Status and Color property read directives, and we've specified procedures for the corresponding write directives. We used procedures to set the property values so that we can update the user interface when the property value changes.

At the end of each property declaration, we've provided a default value. As you might have guessed, this implies that we're going to set those values in the component's constructor, which means we'll need to override it. We've declared an overridden version of the `Create` constructor for just this reason.

Finally, you'll notice that we're overriding the `Paint` method, specifying default values for some inherited properties, and that we're publishing several inherited event properties. The new `Paint` method will allow us to take control of the appearance of the component, the new default property values represent additional work that we'll need to perform in the constructor, and publishing the inherited events gives us the opportunity to customize the component's behavior.

> **NOTE**
>
> It's important to name fields, access methods, and properties in a manner consistent with the standards defined by Borland and published in the *Component Writer's Guide*. The basic guidelines are: Use meaningful names for properties, add an *f* to the names of fields that correspond to properties, and name access methods as `Get` or `Set` plus the property name (as in `SetStatus` and `SetColor`).

As usual, the `Create` constructor calls the inherited version of the constructor (an important step to remember), and then sets the values we've specified as property defaults:

```
constructor TDDHLed.Create (Owner: TComponent);
begin
  inherited Create (Owner);
  // set default values
  fColor := clRed;
  fStatus := lsOn;
  Width := 20;
  Height := 20;
end;
```

The two Set methods follow the standard form: If the new value is really different from the current one, change the value and update the user interface. Otherwise, do nothing:

```
procedure TDDHLed.SetStatus (Value: TDdhLedStatus);
begin
  if Value <> fStatus then
  begin
```

```
    fStatus := Value;
    Invalidate;
  end;
end;

procedure TDDHLed.SetColor (Value: TColor);
begin
  if Value <> fColor then
  begin
    fColor := Value;
    Invalidate;
  end;
end;
```

NOTE

A method like this one is where even a simple component writing tool comes in handy. As you might imagine, you'll write code like this over and over, each time you create a new component!

The `Paint` method is a little more complex than the property methods. First it draws a background circle, which we use as a border, and then an inner circle if the LED is on. To make sure the LED has the correct appearance (they're almost always round), we check the width and height properties to determine the actual diameter of the LED (we use the smaller of the two values). In a future example, we'll show you how to use code to impose a relationship between the width and the height of a component. Here's the `Paint` method:

```
procedure TDDHLed.Paint;
var
  Radius, XCenter, YCenter: Integer;
begin
  // get the minimum between width
  // and height
  if Height > Width then
    Radius := Width div 2 - 2
  else
    Radius := Height div 2 - 2;
  // get the center
  XCenter := Width div 2;
  YCenter := Height div 2;
  // LED border color (fixed)
```

```
Canvas.Brush.Color := clDkGray;
Canvas.Ellipse (
  XCenter - Radius, YCenter - Radius,
  XCenter + Radius, YCenter + Radius);
// led surface
if fStatus = IsOn then
begin
  Canvas.Brush.Color := fColor;
  Radius := Radius - 3;
  Canvas.Ellipse (
    XCenter - Radius, YCenter - Radius,
    XCenter + Radius, YCenter + Radius);
end;
end;
```

Writing a test program for the DdhLed component is very simple. We've placed a Label and a DdhLed component on the main form to simulate a check box (as you can see in Figure 5.3). Clicking either on the label or on the LED changes the DdhLed status.

FIGURE 5.3:

The TestLED program, used to test the TDdhLed component

The code for this example is so simple that we won't bother reviewing it. In fact, to build it you only need to connect the same method to the OnClick event of both components, and in this method change the current status of the DdhLed using an if statement.

You may have noticed that in this simple testing example we've built a compound component (we used a Label and a TDdhLed together). In fact, we could actually turn the two components into a single component which contains the other two. Instead, we've decided to show a similar but different case—combining several TDdhLed components into a TDdhSemaphore component.

We could have extended the DdhLed component by adding custom event handlers (for example, to discriminate between a click on the LED and a click on its border or the rest of the surface of the component). To see this kind of example, study the source code of the TArrow component (and the text that describes it) in the CD's ARROW subdirectory. This example comes from *Mastering Delphi 3* and is duplicated here only for readers who don't own that book. If you've never written a custom event, you may find the TArrow code useful, since we are going to see a custom event in the next example.

A Compound Component: The Traffic Light (or Semaphore)

Now we'll build a component that bundles three DdhLed components and a Timer component together. This is sometimes referred to as a *compound component*. The TDdhSemaphore example component has a number of features that will interest the component developer. Since the code is quite complex, we'll examine it in small chunks. (Of course, you'll find the complete source code on the companion CD.)

In programming, a *semaphore* is an object that synchronizes the behavior of several segments of a program. For instance, multithreaded Win32 programs can use semaphores to coordinate the actions of different threads.

In this example, our TDdhSemaphore class has nothing to do with operating-system semaphores, but instead is an example of a traffic light component, built to demonstrate how you can encapsulate other components within a component, and then make those components work together. Specifically, we'll display three DdhLed components (red, yellow, and green), allow no more than one of them to be "on" at any given time, and then provide an alternate mode where the red DdhLed flashes at an interval specified in a property.

Choosing a Base Class

Here is the first part of the TDdhSemaphore class declaration for the TDdhSemaphore component:

```
TDdhSemaphore = class (TCustomControl)
```

Why did we derive TDdhSemaphore from TCustomControl? When we began researching this component, we first tried embedding another graphical control within the TDdhSemaphore class. However, embedding a graphical control within another graphical control is rather complex since you have to manipulate the parent property in peculiar ways.

Deriving TDdhSemaphore from TWinControl is a bit better, because it provides the proper framework for parenting other components directly. The TWinControl class owns a window, which can directly host the graphical DdhLed components. However, TCustomControl is an even better base class than TWinControl, because it provides painting capabilities similar to the TGraphicControl (such as a Paint method you can override). In contrast, TWinControl provides poorer painting support.

Creating the Embedded Components

First we need to declare the three DdhLed components and build them as we create the semaphore component (in its constructor):

```
type
  TDdhSemaphore = class (TCustomControl)
  private
    // the three traffic lights
    fGreenL, fYellowL, fRedL: TDdhLed;
  ...
constructor TDdhSemaphore.Create (Owner: TComponent);
begin
  inherited Create (Owner);

  // create the LEDs and set their color
  fGreenL := TDDHLed.Create (self);
  fGreenL.Parent := self;
  fGreenL.Color := clLime; // light green

  fYellowL := TDDHLed.Create (self);
  fYellowL.Parent := self;
```

```
fYellowL.Color := clYellow;

fRedL := TDDHLed.Create (self);
fRedL.Parent := self;
fRedL.Color := clRed;
...
```

Next, we need to declare the SemState property. We avoided using the name Color for this property because it might be confusing to the component's users (the property usually has a different role), and also because we want to consider the "off" and "pulse" states. As with the Status property of the DdhLed component, we've based the SemState property on an enumeration:

```
type
  TSemState = (scRed, scGreen, scYellow, scOff, scPulse);
```

Here are the additions to the class declaration, including the SemState property with its read, write, and default specifiers:

```
private
  fSemState: TSemState; // status
protected
  procedure SetSemState (Value: TSemState);
published
  property SemState: TSemState
    read fSemState write SetSemState default scOff;
```

The SetSemState method is more complex than most property-setting methods, in that it calls other private methods of this class (TurnOff, StartPulse, and StopPulse). In fact, besides assigning the new Value for the property, we need to start or stop the Timer (if the SemState property changes to or from scPulse), and change the status of the three embedded DdhLed components.

```
procedure TDDHSemaphore.SetSemState (Value: TSemState);
begin
  if Value <> fSemState then
  begin
    TurnOff;
    if fSemState = scPulse then
      StopPulse;
    case Value of
      scRed: fRedL.Status := lsOn;
      scGreen: fGreenL.Status := lsOn;
      scYellow: fYellowL.Status := lsOn;
      scPulse: StartPulse;
```

```
        // scOff: nothing to do
      end;
      fSemState := Value;
    end;
  end;
```

The `TurnOff` procedure, which we call at the beginning of the `SetSemState` method and at the end of the constructor, sets the `Status` property of all DdhLed components to `lsOff`:

```
procedure TDDHSemaphore.TurnOff;
begin
  fRedL.Status := lsOff;
  fGreenL.Status := lsOff;
  fYellowL.Status := lsOff;
end;
```

The other two methods called by `SetSemState` are `StartPulse` and `StopPulse`, which dynamically create and destroy the Timer that we use to make the red DdhLed flash:

```
procedure TDDHSemaphore.StartPulse;
begin
  fTimer := TTimer.Create (self);
  fTimer.Interval := fInterval;
  fTimer.OnTimer := TimerOnTimer;
  fTimer.Enabled := True;
end;
```

```
procedure TDDHSemaphore.StopPulse;
begin
  fTimer.Enabled := False;
  fTimer.Free;
  fTimer := nil;
end;
```

We also call the `StopPulse` method in the destructor, in case the light is flashing:

```
destructor TDDHSemaphore.Destroy;
begin
  if fSemState = scPulse then
    StopPulse;
  inherited Destroy;
end;
```

The effect of the Timer, and the reason we need it, is to turn the red DdhLed on and off:

```
procedure TDDHSemaphore.TimerOnTimer (Sender: TObject);
begin
  if fRedL.Status = lsOn then
    fRedL.Status := lsOff
  else
    fRedL.Status := lsOn;
end;
```

(You might want to change this behavior to turn on and off the yellow light, if you live in a country where yellow is the pulsing light of a traffic signal.) We added a Timer component reference to the class declaration, as well as one more property, Interval, which we use to set the Timer interval. Here are the new field, property, and method declarations, including the last few methods described:

```
type
  TDdhSemaphore = class (TCustomControl)
  private
    ...
    fTimer: TTimer; // timer for pulse
    fInterval: Integer; // timer interval
    procedure TimerOnTimer (Sender: TObject);
    procedure TurnOff;
    procedure StartPulse;
    procedure StopPulse;
  public
    destructor Destroy; override;
  published
    property Interval: Integer
      read fInterval write SetInterval default 500;
```

Notice that we don't create the Timer in the constructor, but only when we need it (when the SemState is scPulse). If we had chosen to create the Timer in the constructor, we could have used its Interval property and not declared an Interval property for the TDdhSemaphore class. Since the Timer doesn't exist for the life of this component, we'll need to set the internal field, and then copy the value to the embedded component:

```
procedure TDDHSemaphore.SetInterval (Value: Integer);
begin
```

```
    if Value <> fInterval then
    begin
      fInterval := Value;
      if Assigned (fTimer) then
        fTimer.Interval := fInterval;
    end;
  end;
```

Overriding the SetBounds Method

Our program also has to deal with changes to the size of the TDdhSemaphore component. For this component, we basically have three DdhLed components in a column. Accordingly, we need to specify dimensions for the component, or at least its paint area. A user can actually change the Width and Height properties of the component independently, either by using the Object Inspector or by dragging the component's borders. Redefining these properties to resize the three DdhLed components (adjust the Height or Width property for each as the enclosing component changes) would require some work. In fact, it would create many problems, since the property values are actually interrelated.

However, when we examined the VCL source code (and the help file) we discovered that setting any of the TControl's positional properties (Left, Top, Height, and Width) always results in a call to the SetBounds method. Since this is a virtual method, we can simply override it to customize the sizing of the component and the components it contains.

Here are the final additions to the class declaration (including the Paint method, which we discuss in the next section):

```
public
  procedure Paint; override;
  procedure SetBounds (ALeft, ATop,
    AWidth, AHeight : Integer); override;
```

SetBounds defines a minimum size for the component, computes the actual size of the TDdhSemaphore image (which doesn't take up the complete surface of the components, as you can see in Figure 5.4), and sets the size and position of each DdhLed accordingly:

```
procedure TDDHSemaphore.SetBounds (
  ALeft, ATop, AWidth, AHeight : Integer);
var
  LedSize: Integer;
```

```
begin
  // set a minimum size
  if AWidth < 20 then
    AWidth := 20;
  if AHeight < 60 then
    AHeight := 60;
  inherited SetBounds (ALeft, ATop,
    AWidth, AHeight);

  // compute the actual size of the semaphore image
  if AWidth * 3 > AHeight then
    LedSize := AHeight div 3
  else
    LedSize := AWidth;

  // set the LED position and size
  LedSize := LedSize - 2;
  fRedL.SetBounds (1, 1,
    LedSize, LedSize);
  fYellowL.SetBounds (1, LedSize + 3,
    LedSize, LedSize);
  fGreenL.SetBounds (1, LedSize * 2 + 5,
    LedSize, LedSize);
end;
```

FIGURE 5.4:

The TDdhSemaphore image does not take up the full area of the component, but only a portion of it.

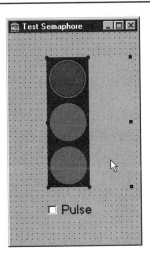

By the way, we could have used the SetBounds method to limit the size of the component to that of the actual image, by modifying the parameters in the inherited SetBounds call:

```
inherited SetBounds (ALeft, ATop,
  LedSize, LedSize * 3);
```

However, this call doesn't do what you might expect, as we'll explain at the end of this chapter (in the section "The Loaded Method").

Painting the Semaphore

Here is the Paint method, which merely delegates the work to the DdhLed components (this is not evident from the source code, because Delphi automatically calls the Paint methods of the three subcomponents):

```
procedure TDDHSemaphore.Paint;
var
  LedSize: Integer;
begin
  // compute the actual size
  // of the semaphore image
  if Width * 3 > Height then
    LedSize := Height div 3
  else
    LedSize := Width;

  // draw the background
  Canvas.Brush.Color := clBlack;
  Canvas.FillRect (Rect (0, 0,
    LedSize, LedSize * 3));
end;
```

Defining Custom Events

Finally, we want to examine the DdhSemaphore component's custom events. Instead of simply redeclaring (sometimes called *surfacing*) standard events, as we did in previous components, we want to define new events. Specifically, we want to create events for clicks on any of the DdhLed components.

As it turns out, this is not only a custom event, it also has a custom event type (that is, a custom method pointer type): TLightClickEvent. Here is the definition of the new data type, marked by the keywords of object to indicate that we are defining a method pointer type instead of a procedural type:

```
type
  TLightClickEvent = procedure (
    Sender: TObject; var Active: Boolean) of object;
```

Notice that in addition to the typical Sender parameter, we've defined a second parameter that's a Boolean value passed by reference. We'll use this parameter to allow the event handler to pass information back to the component (based on some condition determined by the program that uses the component, as we'll see in an example shortly).

To support our custom events, we've added three new TLightClickEvent fields, three methods we are going to use to intercept the TDdhLed component's events, and three new properties for the actual events:

```
type
  TDdhSemaphore = class (TCustomControl)

    ...

  private
    fGreenClick, fRedClick, fYellowClick:
      TLightClickEvent;
    // LED click response methods
    procedure GreenLedClick (Sender: TObject);
    procedure RedLedClick (Sender: TObject);
    procedure YellowLedClick (Sender: TObject);
  published
    // custom events
    property GreenClick: TLightClickEvent
      read fGreenClick write fGreenClick;
    property RedClick: TLightClickEvent
      read fRedClick write fRedClick;
    property YellowClick: TLightClickEvent
      read fYellowClick write fYellowClick;
```

NOTE   There is no technical difference between an event and a property. You define both using the property keyword, the IDE saves both to the DFM file, and both properties and events require storage and *read* and *write* specifications. The fact that events and properties show up in different pages of the Object Inspector is a result of their data type; we'll explore this topic in detail in Chapter 16.

Now let's examine the code for the `GreenLedClick` method. Basically, if we've assigned a method to the corresponding event property, we call that method. What's unusual is that we must provide an initial value for the parameter that we'll pass by reference (the `Status` variable, which becomes the `Active` parameter when you call the method), and then we have to check the final value of the parameter, which might have been changed by the handler for this event:

```
procedure TDDHSemaphore.GreenLedClick (Sender: TObject);
var
  Status: Boolean;
begin
  if Assigned (fGreenClick) then
  begin
    Status := (fGreenL.Status = 1sOn);
    fGreenClick (self, Status);
    if Status then
      SemState := scGreen;
  end;
end;
```

As we mentioned earlier, the `Active` property allows an event handler to return any change of value to the corresponding methods because we used a reference parameter. The rationale behind this approach is that when a user clicks on one of the component's DdhLeds, the program will notify the component to turn that LED on. We won't support the opposite operation, turning off a DdhLed when the user clicks on it, because that would put the DdhSemaphore component in an undefined state. Remember, this is not an event defined for one of the DdhLed components, but an event of the DdhSemaphore component, which acts as a single entity. In fact, the code above changes the `Status` of the traffic light, and not that of an embedded TDdhLed component.

By the way, defining event properties using reference parameters isn't very common in Delphi, but there are several examples in the VCL. The two most common are the `OnCloseQuery` and `OnClose` events of the form. As you have seen, this approach is rather simple to implement, and it makes the component more powerful for the programmers using it. The big advantage is that it requires less code to implement this specific behavior, as we'll see in the next example.

Before we do that, let's review the features of this component by examining the complete class declaration (the complete source code of the component is too long to list here, and is available on the companion CD in the 05\COMPS directory, as usual):

```
type
  TDdhSemaphore = class (TCustomControl)
  private
    // the three traffic lights
    fGreenL, fYellowL, fRedL: TDDHLed;

    fSemState: TSemState; // status
    fTimer: TTimer; // timer for pulse
    fInterval: Integer; // timer interval

    // light click events
    fGreenClick, fRedClick, fYellowClick: TLightClickEvent;

    procedure TimerOnTimer (Sender: TObject);
    procedure TurnOff;
    procedure StartPulse;
    procedure StopPulse;

    // LED click response methods
    procedure GreenLedClick (Sender: TObject);
    procedure RedLedClick (Sender: TObject);
    procedure YellowLedClick (Sender: TObject);

  protected
    // property access methods
    procedure SetSemState (Value: TSemState);
    procedure SetInterval (Value: Integer);

  public
    constructor Create (Owner: TComponent); override;
    destructor Destroy; override;
    procedure Paint; override;
    procedure SetBounds (ALeft, ATop,
      AWidth, AHeight : Integer); override;

  published
    // new properties
    property SemState: TSemState
      read fSemState write SetSemState default scOff;
```

```
property Interval: Integer
  read fInterval write SetInterval default 500;

// inherited properties with defaults
property Width default 30;
property Height default 90;

// custom events
property GreenClick: TLightClickEvent
  read fGreenClick write fGreenClick;
property RedClick: TLightClickEvent
  read fRedClick write fRedClick;
property YellowClick: TLightClickEvent
  read fYellowClick write fYellowClick;
end;
```

Testing the Semaphore

Now that we've built the basic DdhSemaphore component (which still has a minor resizing problem that we'll fix in a later version), let's examine a sample program that tests it. The TestSem example (located on the disk in the Semaph directory) allows a user to turn on one of the DdhLed components of the DdhSemaphore simply by clicking on the appropriate LED. To set the DdhSemaphore to the pulsing state, the user can select a separate check box. You can see the form of this example in Figure 5.5.

To change the current status of the semaphore, we've connected the same handler to the three click events of the component. Here is the code of the handler:

```
procedure TForm1.DDHSemaphore1GreenClick(Sender: TObject;
  var Active: Boolean);
begin
  Active := True;
  CheckBox1.Checked := False;
end;
```

In this case the reference parameter is used to set the new state for the DdhLed in question, and not to check its status. In fact, if the user tries to turn on the DdhLed that's currently on, nothing happens. As you'll recall, the SetSemState method checks to see if the new property value is different from the current one before it does anything. This is the reason we can freely set the value again, without performing another explicit test.

FIGURE 5.5:

The output of the TestSem example, which has very little code simply because it relies on a powerful component

Over-testing properties before assignment (that is, checking values several times before actually changing them) slows down programs considerably and provides a great opportunity for new bugs in a program (such as erroneously checking for the opposite condition so that the value is never set). In reviewing code, we have frequently seen this error in Delphi programs. As the component writer, you are responsible for checking (only once) to see if a value is about to change before proceeding and possibly causing side effects (such as repainting the component).

The remainder of the code responds to changes to the check box:

```
procedure TForm1.CheckBox1Click(Sender: TObject);
begin
  if CheckBox1.Checked then
    DDHSemaphore1.SemState := scPulse
  else
    DDHSemaphore1.SemState := scOff;
end;
```

The only really interesting point of this example program is that when you define a new event handler for one of the click events, Delphi creates a method with this signature (inside the form class definition):

```
procedure DDHSemaphore1GreenClick(
  Sender: TObject; var Active: Boolean);
```

Notice that this is *exactly* the same signature (including formal parameters) as the method pointer type we've defined above, and that the event handler's name is merely the name of the method appended to the component's name! Delphi extracts the signatures of the event handler (including the ubiquitous Sender parameter) from the type definitions.

> **NOTE** We've seen in Chapter 4 how Delphi can access the list of the parameters of a method pointer type, and we'll see in Chapter 13 how to generate a handler for an event manually.

Customizing Buttons

Up to this point, all of the components we've built have been brand-new. Most often, however, you'll probably want to customize an existing component. Often, this implies only simple additions, and there are many approaches to such customizations. We will demonstrate some of these different approaches by customizing the well-known and often-used Button component.

In the following sections, we'll build an *Input* button (which allows the user to change the Caption by typing into it), a *Sound* button (which produces an audio output whenever it's pressed or released), and an *Animated* button (which displays a changing glyph instead of a static one). All these components are quite simple (simpler than the semaphore, anyway), partly because they all inherit the basic capabilities of a Button.

Overriding Message Handlers: The Input Button

Supporting input to a Button component (which creates a very odd and nonstandard user interface) is really very simple. Typically, a Button simply ignores the wm_Char Windows messages that occur when the user presses certain keyword keys. Accordingly, we merely need to process this message to provide the Caption-editing capability.

One way to respond to a message for a given window (whether it's a form or a component) is to create a new *message-response* method that you declare using the message keyword. Delphi's message-handling system makes sure that your message-response method has a chance to respond to a given message before the form or component's default message handler does. As we'll see in the next section, instead of creating a new method you can override an existing virtual method that responds to a given message. (For example, the WmPaint message-response method responds to wm_Paint messages by calling the virtual method Paint.) Below is the complete code of the TDdhInputButton class:

```
type
  TDdhInputButton = class(TButton)
  private
    procedure WmChar (var Msg: TWMChar);
      message wm_Char;
  end;
```

The only new method we've declared is the message-response method for the wm_Char message. In the body of this method, we remove the last character of the caption if the user presses Backspace, and add the new character for any other keypress:

```
procedure TDdhInputButton.WmChar (var Msg: TWMChar);
var
  Temp: String;
begin
  if Char (Msg.CharCode) = #8 then
  begin
    // if backspace, remove last char
    Temp := Caption;
    Delete (Temp, Length (Temp), 1);
    Caption := Temp;
  end
  else
    // add the char
    Caption := Caption + Char (Msg.CharCode);
end;
```

That's it. Now if you place this component on a form, you can type in a new caption as soon as the DdhInputButton has the focus. Notice that pressing the space bar when the input button has the focus produces two effects: The space is added to the caption, but the button is *pressed* as well.

You'll notice that all of the components we've built so far work at design-time as well as at run-time. In other words, you can change the caption of the DdhInputButton as soon as you place it on the form, or you can wait until you run a program that contains the component, and edit the caption while the program is running. Later, we'll describe how you can use the ComponentState property to determine when certain events can occur.

Overriding Dynamic Methods: The Sound Button

Our next component, TDdhSoundButton, plays a sound when you press it, and another sound when you release it. The user specifies each sound by modifying two String properties that name the appropriate WAV files for the respective sounds. Once again, we need to intercept and modify some system messages (wm_LButtonDown and wm_LButtonUp), but instead of handling the messages by writing a new message-response method, we'll override the appropriate *second-level* handlers.

When most VCL components handle a Windows message, they call a *second-level* handler (usually a virtual or dynamic method), instead of executing code directly in the message-response method. This makes it simpler for you to customize the component in a derived class. Typically, a second-level handler will do its own work, and then call any event handler that the component user has assigned.

Here is the code of the TDdhSoundButton class, with the two protected methods that override the second-level handlers, and the two String properties that identify the sound files. You'll notice that in the property declarations, we read and write the corresponding private fields without calling a Get or Set method, simply because we don't need to do anything special when the user makes changes to those properties.

```
type
  TDdhSoundButton = class(TButton)
  private
    FSoundUp, FSoundDown: string;
  protected
    procedure MouseDown(Button: TMouseButton;
```

```
      Shift: TShiftState; X, Y: Integer); override;
    procedure MouseUp(Button: TMouseButton;
      Shift: TShiftState; X, Y: Integer); override;
  published
    property SoundUp: string
      read FSoundUp write FSoundUp;
    property SoundDown: string
      read FSoundDown write FSoundDown;
  end;
```

There are several reasons why overriding existing second-level handlers is generally a better approach than handling straight Windows messages. First, this technique is more sound from an object-oriented perspective. Instead of duplicating the message-response code from the base class and then customizing it, you're overriding a virtual method call that the VCL designers planned for you to override. Second, if someone needs to derive another class from one of your component classes, you'll want to make it as easy for them to customize as possible, and overriding second-level handlers is less likely to induce strange errors (if only because you're writing less code). Finally, this will make your component classes more consistent with the VCL, and therefore easier for someone else to figure out. Here is the code of the two second-level handlers:

```
uses
  MMSystem;

procedure TDdhSoundButton.MouseDown(Button: TMouseButton;
  Shift: TShiftState; X, Y: Integer);
begin
  inherited MouseDown (Button, Shift, X, Y);
  PlaySound (PChar (FSoundDown), 0, snd_Async);
end;

procedure TDdhSoundButton.MouseUp(Button: TMouseButton;
  Shift: TShiftState; X, Y: Integer);
begin
  inherited MouseUp (Button, Shift, X, Y);
  PlaySound (PChar (FSoundUp), 0, snd_Async);
end;
```

In both cases, you'll notice that we call the inherited version of the methods *before* we do anything else. For most second-level handlers, this is a good practice, since it ensures that we execute the standard behavior before we execute any custom behavior.

Next, you'll notice that we call the PlaySound Win32 API function to play the sound. You can use this function (which is defined in the MmSystem unit and is similar to the Win16 API sndPlaySound function) to play either WAV files or system sounds, as the TestSnd example demonstrates. Here is a textual description of the form of this sample program (from the DFM file):

```
object Form1: TForm1
  Caption = 'Sound Button Test'
  object DdhSoundButton1: TDdhSoundButton
    Caption = 'Press for wav files'
    SoundUp = 'up'
    SoundDown = 'down'
  end
  object DdhSoundButton2: TDdhSoundButton
    Caption = 'Press for Windows sounds'
    SoundUp = 'SystemStart'
    SoundDown = 'AppGPFault'
  end
end
```

To run this example, you'll need to make sure that the Up.WAV and Down.WAV files reside in the project directory or in the default path. Otherwise, you'll hear an error sound instead of the sound you've specified in the SoundUp or SoundDown properties.

Compound Components: The Animated Button

The third and final custom Button component we'll create is an animated button. Animating a button means painting its surface dynamically, but a Button component in Delphi has no Canvas, and therefore no drawing surface. There are basically two ways to solve this problem: the first is to make the button owner-draw, as the BitBtn component does; the second is to contain a graphical component on which you can paint inside the Button.

This second approach, embedding a graphical component, is interesting because at design-time Delphi allows only some controls (such as the Panel, the Group Box, the Scroll Box, and the Notebook and Page Control pages) to host other controls. However, at run-time, you can establish *parent* relationships for components in rather peculiar ways.

For example, you can place a PaintBox component inside a button, disable it (otherwise the component will grab the mouse events and prevent the TDdhAni- Button from responding to them), and then start painting into it. In fact, this is exactly what we'll do in the TDdhAniButton class, which also uses an internal Timer component, and an external ImageList component.

When we talk about *internal* components we're referring to components created by the main component; *external* components are those created by the user of the component, placed on the same form, and connected to the main component using a property. For example, in the TDdhAniButton class, the ImageList property (of type TImageList) represents an external component. In contrast, we'll create both the PaintBox and Timer components as internal components.

Here is the declaration of the TDdhAniButton class, with fewer comments than before because it uses no new techniques (other than an external component):

```
type
  TDdhAniButton = class (TButton)
  private
    fImage: TPaintBox;
    fTimer: TTimer;
    fImageList: TImageList;
    fCurrImage: Integer;
    procedure OnTimer (Sender: TObject);
  protected
    // property access methods
    procedure SetImageList (Value: TImageList);
    procedure SetActive (Value: Boolean);
    function GetActive: Boolean;
    procedure SetInterval (Value: Integer);
    function GetInterval: Integer;

    // redefinition of methods
    procedure SetBounds (ALeft, ATop,
      AWidth, AHeight: Integer); override;
    procedure MouseDown (Button: TMouseButton;
      Shift: TShiftState; X, Y: Integer); override;
    procedure MouseUp (Button: TMouseButton;
      Shift: TShiftState; X, Y: Integer); override;
    procedure MouseMove (Shift: TShiftState;
      X, Y: Integer); override;
```

```
// PaintBox event handlers
procedure PaintBoxPaint (Sender: TObject);

public
constructor Create (AOwner: TComponent); override;

published
// image list property,
// based on an external component
property ImageList: TImageList
  read FImageList write SetImageList;
// exported properties of the
// internal timer component
property Active: Boolean
  read GetActive write SetActive default False;
property Interval: Integer
  read GetInterval write SetInterval default 500;
end;
```

As we've already mentioned, this component is related to several other components:

- It creates an internal Timer object (which is a nonvisual component).

- It creates and displays a PaintBox component, which provides a paint surface for the button itself.

- It uses an external ImageList component, which the component user is responsible for creating independently from the component. A user will generally place the external ImageList on the same form, and then connect the two via the ImageList property of the animated button.

Here is the code of the constructor, which creates the two internal components:

```
constructor TDdhAniButton.Create (AOwner: TComponent);
begin
  inherited Create (AOwner);

  // create the paintbox
  fImage := TPaintBox.Create (self);
  fImage.Parent := self;
  fImage.Width := 16;
  fImage.Height := 16;

  {disable it, so that the button can handle
```

```
  its mouse messages directly}
  fImage.Enabled := False;
  // custom paint event handler
  fImage.OnPaint := PaintBoxPaint;

  // create the timer
  fTimer := TTimer.Create (self);
  fTimer.OnTimer := OnTimer;
  fTimer.Enabled := False;
  fTimer.Interval := 500;
end;
```

WARNING Since these internal components have an owner (specified in the constructor), there is no need to free them in a destructor. In fact, trying to free them yourself might lead to an error, as discussed in Chapter 2.

If you examine the SetBounds method, you'll see that we force the fImage PaintBox to stay in the middle of the DdhAniButton. However, there are times when the VCL may call SetBounds before we've created the PaintBox (before the constructor calls the OnCreate event), so we use if Assigned (fImage) to guard against using an uninitialized object reference. We then use a second if Assigned statement to confirm that an image list object is actually associated with the component:

```
procedure TDdhAniButton.SetBounds (
  ALeft, ATop, AWidth, AHeight: Integer);
begin
  inherited SetBounds (ALeft, ATop, AWidth, AHeight);
  // center the paintbox, if it exists
  if Assigned (fImage) then
  begin
    if Assigned (fImageList) then
      fImage.SetBounds (
        (Width - fImageList.Width) div 2,
        (Height - fImageList.Height) div 2,
        fImageList.Width, fImageList.Height)
    else
      fImage.SetBounds (
        Width div 2, Height div 2, 0, 0);
    fImage.Invalidate;
  end;
end;
```

The property access methods are very simple; they either set properties of the Timer subcomponent or change the associated ImageList:

```
procedure TDdhAniButton.SetActive (Value: Boolean);
begin
  fTimer.Enabled := Value;
end;

function TDdhAniButton.GetActive: Boolean;
begin
  Result := fTimer.Enabled;
end;

procedure TDdhAniButton.SetInterval (Value: Integer);
begin
  fTimer.Interval := Value;
end;

function TDdhAniButton.GetInterval: Integer;
begin
  Result := fTimer.Interval;
end;

procedure TDdhAniButton.SetImageList (Value: TImageList);
begin
  if fImageList <> Value then
  begin
    fImageList := Value;
    Caption := '';
    // change the position
    SetBounds (Left, Top, Width, Height);
  end;
end;
```

To paint the current image of the ImageList in the paint box, we've defined an event handler for its OnPaint event (as we did with the DdhSemaphore component, which handled some events of the DdhLed components directly):

```
procedure TDdhAniButton.PaintBoxPaint (Sender: TObject);
begin
  // paintbox OnPaint event handler
  if Assigned (fImageList) then
    fImageList.Draw (fImage.Canvas, 0, 0, fCurrImage);
end;
```

The VCL will automatically call this code when the components needs repainting, but we need to call it ourselves when the Timer elapses (we'll force an update by calling the Repaint method). Therefore, we need another event-handler for the Timer subcomponent:

```
procedure TDdhAniButton.OnTimer (Sender: TObject);
begin
  if Assigned (fImageList) then
  begin
    // update counter and repaint
    Inc (fCurrImage);
    if fCurrImage >= fImageList.Count then
      fCurrImage := 0;
    fImage.Repaint;
  end;
end;
```

The problem we now face is that we need to repaint the image appropriately when the DdhAniButton status changes. Unfortunately, you can't simply override the PaintHandler method of TButton, because the VCL doesn't call this method during state transitions (for example, when you press the *Animate* button and then move the cursor outside its area, the VCL repaints it in the released state, but does not call the PaintHandler method). Instead, we need to handle the mouse-down, -up, and -move messages, ideally by customizing the appropriate secondary handlers:

```
procedure TDdhAniButton.MouseDown (Button: TMouseButton;
  Shift: TShiftState; X, Y: Integer);
begin
  inherited MouseDown (Button, Shift, X, Y);
  // update the image
  fImage.Invalidate;
end;

procedure TDdhAniButton.MouseUp (Button: TMouseButton;
  Shift: TShiftState; X, Y: Integer);
begin
  inherited MouseUp (Button, Shift, X, Y);
  // update the image
  fImage.Invalidate;
end;

procedure TDdhAniButton.MouseMove (Shift: TShiftState;
```

```
      X, Y: Integer);
    begin
      inherited MouseMove (Shift, X, Y);
      // update the image only if dragging
      if MouseCapture then
        fImage.Invalidate;
    end;
```

Notice that in the MouseMove method we update the image only during a dragging or clicking operation (that is, only if the mouse capture is enabled). Otherwise, the user is just moving the mouse over the surface of the DdhAniButton, and it's better not to force a repaint. Repainting would cause a noticeable flicker.

The AniBDemo example shows how to use the TDdhAniButton component. The most complex part of this program is the setup of the TImageList component (which contains the images we'll display). You specify the images at design-time using the special component editor of the ImageList, as you can see in Figure 5.6.

FIGURE 5.6:

The special property editor of the images of an ImageList component in Delphi

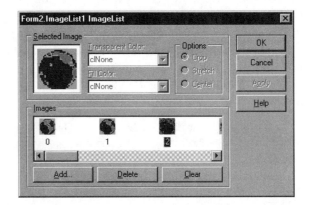

NOTE

Readers of *Mastering Delphi 3* will probably recognize this list of icons from the World2 example in Chapter 11, which used a similar technique to animate a Button. The key difference between the two examples is that now we've put this functionality into a custom component, which you can easily install in the Component palette for use in other programs. The other example hard-coded the behavior into the program. Reusing that code would be tedious and error-prone.

This program has two problems. The first (and most serious) appears if some-one deletes the ImageList component at design-time *after* they've associated it with the DdhAniButton. If this happens, the program will probably experience several errors (such as invalid pointer accesses), since the DdhAniButton compo-nent thinks the ImageList object is still valid. Since this is a rather advanced topic, we'll focus on the solution of this *notification* problem in one of the last sections of this chapter.

The second problem with the DdhAniButton component relates to the `Caption` property: the caption now appears *underneath* the animated image. However, there is no way to remove an existing property from a component, since that would mean that a base class might try to reference a property that no longer existed. In fact, by not allowing you to remove a base class property from a derived class, Delphi is demonstrating a good implementation of object-oriented programming techniques.

Instead, you can use object-oriented techniques to achieve the same thing. As you'll recall, many base classes specify methods as part of an interface, but those methods don't do anything. For those methods, doing nothing is the default action. To eliminate the effect of a property, we can do the same thing: provide an implementation of the property that does nothing. For example, we can provide a dummy field, in this case a string, and define a brand-new read-only property with the same name as the property we want to hide. Instead of using the inher-ited `Caption` property, the Object Inspector (and other parts of our programs) will see the new field:

```
TNoCaptionButton = class (TButton)
private
  fDummy: string;
published
  property Caption: string read fDummy;
end;
```

Actually, you'll also need to reset the caption in an overridden constructor. With this code the property won't show up in the Object Inspector, and you'll be able to refer to the original property (in component methods) as `inherited Caption`. However, this approach is not very good from an OOP perspective, because you cannot apply the same code used to handle any `TButton` object to objects of the new inherited class. This is contrary to OOP inheritance and poly-morphism principles.

One alternative is to create two dummy fields, one for reading, and one for writing:

```
TNoCaptionButton = class (TButton)
private
  fReadString : string;
  fWriteString : string;
published
  property Caption: string
    read fReadString
    write fWriteString;
end;
```

Then you simply let the fWriteString field accept any updates to the property. Since the fReadString field won't change, the displayed property won't change. This approach won't break existing code that assumes the Caption property to be one you can read and write, but it will simply do nothing.

Similarly, you can provide dummy read/write methods for the property that don't update a value at all:

```
TNoCaptionButton = class (TButton)
private
  function GetCaption: string;
  procedure SetCaption(NewCaption: string);
published
  property Caption: string
    read GetCaption
    write SetCaption;
end;
```

The implementation of these dummy methods is rather simple and ensures that the inherited Caption property doesn't contain anything either:

```
function TNoCaptionButton.GetCaption:String;
begin
  inherited Caption := '';
  Result := '';
end;


procedure TNoCaptionButton.SetCaption(NewCaption: string);
begin
  inherited Caption := '';
end;
```

If you try to build this component, you'll see the caption flash as you place a NoCaption component on the form. (The TButton class uses a Windows button control as part of its implementation, and eliminating this flash would require us to write a bit of extra code.) Still, the property-disabling techniques we've shown here will work in most cases.

However, the VCL allows us to follow a completely different approach, an object-oriented approach, which we'll discuss in the next section. This approach offers an even better solution, as it will let us actually solve this problem and not display a property that we don't need.

Using the TCustom... Classes: The Numeric Edit

With the DdhAniButton, we needed to disable a property; this problem is quite common for custom edit boxes. Most often, it occurs when a programmer tries to create an Edit component that allows only numerical input. Such a component should have a Value property instead of the Text property. However, it's not good OOP practice to remove a base class property, so we cannot derive a numeric edit component from TEdit without resorting to the tricks we just mentioned.

Fortunately, the VCL provides us with a solution. The parent class of TEdit, named TCustomEdit, has the same capabilities as TEdit, but doesn't publish its properties. To better understand the relationship between TEdit and TCustomEdit, take a look at the source code for TEdit:

```
type
  TEdit = class(TCustomEdit)
  published
    property AutoSelect;
    property AutoSize;
    property BorderStyle;
    property CharCase;
    // and so on...
    property OnChange;
    property OnClick;
    property OnDblClick;
    property OnDragDrop;
    property OnDragOver;
```

```
    // and so on...
  end;
```

There is nothing to the TEdit class but a list of redeclared properties that were public in the TCustomEdit class, but now become published (that is, visible in the Object Inspector).

Similarly, we can derive our own class from TCustomEdit, one that exports only those properties that we want to make available. At the same time, we can add other new properties. For example, we can derive a TDdhNumEdit class from the TCustomEdit class, publish everything except the Text property, and add a couple of other properties.

We start building this class by adding a first new property, Value, which will contain the number we want to edit:

```
protected
  function GetValue: Integer;
  procedure SetValue (Value: Integer);
published
  property Value: Integer
    read GetValue write SetValue default 0;
```

Notice that we don't create a new field to store this value, because we can use the existing (but unpublished) Text property. To do this we'll simply convert the numeric value to and from a text string. The TCustomEdit automatically paints the information from the Text property on the surface of the component:

```
function TDdhNumEdit.GetValue: Integer;
begin
  // set to 0 in case of error
  Result := StrToIntDef (Text, 0);
end;

procedure TDdhNumEdit.SetValue (Value: Integer);
begin
  Text := IntToStr (Value);
end;
```

The second new property is actually an event. Since we want to filter out non-numeric characters, we'll define an event to activate in case the user enters something other than a number. Here is the declaration of the OnInputError property (we've based it on a predefined method pointer type, TNotifyEvent):

```
private
  fInputError: TNotifyEvent;
published
  property OnInputError: TNotifyEvent
    read fInputError write fInputError;
```

The key element of this component is an override of the KeyPress method, which does exactly what you'd expect:

```
procedure TDdhNumEdit.KeyPress (var Key: Char);
begin
  if not (Key in ['0'..'9']) and not (Key = #8) then
  begin
    Key := #0;
    if Assigned (fInputError) then
      fInputError (self);
  end;
end;
```

This method checks each character as the user enters it, testing for numerals and the Backspace key (which has an ASCII value of 8). We want to allow the user to use Backspace in addition to the system keys (the arrow keys and Del), so we need to check for that value. We don't have to check for the system keys, because the wm_SysChar message doesn't activate the KeyPress method, but is handled by an appropriate message-handling method.

The only other method in the class definition is the constructor, which we use to set the default value:

```
constructor TDdhNumEdit.Create (Owner: TComponent);
begin
  inherited Create (Owner);
  SetValue (0);
end;
```

As usual, we've built a small test program, this time called TestNum. The only interesting part of this program is the definition of event handlers for the new event:

```
procedure TForm1.DdhNumEdit1InputError(Sender: TObject);
begin
  Beep;
end;
```

```
procedure TForm1.DdhNumEdit2InputError(Sender: TObject);
begin
  Inc (ErrorCount);
  if ErrorCount >= 5 then
  begin
    Beep;
    ShowMessage ('Only numbers, please');
    ErrorCount := 0;
  end;
end;
```

In general, it's much better to let the programmer who's using your component decide what to do in case of an error than to define a standard behavior, such as a beep. This way, the programmer can still implement the simple beep, or define a more sophisticated scheme, such as displaying an error message in a dialog box.

Using Collection Properties

You saw in Chapter 3 how to store a list of values into a collection, using the TCollection and TCollectionItem classes. At that time, we mentioned that the role of a collection, by design, is to build a property that contains a list of values. Examples of Delphi collection properties are the TDBGrid component's Columns property and the TStatusLine component's Sections property.

Since we already know about collections, defining a collection property won't be too difficult. (If you haven't read the description of collections in Chapter 3, it's a good idea to do so.) However, to define the collection we must derive a new class from TCollection and another one from TCollectionItem. Since changes to the items in a collection may be important to the enclosing component, these TCollection and TCollectionItem-derived classes will be strongly connected to each other and to that component.

The Collection Items

To simplify the example, the following component, TDdhGraph, uses a collection very similar to the one in Chapter 3. The component can show a series of connected points on the screen, and show a caption for each one. The point class is TDdhPoint (derived from TCollectionItem), and the collection class is TDdhPoints (derived from TCollection). Since the TDdhPoints class uses the TDdhGraph class in its constructor (the classes refer to each other in a circular fashion), we'll need a forward declaration of the class first:

```
type
  TDdhGraph = class; // forward declaration
```

Next, we need to update the TDdhPoint class, which doesn't change much from the previous version:

```
type
  TDdhPoint = class (TCollectionItem)
  private
    fX, fY: Integer;
  public
    Text: string;
    procedure WriteText (Writer: TWriter);
    procedure ReadText (Reader: TReader);
    procedure DefineProperties (Filer: TFiler); override;
    procedure Paint (Canvas: TCanvas);
    procedure Assign (Pt: TPersistent); override;
  published
    property X: Integer read fX write fX;
    property Y: Integer read fY write fY;
  end;
```

The only significant change is to the Paint method; we now want to draw lines between each point, starting with the first:

```
procedure TDdhPoint.Paint (Canvas: TCanvas);
begin
  if Index > 0 then
    Canvas.LineTo (fX, fY);
  Canvas.Ellipse (fX - 3, fY - 3, fX + 3, fY + 3);
  Canvas.TextOut (fX + 5, fY + 5, Text);
  Canvas.MoveTo (fX, fY);
end;
```

You'll notice that we've placed a call to the MoveTo function at the end to set the initial position of the next line, which we'll draw at the beginning of the next call to this paint method (for the next DdhPoint in the collection). You must add this MoveTo call because the TextOut call changes the current drawing position. If you remove the MoveTo line, the Paint method will draw the lines between the points, starting at the end of the text label.

The Custom Collection

The brand-new code derives from the TCollection class:

```
type
  TDdhPoints = class (TCollection)
  private
    fGrid: TDdhGraph;
    function GetItem (Index: Integer): TDdhPoint;
    procedure SetItem (Index: Integer; Value: TDdhPoint);
  protected
    procedure Update (Item: TCollectionItem); override;
  public
    constructor Create (Grid: TDdhGraph);
    function Add: TDdhPoint;
    property Items [Index: Integer]: TDdhPoint
      read GetItem write SetItem; default;
  end;
```

This class basically updates the methods of the parent class, but it uses the TDdhPoint data type for the items. This is quite clear if you look at the code of most of its methods:

```
function TDdhPoints.Add: TDdhPoint;
begin
  Result := TDdhPoint (inherited Add);
end;

function TDdhPoints.GetItem (Index: Integer): TDdhPoint;
begin
  Result := TDdhPoint (inherited GetItem (Index));
end;

procedure TDdhPoints.SetItem (Index: Integer; Value: TDdhPoint);
begin
  inherited SetItem (Index, Value);
end;
```

In contrast, the constructor and the Update method provide a connection between the collection and the class owning it (the constructor call and the fGrid reference forced us to create the forward declaration for the TDdhGraph class):

```
constructor TDdhPoints.Create (Grid: TDdhGraph);
begin
```

```
    inherited Create (TDdhPoint);
    fGrid := Grid;
end;

procedure TDdhPoints.Update (Item: TCollectionItem);
begin
  if Item <> nil then
    fGrid.Invalidate;
end;
```

Basically, we inform the collection of any change to the item collection, and then simply invalidate the component to force a repaint.

The Graph: a Collection of Points

Naturally, the most important part of the component is the TDdhGraph class, which uses the collection as a field and adds several other properties:

```
type
  TDdhGraph = class(TGraphicControl)
  private
    fPoints: TDdhPoints;
    fDefText: string;
    fBorderStyle: TBorderStyle;
    fLinesColor: TColor;
  protected
    procedure SetBorderStyle (Value: TBorderStyle);
    procedure SetLinesColor (Value: TColor);
    procedure MouseDown (Button: TMouseButton;
      Shift: TShiftState; X, Y: Integer); override;
  public
    constructor Create (Owner: TComponent); override;
    destructor Destroy; override;
    procedure Paint; override;
  published
    property Color; // fill color
    property LinesColor: TColor
      read fLinesColor write SetLinesColor
      default clBlack;
    property Font;
    property Align;
    property DefaultText: string
```

```
        read fDefText write fDefText;
      property BorderStyle: TBorderStyle
        read fBorderStyle write SetBorderStyle
        default bsNone;
      // collection property
      property Points: TDdhPoints
        read fPoints write fPoints;
    end;
```

The most important element of the class is the published `Points` property, which will appear in the Object Inspector and provide support for storing and loading the DdhPoint objects in a stream.

WARNING   Although the `Points` property shows up in the Object Inspector, you cannot use it at all. If you try to do so you'll get the error message "Invalid selection 'TDdhPoints' has no owner". In Chapter 12 we'll define a property editor for it, and in Chapter 13 we'll see how to modify the collection to let Delphi use its own internal editor for collection properties .

Here is an example of this property's values (from a DFM file that contains a DdhGraph component):

```
Points = <
  item
    X = 45
    Y = 154
    Text = 'Pt1'
  end
  item
    X = 156
    Y = 112
    Text = 'Pt2'
  end
  item
    X = 224
    Y = 64
    Text = 'Pt3'
  end>
```

As you would expect, we create and destroy the collection in the component's constructor and destructor:

```
constructor TDdhGraph.Create (Owner: TComponent);
begin
  inherited Create (Owner);
  fPoints := TDdhPoints.Create (self);
  fDefText := 'Pt';
  fBorderStyle := bsNone;
  fLinesColor := clBlack;
  // design-time right clicks = left clicks
  ControlStyle := ControlStyle + [csDesignInteractive];
end;

destructor TDdhGraph.Destroy;
begin
  fPoints.Free;
  fPoints := nil;
  inherited Destroy;
end;
```

You'll notice that the last statement of the constructor does something else: It sets a special value for the ControlStyle property. There are two special properties for component writers, used in this example: ControlSyle and ComponentState.

NOTE　In this section, we'll just provide a short introduction to these properties. You can find more information on them in the "Component Status and Style" section later in this chapter. In any case, refer to the Delphi help file for details on the possible values of the ControlSyle and ComponentState properties.

ControlStyle is a *static* value that describes the capabilities of the component to the form designer (that is, to the Delphi development environment). We refer to this value as static because you typically set it in the constructor and don't change it. This component sets the csDesignInteractive flag, which means that at design-time, the control will map any right mouse-button clicks into left-button clicks. This allows a user to edit the control visually at design-time, simply using the right mouse button to perform operations you would normally (at run-time) perform with the left mouse button.

In contrast, the ComponentState property is much more dynamic; it changes to reflect the current status of the component. Component writers use this flag to determine if the component is in some special state and should therefore skip a given action. The two most commonly used states are csLoading, which refers to a state in which the component is loading properties from a stream, and csDesigning, which indicates whether the component is being used at design-time. You can use the csDesigning flag to create a component that behaves differently when it's in the Delphi environment than when it's in a running application.

Adding and Painting Points

If you examine the TDdhGraph source code, you'll notice that we use the csDesignInteractive style to handle the mouse-click messages that add new points to the list at design-time. By default, the right-click operation becomes a left-click operation at design-time (the form designer translates the wm_RButtonDown message into a wm_LButtonDown message). However, since Delphi uses right-clicking at design-time to show a popup menu, we force the user to press the Ctrl key as well, as you'll see in the code below.

The most relevant feature of this component is that each time a user left-clicks within its boundaries, it automatically adds a new TDdhPoint on its surface. Here is the overridden MouseDown method:

```
procedure TDdhGraph.MouseDown (Button: TMouseButton;
  Shift: TShiftState; X, Y: Integer);
var
  Pt: TDdhPoint;
begin
  if (not (csDesigning in ComponentState)) or
    ((csDesigning in ComponentState) and
    (ssCtrl in Shift)) then
  begin
    Pt := fPoints.Add;
    Pt.X := X;
    Pt.Y := Y;
    Pt.Text := Format ('%s%d', [fDefText, fPoints.Count]);
    Invalidate;
  end;
end;
```

The code is quite simple: if we are not in design mode, or if we are in design mode but the user is pressing Ctrl while clicking the mouse, we'll add a new item to the collection. Then we'll set its X and Y properties with the current location. For its Text property, we'll build a name from the value of the DefaultText property and the number of items in the collection.

As soon as the user creates a new point (either at design-time or at run-time), we call the Invalidate method to update the appearance of the component via its Paint method:

```
procedure TDdhGraph.Paint;
var
  I: Integer;
begin
  // values used when drawing the points
  with Canvas do
  begin
    Brush.Color := Color;
    Pen.Color := fLinesColor;
    Pen.Style := psSolid;
    Font.Assign (self.Font);
  end;

  // draw the points
  for I := 0 to fPoints.Count - 1 do
    fPoints.Items[I].Paint (Canvas);

  // conditionally draw a border
  with Canvas do
    // at design-time
    if csDesigning in ComponentState then
    begin
      Pen.Color := clBlack;
      Pen.Style := psDash;
      Brush.Style := bsClear;
      Rectangle (0, 0, Width, Height);
    end
    // at run time
    else if BorderStyle = bsSingle then
    begin
      Pen.Color := clBlack;
      Pen.Style := psSolid;
```

```
      Brush.Style := bsClear;
      Rectangle (0, 0, Width, Height);
   end;
end;
```

This method sets the current colors and font for the output, paints each point, and then draws either a design-time border (made with a dashed line) or a run-time border, if the corresponding property is set.

> **NOTE**
>
> We've buried the core of the painting code in the TDdhPoint class. This is good from an encapsulation perspective, but it gives us only limited control over the process of painting the points. For instance, we might want to hide the lines, make the points bigger, or make other adjustments. To gain this level of flexibility it might be better to "promote" the painting code to the TDdhPoints collection class, or even to the TDdhGraph component class.

Advanced Topics in Building Components

In this chapter so far we've explored many techniques related to building components, but we've left a couple of our examples unfinished. To fix the problems with these components we need to focus on more advanced topics.

First, we'll solve the resizing problem with the DdhSemaphore component by demonstrating the correct way to take advantage of the Loaded method. Then we'll address the issue of deleting an external component that's associated with the DdhAniButton component by examining form designer notifications.

The Loaded Method

As you'll recall from our earlier example, the DdhSemaphore component painted only on a portion of its surface. Since the DdhLed components are always circular, its obvious that the DdhSemaphore component needs to be three times as tall as it is wide, because it contains three LEDs in a column.

First, let's consider redefining the SetBounds method to enforce the *height equals three times the width* rule:

```
procedure TDDHBrokenSem.SetBounds (
  ALeft, ATop, AWidth, AHeight : Integer);
var
  LedSize: Integer;
begin
  // set a minimum size
  if AWidth < 20 then
    AWidth := 20;
  if AHeight < 60 then
    AHeight := 60;

  // compute the actual size of the semaphore image
  if AWidth * 3 > AHeight then
    LedSize := AHeight div 3
  else
    LedSize := AWidth;

  // set component size
  inherited SetBounds (ALeft, ATop,
    LedSize, LedSize * 3);

  // set the LED position and size
  ...
end;
```

This is almost what we need, but not quite. You can find this updated component, TDdhBrokenSem, in the DdhSemaB.PAS unit (in the 05\COMPS directory). With this change, TDdhSemaphore works well at design-time; now when you resize the component by dragging its border, the size of the component always matches the size of the image. Unfortunately, you can't set the Width and Height properties directly from the Object Inspector.

Even more surprising, if you save the component to a DFM file and reload it (or if you cut and paste the component), it will always reappear at the default size. To see this for yourself, load the project, and resize the TDdhBrokenSem component. You'll see that the form resembles the left side of Figure 5.7 at design-time and the right side at run-time. This is obviously wrong. In addition, you'll notice that you can't copy and paste the new component properly (the component "forgets" its height and width). Also notice that if you save and reload the example form, the

TDdhBrokenSem component will reappear at the default size because loading the form doesn't work either.

FIGURE 5.7:

The TestBro example at design-time (on the left) and at run-time (on the right) demonstrates that the new version of the component does not work properly.

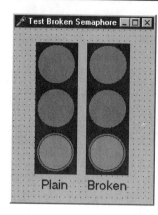 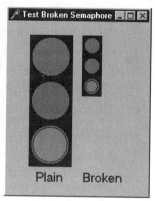

The problem is that when Delphi loads a component from a stream (which also happens during a copy or paste operation), it first creates the component at the default size, and then loads each of the properties in turn. Therefore, Delphi sets the Width and Height properties separately, which forces the SetBounds method above to discard the changes. Accordingly, Delphi displays the component at the default size.

To fix this problem we can modify the SetBounds method further, and execute some special code if the component is loading. When the component is loading its properties from a stream, we do not enforce the relationship between width and height, but assume that the relationship is correct. (This is a relatively safe assumption, because the design-time rules will begin enforcing the relationship as soon as you place the component on a form.) Here is the code for the SetBounds method of the new class (from the DdhSemaL.PAS file):

```
procedure TDdhLoadedSemaphore.SetBounds (
    ALeft, ATop, AWidth, AHeight : Integer);
var
    LedSize: Integer;
begin
    // set a minimum size
    if AWidth < 20 then
        AWidth := 20;
    if AHeight < 60 then
        AHeight := 60;
```

```
// compute the actual size of the semaphore image
if AWidth * 3 > AHeight then
  LedSize := AHeight div 3
else
  LedSize := AWidth;

// set component size
if not (csReading in ComponentState) then
  inherited SetBounds (ALeft, ATop,
    LedSize, LedSize * 3)
else
  inherited SetBounds (ALeft, ATop,
    AWidth, AHeight);

// set the LED position and size
...
end;
```

We're very close to what we want. Unfortunately, it's still possible for the component user to specify invalid values for these properties if they edit the text description of the form. To make the component foolproof, we'll need to override the Loaded method:

```
type
  TDdhLoadedSemaphore = class (TCustomControl)
    ...
  public
    procedure Loaded; override;
```

Delphi calls the Loaded method for each component after it has loaded all the properties for each component of a form. This allows us to execute some specific initialization code to cross-check the values of different properties of the same component (as in this case) as well as properties of different components. Remember that Delphi also calls this method after pasting a component into the form designer.

WARNING   Remember that the VCL doesn't execute this code when you create a component at run-time or at design-time. Only after reading a component's properties from a stream will the VCL call the Loaded method. For this reason, the Loaded method should contain *special property-related initialization code*, and not generic start-up code.

Here is how we'll implement the Loaded method for our semaphore component:

```
procedure TDdhLoadedSemaphore.Loaded;
begin
  // double-check if size is OK
  if (Width * 3) <> Height then
    SetBounds (Left, Top, Width, Height);
end;
```

Now you can use the updated test program (it's in the same directory as the component), or you can build your own test program after installing the final version of the component. At this point, you might want to remove the two older versions of the semaphore component from this chapter's package, and possibly rename the unit and the class name for this final version.

Form Designer Notifications

The other problem we encountered in this chapter related to using an external component (the TDdhAniButton used an external ImageList to hold its images). Suppose you've placed a DdhAniButton component in a form, added an ImageList, and connected the two components using the DdhAniButton component's ImageList property. Now if you delete the ImageList component, the DdhAniButton will contain a pointer to the *nonexistent* object. Obviously, this is something that can cause serious problems both to your program and to the Delphi environment. You can see an example of this type of error (issued by the design-time environment) in Figure 5.8.

Delphi makes solving this and similar interdependence problems relatively easy. One solution is to use the Loaded method to find out if another component still exists. In this case, however, we need to implement the Notification method.

Delphi calls the Notification method when you insert a component or remove one from the form, and so the method is typically most useful to parent and owner components. However, you need to deal with this situation when two components are related (contain references to one another):

```
public
  procedure Notification(AComponent: TComponent;
      Operation: TOperation); override;
```

FIGURE 5.8:

An example of the error caused by removing a component that is connected to a second one

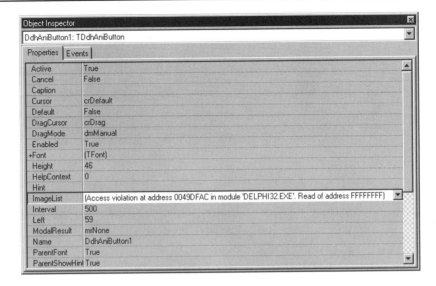

As you can see above, the two parameters identify the component being inserted or removed and the current operation for this component (either opInsert or opRemove). By checking which operation we're performing and whether the component in question (AComponent) is the object we're storing as the fImageList, we can then disconnect the two components by clearing the ImageList property:

```
procedure TDdhAniButton.Notification(
  AComponent: TComponent; Operation: TOperation);
begin
  if (Operation = opRemove) and
     (AComponent = fImageList) then
    SetImageList (nil);
end;
```

Now if you delete the ImageList component while it is connected, nothing bad happens. Remember to use this approach every time you create an external component and connect it to another component via a property. (You'll often do that with data-aware components, as we'll see in Chapter 17.) To make this clearer, we've built a very simple example, with the sole purpose of demonstrating how to use an external component. In this case, the component is an edit box that displays the length of its text in an external label component (as you can see in the demo form of Figure 5.9).

FIGURE 5.9:

An example of a demo form of the CountEdit component at design time. When you change the text of the special edit box, the connected label automatically displays its size.

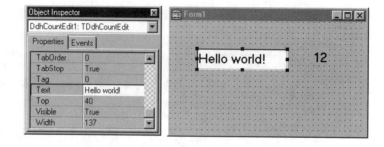

Here's the class declaration, which redefines the Change method to intercept a change in the value of the Text property:

```
type
  TDdhCountEdit = class(TEdit)
  private
    FLabel: TLabel;
    procedure SetCountLabel (Value: TLabel);
  protected
    procedure Notification (AComponent: TComponent;
      Operation: TOperation); override;
    procedure Change; override;
  published
    property CountLabel: TLabel
      read FLabel write SetCountLabel;
  end;
```

The code of the three methods is quite simple: the SetCountLabel method hooks the external component, the Change method uses it (if it exists), and the Notification method removes the connection if necessary.

```
procedure TDdhCountEdit.SetCountLabel (Value: TLabel);
begin
  if Value <> FLabel then
  begin
    FLabel := Value;
    FLabel.Caption := IntToStr (Length (Text));
    FLabel.FreeNotification (self);
  end;
end;
```

```
procedure TDdhCountEdit.Change;
begin
  inherited Change;
  if Assigned (FLabel) then
    FLabel.Caption := IntToStr (Length (Text));
end;

procedure TDdhCountEdit.Notification(AComponent: TComponent;
  Operation: TOperation);
begin
  inherited Notification(AComponent, Operation);
  if (Operation = opRemove) and (AComponent = FLabel) then
    FLabel := nil;
end;
```

What's new in this version of the code is the call to the FreeNotification method within the SetCountLabel procedure. This call is necessary when you connect components from two different forms at design-time. In fact, Delphi will call the Notification method only for actions of a component on the same form. What if we allow the user to connect (at design-time or run-time) to an external component of a different form? We'll be in trouble!

When you call the FreeNotification method of an external component (FLabel) and pass the current component as the parameter (self), you're indicating to the external component that you want it to add our component to the list of components that it will notify when something frees it. To understand how this works, keep in mind that the FreeNotification method is applied to the FLabel component, the external component. Here is the source code of the method for the TComponent class (extracted from the VCL source code):

```
procedure TComponent.FreeNotification (
  AComponent: TComponent);
begin
  if (Owner = nil) or (AComponent.Owner <> Owner) then
  begin
    if not Assigned(FFreeNotifies) then
      FFreeNotifies := TList.Create;
    if FFreeNotifies.IndexOf(AComponent) < 0 then
    begin
      FFreeNotifies.Add(AComponent);
      AComponent.FreeNotification(Self);
    end;
```

```
    end;
  end;
```

Notice that this creates a reverse link as well (to ensure free notification both ways). During destruction, the component notifies all those on its list:

```
destructor TComponent.Destroy;
var
  I: Integer;
begin
  if FFreeNotifies <> nil then
  begin
    for I := 0 to FFreeNotifies.Count - 1 do
      TComponent(FFreeNotifies[I]).
        Notification(Self, opRemove);
    FFreeNotifies.Free;
    FFreeNotifies := nil;
  end;
  ...
```

Component Status and Style

We've already seen that there are some properties related to the style of components and controls and some related to the state. The style properties are properties you'll usually set in the constructor of the component and never change. For this reason you can say that every component of a given class has a fixed style. In contrast, the status of a component typically changes over time during the life of an object.

As we've already seen, there are two style properties, one for generic components (TComponent.ComponentStyle) and the other for controls (TControl.ControlStyle); and two properties for the current status (TComponent.ComponentStatus and TControl.ControlStatus). Below you'll find a list of their possible values (which can be merged because they are set types). You can find the meaning of the various flags in the Delphi online help file, so we won't duplicate it here. However, we've decided to provide the list because there are many new Delphi 3 flags you might want to look up even if you're already aware of these properties in previous versions of Delphi:

```
type
  TComponentStyle = set of (csInheritable, csCheckPropAvail);
```

```
TControlStyle = set of (csAcceptsControls, csCaptureMouse,
    csDesignInteractive, csFramed, csClickEvents,
    csSetCaption, csOpaque, csDoubleClicks, csFixedWidth,
    csFixedHeight, csNoDesignVisible, csReplicatable,
    csNoStdEvents, csDisplayDragImage, csReflector);

TComponentState = set of (csLoading, csReading, csWriting,
    csDestroying, csDesigning, csAncestor, csUpdating,
    csFixups);

TControlState = set of (csLButtonDown, csClicked, csPalette,
    csReadingState, csAlignmentNeeded, csFocusing,
    csCreating);
```

By default, controls use the csCaptureMouse, csClickEvents, csSetCaption, and csDoubleClicks styles. To show you how these and other styles affect the behavior of a component, we've built a somewhat useless example which uses an entirely custom set of styles. We've called the component TDdhSuperNothing, because it's an extended version of the Nothing component:

```
type
  TDdhSuperNothing = class(TCustomControl)
  public
    constructor Create (Owner: TComponent); override;
  published
    property Width default 200;
    property Height default 200;
    property Align;
    property Color;
    property DragMode;
    ...
```

In the constructor of this class we assign a new group of control styles. Notice that we do *not* add the new styles to the default ones, but simply remove the styles set by the base class in the inherited Create call:

```
constructor TDdhSuperNothing.Create (Owner: TComponent);
begin
  // call parent class constructor first
  inherited Create (Owner);
  // set the size
  Width := 200;
  Height := 200;
  // set special styles
```

```
ControlStyle := [csAcceptsControls, csFramed,
    csFixedWidth, csFixedHeight];
end;
```

What's the effect of these styles? As you can see in Figure 5.10 the new control has a three-dimensional frame, and you can place other components in it. The two styles related to the dimensions don't mean you can't resize the component. They mean the component will not scale. To test this effect, the example has a *Scale* button, which calls the form's ScaleBy method. When you press it, everything scales except the new component.

FIGURE 5.10:

The form displayed by the Super-Nothing component's demo program

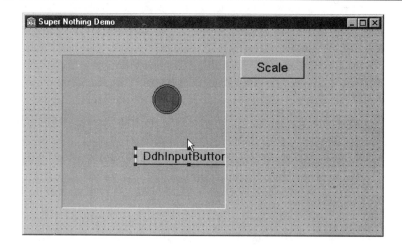

What's Next

This is not the only chapter of the book where we'll discuss components, it is only an introduction to the topic. In the next chapter we'll focus on component distribution, the new package architecture, and writing component help files. Throughout the book we'll explore other topics related to the development of professional-quality components. For example, in Chapter 17 we describe how to build data-aware and database-related components, and in Chapter 8 we build some special Windows components.

In Part III of the book, we'll introduce two topics related to component development—writing property editors (in Chapter 12) and component editors (in Chapter 13)—and we'll use some of the components from this chapter as starting points.

Delphi 3
Packages in Depth

- What Packages Really Are...and What They Are Not

- Packaging Components

- The Package of a Component

- Listing the Package and Their Units

- Preparing a Help File

- Distributing a Package Collection

Now that we've explored designing and building components, let's focus on distributing them. Delphi 3 provides a powerful new technology, *packages*, which you can use to distribute a set of components easily, and also to distribute component libraries (or just simple function and procedure libraries) that programs can use at run-time, thus reducing the size of the main executable file. This technology is similar to the Visual Basic model of using VBRUNxx.DLL to contain common code, in the sense that you can share code among several applications, but with an important difference—you can extend Delphi packages.

We'll start this chapter by focusing on the technical details of package construction, and then focus on information we can access about packages. Finally, we'll cover the development of the help file for a component and the use of the package collection editor. First let's examine some common misconceptions about packages.

What Packages Really Are ... and What They Are Not

Packages, introduced in Delphi 3, are a new and powerful technology for developing and distributing Delphi components, and also for using them in applications. Delphi packages bear a strong resemblance to existing technologies, such as DLLs and the Delphi component libraries of previous versions, but this resemblance is often misleading. In this section, we'll summarize the role of packages and how they differ from these other technologies.

A Package Is a Collection of Components

Packages are generally collections of components. As before, you still create components in separate units, but you can now assemble them using a special package project file, based on the `package`, `contains`, and `requires` keywords. You can use the Package editor and the View Source command to view the Pascal source code of the package. However, keep in mind that a package can also be a collection of units that don't register a component, or it can be a collection of add-on editors and wizards, as we'll see in Part III of the book.

TIP

> To see the source code file of a component package, you can simply open the Package editor and use the Toggle Form/Unit menu item or toolbar button of the Delphi environment. This also toggles between the Package editor and the package source code file.

The package keyword is functionally similar to the library keyword: In both cases the result of compiling the source code is technically a Windows DLL, although you can't use a package as you use a DLL, as you'll see in a moment. Once you've compiled a package there are two ways to use it, depending on its role. You install design packages in the Delphi environment. You'll use run-time packages to contain component code, instead of linking that code directly into the executable file of an application (which is what previous versions of Delphi did).

As you can see in Figure 6.1, you can select package options via two check boxes, offering four possible option combinations:

- If only the *Design package* check box is active, the package source code will contain the {$DESIGNONLY} compiler option. You can install the resulting package in the Delphi environment, but it's not automatically available as a run-time package. Although it's not widely known, you can still use a package of this type at run-time by simply adding it manually to the list of available run-time packages (in the bottom section of the project's Package Options dialog box).

- If only the *Runtime package* option is active, the package source code will contain the {$RUNONLY} compiler option. You can't install the resulting package in the Delphi environment. However, if you install a design package that requires it, Delphi will automatically list it as one of the available run-time packages.

- If both check boxes are active, the package source code will contain neither of the compiler options we just mentioned. You can install the resulting package in the Delphi environment and Delphi will automatically add it to the list of run-time packages.

- If neither of the check boxes are active, the package source code will include both the {$RUNONLY} and {$DESIGNONLY} compiler options. You won't be able to install the resulting package into the Delphi environment, and it won't automatically be added to the list of run-time packages.

FIGURE 6.1:

The main Package Options page of Delphi's Package editor, with the Design Package and Runtime Package check boxes

You can see from this description that the package option check boxes and the compiler flags have a strange relationship: each check box turns off the opposite compiler flag! By selecting the *Runtime package* option you're removing the {$DESIGNONLY} compiler option.

These compiler flags are used only by the Delphi environment. In fact, when you install a package, Delphi does two things:

- It determines whether the package is run-time-only: If this style is present, Delphi aborts the installation. This allows you to distribute third-party run-only packages along with your applications and prevent other developers from using them.

- It determines if the package or one of the packages it requires has the design-only flag: In this case Delphi doesn't add the packages to the list of available run-time packages.

As a rule of thumb, you should build a design-only package for every run-only package you create, as we'll see in an example.

Related Package Files

Another element of confusion concerns the role of the various package-related files. Below we've tried to list them all, indicating what they are used for (and what they are not!):

- A DPK extension denotes the package source code files. These files are necessary to recompile a package. When you open them in the environment, Delphi displays the Package editor.

- A DPL extension denotes a package library. The Delphi environment uses package libraries, and you can use them at run-time. You don't need package libraries to compile and link packages. You'll distribute (or sell) design-time package libraries (DPL files) to other Delphi programmers (along with DCP, DCU, and optionally source code files), and let everyone distribute run-time packages.

- A DCP extension denotes symbolic information for a package. Delphi uses this information to speed up compilation, and to compile and link a run-time package without having the corresponding DCU files.

- A DCU extension denotes compiled Pascal files, as usual. The important thing to note is that Delphi still needs DCU files to statically link components into an executable file.

Don't Use Packages as DLLs

Although a package is technically a DLL, it has a different role in the development of an application. Windows application developers traditionally split an application into an executable file and one or more DLLs so that they can then update only one or the other, without having to ship the entire application again. While you can update the executable of a Delphi 3 package application without redistributing the package, you cannot update the package for that application without also updating the executable.

Underlying this limitation is the fact that every Pascal unit contains version information. This is why you can't, for example, use a unit compiled with Delphi 2 in an application based on Delphi 3 unless you have the unit's source code. If you update only the package of a package application (that is, if you update the interface of one of its units), launching the application will generate an almost incomprehensible error, as shown in Figure 6.2. Actually, Windows usually also shows a second error message, "A device attached to the system is not functioning," which is even harder to understand.

An error message displayed when you execute a package application that was expecting an older version of its package

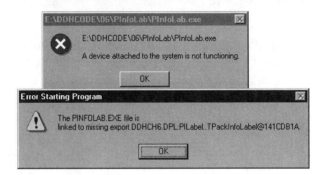

This basically means that when you update a package you should also update any applications that use it. Alternatively, you can rename the package, ensuring that the older version of the application will still find the older version of the package, and that the new version of the application will find the new package. As a result, you'll typically see package names such as MyPack10.DPL, MyPack11.DPL, and so on. Including the version number in the package name makes every one unique, and lets older versions continue to work.

Unfortunately, this approach doesn't allow the user to take advantage of the updates and bug fixes of the new version of the package without downloading everything. The real solution is to use only fairly stable packages at run-time. If you're developing a package and produce a new version every day, simply link its components statically into the executable, and you won't experience any of these problems.

Another situation is even more complex. Some third-party tools might rely on other packages; if two of these tools rely on different versions of the same package, you'll end up either with two copies of the package library, or with an incompatibility problem. It will take some time until Delphi developers understand the role of packages and avoid these problems.

Beware of Duplicated Units

Another problem you might encounter relates to duplicated units. Suppose you write a simple unit with a couple of procedures or functions, call it *Support*, and use it for the development of a component. Now suppose you want to use the

Support unit to build another component, which is part of a different package. As soon as you try to install the second package, you'll get an error indicating that the unit is duplicated.

There are two ways to avoid this problem. The first way is to place the Support unit and other shared units in a third run-time package, used by the other two packages. The second way is to base the second package on the first one. Either way, you'll be introducing a dependency on the Support unit, which will force you to recompile the package that includes the Support if you change it, and will force an update to each of the other packages that require it.

A radically different solution is to rename the unit for each reuse, but in this case you run the risk of fixing a bug in one copy of the unit and not in the other copy; this is worse than the problems we just mentioned.

Packaging Components

Now that we've looked at how packages work with Delphi and Delphi applications, we can focus on a standard approach to package development. As we mentioned earlier, you'll typically want to place components in a run-time package and place the registration code (and any add-on property and component editors) in a design-time package. This doesn't mean that other programmers won't be able to link your components into their executables statically (run-time linking of packages is not even the default option in Delphi). It does mean that you can freely distribute the run-time package without letting other developers install it in Delphi (thereby using your components without paying for them).

To implement this deployment strategy, you should remove all of the `Register` methods from the component units and place them in a separate file, which will be part of the design package. For example, we could take the package we built in the last chapter and update it this way. (Of course, it won't be possible to install the new version along with the original package, because it contains the same units and registers the same component classes!). The registration unit will simply use all the other units and register them with the following call:

```
procedure Register;
begin
  RegisterComponents ('DDHB', [
    TDdhNothing, TDdhLed, TDdhSemaphore,
```

```
        TDdhInputButton, TDdhSoundButton, TDdhAniButton,
        TDdhNumEdit, TDdhGraph, ...]);
    end;
```

Unfortunately, for the components we built in Chapter 5, removing the Register calls from the original units will break the original package. For this reason we've chosen a slightly different approach: We've updated the original package into a run-time package, and saved it with a different name. Here's the resulting source code of the package (without all the compiler options), which we've added to the Comps directory of Chapter 5:

```
package ddhch5rt;

{$DESCRIPTION 'DDH - Chapter 5 Components (Run-time Package)'}
{$RUNONLY}

requires
  vcl30;

contains
  DdhNoth,
  DdhSounB,
  DdhGraph,
  DdhInpuB,
  DdhLed,
  DdhNumEd,
  DdhSemap,
  DdhAnimC,
  DdhAnimB,
  DdhSemaB,
  DdhSemaL,
  DdhCntEd,
  DdhSuper;

end.
```

Because this is a run-time package, even if the Register procedures are there, Delphi won't call them. To install these components, you can now create a corresponding design-time package, which requires the run-time package and includes only the registration unit:

```
package ddhch5dt;
```

```
{$DESCRIPTION 'DDH - Chapter 5 Components (Design time Package)'}
{$DESIGNONLY}

requires
  vcl30,
  ddhch5rt;

contains
  ch5reg;

end.
```

Finally, here's one way of coding the Register procedure (provided you've left the original Register procedures in the component units):

```
unit ch5reg;

interface

procedure Register;

implementation

uses
  DdhNoth, DdhSounB, DdhGraph, DdhInpuB, DdhLed,
  DdhNumEd, DdhSemap, DdhAnimC, DdhAnimB, DdhSemaB,
  DdhSemaL, DdhCntEd, DdhSuper;

procedure Register;
begin
  DdhNoth.Register;
  DdhSounB.Register;
  DdhGraph.Register;
  DdhInpuB.Register;
  DdhLed.Register;
  DdhNumEd.Register;
  DdhSemap.Register;
  DdhAnimC.Register;
  DdhAnimB.Register;
  DdhSemaB.Register;
  DdhSemaL.Register;
  DdhCntEd.Register;
  DdhSuper.Register;
```

```
end;

end.
```

Now, we won't pretend that this is the best way of splitting a single package into a run-time package and a design time package, because it's not. This is just a handy approach that allows you to leave the original source code alone. You should also realize that if you leave the `Register` procedures in the units of a run-time package, it's technically possible to load it with a special-purpose Delphi add-on tool, and use it anyway. Therefore, removing the `Register` calls is an extra measure you can take to forbid the illegal use of a run-time package in the Delphi environment.

The Package of a Component

There's another feature of components we didn't cover in the last chapter, because it relates specifically to packages. In fact, it's not even a feature of components, but of packages in general. Delphi 3 defines a new global variable called `ModuleIsPackage`. You can use this global Boolean variable to determine if a component is executing as part of a run-time package or is statically linked into the executable file of an application. Of course you must perform this test within the component's code, since the `ModuleIsPackage` variable within an application will invariably be `False`.

To demonstrate an interesting way to use this global variable (and a couple of other tricks), we've created a label component that automatically displays information about its executable file and package. Here's the declaration of the component class:

```
type
  TPackInfoLabel = class(TLabel)
  private
    fPackName, fExeName: string;
    fShowIn: Boolean;
    procedure UpdateInfo;
    procedure ShowInfo;
    procedure SetString (Value: string);
    procedure SetShowIn (Value: Boolean);
  public
```

```
    constructor Create (AOwner: TComponent); override;
    procedure Loaded; override;
published
  property PackName: string
    read fPackName write SetString;
  property ExeName: string
    read fExeName write SetString;
  property ShowInCaption: Boolean
    read fShowIn write SetShowIn;
end;
```

The constructor calls the UpdateInfo method when the component is placed on a form at design-time, which displays the application and package information, if it's part of a package. In contrast, the Loaded method calls the UpdateInfo method to update the status of the label after it has been loaded from a DFM file. In this case, Caption information set by the constructor will be replaced by the new value that's generated while loading from the DFM file:

```
constructor TPackInfoLabel.Create (AOwner: TComponent);
begin
  inherited;
  if csDesigning in ComponentState then
    UpdateInfo;
end;

procedure TPackInfoLabel.Loaded;
begin
  UpdateInfo;
end;
```

The information we access is computed by the UpdateInfo method and stored in two local fields, fPackName and fExeName:

```
procedure TPackInfoLabel.UpdateInfo;
begin
  // get exe name
  SetLength (fExeName, 100);
  GetModuleFileName (MainInstance,
    PChar (fExeName), Length (fExeName));
  fExeName := PChar (fExeName); // length fixup

  // get package name
  SetLength (fPackName, 100);
```

```
    if ModuleIsPackage then
    begin
      GetModuleFileName (HInstance,
        PChar (fPackName), Length (fPackName));
      fPackName := PChar (fPackName) // length fixup
    end
    else
      fPackName := 'Not packaged';

    // set label caption
    if fShowIn then
      ShowInfo;
  end;
```

In the method above, you'll notice our use of the `MainInstance` and `HInstance` global variables: the first always refers to the application (the process that's executing the component code), while the second refers to the component's code module (which for packages is a DLL). In this specific case, the design-time value of the `MainInstance` variable is Delphi itself, while the run-time value is the application using the component. Similarly, the `HInstance` variable refers to the component's package library (if you've placed it in a package), or the application using the component (if you haven't placed it in a package). You can see the result in Figure 6.3, which shows the PInfoLab application's form (a form that contains a single PackInfoLabel component), both at design-time and at run-time.

FIGURE 6.3:

The output of the label showing package information at design time (above) and at run-time (below)

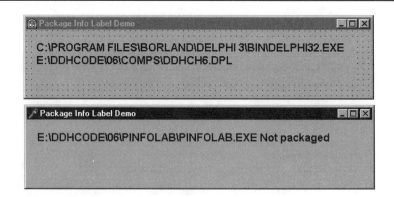

If the `ShowInCaption` property is True, the component displays the process and package information inside its caption:

```
procedure TPackInfoLabel.ShowInfo;
```

```
begin
  Caption := fExeName + ' ' + fPackName;
end;
```

When you set this property, the caption is updated. If you're setting the property to False, the program replaces the process and package information with a default value, the component name:

```
procedure TPackInfoLabel.SetShowIn (Value: Boolean);
begin
  if Value <> FShowIn then
  begin
    fShowIn := Value;
    if FShowIn then
      ShowInfo
    else
      Caption := Name;
  end;
end;
```

You'll notice that the program doesn't update the information at run-time, since after Delphi creates the object and loads the component, the process and package information won't change. A final observation concerns the two filename properties, ExeName and PackName. Logically, these are read-only properties. However, if you define a read-only property, you won't be able to see the property information in the Delphi Object Inspector. To avoid this problem, we add a do-nothing write method for the property. When you change one of the strings from the Object Inspector, the write method ignores the new value:

```
procedure TPackInfoLabel.SetString (Value: string);
begin
  // discard the new value
end;
```

Obviously, this isn't terribly elegant, but it works. In Chapter 13 we'll display this same information inside a component editor and provide a more elegant user interface.

Listing the Packages and Their Units

Besides accessing package information from within a component, you can also do so from a special entry point of the package libraries, the `GetPackageInfoTable` function. This function returns some specific package information that Delphi stores as resources and includes in the package DLL. Fortunately, we don't need to use low-level techniques to access this information, since Delphi 3 provides some high-level functions to manipulate it.

There are basically two functions you can use to access package information:

`GetPackageDescription` returns a string that contains a description of the package. To call this function, you must supply the name of the module (the package library) as the only parameter.

`GetPackageInfo` doesn't directly return information about the package. Instead, you pass it a function that it calls for every entry in the package's internal data structure. In practice, `GetPackageInfo` will call your function for every one of the package's contained units and required packages. In addition, `GetPackageInfo` sets several flags in an Integer variable.

These two function calls allow us to access internal information about a package, but how do we know which packages our application is using? We can determine this by looking at an executable file using low-level functions, but Delphi helps us again by supplying a simpler approach. The `EnumModules` function doesn't directly return information about an application's modules, but allows you to pass it a function, which it calls for each module of the application, the main executable file, and for each of the packages the application relies on.

To demonstrate this approach, we've built a simple example program that displays the module and package information in a TreeView component. Each first-level node corresponds to a module, and within each module we build a subtree that displays the contained and required packages for that module, as well as the package description and compiler flags (`RunOnly` and `DesignOnly`). You can see the output of this example in Figure 6.4.

FIGURE 6.4:

The output of the
PackInfo example,
with the details
of the packages
it uses

In addition to the TreeView component, we've added several other components
to the main form, but hidden them from view: a DBEdit, a Chart, and a Filter-
ComboBox. We added these components simply to include more run-time packages in the application, beyond the ubiquitous Vcl30.DPL. The only method of
the form class is FormCreate, which calls the module enumeration function:

```
procedure TForm1.FormCreate(Sender: TObject);
begin
  EnumModules(ForEachModule, nil);
end;
```

The EnumModules function accepts two parameters. The first is the callback
function (in our case, ForEachModule), and the second is a pointer to a data structure that the callback function will use (in our case, nil, since we didn't need this).
The callback function must accept two parameters, an HInstance value and an
untyped pointer, and must return a Boolean value. The EnumModules function will
in turn call our callback function for each module, passing the instance handle of

each module as the first parameter and the data structure pointer (nil in our example) as the second:

```
function ForEachModule (HInstance: Longint;
  Data: Pointer): Boolean;
var
  Flags: Integer;
  ModuleName, ModuleDesc: string;
  ModuleNode: TTreeNode;
begin
  with Form1.TreeView1.Items do
  begin
    SetLength (ModuleName, 200);
    GetModuleFileName (HInstance,
      PChar (ModuleName), Length (ModuleName));
    ModuleName := PChar (ModuleName); // fixup
    ModuleNode := Add (nil, ModuleName);

    // get description and add fixed nodes
    ModuleDesc := GetPackageDescription (PChar (ModuleName));
    ContNode := AddChild (ModuleNode, 'Contains');
    ReqNode := AddChild (ModuleNode, 'Requires');

    // add information if the module is a package
    GetPackageInfo (HInstance, nil,
      Flags, ShowInfoProc);
    if ModuleDesc <> '' then
    begin
      AddChild (ModuleNode,
        'Description: ' + ModuleDesc);
      if Flags and pfDesignOnly = pfDesignOnly then
        AddChild (ModuleNode, 'Design Only');
      if Flags and pfRunOnly = pfRunOnly then
        AddChild (ModuleNode, 'Run Only');
    end;
  end;
  Result := True;
end;
```

As you can see in the code above, we begin by adding the module name as the main node of the tree (by calling the Add method of the TreeView1.Items object and passing nil as the first parameter). We then add two fixed child nodes, which we store in the ContNode and ReqNode variables declared in the implementation section of this unit.

Next, we call the GetPackageInfo function and pass it another callback function, ShowInfoProc, which we'll discuss shortly. You'll notice that we add the details for the main module (see Figure 6.5), simply because this will provide a list of the application's units. At the end of this function, we add more information if the module is a package, such as its description and compiler flags (we know it's a package if its description isn't an empty string).

FIGURE 6.5:

The PackInfo example also lists the units that are part of the current application.

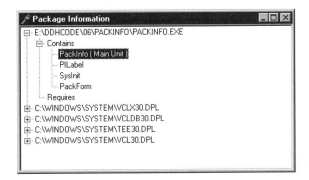

Earlier, we mentioned passing another callback function, the ShowInfoProc procedure, to the GetPackageInfo function, which in turn calls our callback function for each contained or required package of a module. This procedure creates a string that describes the package and its main flags (added within parentheses), and then inserts that string under one of the two nodes (ContNode and ReqNode), depending on the type of the module. We can determine the module type by examining the NameType parameter. Here is the complete code of our second callback function:

```
procedure ShowInfoProc (const Name: string;
    NameType: TNameType; Flags: Byte; Param: Pointer);
var
    FlagStr: string;
begin
    FlagStr := ' ';
    if Flags and ufMainUnit <> 0 then
        FlagStr := FlagStr + 'Main Unit ';
    if Flags and ufPackageUnit <> 0 then
```

```
      FlagStr := FlagStr + 'Package Unit ';
   if Flags and ufWeakUnit <> 0 then
      FlagStr := FlagStr + 'Weak Unit ';
   if FlagStr <> ' ' then
      FlagStr := ' (' + FlagStr + ')';
   with Form1.TreeView1.Items do
      case NameType of
        ntContainsUnit:
          AddChild (ContNode, Name + FlagStr);
        ntRequiresPackage:
          AddChild (ReqNode, Name);
      end;
  end;
```

Here, you'll notice that the Flags parameter doesn't contain flag style information, as the online help seems to imply. If you want to investigate this topic further, examine the SysUtils unit.

Preparing a Help File

Most Delphi developers who create packages will intend to distribute them; and an essential element of distribution software is documentation, particularly the online help. Since the *Component Writer's Guide* online help file (the *CWG*) describes the steps you need to take to create help for your components, we won't duplicate that information here. However, we do want to emphasize three key elements that aren't documented clearly: formatting, the footnote styles, and linking to other Delphi help files.

First, make sure that you use the same formatting, font, style, and size for the text that Delphi uses for the main help. In particular, you should try to use the following settings:

- Use the Keep With Next Paragraph style on paragraphs that contain the page heading and main links. Doing this creates a section that won't scroll out of view on a long help page.

- Use 12 pt Bold Arial for the heading of each page.

- Use 8.5 pt Arial for the main links that appear near the top of each page (Properties, Events, Methods, Example, and so on).

- Use 10 pt Bold Arial for subheadings that describe the body text (Unit, Description, and so on).

- Use 10 pt Bold Arial for headings in popup windows such as the listings of Properties, Methods, and Events.

- Use 8.5 pt Arial for the body text.

These settings will make your help information appear almost identical to the native Delphi help files.

There's unfortunately quite a bit of confusion about the different footnotes that you'll use in a component help file. Here are the footnote styles and their uses:

- The $ footnote: You'll insert this footnote to identify the text that should appear in the Topics Found dialog box or via the Find page of the main help dialog box. This footnote doesn't appear in the body text, and is only an aid to the user when they're searching for information related to a given task or topic. Accordingly, you'll want to add several $ footnotes for a particular page, one for each possible description.

- The # footnote: You'll insert this footnote to create a unique mnemonic identifier for a given page. When you're creating other pages, you'll specify this identifier to tell the help system how to link to this identifier's page.

- The B footnote: You'll use this footnote to create search links that Delphi's built-in help system will locate. These are the words that Delphi displays when the user presses F1. (Make sure you follow the CWG guidelines for naming these identifiers.)

- The K footnote: Use this footnote to create a search entry in the main index. Naturally, you can (and should) create multiple entries for each help topic.

Using this information and the technique described in the CWG, you should be able to bring the user to the correct location in your help file, and link to different topics that you've created.

To link to a topic in the main Delphi help, you'll need to use the `JumpKeyword` macro. (This is not clearly documented in the online help.) For example, if you're writing a help file for the `TDdhAniButton` class and want to link back to the `TButton` class (its base class), you'll create the following macro:

```
!JumpKeyword("DELPHI.HLP", "TButton")
```

You'll place this macro in the same location where you'd normally place a linked page's identifier.

Distributing a Package Collection

Once you've built a package, created its help file, drawn the component bitmaps, and assembled everything else, you are ready to distribute it. Prior to Delphi 3, you had to use a generic installation program, and then ask the users to perform a manual installation of the component to add a given unit to the component library. Delphi 3 automates this process using the Package Collection Editor. (This stand-alone tool doesn't appear in the default program group that the Delphi 3 installation creates, but it does appear on the default Tools menu.) The Package Collection Editor allows you to combine one or more packages, with all their support files, into a single compressed collection file with the extension DCP (Delphi Collection Package).

When you launch the Package Collection Editor, it generates a new, empty collection file. You should begin by saving this file with a new name (and the default PCE extension). Then you can begin to add author information and build the directory list (by pressing the Add button in the main window), as shown in Figure 6.6. In this section, we'll give you some step-by-step instructions for using this powerful tool, because the Delphi manuals and online help files give very limited information about it.

FIGURE 6.6:

The directory information set up for the main node of the package collection

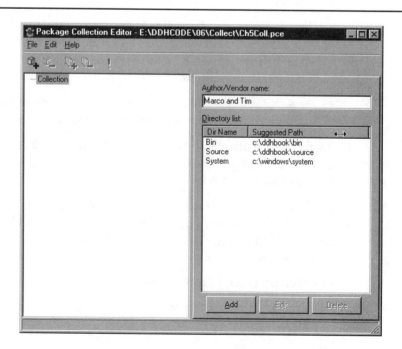

Now you can add packages to the collection file and set the target directories for the various files, including the required executable and library files automatically suggested by the editor, as shown in Figure 6.7. You'll notice that we're placing the run-time package in the windows\system directory. Although this is not strictly mandatory when Windows activates an OLE or ActiveX server (Windows 95 and NT use two different search techniques for the directories of the path), Windows will always check the windows\system directory to find required packages. Therefore, this is the safest approach, even though the windows\system directory tends to have too many files already.

FIGURE 6.7:

The definition of the directories for the main file and the other required files of a design-time package, which relies on a run-time package (saved in the System directory)

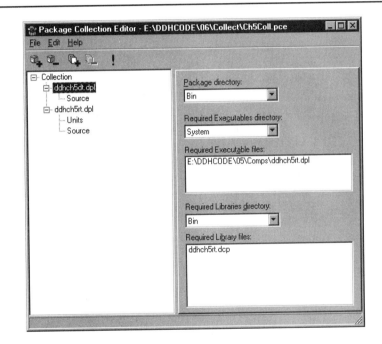

Now you can specify the additional files you want to distribute with the package, usually supplementary units and source code files, but also help files and other support files such as example projects and code. For every group of source code files, you'll add a new package node entry, and then add the files to that node, and check the Optional Group check box.

The Package Collection Editor generates a PCE file, with is nothing more than an INI file in disguise. For example, here is the source code of the Ch5Coll.PCE file.

```
[General]
Author=Marco and Tim

[Directories]
DirCount=3
Dir1Name=Bin
Dir1Path=c:\ddhbook\bin
Dir2Name=Source
Dir2Path=c:\ddhbook\source
Dir3Name=System
Dir3Path=c:\windows\system

[E:\DDHCODE\05\Comps\ddhch5dt.dpl]
PackageDir=0
RequiredExeDir=2
RequiredLibDir=0
Group1=Source
Group1Dir=1
Group1Optional=1
Group1UpdateLib=0
Group1.1=E:\DDHCODE\05\Comps\ch5reg.pas
Group1.2=E:\DDHCODE\05\Comps\ddhch5dt.dpk

[E:\DDHCODE\05\Comps\ddhch5rt.dpl]
PackageDir=2
RequiredExeDir=2
RequiredLibDir=0
Group1=Units
Group1Dir=0
Group1Optional=0
Group1UpdateLib=0
Group1.1=E:\DDHCODE\05\Comps\DdhAnimB.dcu
Group1.2=E:\DDHCODE\05\Comps\DdhAnimC.dcu
Group1.3=E:\DDHCODE\05\Comps\ddhch5.dcu
Group1.4=E:\DDHCODE\05\Comps\ddhch5dt.dcu
Group1.5=E:\DDHCODE\05\Comps\ddhch5rt.dcp
Group1.6=E:\DDHCODE\05\Comps\ddhch5rt.dcu
Group1.7=E:\DDHCODE\05\Comps\DdhCntEd.dcu
Group1.8=E:\DDHCODE\05\Comps\DdhGraph.dcu
Group1.9=E:\DDHCODE\05\Comps\DdhInpuB.dcu
Group1.10=E:\DDHCODE\05\Comps\DdhLed.dcu
Group1.11=E:\DDHCODE\05\Comps\DdhNoth.dcu
```

```
Group1.12=E:\DDHCODE\05\Comps\DdhNumEd.dcu
Group1.13=E:\DDHCODE\05\Comps\DdhSemaB.dcu
Group1.14=E:\DDHCODE\05\Comps\DdhSemaL.dcu
Group1.15=E:\DDHCODE\05\Comps\DdhSemap.dcu
Group1.16=E:\DDHCODE\05\Comps\DdhSounB.dcu
Group1.17=E:\DDHCODE\05\Comps\DdhSuper.dcu
Group2=Source
Group2Dir=1
Group2Optional=1
Group2UpdateLib=0
Group2.1=E:\DDHCODE\05\Comps\ddhch5rt.dpk
Group2.2=E:\DDHCODE\05\Comps\DdhAnimC.pas
Group2.3=E:\DDHCODE\05\Comps\DdhAnimB.pas
Group2.4=E:\DDHCODE\05\Comps\DdhCntEd.pas
Group2.5=E:\DDHCODE\05\Comps\DdhGraph.pas
Group2.6=E:\DDHCODE\05\Comps\DdhInpuB.pas
Group2.7=E:\DDHCODE\05\Comps\DdhLed.pas
Group2.8=E:\DDHCODE\05\Comps\DdhNoth.pas
Group2.9=E:\DDHCODE\05\Comps\DdhNumEd.pas
Group2.10=E:\DDHCODE\05\Comps\DdhSemaB.pas
Group2.11=E:\DDHCODE\05\Comps\DdhSemaL.pas
Group2.12=E:\DDHCODE\05\Comps\DdhSemap.pas
Group2.13=E:\DDHCODE\05\Comps\DdhSounB.pas
Group2.14=E:\DDHCODE\05\Comps\DdhSuper.pas
```

You can find this file in the Collect directory for Chapter 6. Keep in mind that after you've compiled the collection, all the files are stored inside the compressed component collection file, and you won't need to keep the original files in the same directory.

WARNING   To install the Package collection for this chapter (which you can find on the companion CD), you should not only disable the run-time and design-time packages of the Chapter 5 examples, but also remove them from the list of available packages. If you fail to do so, the installation of the collection will stop with an error.

When you finish defining the package collection, you can compile it into the compressed DCP file. Now you can simply distribute the DCP file. Other programmers can then install this package collection by using the standard Install Package menu command, pressing the Add button, and then choosing Package

Collection as the file type. At this step an installation wizard appears, as you can see in Figure 6.8. Before proceeding with the full or the custom installation you can change the default directories by pressing the Directories button.

FIGURE 6.8:

The initial screen of the Install Package Collection Wizard

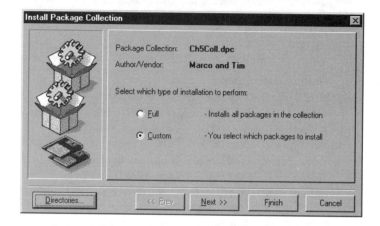

If you choose Custom installation, you'll be able to select which packages to install, and you'll be able to selectively install the optional file groups related to each package (but not those file groups that weren't marked optional). Figure 6.9 illustrates this second step of installing a component collection.

FIGURE 6.9:

The second step of installing a component collection allows you to choose the packages you want to install and to select optional group of files, such as source code files.

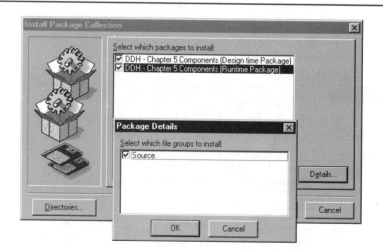

What's Next

Now that we've examined the main topics related to component writing (in the previous chapter), and have discussed in detail using packages to deploy those components, we've completed the first part of the book, which is devoted to Delphi foundations: Object Pascal, VCL, streaming, RTTI, components, and packages.

Now we can move on to a different topic, but we'll use the same approach. The subject of the second part of the book is Windows programming. Even if this isn't a new topic for you, we think you'll find a lot of information in the next chapter. We'll begin by delving into the details of how the windowing and messaging systems work, examining the bare API calls (in case you've never seen them), but we'll also review the internal Delphi messages and the structure of a standard Delphi application.

From that point, we'll move on to build more complex components, such as form extender and application components, and then we'll explore other hot topics, including COM and the Windows shell.

PART II

Delphi and Windows

CHAPTER

SEVEN

The VCL and Windows

7

There are many ways to describe Delphi. One accurate description is "a Windows development environment." Indeed, most people use Delphi to create Windows applications, but in fact, you can use it to build practically any type of Windows code module, including DLLs and ActiveX controls. (The only exception is the development of Windows drivers.)

Unfortunately, the mechanisms that Delphi uses to build Windows code modules quickly and easily aren't immediately obvious. How do Windows messages become Delphi events? How do Delphi applications implement window procedures? What's the relationship between a Delphi form class and the WNDCLASS structure of the corresponding window? This chapter will focus on these and similar questions.

While we'll investigate many Windows API topics, we're not going to discuss merely calling the API functions. We'll examine how Delphi components interact with Windows by carefully reviewing portions of the VCL source code.

In this chapter, we'll frequently refer to the Windows 32-bit API (commonly known as the Win32 API), which is the API common to both Windows 95 and Windows NT. Although there are some minor differences between these two versions of the Win32 API, they're not relevant to the topics we're going to discuss.

First, we'll quickly review Windows API programming in the traditional sense, and demonstrate how you can use Delphi without the benefits of the VCL. If you are fluent in Windows programming from another environment, you might want to skip this section and proceed to "Windows Messages and Delphi Events," where we begin discussing Windows programming from a Delphi perspective.

Windows Applications without the VCL

Few people would consider using Delphi to build applications without taking advantage of its visual design capabilities. Even so, it's instructive to build simple Windows applications without using TForm or any other VCL class. Granted, such an application is extremely small, but you'll have to write a huge amount of code to duplicate the behavior of a simple form-based Delphi application.

If you've never written a Windows application using plain C/C++ or Pascal, using Delphi this way will help you understand how the Windows operating system works. After we build a simple application without using the VCL, we'll show you where the equivalent code appears in the VCL. In some cases, you can use this knowledge in building more powerful Delphi applications and components.

Using Windows API Functions

At the heart of Delphi is its ability to call any Windows API function directly. Or, since the Windows API is basically a collection of functions and procedures within a standard set of DLLs, we might instead say that the ability of Delphi applications to call the exported functions and procedures from a DLL is its crucial capability.

To call an exported function or procedure in a DLL, you need two things: an appropriate function or procedure declaration and an implementation stub that specifies the DLL that contains the function as well as the function's name. For example, if you open the Windows.PAS file (called WinProcs.PAS in Delphi 1.0), you'll find the following:

```
interface

  function WinExec(lpCmdLine: LPCSTR;
    uCmdShow: UINT): UINT; stdcall;

implementation

  function WinExec; external kernel32  name 'WinExec';
```

This declaration describes the parameters and return type as usual, but it also uses the stdcall keyword to indicate that the function uses standard parameter passing, and not the new register parameter-passing technique. In the implementation section, the function stub uses the external keyword to indicate that the code for the function actually lies in another code module, named "kernel32."

In the declaration of the WinExec function above, you've probably noticed that the parameter and return types aren't native Delphi data types. In fact, these are types that are specific to Windows API programming using the C language. Here is a list of the most commonly used Windows types and their Delphi equivalents:

Windows Type	Delphi Type	Description
WCHAR	WideChar	A Unicode character
LPSTR	PAnsiChar	A pointer to a string; corresponds to PChar
LPCSTR	PAnsiChar	A pointer to a constant string
LPWSTR	PWideChar	A Unicode string
LPCWSTR	PWideChar	A Unicode constant string
DWORD	Integer	An unsigned 32-bit value (corresponds to Cardinal)
SHORT	Smallint	A 16-bit value
UINT	Integer	An unsigned 32-bit value (corresponds to Cardinal)
ULONG	Longint	An unsigned 32-bit value
BOOL	LongBool	A 32-bit Boolean value
THandle	Integer	A handle (see the note later in the text)

In addition to the types we've mentioned here, Windows also defines many pointer types, which typically have the same name as the corresponding type preceded by the letter P. For instance, you would refer to a pointer to a double word (DWORD) as a PDWORD. Of course, there are many more type definitions in the Windows unit, including hundreds of record structures. In this table we just wanted to emphasize the correspondence between Pascal data types and the types you use to call Windows API functions.

An important characteristic of the Windows API functions is their use of Hungarian notation for parameters and return types. This notation is a simple set of rules for naming identifiers according to their actual data type. Whether you use this notation for your own functions and procedures or not, it's important to be able to read it because the source code and help files use it to describe and document calling the functions from your code.

Below is a table that contains a short list of the various base type prefixes:

Prefix	Meaning
c	Char
b	Byte (or unsigned character)
n	Integer
sz	PChar, null-terminated string (or string-zero)
f	Boolean
h	THandle
w	Word (this is also a native Delphi type)
dw	DWORD, or unsigned Integer, or Cardinal
fn	Function (generally a function pointer)
x, y	Integer coordinates

In addition to these indicators, Hungarian notation defines other prefixes as modifiers. A *p* in front of any of the above letters indicates a pointer, a *c* indicates "count of" something, and an *l* stands for a long value or pointer (actually, long made sense only in the 16-bit world, because in the Win32 API every pointer is a long pointer, or *lp*). This helps in building a number of composite type names, from which we've extracted some of the most common:

Prefix	Meaning
psz	Pointer to a null-terminated string
lpsz	Long pointer to a null-terminated string
lpfn	Long pointer to a function
cb	Count byte, or the number of bytes
cx, cy	Width and height (relative and not absolute values)

To complete this picture, Microsoft suggests a corresponding Hungarian name for every record type defined in the API. For example, the DrawItemStruct type has a corresponding *dis* type prefix listed in the help file as a comment following the C language type name.

```
typedef struct tagDRAWITEMSTRUCT {   // dis
    UINT  CtlType;
    ...
```

Therefore, an appropriate name for a record of this type would be disMyItem. The dis prefix alerts the reader that this is a DrawItemStruct record. Another important thing to notice is that different handle types use different names, such as hBmp for a bitmap handle, hWnd for a window handle, and so on.

What's a Handle?

It's important at this point to clarify what a handle is. A handle is an integer value that acts as a reference to a location in system memory. Windows uses handles to identify internal objects and data structures.

For example, consider a window. As soon as you create it, Windows assigns it a unique integer value as an identifier. The value doesn't specify a memory address, but instead corresponds to an address that Windows uses to find the memory structure that describes the window. If you need to perform an operation on that window, you'll need to specify the window handle. Because you're not specifying the memory location of the window, Windows is free to move the data structure of the window. You don't need to worry about it, because Windows will update the handle so that it always addresses (indirectly) the correct memory location. Obviously, you must remember to manage handles in much the same way as you'd manage pointers to your own data structures, and Windows provides several API functions to do just that.

In particular, one thing that makes a handle different from a Delphi object reference is that instead of calling a method which has an implicit self parameter, you have to explicitly provide the "object" parameter, which is usually the first parameter of the API function. In that regard, handles are more like references to simple records. Finally, note that many Delphi VCL classes have a run-time Handle property, which stores the window handle that corresponds to a system object managed by the component (such as a window, a windowed control, a menu, a bitmap, an icon, a canvas, and so on).

Writing an API Program in Delphi

Now let's start building a simple Delphi program using only plain Windows API calls. We have named the example PlainApi, and we'll use this program to discuss some important aspects of Windows programming. To write a Windows API program in Delphi, you can simply create an empty project file (or remove the code from an existing one), and write the main body of the program between the begin and end keywords of the project file. This replaces what's known in the C language as the `WinMain` function. Accordingly, you may want to make the program a little more readable (at least to C/C++ programmers) by writing a `WinMain` procedure and calling it within the initialization code of the project file:

```
begin
  WinMain;
end.
```

What will our `WinMain` procedure do? Basically four things: register a window class for the new window, create the window, and start a message processing loop. At the heart of this loop, we'll create a function that responds to the appropriate system messages for our window. This function is generally called a "window procedure," and is the fourth element of our straight Windows API application.

1. The Window Class

The first step is to register the window class. This has nothing to do with a class in the Delphi sense: a window class is simply a data structure of the WNDCLASS or WNDCLASSEX type (Delphi defines these as TWndClass or TWndClassEx), which describes the general behavior of windows of that class. When we're ready to create a window, we will pass the class as a parameter. The window class is really just a blueprint for building the window.

NOTE   Actually, there are two versions of each of these structures in the Win32 API. One of them is indicated by an *A* (for ASCII), the other by a *W* (for Wide or Unicode). Delphi and Windows 95 provide limited support for Unicode characters and strings, so we'll focus on the ASCII version. However, most of the code is fully portable, and some definitions in the Windows.PAS unit determine which version the application will use.

The window class structure defines many characteristics for the windows, but the most important is certainly the window procedure, or *wndproc*, the function that the class's windows will use to respond to system messages:

```
type
  TWndClassExA = packed record // ASCII
    cbSize: UINT; // structure size (version)
    style: UINT; // class style (cs_xxx)
    lpfnWndProc: TFNWndProc; // window procedure
    cbClsExtra: Integer; // class extra bytes
    cbWndExtra: Integer; // window extra bytes
    hInstance: HINST; // application-instance handle
    hIcon: HICON; // window icon
    hCursor: HCURSOR; // window cursor
    hbrBackground: HBRUSH; // background brush
    lpszMenuName: PAnsiChar; // menu resource name
    lpszClassName: PAnsiChar; // class name
    hIconSm: HICON; // Window small icon
  end;
  TWndClassEx = TWndClassExA;
```

You can find a more detailed description of the TWndClass window class record in the Win32 help file under the WNDCLASSEX entry.

As you might have guessed, the two key elements of this record type are the class name and the window procedure. Another important element is the identifier of the application that registered the window class (hInstance). The rest of the fields of this record are basically graphical characteristics: the class style, the extra bytes, the window icon, the small caption icon (hIconSm), the cursor, and the brush used to paint the window's background. We will focus on some of these topics (such as styles and extra bytes) later on in this chapter.

To learn more about the functions you'll use to initialize the graphical elements of a window class, you can look for the following functions in the Help file: LoadIcon, LoadCursor, GetStockObject, and CreateBrush. Here's the initial portion of our WinMain procedure:

```
procedure WinMain;
var
  WndClassEx: TWndClassEx;
begin
  // initialize the window class structure
  WndClassEx.cbSize := sizeOf (TWndClassEx);
```

```
WndClassEx.lpszClassName := 'PlainWindow';
WndClassEx.style := cs_VRedraw or cs_HRedraw;
WndClassEx.hInstance := HInstance;
WndClassEx.lpfnWndProc := @PlainWinProc;
WndClassEx.cbClsExtra := 0;
WndClassEx.cbWndExtra := 0;
WndClassEx.hIcon := LoadIcon (hInstance,
  MakeIntResource ('MAINICON'));
WndClassEx.hIconSm  := LoadIcon (hInstance,
  MakeIntResource ('MAINICON'));
WndClassEx.hCursor := LoadCursor (0, idc_Arrow);;
WndClassEx.hbrBackground := GetStockObject (white_Brush);
WndClassEx.lpszMenuName := nil;
// register the class
if RegisterClassEx (WndClassEx) = 0 then
  MessageBox (0, 'Invalid class registration',
    'Plain API', MB_OK)
else
  ...
```

In the code above, you'll notice that we load an icon named MAINICON. Delphi automatically generates this icon for each application, and places it in the resource file for the project. You can load this resource file by writing

```
{$R *.res}
```

Delphi automatically inserts this code in the project file, so you just need to remember not to delete it. Then, you can load the icon by calling the LoadIcon function. To call this function, you'll first pass the name of the icon (MAINICON in the code above) to the MakeIntResource function, which converts the icon's name string into a number that identifies the correct resource. You'll pass this number to the LoadIcon function.

TIP

For many of the data structures that Microsoft has added to Windows in the last few years, the first parameter contains the size of the structure, which represents a sort of version code. When Microsoft adds new fields to a structure, it adds them to the end, and the size (or version) of the structure changes. However, older programs (if they are well written) will allocate the correct amount of memory, but will only manipulate the fields they understand. This prevents an application from trying to read or write data outside the boundary of the structure.

Once you've initialized the window class structure, you can call the RegisterClassEx function, which returns a special value called an *atom*, an integer value that corresponds to the name of the registered class. If there is an error registering the class, this function returns zero as an error code. If an error occurs, we must skip the rest of the code (if we can't register the main window's class, something catastrophic has happened). It's common to use a plain Exit or Halt function call for this error, instead of an if-then-else statement. Here is an example:

```
if RegisterClassEx (WndClassEx) = 0 then
begin
  MessageBox (0, 'Invalid class registration',
    'Plain API', MB_OK)
  Exit;
end;
```

This is similar to the structure a corresponding C language version of this program would have. Whenever possible, we prefer using language constructs such as an if-then-else statement instead of hard-coded jumps. However, if the code becomes too complex, using Exit might be easier to read.

> **NOTE** Atoms are a bit like system-wide global strings, where each string corresponds to a unique atom. Two applications can therefore refer to the same string by passing each other an atom. That way, they don't have to try to access a common memory location (a string is nothing but a pointer to the memory where the characters of the string reside). In fact, you can almost consider an atom to be a handle to a string. However, the Win32 API also defines *string handles* as a data type for the DDE management library, so the analogy isn't strictly true.

Instead of beginning the WinMain procedure as we did, we could've used the TWndClass type instead of TWndClassEx. For that type, we'd need to call the RegisterClass procedure instead of RegisterClassEx. The effect is similar, but the extended structure (TWndClassEx) defines the size field and a field for the window's small icon.

2. Creating the Window

Once we've defined a window class, we can use it to create a window by calling the CreateWindow or CreateWindowEx functions, using the standard or extended structure. These functions accept similar parameters, but the CreateWindowEx function allows you to specify extended styles for the window. For either function, the key parameter is the class name, which Windows uses to determine how to create the new window. Here's the code that creates a new window, with a short description of each parameter:

```
hWnd := CreateWindowEx (
  ws_Ex_OverlappedWindow, // extended styles
  WndClassEx.lpszClassName, // class name
  'Plain API Demo', // title
  ws_OverlappedWindow, // old styles
  cw_UseDefault, 0, // window position
  cw_UseDefault, 0, // window size
  0, // parent window (if any)
  0, // menu resource handle
  HInstance, // application-instance handle
  nil); // pointer to initialization parameters
```

The old-style and extended-style parameters determine many characteristics of the window's behavior, its relationship with other windows, and its appearance.

You can omit the four position parameters, as we've done here, by letting Windows use a default position and size for the window. The system uses a very simple algorithm to determine the default position, which you can see by launching several copies of this program. Using the value cw_UseDefaults for both the x and cx parameters has the same effect as using the poDefault value for the Position property of a Delphi form. If you examine the other possible values for this property, you'll see the correlation with other possible parameter values in the function call above. Also note that when you use cw_UseDefault for the x parameter, there is no need to specify the y parameter. Windows will ignore it anyway. As usual, refer to the Windows API help file for more details on this function.

NOTE   Notice that the RegisterClassEx and CreateWindowEx functions have no relationship. You can create a window using CreateWindowEx that you registered with RegisterClass, and vice-versa.

After creating the window using CreateWindowEx, we still need to call ShowWindow to display it. Or course, we should do this only if we've successfully created the window. We can check this by examining the return value from CreateWindowEx, the new window handle. Zero indicates that an error occurred, and Windows wasn't able to create the new window:

```
hWnd := CreateWindowEx (...);
if hWnd = 0 then
  MessageBox (0, 'Window not created',
    'Plain API', MB_OK)
else
begin
  ShowWindow (hWnd, sw_ShowNormal);
```

In the code above, we've used the "show normal" parameter of the function to display the window instead of the sw_Minimized or sw_Maximized values. In theory, we should have used the value passed to the application by the system, which you can retrieve by calling the GetStartupInfo API function. (The user can change this value by altering the properties of the icon that launches the application.)

3. The Message Loop

Once we've created the window successfully and displayed it, we can start processing its messages. We'll continue this activity until we're ready to exit (almost every Windows application is based on this type of message processing loop). As we extract system messages for the application, we'll dispatch them to the proper window (by calling the appropriate window procedure). Windows passes information to the application via these messages using a special structure, TMsg (see under MSG in the Windows API Help file):

```
type
  TMsg = packed record
    hwnd: HWND; // destination window
    message: UINT; // message code
    wParam: WPARAM; // additional information
    lParam: LPARAM; // additional information
    time: DWORD; // when the message was posted
    pt: TPoint; // cursor location (when message was posted)
  end;
```

As we'll see shortly, most of this information is important to the window procedures that respond to these messages. However, the last two fields are seldom used. Here is the code for the message loop of our application:

```
var
  Msg: TMsg;
```

```
begin
  ...
  while GetMessage (Msg, 0, 0, 0) do
  begin
    TranslateMessage (Msg);
    DispatchMessage (Msg);
  end;
end;
```

The GetMessage function initializes an Msg record with the information from the top message in the application's message queue (each application has its own queue), and then removes that message. This function returns False only when it retrieves the special wm_Quit message (more on this later). For any other value, it returns True, and therefore continues in the while-do loop.

Inside this loop, we call TranslateMessage to convert some of the lower-level messages into higher-level ones (such as turning key-down and key-up messages into wm_Char messages), and then we dispatch the converted messages to the appropriate window. Since the GetMessage function sets the destination window field in the Msg structure, DispatchMessage simply locates the window information from a system memory area, determines the window procedure for the window, and calls it with the proper parameters.

TIP

It's important to note that when dispatching a message, Windows uses the system information of the *window*, not the information for the window *class*. Although you specify a window procedure in the TWndClass structure when registering the class, Windows copies this information for each window you create. This allows a program to alter the window procedure for a single window without affecting all windows of that window class. We'll describe this process, known as *subclassing*, later in this chapter. Once again, though, remember that the terms *class* and *subclass* relate to Windows data structures in this context, and not to Delphi classes and inheritance.

These three pieces of code—the window class registration, the call to create the window, and the message loop—constitute the main procedure of the program. We've placed this code in a procedure called WinMain, which we then call in the initialization code of the project. Alternatively, you can simply write these three pieces of code in the initialization section.

4. The Window Procedure

The only other code we need to write to complete the PlainAPI example is a window procedure. Window procedures must have the following function signature:

```
function (hWnd: THandle; nMsg: UINT;
  wParam, lParam: Cardinal): Cardinal; export; stdcall;
```

The first parameter is the handle of the window, and the second the message number. The third and fourth parameters contain some additional message data, which varies from message to message. The Messages.PAS unit defines all the Windows messages and some data structures for some of the more complex parameters. Here is a small excerpt from this unit, which shows that the messages are simple integer values:

```
const
  WM_NULL          = $0000;
  WM_CREATE        = $0001;
  WM_DESTROY       = $0002;
  WM_MOVE          = $0003;
  WM_SIZE          = $0005;
  WM_ACTIVATE      = $0006;
  WM_SETFOCUS      = $0007;
  // and about 400 other messages
```

At the very least, a window procedure should provide some termination code, such as posting a wm_Quit message when the system is destroying the main (and only) window:

```
function PlainWinProc (hWnd: THandle; nMsg: UINT;
  wParam, lParam: Cardinal): Cardinal; export; stdcall;
begin
  Result := 0;
  case nMsg of
    wm_Destroy:
      PostQuitMessage (0);
    else
      Result := DefWindowProc (
        hWnd, nMsg, wParam, lParam);
  end;
end;
```

The return value for a window procedure (Result) varies depending on the message you're processing. The simplest approach is to set it to zero, and then use the return value of the `DefWindowProc` call. This function is a default window procedure that provides standard behavior for a window, so you should call it unless you want to override this behavior. If you write the window procedure using the structure above, you're indicating that you want to override the behavior of the window for each message you handle, since we're executing the default code only if we haven't responded to the message earlier in the `case` statement. Occasionally, you may want to call `DefWindowProc` before or after responding to a message, so you can have a mixture of custom and default behavior for the same message:

```
begin
  Result := 0;
  case nMsg of
    wm_xxx:
      // do something, and skip the default
      {specific code}
    wm_yyy:
      // do something, and also the default
      begin
        {specific code}
        Result := DefWindowProc (
          hWnd, nMsg, wParam, lParam);
      end;
    else
      Result := DefWindowProc (
        hWnd, nMsg, wParam, lParam);
  end;
end;
```

As an alternative, some programmers write window procedures that pass each message to the `DefWindowProc` function by default, unless they want to explicitly skip such processing:

```
begin
  Result := 0;
  case nMsg of
    wm_xxx:
      // do something, and skip the default
      begin
        {specific code}
        Exit;
      end;
    wm_yyy:
```

```
      // do something, and also the default
      {specific code}
    end;
    Result := DefWindowProc (
      hWnd, nMsg, wParam, lParam);
  end;
```

When you're choosing one approach over the other, you should consider that most of the time you'll respond to messages entirely with your own code, and rarely handle messages that you want the DefWindowProc to process.

Now let's consider the window procedure for our example. The first version of the window procedure (for the PlainAPI example) responds to the wm_lButton-Down message (which corresponds to the OnMouseDown Delphi event, but only for the left mouse button), and the wm_Paint message (which corresponds to the OnPaint event):

```
function PlainWinProc (hWnd: THandle; nMsg: UINT;
  wParam, lParam: Cardinal): Cardinal; export; stdcall;
var
  hdc: THandle;
  ps: TPaintStruct;
begin
  Result := 0;
  case nMsg of
    wm_lButtonDown:
      MessageBox (hWnd, 'Mouse Clicked',
        'Plain API', MB_OK);
    wm_Paint:
    begin
      hdc := BeginPaint (hWnd, ps);
      Ellipse (hdc, 100, 100, 300, 300);
      EndPaint (hWnd, ps);
    end;
    wm_Destroy:
      PostQuitMessage (0);
    else
      Result := DefWindowProc (hWnd, nMsg, wParam, lParam);
  end;
end;
```

To paint on the surface of the window, as we've done in Figure 7.1, you must first create a *device context*. Device contexts correspond to the TCanvas class in Delphi. If you're using the windows API directly (as we are in this example), you should create a device context every time you want to create some output, and release the device context as soon as you're done with it. In the code above, we use BeginPaint to ask the system to create a device context for painting (something you should generally do only in response to a wm_Paint message). The return value, hdc, is a handle to the new device context. We can use this handle in our paint operations, and then call EndPaint to release the handle (and let the system release the device context).

FIGURE 7.1:

The circle painted by the PlainAPI example, along with the message box displayed when the user clicks on the window

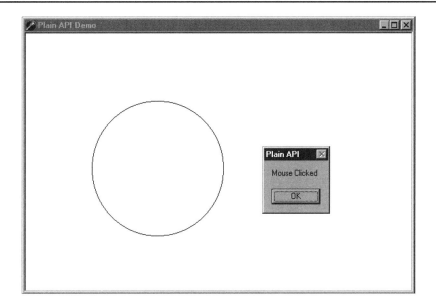

Creating a Control Manually

The previous example was very simple, but it was also instructive. Before returning to Delphi programming, we want to show you one more version (called Plain2) to introduce some topics we will explore later on.

This version will extend the previous program by adding a pushbutton to the window forcing it to stay in the center of the window, and handling the pushbutton's click event. If we decide to use the same name for the window class, and we don't change the window caption, we can simply replace the old window's window procedure with a new version. In the new window procedure, we respond to the wm_Create message (which corresponds to Delphi's OnCreate event) to create the button as a child window inside the main window. We'll also respond to the wm_Size message (which corresponds to the OnResize event) to place the button in the middle of the window, and the wm_Command message (which corresponds to many of the button events and the events of other child windows) to handle clicking the button.

As usual, we've broken this function into manageable pieces and commented the code of each branch of the case statement:

```
const
  id_Button = 100;

function PlainWinProc (hWnd: THandle; nMsg: UINT;
  wParam, lParam: Cardinal): Cardinal; export; stdcall;
var
  Rect: TRect;
begin
  Result := 0;
  case nMsg of
    wm_Create:
      // create button
      CreateWindowEx (0, // extended styles
        'BUTTON', // predefined class
        '&Click here', // caption
        ws_Child or ws_Visible or ws_Border
          or bs_PushButton, // styles
        0, 0, // position: see wm_Size
        200, 80, // size
        hWnd, // parent
        id_Button, // identifier (not a menu handle)
        hInstance, // application id
        nil); // init info pointer
```

We've seen the CreateWindow function before, but here we're using it in a slightly different way. First, you'll notice that we're creating an object from an existing (or preregistered) class instead of a custom class. Windows provides a number of existing controls, including buttons, edit boxes, and list boxes, but also supplies the new Windows 95 common controls such as the tree view and rich edit controls. By simply knowing the correct window class name, you can create such a window.

The new button is a child window of the main window, as indicated by the ws_Child style, the parent parameter, and the use of a button identifier instead of a menu handle. Some of the other style information tells Windows that this is a push button (other button styles include check boxes and radio buttons), it has a border, and that it's visible—even without calling the ShowWindow function.

When we create the button as a child window, we haven't yet specified its position. This isn't a problem, because before showing the main window the system will send the wm_Size message, so we can place the button properly within the main window:

```
wm_Size:
begin
  // get the size of the client region of the main window
  GetClientRect (hWnd, Rect);
  // move the button window
  SetWindowPos (
    GetDlgItem (hWnd, id_Button), // button handle
    0, // zOrder
    Rect.Right div 2 - 100,
    Rect.Bottom div 2 - 40,
    0, 0, // new size
    swp_NoZOrder or swp_NoSize);
end;
```

To determine the client region of the current window (the area we're responsible for), we call the GetClientRect API function. In fact, from this location in the code, all we know about our window is its handle, because we haven't stored any properties along with the window! To center the button we call the SetWindowPos API function, which you can use to size a window and set its position both on the parent window surface (the x and y-axes) and relative to other sibling windows (its z-axis, or z-order). Since we need to set only the x-y position, we use the last parameter of this function to tell it which operations not to perform. This is a rather convoluted way to perform such an operation, but this approach is not uncommon in the Windows API (and one reason most people would rather use a tool like Delphi).

The first parameter of the SetWindowPos function is the handle of the window you want to move (in our case, the button). As we mentioned earlier, we didn't store the button's window handle when we first created it, so we must now retrieve it from the system. One approach is to use the `GetDlgItem` function, which locates an item based on the parent window's handle and the unique identifier of the item. The name of this function is misleading: it should be called *GetChildFromId* or something similar.

NOTE   As a historical note, consider that the names of many Windows API functions and constants still refer to the early times of the Windows API. In the beginning, only dialog boxes could have child windows, and this is the reason for the name GetDlgItem. Other such occurrences of Windows 1.0 names are still quite frequent in the Win32 version (the fourth major version) of this API.

When the user clicks the button, the parent window receives a notification message. The message is `wm_Command`, and its `wParam` and `lParam` indicate which control generated the message (the `Sender` in Delphi event terminology) and what happened. The latter information is called the notification. In complex cases, you'll need to use nested `case` statements to narrow down what happened and where, but here we can use compound `if` statements:

```
wm_Command:
  // if it comes from the button
  if LoWord (wParam) = id_Button then
    // if it is a click
    if HiWord (wParam) = bn_Clicked then
      MessageBox (hWnd, 'Button Clicked',
        'Plain API 2', MB_OK);
```

In Figure 7.2, you can see the output of this program when the user presses the button. As you might expect, the final part of the window procedure is the same as the previous example (and similar to most API programs):

```
wm_Destroy:
  PostQuitMessage (0);
else
  Result := DefWindowProc (hWnd, nMsg, wParam, lParam);
  end;
end;
```

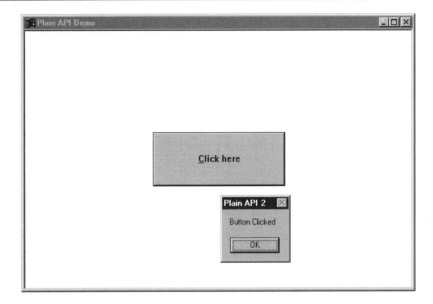

Windows Messages and Delphi Events

Now that we've reviewed Windows programming via straight API calls, we can
start exploring Windows programming from the Delphi perspective. The first
question is how Windows messages correspond to Delphi events. Answering this
question is complicated, and we'll need to examine the internal behavior of the
VCL to understand the details.

Using Windows Procedures within the VCL

In Windows, each window has a corresponding window procedure that
processes its messages. In Delphi, each TWinControl-derived class defines a
MainWndProc that Windows calls to perform message processing. Associating the
class's MainWndProc is complicated, though, because this function must be a
global function, and not a class method.

To solve this problem, Delphi creates something known as an "object instance,"
which is actually a pseudo window procedure that can call the proper MainWnd-
Proc method. Delphi applications actually store object instances in a linked list.

(You can see the source code of this key function, MakeObjectInstance, in the Forms unit.) Each windowed control then stores its corresponding object instance in the FObjectInstance field:

```
constructor TWinControl.Create (
  AOwner: TComponent);
begin
  inherited Create(AOwner);
  FObjectInstance :=
    MakeObjectInstance(MainWndProc);
  ...
```

Delphi uses the MakeObjectInstance return value (a wndproc) to supply the window procedure for the control's window (set in the TWinControl.CreateWnd method). To implement this behavior, Delphi uses a single function, StdWndProc, which pushes the parameters on the stack (to activate the register calling convention) and then calls the MainWndProc method of the Delphi object that corresponds to the window control:

```
function StdWndProc(Window: HWND; Message, WParam: Longint;
  LParam: Longint): Longint; stdcall; assembler;
```

Delphi uses this complex mechanism so that Windows can indirectly call a method of a class, MainWndProc, instead of a global window procedure to handle a message. The MainWndProc method in turn calls the WndProc virtual procedure, a method you can override in your own TWinControl-derived classes:

```
procedure TWinControl.MainWndProc(var Message: TMessage);
begin
  try
    try
      WndProc (Message);
    finally
      FreeDeviceContexts;
      FreeMemoryContexts;
    end;
  except
    Application.HandleException(Self);
  end;
end;
```

You'll notice that this method uses a TMessage class, not the TMsg class we've seen before. The key differences between these classes are that TMessage doesn't store the window handle (it doesn't need to, because the Delphi object stores it), includes the return value as a field, and defines various definitions of a variant record to allow you to access the information more easily (if you are familiar with variant records):

```
type
  TMessage = record
    Msg: Cardinal;
    case Integer of
      0: (
        WParam: Longint;
        LParam: Longint;
        Result: Longint);
      1: (
        WParamLo: Word;
        WParamHi: Word;
        LParamLo: Word;
        LParamHi: Word;
        ResultLo: Word;
        ResultHi: Word);
  end;
```

In fact, the Messages.PAS unit defines many more message records (one for each message type), which makes it easier to access the WParam and LParam fields without having to cast them manually. Here are two examples of such records:

```
type
  TWMCommand = record
    Msg: Cardinal;
    ItemID: Word;
    NotifyCode: Word;
    Ctl: HWND;
    Result: Longint;
  end;

  TWMSetFocus = record
    Msg: Cardinal;
    FocusedWnd: HWND;
    Unused: Longint;
    Result: Longint;
  end;
```

Using these specific message records makes your program more readable, and allows the compiler to do some type checking of the various message fields. Of course, using the wrong message record can cause this mechanism to work against you.

Besides passing the `TMessage` record to the `WndProc` method, the `MainWndProc` method handles any exception the code might raise by activating the `HandleException` method of the `Application` object, which eventually ends up calling the `OnException` handler you've defined, if any. If you don't respond to this event, the `Application` object calls the default `ShowException` method.

As we mentioned earlier, the `WndProc` method is a virtual procedure, so you can easily override it in your classes. In fact, this is the correct approach if you want to write a traditional window procedure inside a Delphi VCL-based application. If you do this, you'll probably want to call the inherited `WndProc` function to let Delphi respond to the message first since it performs several Delphi system actions and then activates the appropriate message handling method of the class.

Overriding WndProc

Now let's create an example that demonstrates how these internal mechanisms work, a program capable of filtering all the messages of a form. We can accomplish this task by overriding the `WndProc` method and then sending information about each message to a list box (in a separate form, to avoid recursion). Here is the resulting `WndProc` method:

```
procedure TForm1.WndProc (var Message: TMessage);
begin
  if not (Message.Msg = Last) then
  begin
    with Form2.Listbox1 do
      ItemIndex := Items.Add (GetMessageName (Message.Msg));
    Last := Message.Msg;
  end;
  inherited WndProc (Message);
end;
```

The only feature of this method you might not expect is the line that stores the number of the last message in the form's `Last` integer field. We do this to ensure that we skip processing this message if we receive it twice in a row.

To make this program work, we need to create Form2 before Form1 (this keeps the application from sending messages to the list box before we've created it). In addition, we need to write a function to convert the various message numbers into a string that describes the message. As we've seen earlier, Delphi defines the various message values as constants in the Messages.PAS unit.

To turn these numbers into the corresponding strings, we've copied a portion of this unit's source code (partially shown in the section "4. The Window Procedure" earlier) and turned the list of constants into the following code:

```
var
  MsgList: TStringList;

  MsgList := TStringList.Create;
  MsgList.AddObject ('wm_Null', TObject($0000));
  MsgList.AddObject ('wm_Create', TObject($0001));
  MsgList.AddObject ('wm_Destroy', TObject($0002));
  MsgList.AddObject ('wm_Move', TObject($0003));
```

This code simply adds objects to a TStringList and casts each integer value as a TObject to create string and message number association. This way, we can search for a given message number to retrieve the corresponding string:

```
function GetMessageName (Msg: Integer): string;
var
  N: Integer;
begin
  N := MsgList.IndexOfObject (TObject(Msg));
  if N >= 0 then
    Result := MsgList.Strings [N]
  else if (Msg >= wm_User) and
      (Msg <= $7FFF) then
    Result := Format (
      'wm_User message (%d)', [Msg])
  else
    Result := Format (
      'Undocumented (%d)', [Msg]);
end;
```

The WProc example combines all this code. In Figure 7.3 you can see its output after we've performed various operations on the target form.

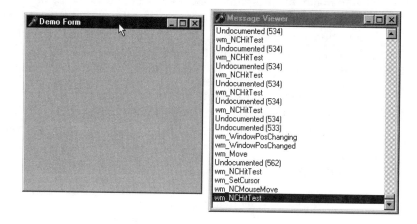

From the WndProc Method to Events

We've just seen how easy it is to override the WndProc method to handle several Windows messages in a rather traditional way. However, to respond to a single message in a Delphi form or component, we can also define an appropriate method, and mark it with the message keyword. In fact, when a message reaches the TControl class's implementation of the WndProc method, that method handles some special cases (for messages that occur during design-time) and then dispatches the message to the message table:

```
procedure TControl.WndProc(
  var Message: TMessage);
var
  Form: TForm;
begin
  if csDesigning in ComponentState then
    ...
  if (Message.Msg >= WM_MOUSEFIRST) and
     (Message.Msg <= WM_MOUSELAST) then
    ...
  Dispatch (Message);
end;
```

Similarly, the TWinControl and TForm classes perform some special preprocessing. Here is the basic format of these methods, which should give you an idea of the types of messages that deserve special attention:

```
procedure TWinControl.WndProc(
  var Message: TMessage);
begin
  case Message.Msg of
    WM_SETFOCUS: ...
    WM_KILLFOCUS: ...
    WM_NCHITTEST: ...
    WM_MOUSEFIRST..WM_MOUSELAST: ...
    WM_KEYFIRST..WM_KEYLAST: ...
    WM_CANCELMODE: ...
  end;
  inherited WndProc(Message);
end;

procedure TForm.WndProc(
  var Message: TMessage);
begin
  with Message do
    case Msg of
      WM_SETTEXT, WM_NCPAINT, WM_NCACTIVATE: ...
      WM_ACTIVATE, WM_SETFOCUS, WM_KILLFOCUS: ...
      WM_WINDOWPOSCHANGING: ...
    end;
  inherited WndProc(Message);
end;
```

Each derived version of WndProc generally (but not always) calls the inherited version, which in turn calls the Dispatch method. This is a method of the TObject class (with source code in assembler), which looks for a *message-response method* in a list of such methods for the current object's class. If the list doesn't contain an appropriate message-response method, Dispatch repeats the search in the parent class. The Dispatch method continues searching up the object's class hierarchy until it either finds an appropriate message-response method or decides there isn't one, in which case it calls the DefaultHandler method instead.

TIP

A message-response method is simply a method that implements the basic behavior for a given message. For example, here's the declaration of a message-response method for the WM_KEYDOWN message:
procedure WMKeyDown(var Message:

TWMKeyDown); message WM_KEYDOWN;

For almost every message in the Win32 API, Delphi declares a method like this, and then calls that method when the Dispatch method receives the corresponding message.

The TObject class defines the DefaultHandler virtual method as a "do-nothing" procedure:

```
procedure TObject.DefaultHandler(var Message);
begin
end;
```

As you move down the class hierarchy toward the various TWinControl classes, you'll find that many of the classes override this method to provide different default-message behavior. For example, in the TControl class, the Default-Handler method processes the wm_GetText, wm_GetTextLength, and wm_SetText messages to implement the Text property for windowed *and* nonwindowed controls. In the TWinControl class, this method calls the window control's default window procedure, unless the handle doesn't yet exist (for messages that occur during construction of the object). Here is the format of this method:

```
procedure TWinControl.DefaultHandler(
    var Message);
begin
    if FHandle <> 0 then
        with TMessage(Message) do
            case Msg of
                // special cases...
            else
                Result := CallWindowProc(FDefWndProc,
                    FHandle, Msg, WParam, LParam);
            end
    else
        inherited DefaultHandler(Message);
end;
```

Obviously, there are many more details to implementing default message-handling behavior, and other classes override these methods. Even so, this overview should help you understand the basics of the message-handling process. If you want to go further, we suggest you examine the VCL source files we've mentioned.

Once the message reaches the appropriate handler or message-response method, the code might generate a corresponding event, as shown in Chapter 3. To implement this, you'll usually find code like this:

```
type
  TWinControl = class(TControl)
    ...
    procedure WMKeyDown(var Message:
      TWMKeyDown); message WM_KEYDOWN;
    function DoKeyDown(var Message:
      TWMKey): Boolean;
    procedure KeyDown(var Key: Word;
      Shift: TShiftState); dynamic;
```

The message-response method (WMKeyDown) calls the internal DoKeyDown method, which handles special cases (omitted in the following source code), and then calls the virtual KeyDown method (a method you can override, as shown in Chapter 5, for a different message). In turn, the KeyDown method activates the component's OnKeyDown event handler:

```
procedure TWinControl.WMKeyDown(var Message: TWMKeyDown);
begin
  if not DoKeyDown(Message) then
    inherited;
end;

function TWinControl.DoKeyDown(var Message: TWMKey): Boolean;
begin
  // code for form key preview (omitted)
  with Message do
  begin
    if not (csNoStdEvents in ControlStyle) then
    begin
      KeyDown(CharCode, ShiftState);
      if CharCode = 0 then
        Exit;
    end;
  end;
```

```
  // other special code (omitted)
end;

procedure TWinControl.KeyDown(
  var Key: Word; Shift: TShiftState);
begin
  if Assigned (FOnKeyDown) then
    FOnKeyDown (Self, Key, Shift);
end;
```

In your forms or components you should either override the WndProc method (to respond to several messages), define direct message-response methods (to implement dramatically different behavior for a single message), or override one of the dynamic *second-level* handlers (to modify slightly different behavior for a message), as illustrated in the KeyDown method above.

Receiving a Message Many Times

To wrap up this section, and to emphasize what we've just discussed, we've written a small example that demonstrates different ways of responding to a single message. By doing so, we'll highlight the flow of the message through the VCL message architecture. We've named this example ManyMess, because it responds to the same message many times.

The example's form contains a list box that we'll use for output, and a button we'll use to clear the list box's contents. This list box doesn't cover the whole client area of the form, because we want to handle left mouse button clicks on the form (the WM_LBUTTONDOWN message), and we want to handle this message in many different ways. In fact, you can respond to this message in five different ways:

- Create an OnMouseDown event-handling method for the form, and check for the left mouse button (this is the standard Delphi approach).

- Define a message-response method for the WM_LBUTTONDOWN Windows message.

- Override the form's WndProc virtual method, and look for the WM_LBUTTONDOWN message.

- Override the form's DefaultHandler virtual method, and look for the WM_LBUTTONDOWN message.

- Override the MouseDown dynamic method, and check for the left mouse button.

Here is the class definition of the form, with the various handlers:

```
type
  TFormManyMess = class(TForm)
    LBox: TListBox;
    Label1: TLabel;
    Button1: TButton;
    procedure FormMouseDown(Sender: TObject;
      Button: TMouseButton; Shift: TShiftState;
      X, Y: Integer);
    procedure Button1Click(Sender: TObject); // clear
  public
    procedure WndProc(var Message: TMessage); override;
    procedure DefaultHandler(var Message); override;
    procedure WmLButtonDown (var Message: TWMMouse);
      message WM_LBUTTONDOWN;
    procedure MouseDown(Button: TMouseButton;
      Shift: TShiftState; X, Y: Integer); override;
  end;
```

The bodies of these methods are very similar. In some of them, we'll check to see if the message is WM_LBUTTONDOWN and in others, we'll check to see if the button being pressed is the left button. It's also interesting to notice how the various methods extract the position of the mouse click; some are easier and some are more convoluted. Here's the code for the five methods:

```
procedure TFormManyMess.FormMouseDown(Sender: TObject;
  Button: TMouseButton; Shift: TShiftState;
  X, Y: Integer);
begin
  if Button = mbLeft then
    LBox.Items.Add (Format ('%s in (%d, %d)',
      ['FormMouseDown', X, Y]));
end;

procedure TFormManyMess.WndProc(var Message: TMessage);
begin
  if Message.Msg = wm_LButtonDown then
    LBox.Items.Add (Format ('%s in (%d, %d)',
      ['WndProc', LoWord (Message.LParam),
      HiWord (Message.LParam)]));
  inherited;
end;
```

```
procedure TFormManyMess.DefaultHandler(var Message);
begin
  with TMessage (Message) do
    if Msg = wm_LButtonDown then
      LBox.Items.Add (Format ('%s in (%d, %d)',
        ['DefaultHandler', LoWord (LParam),
        HiWord (LParam)]));
  inherited;
end;

procedure TFormManyMess.WmLButtonDown (var Message: TWMMouse);
begin
  LBox.Items.Add (Format ('%s in (%d, %d)',
    ['WmLButtonDown', Message.XPos, Message.YPos]));
  inherited;
end;

procedure TFormManyMess.MouseDown(Button: TMouseButton;
  Shift: TShiftState; X, Y: Integer);
begin
  if Button = mbLeft then
    LBox.Items.Add (Format ('%s in (%d, %d)',
      ['MouseDown', X, Y]));
  inherited;
end;
```

TIP   Regardless of what the Delphi documentation says, you can generally call an inherited method without using the method name or any parameter to activate the corresponding method of the parent class with the parameters passed to your method. If you forget to call one of those inherited methods, however, the program won't behave properly (and might even crash).

This example demonstrates the execution order of the various portions of the Delphi message handling system (as you can see in Figure 7.4). Determining which approach you'll use depends on the message you want to handle (not all of the messages are accessible via all five methods). In general, use Delphi event handlers whenever possible (it is easier), use the direct message handler when you have to, and use WndProc when you want to handle several low-level messages in the same way (as in the WndProc example shown before). We don't see any reason to redefine the DefaultHandler, and generally speaking, only a component should override a second-level handler such as the MouseDown method.

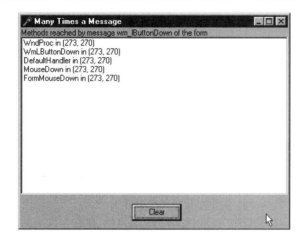

Delphi Message Loop

Now that we've considered how messages reach the event handlers and other methods, we can examine one more area of the application: the message loop. Without this crucial piece of code, Windows messages won't reach the windows of our application.

If you examine the typical project source code of a Delphi application, you'll find the two following lines:

```
Application.CreateForm(TForm1, Form1);
Application.Run;
```

The first statement roughly corresponds to calling the RegisterClassEx and CreateWindowEx functions in a program that calls the Windows API directly. The second statement initiates the message loop. (Actually, the Run method simply calls HandleMessage.) Here's the central code of the Run method:

```
repeat
  HandleMessage
until Terminated;
```

In turn, the HandleMessage method calls ProcessMessage, which looks for a message in the message queue of the application. If there are no messages waiting, HandleMessage calls the Idle method, which displays component hints and activates the OnIdle event. Here's the core of the ProcessMessage method:

```
function TApplication.ProcessMessage: Boolean;
var
  Handled: Boolean;
  Msg: TMsg;
begin
  Result := False;
  if PeekMessage(Msg, 0, 0, 0, PM_REMOVE) then
  begin
    Result := True;
    if Msg.Message <> WM_QUIT then
    begin
      Handled := False;
      if Assigned(FOnMessage) then
        FOnMessage(Msg, Handled);
      if not IsHintMsg(Msg) and not Handled and
        not IsMDIMsg(Msg) and not IsKeyMsg(Msg)
        and not IsDlgMsg(Msg) then
      begin
        TranslateMessage(Msg);
        DispatchMessage(Msg);
      end;
    end
    else
      FTerminate := True;
  end;
end;
```

In this code you can see that Delphi calls the OnMessage event of the Application for each message that reaches this method. As you may know, the message loop doesn't handle all the messages the application receives. This is because in Windows you can either post or send messages, and only posted messages pass through the message queue.

Accordingly, we've modified the ManyMess example of the last section by creating an OnMessage event handler. In ManyMes2, we've added the following OnMessage event handler:

```
procedure TFormManyMess.ApplicationMessage (var Msg: TMsg;
  var Handled: Boolean);
```

```
begin
  if (Msg.Message = wm_LButtonDown) and
      (Msg.hWnd = Handle) then
    LBox.Items.Add (Format ('%s in (%d, %d)',
      ['ApplicationMessage', LoWord (Msg.LParam),
      HiWord (Msg.LParam)]));
  Handled := False;
end;
```

You'll notice that we have to check the destination window, since the application will call this handler for messages to any of the application's windows (including the list box and the button). By setting the Handled parameter to False (at the end of this method) we let the application continue to process the message as usual. If we'd set Handled to True, the application would stop processing this message. Since this is an event handler for the global Application object (which doesn't appear on the Component palette), we must install it *manually* in the form's OnCreate event handler:

```
procedure TFormManyMess.FormCreate(Sender: TObject);
begin
  Application.OnMessage := ApplicationMessage;
end;
```

As you can see in the output shown in Figure 7.5, the application calls the OnMessage event prior to performing any other message processing. Also, you'll notice that this approach (the sixth) is another Delphi-oriented technique. However, as we mentioned earlier, there is an important difference between the use of Application.OnMessage and the use of WndProc: the first intercepts only posted messages, while the latter receives posted *and* sent messages. The next section describes this difference in detail.

Posting and Sending Messages

In a Windows application, you can use two different approaches to deliver a message to an application window (you always address messages to windows):

```
BOOL PostMessage(
  HWND hwnd, // destination window
  UINT uMsg, // message number
  WPARAM wParam, LPARAM lParam); // additional data

LRESULT SendMessage (HWND hwnd, UINT uMsg,
  WPARAM wParam, LPARAM lParam);
```

FIGURE 7.5:

The output of the ManyMes2 example, showing when each message reaches the OnMessage event of the Application object

● A program can post a message (using the PostMessage API function) to politely add it to the message queue of an application. The Boolean return value of this function indicates whether the message reached the queue or not. This function returns False if you supply it with an invalid window handle or if the application's message queue is full. The application's message loop will extract the posted messages from the queue, and will then dispatch them to the proper window.

● A program can send a message (using the SendMessage API function) directly to the proper window procedure. Sending a message this way bypasses the message queue, and corresponds roughly to calling the window procedure directly. The return value from the SendMessage function will be the value returned by the window procedure.

Windows passes messages to applications using both techniques, and determines which technique to use based on the message and the circumstances. For example, Windows uses the SendMessage function whenever it requires an immediate effect or return value. In contrast, Windows uses the PostMessage function to let the various applications handle messages in turn, which improves system multitasking. (In fact, this was the basis for multitasking in 16-bit Windows.)

Plain API applications often send and post messages to their various windows, since this is one of the few techniques you can use to make several windows work together without an object-oriented framework such as the Delphi VCL. Occasionally, programs may also send or post messages to other applications.

For Delphi applications, sending and posting messages directly isn't as common in the code you write, because you can easily access the properties of other components—or even the properties of other forms (windows). However, it's still possible to send and post your own messages, and the VCL does so frequently. In fact, Delphi defines a number of custom messages, and it dispatches them using these techniques.

In addition to the PostMessage and SendMessage API functions, you can use the TControl class's Perform method to initiate an action in another control or form. The Perform method simply calls the WndProc method of the destination object, and turns the various parameters into a TMessage structure:

```
function TControl.Perform(Msg: Cardinal;
  WParam, LParam: Longint): Longint;
var
  Message: TMessage;
begin
  Message.Msg := Msg;
  Message.WParam := WParam;
  Message.LParam := LParam;
  Message.Result := 0;
  if Self <> nil then
    WindowProc (Message);
  Result := Message.Result;
end;
```

As the code above suggests, you can even call an object's WindowProc method directly. However, you should *not* call the Dispatch method directly, since this skips any custom processing for this class and executes only the default handler.

Fundamentally, calling Perform is similar to calling SendMessage. The Perform method is probably faster, but SendMessage allows you to operate on any window (even if it's not created by a Delphi application) once you have the window handle. Since Perform is a method, you can call it only if you have a reference to a valid Delphi control.

Another alternative is to call the SendAppMessage global function (defined in the Controls.PAS unit but not listed in the online help). This function simply sends a message to Application.Handle if it's valid. For this reason the method needs only three parameters:

```
function SendAppMessage(Msg: Cardinal;
  WParam, LParam: Longint): Longint;
```

Besides sending a message to a specific window or component, you can also broadcast a message. For example, you can use the Broadcast method of the TWinControl class to send a message to each of a windowed control's children. Another method, NotifyControls, has a similar effect. In the Windows API you can call the PostMessage function passing the value hwnd_Broadcast as a parameter to post the message to all top-level windows in the system. As an alternative, Windows 95 introduces the similar (but more powerful) BroadcastSystemMessage API function.

The Postman Example

To get a better understand of the posting, sending, and dispatching operations, let's experiment with these operations through a new example called Postman. This is actually an extension of the last example, ManyMes2, although the focus is different. We'll use this example to demonstrate how the handlers in the ManyMes2 example use the various sending or posting techniques, or simulate the left-button-down event.

The form displayed by the Postman program contains a number of buttons, which perform the various sending or posting operations. The first button, labeled Post, simply posts a message and adds a line to the list box:

```
procedure TFormManyMess.ButtonPostClick(Sender: TObject);
begin
  LBox.Items.Add (' -- PostMessage --');
  PostMessage (Handle, wm_lButtonDown,
    0, MakeLong (10, 10));
  PostMessage (Handle, wm_lButtonUp,
    0, MakeLong (10, 10));
end;
```

You'll notice that we must post both the down message and the up message to avoid inconsistent behavior in our application. When the user presses a mouse button, a Delphi form or component captures all the subsequent mouse messages by calling the SetCapture Windows API function. This process terminates when the user releases the mouse button. You can see for yourself the odd behavior of this program if you don't post the second message.

As you can see from the messages in the list box, posting a message has the same effect as generating it by clicking on the form: it activates all six message handlers. In contrast, a sent message (triggered by the *Send* button) doesn't generate the OnMessage event for the Application (as you can see in Figure 7.6):

```
procedure TFormManyMess.ButtonSendClick(Sender: TObject);
begin
  LBox.Items.Add (' -- SendMessage --');
  SendMessage (Handle, wm_lButtonDown,
    0, MakeLong (10, 10));
  SendMessage (Handle, wm_lButtonUp,
    0, MakeLong (10, 10));
end;
```

Calling the Perform method has the same effect as calling SendMessage. The only notable difference is that the syntax of the Perform method doesn't use the window handle:

```
procedure TFormManyMess.ButtonPerformClick(Sender: TObject);
begin
  LBox.Items.Add (' -- Perform --');
  Perform (wm_lButtonDown,
    0, MakeLong (10, 10));
  Perform (wm_lButtonUp,
    0, MakeLong (10, 10));
end;
```

As you may have noticed, we decided to not call the WndProc method directly, simply because the Perform method already does that.

Besides these three "official" techniques to send or post a message, there are two other approaches you can use to activate the OnMouseDown event of the form that you should consider. The first of these is to call the MouseDown *second-level* handler:

```
procedure TFormManyMess.ButtonMouseDownClick(Sender: TObject);
begin
  LBox.Items.Add (' -- MouseDown --');
  MouseDown (mbLeft, [], 10, 10);
end;
```

FIGURE 7.6:

The output of the Postman example. The buttons have been pressed in order, and you can see which handlers are activated in each case.

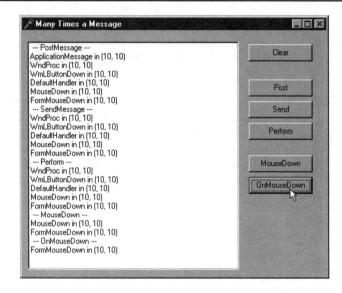

This activates only the MouseDown method and the OnMouseDown event handler, and bypasses the other message-processing methods. The last alternative is to call the event handler directly:

```
procedure TFormManyMess.ButtonOnMouseDownClick(Sender: TObject);
begin
  LBox.Items.Add (' -- OnMouseDown --');
  OnMouseDown (self, mbLeft, [], 10, 10);
end;
```

Exploring Internal Delphi Messages

There are literally thousands of messages moving around in a given Windows application every minute. There are system messages, user-defined messages, registered application messages, and some additional messages defined by Delphi. Part of what Delphi does to simplify Windows programming is to convert some of the Windows messages into various component notifications and messages. This allows you to respond to them using message-response methods and event handlers.

To understand the role of these internal Delphi messages, let's consider the WM_COMMAND message. When a command message reaches a TWinControl, the DoControlMsg method looks for the Delphi object associated with the control that issued the message (found by calling FindWindow), and sends it a pseudo-message by calling Perform:

```
procedure TWinControl.WMCommand(
  var Message: TWMCommand);
begin
  if not DoControlMsg(Message.Ctl, Message)
    then inherited;
end;


function DoControlMsg(ControlHandle: HWnd;
  var Message): Boolean;
var
  Control: TWinControl;
begin
  DoControlMsg := False;
  Control := FindControl(ControlHandle);
  if Control <> nil then
    with TMessage(Message) do
    begin
      Result := Control.Perform(
        Msg + CN_BASE, WParam, LParam);
      DoControlMsg := True;
    end;
end;
```

Like many of the message-response methods, many component classes override the WMCommand method. For example, the TForm class first checks to see if the command is a menu command. If not, it calls the inherited version of the method. The TWinControl version of this method calls the DoControlMsg method to customize command processing further.

In the body of the DoControlMsg method (shown above), you can see that it increases the message number's value by CN_BASE, and then generates a brand new custom message, defined as

```
const
  CN_COMMAND = CN_BASE + WM_COMMAND;
```

Several of the standard controls respond to this custom message, primarily to process notification messages. In a typical Windows application, Windows passes control messages to the control's parent window for processing. In contrast, Delphi sends these notification messages back to the controls (as new message types), suggesting it is their responsibility to process them. For example, here's what a combo box does when its parent form passes it a CN_COMMAND message:

```
procedure TCustomComboBox.CNCommand(
  var Message: TWMCommand);
begin
  case Message.NotifyCode of
    CBN_DBLCLK:
      DblClick;
    CBN_EDITCHANGE:
      Change;
    CBN_DROPDOWN: ...
    CBN_SELCHANGE:
      begin
        Text := Items[ItemIndex];
        Click;
        Change;
      end;
    CBN_SETFOCUS:
      begin
        FIsFocused := True;
        FFocusChanged := True;
        SetIme;
      end;
    CBN_KILLFOCUS:
      begin
        FIsFocused := False;
        FFocusChanged := True;
        ResetIme;
      end;
  end;
end;
```

Some of these events have further side effects. For example, the CBN_DBLCLK notification activates the DblClick dynamic method:

```
procedure TControl.DblClick;
begin
  if Assigned(FOnDblClick) then
```

```
      FOnDblClick(Self);
  end;
```

To summarize, when Windows sends a `WM_COMMAND` message to the parent window of the control, that window redispatches the message to the control itself (as `Msg + CN_BASE`), and the control responds to the notification message and activates the appropriate Delphi event, which is usually processed by the form hosting the control. Similar dispatching operations take place for many other commands. This is how the various derived component classes are able to customize the behavior of a standard Windows control. Delphi, in fact, broadcasts many messages to the child components, using internal component notifications (`cn_xxx`) and component messages (`cm_xxx`).

Responding to these internal messages is not very common in Delphi applications, but it can be very useful for component writers. For demonstration purposes, we'll build examples of their use in plain applications, but this isn't how you'll usually apply them. Delphi defines all internal messages with numbers that do not conflict with Windows messages (their ranges start from `cn_Base` and `cm_Base`). By the way, these messages are not just for windowed controls. You can send them to graphical controls, too.

Seeing Delphi Messages and Notifications

Now let's explore some of the individual Delphi messages and notifications. We've updated the WProc example we built earlier in this chapter to show Delphi notifications, and we've named the updated example DWProc. Actually, adding this capability is quite simple. We've just copied the definitions of the Delphi custom message numbers (primarily found in Control.pas), and updated the MList.PAS file with code such as:

```
MsgList.AddObject ('CM_ACTIVATE',
  TObject(CM_BASE + 0));
MsgList.AddObject ('CM_DEACTIVATE',
  TObject(CM_BASE + 1));
...
MsgList.AddObject ('CN_CHARTOITEM',
  TObject(CN_BASE + WM_CHARTOITEM));
MsgList.AddObject ('CN_COMMAND',
  TObject(CN_BASE + WM_COMMAND));
...
```

You can see the complete source code in the DWProc directory of the companion disk. By examining the source code you can also see the operations performed by the components in the demo form, which happen to generate several custom Delphi messages. The form, with a sample list of messages, is visible in Figure 7.7.

All the messages received by the demo form of the DWProc example are listed in the second form.

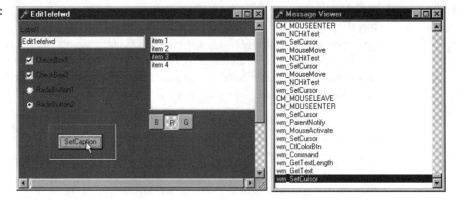

Component Notifications

As we've just seen with the CM_COMMAND message, component notification messages are those sent from a parent form or component to its children. These notifications correspond to messages sent by Windows to the parent control's window, but they're logically intended for the control.

This makes it simple to understand which notification messages correspond to a traditional Windows message: Simply look in the Windows help file for the corresponding Windows message (replace the initial "CN_" with "WM_"). There are several distinct groups of component notification messages:

- General keyboard messages: CN_CHAR, CN_KEYUP, CN_KEYDOWN, CN_SYSCHAR, and CN_SYSKEYDOWN.

- Special keyboard messages used only by list boxes with the lbs_WantKeyboardInput style: cn_CharToItem and cn_VKeyToItem.

- Messages related to the owner-draw technique: cn_MeasureItem, cn_DrawItem, cn_DeleteItem, and cn_CompareItem.

- Messages for scrolling, used only by scroll bar and track bar controls: cn_HScroll and cn_VScroll.

- General notification messages, used by most controls: cn_Command, cn_Notify, and cn_ParentNotify.

- Control color messages in: cn_CtlColorBtn, cn_CtlColorDlg, cn_CtlColorEdit, cn_CtlColorListbox, cn_CtlColorMsgbox, cn_CtlColorScrollbar, and cn_CtlColorStatic. (Delphi 1 and 16-bit Windows offered only the cn_CtlColor message.)

Component Messages

A Delphi component passes *component messages* to other components to indicate any change in its state that might affect those components. Just like component notifications, most of these messages start as Windows messages. However, some of these messages are more complex, higher-level translations, and not simple remappings. Also, components send their own messages as well as forwarding those received from Windows. For example, changing a property value or some other characteristic of the component may necessitate telling one or more other components about the change. Again we can group these messages into categories, and then focus on some of them in more detail:

- Activation and input focus messages are sent to the component being activated or deactivated, receiving or losing the input focus: cm_Activate corresponds to the OnActivate event of forms and of the application; cm_Deactivate corresponds to OnDeactivate; cm_Enter corresponds to OnEnter; cm_Exit corresponds to OnExit; cm_FocusChanged is sent whenever the focus changes between components of the same form. Later, we'll see an example using this last message. Two other messages in this group, declared but not used, are cm_GotFocus and cm_LostFocus.

- Messages sent to child components when a property changes. Here is a list of these messages: cm_VisibleChanged, cm_EnabledChanged, cm_ColorChanged, cm_FontChanged, cm_CursorChanged, cm_Ctl3DChanged, cm_TextChanged, cm_ShowingChanged, cm_IconChanged, cm_ShowHintChanged, and cm_TabStopChanged. Monitoring these messages can help track changes in a property. You might need to respond to these messages in a new component, but it's not likely.

- Messages related to *ParentXxx* properties: cm_ParentFontChanged, cm_ParentColorChanged, cm_ParentCtl3DChanged, and cm_ParentShowHintChanged. These are very similar to the messages of the previous group.

- Notifications of changes in the Windows system: cm_SysColorChange, cm_WinIniChange, cm_TimeChange, and cm_FontChange. Handling these messages is useful only in special components that need to keep track of system colors or fonts.

- Mouse messages: cm_MouseEnter and cm_MouseLeave are sent to the control when the cursor enters or leaves its surface, but these messages are sent by the Application object as low-priority messages; cm_Drag is an important message, and is sent many times during dragging operations. This message has a DragMessage parameter that indicates a sort of submessage, and the address of the TDragRec record that indicates the mouse position and the components involved in the dragging operation. This message isn't that important, because Delphi defines many drag events and drag methods you can override. However, you can respond to cm_Drag for a few things that don't generate an event or method call. This message is sent to find the target component (when the DragMessage field is dmFindTarget); to indicate that the cursor has reached a component (the dmDragEnter submessage), is being moved over it (the dmDragMove submessage), or has left it (the dmDragLeave submessage); when the drop operation is accepted (the dmDragDrop submessage); and when it is aborted (the dmDragCancel submessage).

- Application messages: cm_AppKeyDown is sent to the Application object to let it determine if a key corresponds to a menu shortcut. cm_AppSysCommand corresponds to the wm_SysCommand message. cm_DialogHandle is sent in a DLL to retrieve the value of the DialogHandle property (used by some dialog boxes not built with Delphi). cm_WindowHook is sent in a DLL to call the HookMainWindow and UnhookMainWindow methods. cm_InvokeHelp is sent by code in a DLL to call the InvokeHelp method. You'll rarely need to use these messages yourself.

- Delphi internal messages: cm_DesignHitTest determines whether a mouse operation should go to the component or to the form designer, as we'll see in Chapter 13 (which presents a wizard-like Component Editor). cm_Hittest is sent to a control when a parent control is trying to locate a child control at a given mouse position (if any). cm_CancelMode terminates special operations, such as showing the pull-down list of a combo box. cm_ControlListChange is sent to each control before adding or removing another sibling or child control (controls generally use the Notification method to handle this task, as you saw in Chapter 5, and this message is handled only by DBCtrlGrid components). cm_HintShow is sent to a control just before displaying its hint (only if the ShowHint property is True). cm_MenuChanged is sent after MDI or OLE menu merging operations.

- Messages related to special keys: cm_DialogKey is handled by modal forms and controls that need to perform special actions. cm_DialogChar is sent to a control to determine if a given input key is its accelerator character. cm_WantSpecialKey is handled by controls that interpret special keys in an unusual way (for example, using the Tab key for navigation, as some Grid components do). cm_ChildKey is sent to the parent control to handle some special keys (in Delphi, this message is handled only by DBCtrlGrid components). We'll describe these messages in more detail, and show examples of their use, in the next section.

- Messages for specific components: cm_GetDataLink is used by DBCtrlGrid controls. cm_TabFontChanged is used by the TabbedNotebook components. cm_ButtonPressed is used by SpeedButtons to notify other sibling SpeedButton components (to enforce radio-button behavior). cm_DeferLayout is used by DBGrid components.

- OLE Container Messages: cm_IsToolControl, cm_DocWindowActivate, cm_Release, cm_UIActivate, and cm_UIDeactivate.

- Thread related messages: cm_ExecProc is used to obtain thread synchronization.

Handling Special Keys

Several of the component message groups respond to special keys. We've decided to build an example that responds to this type of message using an approach we suggest you use when exploring the VCL source code. Consider this a typical approach, and keep a GREP utility handy (or use Delphi's own Find in Files command), to search for code that responds to other keys.

As with most of the component messages, the starting point for a special key message is generally a Windows message. For example, if you search the VCL source code for the "cn_KeyDown" string, you'll find the code that responds to the message, but not the code that generates it. Earlier, we saw how some of the VCL code generates component message numbers by adding the value cn_Base to the corresponding Windows message, as was the case with wm_KeyDown. However, if you examine the source code of the TWinControl class's DoKeyDown method, you'll find little code that relates to special keys.

Instead, Delphi uses specific code in its message loop to perform several tests on the messages, such as those that relate to special keys. For instance, the Application object's IsMsgKey method sends the cn_KeyDown message when one of its windows receives a wm_KeyDown message. The TWinControl class's CnKeyDown method uses the following code to respond to this event (we have partially edited and commented the code):

```
procedure TWinControl.CNKeyDown(
  var Message: TWMKeyDown);
var
  Mask: Integer;
begin
  with Message do
  begin
    Result := 1;
    if IsMenuKey(Message) then
      Exit;
    if not (csDesigning in ComponentState) then
    begin
      {check if this is a special child key for the
      parent (handled by TDbCtrlGrid component only)}
      if Perform(CM_CHILDKEY, CharCode,
        Integer(Self)) <> 0 then
          Exit;

      {Mask holds special dialog codes to check for}
      Mask := 0;
      case CharCode of
        VK_TAB:
          Mask := DLGC_WANTTAB;
        VK_LEFT, VK_RIGHT, VK_UP, VK_DOWN:
          Mask := DLGC_WANTARROWS;
        VK_RETURN, VK_EXECUTE, VK_ESCAPE, VK_CANCEL:
          Mask := DLGC_WANTALLKEYS;
      end;
      // original code used "and" instead of "then if"
      // (this updated version seems more readable)
      // see the text below for the description
      if (Mask <> 0) then
        if Perform(CM_WANTSPECIALKEY, CharCode, 0) = 0 then
          if Perform(WM_GETDLGCODE, 0, 0) and Mask = 0 then
            if GetParentForm(Self).Perform (
```

```
                    CM_DIALOGKEY, CharCode, KeyData) <> 0 then
                Exit; // Result := 1
        end;
        Result := 0; // if no Exit code was executed
    end;
  end;
```

The final if statement is the core of this method, so let's examine it in detail. If the key was in one of the groups listed in the case statement (that is, if the mask is not zero), then the component sends the cm_WantSpecialKey message to itself to determine whether to handle the key in a special way. If not, the component asks itself if one of the mask codes corresponds to one of the dialog codes it wants to process (as returned by processing the wm_GtDlgCode message). If not (the character is not among the dialog codes), then the component sends the cm_DialogKey message to its parent form.

The parent form handles some keys such as vk_Tab or the arrow keys (see the CMDialogKey method of the TForm class) and, when it has nothing else to do, broadcasts the message to all of its child controls (in the CmDialogKey method of the TWinControl class), letting them handle special keys.

Only when the wm_Char message reaches the control will this code turn it into a cm_DialogChar message, which is used to identify accelerator keys. This message follows a different path, but after considering how the component messages move, you should be able to investigate this yourself. Now let's consider some examples that use some of these special key-related Delphi messages.

We've built a couple of components, and packaged them in the SpecKey unit (stored in the Comps directory, as usual). The first component is an edit box, which treats the Enter key as if it was the Tab key. To accomplish this we simply respond to the cm_DialogKey message:

```
type
  TTabEdit = class(TEdit)
  protected
    procedure CMDialogKey(var Message: TCMDialogKey);
      message CM_DIALOGKEY;
  end;
```

The code the CmDialogKey method checks for the Enter key's code and sends the parent form the same message, but passes the vk_Tab key code. To halt further processing of the Enter key, we set the result of the message to 1. All this takes place only if the component is enabled:

```
procedure TTabEdit.CMDialogKey(var Message: TCMDialogKey);
begin
  if (Message.CharCode = VK_RETURN) and Enabled then
  begin
    GetParentForm (self).Perform (CM_DialogKey, VK_TAB, 0);
    Message.Result := 1;
  end
  else
    inherited;
end;
```

The second component is a SpeedButton that monitors a special accelerator key (this is useful when the button displays a graphic instead of a caption). This component has a property for the accelerator key, and handles the cm_DialogChar message (not the cm_DialogKey message of the other component):

```
type
  TAccSpeed = class(TSpeedButton)
  private
    fAccKey: char;
  protected
    procedure CMDialogChar(var Message: TCMDialogChar);
      message CM_DIALOGCHAR;
  published
    property AccKey: Char
      read fAccKey write fAccKey;
  end;
```

The cm_DialogChar message is used to check for accelerator keys, and that's what the component does in the CMDialogChar method:

```
procedure TAccSpeed.CMDialogChar(var Message: TCMDialogChar);
begin
  if (Message.CharCode = Word(fAccKey)) and Enabled then
  begin
    Click;
    Message.Result := 1;
  end
  else
    inherited;
end;
```

To test these two components, we've created a package called DdhCh7 and stored it (as usual) in the Comps directory for this chapter. The components appear on the DDHB page of the Component palette, and we use them in a very simple demo program, as you can see in Figure 7.8. Run this program, called SKDemo, and try pressing the Enter key or press Alt+! (typically, you'll need to press Alt+Shift+1, depending on your keyboard), to see the effect. Remember to install the package before you open the program in the Delphi environment.

FIGURE 7.8:

The SKDemo program uses the TTabEdit and TAccSpeed components, which handle some internal Delphi messages related to system keys.

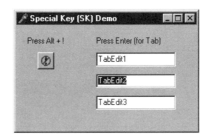

Handling Focus Changes

Now let's build an example that demonstrates how you can respond to focus changes without having to handle the OnEnter event of each component of a form. Our approach will be to respond to Delphi's cm_FocusChanged message, which accepts an Msg parameter that identifies the component that received the focus (the Sender). We've implemented this in a simple program, which shows the name of the component that has the focus in a simple status bar. As an alternative, you could build a component (such as a custom status bar) that displays information about the component that currently has the focus. This is possible because the cm_FocusChanged message is broadcast by a form to each of its child controls. Our example simply intercepts the message in a form:

```
type
  TForm1 = class(TForm)
    Edit1: TEdit;
    Edit2: TEdit;
    Edit3: TEdit;
    StatusBar1: TStatusBar;
  public
    procedure CmFocusChanged (var Msg: TCmFocusChanged);
```

```
        message cm_FocusChanged;
    end;
```

The code of the message is very simple:

```
procedure TForm1.CmFocusChanged (var Msg: TCmFocusChanged);
begin
  StatusBar1.SimpleText := Msg.Sender.Name;
end;
```

The advantage of this approach is that it works independently of the type and number of components you add to the form, and it does so without any special action on your part. You can see the output of this program (FocusChn) in Figure 7.9.

FIGURE 7.9:

The FocusChn example shows the name of the component having the focus in the status bar. The code is completely independent from any components on the form.

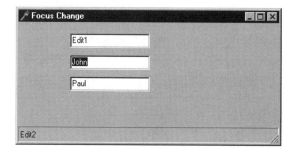

Delphi Forms, Windows Reserved Memory, and Subclassing

Now that we've explored Windows messages and window procedures in depth, there's one last topic to cover: subclassing a window. This is a technique available in the Windows API to change the behavior of an individual window by changing its window procedure. (It has nothing to do with creating a subclass of a form, an object-oriented technique based on inheritance.)

However, before we delve into subclassing, we need to discuss accessing reserved window information, because the subclassing operation is accomplished by modifying some of that information. To that end, let's examine what happens when a Delphi application creates a form (or other windowed component), and how we can interact with this process.

Creating the Window for a Form

The TForm class defines several methods related to the creation of its window in addition to its constructors (Create and CreateNew). In Delphi 2 the methods were actually part of the TForm class, while in Delphi 3 they've been moved to a new base class, TCustomForm. In both cases the methods are the following:

```
protected
  procedure CreateParams(var Params:
    TCreateParams); override;
  procedure CreateWindowHandle(const Params:
    TCreateParams); override;
  procedure CreateWnd; override;

  ...
public
  constructor Create(AOwner: TComponent); override;
  constructor CreateNew(AOwner: TComponent);

  ...
```

These three procedures are closely related. For example, the CreateWnd method calls CreateParams and then calls CreateWindowHandle. CreateParams initializes the creation parameters, later used by CreateWindowHandle. This last method calls the CreateWindowEx API function to actually perform the creation. In between these two calls, the CreateWnd method registers an appropriate window class, by calling the RegisterClass API function. Here is the source code of the CreateWnd method of the TWinControl class, the central piece of the VCL code for the creation of forms and controls windows. As usual, we're presenting a simplified version of the code (you can find the complete source for this method on the CD):

```
procedure TWinControl.CreateWnd;
var
  Params: TCreateParams;
  TempClass: TWndClass;
  ClassRegistered: Boolean;
begin
  CreateParams(Params);
  with Params do
  begin
    FDefWndProc := WindowClass.lpfnWndProc;
    ClassRegistered := GetClassInfo(
      HInstance, WinClassName, TempClass);
    if not ClassRegistered then
    begin
```

```
            WindowClass.lpfnWndProc := @InitWndProc;
            WindowClass.hInstance := HInstance;
            WindowClass.lpszClassName := WinClassName;
            if Windows.RegisterClass(WindowClass) = 0 then
                raise EOutOfResources.CreateRes(SWindowClass);
        end;
        CreationControl := Self;
        CreateWindowHandle(Params);
    end;
end;
```

You can override each of the three virtual functions, but to intervene in the form creation process, it's common to override only the CreateParams method. Inside your revised version of this method you should first call the inherited CreateParams method. Then you can change some of the values of the initialization structure, which defines fields for the various parameters of the CreateWindowsEx API function and a field for the TWndClass structure:

```
type
  TCreateParams = record
    Caption: PChar;
    Style: Longint;
    ExStyle: Longint;
    X, Y: Integer;
    Width, Height: Integer;
    WndParent: HWND;
    Param: Pointer;
    WindowClass: TWndClass;
    WinClassName: array[0..63] of Char;
  end;
```

Later on, the CreateWindowHandle method will use this record:

```
procedure TWinControl.CreateWindowHandle(
  const Params: TCreateParams);
begin
  with Params do
    FHandle := CreateWindowEx(
      ExStyle, WinClassName, Caption, Style,
      X, Y, Width, Height, WndParent, 0,
      WindowClass.HInstance, Param);
end;
```

NOTE For an example of overriding the CreateParams method, see the Transpar program from *Mastering Delphi*, which is available on the companion disk of this book, in the directory for this chapter. This program applies the ws_Ex_Transparent extended window style to the program's main form, which generates a very odd effect.

Obviously, the window class registration information and the window creation parameters play an important role when Delphi creates a form, but most of these fields appear in internal Windows data structures that are accessible at run-time. Tools such as WinSight allow a programmer to see the current values of these fields, but they don't always relate to what we see and do from Delphi. We'll try to bridge this gap with the next example.

Accessing the Reserved Memory of a Window

Although Delphi provides specific properties to retrieve and change most of the form features, in many applications it's important to access and modify some of the internal information of a window or its window class. For this example, called Internal, we've written a tool that's capable of displaying such information for any on-screen window. It's a generic tool you can use to inspect other applications, as you can see in Figure 7.10.

FIGURE 7.10:

The information about Delphi's own main window shown by the Internal example

The foundation of this example is simple: the program calls the GetWindowLong and the GetClassLong API functions to retrieve all the internal values. To access to the information of a specific window, the program tracks the mouse pointer

position and calls the `WindowFromPoint` API function to retrieve the handle of the window under the mouse pointer. This operation takes place continuously if the user has pressed the speed button (and the program has captured the mouse):

```
procedure TFormInternal.SpeedChooseMouseDown(Sender: TObject;
  Button: TMouseButton; Shift: TShiftState; X, Y: Integer);
begin
  MouseCapture := True;
  Capture := True;
end;
```

In the code above, MouseCapture is a VCL property, while Capture is a local field of the form. You'll notice that with this code, the form must capture the mouse input because the *speed* button can't (it isn't a window-based control). During the dragging operation the handle and the caption of the window under the mouse appear in a label of the toolbar panel:

```
procedure TFormInternal.FormMouseMove(Sender: TObject;
  Shift: TShiftState; X, Y: Integer);
var
  hWnd: THandle;
  Title: string;
  Pt: TPoint;
begin
  if Capture then
  begin
    Pt := Point (X, Y);
    Pt := ClientToScreen (Pt);
    hWnd := WindowFromPoint (Pt);
    if hWnd = 0 then
      Exit;
    SetLength (Title, 100);
    GetWindowText (hWnd, PChar (Title), 100);
    LabelTarget.Caption :=
      'Window: ' + IntToHex (hWnd, 8) +
      ' - "' + string (PChar (Title)) + '"';
    if CheckDrag.Checked then
      UpdateData (hWnd);
  end;
end;
```

If you click in the check box, the program displays detailed output, as we'll see in a moment. When you release the mouse button, the program will again locate the window under the mouse pointer, and then mimic releasing the speed button by sending that window a message:

```
procedure TFormInternal.FormMouseUp(Sender: TObject;
  Button: TMouseButton; Shift: TShiftState; X, Y: Integer);
var
  hWnd: THandle;
  Pt: TPoint;
begin
  if Capture then
  begin
    Pt := Point (X, Y);
    Pt := ClientToScreen (Pt);
    hWnd := WindowFromPoint (Pt);
    if hWnd <> 0 then
      UpdateData (hWnd);
    MouseCapture := False;
    Capture := False;
    // release the speed button
    SpeedChoose.Perform (
      wm_LButtonUp, mk_LButton, 0);
  end;
end;
```

In addition to this dragging code (which allows a user to select any window available on the screen), the core of the Internal example is the UpdateData method, which is rather long. The first part of the method extracts the window's class information by calling the GetClassInfo API function, but only after calling GetClassName for the target window (this makes the code simpler than if we called GetClassLong once for each possible flag):

```
procedure TFormInternal.UpdateData (hWnd: THandle);
var
  WndClassName, Title: string;
  WndClass: TWndClass;
  hInst, hwndParent: THandle;
begin
  MemoClass.Lines.BeginUpdate;
  MemoWin.Lines.BeginUpdate;
  try
    SetLength (Title, 100);
    // retrieve the WNDCLASS name
    SetLength (WndClassName, 100);
```

```
hInst := GetWindowLong (hWnd, GWL_HINSTANCE);
GetClassName (hWnd, PChar (WndClassName), 100);
GetClassInfo (hInst, PChar (WndClassName), WndClass);
// show class information
with WndClass, MemoClass.Lines do
begin
  Clear;
  Add ('Class Name: ' + WndClassName);
  Add ('Window Procedure: ' + IntToHex (
    Cardinal (lpfnWndProc), 8));
  Add ('Class Extra Bytes: ' + IntToStr (cbClsExtra));
  Add ('Window Extra Bytes: ' + IntToStr (cbWndExtra));
  Add ('Instance Handle: ' + IntToHex (hInstance, 8));
  GetModuleFileName (hInstance, PChar (Title), 100);
  Add ('Module Name: ' + Title);
  Add ('Icon Handle: ' + IntToHex (hIcon, 8));
  Add ('Cursor: ' + GetCursorName (hCursor));
  Add ('Brush handle: ' + IntToHex (hbrBackground, 8));
  if lpszMenuName <> nil then
    if HiWord (Cardinal(lpszMenuName)) <> 0 then
      Add ('Menu name: ' + PChar (lpszMenuName))
    else
      Add ('Menu ID: ' + IntToStr (LoWord (lpszMenuName)));
  Add (#13);
  Add ('Class styles:');
  Add (GetClassStyles (Style));
end;
// ... continues ...
```

In addition to the information we've extracted from the window class structure, this program also displays the module file name where the window class information actually appears (the GetModuleFileName call). The code related to the menu (the lpszMenuName field) is quite complex, because this pointer to a string field can actually hold either a PChar string or zero in its higher-order 16-bit word and the number of the menu resource in the lower-order 16-bit word.

The final call, GetClassStyles, is an internal method of the program; it examines each of the class style bits to see if they are set and builds a corresponding string:

```
function TFormInternal.GetClassStyles (
  Style: Cardinal): string;
begin
  Result := '';
```

```
  if (cs_bytealignclient and style) = cs_bytealignclient then
    Result := Result + 'ByteAlignClient ';
  if (cs_bytealignwindow and style) = cs_bytealignwindow then
    Result := Result + 'cs_bytealignwindow';
  if (cs_classdc and style) = cs_classdc then
    Result := Result + 'ClassDC ';
  if (cs_dblclks and style) = cs_dblclks then
    Result := Result + 'DblClks ';
  if (cs_globalclass and style) = cs_globalclass then
    Result := Result + 'GlobalClass ';
  // ... and so on ...
end;
```

While the first part of the UpdateData method extracts and displays the window class information, the second part extracts and displays the internal information for a specific window. In addition to calling GetWindowLong with the various parameters, you'll notice that the program uses the GetParent API function. Interestingly, this value and the result of calling

```
GetWindowLong(hWnd, GWL_HWNDPARENT)
```

do not always match. The GetParent function frequently returns the value of the owner window instead of that of the parent. For a main form, for example, the value returned by calling GetWindowLong is the handle of the hidden application window (Application.Handle). In either case, the program displays the caption of the parent window, if any.

Here's the code for the second part of the UpdateData method:

```
// ... UdpateData continues ...
// show window data
with MemoWin.Lines do
begin
  Clear;
  GetWindowText (hWnd, PChar (Title), 100);
  Add ('Window Handle: ' + IntToHex (hWnd, 8));
  Add ('  Title: "' + PChar (Title) + '"');
  Add ('Window Procedure: ' + IntToHex (
    GetWindowLong (hWnd, GWL_WNDPROC), 8));
  Add ('Instance Handle: ' + IntToHex (
    GetWindowLong (hWnd, GWL_HINSTANCE), 8));
  hwndParent := GetWindowLong (hWnd, GWL_HWNDPARENT);
  Add ('Parent/Owner Window: ' + IntToHex (hwndParent, 8));
  if hwndParent <> 0 then
```

```
      begin
        GetWindowText (hwndParent, PChar (Title), 100);
        Add ('  Par/Own Title: "' + PChar (Title) + '"');
      end;
      hwndParent := GetParent (hWnd);
      Add ('Real Parent Window: ' + IntToHex (hwndParent, 8));
      if hwndParent <> 0 then
      begin
        GetWindowText (hwndParent, PChar (Title), 100);
        Add ('  Parent Title: "' + PChar (Title) + '"');
      end;
      if GetParent (hWnd) <> 0 then
        Add ('Child ID: ' + IntToHex (
          GetWindowLong (hWnd, GWL_ID), 8))
      else
        Add ('Menu Handle: ' + IntToHex (
          GetWindowLong (hWnd, GWL_ID), 8));
      Add ('User Data: ' + IntToHex (
        GetWindowLong (hWnd, GWL_USERDATA), 8));
      Add (#13);
      Add ('Window Styles: ' +
        GetWinStyles (GetWindowLong (hWnd, GWL_STYLE)));
      Add (#13);
      Add ('Extended Styles: ' +
        GetWinExStyles (GetWindowLong (hWnd, GWL_EXSTYLE)));
    end;
  finally
    MemoClass.Lines.EndUpdate;
    MemoWin.Lines.EndUpdate;
  end;
end;
```

In the code above, you'll also notice that the result of calling GetWindowLong with the GWL_ID flag can be either a menu handle or a child window identifier, depending on whether the window has a real parent (as returned by the GetParent API). Near the end, you'll notice that we make calls to two local methods which list the window styles (GetWinStyles) and the extended window styles (GetWinExStyles). These two methods have the same structure as the GetClassStyles method we've already shown.

Subclassing a Window

By giving you access to the internal information for a window, the Windows API allows you to change most of this data. By far, the most important characteristic of a window you can change is its window procedure. Changing the window procedure means you change the message response code for the all the messages directed to that window. In Windows, each window typically uses the window procedure of its window class, which keeps the behavior of the windows consistent In a Delphi application, this is generally not true; every window gets its own window procedure.

As you saw earlier in this chapter, you can customize the behavior of a TWin-Control by overriding its WndProc method, or by assigning a new value to the component's WindowProc property. However, in this example we want to focus on generic techniques you can use for any window. We'll subclass a TForm object to help keep things simple. In real-world applications, you'll use this technique to subclass existing windows through a form extender component or the Delphi application window, In the next chapter we'll explore both uses.

The basic mechanism behind subclassing is to provide a new window procedure for a window, and then to call the SetWindowLong API function with the gwl_WndProc flag to install the new window procedure. However, there are at least two alternatives to doing this: you can install a traditional window procedure, or you can install a method of the TWinMethod type. In the Subclass example we'll explore both approaches, starting with the first (and simpler) one.

To subclass a window with a plain window procedure, you must first define a proper function, with the appropriate four parameters and a return value, using the stdcall calling convention:

```
function NewWinProc (Handle: THandle;
  Msg, wParam, lParam: LongInt): LongInt; stdcall;
begin
  if Msg = wm_RButtonDown then
  begin
    Beep;
    SetWindowText (Handle,
      PChar (Format ('Right click in %d, %d', [
        LoWord (lParam), HiWord (lParam)])));
  end;
  // pass call to old window proc
  Result := CallWindowProc (OldWndProc, Handle,
```

```
      Msg, wParam, lParam);
  end;
```

This function contains some specific code to handle the right-button-down window message, and then it calls the original window procedure (stored in the OldWndProc variable when we install the window procedure). For this approach, you'll probably need to rely on the default message response code. Alternatively, you might want to use default processing only for messages you don't handle in the code (for instance, by using an else statement). Below is the code we use to install the window procedure when the user presses the *Procedure* button:

```
procedure TForm1.BtnProcClick(Sender: TObject);
begin
  OldWndProc := Pointer (SetWindowLong
    (Form2.Handle, gwl_WndProc, LongInt (@NewWinProc)));
  BtnProc.Enabled := False;
end;
```

Here, you'll notice that the SetWindowLong call returns the original value of the element you are changing, in this case the old window procedure. As you can see in the code above, the program subclasses the Form2 window. In the new window procedure, there's no specific reference to that window, but simply to the generic Handle parameter. Another important aspect of this example is that the TForm2 class has a custom event handler for OnMouseMove, which will still execute even though we've subclassed the window:

```
procedure TForm2.FormMouseMove(Sender: TObject;
  Shift: TShiftState; X, Y: Integer);
begin
  Caption := Format ('Cursor in %d, %d', [X, Y]);
end;
```

You can see an example of the program's output after the subclassing operation in Figure 7.11. We perform a similar operation using the second button of the main form, but this time we use a more Delphi-oriented approach.

It would be nice to be able to use class methods as window procedures instead of using global functions. Delphi defines the TWndMethod method pointer type for this purpose:

```
type
  TWndMethod = procedure(var Message: TMessage) of object;
```

FIGURE 7.11:

The output in the caption of the Subclass example's second form might be generated by any of three different window procedures.

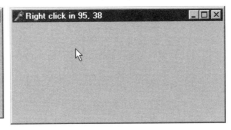

However, Windows requires a function address for a window procedure—not a method address along with the address of the object (the TMethod type and any method pointer type pass this information). To address this problem, Delphi provides the MakeObjectInstance function, which uses an internal data structure to associate a window procedure with a method pointer, and to store the proper parameters (including the value of the object). We saw how Delphi uses this function at the beginning of this chapter, but we haven't used it in a program ourselves.

The important thing to remember is that since this call creates a small internal data structure, for every call to MakeObjectInstance there should be a matching call to FreeObjectInstance, which releases the internal structure. In the Subclass example, we can use a method of the TForm1 class, even if we are subclassing the window of a different class, TForm2:

```
procedure TForm1.NewWinMethod (var Msg: TMessage);
begin
  if Msg.Msg = wm_LButtonDown then
  begin
    Beep;
    SubControl.SetTextBuf (
      PChar (Format ('Left click in %d, %d', [
        LoWord (Msg.lParam), HiWord (Msg.lParam)])));
  end
  else
    Msg.Result := CallWindowProc (OldWndMeth,
      SubControl.Handle, Msg.Msg, Msg.WParam, Msg.LParam);
end;
```

The code is similar to the previous version, although this time the only parameter we're passing is a message structure, which includes all the values (including the result) except the window handle. Since the method is working on a different window, the program saves the subclassed window in the SubControl field of the form. Two other fields are used for the new and the old window procedure:

```
type
  TForm1 = class(TForm)
    ...
  private
    OldWndMeth, NewWndMeth: Pointer;
    SubControl: TWinControl;
  end;
```

All these values are set when the program installs the new window procedure:

```
procedure TForm1.BtnMethClick(Sender: TObject);
begin
  SubControl := Form2;
  NewWndMeth := MakeObjectInstance (NewWinMethod);
  OldWndMeth := Pointer (SetWindowLong (
    SubControl.Handle, gwl_WndProc, Longint (NewWndMeth)));
  BtnMeth.Enabled := False;
end;
```

Naturally, the program must keep track of calling the new window procedure's ObjectInstance to free it when it isn't required any more:

```
procedure TForm1.FormDestroy(Sender: TObject);
begin
  if Assigned (NewWndMeth) then
    FreeObjectInstance (NewWndMeth);
end;
```

Finally, you'll notice that in this example, you can install both window procedures, subclassing Form2 twice. This isn't a problem, since every time the program subclasses the window it stores the current window procedure as the old one, which could be the original window procedure or one provided when subclassing it with the other technique. As we've mentioned earlier, this example is only meant to demonstrate a technique we'll apply in the next two chapters.

What's Next

Now that we've explored the details of Windows API programming and delved into the internals of the windowing system, we're ready to apply this information to Delphi. Although we've already explored some interesting components in this chapter, in the next we'll create a couple of advanced ones, including a form extender and an application component. In the subsequent chapters we'll focus on other Windows topics, such as processes and memory handling, continuing on with the Component Object Model (COM) and shell extensions.

Advanced Window Components

- Building a Form-Extender Component

- Building an Application-Extender Component

- Nonrectangular Controls

- Dragging and Sizing Components at Run-Time

The last chapter introduced the internals of Windows programming. Now we can leverage that information to build some powerful Delphi components. However, before we proceed, we must warn you that the remainder of this chapter assumes that you have a solid understanding of message loops, window procedures, window subclassing, and similar topics.

To begin, we'll build a component that enhances the ways you can interact with a form at design-time. Then we'll create an application component (one that wraps the properties and events of the Application object) and some special windowed controls. Along the way, we'll examine some other details of Windows programming, demonstrate some new API functions, and present some tricks we've learned about developing components.

Some of these components will be useful as is, but the purpose of this chapter is to teach you how to build your own components by extending the basic structure we're presenting. Naturally, you should always evaluate commercial components that have the features or capabilities you want to implement. By spending a little money, you may be able to save a lot of time.

Building a Form-Extender Component

If you derive a new class from TForm and add new properties to that form class, the new properties won't normally show up in the Object Inspector when you try designing a new form with that class. Despite this problem, it's possible to create a special form class that defines new properties, and to display those properties at design-time. In Chapter 15 we'll build an example program that demonstrates this complex process. In this chapter we'll build a nonvisual component that subclasses its owner form and modifies that form's behavior through its own properties.

Since this component is just a demonstration, we won't add every possible feature to it. Instead, we'll add features that demonstrate how a component can provide a new window procedure for its parent form (to modify its behavior); this procedure interacts with the default window procedure for forms. Its features will include changing the background of the form and setting limits for resizing and maximizing.

One Component per Form

For some types of components, it doesn't matter how many you place on a form. For other types, however, it doesn't make sense to allow more than one at a time. The form-extender component falls into this second category. If you allowed more than one on a form, which one would be in control? To avoid this problem, we must find a way to block the creation of a second instance of this component on the same form.

The simplest technique we've found is to override the `Create` constructor so that it searches the owner form's `Components` list for another component of this type. Since we want to block the creation of the component if it's not the first (and interrupt the process of adding it to the form's `Components` list), we must perform this test before calling the inherited version of `Create`:

```
constructor TDdhFormExt.Create (AOwner: TComponent);
var
  I: Integer;
begin
  // create a single instance only
  for I := 0 to AOwner.ComponentCount - 1 do
    if AOwner.Components[I] is TDdhFormExt then
      raise Exception.Create (
        'DdhFormExt component duplicated in ' +
        AOwner.Name);
  // default creation
  inherited Create (AOwner);
  ...
```

If we find a component of type `TDdhFormExt`, we raise an exception, as you can see in Figure 8.1. Since the exception skips the remainder of the constructor body, and the call to `inherited Create` follows the code that raises the exception, we don't have to worry about performing any cleanup of the construction process.

Subclassing the Owner Form

The primary purpose of this component is to provide a new window procedure for its owner form's window. As we discussed in the last chapter, providing a new window procedure for a specific window is called *subclassing*. This is a powerful technique for modifying a window's behavior, and here we'll focus on using this technique inside a component.

The error message
displayed when
you try to add two
copies of the
DhhFormExt com-
ponent to the
same form

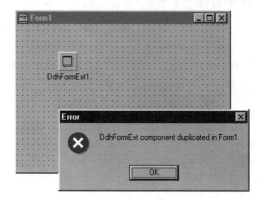

Before we can subclass the owner form's window, we need to acquire the window's handle. Obviously, if we place a form-extender component on a form from inside Delphi, finding the value of the form's handle will be easy. But what if we try to create an instance of this component at run-time? Before we can safely retrieve the form's window handle, we need to check to see if the owner is valid (not Nil); and if the owner is valid, we then test whether it's a form. Here's the code from the Create constructor that implements this test:

```
constructor TDdhFormExt.Create (AOwner: TComponent);
begin
  // check if the owner is a form
  if (Owner = nil) or not (AOwner is TForm) then
    raise Exception.Create (
      'Owner of DdhFormExt component must be a form');
  ...
```

Once we've determined that the owner is valid and is a form, we can retrieve the form's window handle and subclass the window using the MakeObjectInstance technique we introduced in the last chapter for using methods as window procedures. We want to subclass the window at run-time only, and not at design-time:

```
constructor TDdhFormExt.Create (AOwner: TComponent);
begin
  ...
  // from subclassing (run-time only)
  if not (csDesigning in ComponentState) then
  begin
    NewWndProc := MakeObjectInstance (NewWndMethod);
    OldWndProc := Pointer (SetWindowLong (
```

```
        FormHandle, gwl_WndProc, Longint (NewWndProc)));
  end
  else
  begin
    // default values
    NewWndProc := nil;
    OldWndPRoc := nil;
  end;
```

In the code above, you'll notice the pointers to the new and old window procedures, which are fields of our new component class. In addition, you'll notice references to FormHandle (a utility function that retrieves the form's window handle), and NewWndMethod (the method we're inserting as the new window procedure). You'll see the declarations of the new fields and methods in the initial version of the class definition below:

```
type
  TDdhFormExt = class(TComponent)
  private
    // window procedures
    OldWndProc, NewWndProc: Pointer;
  protected
    function FormHandle: THandle;
    procedure NewWndMethod (var Msg: TMessage);
  public
    constructor Create (AOwner: TComponent); override;
    destructor Destroy; override;
  end;
```

The FormHandle method simply casts the owner as a TForm object, and then returns the Handle. We've used this function to make the code easier to read:

```
function TDdhFormExt.FormHandle: THandle;
begin
  Result := (Owner as TForm).Handle;
end;
```

Obviously, the central method of this component is NewWndMethod. By calling MakeObjectInstance with this method, we create a window procedure pointer that's suitable for subclassing. In the body of this method, we'll test for messages that we're interested in intercepting, and pass all other messages to the original window procedure (which we can still access via the OldWndProc pointer):

```
procedure TDdhFormExt.NewWndMethod (var Msg: TMessage);
begin
```

```
case Msg.Msg of
  wm_EraseBkgnd: // handle message
  wm_GetMinMaxInfo: // handle message
end;
// call the default window procedure for every message
Msg.Result := CallWindowProc (OldWndProc,
  FormHandle, Msg.Msg, Msg.WParam, Msg.LParam);
end;
```

Upon destruction, we must remember to release the object instance that provides the new window procedure. However, just in case we weren't able to create it properly, we'll test to see if it's valid:

```
destructor TDdhFormExt.Destroy;
begin
  if Assigned (NewWndProc) then
  begin
    SetWindowLong (FormHandle, gwl_WndProc,
      Longint (OldWndProc));
    FreeObjectInstance (NewWndProc);
  end;
  inherited Destroy;
end;
```

Painting the Form Background

The first feature that we'll implement in our form extender component is a custom background bitmap. We'll paint this bitmap on the form at run-time, tiling it as necessary if the bitmap is smaller than the form. You can see an example of the output in Figure 8.2.

Obviously, we'll want to paint the background bitmap behind any other components, including things like Image components that draw on the form instead of providing their own window. To accomplish this feat, we don't want to respond to the wm_Paint message that the form uses to paint its surface (and to call the OnPaint event handler), we want to respond to the wm_EraseBkgnd message that tells the form window to repaint its background. (By default, the TForm class simply performs a fill operation using the setting from the form's Color property.)

FIGURE 8.2:

The DhhFormExt component can tile multiple copies of a bitmap on the surface of the form hosting it, as shown by the FormExt demo program.

For our component to store the background bitmap, we'll need to add a field for it, and we'll need to provide access to the bitmap via a property. Here are the corresponding changes to the class definition:

```
type
  TDdhFormExt = class(TComponent)
  private
    fBackBitmap: TBitmap;
    procedure SetBackBitmap (Value: TBitmap);
  protected
    procedure BackBitmapChanged (Sender: TObject);
  published
    property BackBitmap: TBitmap
      read fBackBitmap write SetBackBitmap;
  end;
```

We'll create the TBitmap object in the component's constructor using the following code:

```
fBackBitmap := TBitmap.Create;
fBackBitmap.OnChange := BackBitmapChanged;
```

In this code, you'll notice that we've inserted one of the component's methods as an event handler for the bitmap's OnChange event. We'll examine this further in a moment. As you'd expect, we'll destroy the bitmap in the component's destructor:

```
fBackBitmap.Free;
```

Instead of creating a new TBitmap object whenever we need to change the property to use a different image, we'll reuse the same object over and over, and simply change the image the TBitmap object displays. To accomplish this, we must implement an unusual SetBackBitmap method (the method that the Object Inspector will call when you modify the BackBitmap property). Instead of replacing the TBitmap object, we'll take advantage of this class's Assign method, which copies the bitmap data into the object and manages the object's memory (and bitmap handle) accordingly:

```
procedure TDdhFormExt.SetBackBitmap(Value: TBitmap);
begin
  fBackBitmap.Assign (Value);
end;
```

As we mentioned earlier, we've used a method of this component as an OnChange event handler. This is necessary because we're not creating a new TBitmap object when the BackBitmap property changes, and instead need to know if the bitmap image changes. If it does, we need to repaint the entire form to display the new bitmap:

```
procedure TDdhFormExt.BackBitmapChanged (Sender: TObject);
begin
  (Owner as TForm).Invalidate;
end;
```

Now that we've created everything else, we can focus on the code that paints the form's background when the new window procedure intercepts a wm_EraseBkgnd message:

```
procedure TDdhFormExt.NewWndMethod (var Msg: TMessage);
var
  ix, iy: Integer;
  ClientWidth, ClientHeight: Integer;
  BmpWidth, BmpHeight: Integer;
  hCanvas, BmpCanvas: THandle;
begin
  case Msg.Msg of
    wm_EraseBkgnd:
      if (fBackBitmap.Height <> 0) and
        (fBackBitmap.Width <> 0) then
      begin
        ClientWidth := (Owner as TForm).ClientWidth;
        ClientHeight := (Owner as TForm).ClientHeight;
        BmpWidth := fBackBitmap.Width;
        BmpHeight := fBackBitmap.Height;
        BmpCanvas := fBackBitmap.Canvas.Handle;
        hCanvas := THandle (Msg.wParam);
```

```
    for iy := 0 to ClientHeight div BmpHeight do
      for ix := 0 to ClientWidth div BmpWidth do
        BitBlt (hCanvas, ix * BmpWidth, iy * BmpHeight,
          BmpWidth, BmpHeight, BmpCanvas,
          0, 0, SRCCOPY);
    Msg.Result := 1; // message handled
    Exit; // skip default processing
  end;

...
```

NOTE   In the NewWndMethod method we could have used a TCanvas component instead of the hCanvas handle, and we could have called the Draw method of TCanvas instead of the BitBlt API function. Since this is a core method, called many times, we felt it should have been as fast as possible, so (even if there isn't a big difference) we decided to go the low-level way.

It's important to note that we'll execute our painting code only if the width and height of the bitmap are nonzero. By doing so we can verify that the bitmap is valid, and also avoid a potential crash that dividing by zero (in the tiling code) would cause.

At the heart of our background painting code is a pair of nested for loops that traverse the client area of the form, row by row, where the height of the row is the height of the bitmap. To paint each row, the inner for loop divides the client area of the form into cells the width of the bitmap. For each cell, we call the Windows API function BitBlt (the name derives from the term *block transfer*) to copy the bitmap image to the form's surface. The first parameter for this function is the form window's device context (its Canvas in Delphi terms), which the wm_EraseBkgnd message passes via the wParam parameter. The remaining parameters for the BitBlt function determine the size and position of the source and destination bitmaps; you can learn more about them in the Windows API help information.

You'll notice that to speed up the execution of the loop, we've computed all the values we'll need and stored them in local variables. Since accessing properties can be slower than accessing local variables (there may be an access method to call), and performing a typecast (using the as operator) can be slower still, optimizing this code may have a dramatic effect. In addition, you should remember that Windows can generate thousands of messages every minute, so it pays to optimize this type of code.

Finally, the last two lines in this method alert the rest of the message loop that we've handled this message, and then bypass the message processing that normally occurs. If we fail to set the result field to 1 (to announce that we've handled the message), and we don't exit the procedure, the normal message processing will proceed, yielding a strange effect. Our code will paint the bitmap on the background of the form, and then the form's default message handling will replace the bitmap by filling the form's client area with the current Color value.

Tracking the Size of a Form

The final feature of our form-extender component is to limit the size of the owner form during resize operations, and to specify its size and position during Minimize and Maximize operations. All of this data appears within the wm_GetMinMaxInfo message that Windows sends prior to resizing, minimizing, or maximizing a window. (You can find an example of responding to this message using a message-handling method in Chapter 10 of *Mastering Delphi 3*.)

In fact, supporting these operations is quite simple, although it requires a lot of code. First, examine the following additions to the form's class declaration. We've added specific fields for each of the corresponding elements in the MinMaxInfo record type, and properties to expose these fields:

```
type
  TDdhFormExt = class(TComponent)
  private
    fMaximizedWidth: Integer;
    fMaximizedHeight: Integer;
    fMaximizedPosX: Integer;
    fMaximizedPosY: Integer;
    fMinimumTrackWidth: Integer;
    fMinimumTrackHeight: Integer;
    fMaximumTrackWidth: Integer;
    fMaximumTrackHeight: Integer;
  published
    property MaximizedWidth: Integer
      read fMaximizedWidth write fMaximizedWidth
      default 0;
    property MaximizedHeight: Integer
      read fMaximizedHeight write fMaximizedHeight
      default 0;
    property MaximizedPosX: Integer
```

```
      read fMaximizedPosX write fMaximizedPosX
      default 0;
    // and so on 5 more times...
end;
```

NOTE   As an alternative, the private fields of this class could have been placed in a specific TPersistent descendant class, such as TFont. However, since we are going to use this class only inside this component, we decided the limited benefits of this approach (more encapsulation) were not worth the extra effort.

Now the NewWndMethod method needs some code that responds to the wm_Get-MinMaxInfo message. Since Windows sends this message quite often, we've optimized this procedure by checking to see if all the user-set values are zero (the simplest way to accomplish this is to add them all, instead of testing if each of them is zero). If they are, we don't need to respond to the message at all, and can immediately pass the message on to the default window procedure, as shown below:

```
procedure TDdhFormExt.NewWndMethod (var Msg: TMessage);
var
  pMinMax: PMinMaxInfo;
begin
  case Msg.Msg of
    ...
    wm_GetMinMaxInfo:
      if fMaximizedWidth + fMaximizedHeight + fMaximizedPosX +
        fMaximizedPosY + fMinimumTrackWidth + fMinimumTrackHeight +
        fMaximumTrackWidth + fMaximumTrackHeight <> 0 then
      begin
        pMinMax := PMinMaxInfo (Msg.lParam);
        if fMaximizedWidth <> 0 then
          pMinMax.ptMaxSize.X := fMaximizedWidth;
        if fMaximizedHeight <> 0 then
          pMinMax.ptMaxSize.Y := fMaximizedHeight;
        if fMaximizedPosX <> 0 then
          pMinMax.ptMaxPosition.X := fMaximizedPosX;
        if fMaximizedPosY <> 0 then
          pMinMax.ptMaxPosition.Y := fMaximizedPosY;
        if fMinimumTrackWidth <> 0 then
          pMinMax.ptMinTrackSize.X := fMinimumTrackWidth;
        if fMinimumTrackHeight <> 0 then
```

```
      pMinMax.ptMinTrackSize.Y := fMinimumTrackHeight;
  if fMaximumTrackWidth <> 0 then
      pMinMax.ptMaxTrackSize.X := fMaximumTrackWidth;
  if fMaximumTrackHeight <> 0 then
      pMinMax.ptMaxTrackSize.Y := fMaximumTrackHeight;
  Msg.Result := 0; // message handled
  Exit; // skip default processing
end;
```

Notice that at the end of this section, we've set the Result field of the message to 0, which is the correct way to announce that we've handled this particular message. (It's exactly the opposite of what we did when responding to the wm_EraseBkgnd message.) Unfortunately, the Windows API functions aren't very consistent, particularly in terms of return values and parameters of window procedures; so you should always check the Windows API help file to determine the appropriate way to indicate that you've handled a given message.

Building an Application-Extender Component

Now that we've built the form-extender component, we can turn our attention to a component of a completely different type, an application-extender component. Although this isn't strictly a component that demonstrates low-level Windows programming, it will be very useful in customizing Delphi applications because it exposes the properties and events of the global Application object. Along the way, we'll add some extra features to extend its functionality.

> **NOTE**
>
> The reason for creating this component is that the events and properties of the Application object are very useful, but many of them cannot be manipulated at design-time (via the Object Inspector). You must typically set the Application object's property values explicitly in your code, and you have no choice but to use code to assign event handlers to any of the object's events.

One Component per Application

For the form-extender component, we monitored the construction process and aborted it if the owner form already contained a form-extender. In contrast, we'll limit the construction of the application-extender component on an application-wide basis. Once we've created one of these objects, it doesn't make sense to create another.

At first, we considered using a global Boolean variable (called AppCompCreated), set to False in the initialization section of the unit. The component sets it to True in the constructor and to False in the destructor:

```
constructor TDdhAppExt.Create(AOwner: TComponent);
begin
  // check whether already created
  if AppCompCreated then
    raise Exception.Create (
      'Duplicated DdhAppExt component');
  else
    AppCompCreated := True;
  // create the component
  inherited Create(AOwner);
end;

destructor TDdhAppExt.Destroy;
begin
  inherited Destroy;
  AppCompCreated := False;
end;
```

The problem is that this approach doesn't work. Delphi will always call the destructor for an object when you raise an exception inside its constructor. As you try to create a second component the constructor will stop you, but the destructor will set the AppCompCreated variable to False. So the next time you try, you can actually create another copy of the component.

We must use a different technique. As you can see in the code below, we can try to model three states: prior to construction of any objects, after construction of one, and during construction of additional objects. We do this using an integer variable, an object counter (whose value will be 0 prior to the construction of any object, 1 after one instance has been created, and 2 when trying to creating a second instance):

```
var
  AppCompCounter: Integer;

constructor TDdhAppExt.Create(AOwner: TComponent);
begin
  // check whether already created
  Inc (AppCompCounter);
  if AppCompCounter > 1 then
    raise Exception.Create (
      'Duplicated DdhAppExt component');
  inherited Create(AOwner);
end;

destructor TDdhAppExt.Destroy;
begin
  Dec (AppCompCounter);
  inherited Destroy;
end;

initialization
  AppCompCounter := 0;
end.
```

Wrapping TApplication Properties and Events

For each of the properties and events of the TApplication class, we need to create corresponding component properties and events. One approach we could use to store and retrieve this data is to map each of the properties and events to local fields, and then synchronize those fields with the actual values from the Application object at run-time, typically in an overridden version of the Loaded method. However, this technique duplicates information, and if part of the program modifies the Application object directly, our field values will be out of sync.

Instead, we've decided to use a different approach, and write the *get* and *set* methods of our component to access the properties and events of the Application object directly. At run-time, this is a perfect solution. Unfortunately, this doesn't work at design-time, because Delphi itself has a global Application object (and a corresponding window). If we modify the Application object's properties directly at design-time, we'll be modifying Delphi instead of our program!

The solution to this problem is to create a temporary TApplication object, and design our application-extender component to modify that object at design-time instead of the global Application object. At run-time, we'll modify the global Application object's properties and events instead, as shown below:

```
type
  TDdhAppExt = class(TComponent)
  private
    // design-time clone or run-time Application
    CurrApp: TApplication;
    ...

constructor TDdhAppExt.Create(AOwner: TComponent);
begin
  ...
  // application object initialization
  if csDesigning in ComponentState then
  begin
    CurrApp := TApplication.Create (nil);
    CurrApp.Icon := nil;
    CurrApp.Title := '';
    CurrApp.HelpFile := '';
  end
  else
    CurrApp := Application;
end;
```

In the constructor, you'll notice that we initialize the Icon, Title, and HelpFile fields of our temporary TApplication object, CurrApp. These are Application object properties that you can set from the Delphi IDE, so we'll set them to null values.

Now we must write several access methods to map all the properties and events, but the code will be very simple. Here are some examples of the *read* and *write* methods that map the properties and events:

```
// properties

function TDdhAppExt.GetIcon : TIcon;
begin
  Result := CurrApp.Icon ;
end;
```

```
procedure TDdhAppExt.SetIcon (Value: TIcon);
begin
  CurrApp.Icon := Value;
end;

function TDdhAppExt.GetTitle: string;
begin
  Result := CurrApp.Title;
end;

procedure TDdhAppExt.SetTitle(Value: string);
begin
  CurrApp.Title := Value;
end;

// events

function TDdhAppExt.GetOnActivate: TNotifyEvent;
begin
  Result := CurrApp.OnActivate;
end;

procedure TDdhAppExt.SetOnActivate(Value: TNotifyEvent);
begin
  CurrApp.OnActivate := Value;
end;

function TDdhAppExt.GetOnDeactivate: TNotifyEvent;
begin
  Result := CurrApp.OnDeactivate;
end;

procedure TDdhAppExt.SetOnDeactivate(Value: TNotifyEvent);
begin
  CurrApp.OnDeactivate := Value;
end;
```

At this point, we've mapped all the Application object's properties and events, with the exception of the MainFormVisible property. There are two reasons we don't map this last property: First, its value is used only at design-time to determine if the main form should be visible, but the value cannot be used at run-time; second, unless you provide a way to close it, an application with the main window not visible will run forever without displaying any user interface.

Where appropriate, we've set default values for the various properties, and we've used the standard values that Delphi sets for the Application object. Here's the full declaration of the properties and methods that we've mapped from the Application object:

```
type
  TDdhAppExt = class(TComponent)
    ...
  published
    // TApplication properties
    property Icon: TIcon
      read GetIcon  write SetIcon ;
    property Title: string
      read GetTitle write SetTitle;
    property HelpFile: string
      read GetHelpFile write SetHelpFile;
    property HintColor: TColor
      read GetHintColor write SetHintColor
      default clInfoBk;
    property HintPause: Integer
      read GetHintPause write SetHintPause
      default 500;
    property HintShortPause: Integer
      read GetHintShortPause write SetHintShortPause
      default 50;
    property HintHidePause: Integer
      read GetHintHidePause write SetHintHidePause
      default 2500;
    property ShowHint: Boolean
      read GetShowHint write SetShowHint
      default False;
    // TApplication events
    property OnActivate: TNotifyEvent
      read GetOnActivate write SetOnActivate;
    property OnDeactivate: TNotifyEvent
      read GetOnDeactivate write SetOnDeactivate;
    property OnException: TExceptionEvent
      read GetOnException write SetOnException;
    property OnIdle: TIdleEvent
      read GetOnIdle write SetOnIdle;
    property OnHelp: THelpEvent
      read GetOnHelp write SetOnHelp;
```

```
    property OnHint: TNotifyEvent
      read GetOnHint write SetOnHint;
    property OnMessage: TMessageEvent
      read GetOnMessage write SetOnMessage;
    property OnMinimize: TNotifyEvent
      read GetOnMinimize write SetOnMinimize;
    property OnRestore: TNotifyEvent
      read GetOnRestore write SetOnRestore;
    property OnShowHint: TShowHintEvent
      read GetOnShowHint write SetOnShowHint;
  end;
```

Adding Tray Icon Support

Now that we've built the basic functionality of our application-extender component, we've decided to add one extra feature, which is actually quite complex:
tray icon support. Many newer applications display an icon in the Taskbar's tray
area, as the system clock and volume control do, instead of displaying a main
window. Since the basic technique of displaying an icon in the Taskbar tray is
commonly known, we won't discuss the details of the implementation. (If you're
not familiar with these details, review the entry for Shell_NotifyIcon in the
Windows API help file, Chapter 27 of Marco Cantù's *Mastering Delphi 3*, or many
of the freeware examples available on the Internet.)

To call the Shell_NotifyIcon API function, you'll need to prepare a
TNotifyIcon record, and pass it to the function. Accordingly, we'll add a field of
this type to our application-extender component's class declaration, and call it
nid. In addition, we'll need to store an icon that we can display in the Taskbar
tray area, which we create in the component's constructor:

```
constructor TDdhAppExt.Create(AOwner: TComponent);
begin
  ...
  // tray icon initialization
  fTrayIconActive := False;
  fTrayIcon := TIcon.Create;
  fTrayIcon.OnChange := IconChange;

  nid.cbSize := sizeof (nid);
  nid.wnd := CurrApp.Handle;
  nid.uID := 1; // icon ID
```

```
nid.uCallBackMessage := wm_IconMessage;
nid.hIcon := CurrApp.Icon.Handle;
StrLCopy (nid.szTip, PChar('Tip'), 64);
nid.uFlags := nif_Message or
  nif_Icon or nif_Tip;
end;
```

In the constructor, we need to initialize the icon fields and then set the various fields of the TNotifyIcon record. To initialize the icon fields, we set the TrayIconActive property to False, construct the icon, and set the icon's OnChange event handler to one of our component methods. As with the form-extender component, we don't want to recreate the icon each time the user changes it.

To initialize the TNotifyIcon record, we simply retrieve a few of the application object's properties, such as the handle of the application's icon window and the handle of the Application object itself. We'll transfer these values to the nid object's settings, set the uCallBackMessage field to wm_IconMessage, and set the rest of the properties to reasonable default values. In combination, these settings will result in calls to the Application object's window procedure whenever the user interacts with the tray icon.

First, let's examine the various methods that provide tray icon support. Of these, the most important is SetTrayIconActive, which is the write method for the TrayIconActive property:

```
procedure TDdhAppExt.SetTrayIconActive (Value: Boolean);
begin
  if Value <> fTrayIconActive then
  begin
    fTrayIconActive := Value;
    if not (csDesigning in ComponentState) then
    begin
      if fTrayIconActive then
        Shell_NotifyIcon (NIM_ADD, @nid)
      else
        Shell_NotifyIcon (NIM_DELETE, @nid);
    end;
  end;
end;
```

As was the case with the other application-extender features, we display the icon in the tray area only at run-time, not at design-time (to avoid confusing the two versions of the icon). Below you can see the custom icon in the tray area:

The SetTrayIcon and IconChange methods handle changing the icon and updating the tray area display as the icon changes. If the user doesn't provide an icon, we'll use the main form's icon instead of just displaying a gray area:

```
procedure TDdhAppExt.SetTrayIcon (Value: TIcon);
begin
  fTrayIcon.Assign (Value);
end;

procedure TDdhAppExt.IconChange (Sender: TObject);
begin
  if not (fTrayIcon.Empty) then
    nid.hIcon := fTrayIcon.Handle
  else
    nid.hIcon := CurrApp.MainForm.Icon.Handle;
  if fTrayIconActive and
      not (csDesigning in ComponentState) then
    Shell_NotifyIcon (nim_Modify, @nid);
end;
```

The read and write methods for the TrayHint property are even simpler, but they have one important restriction. The TNotifyIcon record defines the hint field as an array of 64 characters. If you try to display more, you'll truncate the hint at best. At worst, you could overwrite important data. Accordingly, we'll limit the hint text to 64 characters:

```
function TDdhAppExt.GetTrayHint: string;
begin
  Result := string (nid.szTip);
end;

procedure TDdhAppExt.SetTrayHint (Value: string);
begin
  StrLCopy (nid.szTip, PChar(Value), 64);
  if fTrayIconActive and
```

```
        not (csDesigning in ComponentState) then
      Shell_NotifyIcon (nim_Modify, @nid);
  end;
```

Now that we've built in support for the tray icon, let's add a popup menu to give the user a better interface. To implement this, we'll create a TPopup menu component and connect it to the DdhAppExt component using the TrayPopup property. Here's the code we use to set the TrayPopup property and to provide a notification mechanism that will remove the popup menu's pointer (a technique we introduced in Chapter 5):

```
procedure TDdhAppExt.SetTrayPopup (Value: TPopupMenu);
begin
  if Value <> fTrayPopup then
  begin
    fTrayPopup := Value;
    if Assigned (fTrayPopup) then
      fTrayPopup.FreeNotification (self);
  end;
end;

procedure TDdhAppExt.Notification(AComponent: TComponent;
  Operation: TOperation);
begin
  inherited Notification (AComponent, Operation);
  if (Operation = opRemove) and (AComponent = fTrayPopup) then
    fTrayPopup := nil;
end;
```

If we want to display our popup menu or perform the default action, we must handle the wm_IconMessage Windows message. By checking the value of the lParam of this message, we determine the correct action to take. Here's the window procedure we'll use, which responds to this message:

```
procedure TDdhAppExt.IconTrayWndProc (var Msg: TMessage);
var
  Pt: TPoint;
begin
  // show the popup menu
  if (Msg.Msg = wm_IconMessage) and
    (Msg.lParam = wm_rButtonDown) and
    Assigned (fTrayPopup) then
  begin
```

```
      SetForegroundWindow (CurrApp.MainForm.Handle);
      GetCursorPos (Pt);
      fTrayPopup.Popup (Pt.x, Pt.y);
  end
  // do the default action
  else if (Msg.Msg = wm_IconMessage) and
    (Msg.lParam = wm_lButtonDblClk) and
    Assigned (fOnTrayDefault) then
  begin
      SetForegroundWindow (CurrApp.MainForm.Handle);
      fOnTrayDefault (self);
  end
  else
    // original window procedure
    Msg.Result := CallWindowProc (OldWndProc,
       CurrApp.Handle, Msg.Msg, Msg.WParam, Msg.LParam);
end;
```

When our window procedure receives the wm_IconMessage message, it either displays the popup menu at the current cursor position (if the lParam value is wm_RButtonDown), or displays the main form's window and calls the component's OnTrayDefault event handler (if the lParam value is wm_LButtonDblClk). This procedure forwards any other messages to the application's original window procedure. Here you can see the popup menu appearing at the current cursor position after we've right-clicked the icon:

We're going to subclass another window to provide the custom tray icon behavior. However, instead of subclassing the main form's window, this time we're subclassing the application window. As before, our application-extender component initiates the subclassing process in its constructor, and cleans up in its destructor:

```
constructor TDdhAppExt.Create(AOwner: TComponent);
begin
   ...
   // subclass the application
   if not (csDesigning in ComponentState) then
   begin
     NewWndProc := MakeObjectInstance (IconTrayWndProc);
```

```
        OldWndProc := Pointer (SetWindowLong (
          CurrApp.Handle, gwl_WndProc, Longint (NewWndProc)));
    end
    else
    begin
      // default values
      NewWndProc := nil;
      OldWndPRoc := nil;
    end;
  end;


  destructor TDdhAppExt.Destroy;
  begin
    // remove the application window procedure
    if csDesigning in ComponentState then
    begin
      // reinstall the original window procedure
      SetWindowLong (CurrApp.Handle, gwl_WndProc,
        Longint (OldWndProc));
      // free the object instance
      if Assigned (NewWndProc) then
        FreeObjectInstance (NewWndProc);
    end;
    ...
  end;
```

You'll notice that we reinstall the original window procedure in the destructor as part of the cleanup process. Since the VCL code does not destroy the Application object and its window until long after destroying the main form, Windows will continue to send it messages until the program terminates. When the program destroys the main form, it will destroy all the form's components, including our application-extender. Since the application-extender creates an object to provide the surrogate window procedure (via the call to MakeObjectInstance), it should also destroy that object in its destructor. However, if we destroy that object without resetting the window procedure, Windows will try to call the new procedure (which no longer exists), and we'll see a serious memory access error.

To complete the picture, here's the full listing of the fields, methods, and properties we added to the component class to support the tray icon management:

```
type
  TDdhAppExt = class(TComponent)
```

```
private
  // window procedures
  OldWndProc, NewWndProc: Pointer;
  // tray support
  fTrayIconActive: Boolean;
  fTrayIcon: TIcon;
  fTrayPopup: TPopupMenu;
  nid: TNotifyIconData;
  fOnTrayDefault: TNotifyEvent;
  procedure IconTray (var Msg: TMessage);
protected
  procedure SetTrayIconActive (Value: Boolean);
  procedure SetTrayIcon (Value: TIcon);
  procedure IconChange (Sender: TObject);
  procedure SetTrayHint (Value: string);
  function GetTrayHint: string;
  procedure SetTrayPopup (Value: TPopupMenu);
  procedure Notification(AComponent: TComponent;
    Operation: TOperation); override;
published
  // tray icon properties
  property TrayIconActive: Boolean
    read fTrayIconActive write SetTrayIconActive
    default False;
  property TrayIcon: TIcon
    read fTrayIcon write SetTrayIcon;
  property TrayHint: string
    read GetTrayHint write SetTrayHint;
  property TrayPopup: TPopupMenu
    read fTrayPopup write SetTrayPopup;
  property OnTrayDefault: TNotifyEvent
    read fOnTrayDefault write fOnTrayDefault;
end;
```

Obviously, you can add more features to make this component more complete. For instance, you may want to provide access to the Application window's system menu, allow the programmer to show or hide the main form based on a property value (instead of calling some Windows API functions), provide a means of selecting a specific INI file or Registry entry, or handle specific system messages (using the new window procedure).

NOTE

In fact, the `Application` object defines an `OnMessage` event that you can use to intercept messages posted to the application window. Unfortunately, the VCL doesn't provide a simple mechanism for responding to messages sent to the Application window. If you try to derive a new class from `TApplication`, you'll find that it creates more problems than it solves. This is why we chose to subclass the application's window in the DdhAppExt component.

Now that we've built the application-extender component, let's use it in a simple example program. We've built one, called AppComp, which sets a special color for the hints, tracks application activation, adds an entry in the tray icon area, and allows users to change the tray icon hint. You can see this example at run-time in Figure 8.3.

FIGURE 8.3:

The AppComp example demonstrates some of the features of the DdhAppExt component.

To give you an idea of how simple the code is for this example, here's a summary of the text description of its main form:

```
object Form1: TForm1
  Caption = 'Application Component Demo'
  object Bevel1: TBevel...
  object Label1: TLabel
    Hint = 'Label1 Component'
    Caption = 'Label1'
```

```
      end
      object Label2: TLabel
        Caption = 'Tray Hint:'
      end
      object cbTray: TCheck box
        Caption = 'Tray Icon'
        State = cbChecked
        OnClick = cbTrayClick
      end
      object Edit1: TEdit
        MaxLength = 63
        Text = 'Tip'
        OnChange = Edit1Change
      end
      object DdhAppExt1: TDdhAppExt
        HintColor = clAqua
        ShowHint = True
        TrayIconActive = True
        TrayIcon.Data = {...}
        TrayHint = 'Here am I, guys!'
        TrayPopup = PopupMenu1
        OnTrayDefault = Message1Click
        OnActivate = DdhAppExt1Activate
        OnDeactivate = DdhAppExt1Deactivate
      end
      object PopupMenu1: TPopupMenu
        object Message1: TMenuItem...
        object About1: TMenuItem...
        object N1: TMenuItem...
        object Close1: TMenuItem...
      end
    end
  end
```

The corresponding code is also quite simple. The activation and deactivation methods change the text and the color of the label, and clicking on the check box or typing in the edit box changes the corresponding properties of the DhhAppExt component:

```
procedure TForm1.DdhAppExt1Activate(Sender: TObject);
begin
  Label1.Caption := 'Active Application';
  Label1.Font.Color := clGreen;
```

```
end;

procedure TForm1.DdhAppExt1Deactivate(Sender: TObject);
begin
  Label1.Caption := 'Inactive Application';
  Label1.Font.Color := clRed;
end;

procedure TForm1.cbTrayClick(Sender: TObject);
begin
  DdhAppExt1.TrayIconActive := cbTray.Checked;
end;

procedure TForm1.Edit1Change(Sender: TObject);
begin
  DdhAppExt1.TrayHint := Edit1.Text;
end;
```

The popup menu item event handlers are even simpler, so we've omitted them from the text of the book. As usual they are available on the companion CD.

Nonrectangular Controls

By default, all windows have a rectangular shape, and so do controls. However, the Win32 API introduced a new feature: nonrectangular windows.

Specifically, you can define a screen region of almost any shape, and then associate that region with a window, by calling SetWindowRgn. This means that the window will paint its surface only within the region, and also that mouse clicks outside the region will be sent to the window behind it.

To better understand how this works, let's consider a very basic example, an elliptical form. Start a new project, and add the following code to the main form's OnCreate event handler:

```
procedure TForm1.FormCreate(Sender: TObject);
var
  hRegion: THandle;
begin
  hRegion := CreateEllipticRgn (0, - Height, Width, Height);
```

```
    SetWindowRgn (Handle, hRegion, True);
end;
```

This makes the window look quite strange, as you can see in Figure 8.4. To make this work even better, however, you should place exactly the same code in the OnResize event handler, to adjust the window's shape every time the size of the window changes. You'll find this code if you examine the RoundWnd example on the companion CD.

FIGURE 8.4:

The semi-elliptical window generated by the RoundWnd example

Of course, you can choose whatever shape you want for the border of the form, provided that the system will be able to adjust the frame of the window to that shape. Besides changing the shape of the window's border, you can also alter the internal area of the window, creating a hole within it. A simple way to do this is to define a region with a polygon that defines a hole. In this case, the region should enclose the entire form, and define the hole by a series of points as shown in Figure 8.5.

The points represented in Figure 8.5 can be coded as follows:

```
uses
    MmSystem;

type
    PtsType = array [0..15, 0..1] of Integer;

const
    Pts: PtsType = ((0, 0), (800, 0), (800, 600),
    (200, 600), (200, 220), (300, 280),
    (265, 205), (350, 117), (205, 170),
    (120, 90), (130, 200), (60, 350), (200, 220),
    (200, 600), (0, 600), (0, 0));
```

```
procedure THoleForm.Button1Click(Sender: TObject);
var
  HRegion1: THandle;
begin
  HRegion1 := CreatePolygonRgn (Pts,
    sizeof (Pts) div 8, alternate);
  PlaySound ('boom.wav', 0, snd_async);
  SetWindowRgn (Handle, HRegion1, True);
end;
```

FIGURE 8.5:

The series of points used by the Hole example to create a hole inside a window

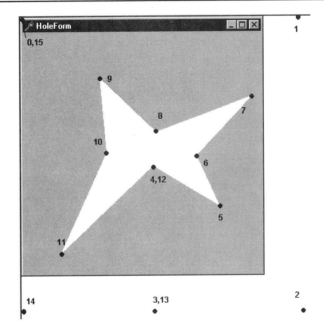

The Hole program executes this code when its button is pressed, and the effect of this operation is to remove the button a user has clicked from the visible area of the form. We've added an explosion sound effect to make the example more fun to use.

You've seen how to apply the SetWindowRgn API function to forms. What is more interesting, however, is to use this technique to create oddly shaped components, as we'll do in the next sections. We'll start with a star-shaped custom control and then build a round owner-drawn button.

A Star Control

Now let's create a star-shaped control. We'll derive it from `TCustomControl`, because this base class provides a window handle and painting support.

First, we must specify the shape of the component. We'll add an array of points to the class declaration; this array will store the positions of the vertices of the star. Each time we resize the control, we'll adjust the values of these points:

```
procedure TDdhStar.SetBounds (ALeft, ATop, AWidth, AHeight: Integer);
var
  HRegion1: THandle;
begin
  inherited;
  // compute points
  Pts [0] := Point (AWidth div 2, 0);
  Pts [1] := Point (AWidth, AHeight);
  Pts [2] := Point (0, AHeight div 3);
  Pts [3] := Point (AWidth, AHeight div 3);
  Pts [4] := Point (0, AHeight);
  Pts [5] := Point (Width div 2, 0);
  // set component shape
  if HandleAllocated then
  begin
    HRegion1 := CreatePolygonRgn (Pts,
      sizeof (Pts) div 8, winding);
    SetWindowRgn (Handle, HRegion1, True);
  end;
end;
```

Inside this procedure, we'll set the component shape only if we've already allocated a window handle for the control. Since we'll call this method from the constructor, when the window handle isn't yet available, performing this test is important. If we don't, we'll generate a run-time error. Unfortunately, this means that the constructor sets the values of the shape points and *then* creates the handle. As a result, the window won't have the correct shape until the size of the component changes, which is when we'll call the `SetWindowRgn` function to adjust the window size. To solve this problem, we'll redefine the component's `CreateHandle` method, and change the window region there too:

```
procedure TDdhStar.CreateHandle;
var
  HRegion1: THandle;
```

```
begin
  inherited;
  HRegion1 := CreatePolygonRgn (Pts,
    sizeof (Pts) div 8, winding);
  SetWindowRgn (Handle, HRegion1, True);
end;
```

If you examine the calls we've made to CreatePoylygonRgn, you'll notice that in both cases we've used the winding style flag. This style creates a closed region. If we'd used the alternate style instead, the center of the star would not be part of the polygonal region.

Similarly, we use the winding style to paint the star shape when the LinesVisible property is True. Otherwise, we simply draw a rectangle larger than the control to ensure that the entire star shape will appear:

```
procedure TDdhStar.Paint;
begin
  Canvas.Brush.Color := clYellow;
  if fLinesVisible then
  begin
    Canvas.Pen.Color := fLineColor;
    Canvas.Pen.Width := fLineSize;
    SetPolyFillMode (Canvas.Handle, winding);
    Canvas.Polygon (Pts);
  end
  else
  begin
    Canvas.Pen.Width := 1;
    Canvas.Rectangle (-1, -1, Width + 1, Height + 1);
  end;
end;
```

Here, you'll notice that we've called the SetPolyFillMode API function using the winding style. This forces the Canvas.Polygon method to use the winding style for it painting operation. The remaining code for the class is quite simple. The class declaration and constructor appear below (you can find the rest of the code on the CD):

```
type
  TDdhStar = class (TCustomControl)
  private
    {data fields for properties}
```

```
      fLineColor: TColor;
      fLineSize: Integer;
      fLinesVisible: Boolean;
      Pts: array [0..5] of TPoint;
    protected
      {set and get methods}
      procedure SetLineColor (Value: TColor);
      procedure SetLineSize (Value: Integer);
      procedure SetLinesVisible (Value: Boolean);
    public
      constructor Create (AOwner: TComponent); override;
      procedure CreateHandle; override;
      procedure SetBounds (ALeft, ATop, AWidth, AHeight:
        Integer); override;
      procedure Paint; override;
    published
      property LineColor: TColor
        read fLineColor write SetLineColor default clBlack;
      property LineSize: Integer
        read fLineSize write SetLineSize default 2;
      property LinesVisible: Boolean
        read fLinesVisible write SetLinesVisible default False;
      property Width default 50;
      property Height default 50;
    end;

constructor TDdhStar.Create (AOwner: TComponent);
begin
  inherited Create (AOwner);
  // set default values
  fLineColor := clBlack;
  fLineSize := 2;
  fLinesVisible := False;
  Width := 50;
  Height := 50;
end;
```

We've built a sample program, StarComp, that uses two star controls, as you can see in Figure 8.6. If you examine the figure closely, you'll notice that the component doesn't hide other components that appear within the points of the star (that is, it's transparent).

FIGURE 8.6:

The StarComp example shows two copies of the DdhStar component, with and without lines.

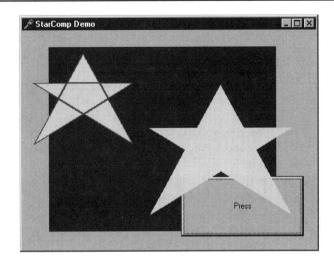

A Round Button

While the star component we've just built is certainly interesting, and it can handle OnClick events, it doesn't provide the visual feedback that you get from clicking a "three-dimensional" button. Instead of adding this support to the star component, we've decided to use the window region technique to define a non-rectangular button. To create this new button class, we'll derived it from TButton, and use owner-draw techniques to define custom painting code for an existing control. As you may know, there's already a class in the VCL that uses this approach, the TBitBtn class. We've used the TBitBtn code as a model for creating our new component.

Let's begin by examining the class declaration, which defines several message-response methods, as well as several overrides of inherited methods:

```
type
  TDdhRoundBtn = class(TButton)
  private
    IsFocused: Boolean;
    FCanvas: TCanvas;
    procedure CNDrawItem(var Msg: TWMDrawItem);
      message cn_DrawItem;
    procedure CMFontChanged(var Msg: TMessage);
      message cm_FontChanged;
```

```
    procedure CMEnabledChanged(var Msg: TMessage);
      message cm_EnabledChanged;
    procedure WMLButtonDblClk(var Message: TWMLButtonDblClk);
      message wm_LButtonDblClk;
  protected
    procedure SetBounds (ALeft, ATop, AWidth, AHeight:
      Integer); override;
    procedure CreateParams(var Params: TCreateParams); override;
    procedure CreateWnd; override;
    procedure SetButtonStyle(ADefault: Boolean); override;
  public
    constructor Create (AOwner: TComponent); override;
    destructor Destroy; override;
  published
    property Color;
    property Width default 100;
    property Height default 50;
    property ParentShowHint;
    property ShowHint;
    property TabOrder;
    property TabStop;
    property Visible;
    property OnEnter;
    property OnExit;
  end;
```

For this class, the constructor sets the size of the component and creates its TCanvas object, which we release in the destructor:

```
constructor TDdhRoundBtn.Create (AOwner: TComponent);
begin
  inherited Create (AOwner);
  SetBounds (Left, Top, 100, 50);
  FCanvas := TCanvas.Create;
end;

destructor TDdhRoundBtn.Destroy;
begin
  inherited Destroy;
  FCanvas.Free;
end;
```

An important feature of this example is the new window style definition for the control, which includes the bs_OwnerDraw style. We specify this style in the overridden CreateParams method:

```
procedure TDdhRoundBtn.CreateParams(var Params: TCreateParams);
begin
  inherited CreateParams(Params);
  with Params
    do Style := Style or bs_OwnerDraw;
end;
```

As you would expect, the CreateWnd and SetBounds methods are similar to the previous example, although this time the region is an elliptical one the same size as the button:

```
procedure TDdhRoundBtn.CreateWnd;
var
  hRegion: THandle;
begin
  inherited CreateWnd;
  hRegion := CreateEllipticRgn (0, 0, Width, Height);
  SetWindowRgn (Handle, hRegion, True);
end;

procedure TDdhRoundBtn.SetBounds (ALeft, ATop,
  AWidth, AHeight: Integer);
var
  hRegion: THandle;
begin
  inherited SetBounds (ALeft, ATop, AWidth, AHeight);
  if HandleAllocated then
  begin
    hRegion := CreateEllipticRgn (0, 0, AWidth, AHeight);
    SetWindowRgn (Handle, hRegion, True);
  end;
end;
```

The most complex part of this component is its drawing method, CNDrawItem. This method must draw the button four ways: in the normal state, in the pressed state, as the default button, and as the focused button. Optimizing this method isn't very easy, but it's quite important because we don't want to repaint the entire component every time something changes. Since we're painting the button using ellipses and arcs, operations that are notoriously slow, optimization is even more important.

Since the code of this method is quite complex, and almost 100 lines long, we'll just show some fragments, along with explanations (as usual, you can find the complete source code in the Comps directory for this chapter). At the beginning of the method, we initialize some local variables using the parameters of the wm_DrawItem Windows message:

```
procedure TDdhRoundBtn.CNDrawItem(var Msg: TWMDrawItem);
var
  OdsDown, OdsFocus, ActionFocus: Boolean;
  Rect: TRect;
begin
  FCanvas.Handle := Msg.DrawItemStruct^.hDC;
  Rect := ClientRect;
  Dec (Rect.Right);
  Dec (Rect.Bottom);
  with Msg.DrawItemStruct^ do
  begin
    OdsDown := itemState and ODS_SELECTED <> 0;
    OdsFocus := itemState and ODS_FOCUS <> 0;
    ActionFocus := ItemAction = oda_Focus
  end;
```

In particular, notice the first line of this method, which sets the component's canvas handle to the canvas handle passed as a parameter. This assignment is fundamental to make this code work properly. It's necessary because CNDrawItem isn't an overridden paint method, but a method called by the button's Paint method after it's performed some initialization. We have to reduce the size of the rectangle because the pixels at the bottom and to the right are not part of the region excluded from the component.

Next, the CNDrawItem method paints the background of the component, but only if we're not performing a focus change:

```
with FCanvas do
begin
  Brush.Color := Color;
  if not ActionFocus then
  begin
    // fill with current color
    Brush.Style := bsSolid;
    FillRect (Rect);
  end;
```

The next step (which we're not showing in a listing) is to draw a black ellipse around the button if it's a default button. At this point, the drawing code that generates the three-dimensional effect is starting to get complex, particularly for the button's pressed state. To draw the pressed state, we paint a white arc on the top and left sides of the button, and black and gray arcs on the bottom and right sides:

```
if OdsDown then
begin
  // draw gray border all around
  Pen.Color := clBtnShadow;
  if not ActionFocus then
    Ellipse (Rect.Left, Rect.Top,
      Rect.Right, Rect.Bottom);
end
else if not ActionFocus then
begin
  // gray border (bottom-right)
  Pen.Color := clWindowFrame;
  Arc (Rect.Left, Rect.Top, Rect.Right, Rect.Bottom, // ellipse
    Rect.Left, Rect.Bottom, // start
    Rect.Right, Rect.Top); // end
  // white border (top-left)
  Pen.Color := clWhite;
  Arc (Rect.Left, Rect.Top, Rect.Right, Rect.Bottom, // ellipse
    Rect.Right, Rect.Top, // start
    Rect.Left, Rect.Bottom); // end
  // gray border (bottom-right, internal)
  Pen.Color := clBtnShadow;
  InflateRect (Rect, -1, -1);
  Arc (Rect.Left, Rect.Top, Rect.Right, Rect.Bottom, // ellipse
    Rect.Left, Rect.Bottom, // start
    Rect.Right, Rect.Top); // end
end;
```

Finally, we'll draw the button's caption and a focus rectangle around the text if necessary:

```
// draw the caption
InflateRect (Rect, - Width div 5, - Height div 5);
if OdsDown then
begin
  Inc (Rect.Left, 2);
  Inc (Rect.Top, 2);
```

```
  end;
Font := Self.Font;
if not ActionFocus then
  DrawText (FCanvas.Handle, PChar (Caption), -1,
    Rect, dt_SingleLine or dt_Center or dt_VCenter);

// draw the focus rectangle around the text
Brush.Style := bsSolid;
Pen.Color:= clBlack;
Brush.Color := clWhite;
if IsFocused or OdsFocus or ActionFocus then
  DrawFocusRect (Rect);
```

This is all the code that's necessary to paint the round button in each of the various states. You can see this code in action (in a couple of different cases) in Figure 8.7. The other methods of the class are quite simple. For example, if the font or the enabled status of the button changes, we call the inherited versions of those methods (to set the appropriate flags), and then repaint the control:

```
procedure TDdhRoundBtn.CMFontChanged(var Msg: TMessage);
begin
  inherited;
  Invalidate;
end;

procedure TDdhRoundBtn.CMEnabledChanged(var Msg: TMessage);
begin
  inherited;
  Invalidate;
end;
```

If you use this component, you'll notice that if you disable the button, we still paint it the same way. You might instead want to gray out the caption; adding support for this change to the CNDrawItem method is fairly simple, but we'll leave that up to you.

Finally, the WMLButtonDblClk method sends a simple wm_LButtonDown message to the component itself (to make it repaint properly), and the SetButtonStyle method saves the default status of the button (the inherited TButton code calls this method when the Default property changes). If you don't override this method, the TButton class will update the window style from bs_PushButton to

Some examples of
round buttons,
from the RoundBut
example

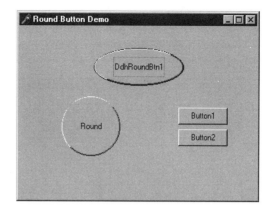

bs_DefPushButton. In both cases it removes the button's owner-drawn style and
forces the system to draw the button as usual (as a rounded rectangle).

```
procedure TDdhRoundBtn.WMLButtonDblClk(
  var Message: TWMLButtonDblClk);
begin
  Perform (WM_LBUTTONDOWN,
    Message.Keys, Longint(Message.Pos));
end;

procedure TDdhRoundBtn.SetButtonStyle (ADefault: Boolean);
begin
  if ADefault <> IsFocused then
  begin
    IsFocused := ADefault;
    Invalidate;
  end;
end;
```

Dragging and Sizing Components at Run-Time

When you're creating a form in the Delphi IDE, you can easily move and resize the
various controls. While your program is running, however, there's no obvious way
to do this. Although there are some other well-known tricks to moving components

at run-time, you might want to show the resize handles (the eight small squares you can drag) that are typically available at design-time only, as you can see in Figure 8.8.

FIGURE 8.8:

The resize handles of a component at design-time, in the Delphi form designer

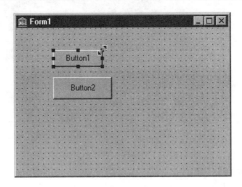

Before we build a run-time resizable component, let's focus on the techniques you can use to move components. The simplest approach is to send a wm_Sys-Command message to the form or component you want to move with the undocumented sc_DragMove flag, defined as

```
const
  sc_DragMove: Longint = $F012;
```

You can send this message only to TWinControl-derived components, and you should do so only in a mouse-down event, since the system captures the mouse at this time (dragging is an operation that makes no sense when the mouse is released). In the MoveComp example you'll find this code, connected to three different controls:

```
procedure TForm1.ControlMouseDown(Sender: TObject;
  Button: TMouseButton; Shift: TShiftState; X, Y: Integer);
begin
  if ssCtrl in Shift then
  begin
    ReleaseCapture;
    (Sender as TWinControl).Perform (
      wm_SysCommand, sc_DragMove, 0);
  end;
end;
```

At the beginning of this method, you'll notice that we test for the Ctrl key in the Shift parameter. If this test is True (the Ctrl key is down), the program allows you to drag the control around the form. Alternatively, you can write the code in the following way (the code below applies to a form, so you can move it by pressing the Ctrl key and dragging the form's surface):

```
procedure TForm1.FormMouseDown(Sender: TObject;
  Button: TMouseButton; Shift: TShiftState; X, Y: Integer);
begin
  if ssCtrl in Shift then
  begin
    ReleaseCapture;
    SendMessage (Handle, wm_SysCommand, sc_DragMove, 0);
  end;
end;
```

Using the Hit Test Message

Another technique you can use to drag or resize a form or component is to respond to the wm_NCHitTest Windows message or the cm_NCHitTest component message. Windows sends the wm_NCHitTest message to determine if a mouse action is over the client area of a window or if it's over one of the special areas of the border (the non-client areas). If you trick Windows into thinking the user has clicked on the window caption, the system will begin dragging the window. If you trick Windows into thinking the user has clicked on the window border, the system will begin resizing the window. If you're not familiar with this message you might want to read its description in Delphi's Windows API help file.

The MoveComp example defines a second form, which responds to the wm_NCHitTest message:

```
type
  TForm2 = class(TForm)
    procedure FormResize(Sender: TObject);
    procedure FormPaint(Sender: TObject);
  private
    MoveRect, TransRect: TRect;
  public
    procedure WmNcHitTest (var Msg: TWmNcHitTest);
      message wm_NcHitTest;
  end;
```

The form defines two special-purpose areas (rectangles), which we update and repaint when the user resizes the window:

```
procedure TForm2.FormResize(Sender: TObject);
begin
  MoveRect := Rect (20, 20,
    ClientWidth - 20, ClientHeight div 2 - 10);
  TransRect := Rect (20, ClientHeight div 2 + 10,
    ClientWidth - 20, ClientHeight - 20);
  Invalidate;
end;

procedure TForm2.FormPaint(Sender: TObject);
begin
  // draw the rectangles
  Canvas.Brush.Color:= Font.Color;
  Canvas.FrameRect (MoveRect);
  Canvas.FrameRect (TransRect);
  // draw the text
  Canvas.Brush.Color:= Color;
  DrawText (Canvas.Handle, 'Move', 4, MoveRect,
    dt_Center or dt_VCenter or dt_SingleLine);
  DrawText (Canvas.Handle, 'Transparent', 11, TransRect,
    dt_Center or dt_VCenter or dt_SingleLine);
end;
```

You can see an example of the resulting form at run-time in Figure 8.9. The key method of this form, however, is the wm_NcHitTest message-response method. After converting the message's mouse coordinates to form coordinates (using the ScreenToClient API function), this method determines if the mouse is in one of the two rectangles, and returns one of the special hit test values: htCaption mimics a mouse operation on the form caption to enable dragging, while htTransparent forwards the mouse operation to one of the other windows of the same application (behind the current window). In fact, if the current mouse position is over one component of Form1, behind Form2, you'll actually click on it *through* Form2. This is very strange behavior, and not what you'd expect. Here is the code:

```
procedure TForm2.WmNcHitTest(var Msg: TWmNcHitTest);
var
  Pt: TPoint;
begin
  Pt := Point (Msg.XPos, Msg.YPos);
  Pt := ScreenToClient (Pt);
```

```
      if PtInRect (MoveRect, pt) then
        Msg.Result := htCaption
      else if PtInRect (TransRect, pt) then
        Msg.Result := htTransparent
      else
        inherited;
    end;
```

FIGURE 8.9:

The second form
of the MoveComp
example can be
moved by drag-
ging the mouse on
the first rectangu-
lar area.

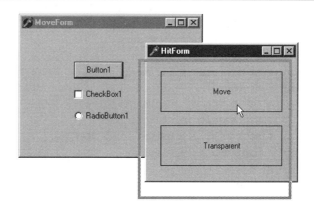

A Component with Drag Handles

As we just mentioned, you can use the wm_NcHitTest message to implement
dragging operations on a component. We've built a simple button component
that allows run-time resizing operations similar to what a form usually provides.
Here is the code for this button:

```
type
  TDdhSizeButton = class (TButton)
  public
    procedure WmNcHitTest (var Msg: TWmNcHitTest);
      message wm_NcHitTest;
  end;

procedure TDdhSizeButton.WmNcHitTest(var Msg: TWmNcHitTest);
var
  Pt: TPoint;
begin
```

```
      Pt := Point (Msg.XPos, Msg.YPos);
      Pt := ScreenToClient (Pt);
      if (Pt.x < 5) and (pt.y < 5) then
        Msg.Result := htTopLeft
      else if (Pt.x > Width - 5) and (pt.y < 5) then
        Msg.Result := htTopRight
      else if (Pt.x > Width - 5) and (pt.y > Height - 5) then
        Msg.Result := htBottomRight
      else if (Pt.x < 5) and (pt.y > Height - 5) then
        Msg.Result := htBottomLeft
      else if (Pt.x < 5) then
        Msg.Result := htLeft
      else if (pt.y < 5) then
        Msg.Result := htTop
      else if (Pt.x > Width - 5) then
        Msg.Result := htRight
      else if (pt.y > Height - 5) then
        Msg.Result := htBottom
      else
        inherited;
  end;
```

The code first checks to see if the cursor is in one of the corners of the button. Then it checks whether the cursor is close to one of the borders. If one of the tests succeeds, the method returns the corresponding hit test value. Otherwise, it lets the base class process the message. This code has two effects: First, it displays the proper resizing cursor as the user moves it over the borders of the control, and second, it allows the user to actually resize the control. You can see an example (the SizeForm demo) in Figure 8.10.

This approach has several drawbacks. First, we don't want to add this code to every component we want to resize. Second, the component doesn't show the familiar resizing handles that users expect. Finally, the user can resize the component at run-time, but cannot move it. To solve these problems we've built the DdhSizerControl component. This component attaches itself to another component that you'll pass as a parameter to its constructor: It doesn't make sense to create it at design-time, so you'll always create it dynamically and attach it automatically to a component.

FIGURE 8.10:

An example of a
button that can be
resized by a user,
the DdhSizeButton
component

Passing an extra parameter to the constructor of the component will make
Delphi issue a warning at compile time. Since a lot of the code is in the
window creation process, we felt it was more reasonable to force the constructor to provide this vital information (the control this component is
attached to) instead of using a property to set this up. Of course, we'll register the component so that it won't be available in the Component palette,
since Delphi won't be able to create it using our nonstandard constructor.

Here's some code (used by the SizeDemo example to handle the OnClick event
of a button) to demonstrate how you'll use it:

```
procedure TForm1.AttachSizer(Sender: TObject);
begin
  TDdhSizerControl.Create (self, Sender as TControl);
end;
```

Now let's examine the new component's class declaration:

```
type
  TDdhSizerControl = class (TCustomControl)
  private
    FControl: TControl;
    FRectList: array [1..8] of TRect;
    FPosList: array [1..8] of Integer;
  public
    constructor Create (AOwner: TComponent;
      AControl: TControl);
    procedure CreateParams (var Params: TCreateParams);
      override;
    procedure CreateHandle; override;
    procedure WmNcHitTest (var Msg: TWmNcHitTest);
      message wm_NcHitTest;
```

```
    procedure WmSize (var Msg: TWmSize);
      message wm_Size;
    procedure WmLButtonDown (var Msg: TWmLButtonDown);
      message wm_LButtonDown;
    procedure WmMove (var Msg: TWmMove);
      message wm_Move;
    procedure Paint; override;
    procedure SizerControlExit (Sender: TObject);
  end;
```

The two array fields store the list of hit test codes and the list of the rectangles where the corresponding resizing handles should appear. Here's the code of the component's constructor:

```
constructor TDdhSizerControl.Create (
  AOwner: TComponent; AControl: TControl);
var
  R: TRect;
begin
  inherited Create (AOwner);
  FControl := AControl;
  // install the new handler
  OnExit := SizerControlExit;
  // set the size and position
  R := FControl.BoundsRect;
  InflateRect (R, 2, 2);
  BoundsRect := R;
  // set the parent
  Parent := FControl.Parent;
  // create the list of positions
  FPosList [1] := htTopLeft;
  FPosList [2] := htTop;
  FPosList [3] := htTopRight;
  FPosList [4] := htRight;
  FPosList [5] := htBottomRight;
  FPosList [6] := htBottom;
  FPosList [7] := htBottomLeft;
  FPosList [8] := htLeft;
end;
```

The constructor saves the associated control in the FControl field, and makes its own size a little larger than that of the target control, so that the resizing handles will be exactly over the associated control's border. After setting its own parent window to that of the target control, the constructor initializes the hit test code array. The new control is a transparent window, but when you create it, it grabs the input focus (after creating its handle):

```
procedure TDdhSizerControl.CreateParams (var Params: TCreateParams);
begin
  inherited CreateParams(Params);
  Params.ExStyle := Params.ExStyle +
    ws_ex_Transparent;
end;

procedure TDdhSizerControl.CreateHandle;
begin
  inherited CreateHandle;
  SetFocus;
end;
```

The reason we monitor the input focus is that we'll automatically destroy the TDdhSizerControl when the user moves the input focus to a different control. We accomplish this by making the component destroy itself when it loses the input focus:

```
procedure TDdhSizerControl.SizerControlExit (Sender: TObject);
begin
  Free;
end;
```

In the constructor, we set the SizerControlExit method as an event handler for the component's OnExit event. In this method, we can call Free for the component directly because the user generally isn't going to install an event handler for a control they've created at run-time.

When the user resizes the control, we reset the positions of the resizing handles:

```
procedure TDdhSizerControl.WmSize (var Msg: TWmSize);
var
  R: TRect;
begin
  R := BoundsRect;
  InflateRect (R, -2, -2);
  FControl.BoundsRect := R;
  // setup data structures
  FRectList [1] := Rect (0, 0, 5, 5);
  FRectList [2] := Rect (Width div 2 - 3, 0,
```

```
      Width div 2 + 2, 5);
  FRectList [3] := Rect (Width - 5, 0, Width, 5);
  FRectList [4] := Rect (Width - 5, Height div 2 - 3,
    Width, Height div 2 + 2);
  FRectList [5] := Rect (Width - 5, Height - 5,
    Width, Height);
  FRectList [6] := Rect (Width div 2 - 3, Height - 5,
    Width div 2 + 2, Height);
  FRectList [7] := Rect (0, Height - 5, 5, Height);
  FRectList [8] := Rect (0, Height div 2 - 3,
    5, Height div 2 + 2);
end;
```

You'll notice that at the beginning of this method, we set the size of the
TDdhSizerControl component to match the size of the SizerControl, minus the
usual border. When it's time to paint the resizing handles or perform the hit test,
we scan the array values using a for loop:

```
procedure TDdhSizerControl.Paint;
var
  I: Integer;
begin
  Canvas.Brush.Color := clBlack;
  for I := 1 to  8 do
    Canvas.Rectangle (FRectList [I].Left, FRectList [I].Top,
      FRectList [I].Right, FRectList [I].Bottom);
end;

procedure TDdhSizerControl.WmNcHitTest(var Msg: TWmNcHitTest);
var
  Pt: TPoint;
  I: Integer;
begin
  Pt := Point (Msg.XPos, Msg.YPos);
  Pt := ScreenToClient (Pt);
  Msg.Result := 0;
  for I := 1 to  8 do
    if PtInRect (FRectList [I], Pt) then
      Msg.Result := FPosList [I];
  // if the return value was not set
  if Msg.Result = 0 then
    inherited;
end;
```

Finally, we'll want to give the user the ability to move the component. To do this we respond to the wm_SysCommand as we've done before (we could have used the htCaption hit test instead). However, the important thing is to handle the wm_Move message, resize the attached control (if necessary), and repaint it properly:

```
procedure TDdhSizerControl.WmLButtonDown (var Msg: TWmLButtonDown);
begin
  Perform (wm_SysCommand, sc_DragMove, 0);
end;

procedure TDdhSizerControl.WmMove (var Msg: TWmMove);
var
  R: TRect;
begin
  R := BoundsRect;
  InflateRect (R, -2, -2);
  FControl.Invalidate; // repaint entire surface
  FControl.BoundsRect := R;
end;
```

Near the end of this method, you'll notice that the call to Invalidate comes before we set BoundsRect (the new control boundaries). This helps to avoid useless flickering of the control. We'll automatically repaint the component when the user moves it, but only if the user moves it to a completely different location. If the previous and new bounding rectangles of the component overlap, Windows won't repaint those areas unless we specifically call Invalidate. This is because of the strange behavior of transparent windows.

NOTE The problems of transparent windows are discussed in Chapter 10 of Marco Cantù's *Mastering Delphi 3*. The Transpar example built in that book is available in the source code of the current chapter. By running this program you'll see the odd behavior of a transparent window.

Finally, keep in mind that this component's package registers the component with no icon (by calling RegisterNoIcon instead of RegisterComponents), so that we won't see it in the Component palette. It should not appear there, because we cannot simply place it on a form (since the constructor requires two parameters), but instead need to create it connected to another control. The SizeDemo example connects the TDdhSizerControl component to three controls in the bottom part of the form, as you can see in Figure 8.11. In particular, notice that this figure is an image of the program at run-time, although a user can move and resize the components as if they were performing these tasks in the Delphi environment at design-time.

FIGURE 8.11:

The DDhSizer-Control component can be attached to other controls to make them moveable and resizable at run-time. Notice the standard resizing handles.

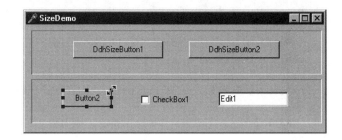

What's Next

In the previous chapter, we reviewed some of the theory behind Windows programming. In this chapter, we moved beyond the theory to apply some complex Windows programming techniques to build special Delphi components. We used subclassing and owner-draw techniques, and we've responded to special-purpose Windows messages to create some useful VCL controls. In the next chapter, we'll continue by examining how Delphi applications use memory, and how you can take advantage of DLLs and other Windows features to share data among different applications.

Then, we'll be ready to delve into one of the more complex and advanced topics of Windows programming: Microsoft's Component Object Model, or COM for short.

CHAPTER

NINE

Processes and Memory

9

In the last two chapters, we discussed the foundations of Windows programming from the API perspective: exploring window classes, windows, messages, subclassing, and so on. In this chapter, we'll return to discussing Windows foundations, primarily with regard to processes (that is, applications). We'll also review how Delphi applications interact with dynamic-link libraries (DLLs); for an introduction to writing DLLs, see *Mastering Delphi 3*.

In considering how the operating system interacts with Delphi processes, we'll also focus on Delphi memory management, and even build some custom memory managers. In the final part of the chapter we'll focus on two techniques you can use to share data between different processes, the wm_CopyData message and memory-mapped files.

Memory Management

It's not easy to review memory management for Delphi applications exhaustively, because there's so much information to consider. First, there's Windows memory management, which on Win32 platforms is fairly simple and robust for applications, but a bit more complex for DLLs. On the application level, there's Delphi's own internal memory management, which is quite complex. While introducing these topics, we'll build small examples to investigate the status of the memory from both perspectives.

In Windows 95 and Windows NT, every application sees its local memory as a single large segment of 4 GB, regardless of the amount of physical memory available. This is possible because the operating system maps the virtual memory addresses of each application into physical RAM addresses, and swaps these blocks of memory to disk as necessary (automatically loading the proper page of the swap file in memory). This single, huge memory segment is managed by the operating system in chunks of 4 KB each, called *pages*.

NOTE Every process has its own private address space, totally separate from the others. This makes the operating system more robust than in the days of 16-bit Windows, when all applications shared a single address space. We'll see in the second part of this chapter, "Passing Data Between Programs," how you can move data between the address spaces of different Win32 applications.

In fact, in both Windows 95 and Windows NT, an application can directly manage only about half of its address space (2 GB), while the other half is reserved for the operating system. Fortunately, 2 GB is usually more than enough.

Another important element of Win32 memory management is virtual memory allocation. Besides allocating memory, a process can simply reserve memory for future use (using a low-level operation called virtual allocation). For example, in a Delphi application, you can use the `SetLength` procedure to reserve space for a string. Delphi does the same thing transparently when you create a huge array. This memory won't be allocated—just reserved for future use. In practice, this means that the memory subsystem won't use addresses in that range for other memory allocations.

Fortunately, most of the memory management, both at the application level and at the system level, is completely transparent to programmers. For this reason, you don't typically need to know the details of how memory pages work, and we won't explore that topic further here. Instead, we'll explore the status of a region of memory, something you might find very useful while writing and debugging an application.

Tracking Global and Local Memory

The Windows API includes a few functions that let us inspect the status of memory. The most powerful of these functions are part of the so-called ToolHelp API (nothing to do with Delphi's own ToolsAPI) and are platform-specific: They are available either on Windows 95 or on Windows NT—but not both. If we want to remain on common ground we can use `GlobalMemoryStatus`, a function that allows us to inspect the status of the memory in the entire operating system. Another function we'll use in our memory inspector program, named `MemStatus`, is `GetHeapStatus`, a Delphi function that tracks the memory status of the current application. As we'll see in a moment, the second function delivers much more useful information.

You use the first function, `GlobalMemoryStatus`, to track global memory consumption in various areas: physical RAM, the page file (or swap file), and the global address space. This function initializes a record of type `TMemoryStatus`, with several parameters:

> `dwMemoryLoad` is a global 0–100 rating, indicating the memory load (it's not a percentage of memory available, and it's not very useful, in our opinion).
>
> `dwTotalPhys` is the amount of physical RAM memory.

dwAvailPhys is the free physical memory (usually there's not much).

dwTotalPageFile is the maximum theoretical size of the page file, which depends on amount of physical RAM memory and free disk space. This is *not* the current size of the swap file, but its maximum size.

dwAvailPageFile is the free portion of the swap file.

dwTotalVirtual is the total amount of memory a process can address.

dwAvailVirtual is the free area of the memory that the process can address, or the available memory addresses.

To demonstrate the use of this function, we've built the MemStatus program. Its form contains a timer component and two string grid controls. (We'll consider the second of these grids in a moment.) The first grid displays TMemoryStatus information and has the following attributes:

```
object StringGrid1: TStringGrid
  ColCount = 2
  DefaultColWidth = 166
  RowCount = 10
  FixedRows = 0
end
```

When the program starts, and every time the timer event fires (by default, every 10 seconds), the application updates the information in the second column. We set the captions of the first column when the program starts. In the following listing (and by looking at the output in Figure 9.1), you can see that in addition to the values in the TMemoryStatus structure, the second column of the first grid displays some extra values computed by the program (such as the RAM and page file load):

```
procedure TForm1.UpdateStatus;
var
  MemStatus: TMemoryStatus;
begin
  MemStatus.dwLength := sizeof (TMemoryStatus);
  GlobalMemoryStatus (MemStatus);
  with MemStatus do
  begin
    // load
    StringGrid1.Cells [1, 0] := IntToStr (dwMemoryLoad) + '%';

    // RAM (total, free, load)
```

```
      StringGrid1.Cells [1, 1] := FloatToStrF (
        dwTotalPhys / 1024,
        ffNumber, 20, 0) + ' Kbytes';
      StringGrid1.Cells [1, 2] := FloatToStrF (
        dwAvailPhys / 1024,
        ffNumber, 20, 0) + ' Kbytes';
      StringGrid1.Cells [1, 3] := IntToStr (100 -
        dwAvailPhys div (dwTotalPhys div 100)) + '%';

      // page file (total, free, load)
      StringGrid1.Cells [1, 4] := FloatToStrF (
        dwTotalPageFile / 1024,
        ffNumber, 20, 0) + ' Kbytes';
      StringGrid1.Cells [1, 5] := FloatToStrF (
        dwAvailPageFile / 1024,
        ffNumber, 20, 0) + ' Kbytes';
      StringGrid1.Cells [1, 6] := IntToStr (100 -
        dwAvailPageFile div (dwTotalPageFile div 100)) + '%';

      // page file (total, used, free)
      StringGrid1.Cells [1, 7] := FloatToStrF (
        dwTotalVirtual / 1024,
        ffNumber, 20, 0) + ' Kbytes';
      StringGrid1.Cells [1, 8] := FloatToStrF (
        dwAvailVirtual / 1024,
        ffNumber, 20, 0) + ' Kbytes';
      StringGrid1.Cells [1, 9] := FloatToStrF (
        (dwTotalVirtual - dwAvailVirtual) / 1024,
        ffNumber, 20, 0) + ' Kbytes';
    end; // with MemStatus
  end;
```

Monitoring this information can be useful, although keeping this window around is not very handy. As an alternative, you can look at (and use) the Mem3 example from *Mastering Delphi 3* and also available on the companion CD's folder for this chapter. This program computes the percentage of free RAM and free swap file space, and it displays this information in a gauge. The advantage is that it shows a summary (using a colored icon) in the tray icon area.

However, our MemStatus program shows some other interesting information in the second string grid component. It uses a second function, GetHeapStatus,

FIGURE 9.1:

The initial output
of the MemStatus
application, which
shows the status
of global memory
in Windows and
the application's
local heap.

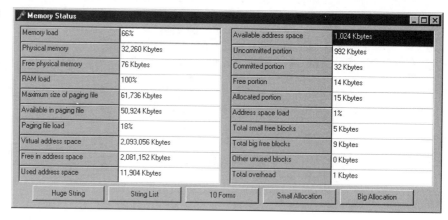

Memory Status				
Memory load	66%	Available address space	1,024 Kbytes	
Physical memory	32,260 Kbytes	Uncommitted portion	992 Kbytes	
Free physical memory	76 Kbytes	Committed portion	32 Kbytes	
RAM load	100%	Free portion	14 Kbytes	
Maximum size of paging file	61,736 Kbytes	Allocated portion	15 Kbytes	
Available in paging file	50,924 Kbytes	Address space load	1%	
Paging file load	18%	Total small free blocks	5 Kbytes	
Virtual address space	2,093,056 Kbytes	Total big free blocks	9 Kbytes	
Free in address space	2,081,152 Kbytes	Other unused blocks	0 Kbytes	
Used address space	11,904 Kbytes	Total overhead	1 Kbytes	

| Huge String | String List | 10 Forms | Small Allocation | Big Allocation |

which keeps track of the status of the application's memory via the Delphi memory manager. The GetHeapStatus function is defined by the System unit (or the ShareMem unit), and returns a structure with the following information:

TotalAddrSpace is the total number of bytes of address space currently available to a program. The value grows as the application requires more memory.

TotalUncommitted is the number of bytes within the address space that haven't been reserved. (This is not the size of the swap file, as the Delphi help suggests.)

TotalCommitted is the number of bytes of address space that have been reserved by the program. The total of the committed and the uncommitted values should always equal the total address space.

TotalAllocated is the number of bytes of address space that your program has actually allocated. This is always smaller than the number of bytes reserved (TotalCommitted).

TotalFree is the number of bytes of the address space that are still free. When this reaches zero, more memory will be given to the program. The total free space is the total of the following three values: FreeSmall, FreeBig, and Unused.

FreeSmall is the total number of free bytes that were previously allocated in small memory blocks. Too many small memory blocks might indicate a memory fragmentation problem.

FreeBig is the total number of free bytes that were previously allocated in big memory blocks. These blocks are easy to reuse in further memory allocations. When you free many small contiguous blocks, they become one single big block.

Unused is the total number of free bytes that the program has never allocated.

Overhead is the number of bytes that the heap manager uses internally to track all the blocks the application dynamically allocates.

HeapErrorCode is an internal error code, not used by our program.

To monitor local memory in the MemStatus program, we created the second string grid component, which has the same properties and layout as the first one, and we added some code to the FormCreate method to insert the value descriptions in the grid's first column. We also added the following code to the UpdateStatus method:

```
procedure TForm1.UpdateStatus;
var
  HeapStatus: THeapStatus;
begin
  ...
  HeapStatus := GetHeapStatus;
  with HeapStatus do
  begin
    StringGrid2.Cells [1, 0] := FloatToStrF (
      TotalAddrSpace div 1024,
      ffNumber, 20, 0) + ' Kbytes';
    StringGrid2.Cells [1, 1] := FloatToStrF (
      TotalUncommitted div 1024,
      ffNumber, 20, 0) + ' Kbytes';
    StringGrid2.Cells [1, 2] := FloatToStrF (
      TotalCommitted div 1024,
      ffNumber, 20, 0) + ' Kbytes';
    StringGrid2.Cells [1, 3] := FloatToStrF (
      TotalFree div 1024,
      ffNumber, 20, 0) + ' Kbytes';
    StringGrid2.Cells [1, 4] := FloatToStrF (
```

```
    TotalAllocated div 1024,
    ffNumber, 20, 0) + ' Kbytes';
  StringGrid2.Cells [1, 5] := IntToStr (
    TotalAllocated div (TotalAddrSpace div 100)) + '%';
  StringGrid2.Cells [1, 6] := FloatToStrF (
    FreeSmall div 1024,
    ffNumber, 20, 0) + ' Kbytes';
  StringGrid2.Cells [1, 7] := FloatToStrF (
    FreeBig div 1024,
    ffNumber, 20, 0) + ' Kbytes';
  StringGrid2.Cells [1, 8] := FloatToStrF (
    Overhead div 1024,
    ffNumber, 20, 0) + ' Kbytes';
  StringGrid2.Cells [1, 9] := FloatToStrF (
    Unused div 1024,
    ffNumber, 20, 0) + ' Kbytes';
end;
```

The program also contains five buttons you can use to test the effect (particularly on the local heap) of different memory allocations. The OnClick event handler code for these buttons should be easy for you to understand. The first button, *Huge String*, allocates a large block of memory for a string field that's a data member of the form's class (in fact, Delphi 3's "garbage collection" feature will destroy a local string as soon as it goes out of scope):

```
procedure TForm1.BtnStringClick(Sender: TObject);
begin
  // 10 megabytes
  SetLength (s, 10000000);
  UpdateStatus;
end;
```

If you click this button you'll see the memory consumption jump to a much higher level; compare Figure 9.2 with Figure 9.1.

The second button, *String List*, creates a new string list, fills it with 1000 strings, and then deletes some of them:

```
procedure TForm1.BtnStringListClick(Sender: TObject);
var
  I: Integer;
begin
  sl := TStringList.Create;
```

FIGURE 9.2:

The status of the local (and global) memory after allocating 10 MB for a string

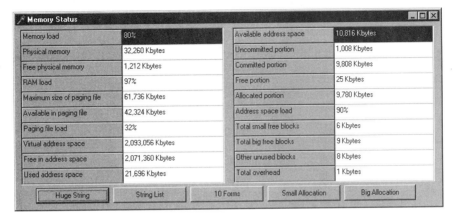

```
  // add one thousand strings
  for I := 0 to 1000 do
    sl.Add ('hello');
  // destroy some of them
  for I := 300 downto 1 do
    sl.Delete (I * 3);
  UpdateStatus;
end;
```

If you keep pressing this button, you'll begin to see memory fragmentation. The amount of free space in the small memory blocks will keep growing and growing, instead of being reused for other memory allocations.

The third button, *10 Forms*, creates several forms, which actually affects the free system resources more than it does free memory:

```
procedure TForm1.BtnFormClick(Sender: TObject);
var
  I: Integer;
begin
  // create ten forms
  for I := 1 to 10 do
    F := TForm.Create (Application);
  UpdateStatus;
end;
```

The last two buttons allocate small and large memory blocks directly. (You'll notice that we have to use the variables by making an assignment, or the optimizing compiler won't perform the allocations.) Pressing these two buttons, you'll see different effects, but in both cases the free memory decreases, increasing the memory address space used by the program:

```
procedure TForm1.BtnSmallAllocClick(Sender: TObject);
var
  P: Pointer;
begin
  GetMem (P, 100);
  Integer (P^) := 10;
  UpdateStatus;
end;

procedure TForm1.BtnBigAllocClick(Sender: TObject);
var
  P: Pointer;
begin
  GetMem (P, 100000);
  Integer (P^) := 10;
  UpdateStatus;
end;
```

In Figure 9.3, you can see the status of system and program memory after the user has pressed each button several times. By comparing this with the two previous illustrations, and by running the program, you'll see that the information Delphi provides about the local heap is much more valuable than the global memory information provided by Windows.

TIP
Try adding more buttons to perform other specific memory allocations, using bigger or smaller memory blocks or strings, and study their effect on the local heap.

Delphi Memory Management

For Delphi programmers, it's important to understand how the operating system manages memory, but it is even more important to understand how Delphi handles its own objects in memory, allocating and deallocating chunks of memory for them.

FIGURE 9.3:

The MemStatus program after each of the buttons has been pressed several times. The program now uses much more memory than it did at startup (see Figure 9.1).

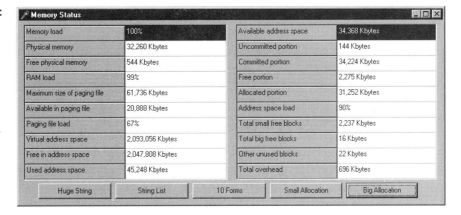

Memory Status				
Memory load	100%	Available address space	34,368 Kbytes
Physical memory	32,260 Kbytes	Uncommitted portion	144 Kbytes
Free physical memory	544 Kbytes	Committed portion	34,224 Kbytes
RAM load	99%	Free portion	2,275 Kbytes
Maximum size of paging file	61,736 Kbytes	Allocated portion	31,252 Kbytes
Available in paging file	20,888 Kbytes	Address space load	90%
Paging file load	67%	Total small free blocks	2,237 Kbytes
Virtual address space	2,093,056 Kbytes	Total big free blocks	16 Kbytes
Free in address space	2,047,808 Kbytes	Other unused blocks	22 Kbytes
Used address space	45,248 Kbytes	Total overhead	696 Kbytes

| Huge String | String List | 10 Forms | Small Allocation | Big Allocation |

In fact, every time a Delphi application creates an object or destroys it, the Delphi memory manager takes over. We've already started exploring its behavior by calling the GetHeapStatus function; as a further exploration, you can create a memory manager, providing your own memory allocation scheme, but that's really a lot of work. The simplest way to build a new memory manager is to rely on the services of the default one provided by Delphi's run-time library, and simply tap into it to keep track of what happens. We'll implement this second type of memory manager in the next example.

Delphi's run-time support system includes two procedures you can use to access the standard memory manager:

```
procedure GetMemoryManager(var MemMgr: TMemoryManager);
procedure SetMemoryManager(const MemMgr: TMemoryManager);
```

The first procedure fills the structure (passed by reference), while the second installs a new memory manager passed to it. Both procedures use the TMemoryManager structure, which includes pointers to three memory manager operations, as you can see from the class declaration:

```
type
  TMemoryManager = record
    GetMem: function(Size: Integer): Pointer;
    FreeMem: function(P: Pointer): Integer;
    ReallocMem: function(P: Pointer; Size: Integer): Pointer;
  end;
```

WARNING We are using the terms "allocating objects" and "destroying objects," but a Delphi application uses the memory manager whenever it needs to allocate a block of memory. This includes memory for global buffers, strings, and many other "memory objects."

A Global Object Counter

To begin, let's build a custom memory manager that maintains a global count of allocated objects. We can write our own versions of the three methods, and thereby keep track of how many times they are called:

```
function NewGetMem (Size: Integer): Pointer;
begin
  Inc (GetMemCount);
  Result := OldMemMgr.GetMem (Size);
end;

function NewFreeMem (P: Pointer): Integer;
begin
  Inc (FreeMemCount);
  Result := OldMemMgr.FreeMem (P);
end;

function NewReallocMem (P: Pointer; Size: Integer): Pointer;
begin
  Inc (ReallocMemCount);
  Result := OldMemMgr.ReallocMem (P, Size);
end;
```

We've declared these functions in the implementation portion of the MemMan unit, which is part of the DelMem1 project. They update three global integer variables declared in the interface portion of the unit, which are therefore accessible by the rest of the program. You'll notice that there's another variable involved, OldMemMgr, a constant that addresses the original memory manager, which we'll use to set the return data for the three functions above:

```
var
  OldMemMgr: TMemoryManager;

const
```

```
NewMemMgr: TMemoryManager = (
  GetMem: NewGetMem;
  FreeMem: NewFreeMem;
  ReallocMem: NewReallocMem);
```

The memory manager is installed when you first load the unit, via the `inital-ization` block. As you might expect, we restore the original memory manager in the `finalization` block, and if our application has allocated more objects than it's destroyed, it displays a warning:

```
initialization
  GetMemoryManager(OldMemMgr);
  SetMemoryManager(NewMemMgr);

finalization
  SetMemoryManager(OldMemMgr);
  if (GetMemCount - FreeMemCount) <> 0 then
    MessageBox (0, pChar (
      'Objects left: ' + IntToStr (GetMemCount - FreeMemCount)),
      'MemManager', mb_ok);
end.
```

We use the `MessageBox` API function to display this dialog because at that point, we don't know which global Delphi objects might already have been destroyed, and the `ShowMessage` function uses the `Application` object. In fact, we should try to install the custom memory manager before the other units initialize, and remove it at the very end. We've done this in the DelMem1 example by simply changing the order of the units in the program source code:

```
program DelMem1;

uses
  MemMan in 'MemMan.pas',
  Forms,
  MemForm in 'MemForm.pas' {Form1};
```

The MemForm unit is a secondary one, which we use to install the new memory manager that keeps track of the number of memory blocks allocated by the application. The DelMem1 example contains a simple main form with a multiline label that shows the current memory status of the application:

```
procedure TForm1.Refresh;
begin
  LblResult.Caption :=
```

```
'Allocated: ' + IntToStr (GetMemCount) + #13 +
'Free: ' + IntToStr (FreeMemCount) + #13 +
'Existing: ' +
  IntToStr (GetMemCount - FreeMemCount) + #13 +
'Re-allocated: ' + IntToStr (ReallocMemCount);
end;
```

We call this method when the application starts, as you can see in Figure 9.4, and also when you click the *Refresh* button. It's interesting to notice that every time you click that button, the application allocates ten new memory blocks. Below is a new version of the Refresh method that saves four of these blocks, creating and destroying six memory blocks for each execution:

```
procedure TForm1.Refresh2;
begin
  LblResult.Caption := Format (
    'Allocated: %d'#13'Free: %d'#13'Existing: %d'#13'Re-allocated %d',
    [GetMemCount, FreeMemCount,
    GetMemCount - FreeMemCount, ReallocMemCount]);
end;
```

FIGURE 9.4:

The initial output of the DelMem1 application, which tracks the number of objects allocated by the Delphi memory manager

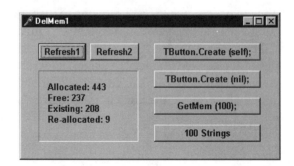

WARNING   When you run this program, notice that to update the output, the program allocates memory objects. In addition, notice that in the output you get a snapshot of the application's memory status before we generated the output! Click the same button at least a couple of times to fully understand its effect.

The four buttons on the right can be used to affect memory status in different ways. The first button allocates a button object with an owner, so that it will be destroyed before the program terminates:

```
procedure TForm1.BtnCreateNilClick (Sender: TObject);
begin
  TButton.Create (nil);
  Refresh;
end;
```

The second button creates a button object, too, but one that doesn't have an owner. If you click the second button, when you close the project you'll be notified that there are five objects left. One is the button itself, and the other objects are those used internally by the button:

```
procedure TForm1.BtnCreateOwnerClick(Sender: TObject);
begin
  TButton.Create (self);
  Refresh;
end;
```

The third button does something similar to the first two, but allocates a memory block using a low-level call. This time, when you close the application you'll be notified of one leftover memory block for each time you clicked the button:

```
procedure TForm1.BtnGetMemClick(Sender: TObject);
var
  P: Pointer;
begin
  GetMem (P, 100);
  Integer (P^) := 0;
  Refresh;
end;
```

Finally, the fourth button creates two strings, and it manipulates one of them in a for loop. Every time you click the button, the memory manager will reallocate the memory for the s1 string 99 times (we thought it should have happened 100 times, but this happens only the first time you press the button):

```
procedure TForm1.Btn100StringsClick(Sender: TObject);
var
  s1, s2: string;
  I: Integer;
```

```
begin
  s1 := 'hi';
  s2 := Btn100Strings.Caption;
  for I := 0 to 100 do
    s1 := s1 + ': hello world';
  Btn100Strings.Caption := s1;
  s1 := s2;
  Btn100Strings.Caption := s1;
  Refresh;
end;
```

A Memory Manager for a Custom Class

In addition to setting up a memory manager for the entire system, you can customize one for a specific class. To accomplish this, you need to override the NewInstance and FreeInstance methods for that class, derived from TObject. The problem is that this operation is possible only in a derived class; you cannot change these methods for an existing VCL class. So while this technique can give you some insight into how your custom classes manage memory, it won't be of much help if you want to inspect or modify existing objects.

Even so, let's build an example class, a simple TButton descendant that counts the allocated objects and keeps track of them in a list. This is the interface of the new MemMan unit of the DelMem2 example:

```
var
  AllocCount, FreeCount: Integer;
  AllocatedList: TList;

type
  TCountButton = class (TButton)
  protected
    class function NewInstance: TObject; override;
    procedure FreeInstance; override;
  end;
```

The two methods simply call the corresponding base-class methods, and then add the object to the list or remove it:

```
class function TCountButton.NewInstance: TObject;
begin
  Inc (AllocCount);
  Result := inherited NewInstance;
```

```
    AllocatedList.Add (Result);
  end;

  procedure TCountButton.FreeInstance;
  var
    nItem: Integer;
  begin
    Inc (FreeCount);
    nItem := AllocatedList.IndexOf (self);
    AllocatedList.Delete (nItem);
    inherited FreeInstance;
  end;
```

The `initialization` block creates the global list, and the `finalization` block destroys it, displaying the usual message in case of objects that haven't been destroyed:

```
  initialization
    AllocatedList := TList.Create;

  finalization
    if (AllocCount - FreeCount) <> 0 then
      MessageBox (0, pChar (
        'Objects left: ' + IntToStr (AllocCount - FreeCount)),
        'MemManager', mb_ok);
    AllocatedList.Free;
  end.
```

As in the previous example, we again display a main form with an output label and a few buttons. We've updated the `Refresh` method as follows:

```
  procedure TForm1.Refresh;
  begin
    LblResult.Caption :=
      'Allocated: ' + IntToStr (AllocCount) + #13 +
      'Free: ' + IntToStr (FreeCount) + #13 +
      'Existing: ' + IntToStr (AllocCount - FreeCount);
  end;
```

There are two buttons on the main form that let you create TCountButton objects, one with and one without an owner. In the Cbutton field of the form, we save the last object we created:

```
  procedure TForm1.BtnCreateNilClick(Sender: TObject);
  begin
```

```
    Cbutton := TCountButton.Create (nil);
    Refresh;
  end;


  procedure TForm1.BtnCreateOwnerClick (Sender: TObject);
  begin
    Cbutton := TCountButton.Create (self);
    Refresh;
  end;
```

The remaining two buttons free either the last object or all of them, respectively. For the *Free All* button we simply traverse the list of objects:

```
  procedure TForm1.BtnFreeLastClick(Sender: TObject);
  begin
    if Assigned (Cbutton) then
    begin
      Cbutton.Free;
      Cbutton := nil;
    end;
    Refresh;
  end;


  procedure TForm1.BtnFreeAllClick(Sender: TObject);
  var
    I: Integer;
  begin
    for I := AllocatedList.Count - 1 downto 0 do
      TCountButton (AllocatedList[I]).Free;
    Cbutton := nil;
    Refresh;
  end;
```

You can see an example of this program's output in Figure 9.5. Again, the technique we're presenting here is interesting; but its usefulness is limited by the fact that you can't use it for existing classes, such as the VCL components. However, this example does suggest a way to go: maintain a list of allocated memory blocks, and use that list to illustrate information about the status of those memory blocks.

FIGURE 9.5:

The output of the DelMem2 example, which counts and keeps track of the objects of a specific class

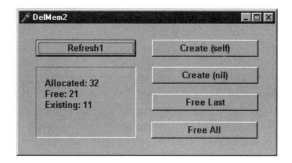

Keeping Track of Objects

Since we don't want to customize each component class to check its own status and track objects of its type in memory, we can try to create a new global memory manager to keep track of the objects. Attempting to use the TList class as a container in the last example, we saw that the allocations and reallocations inside the TList class create a risk of endless recursive calls to the memory manager.

In fact, when we write our own memory manager, we should try to use as few objects as possible, because creating more objects interferes with tracking the allocated objects of our application. The best approach seems to be to create a simple array of pointers. We've made it quite large, but feel free to increase its size if you think it's necessary. The array uses a counter and two support functions to add and remove the memory pointers from the list. Here's the code, extracted from the DdhMMan unit of the DelMem3 example:

```
var
  ObjList: array [1..10000] of Pointer;
  FreeInList: Integer = 1;

procedure AddToList (P: Pointer);
begin
  if FreeInList > High (ObjList) then
  begin
    MessageBox (0, 'List full', 'MemMan', mb_ok);
    Exit;
  end;
  ObjList [FreeInList] := P;
```

```
    Inc (FreeInList);
  end;

  procedure RemoveFromList (P: Pointer);
  var
    I: Integer;
  begin
    for I := 1 to FreeInList - 1 do
      if ObjList [I] = P then
      begin
        // remove element, shifting down the others
        Dec (FreeInList);
        Move (ObjList [I+1], ObjList [I],
          (FreeInList - I) * sizeof (pointer));
        Exit;
      end;
  end;
```

The code the RemoveFromList procedure uses to shift the pointers down in the array is not very elegant, but it should be effective, and it's very fast. Now that we have a list of pointers and the proper support routines, we can update the memory manager's code to add elements to the list:

```
  function NewGetMem (Size: Integer): Pointer;
  begin
    Inc (GetMemCount);
    Result := OldMemMgr.GetMem (Size);
    AddToList (Result);
  end;

  function NewFreeMem (P: Pointer): Integer;
  begin
    Inc (FreeMemCount);
    Result := OldMemMgr.FreeMem (P);
    RemoveFromList (P);
  end;

  function NewReallocMem (P: Pointer; Size: Integer): Pointer;
  begin
    Inc (ReallocMemCount);
    Result := OldMemMgr.ReallocMem (P, Size);
    // remove older object
```

```
      RemoveFromList (P);
      // add new one
      AddToList (Result);
   end;
```

As in the previous examples, we allocate this memory manager in the unit's `initialization` section, and we destroy it in the `finalization` portion, which also contains code (which we've seen before) to test for objects that we haven't destroyed:

```
initialization
   GetMemoryManager(OldMemMgr);
   SetMemoryManager(NewMemMgr);

finalization
   SetMemoryManager(OldMemMgr);
   if (GetMemCount - FreeMemCount) <> 0 then
      MessageBox (0, pChar ('Objects left: ' +
         IntToStr (GetMemCount - FreeMemCount)),
         'MemManager', mb_ok);
   end.
```

Now that we've built the list of objects, we also want to track them, listing all the blocks in memory at a given moment. To do this, we've added a new function to the DdhmMan unit, SnapToFile, which generates a snapshot of the memory manager's pointer list and stores that snapshot in a plain text file. The reason we've used a text file is that once again, this technique has the least impact on memory (compared to using a string list or a stream).

Here's the first draft of the SnapToFile procedure:

```
procedure SnapToFile (Filename: string);
var
   OutFile: TextFile;
   I, CurrFree: Integer;
begin
   AssignFile (OutFile, Filename);
   try
      Rewrite (OutFile);
      CurrFree := FreeInList;
      write (OutFile, 'Memory objects: ');
      writeln (OutFile, CurrFree - 1);
      for I := 1 to CurrFree - 1 do
```

```
    begin
      write (OutFile, I);
      write (OutFile, ') ');
      write (OutFile, IntToHex (
        Cardinal (ObjList [I]), 16));
      writeln (OutFile);
    end;
  finally
    CloseFile (OutFile);
  end;
end;
```

The output for every memory object occupies one line, and consists of the item's index in the memory manager list and the object's memory address. While this is useful, it's certainly not enough information to visualize the status of the application's memory.

A better approach is to determine whether the memory object is actually a Delphi class object. Here's our second version of the internal for loop:

```
var
  Item: TObject;

for I := 1 to CurrFree - 1 do
begin
  write (OutFile, I);
  write (OutFile, ') ');
  write (OutFile, IntToHex (
    Cardinal (ObjList [I]), 16));
  write (OutFile, ' - ');
  try
    Item := TObject(ObjList [I]);
    write (OutFile, Item.ClassName);
    write (OutFile, ' (');
    write (OutFile, IntToStr (Item.InstanceSize));
    write (OutFile, ' bytes)'); }
  except
    on Exception do
      write (OutFile, 'Not an object');
  end;
  writeln (OutFile);
end;
```

The idea behind this code is that when we try to access an object's fields, we expect an exception, which confirms that it isn't an object. Unfortunately, Delphi sometimes produces output with nonsense characters in the name field and a totally random value for the object size. You can see an example of this invalid output in Figure 9.6.

FIGURE 9.6:

The log file produced by the second version of the SnapToFile procedure of the new memory manager lists the objects in memory, but also has some errors.

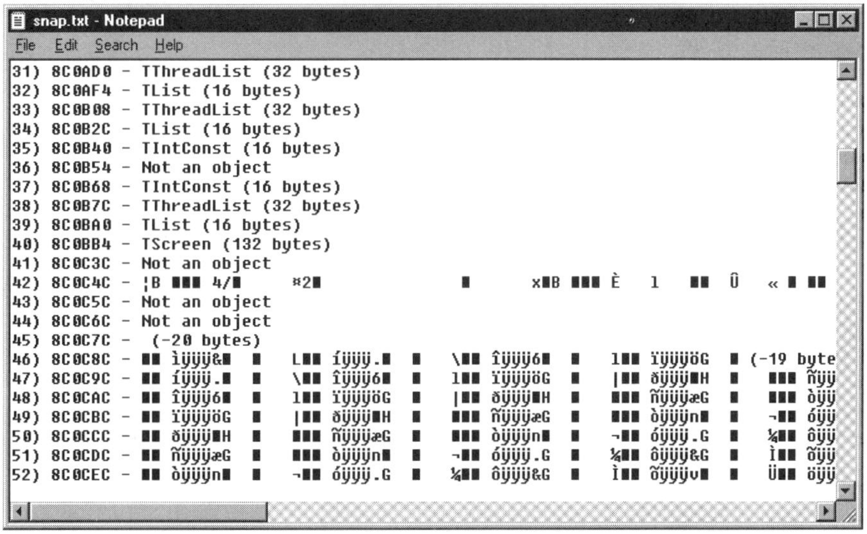

Even adding a test such as

```
if Item is TObject then...
```

doesn't really help. However, after further exploration (including some trial-and-error) we've found an approach that seems reliable. There's no guarantee this approach will work in every circumstance; but even when it raises an exception, that's useful information, because we know that Item isn't an object.

The new version of the code extracts the same information (class name and size) by using the RTTI support available from the TypInfo unit, discussed in Chapter 4. Actually, the final version of the SnapToFile procedure does even more; it displays the name of the component, if any, by searching for the corresponding property, and then displays the name of the unit that defines the class.

Here's the complete source code for this function, a rather long listing, but one that's worth reading (provided you remember the type information and type data from Chapter 4). You'll notice that in this version we've also added information about the local heap provided by the GetHeapStatus function, which you can see in Figure 9.7:

FIGURE 9.7:

The initial portion of the output of the SnapToFile procedure logs the information returned by the GetHeapStatus VCL function.

```
procedure SnapToFile (Filename: string);
var
  OutFile: TextFile;
  I, CurrFree: Integer;
  HeapStatus: THeapStatus;
  Item: TObject;
  ptd: PTypeData;
  ppi: PPropInfo;
begin
  AssignFile (OutFile, Filename);
  try
    Rewrite (OutFile);
    CurrFree := FreeInList;
    // local heap status
    HeapStatus := GetHeapStatus;
    with HeapStatus do
    begin
```

```
      write (OutFile, 'Available address space: ');
      write (OutFile, TotalAddrSpace div 1024);
      writeln (OutFile, ' Kbytes');
      write (OutFile, 'Uncommitted portion: ');
      write (OutFile, TotalUncommitted div 1024);
      writeln (OutFile, ' Kbytes');
      write (OutFile, 'Committed portion: ');
      write (OutFile, TotalCommitted div 1024);
      writeln (OutFile, ' Kbytes');
      write (OutFile, 'Free portion: ');
      write (OutFile, TotalFree div 1024);
      writeln (OutFile, ' Kbytes');
      write (OutFile, 'Allocated portion: ');
      write (OutFile, TotalAllocated div 1024);
      writeln (OutFile, ' Kbytes');
      write (OutFile, 'Address space load: ');
      write (OutFile, TotalAllocated div
        (TotalAddrSpace div 100));
      writeln (OutFile, '%');
      write (OutFile, 'Total small free blocks: ');
      write (OutFile, FreeSmall div 1024);
      writeln (OutFile, ' Kbytes');
      write (OutFile, 'Total big free blocks: ');
      write (OutFile, FreeBig div 1024);
      writeln (OutFile, ' Kbytes');
      write (OutFile, 'Other unused blocks: ');
      write (OutFile, Unused div 1024);
      writeln (OutFile, ' Kbytes');
      write (OutFile, 'Total overhead: ');
      write (OutFile, Overhead div 1024);
      writeln (OutFile, ' Kbytes');
    end;

    // custom memory manager information
    writeln (OutFile); // free line
    write (OutFile, 'Memory objects: ');
    writeln (OutFile, CurrFree - 1);
    for I := 1 to CurrFree - 1 do
    begin
      write (OutFile, I);
      write (OutFile, ') ');
      write (OutFile, IntToHex (
```

```
            Cardinal (ObjList [I]), 16));
        write (OutFile, ' - ');
        try
          Item := TObject(ObjList [I]);
          // type info technique
          if PTypeInfo (Item.ClassInfo).Kind <> tkClass then
            write (OutFile, 'Not an object')
          else
          begin
            ptd := GetTypeData (PTypeInfo (Item.ClassInfo));
            // name, if a component
            ppi := GetPropInfo (
              PTypeInfo (Item.ClassInfo), 'Name');
            if ppi <> nil then
            begin
              write (OutFile, GetStrProp (Item, ppi));
              write (OutFile, ' : ');
            end
            else
              write (OutFile, '(unnamed): ');
            write (OutFile, PTypeInfo (Item.ClassInfo).Name);
            write (OutFile, ' (');
            write (OutFile, ptd.ClassType.InstanceSize);
            write (OutFile, ' bytes)  - In ');
            write (OutFile, ptd.UnitName);
            write (OutFile, '.dcu');
          end
        except
          on Exception do
            write (OutFile, 'Not an object');
        end;
        writeln (OutFile);
      end;
    finally
      CloseFile (OutFile);
    end;
  end;
```

WARNING There is a minor drawback to the code above. When we access the Name property, we might find the name of the component (which is what we're looking for) or the Name of a TFont object used by the component. This unfortunate coincidence in the property names makes the program output look a little strange, as you can see in Figure 9.8. Fortunately, this won't be difficult to fix by writing explicit code to handle objects of the TFont type.

This procedure produces a file with a snapshot of the memory status, including a list of the objects in memory. In the DelMem3 example, we call this procedure when the user clicks a new button on the main form, called *Snap*, which executes the following code:

```
procedure TForm1.BtnSnapClick(Sender: TObject);
begin
  if SaveDialog1.Execute then
  begin
    SnapToFile (SaveDialog1.Filename);
    FormSnap.Memo1.Lines.LoadFromFile (
      SaveDialog1.Filename);
    FormSnap.Show;
  end;
end;
```

When you click this button, the program prompts for a filename for the memory report (although you can usually accept the default filename):

```
object SaveDialog1: TSaveDialog
  DefaultExt = '.txt'
  FileName = 'snap.txt'
  Filter = 'text file (*.txt)|*.txt'
end
```

When the BtnSnapClick method creates the file by calling SnapToFile, it loads the text file into a memo component aligned with the client area of a secondary form, and then displays the form. You can see the effect of this code in Figure 9.8.

FIGURE 9.8:

The DelMem3 example uses a new memory manager to produce a detailed listing of the objects currently in memory, and shows it in a form.

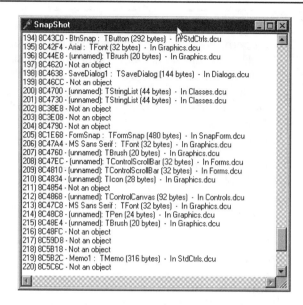

Passing Data between Programs

Both Windows 95 and Windows NT provide each running application with its own virtual address space. This means that two applications cannot interfere with each other by modifying data or code in another's address space, which is good. However, it also means that the two applications cannot easily exchange data, which is not always good. Obviously, this is a dramatic change from 16-bit Windows, where all applications shared memory.

In Win32, there are specific techniques you can use to pass data between programs. You can find discussions of the high-level techniques, such as the use of the Clipboard, Dynamic Data Exchange (DDE), and OLE Automation, in *Mastering Delphi 3*. This book's Chapter 11 shows how to provide file dragging support, and also provides a more in-depth discussion of OLE Automation.

In the remainder of this chapter, we'll focus on low-level techniques, such as the use of the wm_CopyData windows message and memory-mapped files.

Sending Data to an Application

In 32-bit Windows, you can't send the address of a memory block from one application to another, simply because an address in one virtual address space has no meaning in the context of a different address space. To confirm this, we've written a pair of programs, CopyData and GetData, that implement this failed technique. After trying their initial versions, we'll revise them to use the official Win32 technique for exchanging this information.

The CopyData program contains a button that executes the following code:

```
procedure TForm1.Button1Click(Sender: TObject);
var
  Hwnd: THandle;
begin
  // get the handle of the target window
  Hwnd := FindWindow ('TFormGetData', 'GetData');
  if Hwnd <> 0 then
    // send the plain string
    SendMessage (Hwnd, WM_USER, 0,
      Integer (PChar (Caption)))
  else
    // target not found
    ShowMessage ('GetData window not found.');
end;
```

In the SendMessage call, we simply pass the memory address of a character pointer, a PChar. In the receiving program, we've written the following code to receive the message:

```
type
  TFormGetData = class(TForm)
    ...
  public
    procedure UserData (var Msg: TMessage);
      message wm_User;
  end;

procedure TFormGetData.UserData (var Msg: TMessage);
begin
  Edit1.Text := 'Address: ' + IntToHex (Msg.LParam, 16);
  // usually creates a GpFault!!!
  Edit2.Text := 'String: ' + string (PChar (Msg.LParam));
end;
```

This message handler receives the message, displays the address it received in an edit box, and then extracts the string from that address. Well, actually it *tries* to extract the string, and it fails miserably! As you can see in Figure 9.9, the error message indicates that the problem occurred at the memory address shown in the first edit box. This demonstrates that you really can't pass an address between two Win32 applications.

WARNING On some computers, instead of a memory violation, the erroneous program simply returns an odd-looking string, or an empty string. Running one of the two programs in Delphi's debugger (that is, executing it from Delphi) seems to increase the chance of getting the error message.

FIGURE 9.9:

When you click the *Send String* button of the CopyData program, the GetData program generates an memory error, because the pointer passed as a parameter is meaningless in a different memory address space.

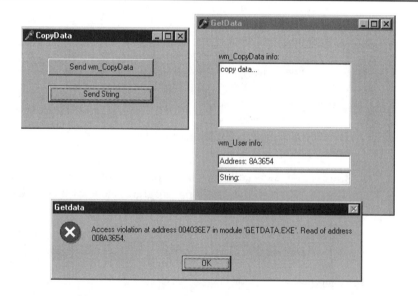

There's a simple solution to this problem. Instead of using a custom message you can use the special wm_CopyData Windows message, which passes the data after performing some special processing behind the scenes. This message requires you to pass the handle of the window that is sending the message, and a pointer to a TCopyDataStruct data structure. This structure has three fields: dwData, which is an extra 32-bit parameter; cbData, which indicates the size of the buffer; and lpData, which is a pointer to the buffer we're passing.

The CopyData program uses this technique to pass some information to the GetData destination application:

```
procedure TForm1.BtnSendCopyDataClick(Sender: TObject);
var
  Cds: TCopyDataStruct;
  Hwnd: THandle;
begin
  // small data (32 bits): top of form
  Cds.dwData := Top;
  // size of data
  Cds.cbData := Length (Caption) + 1;
  // allocate memory for the large block and fill it
  GetMem (Cds.lpData, Cds.cbData );
  StrCopy (Cds.lpData, PChar (Caption));
  // get the handle of the target window
  Hwnd := FindWindow ('TFormGetData', 'GetData');
  if Hwnd <> 0 then
  begin
    // send the message
    if SendMessage (
        Hwnd, WM_COPYDATA, Handle, Cardinal(@Cds)) = 1 then
      // received
      Beep;
  end
  else
    // target not found
    ShowMessage ('GetData window not found.');
  FreeMem (Cds.lpData);
end;
```

As you can see, the BtnSendCopyDataClick method allocates and frees the memory to be passed to the other program, although that is not strictly necessary. It also uses the return value of the message to determine whether the data reached its destination and was properly processed.

On the receiving end, the GetData application receives the wm_CopyData message via a custom message handler. Here's the method:

```
// in TFormGetData
public
  procedure GetCopyData (var Msg: TWmCopyData);
    message wm_CopyData;
```

```
procedure TFormGetData.GetCopyData (var Msg: TWmCopyData);
var
  FromTitle: string;
begin
  Memo1.Clear;
  SetLength (FromTitle, 100);
  GetWindowText (Msg.From, PChar(FromTitle), 100);
  FromTitle := pChar (FromTitle);
  Memo1.Lines.Add ('Message from: ' + FromTitle);
  with Memo1.Lines, Msg.CopyDataStruct^ do
  begin
    Add ('Small data: ' + IntToStr (dwData));
    Add ('Large block size: ' + IntToStr (cbData));
    Add ('String: ' + PChar (lpData));
  end;
  // received (true)
  Msg.Result := 1;
end;
```

The program can easily and directly access all the information from the sender application, producing the output shown in Figure 9.10 (which is far better than the results in Figure 9.9, where we saw a memory access error).

FIGURE 9.10:

The CopyData program can pass any kind of information to the GetData example using the wm_CopyData Win32 message.

By the way, you'll notice that the receiving application should consider the data read-only. It cannot change the string in the sending application's address space, and if it wants to send some data back to the other application, it must do so using another wm_CopyData message. On the positive side, exchanging custom wm_CopyData messages is probably the simplest way two Win32 applications can interact, considering that all the other mechanisms (the Clipboard, DDE, and OLE) are much more complex to set up.

Memory-Mapped Files

An alternative way to share data between Win32 applications is to use memory-mapped files. When Windows 95 and Windows NT load a file into memory (either a data file or an executable), they use a specific global memory area, and then map the application's virtual memory addresses to positions inside this file. In fact, the operating system doesn't load the complete file into memory. It loads only portions of the file, on request. This way the operating system can keep files in memory for fast access, but doesn't need to load them completely.

The important detail that makes this work is that all processes share a global area for memory-mapped files. This is why when two processes load the same module (an application or DLL file), they can actually share its executable code in memory. We can take advantage of this fact by sharing this memory area between processes, without creating a physical file.

You can call the CreateFileMapping API function with a special first parameter to indicate that it should share memory and not a file. The other parameters for this function are somewhat complex to use, but for most of them you can use default values. After you create a mapped file, you can access its memory using a call to another API function, MapViewOfFile. This function returns an application-specific pointer (a pointer that's valid within the address space of that application) to the shared memory block.

Here's the code that our MMapFile example uses to call these two API functions:

```
private
  hMapFile: THandle;
  MapFilePointer: Pointer;

procedure TForm1.FormCreate(Sender: TObject);
begin
  hMapFile := CreateFileMapping (
    $FFFFFFFF, // file handle ... or memory
    nil, // security
    Page_ReadWrite, // access rights
    0, // high memory size
```

```
    10000, // low memory size
    'DdhDemoMappedFile'); // mapped file name
  if hMapFile <> 0 then
    MapFilePointer := MapViewOfFile (
      hMapFile, // handle returned above
      File_Map_All_Access, // access rights
      0, 0, 0) // access the entire mapped file
  else
    ShowMessage ('hMapFile = 0');
  if MapFilePointer = nil then
    ShowMessage ('MapFilePointer = nil');
end;
```

NOTE

The CreateFileMapping function accepts two parameters that indicate the size of the data structure, dwMaximumSizeHigh and dwMaximumSize-Low, instead of a single size parameter. This is necessary because Windows NT files can exceed the 4 GB you can address with a 32-bit value, and reach an astonishing value that's difficult to represent: 16 followed by 18 zeros (that is, 16 billions of billions). Of course, you cannot use the high value of the size if you don't map a physical file.

By creating a *named* memory-mapped file, we allow other programs to share this memory area. All they have to know is the name of the memory-mapped file. To free the appropriate system resources, each program should also free the mapped file when it's through with it:

```
procedure TForm1.FormDestroy(Sender: TObject);
begin
  UnMapViewOfFile (MapFilePointer);
  CloseHandle (hMapFile);
end;
```

Now, instead of creating two different applications and sharing memory between them, we can create two instances of the same application. The effect is exactly the same, because two copies of the same application have different memory address spaces.

The MMapFile application contains two buttons and two edit boxes. The first button copies the text from its edit box to the memory-mapped file, while the second button fetches the data from the memory-mapped file and copies it to the second edit box:

```
procedure TForm1.BtnWriteClick(Sender: TObject);
begin
  StrCopy (PChar (MapFilePointer),
    PChar (EditWrite.Text));
end;

procedure TForm1.BtnReadClick (Sender: TObject);
var
  s: string;
begin
  s := PChar (MapFilePointer);
  EditRead.Text := s;
end;
```

Instead of just running a second copy of this program, it is interesting to run two or three more. Any instance of the program can copy the data to the shared memory region, and the other instances of the program can retrieve that data, as shown in Figure 9.11.

FIGURE 9.11:

The two instances of the MMapFile example share a memory area, and pass information using it. The text of the first edit box in the upper window has been copied into the second edit box in the lower window.

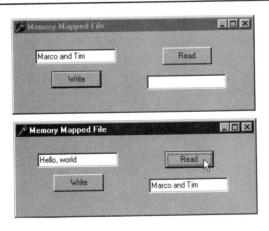

This example works, but you might encounter two problems: synchronizing data access and alerting other instances of changes to the data. You can easily solve the first problem by using one of the many synchronization techniques provided by the Win32 API and wrapped by the SyncObjs VCL unit (available only in the Client/Server Suite version of Delphi).

You can solve the second problem, alerting other instances of data changes, by using a traditional Windows technique: posting a message. Unlike the earlier example, where we tried to pass a data pointer between processes, in this case we'll post an empty message; we'll deliver the data via the memory-mapped file. You can even use that mapped file to store the handles of the windows that you need to notify of the updates.

A Memory-Mapped Graph

To create a more interesting and *almost* practical example, we've built a program that uses a large memory-mapped file to store 100 integer values, logically arranged in a 10×10 grid. We access the memory locations inside the memory-mapped file directly via a pointer, performing the appropriate pointer arithmetic after converting it to a PChar. (In fact, this example is actually more an exercise in pointers than it is in using memory-mapped files.)

The MemGraph example creates a memory-mapped file, using all the parameters for the CreateFileMapping function we used in the last example except the name:

```
procedure TForm1.FormCreate(Sender: TObject);
var
  Address: Pointer;
  X, Y, Total: Integer;
begin
  hMapFile := CreateFileMapping ($FFFFFFFF, nil,
    Page_ReadWrite, 0, 10000, 'DdhMappedFileGraph');
  if hMapFile <> 0 then
    MapFilePointer := MapViewOfFile (hMapFile,
      File_Map_All_Access, 0, 0, 0)
  else
    ShowMessage ('hMapFile = 0');
```

In addition to the 400 bytes of data, the applications that share this memory-mapped file will store their own handles at startup. They'll store this information in the first empty spot of the memory area, after checking to see if other windows have already added their handles there:

```
// FormCreate continued
if MapFilePointer = nil then
```

```
      ShowMessage ('MapFilePointer = nil')
    else
    begin
      // add window to area
      Address := pChar (MapFilePointer) + 400;
      while PInteger (Address)^ <> 0 do
        Address := pChar (Address) + 4;
      PInteger (Address)^ := Handle;
    end;
```

Finally, the FormCreate method initializes a graph with the values from the memory-mapped file. Every column of the graph represents the sum of ten consecutive values:

```
// FormCreate continued
// start up chart
Chart1.Series [0].Clear;
for X := 0 to 9 do
begin
  Total := 0;
  for Y := 0 to 9 do
  begin
    Address := pChar (MapFilePointer) + (X + Y * 10) * 4;
    Inc (Total, PInteger (Address)^);
  end;
  Chart1.Series [0].AddY (
    Total, IntToStr (X+1), clRed);
end;
end;
```

A timer method determines how often we update the data in memory, and in this event handler we increase a random element by a random value:

```
procedure TForm1.Timer1Timer(Sender: TObject);
var
  X, Y: Integer;
  Address: Pointer;
begin
  X := Random (10);
  Y := Random (10);
  Address := pChar (MapFilePointer) + (X + Y * 10) * 4;
  PInteger (Address)^ := PInteger (Address)^ + Random (10);
  Address := pChar (MapFilePointer) + 400;
```

```
  while PInteger (Address)^ <> 0 do
  begin
    PostMessage (PInteger (Address)^, wm_user, 0, 0);
    Address := pChar (Address) + 4;
  end;
end;
```

At the end of this method, the timer scans the upper memory area of the block, and sends the wm_user message to all the window handles it finds. If a window has already been destroyed, there's no problem; if you post a message to a non-existent window, the system will simply throw it away. When the application receives this wm_user message from one of the other instances, it updates the graph:

```
procedure TForm1.WmUser (var Msg: TMessage);
var
  X, Y, Total: Integer;
  Address: Pointer;
begin
  // copy all the data to the graph
  for X := 0 to 9 do
  begin
    Total := 0;
    for Y := 0 to 9 do
    begin
      Address := pChar (MapFilePointer) + (X + Y * 10) * 4;
      Inc (Total, PInteger (Address)^);
    end;
    Chart1.Series [0].YValue [X] := Total;
  end;
end;
```

Not only can you run a copy of this program and see the graph change, you can also start multiple copies of it. Of course, this doesn't make much sense, since you'll see many copies of the same graph.

For this reason, we've written another version of the program, which writes data to the same memory-mapped file, but doesn't read it. Appropriately, we call this program MapWrite. Its form hosts a TrackBar component, which you can use to select the graph column you wish to increase. However, if you run multiple copies of this program, they'll race against each other to update the graph columns, as you can see in Figure 9.12.

FIGURE 9.12:

The output of this only instance of the MapGraph example is updated by the various instances of the MapWrite program in action (visible in the background).

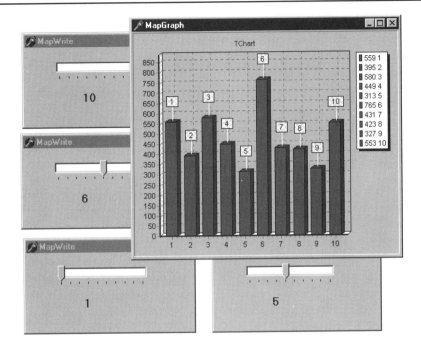

For this program, the FormCreate method creates the memory-mapped file (using the same name) and then simply places the track bar in a random position:

```
procedure TForm1.FormCreate(Sender: TObject);
begin
  hMapFile := CreateFileMapping ($FFFFFFFF, nil,
    Page_ReadWrite, 0, 10000, 'DdhMappedFileGraph');
  if hMapFile <> 0 then
    MapFilePointer := MapViewOfFile (hMapFile,
      File_Map_All_Access, 0, 0, 0)
  else
    ShowMessage ('hMapFile = 0');
  if MapFilePointer = nil then
    ShowMessage ('MapFilePointer = nil');
  // not a listener of messages...
  TrackBar1.Position := 1 + Random (10);
  Label1.Caption := IntToStr (TrackBar1.Position)
end;
```

When the timer event fires, the program uses the fixed X value and a random Y value to update the data in the memory-mapped file, and then posts the update message to the other instances of the application:

```
procedure TForm1.Timer1Timer(Sender: TObject);
var
  X, Y: Integer;
  Address: Pointer;
begin
  X := TrackBar1.Position;
  Y := Random (10);
  Address := pChar (MapFilePointer) + (X + Y * 10) * 4;
  PInteger (Address)^ := PInteger (Address)^ + Random (10);
  Address := pChar (MapFilePointer) + 400;
  while PInteger (Address)^ <> 0 do
  begin
    PostMessage (PInteger (Address)^, wm_user, 0, 0);
    Address := pChar (Address) + 4;
  end;
end;
```

Finally, we've developed a "listener-only" program. The MapGrid example displays the memory-mapped file data in a string grid:

```
procedure TForm1.WmUser (var Msg: TMessage);
var
  X, Y: Integer;
  Address: Pointer;
begin
  // update the grid
  for X := 0 to 9 do
    for Y := 0 to 9 do
    begin
      Address := pChar (MapFilePointer)
        + (X + Y * 10) * 4;
      StringGrid1.Cells [X, Y] :=
        IntToStr (PInteger (Address)^);
    end;
end;
```

This program doesn't use a timer to update the data automatically. Instead, you can click on a cell to refresh its value:

```
procedure TForm1.StringGrid1SelectCell(Sender: TObject;
  Col, Row: Integer; var CanSelect: Boolean);
```

```
var
  Address: Pointer;
begin
  // reset the cell to 0
  Address := pChar (MapFilePointer) + (Col + Row * 10) * 4;
  PInteger (Address)^ := 0;
  // notify all listeners
  Address := pChar (MapFilePointer) + 400;
  while PInteger (Address)^ <> 0 do
  begin
    PostMessage (PInteger (Address)^, wm_User, 0, 0);
    Address := pChar (Address) + 4;
  end;
end;
```

Now you can launch multiple copies of each of the three different applications that share the same memory-mapped file, and see the effect of their continuous interaction. You can see an example of this situation in Figure 9.13, but you should really run these three programs to see their behavior and speed.

FIGURE 9.13:

The MapGrid example shares the same memory-mapped file with the MapWrite and MapGraph applications, and you can run multiple instances of each of them.

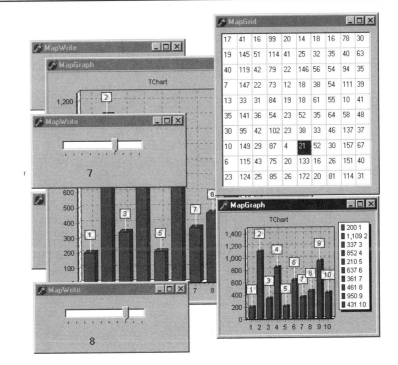

What's Next

In this chapter, we've focused on another fundamental element of Windows programming: memory. We covered some of the theory, but we also built programs that track global memory, track the local heap of each application, and even one that displays a list of the objects allocated by a Delphi program.

In the final section we explored some techniques you can use to share data between Win32 applications. However, even these techniques fall short at times. If you want to write applications that fully interact with other programs and also with the operating system (beyond just sharing a block of memory), you must enter a different world: OLE and COM programming. That is the focus of the next two chapters, the last ones we'll devote to Windows programming issues.

CHAPTER

TEN

10

Delphi and COM

■ Component Software, Delphi, and COM

■ Programming Problems and COM Solutions: Code
Reusability, Language Independence, Implementation
Location, Memory Allocation, Object Lifetime Manage-
ment, Object Orientation, Object Versioning, Location
Transparency, and Location Transparency

■ COM Programming Problems and Delphi Solutions:
Reference Counting, Exception Handling, Class Factory
Implementation, Registration, Type Information Inte-
gration, and Dual Interface Support

The Component Object Model (COM) is one of the most important operating-system developments to emerge from Microsoft. COM is partly a specification for building applications, and partly an implementation in the form of a standard API. Once you've learned COM, your applications will be poised to take advantage of both a well-thought-out component-based software architecture, and *every significant new operating system extension that is being created by Microsoft.*

Many elements of the Windows operating system are now being implemented using COM. For example, the Windows 95 and Windows NT 4.0 shell, the Messaging API or MAPI, the OLE DB database libraries, the DirectX multimedia and gaming extensions, and the ActiveX Internet extensions are each implemented as sets of COM components. In short, you cannot continue to ignore COM. If you do, you'll risk losing touch with the operating system that you're developing applications for: Windows.

This chapter will take a two-pronged approach to introducing COM. The first major section will take you on a tour of programming problems that COM addresses, and show how it provides solutions to these problems. You should read this section from beginning to end, as it will gradually introduce COM concepts within the context of solutions to different programming problems. The second major section will show how Delphi solves a number of COM programming problems. It will introduce Delphi features within the context of solutions to different problems posed by programming in COM. By the end of this chapter, you will understand why the best tool on the market for creating COM applications is Delphi.

NOTE   This chapter and the next were contributed to *Delphi Developer's Handbook* by COM expert John Lam. Although we've made a few changes for stylistic consistency with other chapters and tried to point out where issues Dr. Lam touches upon are addressed elsewhere in the book, these two chapters are essentially an independent discussion of this complex and exciting topic. As noted above, this chapter outlines the problems COM was developed to solve, the mechanisms by which it solves them, and the Delphi tools for implementing COM. Then you'll be ready for Chapter 11's examples of COM components created in Delphi. As you'll see, creating COM components is so easy in Delphi that you would not think there was anything to COM if we showed you how to create them from the outset!

Component Software, Delphi, and COM

This section talks about how COM and Delphi work together to help you create software components. We'll take a look at some of the problems that are solved by software components, contrast the COM and Delphi VCL approaches to these problems, and hopefully clear up some general misconceptions regarding the terminology associated with COM. Experienced COM programmers may want to skip over this section and proceed to the "Programming Problems and COM Solutions" section.

The Holy Grail: Universal Software Components

In this chapter, we will take a close look at the Holy Grail of software development: the creation of universal software components.

What is a universal software component? Ideally, it would allow software developers to create applications by assembling these components using any programming language. The component itself should appear to be a "black box" to its user: just plug and play. Developers could then rapidly assemble software applications from prefabricated building blocks, which in theory would reduce the overall cost of software applications.

The "black box" quality of a universal software component has several aspects:

1. The application developer should not care what programming language was used to create the component, and the component developer should not care what programming language will be using it.

2. The component should be readily reusable, either as a stand-alone component or within composites built from several other components.

3. The component should plug right in and appear to be part of the host operating system.

4. The component should be able to evolve in step with any client code that uses a different version of it and not break that code.

5. The user of these components should not have to write different code to access components that execute in different places.

Sound like a tall order? It is. Many other attempts have been made in the past to create a usable component software architecture. The problems, however, are not merely architectural. It matters little that the *best* technology wins; it is far more important that a usable component software architecture be widely adopted. Thus, it stands to reason that the component software architecture that has the greatest chance of achieving commercial success is the one that is tied to the most popular operating system. In this chapter, we'll look in depth at the component software architecture at the heart of Microsoft Windows: the Component Object Model, or simply, COM.

Delphi Components and the VCL

"But wait," you say, "I'm a *Delphi* developer. Why should I care about COM for component-based software development when I have the VCL?" This is a very good point. COM does not compete with the VCL. If you believe that only Delphi developers will use your software component, then continue to build it as a VCL component. If you want to extend your software component's reach beyond Delphi, then it is time to consider using COM.

Here's another point to consider: Delphi, like any other tool, has its strengths and weaknesses. What if somebody comes along tomorrow with a new software development tool that is as revolutionary compared to Delphi as Delphi was to the tools that preceded it? Then you'd be faced with a very difficult decision: Do you make the jump to the new tool, but face having to port all of your existing code? Or do you continue to program in Delphi and stare enviously at the other side of the fence where the grass is oh-so-green?

If you have built your software components using COM and Delphi, then your code is already portable. You simply switch to the new tool (which more than likely is COM-compliant), and all of your Delphi code moves along with you! If you have built an extensive library of graphical VCL components, Delphi 3's new ActiveX control feature will allow you to convert your VCL components automatically into ActiveX controls (which are really just fancy COM components). Your existing code investment is now safe.

COM Components and ActiveX

Just so there isn't any confusion regarding what the terms *COM*, *OLE*, and *ActiveX* really mean, let's briefly go over the somewhat elusive distinctions between these terms.

COM serves as the foundation of both the OLE and ActiveX technologies. Less glamorous than its better-known cousins, it acts as the plumbing that makes OLE and ActiveX possible. This is a very important point: All of the OLE and ActiveX services are built using the infrastructure provided by COM. By understanding COM, you'll have a far better understanding of what makes OLE and ActiveX possible.

> **NOTE**
>
> For better or worse, there's a new term to contend with: *DCOM,* for *Distributed COM*. Chapter 19 examines DCOM in the context of Delphi database programming and the three-tier database model; but the point to keep in mind here is that it is just another form of COM—nothing has changed with respect to COM itself. There are just more issues to worry about (like security and threading).

The term *OLE* used to mean "Object Linking and Embedding," but has been misused to describe virtually all things built using COM. More recently, however, Microsoft has been using the term to describe just what it originally did: the technology that makes compound documents possible (for example, in-place editing of an Access database within a Word document).

The term *ActiveX* is used to describe the technologies that relate to software components used in Internet applications. ActiveX controls are the most widely encountered variant of these software components. There are also other technologies under the ActiveX banner that warrant closer attention: ActiveX Data Objects (ADO) and ActiveX Document Object technologies are quickly emerging as the software components that will help advance the cause of a browser-based operating system.

Programming Problems and COM Solutions

This section introduces COM programming in terms of the problems that COM was developed to solve. These are perennial programming issues that you most likely have already faced at some point. For each of these problems, you'll see how COM provides a solution. Within each of these topics, you'll learn only a little about COM; but as we proceed, the complete picture will emerge. We'll defer most of the details about implementing COM components and clients until the second half of the chapter, which discusses how Delphi solves COM programming problems.

Code Reusability

Recycling code is an age-old problem in programming. Since programmers are fundamentally lazy creatures, we would like to be able to reuse as much code from previous projects as possible. To this end, a number of features have evolved in operating systems and programming languages to help make reusing code easier and more reliable for developers.

Windows supports extremely efficient code reuse in the form of dynamic link libraries. The code within a DLL is available to any Win32 process that links to it. By maintaining a reference count on all DLLs, Windows ensures that only one copy of a DLL is present in physical memory at any time. In other words, physical memory is committed only when a DLL is referenced for the first time. All subsequent references to that DLL, from the current Win32 process or others, result only in the DLL's reference count being incremented. Through the magic of page table mapping, Windows can make those physical memory code pages appear within the logical address space of any number of Win32 processes, thereby conserving physical memory.

Code reusability within DLLs was a great boon for developers using traditional programming languages such as C or Pascal. While they did introduce their own set of problems, DLLs allowed these developers to create stand-alone libraries of code that could be shared among many applications or among different versions of a single application.

Within a DLL, a developer could make functions available to client applications by exporting those functions by name or ordinal number. Those functions would be exported using a standard calling convention (stdcall in Win32) that would be known to users of that DLL. To make those functions available to other software developers, all the library developer had to do was make the header files (or Delphi units with the proper corresponding declarations) available. The benefits of this approach are obvious. A single DLL can service many clients, thereby conserving memory and creating a natural point of control for all of those clients.

For example, the Win32 API is implemented entirely as a set of DLL-based exported functions. Thus, as Microsoft continues to upgrade particular components of the operating system (ComCtl32.DLL is a great example of this), those new operating-system features are immediately available to all Windows applications. To make the Win32 API accessible to application developers, Microsoft ships the Win32 SDK, which is just a collection of documentation and header files that allow software developers to make use of the functions contained within the Windows system DLLs.

TIP　　To learn more about writing and using DLLs in Delphi you can read Chapter 20 of *Mastering Delphi 3*. Chapter 21 of that book shows how you can export the methods of a class from a Delphi DLL in a custom way (so that only a Delphi program can use them), and how to turn that DLL into a fully COM-compliant library, so that any other program can use them.

While Windows makes it easy to share code contained within DLLs, we cannot share code that resides inside executable files. Calling code inside another Win32 process from within your application is not possible without resorting to methods such as using Windows messages to trigger code inside the other Win32 process. As we will see, COM provides an elegant solution to this problem.

Not wanting to be left out, the compiler writers began adding code-reuse features to their programming languages. One of the reasons object-oriented programming (OOP) was created was to address the need for better support for code reuse from within programming languages. While reusing code within an application written using a single programming language became markedly easier, creating reusable components of code that could be shared using the Windows DLL mechanism became much more difficult.

To understand why the new OOP features make code sharing more difficult, we have to take a closer look at OOP itself. At the heart of OOP is the notion of class. Classes are the primary vehicle for encapsulation, and class inheritance is the primary means for code reuse.

Within each class is a private scope or, to use a modern term, a private *namespace*. In other words, two classes can have identically named functions. To resolve the potential name collision problem, the linker must generate unique names for all member functions of all classes. Unfortunately, the lack of a standard algorithm for generating these unique names creates a problem when we try to share classes from a DLL. If we can solve this name-generation problem, we go a long way toward solving the code reuse problem.

Name Mangling

To make OOP possible in the Windows world, compiler developers had to create unique names for each member function of a class, using a process called, appropriately, "name mangling." These mangled names contain all of the information required to uniquely identify a class's member function within the DLL's class namespace, in much the same way that a filename path uniquely identifies a file within your file system. Thus, for a member function Bar of some class called TFoo, the exported function name for Bar could be TFoo\Bar.

The problem with name mangling is that there is no universal standard. The name mangling conventions for C++ need to be different from those for Delphi because C++ supports the notion of function overloading.

In C++, there can be many functions with the same name that differ only by the function's parameter list. (Actually, name mangling was originally developed for C++ compilers as a way to support function overloading, that is, functions or methods with the same name but different types of parameters.) Thus, the C++ name-mangling algorithm must also include information about the parameter types. The incompatibilities do not end there, however. The different C++ compiler vendors have not agreed on a universal name-mangling convention, which means that a C++ class written by one vendor's compiler cannot be used by code generated by another vendor's compiler!

So how can COM solve the code reuse problem? It solves the problem in two ways. The first is by defining a standard way to represent code in memory, and the second is by defining a standard way to uniquely identify class member functions.

Using a standard way to represent code in memory means that a COM component can be accessed or created by any tool that can generate code compatible with COM's standard. This standard defines the binary layout of a COM component, and it does not tie COM to any particular programming language. It guarantees that a COM component can be accessed from any COM-compliant programming language. It also makes it possible to call a COM component from another Win32 process. This is how COM allows code to be shared from both DLLs and EXEs.

By also defining a *binary* standard for resolving names, as opposed to the DLL mechanism for resolving names, COM guarantees that a COM component can be called from any programming language. This standard also eliminates the possibility of name collisions, because the binary identifiers used in the name resolution process are guaranteed to be unique across all time and space. You no longer have to worry about coming up with unique names for your classes, which is a significant problem in a large multiple-programmer project.

As you'll see in the following sections, COM solves the code reusability problem by addressing related problems such as language independence, implementation location, memory allocation, and object-lifetime management.

Language Independence

Part of the code reusability problem is the requirement that COM components must be portable across many different programming languages. This may sound like a tall order, particularly when we consider that we have different *types* of programming languages. Among the many ways of classifying programming languages, the most relevant in the context of COM support is to group them into those that support the notion of pointers and explicit memory allocation, and those that don't.

Delphi and its Object Pascal language clearly fall into the first category, much like C and C++. As we will soon see, the ability to support pointers is an essential requirement for creating and manipulating COM components. In particular, the ability to create tables of pointers to member functions of a class is the key to making the creation of COM components simple and straightforward.

But what about programming languages that don't support the notion of pointers and explicit memory allocation? These languages are clearly a very important category, including such notables as Visual Basic, Java, and Visual Smalltalk. Are developers using these languages going to be left out in the cold? As it turns out, COM supports them, too!

The key to COM's language independence is that there is a standard mechanism for communicating with COM components: the COM *interface*. You communicate with a COM component using a COM interface, which is a grouping of related functions. This grouping is organized as a table of pointers to those functions, a data structure we can call a *function table* (similar to a *virtual method table*, or *VTable*). There is a separate function table for each COM interface. You call a COM interface member function by using its offset into that interface's function table.

The role of the function table can be made clearer using a simple example. Imagine that we have a simple COM interface called ISimple. It contains three member functions called One, Two, and Three. The function table would contain the 32-bit addresses for those functions, in the order in which they were declared. Therefore, if you wanted to call function One, you would call it by dereferencing the function pointer for the first entry in the function table. If you wanted to call function Two, you would call it by dereferencing the function pointer for the second entry in the function table. For function Three, … You get the point!

The presence of a function table implies a shared responsibility between the caller and the COM component. The COM component is responsible for creating and maintaining the function table, and the caller is responsible for calling a function using the correct offset into the function table. When the caller obtains a reference to the function table, it must know what kind of interface it is getting a reference to. The definition of that interface is what provides the caller with the function table mappings.

This shared responsibility is very similar to that imposed upon us by the Win32 API. Callers of Win32 API functions rely on the Win32 SDK headers to tell them the names of the functions, the DLLs those functions are located in, and the type(s) of parameters each function takes. Analogously, COM interface definitions tell the caller the names, the function table offsets, and the parameter types for each interface member function.

Now that you understand what the role of the function table is, you're probably wondering "how do I use one of these things?" A COM interface is simply a pointer to that interface's function table. So whether you're calling functions using the interface or passing it as a parameter, you're really just manipulating a pointer to that interface's function table.

To recap, a COM interface is simply a pointer to a function table. That function table is itself a table of pointers to functions. Calling a particular member function of a COM interface simply involves calling that function using the correct offset into the function table for that interface. Sounds great. But what about that second category of programming languages—those that don't support pointers and explicit memory allocation?

Programming languages such as Visual Basic or Java can also participate in the COM party. While programmers using those languages cannot explicitly allocate memory or manipulate pointers, the developers who created those programming languages certainly can and do. If the language developers understand how to manipulate COM interfaces in general, they can add support for COM to their programming languages, and they have done so.

What makes it easier for some of these developers to add COM support to their languages is a special COM interface called IDispatch. It allows a caller to refer to a function using its name rather than the function's offset in a function table. This process is known as *dynamic invocation*. It makes it particularly easy for interpreted languages to allow transparent access to a COM component's member functions. For example, you could envision code such as

```
SomeObject.ShowMessageDialog ('Hello World!');
```

It could be translated by the programming language into a call on function ShowMessageDialog, passing a reference to the 'Hello World' string.

If the dynamic invocation method is to be truly universal, it must also use a universal set of data types. This is necessary because different languages use different binary representations for their primitive data types. The binary layout of a Visual Basic string differs from the binary layout of a Delphi string, for example. What is needed is a standard set of data types that all of these programming languages can use as a reference. The data type used in COM's dynamic invocation mechanism is known as a *variant*.

The variant type is a 16-byte packet of data that can assume a number of different types. You can think of it as a Delphi variant record, or a C union. The definition below (extracted from the System unit) shows the different types a variant can assume:

```
type
  TVarData = record
    VType: Word;
    Reserved1, Reserved2, Reserved3: Word;
    case Integer of
      varSmallint: (VSmallint: Smallint);
      varInteger:  (VInteger: Integer);
      varSingle:   (VSingle: Single);
      varDouble:   (VDouble: Double);
      varCurrency: (VCurrency: Currency);
      varDate:     (VDate: Double);
      varOleStr:   (VOleStr: PWideChar);
      varDispatch: (VDispatch: Pointer);
      varError:    (VError: Integer);
      varBoolean:  (VBoolean: WordBool);
```

```
    varUnknown:    (VUnknown: Pointer);
    varByte:       (VByte: Byte);
    varString:     (VString: Pointer);
    varArray:      (VArray: PVarArray);
    varByRef:      (VPointer: Pointer);
end;
```

The variant type is also self-describing, so you can (and should) always ask a variant what type it is. Delphi includes special routines for the variant type, including VarType, which returns the type of a variant, and VarToStr, which returns a string representation of the variant (if any). On the companion CD you can find a sample program called Varia, which uses these and other variant type routines to display information about a variant variable, as you can see in Figure 10.1.

FIGURE 10.1:

The Varia example allows you to assign values of different types to a variant, and also to convert them back and forth.

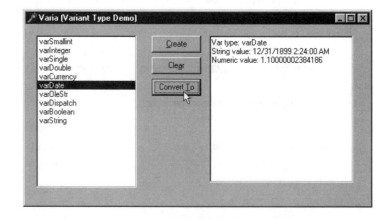

Besides assigning values of different types to the variant, the program allows you to convert the current variant to a different variant type, using the VarAsType routine. Of course, the conversion is not always successful, and might well lose significant digits; for example, try converting a date variant into an integer variant and then back to a date variant.

Variants also have the advantage of being a fixed size. Therefore, when variants are passed as parameters for dynamically invoked functions, they can be passed as simple arrays. However, there is a performance penalty that must be paid for converting data types to and from variants, and allocating the memory for the variant array from the global heap. Passing parameters on the call stack is far more efficient in both time and space.

The technology that allows you to call a COM component's member function by name was important enough to warrant its own name. It is known as *Automation* (formerly *OLE Automation*). Automation was created primarily as a means for Visual Basic to manipulate and talk to COM components. As a published specification, it now means that most programming languages today have the ability to talk to COM components.

NOTE   You'll see examples of Automation in the next chapter.

To summarize this section, you have now seen that COM uses the notion of interfaces to allow developers working in different programming languages to access the same COM component. Interfaces represent a language-independent binary standard. Using regular COM interfaces, a programming language that can manipulate pointers can directly access a COM interface's member functions through its function table. Using the IDispatch interface, a COM component's member functions can be accessed by name from programming languages that do not allow pointers. As you can see, this represents the best of all worlds, a universality that allows practically all programmers to access the rich functionality of COM.

But how do you obtain a reference to one of these COM interfaces? This will be answered in the next section, where we explore how to find and instantiate a COM component.

Implementation Location

How do you find the container of the code that you want to get at? This is a problem that has always plagued software developers. In the COM world, that container can be either an EXE or a DLL. In the Windows world, that container can only be a DLL. Let's first look at the problem from the perspective of DLLs.

Before Windows can load the DLL that you want, it has to be able to locate it. Windows currently relies on the fully qualified path to a DLL to identify it within the file system. Sometimes you want your DLL to be in an arbitrary directory on your computer; sometimes it makes sense for it to be in the Windows system directory. However, the only way Windows can load that DLL is if it resides somewhere along your system path.

Unfortunately, the system path is a finite resource. If there isn't enough room in the system path string to add the path to the directory where your DLL resides, Windows cannot find the DLL that you're looking for. This is a particularly serious problem when you're building components using Delphi; all of your components must reside in the same directory or you risk running out of path space.

An additional drawback is performance. Ideally you would like to have Windows find and load the code that your application needs right away. However, using the system path to find your DLL requires asking the file system to look in many directories. The file system is not particularly good at doing this quickly.

The problem becomes even more difficult if you want to connect to code that runs on *another computer*. To do this, you'll have to learn all of the arcane details of Remote Procedure Calls (RPC). Unfortunately, RPC is a completely different programming model than you would use to find a piece of code on *your* computer. Wouldn't it be great if there were a single method that you could reliably use to find code regardless of where it may reside?

As you may guess, COM provides a unified way to connect any piece of code, regardless of its location. However, what you first need is a way to uniquely identify the particular COM component that contains the code you would like to connect to.

COM introduces the concept of a *Globally Unique Identifier*, or GUID (pronounced *goo-id*, or *gwid* if you prefer), to identify COM entities. A GUID is a 128-bit number that is guaranteed to be unique across time and space. To generate a GUID, you call the COM API function CoCreateGuid, which generates a GUID for you using a complex algorithm that makes use of your network card's Ethernet address, your system clock, and a number of other highly variable system states.

> **NOTE** The NewGuid example from *Mastering Delphi 3* creates new GUIDs and adds them to a memo component, so that a user can copy them. That program (along with its simple source code) is available also on the companion CD of this book, in the current chapter's folder. As noted later on, however, in the Delphi editor you can simply press the Ctrl+Shift+G combination to obtain a new GUID.

There are several classes of GUIDs, including Interface Identifiers (IIDs), Class Identifiers (CLSIDs), and others. An important point to remember is that all these identifiers are GUIDs. There are no special numerical ranges that have been preassigned for particular types of GUIDs. They have been assigned different types to allow your compiler to enforce type safety (for example, to prevent you from passing a CLSID to a function that expects an IID).

A CLSID is a type of GUID that is used to uniquely identify a particular COM component. To create an instance of a particular COM component, you can call the COM API function CoCreateInstanceEx, which has the following function signature:

```
function CoCreateInstanceEx(const clsid: TCLSID;
   unkOuter: IUnknown; dwClsCtx: Longint;
   ServerInfo: PCoServerInfo; dwCount: Longint;
   rgmqResults: PMultiQIArray): HResult; stdcall;
```

When you pass it the CLSID for the COM component that you would like to create, CoCreateInstanceEx will create the COM component for you.

So how does CoCreateInstanceEx map a CLSID to the DLL that contains the COM component in question? The answer lies in the Windows Registry. All COM components must register their CLSID and their location with the Registry. CoCreateInstanceEx looks up the COM component's CLSID in the Registry and retrieves the full path to the DLL that contains the COM component you're looking for. This path is stored in a subkey called InprocServer32, which is found under the object's CLSID key. Figure 10.2 shows an example.

FIGURE 10.2:

An example of the Registry keys for the Control Panel COM object, seen in the Windows RegEdit application

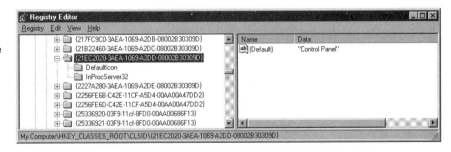

Up until now, we have been talking exclusively about COM components that reside in DLLs. As noted in the Code Reusability section, you can connect to a COM component in another Win32 process. You do so by simply specifying CLSCTX_LOCALSERVER in the dwClsCtx parameter of CoCreateInstanceEx. This function looks in the Registry as usual, but it looks for a path to a Windows EXE file in the LocalServer32 subkey of the COM server's CLSID key.

The ServerInfo structure is one of the other parameters that you can pass to CoCreateInstanceEx. This structure allows you to identify the computer where you want to create the COM component. The combination of the CLSID and the ServerInfo structure will allow you to identify and obtain a reference to any COM component on any computer on the network.

We'll defer discussion of how the COM component is actually created to the next section. Once CoCreateInstanceEx has found the DLL or EXE that contains a particular COM component, all of its work is done.

The final piece of the puzzle is obtaining a reference to a particular COM interface. As hinted above, its Interface Identifier or IID identifies a COM interface. Also recall that a COM interface is merely a pointer to the function table for that COM interface. To request a particular COM interface, you'll need to pass along a reference to its IID and a reference to a pointer that will ultimately hold the pointer to that interface's function table.

The PMultiQIArray structure is what makes it possible to obtain a number of COM interface references. Its structure is defined as follows:

```
PMultiQI = ^TMultiQI;
TMultiQI = record
  IID: PIID;
  Itf: IUnknown;
  hr: HRESULT;
end;

PMultiQIArray = ^TMultiQIArray;
TMultiQIArray = array [0..65535] of TMultiQI;
```

PMultiQIArray is simply an array of TMultiQI records. When you supply a TMultiQI record with an IID and an interface reference, CoCreateInstanceEx will return to you a reference to the interface that you requested in the Itf data member. Since the PMultiQI data structure is an array, you can pass more than one IID and interface reference pair. As we will see later, the Microsoft designers made it an array so that a single COM component can implement multiple interfaces.

You may have noticed that there was a third data member in the TMultiQI record. Simply called an HRESULT, it represents a standard COM return value type that indicates success or failure. Always try to return an appropriate HRESULT value from all of your COM functions. You will find that Microsoft has defined a large number of sensible error codes for you already.

> **TIP**　Delphi has defined most of the HRESULT values. They all begin with the letter E and an underscore (for example, E_NOINTERFACE). Take a look at the Windows.PAS file in the Source\RTL\Win subdirectory of your Delphi directory.

To summarize what we have learned up to now, we know that we can communicate with any COM component through a COM interface. We know that we can get a reference to a COM component's interface by calling CoCreateInstanceEx. We also know that CoCreateInstanceEx solves the implementation location problem for us by letting us find the implementation of any COM component using its CLSID and the identity of the computer on which it is located. Now we're getting somewhere! We no longer have to worry about system paths, or about modifying Autoexec.BAT files!

Now that we know how to get a reference to a COM interface, we can turn our attention to a number of still-unanswered questions. First, how does the code within CoCreateInstanceEx actually create our COM component? Second, how do we write the code for our own COM component? We will encounter the answer to the first question in the following section, and the answer to the second question in the "Object Lifetime Management" section.

Memory Allocation

There are two general problems with memory allocation that most programmers face at some point. The first occurs when we are creating objects: How much memory do we need to allocate for the object, and who owns that memory? The second problem involves ownership of blocks of heap-allocated memory that are passed around as parameters: Is the caller or the called function responsible for freeing the memory? We will examine each of these difficult problems in turn and show how COM provides a workable solution to both of them.

Why is ownership of the memory of the COM component a problem? Let's first consider what we have to know before we can create a simple object in Delphi.

The first thing that Delphi must figure out is how much memory to allocate. This implies that we need to know the exact size of the object. This is not much of a problem in Delphi; before you can use an object, you must have the class definition handy. The class definition must either be in the same unit, or be referenced by a uses clause within the unit.

For Delphi to calculate the size of the object, it must add up the total number of bytes required by the private, public, protected and published data members in the class. The problem is that if you change the implementation of your class, you are likely to be adding or removing private data members, thereby changing the size of an instance of your class. Once you have done this, all of the code that uses your class must be recompiled. While this is not a big deal for classes that are contained entirely within a single application, it becomes a *huge* problem when you have a published library of code with many client applications depending on it. You don't want to force a recompilation of all of those clients every time you change the implementation of one of your objects!

In other words, the need to know the size of an object that you are creating effectively weakens the encapsulation of that class. It is no longer a "black box" to the outside world. In object-oriented programming, the way you can separate the creation of an object from its implementation is through some form of a *factory pattern*.

Object Patterns

If you haven't read about the role of patterns in object-oriented programming yet, you really owe it to yourself to read up on this extremely valuable topic. Essentially, a *pattern* in the context of programming languages is a broad conceptual template for performing some task. One of the important benefits of approaching programming in terms of object patterns is that the concept provides a common vocabulary developers can use to describe problems and their solutions. For example, a *factory pattern* indicates a class used to create an object of another class. Where appropriate, this chapter and the next describe certain aspects of COM as being representative of this pattern or that pattern. When you have an opportunity to read up on those patterns, you'll gain a deeper insight into why COM was implemented in the way it was.

The best source of information about patterns is

Erich Gamma et al., *Design Patterns: Elements of Reusable Object-Oriented Software* (Addison Wesley, 1995, 1997). This is the book that ignited today's popular interest in object patterns. It identifies many of the recurring patterns in object-oriented programming and describes their applications and the motivations behind them.

A COM component's class factory is responsible for creating the component. There is a separate class factory for each CLSID. Since all information about the size of the COM component is contained inside the class factory, and the class factory is responsible for allocating the memory for the COM component, the caller effectively needs to know absolutely nothing about the details of the COM component's creation!

As you would expect, the way you communicate with a COM component's class factory is through a COM interface. The IClassFactory COM interface is defined as follows:

```
IClassFactory = interface(IUnknown)
  ['{00000001-0000-0000-C000-000000000046}']
  function CreateInstance (const unkOuter: IUnknown;
    const iid: TIID; out obj): HResult; stdcall;
  function LockServer (fLock: BOOL): HResult; stdcall;
end;
```

By repeatedly calling the CreateInstance member function of the IClassFactory interface, you can create as many instances of a particular COM component as you wish. You can see that the CreateInstance function takes a reference to an interface identifier and returns a pointer to that interface in the obj out parameter.

We can now fill in the blanks in our earlier discussion of how a COM component is created using the CoCreateInstanceEx function. We saw that CoCreateInstanceEx discovers the path to the DLL or EXE that contains a particular COM component by looking up that component's CLSID in the Registry. Once it has determined what file the COM component is located in, the function must then create an instance of that COM component.

Not surprisingly, before it creates the COM component, it requests and receives a reference to the IClassFactory interface of that COM component's class factory. Using the class factory reference, it calls its CreateInstance member function to create an instance of the COM component. The final piece of the puzzle fits into place when we consider how CoCreateInstanceEx obtains a pointer to a COM component's IClassFactory interface from the DLL or EXE.

All COM components and their associated class factories are housed inside COM servers. A COM server, as alluded to earlier, can be either an EXE or a DLL. In the case of a DLL-based server, CoCreateInstanceEx calls an exported function called DllGetClassObject. This function is prototyped as follows:

```
function DllGetClassObject (const CLSID, IID: TGUID;
  var Obj): HResult; stdcall;
```

As you can see, CoCreateInstanceEx passes this function the CLSID of the COM component that it wants to receive and the IID of the class factory interface (also known as an *activation interface*) that it wants to retrieve. In the case of an EXE-based server, the startup code of that server registers all of its class factories with the COM libraries by using the COM API function CoRegisterClassObject. In this case CoCreateInstanceEx looks up the CLSID of the COM component that it wants to create from the table of registered class factories in the COM libraries. In either case, the way you call CoCreateInstanceEx is exactly the same.

Let's now consider the problem associated with passing around blocks of shared memory. It usually manifests itself when you are passing around pointers to objects as function parameters. A simple example will help illustrate this point.

Suppose you have an exported procedure within a DLL called PrintData. You want to be able to call this procedure asynchronously and continue execution within your application. The PrintData function creates a worker thread to actually print the data. Also, in the interest of efficiency, you don't want to copy all of the data that is passed in. Let's say that the procedure is prototyped as follows:

```
procedure PrintData (Data: PByte): Boolean; stdcall;
```

However, what happens to the data that was passed to PrintData?

The code in the DLL must have its own memory allocator, since it can't be sure that the code calling it will be written in Delphi. The code that created the block of memory that was passed to the PrintData function also must have its own memory allocator. A memory allocator cannot free memory that it did not allocate. The ideal solution would be to have a neutral third party allocate and free the data being passed between functions.

COM acts as the neutral third party to solve the memory allocation problem. It provides memory allocation services through a COM interface called IMalloc, which is defined as follows:

```
IMalloc = interface(IUnknown)
  ['{00000002-0000-0000-C000-000000000046}']
  function Alloc (cb: Longint): Pointer; stdcall;
  function Realloc (pv: Pointer; cb: Longint): Pointer; stdcall;
  procedure Free (pv: Pointer); stdcall;
  function GetSize (pv: Pointer): Longint; stdcall;
  function DidAlloc (pv: Pointer): Integer; stdcall;
  procedure HeapMinimize; stdcall;
end;
```

You can obtain a reference to the COM library's implementation of the `IMalloc` interface by calling the COM API function `CoGetMalloc`. If you allocate memory blocks using the `Alloc` member function of `IMalloc`, you can be assured that those memory blocks can be freed by any other code that has a reference to an `IMalloc` interface. In our example, `PrintData` will call the `Free` member function of the `IMalloc` interface when it is finished printing the data, or when it encounters a fatal error while printing the data. This ensures that there is no leakage of resources during the printing of the data.

At this point, we now understand the details behind the creation of a COM component, and how COM acts as a neutral third party to assist in passing blocks of memory around. We understand why COM components have to be created this way: to solve the problems of code reusability, language independence, and memory allocation. Now we are ready to examine the details involved in writing our own COM components. One of the first things that we have to worry about when writing a COM component is how to manage the lifetime of that object.

Object Lifetime Management

When we start building our own COM components, we have to consider some additional problems. Ideally, we would like to allow the client code to maintain several references to a single instance of our COM component. We would also like the COM component to go away automatically when the client is done using it. This can be done through a technique known as *reference counting*.

Reference counting is a well-known object pattern. In various books on the topic, it has been described as both a handle class idiom and a proxy pattern. This object pattern allows an object to track the number of clients that currently have a reference to it. Every time a client obtains a reference to the object, the object increments its own reference count. Every time a client relinquishes its reference to an object, the object decrements its own reference count. Once its reference count drops to zero, the object can automatically destroy itself.

The requirement that the object manage its own lifetime is an important aspect of COM. For an object to be truly a black box, the code using that object cannot have any knowledge about other client programs that may be using the object. Therefore, if it were up to the client to explicitly destroy a COM component after it's done with it, that same COM component could not be used to service multiple clients. Reference counting gives a COM component far more flexibility than would be possible in a model where the client must explicitly destroy the COM component.

This reference counting model is very similar to the model that Windows uses to manage the lifetime of a DLL. The first reference to a DLL causes that DLL to be loaded into physical memory. (Memory management for DLLs was partially discussed in the last chapter, and more completely in Chapter 20 of *Mastering Delphi 3*.) Subsequent references to that DLL do not cause any more copies of it to be loaded; Windows simply increments the reference count of that DLL. As each reference to the DLL is removed, Windows decrements that DLL's reference count. Only when the reference count for the DLL has reached zero does Windows consider unloading the DLL from physical memory.

Clearly, reference counting is a property that all COM components must have. Since all access to a COM component must occur through interfaces, it is not surprising that all reference counting is done through a COM interface. This interface is called IUnknown and is defined as follows:

```
type
  IUnknown = interface
  public
    function QueryInterface (const iid: TIID;
      var obj): HResult; stdcall;
    function AddRef: Longint; stdcall;
    function Release: Longint; stdcall;
  end;
```

The member functions AddRef and Release handle all of the reference-counting details for your COM component. They both return an integer value that represents the new reference count for the COM component after the call. Typically, they are implemented as follows:

```
function TComObject.AddRef: Integer;
begin
  Inc (FRefCount);
  Result := FRefCount;
end;

function TComObject.Release: Integer;
begin
  Dec (FRefCount);
  if FRefCount = 0 then
  begin
    Destroy;
    Result := 0;
```

```
    Exit;
  end;
  Result := FRefCount;
end;
```

It is the client code's responsibility to correctly AddRef and Release interface pointers to a COM component. A very common source of resource leaks is failing to decrement the reference count for a COM component when you are finished using its services. The following set of rules will help you decide when to call AddRef and when to call Release:

Out parameters: Always increment the reference count of an object when returning its reference as an out parameter of a function. For example, the following function returns a reference to an interface pointer that has been previously saved in a small cache (the FCachedObjectInterface field):

```
procedure GetCachedObject (out ObjectInterface: IUnknown)
begin
  ObjectInterface := FCachedObjectInterface;
  ObjectInterface.AddRef;
end;
```

In parameters: When passing an interface reference to a function, you don't need to explicitly change the COM component's reference count by calling AddRef or Release. The lifetime of the COM component is controlled by the code that is calling that function, so you don't need to worry about this case.

In-out parameters: In general, using a single parameter to handle two duties is a bad thing. However, if you must force a single parameter to perform two functions, make sure that you call Release on the referenced interface before you overwrite that interface reference with a new value. The following example will illustrate this case:

```
procedure GetCachedObject (out ObjectInterface: IUnknown)
begin
  ObjectInterface.Release;
  ObjectInterface := FCachedObjectInterface;
  ObjectInterface.AddRef;
end;
```

Global variables: If you are storing an interface reference in a global variable (or a data member of a class), make sure that you increment the reference count on that reference. Unfortunately, the responsibility rests with you to ensure that the reference count is correctly maintained on that global variable. In other words, the reference count should be incremented only the first time that global variable is set, and it must be decremented when that global variable goes out of scope.

In this section, we learned that a COM component implements reference counting through the IUnknown interface. By using its reference count, a COM component can manage its own lifetime. This allows multiple clients to share the services of the same COM component without requiring that those clients have any knowledge of each other.

TIP In the case of in-process COM, which that doesn't cross any thread boundaries, the client application does manage the lifetime of a COM component. However, this is not strictly the case in out-of-process or remote COM. The interface stub component that is required for location transparency actually manages the lifetime of the COM component. This means that your COM component can still be "alive" even though there may be no outstanding references to it!

However, there is still one additional member function of the IUnknown interface that we have not talked about: QueryInterface. Up until now, we have only been looking at how black-box COM components can be created, managed, and destroyed. This is hardly object-oriented programming. However, by considering the role of QueryInterface, we will see how it transforms what we know about COM into a truly object-oriented framework.

Object Orientation

In this section, we'll explore how COM solves the code reusability problem for object-oriented programming languages. Up until now, we have seen that COM allows you to get access to COM components without regard to their location. We have also seen that COM components are truly black-box objects. In the last section, we saw that a COM component can service multiple clients and manage its own lifetime. If these features were all that COM had to offer, COM would provide only marginal advantages over the code reusability that DLLs already offer. For COM to be truly usable with today's object-oriented languages, it must also be object-oriented.

The classic textbook definition of object orientation is a style of programming that enforces encapsulation and provides a means toward polymorphic behavior. An auxiliary benefit of object-oriented programming is that it also makes it relatively easy to reuse families of related code. So, let's see if COM passes the two fundamental tests of object-orientation: encapsulation and polymorphism.

The first thing to consider is whether COM offers encapsulation. We hope that by now you're convinced that COM components are truly encapsulated. There is absolutely no way to manipulate a data member within a COM component without first going through some kind of COM interface member function. COM components manage their own memory, their own creation, and their own destruction. All of these implementation details are effectively hidden from you. In effect, COM forces you to program to an interface rather than an implementation, thereby freeing you from dependencies between your client code and the COM components that it uses.

The second aspect of object orientation is polymorphism. This allows you to substitute objects that have identical interfaces at run-time. As mentioned earlier, a COM component can have more than one COM interface. Along with the restriction that you can only communicate with a COM component through COM interfaces, this effectively guarantees that two COM components that have a common set of interfaces can always be interchanged. In other words, those two COM components are *polymorphic*.

Since one of the key features of a COM component is that it can have more than one COM interface, there has to be a mechanism for obtaining a reference to any COM interface of a particular object. The QueryInterface function of IUnknown allows us to do just this. It is prototyped as follows:

```
function QueryInterface (const iid: TIID;
  var obj): HResult; stdcall;
```

To get a reference to any other interface, call the QueryInterface function and pass it the IID of the interface to which you want a reference, and the interface variable that will hold the COM interface reference. Note that the QueryInterface function returns the standard HRESULT return type, meaning that this function can fail gracefully. In other words, if you cannot find a particular interface, your application code can either fail gracefully or try to find another interface to communicate with the COM component.

If you had to hold on to a separate pointer to the IUnknown interface for a COM component just to perform QueryInterface calls, COM would be less flexible than it actually is. What if someone passed you a reference to a COM component's ISimple interface, but forgot to pass you a reference to that component's IUnknown interface? You'd never be able to get to any other interface for that component!

So that we won't always have to pass a reference to a COM component's IUnknown interface along with any other interface reference being passed as a parameter, the designers of COM chose to use *interface inheritance* to solve this problem. All COM interfaces must derive from IUnknown; thus, the COM component that implements a particular interface must support the QueryInterface, AddRef, and Release functions for that interface. Therefore, the client code is always assured of having access to the QueryInterface functionality for that COM component, regardless of which interface it currently has a reference to.

WARNING Interface inheritance is not the same as implementation inheritance. In Delphi terms, you can think of a COM interface as being a purely abstract base class, which is a class that consists entirely of abstract virtual or abstract dynamic functions. A purely abstract base class has no implementation, and deriving from that class does not inherit any code.

Let's summarize the role that QueryInterface plays in making COM truly object-oriented. It allows client code to discover at run-time what interfaces a COM component implements. If it fails to find the interface that it is looking for, it can either fail gracefully or attempt to request a different interface. Also, QueryInterface must be implemented by all interfaces that are supported by a COM component because all COM interfaces must derive from IUnknown.

So far we have taken a whirlwind tour of some of the basic features of COM. We now understand that COM is object oriented because it allows COM components to exhibit polymorphic behavior. In discussing the memory management and lifetime management issues, we saw that COM components are very tightly encapsulated. They are truly "black box" components, whose implementation is completely hidden from us.

In the sections ahead, we will look at some of the additional features that naturally result from the core features of COM. This will allow us to expand the scope of our discussion to show how COM can solve a number of additional real-life programming problems.

Object Versioning

Another common problem that faces software developers is the need to revise shared objects. If you are building a library of these objects, even fairly minor changes to one object will require you to recompile all of the clients that use those objects. While you can use any number of object patterns to solve this problem, any implementation of those patterns would be tied to the programming language that you used to create it.

In an ideal world, you would have "versionable" binary objects that could be used by any programming language. Simply by requesting a particular version of an object, you would gain access to all of the functionality provided by that version.

COM provides most of the answers to the object versioning problem. Because all access to a COM component must occur through one or more of that object's COM interfaces, it is not surprising that COM interfaces provide the mechanism that makes object versioning possible.

The key to versionable COM interfaces is a rule that we have not discussed until now: A COM interface, once published, is immutable. In other words, once you have code in the field that makes use of a particular COM interface you have defined, you *cannot make any changes to it whatsoever*. By following this simple rule, you will be guaranteed that every time a piece of code requests a particular COM interface using its IID, it will be assured of getting what it expects.

But what if you want to add functionality to a published interface? You do so by deriving a new interface from the existing interface, and giving that new interface its own unique IID. Here's an example from Microsoft's own experience.

The basic IClassFactory interface for creating COM components is very simple, but it does the job of creating COM components. However, what if you wanted to restrict who can create your COM component, perhaps making sure that they have a valid license to execute the code in your COM component? To solve this problem, Microsoft created a new COM interface called IClassFactory2, derived from IClassFactory, which adds a number of new functions that allow it to implement some additional licensing features:

```
IClassFactory2 = interface(IClassFactory)
  ['{B196B28F-BAB4-101A-B69C-00AA00341D07}']
  function GetLicInfo (var licInfo: TLicInfo):
    HResult; stdcall;
  function RequestLicKey (dwResrved: Longint;
    out bstrKey: WideString): HResult; stdcall;
```

```
function CreateInstanceLic (const unkOuter: IUnknown;
  const unkReserved: IUnknown; const iid: TIID;
  const bstrKey: WideString; out vObject):
  HResult; stdcall;
end;
```

In addition to the `CreateInstance` and `LockServer` functions of `IClassFactory`, the `IClassFactory2` interface adds the `GetLicInfo`, `RequestLicKey`, and `CreateInstanceLic` member functions. Keep in mind, however, that the object that implements this interface must provide implementation for *all* functions of `IClassFactory2`, including the `IClassFactory` member functions.

We have learned that COM interfaces make object versioning possible. By adding additional COM interfaces to an existing COM component and distributing this new version to all of your users, you can incrementally add new functionality to your library of code without breaking any existing code that depends on that library. While COM's interface-based versioning allows you to add new functionality to an existing COM component, it does not solve all component versioning problems.

Component Versioning and Bug Fixes

An additional component versioning problem arises from the bug fixes and new versions that inevitably must be released for COM components in the field. Existing users of the COM component may have code in place that depends on the buggy behavior of the existing COM component. By releasing a new COM component that "fixes" those bugs, you might be breaking code that depended on your older, less reliable COM component! As application writers use more and more third-party COM components, this problem will only become greater in the future.

To distribute an application with confidence, we must be able to depend on connecting to a particular binary version of a COM component. Unfortunately, as a user installs other applications on their computer, and newer versions overwrite older versions, your application can no longer connect to that older binary version. You cannot simply hide the DLLs or EXEs that house those third-party COM components in a private subdirectory, because newer versions will overwrite the CLSID entries in the Registry that point to those DLLs and EXEs. The next time someone tries to create a COM component with that CLSID, it will create the latest binary version on your machine, not the one in your private subdirectory! This problem currently lacks a solution.

Location Transparency

Imagine that you have just finished writing some software components that provide services for one of the applications that your company produces. During the first go-around, you have placed all of your software components in a DLL, because you had foreseen that some code might be reusable in other applications that your company produces. Other developers in your company take notice of the code you have created and marvel at its elegance. They begin adding features to their applications to take advantage of your code. But then all of a sudden, a change in the application requirements forces you to implement your code in an EXE that resides on another computer. What do you do now? What do you tell your fellow developers who have invested time and effort in their own applications to add new features that rely on your code?

If you were using COM to create your software components, you would just sit back and smile. You would send some e-mail around to your fellow software developers, and tell them how to get the name of the computer on which your software components reside. Then you'd go back to worrying about other, more difficult software problems . . .

Does this scenario sound far-fetched? Even though you may not have faced this problem yet, you most likely will face it eventually as more of our computers become networked. The concept of delegating responsibility to one or more computers on a network to provide a set of common services is likely to be a popular design in the future. So how does COM free your code from caring about *where* a software component resides?

There are three types of function calls that must be considered. The first is an in-process call, or the case of a DLL server. The second is an out-of-process call, or the case of an EXE server. The third is a remote call, or the case of an EXE server that runs on another computer. The first case involves crossing no boundaries at all, and the next two cases involve crossing some kind of operating system boundary. Out-of-process calls must cross a Win32 process boundary, and remote calls must cross a network boundary.

The feature of COM that allows you not to care about where a software component resides is known by the lofty title of *local-remote transparency* or simply *location transparency*. There are two general problems that location transparency must solve for you:

- Locating the function's code, regardless of whether it is local or remote

- Passing parameters to the function and returning the function result to you, regardless of whether it is local or remote

The magic of COM is its ability to make all COM function calls, regardless of whether they are in-process or not, *appear to be* in-process. Since all COM interface function calls must occur via that interface's function table, this is a natural control point that can be manipulated by the COM libraries.

The COM libraries make the COM interface of an out-of-process or remote object appear to be in-process by transparently creating an *interface proxy object* in the process space of the application making the call. When the application calls one of the COM interface's functions, it pushes the function's parameters onto the stack as usual, and invokes that function using its offset into the function table. Rather than directly calling the COM component's code, as would be the case for an in-process COM component, the application calls functions in the interface proxy object! The COM libraries have modified the interface's function table to point to functions in the proxy object rather than functions in the remote COM component.

The interface proxy object contains code that knows how to call the actual COM component. Remember that a function address in a different Win32 process has no meaning outside that process. Similarly, a function address in a Win32 process running on a different computer has no meaning outside that process. So how does the proxy object code actually communicate with the COM component if it resides in another Win32 process or another computer?

An interface proxy object must have a corresponding *interface stub object*. These objects are always found in pairs. The interface stub object is created within the process space of the out-of-process or remote COM component. Since these objects are created in pairs, they also know how to communicate with each other. Interface proxy-stub object pairs in different Win32 processes on the same computer communicate with each other using Local Procedure Calls (LPCs). Interface proxy-stub object pairs on different computers communicate with each other using RPC calls.

An interface proxy-stub pair is responsible for transporting function parameters between themselves. This process is commonly referred to as *marshaling* the function parameters. While this seems like a rather simple task, it turns out to be a very complex problem.

The complexity arises from the requirement that the marshaling code faithfully re-create all of the function parameters in an entirely new process space. For example, if the function parameter contains a pointer to an array of pointers to blocks of memory of different sizes, the marshaling code must create an image of all of this information in the other COM component's process space! Since it cannot be guaranteed that you will be able to re-create those parameters at the same logical addresses, the marshaling code must know enough about the data to perform some kind of manipulation on that data.

As an example, imagine what would be involved in marshaling a linked list of data from one process space to another. The individual nodes would have to be re-created in the other process space, and the addresses of those nodes would have to be fixed up by the marshaling code. It would be unreasonable to expect this process to occur transparently; hence the need for *marshaling* code.

There are two ways to implement marshaling. One is to create your interface definitions using the Interface Definition Language (IDL), and use the Microsoft IDL compiler (MIDL.EXE) to generate C source code files that you can compile into a DLL. This process is known as *standard marshaling*. The other is to implement the `IMarshal` COM interface in your COM component in a process known as *custom marshaling*. A detailed discussion of these topics is beyond the scope of this book. For more information, please see the references at the end of this chapter.

Fortunately, in the vast majority of cases, you won't be passing such complex data structures between processes. If you make all of your COM interfaces Automation-compatible, and provide a binary description of those interfaces, COM will automatically marshal your parameters for you! So how exactly can COM perform this automatic marshaling magic? By using some additional information that describes a COM object's interfaces. This information is known as a *type library*, and we'll examine it in the following section.

Object Descriptions

One of the most time-consuming problems that you encounter when you are confronted by a new and unfamiliar piece of code is *where is the documentation?* In the world of software components, this becomes a particularly serious problem. Faced with a bewildering mass of components that may or may not ship with source code to study, the poor software developer has to discover which component best suits a project's needs. Enter the self-describing component.

In a world where components are everywhere, component browsers become an increasingly important tool in the developer's toolbox. In the world of COM components, there are several component browsers you can choose from. One of the best-known is the OLE/COM Object Viewer, which ships with the Win32

SDK and various Microsoft tools. If you don't have a copy installed on your computer already, you can freely download it from Microsoft at this address:

`www.microsoft.com/oledev/olecom/oleview.htm`

The OLE/COM Object Viewer relies on several sources of information to provide a unified way to browse the COM components installed on your computer. It makes extensive use of your Windows Registry, as well as additional information stores known as type libraries.

A type library can contain a rather complete description of one or more COM components. However, since most of the information contained within a type library is optional (the type library itself is an optional part of a COM component), the creator of the COM component largely determines the quality of information. A carefully constructed type library can yield volumes of information to the user of a COM component.

A type library contains a hierarchical organization of information. It describes the capabilities of one or more COM components. For each COM component, it describes all of the supported interfaces. For each interface, it describes all of the member functions. For each member function, it describes all of the parameters and their types. Taken in its entirety, a type library can be considered a language-independent header file.

There are many uses for type libraries. Development tools can use the information contained within a type library to generate language-specific header files automatically. Integrated development environments can use the help file links contained within the type library to provide context-sensitive help. The COM libraries use type libraries to provide automatic marshaling of Automation-compatible interfaces. In short, a COM component that is described by a type library can be more easily integrated into its environment.

How do you create a type library? There are currently two Microsoft tools (MkTypLib.EXE and MIDL.EXE) that can be used. Both of these tools ship with the Win32 SDK, and can convert a source file written in a language-neutral format into the type library binary format. The MkTypLib compiler takes Object

Definition Language (ODL) files as input, and the MIDL compiler can take either ODL or Interface Definition Language (IDL) files as its input.

These two file formats are essentially incompatible. However, existing type library descriptions in ODL can be compiled by recent (3.00.44 or greater) versions of the MIDL compiler. For current and future projects, however, Microsoft recommends using IDL, which can also be compiled by the MIDL compiler. MkTypLib is provided only for backward compatibility for older tools that may depend on its existence.

A sample IDL file for the AutoTextEntry interface of Microsoft Word 8.0 is shown below:

```
[
  uuid(00020936-0000-0000-C000-000000000046),
  version(8.0),
  helpcontext(0x00000936),
  dual,
  nonextensible
]
dispinterface AutoTextEntry {
  properties:
  methods:
    [id(0x000003e8), propget, helpcontext(0x093603e8)]
    Application* Application();
    [id(0x000003e9), propget, helpcontext(0x093603e9)]
    long Creator();
    [id(0x000003ea), propget, helpcontext(0x093603ea)]
    IDispatch* Parent();
    [id(0x00000001), propget, helpcontext(0x09360001)]
    long Index();
    [id(0x00000002), propget, helpcontext(0x09360002)]
    BSTR Name();
    [id(0x00000002), propput, helpcontext(0x09360002)]
    void Name([in] BSTR rhs);
    [id(0x00000003), propget, helpcontext(0x09360003)]
    BSTR StyleName();
    [id(00000000), propget, helpcontext(0x09360000)]
    BSTR Value();
    [id(00000000), propput, helpcontext(0x09360000)]
    void Value([in] BSTR rhs);
    [id(0x00000065), helpcontext(0x09360065)]
    void Delete();
    [id(0x00000066), helpcontext(0x09360066)]
```

```
Range* Insert( [in] Range* Where, [in, optional]
  VARIANT* RichText);
};
```

We used the OLE/COM Object Viewer to generate this file from Word 97's type library.

The `AutoTextEntry` interface is defined as a `dispinterface`, which is an Automation-compatible interface. All of its methods are defined, along with member properties of that interface, as either `propget` or `propput` functions (these are very similar to the read and write directives for a Delphi property).

You can also see some of the attributes described earlier. For example, the `help-context` attribute links each function listed in the interface to a specific help file topic. A full discussion of IDL is well beyond the scope of this brief introduction. For further information, see the IDL documentation in the Microsoft Developer Network Library, which can also be found on the Web at `www.microsoft.com/msdn`.

> **NOTE**
>
> As we'll see shortly, these Microsoft tools are not the only way to create a type library. You can also use some Borland tools included in Delphi, particularly the visual Type Library Editor. In this case you don't have to use a definition language, and creating a type library becomes much easier.

COM Programming Problems and Delphi Solutions

While COM provides a lot of solutions to common programming problems, it introduces a number of programming problems itself. Most of them are of the bookkeeping variety. Many opportunities for bugs can arise from the strict requirements that COM components must adhere to.

We will see in this section how Delphi 3 provides a number of solutions that eliminate most of the grunt work and bookkeeping duties that have commonly been associated with COM programming in general. These problems are the greatest single source of bugs in COM programming. By making COM programming easier and more accessible, Delphi 3 also makes it easier to create robust COM components.

Reference Counting

The reference counting problem has two aspects. First, your application code that uses COM components is responsible for maintaining those objects' reference counts. On the other side, any code that you write for your COM component must correctly implement the AddRef and Release functions for all interfaces implemented by your COM component. While this code is not particularly difficult to write, failing to implement it correctly in all cases will result in hard-to-find bugs in your applications.

Delphi solves the reference count problem by effectively removing it from your consideration. If you use Delphi's COM features correctly, you should never have to worry about reference counts in either the client code that you write or the COM components that you create. Intrigued? Read on.

Any application code that you write must call AddRef and Release in all of the appropriate places. Failure to do so can result in the leakage of COM components, or in general protection faults from trying to call Release on a component that has already destroyed itself. Delphi solves this problem by introducing *interface references* to the Object Pascal language.

Delphi uses interface references to solve the reference count problem for application code. Every interface reference must have an interface definition. A COM interface is defined in Delphi using the interface keyword. For example, here is the definition of the IMalloc COM interface:

```
type
  IMalloc = interface (IUnknown)
    ['{00000002-0000-0000-C000-000000000046}']
    function Alloc (cb: Longint): Pointer; stdcall;
    function Realloc (pv: Pointer; cb: Longint):
      Pointer; stdcall;
    procedure Free (pv: Pointer); stdcall;
    function GetSize (pv: Pointer): Longint; stdcall;
    function DidAlloc (pv: Pointer): Integer; stdcall;
    procedure HeapMinimize; stdcall;
  end;
```

As you can see, the interface keyword also allows you to specify the IID of the interface. By using the information contained in the interface definition, Delphi has everything that it needs to simplify your manipulation of COM interfaces.

To illustrate how interface references solve the reference count problem, let's draw an analogy with the way Delphi currently manipulates strings. A Delphi string points to a reference-counted block of memory that is allocated on the heap. When you manipulate a Delphi string, you don't give any thought whatsoever to issues such as memory leakage or reference counting, right? The compiler handles all of those issues for you transparently.

Let's consider some of the issues that relate to strings, and see how interface references behave in exactly the same way. There are a number of areas that we will look at: what happens during an assignment, what happens when interface references go out of scope, and what happens when you pass an interface reference by reference.

When you assign one string to another, as in String1 := String2, Delphi generates some additional code for you. The pseudocode that represents what Delphi actually generates looks like this:

```
if Assigned (String1) then
   String1.DecrementReferenceCount;
String1.Pointer := String2.Pointer;
if Assigned (String1) then
   String1.IncrementReferenceCount;
```

The DecrementReferenceCount function will free the memory allocated to the string when the number of outstanding references to it reaches zero.

Similarly, if you are assigning one COM interface reference to another, as in Interface1 := Interface2, Delphi also generates some additional code for you:

```
if Assigned (Interface1) then
   Interface1.Release

Interface1.Pointer := Interface2.Pointer;

if Assigned (Interface1) then
   Interface1.AddRef;
```

By generating this additional code behind the scenes, Delphi effectively prevents an assignment from overwriting an existing interface reference. If an existing interface reference were overwritten, the object that it referred to would "live forever" and never be destroyed; it would be a resource leak.

The next point to consider is the scope of the string variable or interface reference. When a string or interface reference goes out of scope, Delphi generates some code to decrement the reference count for that string or interface reference. Therefore, there is always code generated at the end of a function that uses a string or interface reference. For example, consider the following procedure Foo, which declares a string variable called s and an IUnknown interface reference called unk:

```
procedure Foo;
var
  s: String;
  unk: IUnknown;
begin
  { some code that uses s and unk }
end;
```

Simply by assigning a value to these variables, we instruct Delphi to generate s.IncrementReferenceCount and unk.AddRef calls. Then, regardless of whether the procedure terminates normally, or as the result of an exception, the following lines of pseudocode will always be executed:

```
if Assigned(s) then
  s.DecrementReferenceCount;
if Assigned(unk) then
  unk.Release;
```

Once again, this code guarantees that an interface reference will never be left dangling, and thereby protects you from the resource leak that would otherwise result.

When we discussed COM's reference counting rules, we saw that there was a special rule for in/out parameters: you must decrement the reference count for the in parameter before you reassign it to another value. Delphi enforces this reference counting rule for its interface references with a little help from a new keyword called, appropriately, out. For example, consider the following fragment of code. We will be calling the functions GetCachedObject1 and GetCachedObject2, which are prototyped as follows:

```
procedure GetCachedObject1 (out ObjectInterface: IUnknown);
procedure GetCachedObject2 (out ObjectInterface: IUnknown);
```

We call them from the following code fragment:

```
var
  intf: IUnknown;
begin
  GetCachedObject1 (intf);
  GetCachedObject2 (intf);
end;
```

Behind the scenes, Delphi is generating this code for those function calls:

```
if Assigned (intf) then
  intf.Release;
GetCachedObject1 (intf);
if Assigned (intf) then
  intf.Release;
GetCachedObject2 (intf);
```

This effectively prevents your interface references from being overwritten by code that fails to release interface references passed in as in/out parameters.

Moving to the other side of the fence, let's consider how Delphi helps with the implementation of reference counting for your COM interfaces.

The key to implementing a Delphi COM component is the TComObject base class. This class contains Delphi's implementation of the IUnknown interface. The base class is only half of the story, however. Delphi also natively supports COM interfaces at the compiler level through an extension to the class keyword. You can create COM components that support any number of interfaces simply by listing them after the class keyword. Consider the following example of a COM component that implements the COM interfaces IShellExtInit and IContextMenu:

```
TContextMenu = class (TComObject,
  IShellExtInit, IContextMenu)
public
  { IShellExtInit member function }
  function Initialize (pidlFolder: PItemIDList;
    lpdobj: IDataObject; hKeyProgID: HKEY):
    HResult; stdcall;

  { IContextMenu member functions }
  function QueryContextMenu(Menu: HMENU;
    indexMenu, idCmdFirst, idCmdLast, uFlags: UINT):
    HResult; stdcall;
  function InvokeCommand (var lpici: TCMInvokeCommandInfo):
HResult; stdcall;
  function GetCommandString (idCmd, uType: UINT;
    pwReserved: PUINT; pszName: LPSTR; cchMax: UINT):
    HResult; stdcall;
end;
```

The extensions to the class keyword allow you to derive the class TContextMenu from the TComObject class, and they instruct the compiler to generate code to support the `IShellExtInit` and `IContextMenu` interfaces. Both `IShellExtInit` and `IContextMenu` are defined as Delphi interface references. The compiler uses the interface reference definition to generate the function tables for those interfaces. It also uses the interface reference definition to force you to implement all of the member functions for those interfaces. Since you are claiming to support both of these interfaces, the rules of COM state that you *must* provide an implementation for all of the member functions of those COM interfaces. However, since Delphi provides an `IUnknown` implementation for you in the `TComObject` base class, you don't have to worry about those functions.

The great thing about Delphi's implementation of `IUnknown` in `TComObject` is that you no longer have to worry about reference counting issues in any of your COM components! Even though your `TContextMenu` COM component supports three COM interfaces, `IUnknown`, `IShellExtInit`, and `IContextMenu`, you don't have to worry about implementing `AddRef`, `Release`, and `QueryInterface` separately for each of these interfaces. The default implementation in `TComObject` handles the `IUnknown` implementation for you automatically!

To summarize, Delphi uses interface references to implement automatic support for reference counting in client applications. Similar to Delphi's reference-counted strings, these interface references are automatically resource-protected. In your own COM components, Delphi also provides a default reference counting implementation in the `TComObject` base class; this class is used to create all Delphi COM components. The compiler uses interface references to generate the function table for each COM interface and to enforce the COM requirement that all interface member functions be implemented.

Reference Counting in Action

Since it is very important for you to understand the reference counting mechanism of COM in detail, here is a practical example.

The COM server we're going to implement is a simple extension of an example from *Mastering Delphi 3*. Of particular interest is that it warns the user when it is being destroyed, thanks to a `MessageBox` call in its destructor. The interface implemented by this server also includes a method that returns the reference count:

```
type
  INumber = interface
    ['{ECD5DAE3-1D37-11D1-854E-444553540000}']
    function GetValue: Integer; stdcall;
```

```
    procedure SetValue (New: Integer); stdcall;
    procedure Increase; stdcall;
    function RefCount: Integer; stdcall;
  end;
```

The code for the class of the server that implements this interface is trivial; we only need to look at the class definition and two of its methods:

```
type
  TDllNumber = class (TComObject, INumber)
  private
    Value: Integer;
  public
    function GetValue: Integer; virtual; stdcall;
    procedure SetValue (New: Integer); virtual; stdcall;
    procedure Increase; virtual; stdcall;
    function RefCount: Integer; stdcall;
    procedure Initialize; override;
    destructor Destroy; override;
  end;

destructor TDllNumber.Destroy;
begin
  inherited;
  MessageBox (0,
    PChar ('Object ' + IntToStr (Value) + ' Destroyed'),
    'TDLLNumber', mb_OK);
end;

function TDllNumber.RefCount: Integer;
begin
  Result := inherited RefCount;
end;
```

Once you have compiled this COM server (called FirstCom) and registered it using Delphi's Run ➤ Register ActiveX Library command, you can move to the demo program (called RefCount). The main form of this program has three simple buttons. The first is used to create a brand new TDllNumber COM object, while the other two add a reference to the object (assigning it to INum2 or INum3):

```
procedure TForm1.Button1Click(Sender: TObject);
begin
```

```
    INum1 := CreateComObject (
      CLSID_TDllNumber) as INumber;
    INum1.SetValue (Random (1000));
  end;

  procedure TForm1.Button3Click(Sender: TObject);
  begin
    INum2 := INum1;
  end;
```

With this code you can replace the current INum1 COM object with a new one. Assigning a new object to INum1 decreases the reference count of the previous object. If there were no other references to it, that object is immediately destroyed; this is confirmed by the server itself, which displays a warning message box. If INum2 or INum3 refers to the same object, this won't be destroyed until you remove all of the references to it by assigning INum2 or INum3 to other objects.

A timer component updates the description of the three interface variables, which might refer to the same COM object or different ones:

```
  procedure TForm1.Timer1Timer(Sender: TObject);
  begin
    if Assigned (INum1) then
      Label1.Caption := Format (
        '%s: Value = %d; RefCount = %d',
        ['Num1',
        INum1.GetValue,
        INum1.RefCount])
    else
      Label1.Caption := 'INum1 not assigned';
    // same code for Num2 and Num3...
  end;
```

From the output of this program, illustrated in Figure 10.3, you can see the status of the three references; the labels use the value of the object as a sort of ID. Try playing with this program, pressing the various buttons in all the possible sequences, and adding new features until you fully grasp how COM reference counting works.

FIGURE 10.3:

The output of the RefCount example with two objects in memory, and two variables referring to the same object

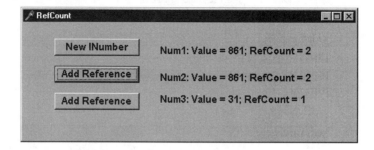

QueryInterface Implementation

Implementing QueryInterface in your client applications and in your COM components is somewhat easier than implementing reference counting correctly, but it is still a chore. Delphi provides support for QueryInterface on both the client side and the COM component side.

On the client side of things, Delphi provides support for QueryInterface calls through the as operator. Those of you who are familiar with dynamic typecasting using Delphi will be right at home with the as operator.

In most Delphi programming, the as operator is used to attempt to cast one class to another. By using RTTI, Delphi attempts to verify at run-time that the cast can be legally made. If the cast is legal, the as operator returns an appropriately cast reference to the object. If the cast cannot be made, Delphi raises an exception.

NOTE   See Chapter 4 if you need a refresher on run-time type information (RTTI).

When it's used in conjunction with interface references, the as operator attempts to return a reference to another interface by calling QueryInterface on the specified interface reference. For example, the CreateComObject helper function normally returns an IUnknown interface reference to a newly created COM component. However, we can use the as operator to cast that interface to the interface we really want. Consider the following code:

```
var
  contextMenu: IContextMenu;
begin
```

```
try
  contextMenu := CreateComObject (CLSID_TContextMenu) as
    IContextMenu;
  { code that uses contextMenu }
except
  ShowMessage ('Cannot retrieve IContextMenu!');
end;
end;
```

We are using the as operator to cast the IUnknown interface reference returned by CreateComObject to an IContextMenu interface reference. If the CLSID_TContext-Menu COM component doesn't support the IContextMenu interface, Delphi raises an exception and executes the ShowMessage function in the exception handler. The benefits are obvious when you consider the code that would otherwise have to be written to perform the same typecasting:

```
var
  unk: IUnknown;
  contextMenu: IContextMenu;
begin
  unk := CreateComObject (CLSID_TContextMenu);
  if unk.QueryInterface (IContextMenu, contextMenu) =
    S_OK then
  begin
    { code that uses contextMenu }
  end
  else
  begin
    { code that handles the error }
  end;
end;
```

The code that uses the as operator is much clearer in its intent and purpose.

NOTE   If you're interested in the details behind how Delphi implements QueryInterface, take a look at the TObject.GetInterface function declared in the System unit.

When creating COM components, `TComObject` and the `class` keyword team up to provide you with an automatic `QueryInterface` implementation. Consider the COM component that we looked at in the reference counting section:

```
TContextMenu = class (TComObject,
    IShellExtInit, IContextMenu)
```

The compiler uses the IID information contained in the class references `IShellExtInit` and `IContextMenu` to build a table of COM interfaces that are supported by `TContextMenu`. This table is then used to drive the `QueryInterface` implementation provided by `TComObject`.

In summary, Delphi provides a rather complete implementation of `QueryInterface` for you. When writing client application code that manipulates a COM component, just use the as operator to obtain new interfaces from the COM component. Delphi's exception handling mechanism automatically takes care of the failure cases for you. When implementing COM components, don't worry about it at all. Simply by defining your COM component, you have done all of the work that is required to implement `QueryInterface`!

Exception Handling

One of the nicest features in Delphi is its simple support for exception handling. However, exceptions raised across interface boundaries are strictly forbidden in COM. The COM specification states that "it is strictly illegal to throw an exception across an interface invocation; all such cross-interface exceptions which are thrown are in fact bugs in the offending interface implementation."

When you stop to think about it, this restriction makes sense. There is no way you can know what language was used to write the code that is calling your COM component. Furthermore, the COM specification states that you shouldn't care what language the code was written in. Unfortunately, exception-handling implementations are not guaranteed to be portable across different programming languages. Therefore, COM must take the restrictive position that *all* cross-interface exceptions must be forbidden.

There are two aspects to the exception-handling problem that we need to consider. The first is what to do within interface member functions, and the second involves what to do in the client code when a call to an interface member function fails.

When considering the interface member function problem, we need to remember that exceptions are used to varying degrees by Delphi programmers. The code within your interface member functions could be calling other functions you have implemented that raise their own exceptions. That code may also be calling Delphi run-time code that can raise its own exceptions. In short, even if *you* don't use exceptions, Delphi does. This means that you have to protect yourself from accidentally throwing an exception across an interface boundary. So how do we resolve this problem?

Here is a rule of thumb to prevent exceptions from leaking across an interface boundary: *always protect your interface member function with a try/except block.* There is a case that we will see later where Delphi creates this for you automatically, but the responsibility rests upon you for the majority of interface member functions.

The following is a piece of skeleton code that has been extremely useful in converting Delphi exceptions into COM exceptions:

```
try
  Result := S_OK;
  { Code that can raise an exception }
except
  on E: EOleSysError do
    Result := E.ErrorCode;
else
  Result := E_Unexpected;
end;
```

The exception handling code will automatically convert all Delphi OLE-based exceptions into the appropriate HRESULT value, since the error code for all EOleSysError exceptions *is* an HRESULT value. You could add further code to convert, for example, EOutOfMemory exceptions into E_OutOfMemory return values. The important point, regardless, is that the Delphi exception will always be caught.

NOTE   Delphi automatically generates a similar block of code on your behalf when you use the *safecall* calling convention. It is described in more detail in the next chapter.

Let's now consider how we can gracefully handle interface member function calls that fail. In traditional COM programming, the error handling was usually spread liberally throughout your code in blocks like this one:

```
if not Succeeded (AInterface.ShowMessage ('Hello World')) then
begin
  { failure case }
```

```
{ Break or Exit function }
end;
```

This is very similar to code that we used to write in the days before exception handling. A better alternative would be to convert a failed interface member function call into a Delphi exception transparently.

Delphi supplies a very useful function in the ComObj unit, called OleCheck, to help you handle failed interface member function calls. You simply pass the OleCheck procedure the HRESULT value that was returned from an interface member function call. For example, the code in the function block above would simplify into:

```
OleCheck (AInterface.ShowMessage ('Hello World'));
```

If the return value of the AInterface.ShowMessage call does not equal S_OK, then OleCheck raises an EOleSysError exception and sets the ErrorCode of that exception to the return value. This allows you to handle the exception where it makes the most sense to handle it, just as in the rest of your Delphi code.

To summarize, there are two distinct issues in the exception-handling problem. To handle exceptions that may be thrown inside your COM components, you must write exception-handling code in your interface member functions to catch all exceptions that would otherwise leak across the interface boundary. The skeleton code that is provided in this section should handle most of these cases correctly. On the client side, use the OleCheck helper procedure to convert failed interface member function calls into Delphi exceptions automatically.

Class Factory Implementation

Class factory code, like (for example) the Windows loader and the code that initializes your DLLs, is code that definitely should be hidden from programmers using it. While there are cases where you would want to write your own class factories, Delphi provides a default implementation that should handle most of your needs.

Delphi creates class factories on your behalf using a class called TComClassFactory. All you have to do is declare an instance of a TComClassFactory class in the initialization section of your COM component's unit:

```
initialization
  TComObjectFactory.Create (ComServer,
    TMyComObject, Class_MyComObject, 'MyComObject',
  'Sample COM component', ciMultiInstance);
```

This code creates an instance of a class factory object that will create only COM components of the Delphi class TMyComObject.

The Class_MyComObject parameter is actually of type TGUID, and is declared as follows:

```
Class_MyComObject:
  TGUID = '{6C862F81-DE8E-11D0-80B1-000021617139}';
```

Delphi uses this CLSID in its registration implementation and to bind incoming calls from the COM libraries to the correct class factory.

> **TIP**
>
> As already mentioned, to get Delphi to generate a GUID for you, just press Ctrl+Shift+G! Remember to strip off the square brackets that surround the GUID that is generated (the brackets are added by Delphi so that the generated GUID will be compatible with the interface keyword).

The ciMultiInstance parameter instructs Delphi to allow multiple instances of TMyComObject to be created. If you use ciSingleInstance instead, Delphi will allow users to create only a single instance of that COM component. You can also use ciInternal, which instructs Delphi to disallow external creation of that COM component. In other words, the COM component will only be created and used within the COM server itself.

Finally, the ComServer parameter is what Delphi uses to hide some of the ugliest code from your view. Remember how COM components can be packaged inside either a DLL- or an EXE-based server? The mechanisms that the COM libraries use to find the class factories for your COM component are quite different in each case. However, Delphi hides these details from you in the ComServer global object.

Registration

Registration is an issue that you will eventually have to deal with in creating COM components. When we discussed how COM solves the implementation location problem, you saw how a COM component must be registered in the Windows Registry. Fortunately, you don't have to deal with all of those bookkeeping details yourself; Delphi provides a handy default implementation for you.

Exporting the DllGetClassObject Function

A DLL-based COM server uses the exported function DllGetClassObject to map incoming calls from the COM libraries to the appropriate class factory. The DllGetClassObject function is prototyped as follows:

```
function DllGetClassObject (
   const CLSID, IID: TGUID; var Obj):
   HResult; stdcall;
```

It maps the incoming CLSID and IID to an internally managed list of registered class factory objects. If it finds the appropriate class factory, it returns a reference to the interface specified by the IID parameter in the Obj out parameter.

An EXE-based COM server, on the other hand, cannot export any member functions at all. This is a Windows restriction. To get around this problem, the COM server must register its class factory objects with the COM libraries, which then assume the functionality of the DllGetClassObject function. Delphi automatically registers your EXE server's class factory objects using the COM API function CoRegisterClassObject.

A side effect of the dual nature of the ComServer global object is that the ComServ unit cannot be included in a Delphi package. This means you cannot create COM components that can be exported from a Delphi package. This poses a problem when you create Delphi components that rely on additional COM helper objects. Those helper objects must be placed in their own ActiveX Library project.

One of the optional requirements in the COM specification is that COM servers contain the code required to register their COM components with the system Registry. At the very least, a COM component that supports this self-registration capability must be able to create the key entries that allow the COM libraries to locate the code for a particular CLSID. Delphi's list of class factory objects contains all of the information required to register those objects with the system Registry.

Delphi implements all of the registration services for you automatically. All you have to do is include the ComServ unit. As with the class factory implementation, the global ComServer object abstracts the details of whether your COM components are packaged inside a DLL or an EXE.

NOTE   DLL-based COM servers use a pair of exported functions called DllRegisterServer and DllUnregisterServer. A setup program can call these exported functions using a LoadLibrary/GetProcAddress call to register the COM server. You can register ActiveX servers that you have created in Delphi simply by selecting Register ActiveX Server from Delphi's Run menu. An EXE-based COM server, on the other hand, must use a command-line argument to tell it whether to register itself. To register an EXE-based COM server, simply run it with /regserver or /Register in the command line. Conversely, running it with /unregserver or /Unregister on the command line causes the server to remove itself from the Windows Registry.

If your COM component knows how to register itself, then it stands to reason that it should also know how to unregister itself from the Windows Registry. Once again, the ComServer object provides you with a default implementation for the unregistration code.

There are times, however, when you would like to add your own registration code. The ComServ unit does not easily let you hook into the registration process. In this section, I'll describe a mechanism that will let you "override" Delphi's registration implementation for DLL-based COM servers.

If you use Delphi's Object Repository to create a new ActiveX Library project, it will create a new library file that contains the following code:

```
library Project1;

uses
  ComServ;

exports
  DllGetClassObject,
  DllCanUnloadNow,
  DllRegisterServer,
  DllUnregisterServer;

end.
```

Rather than using the DllRegisterServer implementation contained within the ComServ unit, you can implement the DllRegisterServer function within your

own application. To do so, just create a new unit that implements the DllRegister-
Server and DllUnregisterServer functions. However, since the ComServ unit must
still be used in your project, you must explicitly scope the DllRegisterServer and
DllUnregisterServer exported function names.

The following code snippet shows the implementation of the DllRegisterServer
and DllUnregisterServer functions inside a unit called uRegister:

```
function DllRegisterServer: HResult;
begin
  Result := S_OK;
  try
    ComServer.UpdateRegistry (True);
    { Insert custom registration code here }
  except
    Result := E_Fail;
  end;
end;

function DllUnregisterServer: HResult;
begin
  Result := S_OK;
  try
    { Insert custom unregistration code here }
    ComServer.UpdateRegistry(False);
  except
    Result := E_Fail;
  end;
end;
```

You clearly have the option of updating the Registry before or after Delphi's
default implementation via the ComServer.UpdateRegistry function call. However,
it is arguably better to let Delphi do most of the work constructing the Registry
keys before adding the additional keys that you want. On occasion, you will have
to add additional subkeys under the CLSID keys that Delphi generates for your
COM components.

TIP   One use for custom registration is the requirement that shell extension
objects must support the Apartment threading model. This requires the
addition of a subkey under the COM component's CLSID key with a name
of Threading Model and a value of Apartment. We'll see an example of the
use of the Apartment model in the next chapter.

Remember that we must explicitly scope the name of an exported function to avoid confusion with the identically named functions in the ComServ unit. Here's how the code in the library file would look after we explicitly scope our function names:

```
exports
  DllGetClassObject,
  DllCanUnloadNow,
  uRegister.DllRegisterServer,
  uRegister.DllUnregisterServer;
```

You can find the complete code for custom registration on the CD-ROM in the project called CustomReg.

You have now seen how Delphi provides a default implementation for self-registering COM servers. If you use Delphi's implementation, it provides registration services for both DLL- and EXE-based COM servers. On the other hand, if you must implement your own custom registration code, you can use the simple piece of code presented in this section to intercept Delphi's default implementation for DLL-based COM servers.

Type Information Integration

Delphi's type information integration solves an important problem in COM: How do you create self-describing COM components? As we discussed earlier, in the object description section, developers have to learn either ODL or IDL, and feed these source code files through the MIDL compiler to generate the type libraries. But why should you have to learn a new language to create type libraries when you are programming in Delphi?

To solve that problem, Borland added two-way tool support for type libraries into Delphi 3. Delphi's new Type Library Editor makes it a snap to create type libraries for Automation-compatible COM components. We'll use the Type Library Editor in the next chapter. To open it, choose File ➢ New ➢ ActiveX ➢ Type Library. Figure 10.4 shows a screen shot.

The Type Library Editor allows you to create and maintain type library files. Behind the scenes, Delphi creates a separate unit that contains all of the Delphi-specific definitions for your type library's COM components. Delphi automatically creates the interface reference definitions and extracts the relevant constants from the type library. It even builds a number of useful helper class functions with which you can easily create the COM components referenced in the type library.

FIGURE 10.4:

The new Type
Library Editor in
Delphi 3 makes
building
Automation-
compatible COM
components a snap.

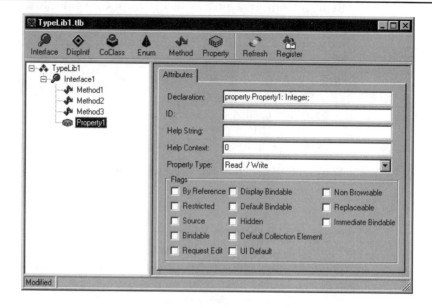

What happens if you want to use a COM component that wasn't created using Delphi? As long as you have a type library for that COM component, Delphi can convert it into a Delphi unit for you. Simply select the Import Type Library command from the Project menu, enter the path to the type library, and Delphi will do the rest!

Dual Interface Support

In the section on language independence, we saw how languages that don't support the notion of pointers or explicit memory allocation can manipulate COM interfaces. The mechanism that we explored is called dynamic invocation, and it allows a caller to refer to a COM interface member function by name rather than through its offset in the interface's function table. However, dynamic invocation does not come without a cost.

As we discussed earlier, the dynamic invocation mechanism cannot possibly make a function call as quickly as calling that function using an offset into a function table with the parameters on the stack. The IDispatch interface defined below takes care of the explicit conversion of a function name to an actual function address:

```
IDispatch = interface(IUnknown)
  ['{00020400-0000-0000-C000-000000000046}']
  function GetTypeInfoCount(out Count: Integer):
    Integer; stdcall;
  function GetTypeInfo(Index, LocaleID: Integer;
    out TypeInfo): Integer; stdcall;
  function GetIDsOfNames(const IID: TGUID; Names: Pointer;
    NameCount, LocaleID: Integer; DispIDs: Pointer):
    Integer; stdcall;
  function Invoke(DispID: Integer; const IID: TGUID;
    LocaleID: Integer; Flags: Word; var Params;
    VarResult, ExcepInfo, ArgErr: Pointer): Integer; stdcall;
end;
```

The member function GetIDsOfNames takes care of converting the function name to an integer value known as a DispID. The DispID is used in the Invoke function to call the function in question.

As you can see, calling a function by name involves calling two separate functions in the IDispatch interface. If the COM component that you are talking to lives in another Win32 process or on another computer, you have just performed two round-trip function calls to invoke a single function. Clearly, the function call overhead is something that can be optimized.

A dual interface combines the best features of a regular COM interface (like IUnknown) with the dynamic invocation capabilities of the IDispatch interface. A COM component that implements all of its COM interfaces as dual interfaces can be called by clients that only understand dynamic invocation (like earlier versions of Visual Basic and Delphi). It can also be called by clients that know how to make calls on native COM interfaces by using offsets in the dual interface's function table. This gives the creator of the COM component the greatest amount of accessibility to potential users.

So what exactly is a dual interface? It's a COM interface that is derived from IDispatch, rather than IUnknown. The implementation of the IDispatch portion of the dual interface will dispatch function calls to the dual interface's member functions the same way that it always has. However, for those clients who know the layout of the dual interface's function table (using an interface reference in Delphi, for example), they can make calls directly using offsets into the function table. This avoids the overhead that is normally associated with dynamic invocation, while preserving the dynamic dispatch capabilities of IDispatch.

For example, suppose you want to create a dual interface that has two member functions: Foo and Bar. You would declare the dual interface in Delphi as follows:

```
IDualInterface = interface (IDispatch)
  ['{47EB8811-F23A-11D0-BA31-00A024332816}']
  function Foo: HResult; safecall;
  function Bar: HResult; safecall;
end;
```

There are seven methods in the IDispatch interface. Pointers to these functions will occupy positions 0 through 6 in the interface's function table. The functions Foo and Bar occupy positions 7 and 8. The implementation of the GetIDsOfNames function in IDispatch will map the text strings Foo and Bar to an arbitrary set of DispIDs. The Invoke function will map those DispIDs to entries 7 and 8 in the function table.

How does the user of a COM component discover the layout of its dual interfaces? By reading the component's type library.

If you had to implement the IDispatch functions for your dual interface, and manually generate the mappings described above, dual interfaces might be more trouble than they are worth. However, Delphi 3 makes it remarkably simple to create a dual interface COM component: simply derive the class that implements your COM component from TAutoObject rather than from TComObject! Delphi's IDispatch implementation in TAutoObject takes care of the implementation of your dual interfaces for you.

Creating dual-interface COM components is even easier if you use Delphi's Object Repository to select the Automation Object Wizard. In the next chapter, we will create an Automation object that supports dual interfaces.

What's Next

This chapter has attempted to provide a reasonably complete introduction to COM by considering the programming problems that COM solves. Building on that introduction, we saw how Delphi solves a number of programming problems that COM introduces.

In the next chapter, we will build a number of COM components and COM applications to demonstrate how the various Delphi COM features that we explored in this chapter fit together. Hopefully, by the end of this section you'll see how Delphi and COM form a potent combination that can be used to create both COM components and COM client applications.

Here's a list of some additional references and resources that you'll want to look at to round out your knowledge of COM:

> The COM Specification. This is a must-read for any serious COM programmer. You can download it from Microsoft at
>
> ```
> http:www.microsoft.com/oledev
> ```
>
> Dale Rogerson, *Inside COM* (Microsoft Press, 1997). This is a very good introduction to the inner workings of COM, and how to use some of the more advanced features of COM (aggregation, multithreading). It's written for C++ programmers.
>
> David Chappell, *Understanding ActiveX and OLE* (Microsoft Press, 1996). A very clear and concise overview of the various OLE and ActiveX technologies. Not much code, but a fantastic overview of a large body of technologies.
>
> Don Box, *COM: The Distributed Object Programming Model* (Addison-Wesley, 1998). This is a book on how to "live the COM lifestyle," as told by one of its most ardent practitioners. The focus here is on the *why* of COM as opposed to the nuts-and-bolts of how to implement COM.
>
> Kraig Brockschmidt, *Inside OLE* Second Edition (Microsoft Press, 1995). The original bible of all things COM and OLE. Many topics that are not covered elsewhere (particularly the details of how Object Linking and Embedding works) can be found here.
>
> The `www.IUnknown.com` Web site, which Dr. Lam maintains to serve as a focal point for discussions on COM development. His *PC Magazine* articles will all be reprinted on this Web site, and you'll find an up-to-date collection of links to useful COM resources on the Internet.

CHAPTER

ELEVEN

11

Applying COM

- Adding Scripting Support to an Application

- The safecall Calling Convention

- OLE Drag-and-Drop

- The Dispatch Interface

- Working with Type Libraries

- A Context-Menu Handler

This chapter's objective is to provide a number of concrete examples that illustrate the principles discussed in the previous chapter. We'll examine a couple of applications of COM that should provide the motivation to begin using COM in your own work.

The first example shows off the power of Automation by making an existing application scriptable. Before COM became available, one of the problems that developers had to face when building applications was building a mechanism that allows them to automatically test those applications. Often it involved writing specialized code that would read in test scripts and execute them on the fly. This was necessary because of a limitation imposed by Win32 processes: you cannot call a function that resides in another Win32 process!

However, as we learned in the last chapter, one of the key features of Automation is that it can let you export functions from a Win32 process. In Chapter 10, we noted that Automation was flexible in this regard because you did not have to write specialized code to marshal parameters between Win32 processes. Simply by exposing the capabilities of your applications as Automation objects, you enable outside applications (such as a testing application) to script the behavior of your application!

The second example shows how you can integrate your application with the Win32 shell. We'll take a typical Delphi application and add drag-and-drop integration with Explorer, in addition to a shell context menu. However, in contrast to the first example where there are alternate ways of achieving the end result, you *must* use COM to integrate your application with the Win32 shell.

In both cases, we'll be extending a simple Delphi application: a basic word processor called SimpleWord. It uses a Win32 Rich Edit control to hold the text, and a number of stock Delphi components to round out the user interface. It allows you to load, save, and print your rich-text format files; and we'll extend these commands by using COM.

Scripting an Application

In this section, we'll add scripting capabilities to our basic word processor. SimpleWord supports the following operations:

- Load a rich text format (RTF) file.
- Save an RTF file.

- Save an RTF file under a different name.

- Print the currently loaded RTF file.

- Copy the current text selection to the Clipboard.

- Paste the current Clipboard contents into the file.

We are going to expose these capabilities to a scripting application, along with some of the more rudimentary operations that involve moving the cursor position and selecting regions of text (for the Clipboard operations). Finally, we'll build a controller application that exercises our new scriptable application.

The code in this section will illustrate several important new features introduced by Borland in Delphi 3: building Automation servers and building Automation controllers.

The SimpleWord Application

Before we begin adding scripting support to our basic word processor application, let's take a quick look at how its features are implemented. You can find the complete source code on the CD; here we'll examine only the parts that will be pertinent to our discussions later on.

The skeleton of the word processor application was generated using Delphi's Application Wizard. It created the main application form, its main menu, a status bar, a tool bar, and a skeleton framework to which we can add our application-specific functionality. To add functionality, we dropped a TRichEdit component onto the client area of the form, and set its Align property to Client, as you can see in Figure 11.1. The Application Wizard added all of the components and code required to activate the various common dialog boxes (Open, Save, Print and Print Setup) for us already, so all we have to do is add the code that orchestrates the behavior of these components.

Here is the code for loading and saving our rich-text files. The Application Wizard generated most of it; the code we added is marked with // *Added* comments:

```
procedure TMainForm.FileOpen(Sender: TObject);
begin
  if OpenDialog.Execute then
  begin
    FCurrentFileName := OpenDialog.FileName;
```

FIGURE 11.1:

The form of the first version of the SimpleWord example (SimpleW1) at design time

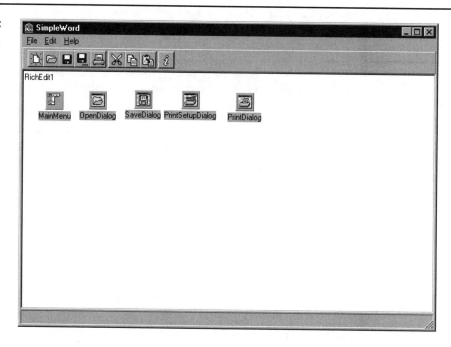

```
      RichEdit1.Lines.LoadFromFile( FCurrentFileName ); // Added
   end;
end;


procedure TMainForm.FileSave(Sender: TObject);
begin
  RichEdit1.Lines.SaveToFile( FCurrentFileName ); // Added
end;


procedure TMainForm.FileSaveAs(Sender: TObject);
begin
  if SaveDialog.Execute then
  begin
    FCurrentFileName := SaveDialog.FileName;
    RichEdit1.Lines.SaveToFile( FCurrentFileName ); // Added
  end;
end;
```

Similarly, we added print functionality by modifying the `Print` method of `TMainForm`:

```
procedure TMainForm.FilePrint(Sender: TObject);
begin
  if PrintDialog.Execute then
    RichEdit1.Print( FCurrentFilename ); //Added
end;
```

The Clipboard operations were equally straightforward:

```
procedure TMainForm.EditCut(Sender: TObject);
begin
  RichEdit1.CutToClipboard; // Added
end;

procedure TMainForm.EditCopy(Sender: TObject);
begin
  RichEdit1.CopyToClipboard; // Added
end;

procedure TMainForm.EditPaste(Sender: TObject);
begin
  RichEdit1.PasteFromClipboard; // Added
end;
```

Before we begin to modify the SimpleWord application, you should compile and build the application for yourself to see it in action. You can find the source code files in the SimpleW1 subdirectory of the current chapter on the companion CD.

Adding Scripting Support

We would like to expose a number of commands from our application. The first category comprises the high-level commands:

- Open
- Save As
- Save
- Print
- Cut

- Copy

- Paste

The second category involves a number of lower-level commands that allow us to reposition the cursor within the RichEdit component:

- Home

- Select All

- Select

We will export these commands from SimpleWord in an Automation object. By creating an instance of the SimpleWord Automation object, we will also be creating an instance of the SimpleWord application.

NOTE   Keep in mind that the SimpleWord Automation object is just a COM component. This means that you never have a reference to the Automation object itself; you just have a reference to one of the object's interfaces.

An Automation object can have any number of interfaces. In our case, we will implement only one interface, which contains all of the commands we want to make scriptable. Since we want to ensure that our Automation object has a minimal impact on our application, it delegates all of its functionality to code contained within the application itself.

Our Automation object is an example of a local server (one that runs in its own process space). As discussed in Chapter 10, Delphi encapsulates the differences between an in-process and a local Automation object in the ComServ unit. In the next section, we'll take a closer look at the details of creating a local server and see what Delphi is doing for us behind the scenes.

Creating Automation Objects

To create a new Automation object, all you have to do is run the Automation Object Wizard. Open Delphi's Object Repository by selecting New from the File menu. Select the ActiveX page and double-click on the Automation Object Wizard (see Figure 11.2).

FIGURE 11.2:

Delphi's Object Repository shows the different ActiveX objects that you can create.

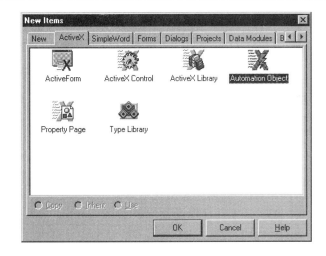

The Automation Object Wizard will prompt you for the name of the Automation Object you will be creating and the type of instancing you want to allow:

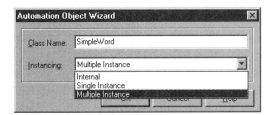

The Automation Object Wizard offers three instancing options:

Multiple Instance: Allows any number of Automation objects to be created.

Single Instance: Allows only a single Automation object to be created.

Internal: Disallows external creation of the Automation object.

In most cases, you'll select multiple instancing. Once you have entered the class name (`SimpleWordObject` in our case) for your new Automation object in the Wizard, Delphi will generate a skeleton unit that contains some prefabricated code for creating your new Automation object. There are three important bits of code that Delphi has generated for you.

The first is the declaration of the Automation object's class. In our example, the declaration looks like this:

```
TSimpleWordObject = class (TAutoObject, ISimpleWordObject)
  ...
end;
```

Delphi has derived a new class from the TAutoObject base class, which is implemented in the ComObj unit. TSimpleWordObject also implements the ISimpleWordObject interface, which is declared in the SimpleWord_TLB unit. This unit is automatically generated and maintained by Delphi's Type Library Editor, and we'll be taking a closer look at it in the following section.

The second piece of code that is generated for you is the declaration of the class factory in the initialization section of the unit:

```
initialization
  TAutoObjectFactory.Create(ComServer, TSimpleWordObject,
    Class_SimpleWordObject, ciMultiInstance);
```

This creates a new class factory object whose sole purpose is to create instances of TSimpleWordObjects. It also registers itself with Delphi's class factory framework.

Note the unusual syntax that is used in the creation of this object. Delphi does not store the return value of the call to the TAutoObjectFactory.Create constructor! Instead, the code in the constructor registers itself with the global ComClassManager object, which maintains a singly linked list of all class factory objects. The key line of code that does this registration is shown below (extracted from the code in the TComClassFactory.Create constructor):

```
ComClassManager.AddObjectFactory(Self);
```

The final piece of code that is generated for you is the SimpleWord_TLB unit. It's worth your while to look at the code that Delphi generates in this unit. In particular, there are two helper class functions that help you create instances of your Automation object. Here are the ones that are found in the SimpleWord_TLB unit:

```
class function CoSimpleWordObject.Create: ISimpleWordObject;
begin
Result := CreateComObject(Class_SimpleWordObject) as
  ISimpleWordObject;
end;

class function CoSimpleWordObject.CreateRemote(
  const MachineName: string): ISimpleWordObject;
```

```
begin
  Result := CreateRemoteComObject(MachineName,
    Class_SimpleWordObject) as ISimpleWordObject;
end;
```

> **NOTE**
> A *class function* is one that does not require an instance of an object to operate on.

The CoSimpleWordObject.Create function allows you to create instances of the SimpleWordObject Automation object on your local computer. If you wish to create an instance of a SimpleWordObject on another computer, just use the CoSimpleWordObject.CreateRemote function. It takes a MachineName as a parameter, which can be a UNC (Universal Naming Convention) name, a DNS (Domain Name System) name, or an IP address. All of the details of calling either CoCreateInstance (in the local case) or CoCreateInstanceEx (in the remote case) are hidden from you in these two class functions.

Delphi's Type Library Editor

Now that you have finished creating the skeleton of an Automation object using the Automation Wizard, you should see Delphi's new Type Library Editor in the foreground (Figure 11.3). You should always use the Type Library Editor to define and edit your Automation interfaces. Delphi uses its two-way tools technology to generate the source code automatically and maintain it.

Let's begin our examination of the Type Library Editor by adding a couple of the member functions that we will be implementing in our Automation object. First we'll add the NewFile function, which creates a new, empty file in SimpleWord. Select the ISimpleWordObject interface in the left pane of the Type Library Editor and click on the Method button on the toolbar. The Type Library Editor creates a new procedure, called Method1, and positions the cursor in the Declaration field of the Attributes tab in the right pane of the editor. Just replace Method1 with NewFile in that field. Click on the *Refresh* button to force the editor to generate some code for you.

There are several places where the Type Library Editor will generate the resulting code. The first is in the SimpleWord_TLB file, where it will add code to both the interface and the dispinterface declarations.

Delphi's Type
Library Editor makes
it easy for you to
create type libraries
for your Automation
objects.

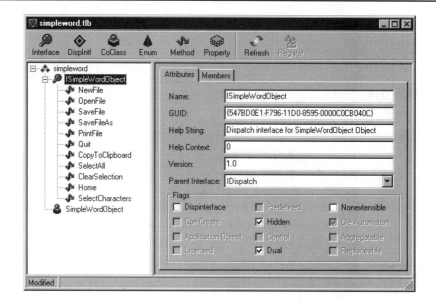

The type library editor added the commented line of code to the `interface` declaration:

```
ISimpleWordObject = interface(IDispatch)
  ['{547BD0E1-F796-11D0-8595-0000C0CB040C}']
  ...
  procedure NewFile; safecall; // Added
  ...
end;
```

The `safecall` keyword informs Delphi that this function will be called using a special calling convention known as `safecall`. The `safecall` calling convention is an important concept in Delphi's Automation implementation, and we'll discuss its details in the next section.

Delphi's Type Library Editor added the commented line of code to the `dispinterface` declaration:

```
ISimpleWordObjectDisp = dispinterface
  ['{547BD0E1-F796-11D0-8595-0000C0CB040C}']
  procedure NewFile; dispid 1; // Added
end;
```

Rather than specifying a calling convention, the `dispinterface` declaration contains the `dispid` for the `NewFile` procedure. Remember that "conventional" Automation controllers use the `dispid` to perform late binding via the `IDispatch.Invoke` function. By packaging the `dispid` in the `dispinterface` declaration, Delphi avoids having to call the `IDispatch.GetIDsOfNames` function to obtain the `dispid` prior to calling the `IDispatch.Invoke` function.

The final place where the Type Library Editor generates code on your behalf is in the unit that implements the Automation object. In this case, it's the Simple-WordObject unit of the SimpleW2 directory of the companion CD. It adds the following line to the class declaration:

```
procedure NewFile; safecall;
```

It also creates an empty procedure block in the implementation section of the unit:

```
procedure TSimpleWordObject.NewFile;
begin

end;
```

This saves you quite a bit of typing when implementing your Automation object's methods.

NOTE   The Type Library Editor will only reverse changes to the type library file. For example, if you try to delete the `NewFile` method that you created in the Type Library Editor, it will only remove the declarations from the SimpleWord_TLB file. You'll have to manually remove the code that it generated in the SimpleWordObject unit.

So far, we have not talked about function parameters or their types. As we mentioned in the last chapter, Automation strikes a necessary compromise between flexibility and scope by defining a single "universal" type called a variant. All Automation object parameters must be variant compatible. This restricts us to using the following Delphi types as Automation method parameters: `SmallInt`, `Integer`, `Single`, `Double`, `Currency`, `TDateTime`, `WideString`, `IDispatch`, `WordBool`, `OleVariant`, `SCode`, `TColor`, `Byte`, `TSafeArray`, and `IUnknown`. You are free to use standard Delphi `var` and `const` directives to signify pass-by-reference. The Type Library Editor enforces this restriction, and will not allow you to enter parameter types that are not Automation-compatible.

As a concrete example, let's use the Type Library Editor to add the `OpenFile` method to our SimpleWordObject. Click on the Method button to create a new method, and type the following in the Declaration field:

```
procedure OpenFile (const FileName: String);
```

When you click on the *Refresh* button, however, you'll notice that the type library editor is displaying "Invalid parameter type: String" in its status bar. Change the `String` type to `WideString`, and the Type Library Editor will generate the correct declarations for the function.

> **NOTE** The Automation string type is a special Unicode string. In Unicode, each character is represented by a 16-bit value. Automation strings are also known as BSTRs or Basic Strings. Delphi provides native support for BSTRs through its `WideString` type.

What if you want to create a function that returns a value? As long as the return value is an Automation-compatible type, you can declare the Automation method as a `function` instead of a `procedure`. Let's add the `IsDirty` function to the Automation object. Click on the Method button to create a new method, and type the following into the Declaration field:

```
function IsDirty: WordBool;
```

The safecall Calling Convention

The `safecall` calling convention was designed to simplify error handling in your Automation object member functions. It does so by automatically catching all of the exceptions that are raised within the context of a `safecall`-protected function. Delphi generates code that intercedes on your behalf to automatically convert Delphi exceptions into `HRESULT` error codes, and it extracts the information from the exception object to construct an error context object that can be queried using the `IErrorInfo` interface.

The first thing that `safecall` does is to force the function to return an `HRESULT` value. Remember that *all* COM interface member functions must return an `HRESULT` value (except for the `IUnknown.AddRef` and `IUnknown.Release` functions, which must return long integers). Even though you have defined `NewFile` as a procedure, Delphi actually defines the function as follows:

```
function NewFile: HRESULT;
```

In the case where you are defining a `function` rather than a `procedure`, Delphi must do some additional work. Consider the `IsDirty` function that we added above:

```
function IsDirty: WordBool; safecall;
```

An Automation parameter can be marked with the `retval` attribute in IDL. This means that Delphi is actually passing the return value of the `IsDirty` function in the parameter list. You will never notice this in your code because the Automation controller code will automatically convert a parameter that has the `retval` attribute into the return value of a function.

The second thing that `safecall` does is to create an implicit `try/except` block around all of the code within the body of your procedure. As discussed in the previous chapter, throwing exceptions across COM interface boundaries is strictly forbidden. Within this `try/except` block, Delphi will automatically convert error codes into the corresponding `HRESULT` error codes for you.

Delphi's compiler generates some special code for functions that use the `safecall` calling convention. When an exception is thrown within the protected function, this code implicitly calls the `SafeCallException` virtual function, defined in `TObject`. In the ComObj unit, `TComObject` overrides this virtual function and delegates the call to the `HandleSafeCallException` function shown below:

```
function HandleSafeCallException(ExceptObject: TObject;
  ExceptAddr: Pointer; const ErrorIID: TGUID;
  const ProgID, HelpFileName: WideString): HResult;
var
  E: TObject;
  CreateError: ICreateErrorInfo;
  ErrorInfo: IErrorInfo;
begin
  Result := E_UNEXPECTED;
  E := ExceptObject;
  if CreateErrorInfo(CreateError) = S_OK then
  begin
    CreateError.SetGUID(ErrorIID);
    if ProgID <> '' then
      CreateError.SetSource(PWideChar(ProgID));
    if HelpFileName <> '' then
      CreateError.SetHelpFile(PWideChar(HelpFileName));
    if E is Exception then
    begin
      CreateError.SetDescription(PWideChar(
```

```
          WideString(Exception(E).Message)));
      CreateError.SetHelpContext(Exception(E).HelpContext);
      if (E is EOleSysError) and
          (EOleSysError(E).ErrorCode < 0) then
        Result := EOleSysError(E).ErrorCode;
    end;
    if CreateError.QueryInterface(IErrorInfo,
        ErrorInfo) = S_OK then
      SetErrorInfo(0, ErrorInfo);
  end;
end;
```

This function does two very useful things for you. First, it implements support for generic COM error context objects. Well-behaved Automation client applications will typically call the GetErrorInfo COM API function to retrieve the IErrorInfo interface when function calls return an HRESULT error code. They can then call the various member functions of IErrorInfo (shown below) to obtain more detailed information about the cause of the error.

```
type
  IErrorInfo = interface(IUnknown)
    ['{1CF2B120-547D-101B-8E65-08002B2BD119}']
    function GetGUID(out guid: TGUID): HResult; stdcall;
    function GetSource(out bstrSource: WideString):
      HResult; stdcall;
    function GetDescription(out bstrDescription: WideString):
      HResult; stdcall;
    function GetHelpFile(out bstrHelpFile: WideString):
      HResult; stdcall;
    function GetHelpContext(out dwHelpContext: Longint):
      HResult; stdcall;
  end;
```

The HandleSafeCallException function creates a generic COM error-context object by calling the COM API function CreateErrorInfo and retrieving the COM component's ICreateErrorInfo interface. It then uses this interface to initialize the error-context object's state with the information contained within the Delphi exception object.

The second thing that HandleSafeCallException does is to return the appropriate HRESULT error code for a safecall function or procedure. The default HRESULT error code for a Delphi exception is E_UNEXPECTED. If the Delphi exception object happens to be an EOleSysError object, then HandleSafeCallException returns the ErrorCode field of the EOleSysError object (which is itself an HRESULT value). Note the similarities between this code and the generic try/except code presented in Chapter 10.

This mechanism essentially allows Delphi to "throw exceptions" across an interface boundary. Well-behaved OLE Automation controllers such as Visual Basic or Delphi itself will report the extended error information contained in the error-context object to the client application.

The Scripting Object

The rest of the code for the scripting object is excerpted below. The key thing to note is that TSimpleWordObject does not actually implement any of these functions. It simply delegates all of the functionality back to the code that is contained within the SimpleWord application itself. This ensures that we have minimal impact on the application; when we execute TSimpleWordObject, we are actually exercising the code in the SimpleWord application. Here are some of the methods of this class (a few others have been omitted):

```
procedure TSimpleWordObject.CopyToClipboard;
begin
  MainForm.EditCopy (Self);
end;

procedure TSimpleWordObject.NewFile;
begin
  MainForm.FileNew (Self);
end;

procedure TSimpleWordObject.OpenFile (
  const FileName: WideString);
begin
  MainForm.FileOpen (FileName);
end;

procedure TSimpleWordObject.PrintFile;
begin
  MainForm.Print;
end;

procedure TSimpleWordObject.Quit;
```

```
begin
  MainForm.FileExit (Self);
end;

procedure TSimpleWordObject.SaveFile;
begin
  MainForm.FileSave (Self);
end;

procedure TSimpleWordObject.SaveFileAs(
  const FileName: WideString );
begin
  MainForm.FileSaveAs (FileName);
end;
```

Building a Scripting Client

The scripting client application, called Script, will exercise most of the features of the SimpleWord application. It is an example of a Delphi Automation controller that uses interface references to manipulate a dual-interface Automation object. This section looks at the various kinds of Automation controllers you can create using Delphi, and you'll see how to use Delphi's type library import facility to simplify the task of controlling an Automation application.

Automation Controllers

Delphi allows you to build two kinds of Automation controllers. One uses late binding exclusively, and is implemented using the variant keyword introduced in Delphi 2. The other uses early binding via a dispinterface or an interface reference. Both of these early-binding techniques were introduced in Delphi 3.

Late binding, as discussed in Chapter 10, involves calling IDispatch.GetIDs-OfNames followed by IDispatch.Invoke for each function invocation that the client application wishes to make. Early binding, on the other hand, involves bypassing the requirement to call the IDispatch.GetIDsOfNames function, and instead calling IDispatch.Invoke directly in the case of a conventional Automation interface. Early binding can also imply that the function is called using its function table offset in the case of a dual interface.

The kind of Automation controller that your client application will implement depends largely on the Automation object that you are trying to control. Let's consider the three types of Automation objects you are likely to encounter.

The antique: This Automation object does not have a type library associated with it, and only exports `IDispatch` interfaces. In this case, you have no choice but to use the `variant`-style automation controller.

Last year's model: This Automation object does have a type library that you can import into your Delphi application. However, it only understands calls via its `IDispatch` interface. In this case, you can use the `dispinterface` interface reference in your code, and bypass the need to call `IDispatch.GetIDsOfNames`.

The hot rod: This is the Automation object that everybody wants to control. Not only does it export a type library, it also supports dual interfaces, the "hot rod" interface of Automation objects. You can import this object's type library into Delphi, and use the type library's defined interfaces to make calls using function table offsets and thus bypass the need to call `IDispatch.Invoke`.

Importing Type Libraries

Delphi makes it very easy to import another application's type library for use in your own applications. If you create a new project, and select Import Type Library from Delphi's Project menu, you'll see a list of all the registered type libraries on your computer, as shown in Figure 11.4.

Delphi enumerates all of the Registry keys under the `HKEY_CLASSES_ROOT\TypeLib` key in the Registry to generate this list. If you can't find the type library that you're looking for in this list, chances are it isn't registered.

Type library files can be stand-alone TLB files; they can also be bound as Windows resources to DLL and EXE files. If you can't find the type library that you're looking for, try using the Import Type Library applet to examine the DLL and EXE files of the application that you're inspecting. Click on the Add button in the Import Type Library dialog to inspect individual files.

Examining an extensive type library such as the one defined by PowerPoint 97 can provide some interesting insights into possible uses for a type library. For

FIGURE 11.4:

Delphi's Import Type
Library dialog
shows a list of all
registered type
libraries.

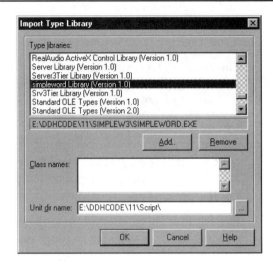

example, PowerPoint defines all of the constants that can be used by application programmers within its type library. Here's an excerpt from the type library file generated from the PowerPoint 97 type library on one computer:

```
{ PpWindowState }

ppWindowNormal = 1;
ppWindowMinimized = 2;
ppWindowMaximized = 3;
```

This is an example of an Automation *enumeration*. You can define your own enumerated constants by clicking on the Enum toolbar button in Delphi's Type Library Editor.

Take some time to browse through the rest of this and other type libraries. You'll discover that Delphi generates many other attributes and keywords that we don't have time to cover in this chapter. These type library examples should also give you some insights into how you can make better use of type libraries in your own projects.

The Scripting Client

The scripting client application, called Script, exercises two of the main features of the SimpleWord application. The first feature is copying to the Clipboard. The client application will create an instance of the SimpleWordObject, open the file that you specify, select all of its text, and copy that text to the Clipboard. The second feature is printing the document that you specify. The client creates an instance of the SimpleWordObject, opens the file that you specify, and prints that file to the current printer.

The scripting client uses the SimpleWordObject type library. In our case, we just include that unit in the uses clause of the scripting client. You could also use the Import Type Library functionality in Delphi to construct your own type library unit dynamically from the SimpleWordObject type library file.

The scripting client application has a simple user interface that consists of an edit control that accepts a filename from the user, and three buttons labeled *Select File*, *Copy File*, and *Print File*:

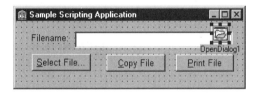

The code that implements each of the features is contained in the OnClick event handler for each of the buttons. The code that copies the file to the Clipboard is shown below; you can see the results in Figure 11.5:

```
procedure TMainForm.btnCopyClick(Sender: TObject);
var
  simpleWord: ISimpleWordObject;
begin
  simpleWord := CoSimpleWordObject.Create;
  with simpleWord do
  begin
    OpenFile( Edit1.Text );
    SelectAll;
    CopyToClipboard;
  end;
end;
```

In this code we create a new instance of the SimpleWordObject by calling the class function CoSimpleWordObject.Create. We then enclose all of the operations on the ISimpleWordObject interface within a with/do block, and perform each of

FIGURE 11.5:

The Script application can be used to copy an RTF file into the Clipboard and then paste it into a word processor.

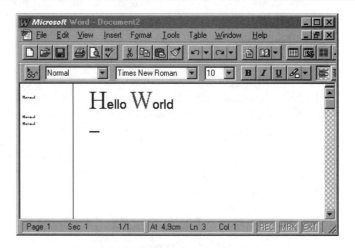

the operations that you would expect: OpenFile, SelectAll, and CopyToClipboard. Similarly, the code that prints the file to the Clipboard is shown below:

```
procedure TMainForm.btnPrintClick(Sender: TObject);
var
  simpleWord: ISimpleWordObject;
begin
  simpleWord := CoSimpleWordObject.Create;
  with simpleWord do
  begin
    OpenFile( Edit1.Text );
    PrintFile;
  end;
end;
```

You can find all of the code that implements the Automation-enabled SimpleWord application and the scripting application in the SimpleW2 and Script subdirectories on the CD.

Extending an Application

Well-behaved Win32 applications integrate themselves into the Windows shell. Applications that work with documents should provide users with several ways to open files. Typically, they support drag-and-drop on the Windows desktop, and they add a context menu so that users can right-click a document to open the application.

Not surprisingly, the Windows shell (for all of the current 32-bit versions of Windows: 95, 98, NT 4.0, and NT 5.0) is largely built from and extended using COM components. Since COM components are added and removed using Registry keys, it does not take much additional support on the part of Windows to allow specially registered COM components to extend the Windows shell.

In this section, we'll add support for drag-and-drop and shell context menus to our SimpleWord word processor. Our drag-and-drop support is quite flexible: it is implemented entirely as a Delphi VCL component and an ActiveX library. You'll be able to add drag-and-drop functionality to any of your applications simply by dropping the drag-and-drop component onto your application's main form.

The context menu support is implemented in its own ActiveX library. The code in the library can provide context menu support for multiple applications and multiple file extensions. It communicates with the SimpleWord application using the command line.

Drag-and-Drop

In this section, we'll take a closer look at the drag-and-drop support that we'll be adding to the SimpleWord application, in the SimpleW3 version. For maximum flexibility, the bulk of the drag-and-drop code is implemented within a VCL component, named `TDropComponent`, that can simply be dropped onto your application's main form.

Using the drag-and-drop component is very straightforward. By setting the `DropWindow` property of the drag-and-drop component, you set the window upon which you would like to enable drag-and-drop. You can set `DropWindow` to any `TWinControl`-derived component on your form. When the user drops a file onto the drop-enabled window, the `DropNotification` event will fire, and the component will pass you the full path to the file that was just dropped on the window.

The component also illustrates a number of very interesting techniques in Delphi component programming. Before we can start discussing how to implement a drag-and-drop component, we should first take a quick overview of the theory behind OLE drag-and-drop.

OLE Drag-and-Drop Theory

There are two general issues that we have to be concerned about with drag-and-drop. The first is how individual applications can register with the operating system to receive drag-and-drop notifications. The second is how the data (the list of filenames) is passed around between applications. Both of these problems are good examples of how COM can be used to solve the problem of interprocess communications.

There is a very clear separation of responsibility between the application and the Windows shell when it comes to handling drag-and-drop. The application is responsible for providing feedback to the user whenever the user drags a shell object over the application. This feedback is expressed through the shape of the mouse pointer as the user drags the file over the application. On the other hand, the Windows shell bears the responsibility for notifying each application when the user drags a file over it.

Since the responsibility is shared in this fashion, the drag-and-drop design is extremely flexible. The Windows shell does not have to know anything at all about what file types can be dropped onto a given application. Instead, each application is responsible for knowing what file types it can accept in a drag-and-drop operation. How it determines this can be quite sophisticated, and is not necessarily based upon the filename or the file extension. An application can actually open up a file and inspect its contents before deciding whether to allow the user to drop the file!

The application is also responsible for providing the user with a visual cue about whether a drop operation is permitted or not. This cue is typically a circle with a backslash when a drop operation is not allowed, and some kind of icon that represents a file being dropped when the drop operation is approved. To accomplish this, the shell must communicate with the application's code throughout the drag-and-drop process. Since the shell is built using COM components, it should not be surprising that the application code that communicates with the shell is housed inside a COM component.

The COM component that provides user interface feedback to the shell must implement the IDropTarget interface:

```
type
  IDropTarget = interface(IUnknown)
    ['{00000122-0000-0000-C000-000000000046}']
    function DragEnter(const dataObj: IDataObject; grfKeyState:
      Longint; pt: TPoint; var dwEffect: Longint): HResult;
      stdcall;
    function DragOver(grfKeyState: Longint; pt: TPoint;
      var dwEffect: Longint): HResult; stdcall;
    function DragLeave: HResult; stdcall;
    function Drop(const dataObj: IDataObject; grfKeyState:
      Longint; pt: TPoint; var dwEffect: Longint): HResult;
      stdcall;
  end;
```

The shell calls the DragEnter member function whenever a file is initially dragged over the application. It passes a reference to an IDataObject interface that the application can query to discover the filenames that are being dropped onto the application. Data objects are an important aspect of COM, and the next section discusses them in detail. For the time being, just remember that they represent a standard way for applications to pass structured data around.

The workhorse function of IDropTarget is DragOver. Its role is to provide feedback to the shell throughout the drag operation. It returns DropEffect_None in the dwEffect parameter if a drop operation is not permitted. If a drop operation is allowed, it will return the appropriate value, DropEffect_Copy, DropEffect_Move, or DropEffect_Link, in the dwEffect parameter.

If the user changes the context of the drop operation by pressing the Shift, Ctrl, Alt, or any combination of those keys, it will be reflected in the grfKeyState parameter that is passed into the DragOver function. The function can then decide which dwEffect value to return in the dwEffect parameter.

Finally, the shell calls the Drop function when the user releases the mouse button—unless the DragOver function signals that a drop operation is not allowed. (This simplifies the programming model at your end.) In response to this function call, the application can take whatever actions are necessary to open the file or files.

Data Objects

Data objects are COM components that can render data in various application-specific formats. They share one thing in common: they all implement the IDataObject interface:

```
type
  IDataObject = interface(IUnknown)
    ['{0000010E-0000-0000-C000-000000000046}']
    function GetData(const formatetcIn: TFormatEtc;
      out medium: TStgMedium): HResult; stdcall;
    function GetDataHere(const formatetc: TFormatEtc;
      out medium: TStgMedium): HResult; stdcall;
    function QueryGetData(const formatetc: TFormatEtc):
      HResult; stdcall;
    function GetCanonicalFormatEtc(const formatetc: TFormatEtc;
      out formatetcOut: TFormatEtc): HResult; stdcall;
    function SetData(const formatetc: TFormatEtc;
      var medium: TStgMedium; fRelease: BOOL): HResult; stdcall;
    function EnumFormatEtc(dwDirection: Longint;
      out enumFormatEtc: IEnumFormatEtc): HResult; stdcall;
    function DAdvise(const formatetc: TFormatEtc; advf: Longint;
      const advSink: IAdviseSink; out dwConnection: Longint):
      HResult; stdcall;
    function DUnadvise(dwConnection: Longint): HResult; stdcall;
    function EnumDAdvise(out enumAdvise: IEnumStatData):
      HResult; stdcall;
  end;
```

While this interface may look intimidating, the only function we'll need to be concerned about is the GetData function.

The GetData function is responsible for rendering the data in a suitable format for an application. It takes two parameters: formatetcIn and medium. The formatetcIn parameter defines what format you want the data object to render the information in. The medium parameter tells the data object what kind of storage structure you want the data object to render that data into.

Both of these parameters are required to implement delayed rendering. Delayed rendering is an extremely powerful technique because the data does not need to be transferred until it is absolutely necessary. This can dramatically improve the perceived performance of an application, since you don't need to pre-render the data in all of the formats that you *think* another application may want. Instead, you pass the other application a data object, and allow that application to request the appropriate data format.

In our case, we are interested in the cf_HDrop format type. Not coincidentally, the name of this format is very similar to that of a Clipboard data format, since in this regard data objects can be thought of as individual Clipboard objects. By calling the GetData function and specifying cf_HDrop as the desired data format, we can ask the data object to render us a list of all of the files that are being dragged around by the user.

The other important parameter of the GetData function is the medium structure. This is a TStgMedium structure that is declared as a variant record:

```
TStgMedium = record
  tymed: Longint;
  case Integer of
    0: (hBitmap: HBitmap; unkForRelease: Pointer{IUnknown});
    1: (hMetaFilePict: THandle);
    2: (hEnhMetaFile: THandle);
    3: (hGlobal: HGlobal);
    4: (lpszFileName: POleStr);
    5: (stm: Pointer{IStream});
    6: (stg: Pointer{IStorage});
  end;
end;
```

WARNING   To be more precise, there are two different definitions of the TStgMedium record, one in the Ole2 unit, and the one above in the ActiveX unit. The differences between the two are minimal: In the definition of the Ole2 unit there are the data types here in braces instead of generic pointers.

As you can see, there is a wide range of storage data structures and media into which the data can be rendered. In contrast to the Windows Clipboard, which only allows you to transfer data in global memory, a data object can render the data in global memory, in a COM stream or storage object, or even in a file. This flexibility can be very useful in cases where the data being transferred is very large and making a copy of that data in memory would be prohibitively time-consuming.

This concludes our discussion of the theory of data objects and OLE drag-and-drop. You'll find extensive coverage of these topics in *Inside OLE*, by Kraig Brockschmidt (Microsoft Press). Next, we'll turn our attention to implementing drag-and-drop functionality using Delphi.

COM Components and VCL Components

There are two parts to our drag-and-drop implementation: the COM component that implements the IDropTarget interface, and the VCL component that we will drop onto our application's main form. However, a restriction in Delphi's implementation of COM will prevent us from putting both of these parts into the same container.

The restriction is caused by the way in which Delphi packages its components. When you create a Delphi component, you will typically use the Component Wizard to generate a skeleton component. Once you have finished writing and testing your component, you will want to install that component onto your Component palette. Starting in Delphi 3, a component can appear on the Component palette only if it is part of a package. This is the source of the problem.

A Delphi package is essentially just a Windows dynamic link library. Unfortunately, you cannot export DLL-based COM components from a Delphi package. A compiler directive in the ComServ unit prevents it from being included in a package.

To work around this problem, we placed the COM component that implements IDropTarget in its own ActiveX library. We pulled out all of the common declarations that would be required by both the component and the COM component and placed them in a unit (Interfaces in the ComLibrary application) that could be included in both the Delphi package and the ActiveX library. We suggest that you do the same in your own code if you encounter this situation in COM programming projects.

With that introduction out of the way, we are ready to look at the code. First, we'll examine the COM component that implements IDropTarget.

The COM Component

The TDropTarget component is housed in an ActiveX Library, which you can find in the ComLibrary directory of the companion CD. We used the ActiveX Library Wizard to generate a skeleton ActiveX library for the code in this section. You'll find the code for the COM object in the COM Library subdirectory on the CD.

Let's take a look at the code in the DropTarget unit. The following line declares the TDropTarget class:

```
TDropTarget = class (TComObject,
  IDropTarget, IInitDropTarget)
```

This declares TDropTarget to be derived from the TComObject class and to implement the IDropTarget and IInitDropTarget interfaces.

We need the IInitDropTarget interface because our COM component must be initialized before it can be used. One of the things missing in COM components is the concept of a constructor, where we traditionally initialize an object's state. However, we can achieve much the same effect through an initialization interface such as IInitDropTarget.

NOTE Another way that an object's state can be initialized is through its class factory. Rather than requesting IClassFactory or IClassFactory2 when calling CoGetClassObject, you can request a custom *activation interface* from the class factory. However, this requires that you implement custom class factories.

The IInitDropTarget interface is declared below:

```
type
  IInitDropTarget = interface( IUnknown )
    ['{DB232EA2-E1C4-11D0-80B1-000021617139}']
    function AllowMultipleFiles( Value: Boolean ): HResult;
      stdcall;
    function Enabled( Value: Boolean ): HResult; stdcall;
    function SetDropTargetInstance(
      const DropTarget: TCustomDropComponent): HResult; stdcall;
  end;
```

Notice some of the differences between the declaration of this interface and the Automation interfaces that we declared earlier in this chapter. All of the methods of IInitDropTarget are declared as functions that return an HResult return value. They use the stdcall calling convention as opposed to the safecall calling convention that was used in Automation.

WARNING You must tag all COM interface member functions with the stdcall calling convention. If you fail to do so, your COM interfaces will not work correctly. Remember that the default calling convention in Delphi is register, not stdcall.

The member functions of IInitDropTarget allow us to set and change the state of the DropTarget object. By calling AllowMultipleFiles, we can tell the DropTarget object whether we want to allow more than one file to be dropped onto the application. By calling the Enabled function, we can turn on and off the application's drag-and-drop capability. The SetDropTargetInstance member function is called when the DropTarget object is first initialized, so that it knows which VCL component to collaborate with.

The rest of the declaration of TDropTarget is shown below:

```
TDropTarget = class (TComObject, IDropTarget, IInitDropTarget)
private
  FAllowMultipleFiles: Boolean;
  FDropComponent: TCustomDropComponent;
  FEnabled: Boolean;
  FState: TDropState;
  function GetKeyState (grfKeyState: Longint): DWORD;
public
  procedure Initialize; override;

  { IDropTarget methods }
  function DragEnter (const dataObj: IDataObject;
    grfKeyState: Longint; pt: TPoint; var dwEffect: Longint):
    HResult; stdcall;
  function DragLeave: HResult; stdcall;
  function DragOver (grfKeyState: Longint; pt: TPoint;
    var dwEffect: Longint): HResult; stdcall;
  function Drop (const dataObj: IDataObject;
    grfKeyState: Longint; pt: TPoint;
    var dwEffect: Longint): HResult; stdcall;

  { IInitDropTarget methods }
  function AllowMultipleFiles (Value: Boolean):
    HResult; stdcall;
  function Enabled (Value: Boolean): HResult; stdcall;
  function SetDropTargetInstance (
    const DropTarget: TCustomDropComponent): HResult; stdcall;
end;
```

You'll notice that we override the Initialize virtual function of TDropTarget. You will override this member function when you need to initialize your COM component. Since you cannot pass any parameters to this procedure, its usefulness is limited. However, we can use it to initialize the initial state of the FState data member that tracks the current state of TDropTarget:

```
procedure TDropTarget.Initialize;
begin
  FState := dsNone;
  inherited Initialize;
end;
```

You can think of Initialize as a constructor that takes no arguments.

The first IDropTarget function that we will consider is the DragEnter function:

```
function TDropTarget.DragEnter (const dataObj: IDataObject;
  grfKeyState: Longint; pt: TPoint; var dwEffect: Longint):
  HResult;
```

Remember that this is the function that is called immediately after the user initially drags a file over the window that our DropTarget component is monitoring. The role of this function is to inspect the contents of the data object whose IDataObject interface is being passed to us in the dataObj parameter.

The DragEnter function validates the contents of the data object using two tests. It must first determine the number of files in the data object by asking the data object to render the data in the CF_HDROP format. Setting the cfFormat (Clipboard format) field of the formatEtc structure to CF_HDROP accomplishes this. In addition, we also must request that the data object render the data in global memory by setting the tymed (type of medium) field to TYMED_HGLOBAL:

```
with formatEtc do
begin
  cfFormat := CF_HDROP;
  ptd := nil;
  dwAspect := DVASPECT_CONTENT;
  lindex := -1;
  tymed := TYMED_HGLOBAL;
end;
```

We then call the IDataObject.GetData function and pass it the information contained in the formatEtc structure:

```
OleCheck (dataObj.GetData (formatEtc, medium));
```

When the function returns, it will have filled in the fields of the medium structure. We'll use this structure to examine the data that was rendered by the data object.

The shell provides a function called `DragQueryFile` that parses the data that was rendered by the data object. It returns the filenames to us one at a time, and is prototyped as follows:

```
function DragQueryFileA (Drop: HDROP; FileIndex: UINT;
    FileName: PAnsiChar; cb: UINT): UINT; stdcall;
```

The `Drop` parameter is the handle to the global block of memory that was passed to us by `GetData` in the `medium.hGlobal` parameter. We can use the `FileIndex` parameter to specify the index of the file, or pass in –1 to get the number of files.

The following lines of code determine how many files are contained in the data object. If the number of files is greater than one and the `FAllowMultipleFiles` data member is `False`, it disallows any further drop operations using this data object by setting the `FState` data member to `dsDisallow`. Otherwise, it checks the state of the Shift, Ctrl, and Alt keys on the keyboard by calling the `GetKeyState` helper function, which returns the appropriate drop effect code (in our case we only return `COPY`) and sets the `FState` data member to `dsEntered`:

```
try
  count := DragQueryFile (medium.hGlobal, -1, @buffer [1],
    MAX_PATH);
finally
  ReleaseStgMedium (medium);
end;

if (count > 1) and (not FAllowMultipleFiles) then
begin
  dwEffect := DROPEFFECT_NONE;
  FState := dsDisallow;
end
else
begin
  dwEffect := GetKeyState (grfKeyState);
  FState := dsEntered;
end;
```

The `DragOver` member function is called repeatedly by the shell, whenever the user changes the context of the drag operation by pressing a different combination of the Shift, Ctrl, and Alt keys. When this happens, the `DragOver` function is called by the shell to determine the type of feedback it should display.

The code that implements DragOver is very similar to the code that is used in DragEnter:

```
function TDropTarget.DragOver(grfKeyState: Longint; pt: TPoint;
  var dwEffect: Longint): HResult;
begin
  Result := S_OK;
  dwEffect := DROPEFFECT_NONE;
  if not FEnabled or (FState = dsDisallow) then
    Exit;

  dwEffect := GetKeyState (grfKeyState);
end;
```

This code checks the current state of the drag operation by examining the FState data member to determine whether we should provide any feedback to the user. The default return value is DropEffect_None; otherwise, it calls the GetKeyState helper function, which examines the Ctrl, Shift, and Alt key states to return the appropriate feedback.

When the user releases the left mouse button, all of the action can then take place. The shell calls the IDropTarget.Drop function, and passes it the data object once again:

```
function TDropTarget.Drop (const dataObj: IDataObject;
  grfKeyState: Longint; pt: TPoint; var dwEffect: Longint):
  HResult;
begin
  Result := S_OK;
  if not FEnabled then
    Exit;

  dwEffect := GetKeyState (grfKeyState);
  FDropComponent.Drop (dataObj, dwEffect);
end;
```

The function simply determines the current state of the Shift key by calling the GetKeyState private helper function, and it passes this information, along with the IDataObject interface reference, to the VCL component for final processing.

The VCL Component

The TDropComponent component links the COM component to your application code. By setting the DropWindow property of the component, you can enable any TWinControl-derived Delphi component to receive drop events. TDropComponent also initializes the COM component and fires a Delphi event when the user drops a file on the DropWindow component's window.

TDropComponent is derived from TComponent, so it is not a visual component:

```
type
  TCustomDropComponent = class( TComponent )
  private
    FAllowMultipleFiles: Boolean;
    FFileNames: TStringList;
    FDropNotification: TDropNotification;
    FDropTarget: IDropTarget;
    FDropWindow: TWinControl;
    FEnabled: Boolean;
    FInstance: Pointer;
    FWnd: HWND;
    FWndProc: Pointer;
    procedure SetAllowMultipleFiles (Value: Boolean);
    procedure SetDropWindow (ADropWindow: TWinControl);
    procedure SetEnabled (Value: Boolean);
  protected
    procedure DoDropNotification (
      const FileNames: TStringList); virtual;
    procedure Loaded; override;
    procedure Notification (AComponent: TComponent;
      Operation: TOperation); override;
    procedure SubWndProc (var Message: TMessage);
    property AllowMultipleFiles: Boolean
      read FAllowMultipleFiles write SetAllowMultipleFiles
      default False;
    property DropNotification: TDropNotification
      read FDropNotification write FDropNotification;
    property DropWindow: TWinControl
      read FDropWindow write SetDropWindow;
    property Enabled: Boolean
      read FEnabled write SetEnabled default True;
  public
    constructor Create (AOwner: TComponent); override;
```

```
  destructor Destroy; override;
  procedure Drop (const DataObject: IDataObject;
    const dwEffect: Integer); virtual;
end;
```

We follow standard Delphi component conventions by first deriving this component as a TCustomDropComponent component and then deriving the TDropComponent class from it to handle property publishing.

Much of this component uses standard Delphi component building techniques that are discussed in Chapter 5. However, there are a couple of component-building tricks that warrant closer inspection.

The Protected Access Technique

For our drag-and-drop component, we must be able to access the DefWndProc property of a TWinControl-derived component. Unfortunately, this property is declared as protected in the TWinControl declaration in the Controls unit. This is where the first pattern exerts its influence.

The *protected access* technique (introduced in Chapter 1) clearly falls into the category of a "hack," but is invaluable in those rare cases when you truly need it. It is based on the implicit "friendship" that exists between classes declared within the same unit. Any class can access the protected data members of any other class that is declared within the same unit. Since we will be exploiting this behavior to circumvent Delphi's type protection system, this must be called a "hack."

To apply the protected access pattern you must subclass, in the interface section of your unit, the class to which you want access. You should give the new subclass a name that clearly denotes its purpose; in this case we called our subclass THackWinControl:

```
THackWinControl = class( TWinControl )
end;
```

Whenever you need to gain access to a TWinControl object's protected property or method, simply cast the object into a THackWinControl object:

```
FWndProc := THackWinControl(FDropWindow).DefWndProc;
```

As long as this is a legal cast—that is, as long as FDropWindow is derived from TWinControl—this hack will allow you to bypass Delphi's type protection system.

> **NOTE**
>
> You should not use the protected access technique indiscriminately. You should only use it as a last resort. For example, you can use it when you don't have access to the source code for the class whose protected property or method you need access to. You'll also use it when you need access to a protected property or method that is supplied by Delphi itself.

Why did we need to gain access to the DefWndProc property of TWinControl in the first place? To answer this question, we need to consider the life cycle of TDropComponent.

TDropComponent is created at the same time as all of the other components on the form. When TDropComponent is created at run-time, Delphi will call the SetDropWindow property-assignment procedure of TDropComponent, where we perform some run-time initialization:

```
procedure TCustomDropComponent.SetDropWindow(
    ADropWindow: TWinControl);
begin
  if Assigned (FDropWindow) then
    RevokeDragDrop (FDropWindow.Handle);

  if Assigned (ADropWindow) then
  begin
    FDropWindow := ADropWindow;
    RegisterDragDrop (FDropWindow.Handle, FDropTarget);

    // Hook the window procedure of the component to receive
    // notifications when the actual HWND is destroyed.
    FWnd := FDropWindow.Handle;
    FWndProc := THackWinControl(FDropWindow).DefWndProc;
    THackWinControl(FDropWindow).DefWndProc :=
      MakeObjectInstance (SubWndProc);
  end;
end;
```

In `SetDropWindow`, we examine the `DropWindow` property of the component. If it was assigned (usually at design-time) to a `TWinControl`-derived component on the same form, we register that component's window handle with the shell libraries by calling `RegisterDragDrop`. However, this is where the trouble lies.

Delphi will inform us when the component referenced by `DropWindow` is destroyed. Typically, you handle these notifications by overriding the `Notification` virtual procedure that is initially defined in `TComponent`. Unfortunately, Delphi only calls this procedure *after* it has destroyed the component's window handle! We need to receive a notification that the component is being destroyed *before* its window handle is destroyed so that we can call the `RevokeDragDrop` function with a valid window handle. Failure to do so will result in a memory leak.

If you create your own component, you can receive a notification message prior to the destruction of its window handle by registering a message handler for the `wm_Destroy` message. In our case, however, we would like to receive notification of a window handle's destruction for *any* `TWinControl`-derived component. This requirement rules out deriving a new class at compile-time so that we can register a `wm_Destroy` message handler. The standard windows programming technique for *dynamically* registering message handlers is to subclass that `TWinControl` component's window procedure.

To subclass another component's window procedure, we require access to the `DefWndProc` property for that component. By using the protected access pattern to gain access to the `DefWndProc` property, we can register a new window procedure, `SubWndProc`, in place of the default window procedure for that component:

```
FWnd := FDropWindow.Handle;
FWndProc := THackWinControl(FDropWindow).DefWndProc;
THackWinControl(FDropWindow).DefWndProc :=
  MakeObjectInstance( SubWndProc );
```

This allows us to receive *all* Windows messages destined for the subclassed component's window *before* the subclassed component gets a chance to dispatch them.

The MakeObjectInstance Function

However, there's an additional problem. We would like that window procedure to be a member function of the component itself. That is, the window procedure must have access to the internal state of the component it is associated with. If there are four drag-and-drop components on a form, each component must have its own window procedure, rather than sharing a single window procedure that would be implemented as a regular function in the TDropComponent's unit.

To understand this problem better, let's take a look at the difference between a regular function and a function that is the member of a class. A Windows procedure is an example of a regular function. Windows will call the registered Window procedure for a window each time a Windows message is dispatched to that window. On the other hand, a class member function has an implicit Self parameter passed as its first parameter. So, how do we make Windows call a class member function, even though it requires the Self parameter to be the first parameter?

The solution to this problem, and the topic of our second technique, is to use the MakeObjectInstance helper function in Delphi:

```
THackWinControl(FDropWindow).DefWndProc :=
    MakeObjectInstance (SubWndProc);
```

MakeObjectInstance will convert a TWndMethod procedure into a callback function by dynamically creating a *thunk* procedure. TWndMethod is a standard Windows procedure that is declared as follows:

```
TWndMethod = procedure (var Message: TMessage) of object;
```

Delphi uses MakeObjectInstance to export its own Windows procedures from TForm-derived components. Therefore, it is not surprising that MakeObjectInstance is declared in the Forms unit.

NOTE   A *thunk* is a special piece of code that is dynamically generated. Its purpose is to perform some kind of implicit conversion. Windows uses thunks extensively to allow 16-bit applications to call API functions that are implemented in 32-bit code. In our case, the thunk generated by MakeObjectInstance adds a Self parameter to the call stack before calling SubWndProc in our component. For details, look at the implementation of MakeObjectInstance in Delphi's Forms unit.

Our special Windows procedure looks for wm_Destroy messages sent to our subclassed component. Once it encounters one, it calls RevokeDragDrop using that component's window handle, and saves the address of our special thunk procedure for later removal via a FreeObjectInstance call in TCustomDropComponent's destructor:

```
procedure TCustomDropComponent.SubWndProc (
```

```
    var Message: TMessage);
begin
  with Message do
  begin
    if Msg = WM_DESTROY then
    begin
      OleCheck (RevokeDragDrop (FWnd));
      FInstance := Pointer (GetWindowLong (FWnd, GWL_WNDPROC));
    end;
    Result := CallWindowProc (FWndProc, FWnd, Msg,
      WParam, LParam);
  end;
end;
```

Otherwise, its default behavior is to call the real window procedure for the sub-classed component by passing the CallWindowProc function the address of the component's original window procedure.

Interactions

TDropComponent interacts with the DropTarget component on several levels. One level is passing state changes through to the DropTarget component so that it knows whether to enable drag-and-drop, or to allow multiple files to be dropped.

These state changes are implemented in a very straightforward manner. Whenever the developer changes the state of one of the published properties of TDropComponent—AllowMultipleFiles or Enabled—the appropriate property write handler is called. Here is all of the code involved in a call to SetAllow-MultipleFiles; both the code for the VCL component and the COM component are shown as an example of how to pass state information along to a COM object:

```
// TDropComponent VCL code
procedure TCustomDropComponent.SetAllowMultipleFiles (
  Value: Boolean);
var
  initDropTarget: IInitDropTarget;
begin
  if Value <> FAllowMultipleFiles then
  begin
    FAllowMultipleFiles := Value;
    if Assigned (FDropTarget) then
```

```
    begin
      initDropTarget := FDropTarget as IInitDropTarget;
      initDropTarget.AllowMultipleFiles (Value);
    end;
  end;
end;

// DropTarget COM code
function TDropTarget.AllowMultipleFiles (
  Value: Boolean): HResult;
begin
  FAllowMultipleFiles := Value;
  Result := S_OK;
end;
```

We use a cached FDropTarget interface reference data member to acquire a reference to the IInitDropTarget initialization interface. Notice the use of the as operator to convert the IDropTarget interface reference to an IInitDropTarget interface reference. The code then calls the AllowMultipleFiles member function to pass along the new value.

The most important interaction that occurs between the COM component and TDropComponent is, of course, the Drop event. As you saw in the section discussing the COM component, the function call that makes it all happen is this:

```
FDropComponent.Drop (dataObj, dwEffect);
```

We pass along a reference to the IDataObject interface, and give the VCL component an indication of whether this is a Move, Copy, or Link event.

The workhorse function in TDropComponent is the Drop function:

```
procedure TCustomDropComponent.Drop (const DataObject:
  IDataObject; const dwEffect: Integer);
var
  buffer: String;
  count, i: Integer;
  formatEtc: TFormatEtc;
  medium: TStgMedium;
begin
  FFileNames.Clear;
  SetLength (buffer, Max_Path);

  with formatEtc do
```

```
begin
  cfFormat := cf_HDrop;
  ptd := nil;
  dwAspect := dvAspect_Content;
  lindex := -1;
  tymed := Tymed_HGlobal;
end;
OleCheck (DataObject.GetData (formatEtc, medium));

try
  count := DragQueryFile (medium.hGlobal, -1,
    @buffer[1], Max_Path);
  for i := 0 to count - 1 do
  begin
    DragQueryFile (medium.hGlobal, i, @buffer[1], Max_Path);
    FFileNames.Add (String(PChar(buffer)));
  end;
finally
  ReleaseStgMedium (medium);
end;
DoDropNotification (FFileNames);
end;
```

Within the Drop function, we're building a TStringList object that contains all of the dropped filenames.

Most of the code is very straightforward, except for the use of a string variable as a buffer. The DragQueryFile function requires a fixed-size buffer of at least Max_Path bytes. A handy way to allocate such a buffer is to use the SetLength function on a Delphi string. SetLength will set aside the number of bytes that you specify within the Delphi string, and you can then pass the address of the first character of the string for use as the address of the fixed-length buffer.

Once the function has built up a list of filenames, it releases the storage medium where the filename list was originally rendered by the data object. It then triggers the Delphi event by calling the DoDropNotification virtual function.

TIP   It is a very good idea to use a virtual (or dynamic) function to fire your Delphi component's events. This allows developers who subclass your component to intercept the event-firing sequence within their own code.

The complete source code of the component and the Delphi package hosting it are available in the same ComLibrary directory hosting also the ActiveX library used by the component. The two projects, in fact, share the file Interfaces.PAS.

Dragging in Action

The third version of the SimpleWord example, available in the SimpleW3 directory, uses the new component to support file dragging. Here are the properties of the component:

```
object DropComponent1: TDropComponent
  AllowMultipleFiles = False
  DropNotification = DropComponent1DropNotification
  DropWindow = SpeedBar
end
```

As you can see, the component allows a user to drag one file onto the SpeedBar panel (in fact, trying to use the component with the RichEdit control doesn't work properly; we are not sure why). Responding to this event, the dragged file is opened in the RichEdit control:

```
procedure TMainForm.DropComponent1DropNotification(
  Sender: TObject; const FileNames: TStringList);
begin
  FCurrentFileName := FileNames [0];
  RichEdit1.Lines.LoadFromFile (FCurrentFileName);
  Caption := APP_NAME + ' - ' + FCurrentFileName;
end;
```

You can see an example of the dragging cursor, indicating that we can perform the operation, in Figure 11.6.

The Context-Menu Handler

A shell context-menu handler is a prototypical example of a Windows shell extension. Shell extensions allow you to integrate your application into the Windows desktop environment in a number of ways. The shell extensions that you can create are:

> **Context-menu handlers:** Allow you to register custom right-click menus for certain application types.

FIGURE 11.6:

The cursor of the toolbar panel of the SimpleW3 example indicates that you can drop files onto it.

Copy-hook handlers: Allow you to validate file operations such as copy, remove and delete.

Icon handlers: Allow you to specify the icon that is associated with a particular file. You may want different icons for files with the same file extension, such as the CPL files that make up the applets in the Control Panel.

Drag-and-drop handlers: Allow you to display a context menu when the user drops the files at a new location. This is much like the behavior that you get when you drop a set of files with the Ctrl and Shift keys pressed.

Property sheet handlers: Display a property sheet for a particular file type when the user selects the Properties menu option on the context menu.

Drop target handlers: Allow you to specify an action to be performed when the user drops a file onto another file (for example, adding files to an existing ZIP archive).

Data object handlers: Allow you to create a custom data object that represents your file type that is being dragged around. When the user drops your file onto an application that knows your file type, it can ask your custom data object to render data for that file type in a specialized format.

Windows shell extensions share a number of things in common. They all must be implemented as DLL-based COM components. They all must implement the `IShellExtInit` interface, and they all must be housed in Apartment-threaded

COM servers. Outside of those common features, it is the type of COM interface that a shell extension implements, and how it is registered in the Windows Registry that determines its functionality.

The Architecture of Explorer

Before we delve into the details of how a shell extension is implemented, we have to take a quick look at how the Windows shell itself is implemented. The shell runs within its own Win32 process, and is started up when you run Explorer.EXE. Each window that is created by Explorer.EXE (including the main desktop window) runs within its own Win32 thread.

A consequence of this design is that each shell extension that the shell creates on your behalf will be created from within its own thread of execution. For example, when you right-click on a file within an Explorer window, the context menu objects that Explorer creates to build the context menu you see on the screen are all created by that Explorer window's controlling thread.

Does this mean that your COM components must be thread-safe? Well, yes and no. We'll take a very brief look at COM threading models in the following section, and you'll see how COM actually simplifies things on your behalf.

COM Threading Models

As far as Windows 95 is concerned, there are two threading models supported by COM: the default model, which is no-threading, and the single-threaded Apartment model. Under Windows NT 4.0 and Windows 95 with the DCOM extensions installed, there is an additional threading model, the multithreaded Apartment model.

The role of these threading models in COM is conceptually similar to the role that interfaces play in COM. Both represent a binding contract between a client application and a COM component.

Both the client application and the COM component must declare their threading model to COM when they are initialized. Their threading model defines what steps the COM libraries will take to protect your code from the perils of multithreaded application writing. Let's take a look at the COM threading models in the order of most to least protection:

- The default COM threading model is the most restrictive model. The COM libraries assume that your code was written without any provisions for multiple threads; your code is not considered to be *thread-safe*. To protect your code, the COM libraries step in to ensure that all incoming calls on your COM component's interfaces will be made from the same thread of execution. By doing so, the COM libraries allow you to run code that has no concept of multiple threads of execution within a multithreaded environment such as the Windows shell.

- The Apartment threading model relaxes these assumptions somewhat. By declaring this threading model, your code is telling COM that it agrees to behave according to a particular code of conduct. There are similar sets of rules for the COM component/server and the client application. We will look at the server side of the picture first.

A COM component belonging to an apartment-threaded COM server declares to the COM libraries two things. The first is that it is thread-aware. If there are any shared data members that the COM component is manipulating, it promises to take steps to protect these data members from concurrent access. Typically, this is accomplished using various operating-system synchronization primitives such as critical sections or mutexes. The second is that the COM component's server has taken steps to protect itself from concurrent accesses; as any thread can create the COM component, and many threads can attempt to create that COM component at any given moment. Once created, however, the COM component can only be called within the thread that it was created on. This second condition implies that the code for the COM component need not be thread-safe, and that the instance data of that component is protected from concurrent access by COM. This condition simplifies the programming model by requiring only that the class factory code in the COM server and the code that accesses shared data members be thread-safe. A COM client application that declares to the COM libraries that it is apartment-threaded must also live up to its end of the contract. Typically, it will call `CoInitialize` from its main thread to declare this fact to COM.

As far as COM is concerned, the thread that calls `CoInitialize` is the *only* thread that lives inside that apartment (hence the name *single*-threaded apartment). In order for method calls to be dispatched to this apartment from other apartments, COM must ensure that all method calls originate on this thread. To do so, COM posts private Windows messages to this thread to dispatch those method calls. Therefore, any thread that declares itself to be apartment-threaded must regularly service its message queue by calling `GetMessage` and `Dispatch-Message`. Also, when it creates a COM object, it must *always* call that COM object from that thread of execution!

If it *must* call that COM object from another thread, it must marshal that interface pointer to the other thread by using the COM API function with the world's longest name: `CoMarshalInterThreadInterfaceInStream`. The details of how to do this are beyond the scope of this chapter. For more details, see Dale Rogerson's *Inside COM* (Microsoft Press, 1995).

> **WARNING** As this book goes to press, there are a couple of known bugs in Delphi 3's implementation of its COM servers with respect to Apartment-threaded COM components. The global state of the server is not protected correctly in Delphi's class factory implementation. This global state could potentially become corrupted by multiple concurrent thread accesses.

The Code

The context menu code is housed within an ActiveX library, called ContextMenu and available in a subdirectory with the same name. This library contains Delphi's implementation of the class factory code. This code is thread-safe, so the context menu COM component can be labeled as an apartment-threaded object. This is essential, since the shell code will not create a shell extension object that is not labeled as apartment-threaded.

COM components label themselves as apartment-threaded by using a Registry entry. Since Delphi does not label COM components as being apartment-threaded by default, we will have to add the label ourselves. To do this, all we have to do is add a Registry value called "ThreadingModel" and set its value to "Apartment."

The previous chapter proposed one way you could globally override the `DllRegisterServer` exported function (as shown in the CustReg example). In this chapter, you'll see another way you can add your own custom Registry entries.

Delphi provides a mechanism for creating custom Registry entries by allowing you to create your own custom class factory objects. To do so, you will have to derive a new class from `TComObjectFactory`:

```
TContextMenuFactory = class (TComObjectFactory)
public
  procedure UpdateRegistry (Register: Boolean); override;
end;
```

Note that we are overriding the UpdateRegistry virtual function. Within this function, we can include the code to add our own Registry entries:

```
procedure TContextMenuFactory.UpdateRegistry (
  Register: Boolean);
begin
  inherited UpdateRegistry (Register);

  // Register our global context-menu handler
  if Register then
  begin
    CreateRegKey ('*\ShellEx\ContextMenuHandlers\SimpleWord',
      '', GUIDToString (Class_ContextMenu));
    CreateRegKey ('CLSID\' + GUIDToString (ClassID) + '\' +
      ComServer.ServerKey, 'ThreadingModel', 'Apartment');
  end
  else
  begin
    DeleteRegKey ('*\ShellEx\ContextMenuHandlers\SimpleWord');
  end;
end;
```

The UpdateRegistry function takes a single parameter, Register, which signifies whether we are adding or removing Registry entries.

Our code has to add two Registry entries. The first entry tags our COM component as implementing the Apartment threading model. The second registers our COM component as a context-menu handler. We use the helper functions CreateRegKey and DeleteRegKey that are defined in the ComObj unit to create and remove the Registry entries. Before adding our own keys, however, we give Delphi an opportunity to add its own Registry entries by calling the inherited UpdateRegistry function prior to executing any of our own code.

One of the tenets of Registry modifications is that your code should not modify any Registry keys that you did not create. Since Delphi creates the Registry entry under the HKEY_CLASSES_ROOT\CLSID key, Delphi also is responsible for deleting that key, and all keys underneath that key. This is why we have the line of code that adds the *ThreadingModel = Apartment* value to the Registry, but we don't have a line of code that deletes that value. Delphi will delete that Registry value for us automatically. The only Registry key that we are responsible for adding and deleting is HKEY_CLASSES_ROOT*\ShellEx\ContextMenuHandlers\SimpleWord.

As in the other COM components that we created earlier, we declare our context-menu handler class by subclassing the TComObject base class provided by Delphi:

```
TContextMenu = class (TComObject, IShellExtInit, IContextMenu)
private
  FFileName: String;
  function BuildSubMenu (Menu: HMENU; IndexMenu: Integer;
    var IDCmdFirst: Integer): HMENU;
protected
  function IShellExtInit.Initialize =
    IShellExtInit_Initialize;
public
  { IShellExtInit members }
  function IShellExtInit_Initialize (pidlFolder: PItemIDList;
    lpdobj: IDataObject; hKeyProgID: HKEY): HResult; stdcall;
  { IContextMenu }
  function QueryContextMenu (Menu: HMENU; indexMenu,
    idCmdFirst, idCmdLast, uFlags: UINT): HResult; stdcall;
  function InvokeCommand (var lpici: TCMInvokeCommandInfo):
    HResult; stdcall;
  function GetCommandString (idCmd, uType: UINT; pwReserved:
    PUINT; pszName: LPSTR; cchMax: UINT): HResult; stdcall;
end;
```

A context menu COM component must implement the IShellExtInit and IContext-Menu interfaces. In the case of this COM component, we don't need to do any special initialization, so we can do without a special initialization interface here.

One line of code in the class declaration deserves special attention:

```
function IShellExtInit.Initialize = IShellExtInit_Initialize;
```

Earlier, we mentioned that you could override the TComObject.Initialize function to do any special initialization that might be required by your application. What happens if one of the COM interfaces that your COM component implements also has a member function called Initialize?

Single-inheritance languages such as Delphi have not had problems like this in the past. However, with the addition of interfaces, we need a mechanism to resolve the function name ambiguity (a process commonly known as *disambiguation*). The line of code above performs the disambiguation service for you. It renames the Initialize member function of IShellExtInit to IShellExtInit_Initialize.

It's a good idea to include the interface name in the new function name, as this makes your code more understandable.

There are two ways you can register a context-menu handler: for a specific file extension, or as a global context-menu handler. In our case, we registered our context-menu handler as a global handler. This means that the Windows shell will always load and call our context-menu handler, regardless of the file being right-clicked on.

Since our code is always called on a right-click, we can build some code that filters out the filename extensions to activate our handler. This is the role of the code in the initialization and finalization sections. The code in the initialization section creates a list of filename extensions that our context-menu handler will respond to:

```
GFileExtensions := TStringList.Create;
GFileExtensions.Add ('.PAS');
GFileExtensions.Add ('.RTF');
```

In the finalization section, we have some additional code that cleans up our TStringList object:

```
GFileExtensions.Free;
```

Our context-menu handler is activated when the shell calls CoCreateInstance and creates a new instance of our context-menu handler. The first function that the shell calls is the Initialize member function of the IShellExtInit interface. It passes a reference to the IDataObject interface for the shell-created data object that contains the list of filenames for which the shell is creating a context-menu handler.

NOTE   The shell allows you to create context-menu handlers for several selected files. Logically, you should present only the menu items that are common to all of the selected file types. This would require some additional code that determines what commands are associated with what file extensions. For simplicity, however, our context-menu handler will only support single-selection.

The IShellExtInit_Initialize method of TContextMenu function asks the data object to render a list of filenames. As mentioned in the note, the code does not support multiple-selection, so if more than one filename is present in the list of files, the function exits with an error. Otherwise, it retrieves the lone filename in the list and saves it in a unit-level variable that we will use later. This code is shown below:

```pascal
function TContextMenu.IShellExtInit_Initialize (
  pidlFolder: PItemIDList; lpdobj: IDataObject;
  hKeyProgID: HKEY): HResult;
var
  buffer: String;
  count: Integer;
  formatEtc: TFormatEtc;
  medium: TStgMedium;
begin
  Result := E_FAIL;

  if Assigned (lpdobj) then
  begin
    with formatEtc do
    begin
      cfFormat := cf_HDrop;
      ptd := nil;
      dwAspect := dvAspect_Content;
      lindex := -1;
      tymed := Tymed_HGlobal;
    end;

    SetLength (buffer, Max_Path);
    OleCheck (lpdobj.GetData (formatEtc, medium));
    try
      count := DragQueryFile (medium.hGlobal, -1,
        @buffer[1], Max_Path);
      if count > 1 then
        Exit;

      DragQueryFile (medium.hGlobal, 0, @buffer[1], Max_Path );
      GFileName := PChar (buffer);
      Result := S_OK;
    finally
      ReleaseStgMedium (medium);
    end;
  end
  else
    Result := e_InvalidArg;
end;
```

NOTE

Always remember to release the storage medium structure that you obtained from the IDataObject.GetData function. The best way to do this is to place the call to ReleaseStgMedium in a try/finally block. In the case of our code, which asked the GetData function to render the data in a global block of memory, ReleaseStgMedium calls the GlobalFree API function on the hGlobal parameter of the medium structure.

When the user right-clicks on a file in an Explorer window, the shell looks up in the Registry all of the context-menu handlers that are appropriate for that file's extension. The shell then proceeds to instantiate each of those context-menu handler objects and calls each handler's IShellExtInit.Initialize and IContextMenu. QueryContextMenu functions. One thing to keep in mind is that there are no guarantees about the order in which the shell will call each handler.

The QueryContextMenu function creates a menu handler for the filenames specified in the data object. In our case, the IShellExtInit.Initialize function extracted a single filename from the data object and stored it in the FFileName data member for us. The code in QueryContextMenu simply validates this filename's extension against the list of possible filename extensions stored in GFileExtensions:

```
function TContextMenu.QueryContextMenu (Menu: HMENU;
  indexMenu, idCmdFirst, idCmdLast, uFlags: UINT): HResult;
var
  extension: String;
  i: Integer;
  idLastCommand: Integer;
begin
  Result := e_Fail;
  idLastCommand := idCmdFirst;

  extension := UpperCase (ExtractFileExt (FFileName));

  for i := 0 to GFileExtensions.Count - 1 do
    if extension = GFileExtensions [i] then
    begin
      BuildSubMenu (Menu, indexMenu, idLastCommand);
      // Return value is number of items added to context menu
      Result := idLastCommand - idCmdFirst;
      Exit;
    end;
end;
```

If the filename is validated, we call the `BuildSubMenu` function to actually build the context menu.

Part of the design of the `QueryContextMenu` function is to allow context-menu handlers to insert menus into an existing menu that was created by the shell. Some of the menu commands (such as the Properties command) are implemented entirely by the shell. To prevent command identifier collisions, the shell assigns command identifier ranges to each context-menu handler. The `idCmdFirst` parameter tells the context-menu handler the lowest command identifier that it can use, and the `idCmdLast` parameter specifies the highest command identifier.

For the return value of the `QueryContextMenu` function, we must return to the shell the total number of menu items that we added to the context menu. The shell takes note of the command ID ranges for each of the context-menu handlers that it calls, and calls them back using *offsets* into each menu handler's command ID range.

Whereas `QueryContextMenu` determines whether we should be creating a context menu for a particular filename extension, `BuildSubMenu` actually builds the context menu in question. It assembles the menu information stored in the `MenuCommandStrings` array into a set of menu items that will be inserted into the context menu:

```
function TContextMenu.BuildSubMenu (Menu: HMENU;
  IndexMenu: Integer; var IDCmdFirst: Integer): HMENU;
var
  i: Integer;
  menuItemInfo: TMenuItemInfo;
begin
  if Menu = 0 then
    Result := CreateMenu
  else
    Result := Menu;

  // Build the menu items here
  with menuitemInfo do
  begin
    cbSize := SizeOf( TMenuItemInfo );
    fMask := miim_CheckMarks or miim_Data or miim_Id
      or miim_State or miim_SubMenu or miim_Type;
    fType := mft_String;
    fState := mfs_Enabled;
    hSubMenu := 0;
```

```
    hbmpChecked := 0;
    hbmpUnchecked := 0;
  end;

  for i := 0 to High (MenuCommandStrings) do
  begin
    menuitemInfo.dwTypeData := PChar (MenuCommandStrings [i]);
    menuitemInfo.wID := IDCmdFirst;
    InsertMenuItem (Result, IndexMenu + i, True, menuItemInfo);
    Inc (IDCmdFirst);
  end;
end;
```

As the function adds additional menu commands to the context menu referenced by the Menu parameter, the IDCmdFirst parameter is incremented each time. QueryContextMenu uses this value to count the number of menu commands added to the context menu. You can see the new menu items created by this and other registered shell extensions in Figure 11.7.

FIGURE 11.7:

This context menu handler has several custom items added by our ContextMenu library and other shell extensions.

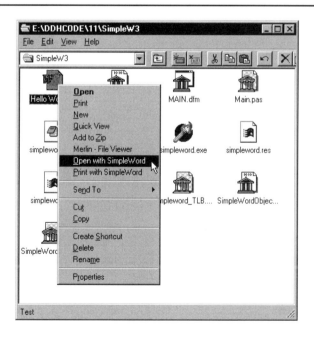

When the user selects a menu command from the context menu, the TContextMenu.InvokeCommand function is called:

```
function TContextMenu.InvokeCommand (
  var lpici: TCMInvokeCommandInfo): HResult;
var
  idCmd: UINT;
begin
  if HiWord (Integer (lpici.lpVerb)) <> 0 then
    Result := e_Fail
  else
  begin
    idCmd := LoWord (lpici.lpVerb);
    Result := S_OK;
    case idCmd of
      0:
        ShellExecute (GetDesktopWindow, nil, sw_Path,
          PChar('"' + FFileName + '"'), nil, sw_Show);
      1:
        ShellExecute (GetDesktopWindow, nil, sw_Path,
          PChar('/P "' + FFileName + '"'), nil, sw_Show);
      else
        Result := e_Fail;
    end;
  end;
end;
```

Within this function is a case statement that dispatches the commands. As mentioned earlier, the command identifiers that are passed back from the shell represent *offsets* into the command-identifier range that the shell assigned. Therefore, we dispatch the command identifiers using indexed values that begin at zero.

Currently the context-menu handler dispatches commands to the SimpleWord application by using the ShellExecute API function. If we are opening a file for inspection, we simply pass the fully qualified path to the file on the command line. If we want SimpleWord to print the file in question, we pass a /P switch on the command line in addition to the fully qualified path to the file.

> **WARNING** In the code, the fully qualified path is stored in the sw_Path variable. You should modify this path name depending on the directory where you've copied the third version of the SimpleWord example. In the source code the path is 'c:\ddhcode\11\simplew3\simpleword.exe'.

You could also use Automation to create a new instance of a `SimpleWordObject`, as we did in our Automation scripting application. However, the role of a context-menu handler is such that it is used only to *launch* another application to perform a task. It shouldn't be used to control the lifetime of that application. In fact, the application will shut down as soon as the reference to the `ISimpleWordObject` interface goes out of scope. You could keep it around permanently by simply incrementing the reference count of the `SimpleWordObject`, but Delphi will warn the user when they manually shut down the SimpleWord application.

You can, however, use Automation to implement the Print command. Since the Print command starts up SimpleWord to print the desired file and immediately returns, it would be a good candidate for implementation through Automation. Based on what you've learned, that should be a straightforward exercise.

What's Next

This chapter has provided a number of concrete examples of COM applications, touching upon various topics of interest along the way.

In the scripting example, where we added Automation-scripting to the SimpleWord application, we discussed some of the details behind how Automation objects were implemented. We also discussed the `safecall` calling convention and type libraries.

In adding drag-and-drop capability to the SimpleWord application, we also discussed some of the issues involved in getting COM components and VCL components to cooperate. You saw how to use activation interfaces to initialize your COM components.

Finally, in adding context-menu support to the SimpleWord application, we discussed the general issues involved in building shell extension COM objects, including the different threading models in COM and how the Apartment threading model specifically relates to the way the Windows shell operates.

Hopefully, this chapter has given you the motivation, and some additional information, to help you in your COM travels. There is always more to read, so here's a brief bibliography of other books that you should consider reading to learn more about the intricacies of COM, DCOM, and Windows shell programming:

The COM Specification. Available at `http://www.microsoft.com/oledev`.

Dale Rogerson, *Inside COM*, Microsoft Press, 1997

Kraig Brockschmidt, *Inside OLE 2nd Edition*, Microsoft Press, 1995

David S. Platt, *The Essence of OLE with ActiveX*, Prentice Hall, 1997

Nancy Winnik-Cluts, *Programming the Windows 95 User Interface*, Microsoft Press, 1995

David Chappell, *Understanding ActiveX and OLE*, Microsoft Press, 1996

Richard Grimes, *Professional DCOM Programming*, Wrox Press, 1997

This was also our last chapter devoted to Windows programming. We've covered the foundations of Windows programming in Delphi, plus a number of advanced topics. But now it is time to move to a completely different area of Delphi programming: customizing the development environment with property and component editors, wizards, and many other techniques.

PART III

Extending the
Delphi Environment

CHAPTER

TWELVE

12

Property Editors

Writing components is one of the most important ways you can customize the Delphi development environment. However, if you want to make your new components easy to use you can go a step further: Customize the Object Inspector.

The primary purpose of the Object Inspector is to allow you to edit and view properties. Which editor the Object Inspector will use depends on the data type of the property, but it is possible to provide custom editors for different properties of the same type, or to use a special-purpose property editor for a given property of a given component. We'll discuss this topic again when we examine the `RegisterPropertyEditor` function.

Although the standard Delphi property editors are very powerful, at times you will need to use a special editor to operate on very complex properties, or on more than one property at a time. In addition, Delphi programmers know that some components display a SpeedMenu when you right-click them. Typically, this menu provides customized options for the component, and frequently launches a special type of extension to the IDE known as a *component editor*. Accordingly, writing a component editor usually means adding special options to the SpeedMenu when the user selects your component. The next chapter shows how to create component editors.

However, you can do far more to customize the Delphi environment than simply creating new property and component editors. In Chapters 14 and 15, we'll discuss creating your own Delphi wizards and version control systems. In each case, keep in mind that these techniques provide ways to extend the Delphi development environment, perhaps in ways even Borland couldn't foresee. We'll begin by creating some complex property editors that actually extend the Delphi environment, and then expand on this topic in following chapters.

Introducing Property Editors

As a Delphi programmer, you've already used a property editor. Each time you interact with the Object Inspector, you're using one or more property editors. It's easy to recognize that when the Object Inspector displays an editor in a dialog box (an ellipsis button on the right of the property-editing area will typically open this type of property editor). However, property editors are also in action when you view or edit simple values. In fact, without property editors, the Object

Inspector can't do anything. Put a different way, property editors aren't simply a way to extend the Object Inspector, they're an integral and fundamental part of this tool.

The TPropertyEditor Class

What, then, is a property editor? Technically, it's a subclass of the TPropertyEditor class, which is documented in the DsgnIntf.PAS file (the name stands for "Design Interface"). Below is the public interface of the class:

```
type
  TPropertyEditor = class
  public
    destructor Destroy; override;
    procedure Activate; virtual;
    function AllEqual: Boolean; virtual;
    procedure Edit; virtual;
    function GetAttributes: TPropertyAttributes; virtual;
    function GetComponent(Index: Integer): TPersistent;
    function GetEditLimit: Integer; virtual;
    function GetName: string; virtual;
    procedure GetProperties(Proc: TGetPropEditProc); virtual;
    function GetPropType: PTypeInfo;
    function GetValue: string; virtual;
    procedure GetValues(Proc: TGetStrProc); virtual;
    procedure Initialize; virtual;
    procedure Revert;
    procedure SetValue(const Value: string); virtual;
    function ValueAvailable: Boolean;

    property Designer: TFormDesigner
      read FDesigner;
    property PrivateDirectory: string
      read GetPrivateDirectory;
    property PropCount: Integer
      read FPropCount;
    property Value: string
      read GetValue write SetValue;
  end;
```

Many of the public methods (and some of the protected ones) are useful for accessing the value of the current property or other information related to the selected component(s). As you look over these methods, keep in mind that in many cases you can use the Object Inspector (and hence a property editor) to edit the same property of several components at the same time.

Not all of these methods will be useful if you want to write your own property editors, but if you're curious, you can find a description of their use in the *Component Writer's Guide* and in the source code comments in DsgnIntf.PAS (if you have the VCL source code). Instead of discussing each of these methods, we'll focus on the methods you'll most often override or call when you write your own property editors.

> **NOTE**
>
> There is only one minor difference between the Delphi 2 and Delphi 3 implementations of the TPropertyEditor class: In version 3.0, the GetComponent method returns a TPersistent object instead of a TComponent object.

Standard Delphi Property Editors

Before we start building our own property editors, let's review Delphi's documented property editors. (In fact, Delphi uses several undocumented property editors, such as the TDataFieldProperty and TDataSourceProperty editors defined in the DBReg unit. However, since these property editors have very specific purposes, they don't work particularly well as base classes for new property editors, so we won't discuss them in more detail.) You can find the complete source code for the documented property editors in DsgnIntf.PAS. Studying this file will prove very useful, and may teach you more (at this point) than looking at other examples.

> **NOTE**
>
> Delphi's default editors are difficult to surpass in terms of their integration with the design environment. For this reason, you'll want to keep the DsgnIntf.PAS file handy when you're building your own property editors. On the other hand, the default property editors aren't perfect. In many cases, you'll find that the source code for these editors accesses the private data of the parent classes directly (which is legal within the same unit). Unfortunately, this means you may not be able to access that information when you write your own property editors (since you'll be creating a separate unit).

The property editors form a class hierarchy, derived from `TPropertyEditor`, as you can see in Figure 12.1. Here is a summary of the capabilities of the various basic editors:

`TOrdinalProperty`: All of the ordinal-property editors, such as those for integer, character, and enumerated properties, descend from the `TOrdinalProperty` class. This is a base class for other property editors, and not one that Delphi will use directly.

`TIntegerProperty`: This is the property editor for `Byte`, `Word`, `Integer`, and `LongInt` properties, as well as user-defined subranges of these types. You can enter values using decimal or hexadecimal (using the $ notation) values.

`TCharProperty`: This is the editor for `Char` properties and for subranges of `Char`, such as `'A'..'Z'`. Don't confuse this with the `TStringProperty` editor. You can enter characters directly or you can specify their ordinal value (using the # or #$ notation).

`TEnumProperty`: This is the property editor for any enumerated type or a subrange of an enumerated type. All of the possible values appear in an alphabetized drop-down list, or you can cycle through each value by double-clicking on the property value.

`TFloatProperty`: This is the editor for all floating-point numbers, including `Single`, `Double`, `Extended`, `Comp`, and `Currency`. (You can't use the `Real` type for component properties. If you try, the Object Inspector will generate a protection fault as soon as it tries to display the property.) You can enter values in fixed or scientific notation.

`TStringProperty`: This is the editor for `String` properties, including strings of specified length, such as `string[20]`. It supports the `AnsiString` and `ShortString` types. If you specify a length for the string (as part of the property definition), this editor will limit entries to that length. For both `AnsiString` and `ShortString` properties, this editor will limit the entry to 255 characters.

`TSetProperty`: This is the main editor for all set types. This editor doesn't allow you to edit the set directly (you can't simply type new set values), but instead creates a list of `TSetElementProperty` objects for each element in the set.

`TSetElementProperty`: This is a property editor for the subproperties of sets. This editor displays all set elements as Boolean values. (An element either belongs to the set or it doesn't.) You can toggle a set element by double-clicking its value.

TClassProperty: This is the default editor for instances of a class. This editor displays the name of the object's class and creates the appropriate subproperty objects for each of the class's properties. The editor for a subproperty can be any of the editors for plain properties, listed here.

TComponentProperty: This is the editor for references to other components on the same form. For a given property type, this editor displays a drop-down list of all the form's components of the same type (or a compatible subtype). You can cycle through the list of compatible components by double-clicking the property value.

TMethodProperty: This is the property editor for method pointers, most notably for events. If you enter a method name, this editor will either create a new form method of that name or will find an existing method of that name. If you double-click the property value, this editor will automatically generate a new form method whose name is based on the component name and the event name. In addition, this property editor will display a list of all the current form methods that match the event type.

TColorProperty: This is the property editor for color properties. If an appropriate color constant exists, this editor will display it. Otherwise, it displays the color in hexadecimal format. You can view all of the defined color constants in a drop-down list, or you can double-click the property value to display the standard Windows color-selection dialog box.

TFontProperty: This is the editor for the subproperties of fonts (Height, Name, Style, and so on). You can edit the subproperties directly, or you can double-click the property value to display the standard Windows font dialog box.

TFontNameProperty: This is the property editor for the Name subproperty that the TFontProperty editor displays. It gathers the names of all the current fonts in the system and displays them in a drop-down list. You can cycle through the list of available fonts by double-clicking on the property value.

FIGURE 12.1:

Here's the VCL hier-
archy of property
editor classes, as
shown by the
VclHiera program we
built in Chapter 1.

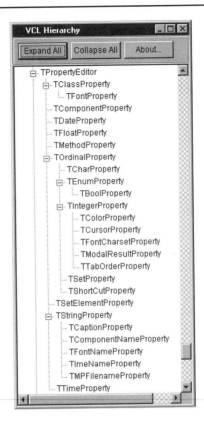

You'll notice that the property editor class names all end in "Property."
Although this may seem odd at first (since the class doesn't represent a
property but an editor for that property), this is a widespread convention.
Similarly, you'll want to use "PE" as a prefix for source files that define
only property editors.

Writing Property Editors

With this introduction, you can start writing your own property editors. To do
this you need to choose an existing property editor class to use as a base class

(use the TPropertyEditor class only if you want to write more code), and install it by calling the RegisterPropertyEditor method inside a Register procedure.

The code for a property editor can be very simple: derive a new class, override one or two methods, and you're done. For example, we might extend the string property editor by writing a string editor that forces the text to be uppercase. To do this, all we need to do is override the GetValue and SetValue methods of the TStringProperty subclass. Here is the declaration of the class:

```
type
  TUpperProperty = class (TStringProperty)
  public
    function GetValue: string; override;
    procedure SetValue (const Value: string); override;
  end;
```

And here is the code for the methods:

```
function TUpperProperty.GetValue: string;
begin
  // show the value as uppercase
  Result := UpperCase (inherited GetValue);
end;

procedure TUpperProperty.SetValue (const Value: string);
begin
  // force the string to uppercase when saving
  inherited SetValue (UpperCase (Value));
end;
```

First, each method calls the inherited version. Then, they convert the value to uppercase using the UpperCase library function.

NOTE   This property editor doesn't restrict the entry to uppercase, it merely displays the string in uppercase inside the Object Inspector, and then stores the characters as uppercase if you change their value. If you don't change the string's value, the stored text might be mixed case, but the new property editor will always display it as all-uppercase.

Typically, you'll call the RegisterPropertyEditor procedure from a global Register procedure in the unit that defines the property editor (similar to calling RegisterComponent). This procedure has four parameters: the data type of the property, the component class that defines the property (if you want to restrict it to a single component), the property name (if you want to restrict it to a specific property), and the property editor's class name:

```
procedure RegisterPropertyEditor(
  PropertyType: PTypeInfo; ComponentClass: TClass;
  const PropertyName: string; EditorClass: TPropertyEditorClass);
```

The first parameter is of type `PTypeInfo`. This data type was covered in Chapter 4; the important thing to remember here is that you can use a special function, `TypeInfo`, to extract type information from a data type. The second and third parameters allow you to determine whether the Object Inspector will try to use a property editor for a given component type and property.

If the `ComponentClass` parameter is `nil`, the Object Inspector will consider the editor for any component. This is the most general way to specify the component type; it basically tells the Object Inspector to ignore the component's type when considering whether this editor matches a given property type. If you specify a class name, the Object Inspector will check for type compatibility between that class and the selected component. If the types are compatible (that is, if the component type matches exactly or is derived from the class specified in `ComponentClass`), the Object Inspector will consider it an acceptable editor for that component.

The third parameter, `PropertyName`, allows you to restrict a property editor to a specific property. (To restrict a property editor to a given property, you must supply a `ComponentClass` that is not `nil`.) If you supply a property name, the property of the selected component must match the `PropertyName` exactly for the Object Inspector to use the property editor. If you don't want to specify a property (that is, if you want to use this property editor for any property of the given `PropertyType`), specify an empty string as the `PropertyName` parameter.

Choosing Property Editors

To edit a particular property, the Object Inspector will choose the first property editor that provides an acceptable match for that property. To do so, it calls the `GetEditorClass` function (which appears in the DsgnIntf.PAS unit) to search a linked list of property editor descriptions. This function applies a series of tests to each property editor description (designated as P in the source code), comparing them against a description of the current property of the selected component (designated as `PropInfo` in the source code). Below, we'll walk through some of the source code for this function.

The first test checks the selected component's property type against the editor's property type :

```
if ((P^.PropertyType = PropInfo^.PropType) or
    ((PropType^.Kind = tkClass) and
     (P^.PropertyType^.Kind = tkClass) and
     GetTypeData(PropInfo^.PropType)^.
       ClassType.InheritsFrom
       (GetTypeData(P^.PropertyType)^.ClassType)))
```

If the property type matches, *or* if the component's property is a class property *and* the property editor applies to a class property, *and* it applies to that class (or one of its base classes), the Object Inspector considers the property editor compatible for that property type.

The second test involves the property editor's ComponentClass field:

```
and {...continuing the test...}
    ((P^.ComponentClass = nil) or
     (ComponentClass.InheritsFrom(P^.ComponentClass)))
```

If this field is nil, the Object Inspector considers the property editor compatible for any component. If the property editor's ComponentClass field isn't nil, the Object Inspector checks to see if the selected component is of the class specified in the ComponentClass field, or derives from that class.

The Object Inspector applies the third test, checking the property name, only if the ComponentClass field isn't nil:

```
and ((P^.PropertyName = '') or
     (CompareText(PropInfo^.Name, P^.PropertyName) = 0))
```

If it's non-nil, the property name of the selected component must match the PropertyName field of the property editor exactly.

If a given property editor passes each of the three tests, the Object Inspector will try to determine if it has already found a property editor description (designated as C in the source code) that represents a better match for the selected component's property (if C is nil, the function hasn't yet found a matching property editor description):

```
then
    if (C = nil) or
        (C^.ComponentClass = nil) and
        (P^.ComponentClass <> nil)) or
        ((C^.PropertyName = '') and
```

```
          (P^.PropertyName <> ''))
    then C := P;
```

To qualify as a better match, a property editor must specify a component class *and* the previous best match must contain nil for its ComponentClass field. (In other words, a property editor registered for the TComponent class will represent a better match than one registered using nil for the ComponentClass parameter.) *Or*, if a property editor specifies a property name *and* the previous best match didn't, the Object Inspector considers it a better match.

As you can imagine, there may be several property editors in the linked list that would apply equally well to a given component's property. As the previous paragraphs imply, the Object Inspector chooses the first property editor that matches the PropertyType, ComponentClass, and PropertyName fields. If the first property editor in the linked list is compatible for each of these fields, the Object Inspector will use that editor, and will ignore all of the others in the linked list, whether they also qualify for the selected component or not.

For each property that's currently visible, the Object Inspector will use these tests to determine the appropriate property editors to use, and will then use them to display the property values. At any given time, the Object Inspector may be displaying 20 to 30 properties, and will therefore search the entire linked list of property editors for each of these properties. Fortunately, the code that performs these tests is very efficient. Otherwise, you'd see a noticeable lag as the Object Inspector performs this exhaustive search.

Registering a Property Editor

Here's a possible version of the registration procedure for the uppercase string property editor we've just described:

```
RegisterPropertyEditor (TypeInfo ( string),
    nil, '', TUpperProperty);
```

This procedure assigns the TUpperProperty editor to every string property (we didn't specify a property name, so it applies to all) of any component.

Alternatively, you could apply this editor to any Caption property by rewriting the procedure this way:

```
RegisterPropertyEditor (TypeInfo (TCaption),
    TComponent, 'Caption', TUpperProperty);
```

In this version, you'll notice that we've specified a component class, TComponent. As we mentioned earlier, if you want to specify a property name, you must supply a component class name. However, since all components must have TComponent at some point in their ancestry, Delphi will consider this editor for any component that has a Caption property.

To avoid confusion, we'll apply the TUpperProperty editor only to a particular property (Caption) of a particular component class (TDdhDummyButton). The component is one we've created specifically to test this property editor:

```
// special button component to test
// the TUpperProperty editor
type
  TDdhDummyButton = class (TButton)
  end;
```

Naturally, there are the two related registration procedure calls:

```
procedure Register;
begin
  RegisterComponents ('DDHB', [TDdhDummyButton]);
  RegisterPropertyEditor (TypeInfo (TCaption),
    TDdhDummyButton, 'Caption', TUpperProperty);
end;
```

You'll notice that we use TCaption as the property type instead of String. You must always specify the exact property type when registering a property editor.

Property Editor Attributes

Instead of starting with a detailed list of the TComponentEditor class methods, and then showing some ready-to-use examples, we'll follow a different approach. We'll start with simple examples of the various types of property editors, then build some more complex examples.

One of the most important methods of this class, and one you'll often override, is GetAttributes. This method allows a property editor to inform the Object Inspector of its own capabilities, and then determine which other methods Delphi will call.

The GetAttribute method can set one or more values of the TProperty-Attributes set. Here's the type declaration:

```
type
  TPropertyAttribute = (paValueList, paSubProperties,
    paDialog, paMultiSelect, paAutoUpdate
    paSortList, paReadOnly, paRevertable);
  TPropertyAttributes = set of TPropertyAttribute;
```

By studying these values in detail, and seeing examples of each of them, we'll explore most of the capabilities of property editors.

Displaying a List of Possible Values

The paValueList flag indicates that the property editor will display the possible values in a drop-down list. By default, Delphi displays a similar list of values for enumerated properties and lists of components of a given data type (such as when one component refers to another component, as the animated button in Chapter 5 did). There are specific property editors to display lists of cursors, colors, the names of all the installed fonts, and all available databases or tables.

We can design our own property editor to display a similar list of values by merely redefining the GetValues method (notice the final *s*: the GetValue method, without the final *s*, has a totally different role!). For example, we can write an editor to suggest (but not enforce) a numeric value from a list:

```
type
  TNumListProperty = class (TIntegerProperty)
  public
    function GetAttributes: TPropertyAttributes; override;
    procedure GetValues(Proc: TGetStrProc); override;
  end;
```

Here is the code for these functions:

```
function TNumListProperty.GetAttributes: TPropertyAttributes;
begin
  Result := [paValueList];
end;

procedure TNumListProperty.GetValues(Proc: TGetStrProc);
var
  I: Integer;
```

```
begin
  I := 10;
  while I <= 300 do
  begin
    Proc (IntToStr (I));
    I := I + 10;
  end;
end;
```

You'll call the method addressed by the Proc pointer parameter once for each value you want to add to the list, and pass the value you want as a string. Below is the declaration for this method pointer type:

```
type
  TGetStrProc = procedure(const S: string) of object;
```

Now, we can use this editor to help programmers size a component by registering the property editor for the TDdhDummyButton class's Width and Height parameters:

```
RegisterPropertyEditor (TypeInfo (Integer),
  TDdhDummyButton, 'Width', TNumListProperty);
RegisterPropertyEditor (TypeInfo (Integer),
  TDdhDummyButton, 'Height', TNumListProperty);
```

You can see an example of this editor in action in Figure 12.2.

FIGURE 12.2:

The TNumList-Property editor displays possible integral values in a list.

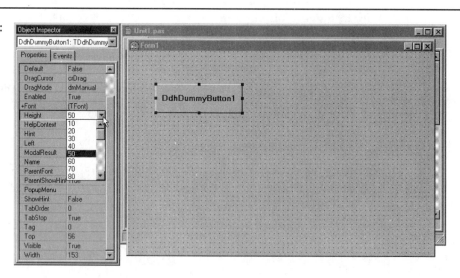

All the editors discussed in this section appear in the PEParade.PAS source file, installed in the package for this chapter (the file DdhPk12.DPK). The source code files of the package and the editors it installs are in the Comps directory of this chapter, as usual. If you install this package, you'll be able to use each of these property editors, which work in combination with the corresponding dummy components.

Sorting the List

Along with the paValueList flag, you can use the paSortList flag to indicate that the Object Inspector should sort the values returned by GetValues. This is the default behavior for many property editors, including those for enumerations, set elements, components, methods, and font names. However, some property editors don't organize the list items alphabetically. For instance, the editor for Color properties groups color values logically, not alphabetically.

A Read-Only Value

The paReadOnly flag indicates that the user won't be able to edit applicable properties from within the Object Inspector. For example, to edit a Color property, you can enter a value or constant directly in the Object Inspector, choose one of the values from the drop-down list, or double-click the property value to display the standard color-selection dialog box. If you didn't want the user to be able to enter color values or constants in the Object Inspector, you could create a compatible property editor for Color properties, and specify the paReadOnly flag. You would, however, be able to change the value by selecting a new value from the drop-down list or from the color-selection dialog box.

Basically, you can use this flag in conjunction with the paValueList flag to make the selection from the list or an alternate editor compulsory. As a weird example, suppose your *dummy* buttons (the component we wrote earlier to demonstrate the property editors) can display a hint string from a limited choice of predefined hints. The class definition is almost the same as for the first property editor:

```
type
  THintListProperty = class (TStringProperty)
  public
```

```
function GetAttributes: TPropertyAttributes; override;
procedure GetValues(Proc: TGetStrProc); override;
end;
```

The GetAttributes method now sets several flags to make selecting from a sorted drop-down list compulsory:

```
function THintListProperty.GetAttributes: TPropertyAttributes;
begin
  Result := [paValueList, paReadOnly, paSortList];
end;
```

The GetValues method adds some values to the list, and then does something interesting at the end:

```
procedure THintListProperty.GetValues(Proc: TGetStrProc);
begin
  Proc ('Press the button, please');
  Proc ('You are kindly requested to press me');
  Proc ('I''m a button');
  Proc ('Do NOT press me!');
  Proc ('The ' + (GetComponent(0) as TComponent).Name
    + ' button');
end;
```

In addition to accessing the value of the current property (with GetValues or other specific access functions for the different data types), a property editor can retrieve a reference to the current component by calling the GetComponent method. The parameter indicates which component to retrieve if the user is editing more than one component's property at a time (more on this later, when we discuss the paMultiSelect flag). Passing zero to this method returns the first component in the list of current components. (If the user is editing a single component, the first component will be the only one in the list.) Since the return type of GetComponent is TPersistent, you must cast it to TComponent to access the component's properties.

TIP

If you access the current component inside a property editor, you might need to cast the component reference to a specific type, such as TButton. However, this is possible only if you've installed this property editor for a specific component type.

Here is the registration function for the THintListProperty editor:

```
RegisterPropertyEditor (TypeInfo (string),
    TDdhDummyButton, 'Hint', THintListProperty);
```

You can see the list of hints in the drop-down list that appears in Figure 12.3. In this figure, you'll notice that the Object Inspector limits the width of the drop-down list to the width of the Object Inspector window's client area. This is a display problem, and doesn't affect the text that the THintListProperty editor stores in a Hint property.

FIGURE 12.3:

The THintList-Property editor displays several predefined hint messages in a list.

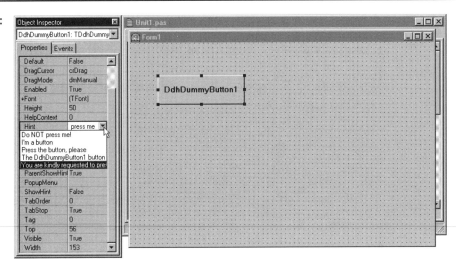

Displaying Subproperties

The paSubProperties flag indicates that a property can display subproperties in the Object Inspector. This type of property displays a plus sign to indicate that you can expand it to display the subproperties directly in the Object Inspector. When you double-click this type of property, Delphi will call the GetProperties method to return a list of subproperties.

By default, Delphi will display subproperties for class properties that are not components themselves. The class property editor (TClassProperty), simply lists the properties of the class (for example a TFont, a TPen, a TBrush, a TScrollBar) and displays the value for each of those properties. In contrast, the component property editor lists compatible external components (such as other components on the form) in a drop-down list. To make the class property editor work, you just need to add the proper published properties to your custom components.

More importantly, we'd like to point out that you can use subproperties for purposes other than displaying property values from another component. One example of this is a *set* property, which displays a list of possible set values and treats them as individual items.

At this point, you may wonder, "Is it possible to display custom subproperties in your own property editor the same way the native Delphi property editors do?" The answer is yes, and no. Yes, there is a way to do this, but no, you can't accomplish it in the same way that Delphi does. Unfortunately, both techniques (Delphi's and ours) are rather complex. If you're not interested in displaying your own subproperties, you may want to skip the next two sections.

Showing Subproperties the Delphi Way (You Can't Do This)

After looking at the limited documentation for property editors and studying the DsgnIntf.PAS file, we determined that writing property editors that display subproperties requires a two-level approach. First, you need to create a property editor that has the paSubProperties attribute. Second, this editor needs to define a GetProperties method, which creates a property editor for each subproperty:

```
type
  TSubColorProperty = class (TColorProperty)
  public
    function GetAttributes: TPropertyAttributes; override;
    procedure GetProperties(Proc: TGetPropEditProc); override;
  end;
```

In this example we want to show the red, green, and blue components of a color as subproperties of the Color property. To begin, we add the paSubProperties flag to the attributes and disable the paMultiSelect flag (this helps us avoid problems later on):

```
function TSubColorProperty.GetAttributes: TPropertyAttributes;
begin
  Result := inherited GetAttributes +
    [paSubProperties] - [paMultiSelect];
end;
```

The GetProperties method accepts a procedural type as parameter. This is necessary because our property editor will receive the address of a procedure that adds new properties to the Object Inspector. We'll need to create the subproperty editor and then pass each one to this procedure. Here is the type declaration of the procedural type:

```
TGetPropEditProc = procedure(Prop: TPropertyEditor) of object;
```

Here is a rough outline of the method:

```
procedure TSubColorProperty.GetProperties(Proc: TGetPropEditProc);
var
  ElementIndex: Integer;
begin
  for ElementIndex := 0 to 2 do
    Proc (TColorElementProperty.Create (ElementIndex, ...));
end;
```

In the body of this method, we need to create each subproperty and pass a parameter to each constructor to give the editors unique identifiers. Later, each editor will use its identifier to determine which color it's displaying.

Following this logic further, here's one approach we could take to writing the class for the subproperty editor:

```
type
  TColorElementProperty = class (TIntegerProperty)
  private
    fElement: Integer;
  public
    constructor Create (Element: Integer;
      Designer: TFormDesigner; PropCount: Integer);
    function GetName: string; override;
    function GetValue: string; override;
    procedure SetValue(const Value: string); override;
  end;
```

We override GetName because we need to supply a proper name for each of the subproperties:

```
function TColorElementProperty.GetName: string;
begin
  case fElement of
    0: Result := 'Red';
    1: Result := 'Green';
```

```
    2: Result := 'Blue';
  end;
end;
```

The value for each subproperty is the amount of the specific color, which we can extract by using the GetRValue, GetGValue, and GetBValue library functions.

However, before doing this conversion we need to transform the Delphi color (a TColor object) into an RGB color value (a standard Windows color) using the ColorToRGB function. Of course, we need to convert this to a string value for display, which we'll do by performing a final IntToStr conversion:

```
function TColorElementProperty.GetValue: string;
begin
  case fElement of
    0: Result := IntToStr (GetRValue (ColorToRGB (GetOrdValue)));
    1: Result := IntToStr (GetGValue (ColorToRGB (GetOrdValue)));
    2: Result := IntToStr (GetBValue (ColorToRGB (GetOrdValue)));
  end;
end;
```

To set the value we impose a limit first, then get the original subproperty value, and finally, replace the amount of red, green, or blue in the color with the new value. We can use the RGB function to set the new value from the three basic colors—the current value plus two values retrieved from the current color:

```
procedure TColorElementProperty.SetValue(const Value: string);
var
  Val: Integer;
  Col: TColor;
begin
  // get the value
  Val := StrToInt (Value);
  // impose a limit
  if Val < 0 then
    Val := 0;
  if Val > 255 then
    Val := 255;
  // get the 'older' color
  Col := ColorToRGB(GetOrdValue);
  case fElement of
    0: SetOrdValue (RGB (
      Val, GetGValue (Col),  GetBValue (Col)));
```

```
    1: SetOrdValue (RGB (
       GetRValue (Col), Val,  GetBValue (Col)));
    2: SetOrdValue (RGB (
       GetRValue (Col), GetGValue (Col),  Val));
  end;
end;
```

So far, this approach seems to be working quite well, but we also have to write a constructor for the subproperty class. The most reasonable way to write it is the following:

```
constructor TColorElementProperty. Create (
  Element: Integer; Designer: TFormDesigner;
  PropCount: Integer);
begin
  inherited Create (Designer, PropCount); // error!
  fElement := Element;
end;
```

Unfortunately, the TPropertyEditor class has a private (*ugh!*) constructor. We don't know the reason for this approach; it's probably a form of protection since this means Delphi programmers can write their own property editors (which the Object Inspector creates), but cannot *create* them inside an add-on tool. We don't know whether imposing this limit is a reasonable thing to do. What we *do* know is that the same level of protection would be available by declaring the constructor as *protected!* In any case, the private constructor means that we cannot write a subproperty editor using the same code Delphi uses.

If we can't call the default constructor for a property editor, we might try to mimic it (since we have access to the VCL source code). However, we need to set the value of some of the base class's private fields (in particular, FDesigner and FPropCount), which you can access only via published, read-only properties. These properties and some other private fields are used a lot by other nonvirtual methods as well, so we can't just trick the system by adding corresponding fields to our derived class. We need to set these fields with the correct data, and to do so, we need a constructor that's not private.

Hacking Our Way to Subproperties

After a great deal of trial and error, we found a solution. It may not be the best solution, but it works. At the core of this approach is the fact that we need to create a class that some internal Delphi code will use. The main problem is that we know Delphi will access some private fields of the class using methods we cannot modify. Since, as we just discovered, we can't change the behavior of the class using OOP techniques, we must resort to some hacking.

Our approach will be to create a clone of the original class, adding new data at the end (so that the original memory layout is unaffected) and changing only virtual functions, since the other functions will be unaffected. To accomplish this, we'll need to write a brand new property editor class, but not one derived from TPropertyEditor. To duplicate the structure and behavior of the original property editor class, we can simply copy and paste the original source code, editing it in a few limited places. This class won't be type-compatible with a normal property editor (because of the inheritance rules), but it will be identical in structure (up to the point where we add new data members). The Pascal compiler won't accept this clone class directly, but we can force it to do so using typecasting.

Here is the structure of the new class, for the most part a clone of the TPropertyEditor class. The only changes we've made relate to the new parameters in the constructor:

```
type
  THackColorElementProperty = class
  private
    FDesigner: TFormDesigner;
    FPropList: PInstPropList;
    FPropCount: Integer;
    fElement: Integer;
    function GetPrivateDirectory: string;
    procedure SetPropEntry(Index: Integer; AInstance: TComponent;
      APropInfo: PPropInfo);
  protected
    constructor Create(Element: Integer; ADesigner: TFormDesigner;
      AInstance: TComponent; APropInfo: PPropInfo);
    function GetPropInfo: PPropInfo;
    function GetFloatValue: Extended;
    function GetFloatValueAt(Index: Integer): Extended;
    function GetMethodValue: TMethod;
    function GetMethodValueAt(Index: Integer): TMethod;
    function GetOrdValue: Longint;
    function GetOrdValueAt(Index: Integer): Longint;
    function GetStrValue: string;
    function GetStrValueAt(Index: Integer): string;
    function GetVarValue: Variant;
```

```
      function GetVarValueAt(Index: Integer): Variant;
      procedure Modified;
      procedure SetFloatValue(Value: Extended);
      procedure SetMethodValue(const Value: TMethod);
      procedure SetOrdValue(Value: Longint);
      procedure SetStrValue(const Value: string);
      procedure SetVarValue(const Value: Variant);
    public
      destructor Destroy; override;
      procedure Activate; virtual;
      function AllEqual: Boolean; virtual;
      procedure Edit; virtual;
      function GetAttributes: TPropertyAttributes; virtual;
      function GetComponent(Index: Integer): TComponent;
      function GetEditLimit: Integer; virtual;
      function GetName: string; virtual;
      procedure GetProperties(Proc: TGetPropEditProc); virtual;
      function GetPropType: PTypeInfo;
      function GetValue: string; virtual;
      procedure GetValues(Proc: TGetStrProc); virtual;
      procedure Initialize; virtual;
      procedure Revert;
      procedure SetValue(const Value: string); virtual;
      function ValueAvailable: Boolean;

      property Designer: TFormDesigner
        read FDesigner;
      property PrivateDirectory: string
        read GetPrivateDirectory;
      property PropCount: Integer
        read FPropCount;
      property Value: string
        read GetValue write SetValue;
    end;
```

Of course, most of the implementation code is identical to that of the TProperty-Editor class, but there are some interesting differences. First, we'll use the code of the GetName, GetValue, and SetValue methods of the TColorElementProperty class described in the previous section. Now we can focus on the constructor, which contains the trickiest code.

The original constructor sets the FDesigner and FPropCount fields with the parameters, and allocates memory for an FPropList object. Setting the FDesigner field is simple, because this is an identifier we have access to in the property editor. The rest of the method is more complex:

```
constructor THackColorElementProperty.Create(
  Element: Integer; ADesigner: TFormDesigner;
  AInstance: TComponent; APropInfo: PPropInfo);
begin
  // store the value
  FDesigner := ADesigner;
  // there is only one component
  FPropCount := 1;
  GetMem (FPropList, 1 * SizeOf(TInstProp));
  // with the following description
  with FPropList^[0] do
  begin
    Instance := AInstance;
    PropInfo := APropInfo;
  end;
  // this is the editor code
  FElement := Element;
end;
```

What are fPropCount and fPropList? Judging by their names, they seem to represent a number of properties and a list of properties, and a look at the VCL source code clearly reveals that the value of fPropCount parallels the number of items of the FPropList. However, examining the type definition of the FPropList field, we were surprised: it's not a list of properties, but a list of components and type information about the current property. Further investigation revealed that this is the list of components that the Object Inspector is currently manipulating.

In this case, we're editing only one component (we've disabled the paMultiSelect flag), so we can set fPropCount to 1, allocate memory for one item of the property list, and initialize it with a reference to the current component and its property data type information (PropInfo). We'll pass these values to the constructor when we create the editors (this was a method we left unfinished in the previous section):

```
procedure TSubColorProperty.GetProperties(Proc: TGetPropEditProc);
var
  I: Integer;
begin
```

```
for I := 0 to 2 do
  Proc (TPropertyEditor (THackColorElementProperty.Create (
    I, Designer, GetComponent (0), GetPropInfo)));
end;
```

Well, this was a lot of work, but the effect was really worth the effort. As you can see in Figure 12.4, you can use the color property editor as before (looking at the list of values, or double-clicking an item to open up the editor), or expand it to view *RGB color* subproperties. Notice that you can continue to view a color as a number or a name, but you can also view the actual values of the subcolors. By setting the subcolors properly (try using 0, 128, and 255), you can successfully define a color that corresponds to one of the predefined color constant names.

FIGURE 12.4:

You can use the color subproperties editor to display color information in several different formats.

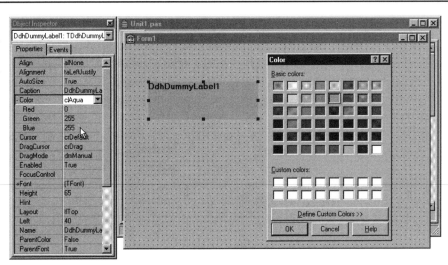

Displaying a Dialog Box

The paDialog flag tells the Object Inspector to display an ellipsis button next to the value of the property. When the user presses this button, the Object Inspector will call the property editor's Edit method, which typically displays a dialog box.

Providing a custom editor for a specific property is probably the most common reason for writing your own property editor. Custom property editors can be very complex (if you want them to be), but it's easy to build a simple one in Delphi since you can use the visual environment to build the dialog box that the property editor will display.

For our first example of a custom property editor, we'll create a *spin editor* for integers. We can't integrate it in the Object Inspector (since there's no approved technique for determining the type of button the Object Inspector will display), but we'll instead display a simple dialog box with an UpDown button and an Edit component. You can see the form at design-time in Figure 12.5.

FIGURE 12.5:

You'll use this form as the dialog box of the new integer property editor.

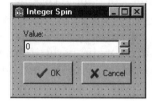

This dialog box contains two BitBtn buttons where we've set the Kind property to bkOK and bkCancel, the UpDown component connected to the Edit component, and other standard properties. Here are the key elements of the form description:

```
object SpinForm: TSpinForm
  BorderStyle = bsToolWindow
  Caption = 'Integer Spin'
  object Label1: TLabel
    Caption = 'Value:'
  end
  object Edit1: TEdit
    Text = '0'
  end
  object BitBtn1: TBitBtn
    Kind = bkOK
  end
  object BitBtn2: TBitBtn
    Kind = bkCancel
  end
  object UpDown1: TUpDown
    Associate = Edit1
    Min = 0
    Increment = 2
    Position = 0
  end
end
```

Once you've set the properties as suggested, the form requires no code. The initialization code, in fact, is in the property editor:

```
type
  TDialogIntProperty = class (TIntegerProperty)
  public
    function GetAttributes: TPropertyAttributes; override;
    procedure Edit; override;
  end;
```

Here's the implementation of these methods (we'll discuss the flag paMultiSelect in the next section):

```
function TDialogIntProperty.GetAttributes:
  TPropertyAttributes;
begin
  Result := [paDialog, paMultiSelect];
end;

procedure TDialogIntProperty.Edit;
var
  PEForm: TSpinForm;
begin
  PEForm := TSpinForm.Create (Application);
  try
    PEForm.UpDown1.Position := GetOrdValue;
    if PEForm.ShowModal = mrOK then
      SetOrdValue (PEForm.UpDown1.Position);
  finally
    PEForm.Free;
  end;
end;
```

As you can see, the Edit method calls the default GetValue and SetValue methods, inherited from the TIntegerProperty parent class, to get the initial value and the set the final value if the user presses the OK button of the dialog box. If the user presses the Cancel button, we leave the value alone.

As before, we need to register this property editor. This time, we'll register it as an editor for any integer property of the TDdhDummyLabel class:

```
RegisterPropertyEditor (TypeInfo(Integer),
  TDdhDummyLabel, '', TDialogIntProperty);
```

Now when you place a DdhDummyLabel component on a form, you'll see an edit button (the small button with an ellipsis) for each integer property. If you click this button, you'll see the Integer Spin dialog box, as shown in Figure 12.6.

Here's the Integer Spin dialog box in action.

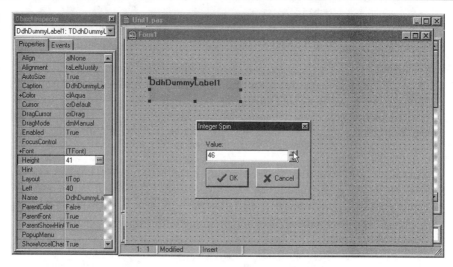

> **NOTE**
>
> Be sure to use exception handling in property editors (to avoid memory leaks), as we've shown in the example above. This is a particularly important technique to use for handling error conditions yourself. However, keep in mind that when a user error occurs (for example, "input is not compatible with the data type"), you should also use exceptions to inform the Object Inspector that something is wrong. For instance, the TIntegerProperty editor raises an exception when the user enters characters or a value that's too big.

Editing Properties for Multiple Components

The paMultiSelect flag indicates that a property editor can manipulate several components at the same time. This happens when the user Shift-selects more than one component and then views the group of components in the Object Inspector. The Caption and positional properties are typical multiple-selection properties, while obviously the Name property is not.

To see an example of a multiple-selection property you can refer to the previous example, which used this flag in addition to the paEdit flag. If you select two Ddh-DummyLabel components and the integer properties are visible, the Object Inspector will display the property value if that value is the same in both components. In contrast, the Object Inspector will never display the Height and Width properties for more than one DdhDummyButton because they use a property editor (the one that displays the list of integer values) that doesn't have the paMultiSelect attribute.

When the Object Inspector creates a property editor that contains this flag, it calls the editor's AllEqual method to determine if the property value is the same in each of the currently selected components. In most cases, the default behavior of this method is adequate, and you can rely on the inherited version to do the correct thing. The only time you might want to override the AllEqual method is when you derive a new property editor directly from the TPropertyEditor class. As you might imagine, the default property editors do a good job of overriding this method.

We'll override the AllEqual method in some future examples. However, to show how this method works, and how you should access several components at the same time, here is the code for the TOrdinalProperty class's implementation of this method:

```pascal
function TOrdinalProperty.AllEqual: Boolean;
var
  I: Integer;
  V: Longint;
begin
  { start by assuming values differ }
  Result := False;
  { if there are multiple values... }
  if PropCount > 1 then
  begin
    { get first value }
    V := GetOrdValue;
    { compare with every other value }
    for I := 1 to PropCount - 1 do
      if GetOrdValueAt(I) <> V then
        { if any are different, return False }
        Exit;
  end;
  { if we get here, all were equal }
  Result := True;
end;
```

Automatically Updating Properties

The paAutoUpdate flag indicates that we want the Object Inspector to update the property value continuously while the user is editing it. The most obvious example of this is the Caption property: while you type a new caption, the Object Inspector updates the Caption immediately.

Of course, this behavior is something you generally don't want. For instance, suppose you created a property editor for the Top property, and set the paAuto-Update flag as one of its attributes. If you wanted to enter **100** as a new position, the component would move to the top of the form when you entered the **1**, then move down nine pixels when you entered the **0**, and then finally move down another 90 pixels when you entered the last **0**. Although this doesn't make much sense, here's the implementation of such a property editor (again, this is from the PEParade.PAS file):

```
type
  TAutoIntegerProperty = class (TIntegerProperty)
  public
    function GetAttributes: TPropertyAttributes; override;
  end;

function TAutoIntegerProperty.GetAttributes:
  TPropertyAttributes;
begin
  Result := inherited GetAttributes + [paAutoUpdate];
end;
```

The GetAttributes method simply adds the paAutoUpdate flag to the existing attributes. The rest of the code of the property editor remains unchanged. We can then install this editor for a few selected properties of one of our dummy components:

```
RegisterPropertyEditor (TypeInfo(Integer),
  TDdhDummyLabel, 'Top', TAutoIntegerProperty);
RegisterPropertyEditor (TypeInfo(Integer),
  TDdhDummyLabel, 'Left', TAutoIntegerProperty);
```

If you install this editor, using the Top and Left properties of the DdhDummyLabel component will become an interesting visual exercise! However, keep in mind that you can't use an empty string as a value for this property (not even to delete the current value), because that's invalid. You'll have to replace the current value with another one—not delete it and then type a new value.

This empty-string issue is an example of the problems you face with the paAutoUpdate flag. In other situations, the problems can be even worse. In only a few cases is the paAutoUpdate flag handy, so it's not used often by Delphi.

Revertable Changes

Finally, the paRevertable flag indicates that the property editor can surface the value *inherited* from a parent form class, by using the Object Inspector's Revert To Inherited command on the SpeedMenu. This operation makes sense only when you're using visual form inheritance.

Real-World Property Editors

In the first half of this chapter, we've explored some property editor capabilities by examining the basics and exploring different styles and attributes. We haven't used each and every method of the TPropertyEditor class, but we've seen how to override most of the virtual ones.

Now we want to build some more complex property editors—primarily ones that display dialog boxes. We'll focus on real-world uses for these editors and on stressing the capabilities of such an editor. We'll start with an editor for the sound button from Chapter 5, and then write an editor for the collection property we also defined in that chapter. After these two real-world examples, we'll examine editors capable of manipulating multiple components and displaying other system information.

A Sound Editor (for the Sound Button)

The sound button we built in Chapter 5 had two sound-related properties: SoundUp and SoundDown. These were actually strings, so we were able to display them in the Object Inspector using the TStringProperty editor. However, typing the name of a system sound or of an external file is not very user-friendly, and it's a bit error-prone.

When you need to select a file for a string property, you can reuse an existing property editor, the TMPFilenameProperty class. All you have to do is register this editor for a property:

```
RegisterPropertyEditor (
   TypeInfo (string), TDdhSoundButton,
   'SoundUp', TMPFileNameProperty);
RegisterPropertyEditor (
   TypeInfo (string), TDdhSoundButton,
   'SoundDown', TMPFileNameProperty);
```

This editor allows you to select a file for the sound, but we want to be able to select system sounds as well. For this reason, instead of using this simple approach we'll build a more complex property editor. Our editor for sound strings allows a user to either choose a value from a drop-down list or display a dialog box from which you can load and test a sound (from a sound file or a system sound). This property editor combines both the paValueList and the paDialog attributes, but also allows direct editing (as the TColorProperty does):

```
function TSoundProperty.GetAttributes:
  TPropertyAttributes;
begin
  // allow direct editing and multiple selection
  Result := [paDialog, paMultiSelect,
    paValueList, paSortList];
end;
```

Here's the complete class declaration, which overrides the GetAttributes, GetValues, and Edit methods:

```
type
  TSoundProperty = class (TStringProperty)
  public
    function GetAttributes: TPropertyAttributes; override;
    procedure GetValues(Proc: TGetStrProc); override;
    procedure Edit; override;
  end;
```

The GetValues method returns a default list of system values (taken from Windows 95):

```
procedure TSoundProperty.GetValues(Proc: TGetStrProc);
begin
  // provide a list of system sounds
  Proc ('Maximize');
```

```
      Proc ('Minimize');
      Proc ('MenuCommand');
      Proc ('MenuPopup');
      Proc ('RestoreDown');
      Proc ('RestoreUp');
      Proc ('SystemAsterisk');
      Proc ('SystemDefault');
      Proc ('SystemExclamation');
      Proc ('SystemExit');
      Proc ('SystemHand');
      Proc ('SystemQuestion');
      Proc ('SystemStart');
      Proc ('AppGPFault');
      Proc ('[DoubleClick for dialog]');
    end;
```

TIP

A better approach would be to extract these values from the Windows Registry, where all these names are listed.

Providing a drop-down list of values *and* a dialog box for editing a property causes a problem: the Object Inspector will display the arrow button that indicates a drop-down list instead of displaying the ellipsis button to indicate that a dialog box editor is available. To overcome this problem we've added a bogus entry to the list, which you can see as the last value above. This is a hint for the user—a line the user shouldn't select. You can see an example of the effect in Figure 12.7.

The Edit method is very straightforward, as it simply creates and displays a dialog box. You'll notice that we could have just displayed the File Open dialog box directly, but we decided to add an intermediate step to allow the user to test the sound. This is similar to what Delphi does with graphic properties: You open the preview first, and load the file only after you've confirmed that it's correct. The most important step is to load the file and test it before you apply it to the property. Here is the code of the Edit method:

```
procedure TSoundProperty.Edit;
begin
  SoundForm := TSoundForm.Create (Application);
  try
    SoundForm.ComboBox1.Text := GetValue;
    // show the dialog box
    if SoundForm.ShowModal = mrOK then
```

```
            SetValue (SoundForm.ComboBox1.Text);
        finally
            SoundForm.Free;
        end;
    end;
```

The form this method displays is quite simple: a ComboBox displays the same values returned by the GetValues method, and four buttons allow you to open a file, test the sound, and terminate the dialog box by accepting the values or canceling. You can see an example of the dialog box at design-time in Figure 12.8.

FIGURE 12.7:

The odd entry in the list of sounds provides a hint for the user (since there is no ellipsis button in the Object Inspector to indicate that a dialog box is available).

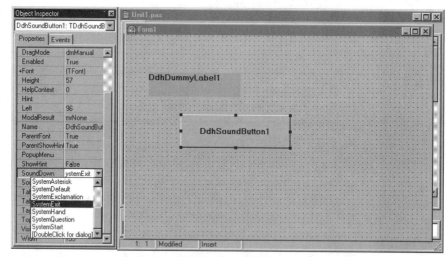

FIGURE 12.8:

The sound property editor's form displays a list of available sounds.

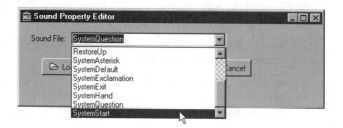

The first two buttons of the form have two simple methods assigned to their OnClick event:

```
procedure TSoundForm.SpeedButton1Click(Sender: TObject);
begin
  if OpenDialog1.Execute then
    ComboBox1.Text := OpenDialog1.FileName;
end;

procedure TSoundForm.PlayClick(Sender: TObject);
begin
  PlaySound (PChar (ComboBox1.Text), 0, snd_Async);
end;
```

Unfortunately, we've not found a simple way to determine whether a sound is valid. The PlaySound function returns an error code only if it can't find the default system sound (which it attempts to play if it can't find the system sound or sound file); otherwise it plays the default system sound but provides no feedback that an error occurred. PlaySound looks for the sound in the Registry first, and if it doesn't find the sound there, checks to see if the specified sound file exists.

Finally, here's the code we use to register this editor with Delphi. You'll notice that we install this editor for only two properties of the TDdhSoundButton component (which you should include in a uses clause to compile this code):

```
procedure Register;
begin
  RegisterPropertyEditor (TypeInfo(string),
    TDdhSoundButton, 'SoundUp', TSoundProperty);
  RegisterPropertyEditor (TypeInfo(string),
    TDdhSoundButton, 'SoundDown', TSoundProperty);
end;
```

Editing a Collection of Points

A typical case in which you absolutely need to write a property editor is when you define collection properties, because there's no predefined editor for this type of property. If you don't create an editor for a collection property, Delphi will use the TClassProperty editor for that collection (not the TComponentProperty editor it uses for external components). TClassProperty has the paSubProperties flag set, but is capable of displaying automatically only published subproperties, not collections.

As an example, we'll build a property editor for the TDdhPoints collection of the TDdhGraph component that we created in Chapter 5. This component displays a series of points, and connects the points together with straight lines. To store the points, we've created a Points property, which represents a TDdhPoints collection of TDdhPoint objects.

> **NOTE**   This property editor won't allow you to create new TDdhPoint objects, but will instead allow you to edit existing points in a TDdhPoints collection. We've done this to help simplify the example. To test this property editor, you can open the TestGr project (in the Graph directory) that we showed in Chapter 5, after installing the new editor.

We'll base the editor for this collection property on a dialog box, and we'll therefore define the following class:

```
type
  TPointsProperty = class (TClassProperty)
  public
    function GetAttributes: TPropertyAttributes; override;
    procedure Edit; override;
  end;
```

The attributes should be those of the parent class, minus the paSubProperties flag, and plus the paDialog flag:

```
function TPointsProperty.GetAttributes:
  TPropertyAttributes;
begin
  Result := inherited GetAttributes +
    [paDialog] - [paSubProperties];
end;
```

Before examining the code of the Edit method, let's take a look at the dialog box form. We've based this particular editor on a TStringGrid component, with several lines and three columns to host the values of each point (X, Y, and Text), plus the usual buttons, as you can see in Figure 12.9.

Here's a summary of the key property settings of the TPointsForm class (from the DFM file):

```
object PointsForm: TPointsForm
  BorderStyle = bsDialog
  Caption = 'Points Editor'
```

```
object Grid1: TStringGrid
  ColCount = 3
  FixedCols = 0
  RowCount = 10
  FixedRows = 0
  Options = [goFixedVertLine, goFixedHorzLine,
    goVertLine, goHorzLine, goRangeSelect,
    goEditing]
  OnGetEditMask = Grid1GetEditMask
end
object BitBtn1: TBitBtn
  Kind = bkOK
end
object BitBtn2: TBitBtn
  Kind = bkCancel
end
end
```

FIGURE 12.9:

The point list property editor's form contains a StringGrid and two BitBtn components.

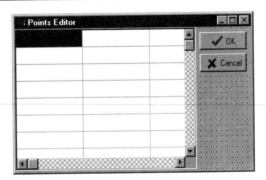

The only code for this form is the handler for the OnGetEditMask event of the Grid1 string grid component:

```
procedure TPointsForm.Grid1GetEditMask (
  Sender: TObject; ACol, ARow: Longint;
  var Value: string);
begin
  if ACol < 2 then
    Value := '9999;0; '
  else
    Value := '';
end;
```

Basically, we want to be able to enter only numbers in the first two columns (column 0 and column 1), and any text string in the third one. Now that we've created this form, we can consider the property editor's `Edit` method. Since this particular method is quite long, we'll break it into pieces to describe it. Here's the initialization code:

```
procedure TPointsProperty.Edit;
var
  Pts: TDdhPoints;
  I: Integer;
begin
  PointsForm := TPointsForm.Create (Application);
  try
    // access the property
    Pts := TDdhPoints (GetOrdValue);
    with PointsForm.Grid1 do
    begin
      // set the number of rows
      RowCount := Pts.Count;
      // set the width of the three columns
      ColWidths [0] := 50;
      ColWidths [1] := 50;
      ColWidths [2] := ClientWidth - 104;
      // copy the values
      for I := 0 to Pts.Count - 1 do
      begin
        Cells [0, I] := IntToStr (Pts.Items [I].X);
        Cells [1, I] := IntToStr (Pts.Items [I].Y);
        Cells [2, I] := Pts.Items [I].Text;
      end; // for
    end; // width
```

To initialize the form we first retrieve the data from the collection. To do so, we can use the `GetOrdValue` method, which returns the ordinal value of the property. For this property, the ordinal value is simply the memory address of the object, so we can cast it back to the original type by writing `TDdhPoints (GetOrdValue)`.

At this point, we can scan the point collection and store the values in the string grid after we've set the size of the columns (something we can do only at run-time) and the proper number of rows.

Having initialized the dialog box, we can show it and then save the updated values of the grid back to the collection (actually, we don't test whether the values have been updated but simply save them when the user clicks OK):

```
// show the dialog box
if PointsForm.ShowModal = mrOK then
begin
  with PointsForm.Grid1 do
    for I := 0 to Pts.Count - 1 do
    begin
      Pts.Items [I].X := StrToIntDef (Cells [0, I], 0);
      Pts.Items [I].Y := StrToIntDef (Cells [1, I], 0);
      Pts.Items [I].Text := Cells [2, I];
    end;
  // indicate that the component data
  // has changed and should be saved
  Designer.Modified;
  // updates the user interface of the component
  (GetComponent(0) as TDdhGraph).Invalidate;
end;
finally
  PointsForm.Free;
end;
end;
```

Notice the two lines that we execute after we've updated the data. By calling the Modified method of the Designer object (Designer is a property of the TPropertyEditor class), we notify the designer that we've changed some of its data. Typically, you notify the designer by calling the SetValue method, but in this case we update the data without calling this method since we don't create a new object (we simply update the current one). If you call the Modified method, the form designer will know its data has changed, and will ask if you want to save the data when you close the form.

However, calling Modified has no impact on the user interface of the designer. Accordingly, we have to call the designing form's Invalidate method to update it, or, even better, we could invalidate the component at design-time. To access the current component we can use the GetComponent function and pass zero as the parameter. We have to cast the return value to a windowed control type, or a specific data type, for which we can then call Invalidate.

WARNING   If you look at the code, it seems that the component should be able to update itself automatically (since we change some of its data and end up calling an Invalidate method), but that's not the case. Unfortunately, this isn't the first time we've found that you need to explicitly add code to update the user interface of a component at design-time.

As usual, we need to provide a registration procedure at the end of the unit:

```
procedure Register;
begin
  RegisterPropertyEditor (TypeInfo(TDdhPoints),
    TDdhGraph, 'Points', TPointsProperty);
end;
```

Once you've installed this property editor (located in the PEPoints file), you can display the points in the TDdhPoints collection property of a TDdhGraph component. As we mentioned earlier, the TestGr.DPR project contains this component and displays several points at design-time (we created them at run-time and saved the resulting points to the DFM file). Figure 12.10 shows our new Points Editor dialog box with the positional values of each TDdhPoint in the collection.

FIGURE 12.10:

The point collection property editor displays detailed information about each point in the list.

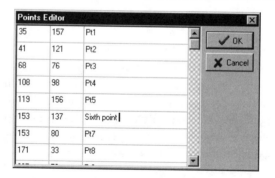

Accessing Other Components: The Comparative Name Editor

Up to now, we've examined property editors that manipulate a specific property of one or more selected components. Now we'll move in a completely different direction, and build a property editor that displays the value of a given property for each component on a form—even if you haven't selected any other components.

This can be particularly useful when you need to set a value that affects the same property on other components, such as the Tag, TabOrder, Hint, and Name properties. We'll call these *comparative* property editors.

TIP The fact that no standard editor in Delphi uses this approach *visually* doesn't mean it isn't a good idea. In fact, editing a property such as Tag might affect the same property of other components on the form, making it much faster to edit multiple values. As we'll see again in the future, it's possible and interesting to use hooks provided by Borland to customize Delphi in ways that were not foreseen by its developers.

Here's the property's class definition and the simple GetAttributes method:

```
type
  TNameProperty = class (TStringProperty)
  public
    function GetAttributes: TPropertyAttributes; override;
    procedure Edit; override;
  end;

function TNameProperty.GetAttributes:
  TPropertyAttributes;
begin
  Result := [paDialog];
end;
```

The dialog box of this property editor is based on the form in Figure 12.11, which contains an Edit component (the actual editor), two ListBox components that will display component names, and two Buttons. The first list box will display the names of all the components on the current form, and the other list box will display only the names of the components from the same class as the currently selected component. The two buttons allow the user to set or reject changes.

FIGURE 12.11:

The Name compara-
tive property editor's
form uses two ListBox
components and
three Buttons.

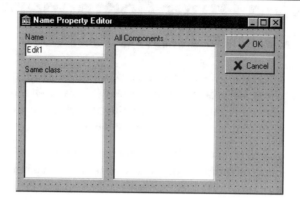

When the user types a name in the edit box, the editor checks to see if this is a
valid identifier, turning the color of the background of the edit box to red if not:

```
procedure TNameForm.Edit1Change(Sender: TObject);
begin
  if IsValidIdent (Edit1.Text) then
    Edit1.Color := clWindow
  else
    Edit1.Color := clRed;
end;
```

When the user leaves the edit box and repeats the test, we show an error message
and move the focus back to the edit box:

```
procedure TNameForm.Edit1Exit(Sender: TObject);
begin
  if not IsValidIdent (Edit1.Text) then
  begin
    ShowMessage ('The new name is an illegal identifier');
    Edit1.SetFocus;
  end;
end;
```

TIP

Using the ShowMessage procedure inside a property editor has a nice side-
effect. The caption of the dialog box displays the name of the current
application, which in this case is Delphi itself. We mention this to remind
you of the tight integration of this code with the Delphi environment.

The only other method of this form is the one that responds to the OnClick event of both list boxes by copying the name of the current list item to the edit box (of course, a user will need to edit the name once it appears in the Edit control since Delphi won't allow two components on a form to have the same name):

```
procedure TNameForm.ListSameClick(Sender: TObject);
begin
  with Sender as TListbox do
    Edit1.Text := Items [ItemIndex];
end;
```

The code above should come in handy if you use a complex prefix for naming all components of the same type: Once you've created one component of a given type on a form, you can use its name as a starting point for the name of other components of the same type.

Here's the property editor's Edit method, which initializes and shows the form we've just defined:

```
procedure TNameProperty.Edit;
var
  PeForm: TNameForm;
  TheComponent: TComponent;
  TheForm: TForm;
  I: Integer;
begin
  PeForm := TNameForm.Create (Application);
  try
    PeForm.Edit1.Text := GetValue;
    // fill the listboxes
    TheComponent := GetComponent (0) as TComponent;
    if TheComponent is TForm then
      TheForm := TForm (TheComponent)
    else
      TheForm := (TheComponent.Owner) as TForm;
    for I := 0 to TheForm.ComponentCount - 1 do
    begin
      PeForm.ListAll.Items.Add (TheForm.Components[I].Name);
      if TheForm.Components[I] is TheComponent.ClassType then
        PeForm.ListSame.Items.Add (TheForm.Components[I].Name);
    end;
    if PeForm.ShowModal = mrOK then
      SetValue (PeForm.Edit1.Text);
```

```
finally
    PeForm.Free;
  end;
end;
```

As you can tell, this method is somewhat complex. Basically, our aim is to retrieve a reference to the form that contains the current component, which we store in the TheForm variable. Since a form has a name, too (at design-time), the form could itself be the current component, or it could be the owner of the current component. To locate the form, we'll simply check to see if the data type of the current component is TForm or not. Once we have a reference to the form, we simply scan its Components property array, add the name of each component to the ListAll list box, and then add the name of each component of the same class as the current one to the ListSame list box.

Finally, here is the registration code:

```
procedure Register;
begin
  RegisterPropertyEditor (TypeInfo(TComponentName),
    TComponent, 'Name', TNameProperty);
end;
```

This installs the property editor system-wide in Delphi. In Figure 12.12, you can see an example of its use.

FIGURE 12.12:

The Name comparative property editor displays the names of all the components on a given form, and identifies components of the same class.

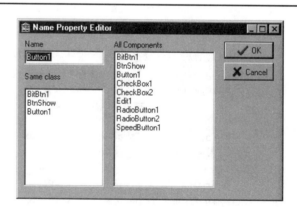

It's possible to extend this comparative editor further by allowing it to change the Name property of any component on the form. This is something we don't suggest for the Name property, but it can come handy for other properties, such as Tag. This is demonstrated by the next example.

Editing Several Components at Once

Now let's build an editor for the Tag property of components the user has selected, which allows the user to set the individual values of this property for each of the components. The code of this example is actually quite simple. The property editor displays a dialog box, which will be available whenever the user selects multiple components:

```
type
  TTagMultiProperty = class (TIntegerProperty)
  public
    function GetAttributes: TPropertyAttributes; override;
    procedure Edit; override;
  end;

implementation

function TTagMultiProperty.GetAttributes:
  TPropertyAttributes;
begin
  Result := [paDialog, paMultiSelect];
end;
```

The editor itself is based on a form that contains a ListBox component (which we'll use to show the names of the selected components and the value of their tag property), as you can see in Figure 12.13. We fill this inside the form's UpdateList method:

```
procedure TTagForm.UpdateList;
var
  I: Integer;
begin
  // fill the listbox
  ListBoxTags.Items.Clear;
  for I := 0 to Pe.PropCount - 1 do
    with Pe.GetComponent (I) as TComponent do
      ListBoxTags.Items.Add (
        Format ('%s: %d', [Name, Tag]));
end;
```

The dialog box of the
editor for the Tag
property of multiple
components,
TTagMultiProperty

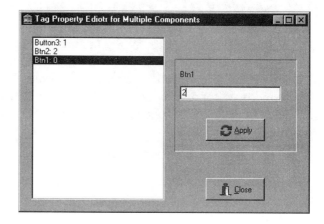

In this method, Pe is a local field of the form, which contains a reference to the
property editor. This is actually the declaration of the form:

```
type
  TTagForm = class(TForm)
    ListBoxTags: TListBox;
    EditTag: TEdit;
    LabelComp: TLabel;
    BtnApply: TBitBtn;
    BtnClose: TBitBtn;
    Bevel1: TBevel;
    procedure ListBoxTagsClick(Sender: TObject);
    procedure BtnApplyClick(Sender: TObject);
  public
    Pe: TTagMultiProperty;
    procedure UpdateList;
  end;
```

NOTE   In the UpdateList method, you'll notice that we use the TProperty-
Editor class's PropCount property. This property holds the number of
properties we're editing, which in fact represents the number of components we're editing. The method's name is a little misleading (it should
probably be something like *CompCount*), but you can indeed access the
various components (with the GetComponent method) by passing indices
from 0 to PropCount – 1.

Elsewhere on this form, a label and an edit box display information for the current component. We'll update this information each time the user selects a new item from the list box:

```
procedure TTagForm.ListBoxTagsClick(Sender: TObject);
begin
  with Pe.GetComponent (ListBoxTags.ItemIndex)
    as TComponent do
  begin
    LabelComp.Caption := Name;
    EditTag.Text := IntToStr (Tag);
  end;
end;
```

If the user clicks the Apply button, we'll change the value of the component directly, and then update the list and notify the form designer that we've modified the value of a property:

```
procedure TTagForm.BtnApplyClick(Sender: TObject);
begin
  with Pe.GetComponent (ListBoxTags.ItemIndex)
      as TComponent do
    Tag := StrToInt (EditTag.Text);
  UpdateList;
  Pe.Designer.Modified;
end;
```

Since we update the components immediately, when a user clicks the *Close* button we have nothing left to do. Accordingly, we can simply set the button's ModalResult property to mrOk (or any other value except mrNone), and write no code for it.

The Edit method of the property editor has little to do besides creating the form, initializing the ListBox, selecting the first ListBox item in the Label and Edit controls, and then displaying the form modally:

```
procedure TTagMultiProperty.Edit;
var
  PeForm: TTagForm;
begin
  PeForm := TTagForm.Create (Application);
  PeForm.Pe := self;
  try
    // update the list
```

```
      PeForm.UpdateList;
      // select and show the first item
      PeForm.ListBoxTags.ItemIndex := 0;
      PeForm.ListBoxTagsClick (self);
      // show the form
      PeForm.ShowModal;
   finally
      PeForm.Free;
   end;
end;
```

In this method, the only unusual step occurs when we set the Pe field of the form with the component editor.

As usual, we need to provide a registration procedure. Here, we've used TComponent as the component class to make this property editor available for all component types:

```
procedure Register;
begin
   RegisterPropertyEditor (TypeInfo(LongInt),
      TComponent, 'Tag', TTagMultiProperty);
end;
```

What's Next

One way to look at property editors is to consider them hooks into the Delphi environment. Other hooks you're probably familiar with are component editors, wizards, and version control systems. You can use each of these Delphi extensions for its original purpose, or take advantage of the hook interfaces for other purposes.

What can you do with a hook into Delphi? The source code of the VCL (particularly the files in the Source\ToolsAPI directory) lists many internal objects you can access: the form designer, the editor, the menu, and the component library, just to name a few. One object that's particularly interesting is the ToolServices global object we'll discuss in Chapters 14 and 15 (along with a more systematic description of the available system objects and information). What's important to notice is that this functionality is available at design-time only: Your stand-alone programs cannot interact with Delphi the same way these system extensions do, because they're strictly tied to the Borland environment.

Generally, property editors are less appropriate for retrieving information from the IDE. This is because they are meant to interact with specific properties. In contrast, component editors and experts are better suited for interacting with the environment or with elements other than individual properties. We'll look at component editors in the next chapter.

CHAPTER
THIRTEEN

13

Component Editors

- Writing a Component Editor

- Creating a New Event Handler

- Using the ToolServices Methods

- A "Wizard-Like" Component Editor

- Editing with the Object Inspector

- Editing Collection Items

Besides associating specific editors with component properties, we can create an editor for a component as a whole. Delphi makes it possible to use the form designer and its SpeedMenu to activate our editors, which in this case are called component editors.

You've almost certainly used component editors already, though you may not have been aware of it. The two most common examples are the Menu Designer for the TMainMenu and TPopupMenu component classes, and the Fields Editor for the TTable and TQuery components. These component editors manipulate public, run-time only properties, which aren't available from the Object Inspector, and which are quite complex in their internal structure. If you have a similar need to edit such properties in your own components, you can write a component editor to handle the task. Not surprisingly, in Delphi, writing a component editor is very simple.

Writing a Component Editor

To write a custom component editor you must derive it from the TComponentEditor class. This class allows you to add items to the context menu of a particular type of component, customize the default action for that component (invoked by double-clicking on it), and copy the component to the Clipboard along with some additional information. As you might expect from the last chapter's discussion of property editors, you'll have to register the component editor. In this case, you have to use the RegisterComponentEditor procedure.

Besides using custom editors for particular components, Delphi provides a common component editor whose class is TDefaultEditor (a descendant of the TComponentEditor class). This component editor adds no special menu items but does define a default action: it opens the unit for the current form and advances the cursor to an appropriate form method. If the method doesn't already exist, the TDefaultEditor object will create one for you. In addition, it assigns the form methods to the OnCreate, OnClick, or OnChange event properties (whichever property is appropriate for the component).

Here is the source code for the public portion of the TComponentEditor class:

```
type
  TComponentEditor = class
  public
```

```
constructor Create(AComponent: TComponent;
  ADesigner: TFormDesigner); virtual;
procedure Edit; virtual;
procedure ExecuteVerb(Index: Integer); virtual;
function GetVerb(Index: Integer): string; virtual;
function GetVerbCount: Integer; virtual;
procedure Copy; virtual;
property Component: TComponent read FComponent;
property Designer: TFormDesigner read FDesigner;
end;
```

The Component property refers to the current component (the one for which the component editor was invoked), and the Designer property to the form designer. Delphi will call the component editor's Edit method when the user double-clicks the component. It will call the GetVerbCount and GetVerb methods to create the SpeedMenu for the component; it will call the ExecuteVerb method when the user selects a menu item; and it will call the Copy method to copy the component to the Clipboard.

By overriding these methods, you can customize the behavior of a component editor, as we'll see in the next sections. Of course, you must register component editors just as you registered the property editors. The RegisterComponentEditor procedure accepts two parameters, the component class type and the component editor's class type:

```
procedure RegisterComponentEditor(
  ComponentClass: TComponentClass;
  ComponentEditor: TComponentEditorClass);
```

TIP

Although it is not clearly documented, if you pass a base class as the ComponentClass parameter instead of an actual component class, the base class's subclasses will use this component editor unless a specific editor has been assigned to a particular component class. For example, if you register a component editor for the TComponent class, Delphi will use it instead of the TDefaultEditor component editor.

To explore the capabilities of component editors, we've written three simple examples. The source code of these three component editors is available in the Comps directory on the companion CD, along with the other source code files that are part of the package for this chapter.

> **NOTE** The filenames of the units containing component editors begin with the letters CE, just as the property editors in Chapter 12 were marked with the prefix PE.

Adding Verbs to the SpeedMenu

The first component editor we'll write simply adds a verb to a component's SpeedMenu, and displays an About box when the user selects that item. When we add only one item to the menu, the selection of this menu item becomes the default action, which in this case means that double-clicking on the component (an edit control derived from TEdit) will display the About box. Here is the class declaration:

```
type
  TCeAbout = class (TComponentEditor)
    function GetVerbCount: Integer; override;
    function GetVerb(Index: Integer): string; override;
    procedure ExecuteVerb(Index: Integer); override;
  end;
```

And here is the code of the three methods:

```
function TCeAbout.GetVerbCount: Integer;
begin
  Result := 1;
end;


function TCeAbout.GetVerb (Index: Integer): string;
begin
  if Index = 0 then
    Result := '&About this component...';
end;


procedure TCeAbout.ExecuteVerb (Index: Integer);
begin
  if Index = 0 then
    MessageDlg ('A dummy edit box, from an example'#13 +
      'of the book "Delphi Developer''s Handbook"',
      mtInformation, [mbOK], 0);
end;
```

We add one new menu item (or verb), which uses an index of 0. In the other two methods, we check this menu index and either return the string (with the proper ampersand character and ellipsis), or execute the action. Here is the registration procedure, which associates the component editor (as usual) with a specific component class:

```
RegisterComponentEditor (TDdhDummy1Edit, TCeAbout);
```

You can see the component menu and its effect in Figures 13.1; its message box looks like this:

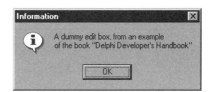

These illustrations were taken from the DemoCed example, which you'll find in the directory of the same name. However, there's no reason to run this program: What's important is what happens when you open it in the Delphi environment. Of course, you first need to install the package for this chapter, which registers the new component editors and the related components.

FIGURE 13.1:

The custom menu item added by the TCeAbout component editor to the local menu of the form when a specific component is selected.

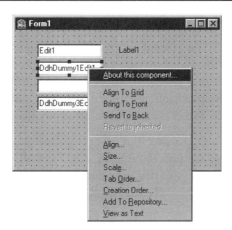

Editing a Component

Besides adding items to the form designer's SpeedMenu when the user selects a component, a component editor can also change the default action that is executed when you double-click on the component.

The default action for a component editor can be anything you like. For example, we've noticed that it's rather annoying to have to remove the text from an Edit component after you've created it, so we've written a component editor that clears the default text when you double-click on an Edit component. Here is the class declaration:

```
type
  TCeEditText = class (TComponentEditor)
    procedure Edit; override;
  end;
```

This editor is quite simple because we're not adding any items to the SpeedMenu. As you might expect, the implementation code is very simple, as well:

```
procedure TCeEditText.Edit;
begin
  (Component as TEdit).Text := '';
end;
```

Showing a Dialog Box

Usually, a component editor adds at least one item to the component's SpeedMenu, and assigns the menu item's action to the double-click event. This is what the next example does. Since the component's Name is a very important property, it may be appropriate to create a component editor for it. By doing so, we'll reuse the code of the Name property editor shown earlier in this chapter.

What's interesting in the next example is that we can subclass an existing component editor (TCeAbout), and add capabilities without compromising the inherited ones. You can use a similar approach (and reuse this code) in your own property editors. Here is the class, with the commonly overridden methods:

```
type
  TCeNameDialog = class (TCeAbout)
    procedure Edit; override;
    function GetVerbCount: Integer; override;
    function GetVerb(Index: Integer): string; override;
```

```
      procedure ExecuteVerb(Index: Integer); override;
    end;
```

The GetVerbCount method alerts Delphi to the fact that this component editor will display one more item than the parent class displays:

```
function TCeNameDialog.GetVerbCount: Integer;
begin
  Result := inherited GetVerbCount + 1;
end;
```

Now, if the index of the menu item of the GetVerb and ExecuteVerb methods is less than the number of items implemented by the parent class, we need to call the corresponding parent class method. Otherwise, we'll execute some code of our own. Now we display two custom menu items in the component's SpeedMenu, as you can see in Figure 13.2. This may be easier to understand in code than in words:

```
function TCeNameDialog.GetVerb (Index: Integer): string;
begin
  if Index < inherited GetVerbCount then
    // base class editor verb
    Result := inherited GetVerb (Index)
  else
    // verbs of this editor
    if Index = inherited GetVerbCount then
      Result := '&Edit Name...';
end;

procedure TCeNameDialog.ExecuteVerb (Index: Integer);
begin
  if Index < inherited GetVerbCount then
    inherited ExecuteVerb (Index)
  else
    if Index = inherited GetVerbCount then
      Edit;
end;
```

The significant code for this example is in the Edit method, which displays the form that we designed for the Name property editor in the last chapter, and then executes a very similar section of code. The main difference is that now we can refer to the current component by using the component editor's Component property, instead of having to use the GetComponent method.

FIGURE 13.2:

The TCeNameDialog
component editor adds
a custom menu item to
the local menu. The
other custom menu
item, instead, is added
by the base class.

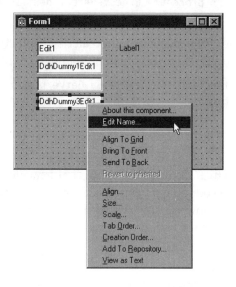

```
procedure TCeNameDialog.Edit;
var
  PeForm: TNameForm;
  TheForm: TForm;
  I: Integer;
begin
  PeForm := TNameForm.Create (Application);
  try
    PeForm.Edit1.Text := Component.Name;
    // fill the list boxes
    TheForm := (Component.Owner) as TForm;
    for I := 0 to TheForm.ComponentCount - 1 do
    begin
      PeForm.ListAll.Items.Add (TheForm.Components[I].Name);
      if TheForm.Components[I] is Component.ClassType then
        PeForm.ListSame.Items.Add (TheForm.Components[I].Name);
    end;
    if PeForm.ShowModal = mrOK then
      Component.Name := PeForm.Edit1.Text;
  finally
    PeForm.Free;
  end;
end;
```

To make this code work, the package containing this editor requires the package of the last chapter, DdhPk12. For this reason, you should add that package to the Requires page of the Package Editor.

TIP   You might be tempted to add the same unit, defining the form of the name property editor, to both packages, but you cannot. If two different packages include the same unit, Delphi won't allow you to install both of them at the same time.

Advanced Component Editors

Beyond the simple editors we've written up to now, you can create component editors that allow you to interact with the system in more complex ways and provide advanced capabilities. As we did with property editors, we can consider component editors as hooks into the Delphi system, and use that interface for purposes beyond those Borland intended.

In this section we'll present three examples of advanced component editors: an editor that lets you jump to a particular event handler (creating the handler if necessary) as the default property editor does; one that adds a Delphi system command to the menu of each and every component; and a complex component editor that provides a "wizard" user interface.

Creating New Event Handlers

The TDefaultEditor class has the ability to add event-handling methods to the current form's unit to handle a component's default event (OnCreate, OnClick, or OnChange, depending on which event is first in the class declaration). Suppose you want to mimic this capability, but you want to create a different event handler. Is it possible? Of course. Is it simple? Not at all. You won't need to create a great deal of code, but the code you will write is quite complex.

If you look at the TDefaultEditor code in the file DsgnIntf.PAS, you'll find that it creates a property editor and then uses the capabilities of this object to create the default event-handling methods. Since the constructor of this class is private, we must follow a different approach, basically duplicating the code of the TMethod-Property property editor class. Actually, we've modified the code somewhat to simplify it.

The key to this code is in a series of calls to TFormDesigner methods. We've already used the Designer property, calling its Modified method to alert Delphi about changes in the form. The Designer property contains a reference to a TFormDesigner object. Before going further, we need to examine this class in depth. Here is the public interface of the class with the methods rearranged according to each one's purpose:

```
type
  TFormDesigner = class(TDesigner)
  public
    // form and unit method operations
    function CreateMethod(const Name: string;
      TypeData: PTypeData): TMethod; virtual; abstract;
    function GetMethodName(const Method: TMethod):
      string; virtual; abstract;
    procedure GetMethods(TypeData: PTypeData;
      Proc: TGetStrProc); virtual; abstract;
    function MethodExists(const Name: string): Boolean;
      virtual; abstract;
    procedure RenameMethod(const CurName,
      NewName: string); virtual; abstract;
    procedure ShowMethod(const Name: string);
      virtual; abstract;
    function MethodFromAncestor(const Method: TMethod):
      Boolean; virtual; abstract;

    // directory information
    function GetPrivateDirectory: string;
      virtual; abstract;

    // selecting and deselecting components
    procedure GetSelections(List: TComponentList);
      virtual; abstract;
    procedure SelectComponent(Instance: TPersistent);
      virtual; abstract;
    procedure SetSelections(List: TComponentList);
      virtual; abstract;
    function GetComponent(const Name: string):
      TComponent; virtual; abstract;
    function GetRoot: TComponent; virtual; abstract;

    // components: creating and other operations
```

```
function CreateComponent(
  ComponentClass: TComponentClass; Parent: TComponent;
  Left, Top, Width, Height: Integer): TComponent;
  virtual; abstract;
function IsComponentLinkable(Component: TComponent):
  Boolean; virtual; abstract;
procedure MakeComponentLinkable(Component: TComponent);
  virtual; abstract;
procedure Revert(Instance: TPersistent;
  PropInfo: PPropInfo); virtual; abstract;

// component names
function UniqueName(const BaseName: string):
  string; virtual; abstract;
procedure GetComponentNames(TypeData: PTypeData;
  Proc: TGetStrProc); virtual; abstract;
function GetComponentName(Component: TComponent):
  string; virtual; abstract;

// new Delphi 3 methods
function GetIsDormant: Boolean; virtual; abstract;
property IsDormant: Boolean read GetIsDormant;

function HasInterface: Boolean; virtual; abstract;
function HasInterfaceMember(const Name: string): Boolean;
  virtual; abstract;
procedure AddInterfaceMember(const MemberText: string);
  virtual; abstract;
end;
```

There are many capabilities in this class, including manipulating form methods (as we'll see in the next example), selecting, deselecting, and creating components, and more. The online *Component Writers' Guide* lists the class's basic capabilities, but it doesn't give any concrete examples of how to use them. We'll use some of these methods in future chapters, so here we won't summarize what they do. In most cases, a method's name indicates what it does.

Our latest component editor class declaration is as simple as it can be:

```
type
  TCeShowOnEnter = class (TDefaultEditor)
    procedure Edit; override;
  end;
```

The Edit method searches to see if an event handler for the OnEnter event exists. This is actually quite simple since we only need to reference the current component and test the appropriate event property. To make the code easier to read, we save this method pointer in a temporary TNotifyEvent variable (this is the method pointer type for the OnEnter event):

```
procedure TCeShowOnEnter.Edit;
var
  EventName: string;
  EnterEvent: TNotifyEvent;
begin
  EnterEvent := (Component as TEdit).OnEnter;
  // if an OnEnter event handler exists
  if Assigned (EnterEvent) then
    ...
```

TIP   You cannot write the test using the syntax if EnterEvent < > nil because this resembles calling the EnterEvent method and the compiler complains about the missing parameters. At times it is difficult to force the compiler into using a method pointer without calling the corresponding method.

If the event handler is assigned, we can use the designer's GetMethodName method (see the class TFormDesigner above) to retrieve its name, and then call the ShowMethod method to jump to the appropriate location in the editor:

```
EventName := Designer.GetMethodName (TMethod (EnterEvent))
Designer.ShowMethod (EventName);
```

It is important to retrieve the current name and not try to invent one, because a programmer can assign any name to an event handler instead of the default.

As you might imagine, things get more complex when you want to create the new event-handling method. For instance, notice that the TFormDesigner class's CreateMethod method requires a strange second parameter:

```
function CreateMethod(const Name: string;
  TypeData: PTypeData): TMethod;
```

It's rather simple to come up with the method name, since we can follow the standard Delphi approach of combining the event name (minus the initial "On") to the component name. The second parameter of the CreateMethod function above uses run-time type information (RTTI), discussed in Chapter 4. As you saw in that chapter, the *run-time type information* is associated with each class type, and can be accessed using the ClassInfo method. To get *property information* about a specific property we can write something like:

```
ppi := GetPropInfo (Component.ClassType.ClassInfo, 'OnEnter')
```

This function returns a data structure that contains the PropType member. Once we have this property type data we can call the GetTypeData function

```
GetTypeData (ppi.PropType^)
```

to return a pointer to the type data, which is exactly what we were looking for.

NOTE   As you might recall from Chapter 4, the type information for a method pointer type includes the type and the name of each parameter. This information is used by the form designer to generate the proper signature for the event handler.

To summarize, here is the code of the last part of the Edit method of the TCeShowOnEnter class:

```
var
  ppi: PPropInfo;
...
  else // the event is not assigned...
  begin
    // make up a name
    EventName := Component.Name + 'Enter';
    // access to the property information
    ppi := GetPropInfo (
      Component.ClassType.ClassInfo,
      'OnEnter');
    // generate the method and assign it
    EnterEvent := TNotifyEvent (
      Designer.CreateMethod (
        EventName,
        GetTypeData (ppi.PropType^)));
    // store the new value
    (Component as TEdit).OnEnter := EnterEvent;
    Designer.Modified;
    Designer.ShowMethod (EventName);
  end;
```

NOTE

In this code we make up a method name, but it is remotely possible that the name is already used by a different event handler. You might add to the code above a check on the name duplication, by using the UniqueName method of the TFormDesigner class. If the method name already exists, you can add a number or an underscore to the tentative name, and then check for uniqueness again in a while loop.

At the end, we need to save a method pointer for the new event handler in the component's OnEnter event property. Then we need to call Designer.Modified (to alert Delphi to the change and allow automatic saving of the unit), and then jump to this new method by calling ShowMethod. You can see the effect of this component editor in Figure 13.3. Finally, here's the usual registration procedure, based again on a dummy Edit component:

```
procedure Register;
begin
  RegisterComponents ('DDHB', [TDdhDummy4Edit]);
  RegisterComponentEditor (TDdhDummy4Edit, TCeShowOnEnter);
end;
```

FIGURE 13.3:

When you double-click on a TDdhDummy4Edit component, the component editor creates a new OnEnter event handler.

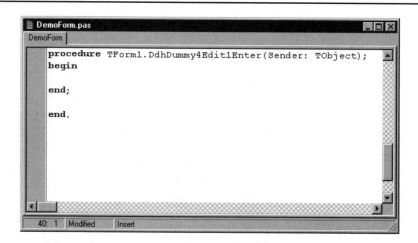

An Editor for Every Component

As usual, after some basic examples we want to delve deeper. For the next example, we'll attach a component editor to each and every component that doesn't have a specific property editor, and add a couple of Delphi system commands to each component's SpeedMenu. In particular, we'll add menu items such as Save Form and Run. To add these capabilities to a component editor, we'll need to enter the ToolServices realm.

When you're writing Delphi extensions and add-ins (such as wizards, property editors, and component editors), you can access many system capabilities through the global ToolServices object. This is a global object that's available only to add-ins and not to programs (even if Delphi is running). The TIToolServices class is documented in the file ToolIntf.PAS, in the ToolsAPI Delphi source code directory. Actually, in addition to the source code, there is some reasonable (although limited) documentation, included as comments in the source code.

NOTE We've tried to avoid duplicating the information provided by these lengthy comments, just as we've tried to avoid reproducing information already available in the Delphi help file. We suggest you keep the VCL source code files at hand, and possibly even print them. This reference material will complement what you can find in this book.

The ToolServices global object provides methods for different tasks in the following areas:

Project and file handling: You can open, close, and save a project. Likewise, you can open, close, save, and reload a file.

Module creation: You can create new modules (a unit, or a unit and a corresponding form file) or generate a new, unique module identifier.

Access to project information: This includes the project name, the number of units, the name of each unit, the number of forms, the name of each form, and the current file.

Access to VCL information: This includes the number of modules, the name of each module, the number of components installed by each module, and the name of each component.

Virtual file system operations: You can register and unregister a new file system, and then access it. A virtual file system is a mechanism for mapping file operations onto data structures that are not file-based. Chapter 15 briefly describes an example.

Interface access: This includes module interfaces, form interfaces, and main menu interfaces. In each case, you can obtain a pointer to internal Delphi objects, and you can then call methods of those objects.

Notifications: You can register and remove add-in notifiers, which allow you to specify a procedure that Delphi will call whenever a given event occurs. Some of the events you can create notifiers for are loading and saving files, and opening and closing projects. Notifiers are very important for integrating Version Control Systems (or VCS) with Delphi (see Chapter 15 for some examples).

Some Pascal string- and error-handling functions: These methods should be used only when you write a Delphi add-in in a language other than Pascal (for example, C++).

A configuration access function: Helps access Registry information.

Extensions: These are new features added in Delphi 3, which offer access to the module create and project create interfaces (discussed in the next chapter) and to an extended add-in notifier.

NOTE   TIToolServices is not an Object Pascal class in the traditional sense. Along with most of the other Delphi interfaces, it is an interface. This is basically a function with all its methods declared as `virtual abstract`, and not directly implemented. This means the actual code is in an external DLL, and might be written in Object Pascal, or C++, or other OOP languages. (*Mastering Delphi 3* shows how to write a DLL that exports an object). Note that all the so-called "interface" classes of the ToolsAPI inherit from the TInterface class, but they are not based on the `interface` keyword available in Delphi 3.

As we've just mentioned, the TIToolServices class is declared in the Tool-Intf.PAS file. However, in that file there is no sign of how you can access an object of that class. But if you look at the interface file for Delphi wizards (more about this in the next chapter), ExptIntf.PAS, you'll find the following line:

```
var
    ToolServices: TIToolServices = nil;
```

This means that a ToolServices global object is available if you include both files in a uses statement. By the way, you'll notice that the statement above assigns the object a value of nil. Delphi initializes this variable for you when it launches, but you may want to check the value of this object before using it, as a precaution.

Now that we know how to access the ToolServices object and have a rough idea of its services, we can complete our next component editor. We'll implement three different kinds of operations, just to give you some ideas. However, before examining the implementation details, here is the new class declaration, which inherits from TDefaultEditor the default double-click Edit action:

```
type
  TAddInEditor = class (TDefaultEditor)
    function GetVerbCount: Integer; override;
    function GetVerb(Index: Integer): string; override;
    procedure ExecuteVerb(Index: Integer); override;
  end;
```

The class adds three verbs (that is, three menu items), to the component's Speed-Menu either by returning the number 3 (as we'll do) or adding 3 to the number of menus of the parent class (as we've done in previous examples). There is really no difference, in this specific case. The three verbs are returned in each case by the GetVerb method:

```
function TAddInEditor.GetVerbCount: Integer;
begin
  Result := 3;
end;

function TAddInEditor.GetVerb(Index: Integer): string;
begin
  case Index of
    0: Result := 'Component &Module...';
    1: Result := '&Run';
    2: Result := '&Save...';
  end;
end;
```

The simplest code is that of the Save operation:

```
procedure TAddInEditor.ExecuteVerb(Index: Integer);
begin
  case Index of
    2: begin
```

```
    if Assigned (ToolServices) then
      ToolServices.SaveFile (
        ToolServices.GetCurrentFile)
    else
      ShowMessage ('ToolServices not found');
  end;
  ...
```

When you call the SaveFile method of ToolServices, Delphi asks if you're sure you want to save the file:

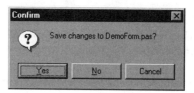

If you choose to save the file and the unit has a default name (such as Unit1), you'll see the Save File common dialog box. If the file hasn't changed since the last time you saved it, Delphi simply ignores the request.

Next we'll examine the implementation of the Component Module command. This command shows the name of the module that registered the component. This may be useful if you're not sure which source file defines a particular component, and you want to examine the component's source code. Unfortunately, this may not be the module that defines the component, because many component registration procedures are placed in separate units; so the value of the information we retrieve is somewhat limited. However, at the very least, we might be able to determine whether a component is a standard Delphi component or a third-party product.

Since we know nothing about the component except its name, we must scan each installed module by searching for the component in a nested for loop. We've created a specific function to accomplish this task.

```
function GetCompModuleName (CompName: string): string;
var
  nComp, nMod: Integer;
begin
  Result := 'Module not found !?';
  for nMod := 0 to ToolServices.GetModuleCount - 1 do
    for nComp := 0 to
        ToolServices.GetComponentCount (nMod) - 1 do
```

```
    if CompareStr (
      CompName, ToolServices.
      GetComponentName (nMod, nComp)) = 0 then
    begin
      Result := ToolServices.GetModuleName (nMod);
      Exit;
    end;
end;
```

We'll call this function when the user selects the corresponding SpeedMenu item of the component editor:

```
case Index of
  0: begin
    if Assigned (ToolServices) then
      ShowMessage (GetCompModuleName (
        Component.ClassName))
    else
      ShowMEssage ('ToolServices not found');
  end;
```

The effect, though not spectacular, is that the name of the module appears in a small message box:

Finally, we'll examine the code that implements the Run menu command. To send a shortcut key to Delphi, you can simply use a Windows message! Here is the code:

```
case Index of
  1: PostMessage (FindWindow ('TAppBuilder', nil),
      wm_KeyDown, VK_F9, 0);
```

TAppBuilder is the class name of the Delphi main window. What we've done is post a Windows wm_KeyDown message to this window, with the code of the F9 key as its parameter. To Delphi, this appears to be a keystroke entered at the keyboard.

As we saw in Chapter 7, sending a fake message to a window has exactly the same effect as the original operation, including user input operations. In the next chapter, you'll see another technique you can use to activate a Delphi menu item directly (the code is in the Rebuild Wizard example).

The registration procedure for this component editor is a bit different from any of the others we've used so far:

```
RegisterComponentEditor (TComponent, TAddInEditor);
```

This time, you'll notice that we're passing TComponent as the class for this component editor. As we suggested earlier, doing this tells Delphi to apply this component editor to any component that doesn't have its own editor (Delphi would otherwise use the TDefaultEditor component editor). This is still far from perfect, because you might want to be able to add some commands to the local menu of the form designer, for every possible component. Chapter 15 shows how to do this.

A "Wizard-Like" Component Editor

The most common form of component editor is one that displays a multipage property dialog box. This is a very common interface for ActiveX controls, and is appropriate for component editors too. Similarly, ActiveX controls frequently use experts (also called wizards) to set their values and properties. These are still multipage dialogs, but they tend to be easier to use because they guide you from page to page, with a flow that depends on your previous selections. To complete our overview of component editors, we want to build this type of tool: a component editor that has the user interface of a wizard, although technically, it's not. We'll discuss wizards in detail in the next chapter.

We'll build this complex editor in two steps. First, we'll build a stand-alone program that displays the editor/expert form. Then, we'll connect the form to the component editor, provide some initialization code, and focus on a couple of implementation problems. The editor we'll build will allow the user to create new points or move existing points in the Graph component we discussed at length in Chapter 5 and in the last chapter.

We'll base the form of this example on a Notebook with no page tabs. To move from one page to another, we'll use several SpeedButtons. We'll discuss this example one page at a time, but you need to know at the outset that the last page will contain a preview of the graph using a component variable named DdhGraph1. All the operations that we do in the form modify the properties of this preview component. The stand-alone program we've used to build the form is named DemoExp.

As you can see in Figure 13.4, the first page contains the default text for the point captions and a button that selects the caption font. The button has some very simple code attached:

```
procedure TFormCeExp.ButtonFontClick(Sender: TObject);
begin
  if FontDialog1.Execute then
    DdhGraph1.Font := FontDialog1.Font;
end;
```

FIGURE 13.4:

The first page of the Graph Component Expert displays some general information.

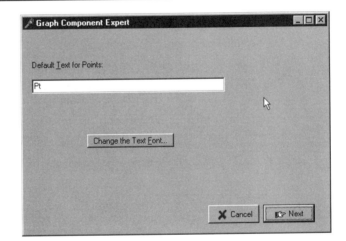

Clicking the *Next* button updates the default text in the preview graph and moves to the next page:

```
procedure TFormCeExp.BtnNext1Click(Sender: TObject);
begin
  with Notebook1 do
    PageIndex := PageIndex + 1;
  DdhGraph1.DefaultText := EditDefText.Text;
end;
```

The second page contains a ColorGrid component that we use to set the background and line color of the graph:

```
procedure TFormCeExp.BtnNext2Click(Sender: TObject);
begin
  with Notebook1 do
    PageIndex := PageIndex + 1;
  DdhGraph1.Color := ColorGrid1.BackGroundColor;
  DdhGraph1.LinesColor := ColorGrid1.ForeGroundColor;
end;
```

This second page also contains a *Previous* button, which simply moves back to the previous page of the notebook:

```
procedure TFormCeExp.BtnPrevClick(Sender: TObject);
begin
  with Notebook1 do
    PageIndex := PageIndex - 1;
end;
```

As you can see in Figure 13.5, the third page allows you to specify how many new points to add to the graph (the possible range of values is 1 to 20, as indicated by the properties of the UpDown component) and contains a check box specifying whether to delete existing points. Here the code becomes a bit more complex:

```
procedure TFormCeExp.BtnNext3Click(Sender: TObject);
var
  I: Integer;
begin
  // remove existing points
  if CheckBoxRemove.Checked then
    DdhGraph1.Points.Clear;
  // add the new points
  for I := 1 to UpDownNPts.Position do
    DdhGraph1.Points.Add;
  // reset controls
  UpDownNPts.Position := 0;
  CheckBoxRemove.Checked := False;
  // set the total points and the current one
  nTotPts := DdhGraph1.Points.Count;
  nCurPt := 0;
  // get the data of the first point
  GetCurrentPt;
  // bug fix....
```

```
UpDownX.Position := DdhGraph1.Points[0].X;
UpDownY.Position := DdhGraph1.Points[0].Y;
EditX.Text := IntToStr (UpDownX.Position);
EditY.Text := IntToStr (UpDownY.Position);
// move to next page
with Notebook1 do
  PageIndex := PageIndex + 1;
end;
```

FIGURE 13.5:

The third page of the Graph Component Expert determines the number of points in the graph.

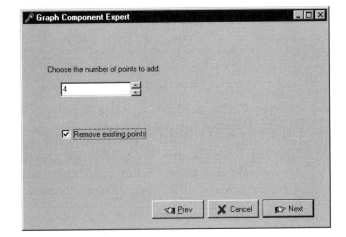

This method removes the existing points, and then adds the new ones as specified by the corresponding CheckBox and UpDown components. You'll notice that we reset the settings of these two components to allow a user to return to this page and then proceed again without any side effect.

Next, we set the values of the nTotPts and nCurPt fields of the form. We use these two Integer values to track the current point we're editing. As you'll see in a moment, we use a single Notebook page to edit each of the points, one after the other. The nCurPt field refers to the index of the current point, beginning with zero for the first item. Once we've set this value, we call the GetCurrentPt method, which transfers the current point's values to the controls of the next Notebook page. The next four statements simply set the same values again, which fixes a bug in the UpDown component. Finally we move to the fourth page, which you can see in Figure 13.6.

FIGURE 13.6:

We'll use the fourth page of the Graph Component Expert to edit the values of each point.

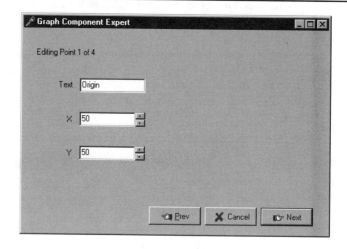

When we reach this page, the GetCurrntPt method will have already initialized the page's components, using the data for the first point. This is important because this component editor will allow you to modify existing points as well as create new ones. Here is the code for GetCurrntPt:

```
procedure TFormCeExp.GetCurrentPt;
begin
  // point number
  LabelPt.Caption := Format (
    'Editing Point %d of %d',
    [nCurPt + 1, nTotPts]);
  // point data
  EditText.Text := DdhGraph1.Points[nCurPt].Text;
  if EditText.Text = '' then
    EditText.Text := DdhGraph1.DefaultText +
      IntToStr (nCurPt + 1);
  UpDownX.Position := DdhGraph1.Points[nCurPt].X;
  UpDownY.Position := DdhGraph1.Points[nCurPt].Y;
end;
```

The only unusual thing to notice in this method is that if the point has no caption we add the default one, just as the component does when a user clicks on it at run-time. If the user clicks the *New* button, we save the values of the current point and advance to the next point instead of moving to the next page.

When the user advances past the last point in the list, we move to the final page of the Notebook:

```
procedure TFormCeExp.BtnNextPtClick(Sender: TObject);
begin
  SetCurrentPt;
  // go to the next point...
  Inc (nCurPt);
  if nCurPt < nTotPts then
    GetCurrentPt
  else
    // ... or the next page
    with Notebook1 do
      PageIndex := PageIndex + 1;
end;
```

The SetCurrentPt method performs the complementary operation to GetCurrentPt by storing the new values for the current point:

```
procedure TFormCeExp.SetCurrentPt;
begin
  // update the data...
  DdhGraph1.Points[nCurPt].Text := EditText.Text;
  DdhGraph1.Points[nCurPt].X := UpDownX.Position;
  DdhGraph1.Points[nCurPt].Y := UpDownY.Position;
end;
```

As you would expect, the user can keep moving back to previous points until they attempt to move prior to the first point in the list:

```
procedure TFormCeExp.BtnPrevPtClick(Sender: TObject);
begin
  SetCurrentPt;
  // go to the previous point...
  Dec (nCurPt);
  if nCurPt >= 0 then
    GetCurrentPt
  else
    // ... or the previous page
    with Notebook1 do
      PageIndex := PageIndex - 1;
end;
```

When the user reaches the last page, we display the preview of the Graph component (see Figure 13.7), which contains all the new and existing points. From this page, the user can continue to add new points by clicking on the graph component, and can edit those points further by clicking the *Previous* button. Since the user might have added new points, we must reset the nTotPts and nCurPt variables:

```
procedure TFormCeExp.BtnPrev5Click(Sender: TObject);
begin
  // update the points, which might
  // have changed in the DdhGraph
  nTotPts := DdhGraph1.Points.Count;
  nCurPt := nTotPts - 1;
  GetCurrentPt;
  with Notebook1 do
    PageIndex := PageIndex - 1;
end;
```

FIGURE 13.7:

The fifth and last page of the Graph Component Expert contains the Graph preview.

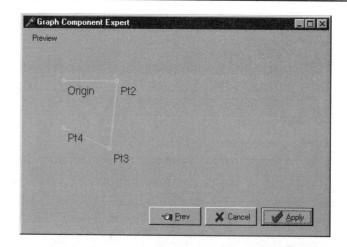

You can see how this form works (and check the nCurPt mechanism, which uses a single page of the Notebook to display each point in the graph) by running the DemoExp example. Keep in mind that this example is merely a tool we've used to debug the form. We've left it in the source file of the component editor just to document the construction of the component expert.

Now that the form is complete, we can examine the code of the component editor. The structure of the class is the same as before, as it overrides the GetVerbCount and GetVerb methods:

```
type
  TCeExpert = class (TComponentEditor)
    function GetVerbCount: Integer; override;
    function GetVerb(Index: Integer): string; override;
    procedure ExecuteVerb(Index: Integer); override;
  end;

implementation

function TCeExpert.GetVerbCount: Integer;
begin
  Result := 1;
end;

function TCeExpert.GetVerb (Index: Integer): string;
begin
  if Index = 0 then
    Result := 'Graph Component &Expert...';
end;
```

The only unusual code is in the ExecuteVerb method. In this method, we must create the form, initialize the form data and its preview component, and show the form modally. If the user clicks the *Apply* button (which has mrOK as the value of its ModalResult property), we retrieve the new values:

```
procedure TCeExpert.ExecuteVerb (Index: Integer);
begin
  if Index = 0 then
  begin
    FormCeExp := TFormCeExp.Create (Application);
    try
      with Component as TDdhGraph do
      begin
        // initialize the target component
        FormCeExp.DdhGraph1.DefaultText := DefaultText;
        FormCeExp.DdhGraph1.Font := Font;
        FormCeExp.DdhGraph1.LinesColor := LinesColor;
        FormCeExp.DdhGraph1.Points.Assign (Points);
        // initialize the editors
```

```
          FormCeExp.EditDefText.Text := DefaultText;
          FormCeExp.FontDialog1.Font := Font;
        end;
        // show the modal form
        if FormCeExp.ShowModal = mrOK then
          // retrieve the results
          with Component as TDdhGraph do
          begin
            // set the properties of the target component
            DefaultText := FormCeExp.DdhGraph1.DefaultText;
            Font := FormCeExp.DdhGraph1.Font;
            Color := FormCeExp.DdhGraph1.Color;
            LinesColor := FormCeExp.DdhGraph1.LinesColor;
            Points.Clear;
            Points.Assign (FormCeExp.DdhGraph1.Points);
            Repaint;
            Designer.Modified;
          end;
      finally
        FormCeExp.Free;
      end;
    end;
  end;
```

In this method, the TCollection class's Assign method comes in handy since
it copies the values of each item of a collection. The only shortcoming to this
approach is that this method adds new items to the existing ones (instead of
replacing them), so we need to clear the collection before we copy the items back
to the component. At the end we set the designer's Modified flag to notify Delphi
that the data has changed, and to call the component's Repaint method to update
its output.

This ends the code of the component editor. However, if we register this editor
in the usual way by writing

```
procedure Register;
begin
  RegisterComponentEditor (TDdhGraph, TCeExpert);
end;
```

we'll find that when we right-click on the component—nothing happens. Not
only do we not see our component editor menu command, we don't even see the
standard local menu of the form designer!

The problem is a result of using the csDesignInteractive component style, which transforms all right-mouse-button design-time operations into left-button messages for the component. If you'll recall, we did this to add new points at design-time by right-clicking on the component while pressing the Ctrl key. To refresh your memory, here is the relevant code:

```
procedure TDdhGraph.MouseDown (Button: TMouseButton;
  Shift: TShiftState; X, Y: Integer);
var
  Pt: TDdhPoint;
begin
  if (not (csDesigning in ComponentState)) or
    ((csDesigning in ComponentState) and
    (ssCtrl in Shift)) then
  begin
    // add a point...
```

But if you enable the csDesignInteractive component style, the form designer won't be able to use the right mouse button. Accordingly, some Delphi components with design-time mouse capabilities (such as the THeader control) demonstrate similar behavior, and do *not* display the local menu.

However, other Delphi components (such as some of the grid components) allow both design-time operations *and* a local menu. How is this possible? You must first remove the csDesignInteractive flag and use an internal Delphi message instead. Delphi sends the cm_DesignHitTest message to components at design-time to determine whether they should receive the mouse messages or send them on to the form designer. If you set the Result field of the message to a nonzero value, it indicates that the component should receive the mouse-click messages.

Instead of altering the TDdhGraph component to deal with this situation, we've derived a new class from it, called TDdhDesignGraph, which redefines the constructor and handles that specific Delphi internal message:

```
type
  TDdhDesignGraph = class(TDdhGraph)
  public
    constructor Create (Owner: TComponent); override;
    procedure CmDesignHitTest (var Msg: TWMMouse);
      message cm_DesignHitTest;
  end;
```

The constructor simply calls the inherited constructor and then removes the csDesignInteractive style that was added by the parent class. The CmDesignHit-Test method returns a value of 1 if the Ctrl key is down during the mouse event (to indicate that this is a message for the component), and returns zero otherwise (to indicate the message should go to the form designer). If the Ctrl key isn't down, the component passes the mouse messages to the form designer to display the local menu, which contains the component expert command.

```
constructor TDdhDesignGraph.Create (Owner: TComponent);
begin
  inherited Create (Owner);
  // remove the flag...
  ControlStyle := ControlStyle -
    [csDesignInteractive];
end;

procedure TDdhDesignGraph.CmDesignHitTest (
  var Msg: TWMMouse);
begin
  if (Msg.Keys and mk_Control) <> 0 then
    // interactive design
    Msg.Result := 1
  else
    // default designer behavior
    Msg.Result := 0;
end;
```

Now, as before, we need to register the new component and the component editor for the new component. Here is the final registration code of the CeExp unit:

```
procedure Register;
begin
  RegisterComponents ('DDHB', [TDdhDesignGraph]);
  RegisterComponentEditor (TDdhGraph, TCeExpert);
  RegisterComponentEditor (TDdhDesignGraph, TCeExpert);
end;
```

When you install the component and its editor, you'll be able to use interactive design *and* respond to mouse clicks, as you can see in Figure 13.8.

FIGURE 13.8:

The TDdhDesignGraph component displays its local menu with the component editor/ expert menu item.

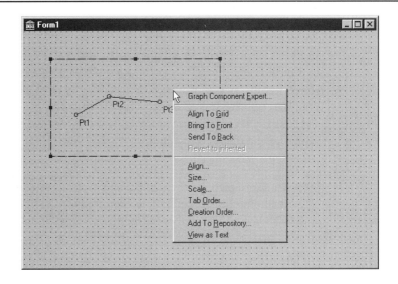

NOTE

In Chapter 7, we discussed Windows message in general, and Delphi internal messages specifically. In particular, we described the role of internal Delphi messages, and saw examples of their use. Currently, these internal messages are not well documented by Borland.

Editing with the Object Inspector

When you want to edit a specific "subobject," such as a point on our example's graph, you can select it in the Object Inspector instead of building your own custom editor. Consider Delphi's Menu Designer: When you select a menu item in it, the corresponding component is selected in the Object Inspector. To accomplish this selection, you can use the SelectComponent method of the TFormDesigner class.

Editing Collection Items

Unfortunately, this technique cannot be used with the TDdhPoints collection we built in Chapter 3. To select an object in the Object Inspector, Delphi requires an owner of the object. While components have an Owner property, persistent objects don't. For this reason we need to override the GetOwner method of the TCollection and TCollectionItem classes. While we are doing that, we can also override the GetDisplayName property of the collection item, to provide a custom display name for the Object Inspector.

<blockquote>
NOTE

The GetOwner property of collections and collection items, along with the technique described in this section, have been introduced by Borland in Delphi 3 and are not applicable to older versions of the environment.
</blockquote>

Here is the updated definition of the collection and collection item classes, which you can find in the DdhEdCol unit (in the Comps directory of the current chapter) on the companion CD:

```
type
  TDdhEdPoint = class (TCollectionItem)
  private
    fX, fY: Integer;
  public
    Text: string;
    procedure WriteText (Writer: TWriter);
    procedure ReadText (Reader: TReader);
    procedure DefineProperties (Filer: TFiler); override;
    procedure Paint (Canvas: TCanvas);
    procedure Assign (Pt: TPersistent); override;
    procedure SetX (Value: Integer);
    procedure SetY (Value: Integer);
    /// new methods ///
    function GetDisplayName: string; override;
    function GetOwner: TPersistent; override;
  published
    property X: Integer
      read fX write SetX;
    property Y: Integer
      read fY write SetY;
  end;
```

```
TDdhEdPoints = class (TCollection)
private
  fGrid: TDdhEdGraph;
  function GetItem (Index: Integer): TDdhEdPoint;
  procedure SetItem (Index: Integer; Value: TDdhEdPoint);
protected
  procedure Update (Item: TCollectionItem); override;
public
  constructor Create (Grid: TDdhEdGraph);
  function Add: TDdhEdPoint;
  /// new method ///
  function GetOwner: TPersistent; override;
  property Items [Index: Integer]: TDdhEdPoint
    read GetItem write SetItem; default;
end;
```

As you can see, we've added these methods to some brand-new classes, and connected them to a new component class, TDdhEdGraph, very similar to the previous versions. The three new methods have the following simple code:

```
function TDdhEdPoint.GetDisplayName: string;
begin
  Result := Format ('Point %s [%d]',
    [Text, Index]);
end;

function TDdhEdPoint.GetOwner: TPersistent;
begin
  Result := (Collection as TDdhEdPoints).fGrid;
end;

function TDdhEdPoints.GetOwner: TPersistent;
begin
  Result := fGrid;
end;
```

The DdhEdCol unit also includes a standard component editor, called TCeCollEdit, which has the usual GetVerbCount, GetVerb, and ExecuteVerb methods. The first two are used to add a single menu item to the form designer speed menu, while the third opens a custom editor form:

```
procedure TCeCollEdit.ExecuteVerb (Index: Integer);
begin
  if Index = 0 then
```

```
    begin
      if not Assigned (PointsListForm) then
      begin
        PointsListForm := TPointsListForm.Create (Application);
        PointsListForm.Desinger := Designer;
        PointsListForm.Graph := Component as TDdhEdGraph;
      end;
      PointsListForm.Show;
    end;
  end;
```

This method copies the Designer and the graph component into two fields of the new PointsLineForm, and then shows the form (which destroys itself when it is closed). This form is completely covered by a list box, which is updated every time the form is activated:

```
procedure TPointsListForm.FormActivate(Sender: TObject);
var
  I: Integer;
begin
  PointsListForm.ListBox1.Clear;
  for I := 0 to Graph.Points.Count - 1 do
    PointsListForm.ListBox1.Items.Add (
      Graph.Points.Items [I].GetDisplayName);
end;
```

Now, when a user double-clicks on one of the items, we can select the corresponding object of the collection in the Object Inspector, with this simple call to the SelectComponent method:

```
procedure TPointsListForm.ListBox1DblClick(Sender: TObject);
begin
  Desinger.SelectComponent (
    Graph.Points [Listbox1.ItemIndex]);
end;
```

Figure 13.9 shows an example of this editor with the collection item selected in the Object Inspector.

However, once you've defined the GetOwner function of a collection and of its items, you can avoid writing a custom editor. Delphi automatically uses an internal collection property editor for the property. You can use this editor to select each item of the collection in the Object Inspector, and to add new items or remove existing ones. Figure 13.10 shows an example of this default editor in action.

FIGURE 13.9:

The TCeCollEdit component editor selects an item of a collection in the Object Inspector.

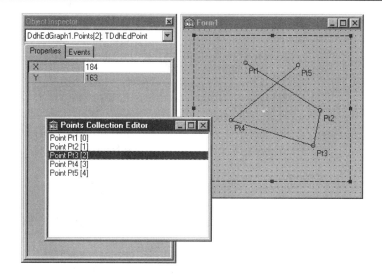

FIGURE 13.10:

Once you've properly defined a collection, Delphi enables the default collection property editor for it.

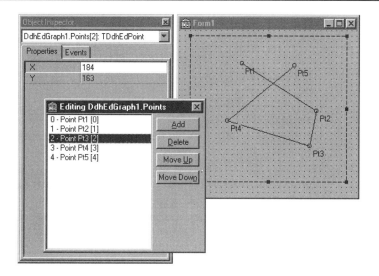

Selecting Components with a Menu

Since using the Object Inspector to edit subcomponents is a very important technique, we decided to build a second example to show it. This example is a property editor for a special component that allows you to list either all the components of a form at design-time or only the nonvisual components. In this case the only role of the component is to enable the component editor; we could have applied a similar technique to the component editor of generic components we built before.

This example also demonstrates another feature: It creates a component editor with a variable number of menu items, which depends on the status of the form itself. Here is a first version of the component and its editor, which lists in the local menu all the components of the form:

```
type
  TDdhCollect = class (TComponent);

  TDdhCollectEditor = class (TComponentEditor)
  public
    function GetVerbCount: Integer; override;
    function GetVerb(Index: Integer): string; override;
    procedure ExecuteVerb(Index: Integer); override;
  end;

function TDdhCollectEditor.GetVerbCount: Integer;
begin
  Result := Designer.Form.ComponentCount
end;

function TDdhCollectEditor.GetVerb (Index: Integer): string;
begin
  Result := Designer.Form.Components [Index].Name
end;

procedure TDdhCollectEditor.ExecuteVerb (Index: Integer);
begin
  (Designer as TFormDesigner).SelectComponent (
      Designer.Form.Components [Index])
end;

procedure Register;
begin
  RegisterComponents ('DDHB', [TDdhCollect]);
  RegisterComponentEditor (TDdhCollect, TDdhCollectEditor);
end;
```

This first version of the TDdhCollectEditor component editor simply uses the information stored in the form connected to the designer, and the form's Component-Count and Components properties. The relevant code is in the ExecuteVerb method, which calls SelectComponent to activate it in the Object Inspector. You can see this editor in action (and the complete list of components of a form at design time) in Figure 13.11.

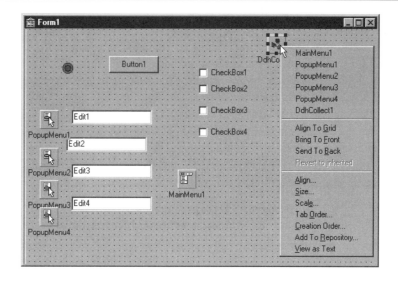

To make this component a little more useful, and to demonstrate some further problems related to the development of component editors, we've added the capability to show only the nonvisual components of the form. What you might do is to scan the list of the components of the design-time form in each of the three methods of the component editor, looking for types that aren't derived from TControl. However, this approach might slow down the execution slightly. As a better alternative, the first time we scan the component list we can save the relevant information in a string list, storing the component reference as well. The problem is deciding where to declare the string list, where to create it, and where to destroy it. The component editor object, in fact, is created and destroyed by Delphi, and you have very little control over these operations and know very little about their sequence and timing. As an alternative you might want to declare a local variable in the unit defining the component editor class, but we have no guarantee that Delphi won't create two instances of the editor if you have two components in two different forms. Sharing the same data structure, in fact, might create some trouble.

A reasonable solution is to attach the data to the fake component we are connecting to the editor. This solves the memory allocation problems, since we can easily control the construction and destruction of the component, and it allows us to have multiple components with multiple editors in different forms at the same time.

With this idea in mind, here is the updated code for the component class, which stores the kind of list displayed in a property, and the temporary list of nonvisual components in a string list:

```
type
  TDdhCollect = class (TComponent)
  private
    FAllComps: Boolean;
    FComps: TStringList;
  public
    constructor Create (AOwner: TComponent); override;
    destructor Destroy; override;
  published
    property AllComps: Boolean
      read FAllComps write FAllComps default False;
  end;

constructor TDdhCollect.Create (AOwner: TComponent);
var
  I: Integer;
begin
  // create a single instance only
  for I := 0 to AOwner.ComponentCount - 1 do
    if AOwner.Components[I] is TDdhCollect then
      raise Exception.Create (
        'Component already available in ' + AOwner.Name);
  // construction
  inherited Create (AOwner);
  FAllComps := False;
  if csDesigning in ComponentState then
    FComps := TStringList.Create
  else
    FComps := nil;
end;
```

```
destructor TDdhCollect.Destroy;
begin
  FComps.Free;
  inherited;
end;
```

Now the code of the component editor gets a little more complex, and becomes strictly related to the component itself (which stores the data). Here is the first method, which creates the list of nonvisual components:

```
function TDdhCollectEditor.GetVerbCount: Integer;
var
  I: Integer;
begin
  with Component as TDdhCollect do
  begin
    if FAllComps then
      Result := Designer.Form.ComponentCount
    else
    begin
      FComps.Clear;
      for I := 0 to Designer.Form.ComponentCount - 1 do
        if not (Designer.Form.Components [I] is TControl) then
          FComps.AddObject (Designer.Form.Components [I].Name,
            Designer.Form.Components [I]);
      Result := FComps.Count;
    end;
  end; // with
end;
```

The code we looked at earlier is intertwined with the new code in the other two methods, which rely on the list of components. We took this approach because you cannot add a new component to a form at design-time while you are displaying the local menu for a specific component.

```
function TDdhCollectEditor.GetVerb (Index: Integer): string;
begin
  with Component as TDdhCollect do
    if FAllComps then
      Result := Designer.Form.Components [Index].Name
    else
      Result := FComps.Strings [Index];
end;
```

```
procedure TDdhCollectEditor.ExecuteVerb (Index: Integer);
begin
  with Component as TDdhCollect do
    if FAllComps then
      (Designer as TFormDesigner).SelectComponent (
        Designer.Form.Components [Index])
    else
      (Designer as TFormDesigner).SelectComponent (
        FComps.Objects [Index] as TComponent);
end;
```

In general, property editors and component editors should be used to interact with a specific property or a specific component. For more generic design-time operations, you should generally think about building a wizard or using one of the other advanced techniques described in the next two chapters.

What's Next

In this chapter you've seen how to build component editors and use them to customize the default behavior of the Delphi environment. All of the functionality is made possible by the ToolsAPI, which we've partially explored. In the next two chapters we'll look at two other ways of extending Delphi: wizards and Version Control System (VCS) integration.

Although this book won't discuss each and every one of the ToolsAPI interfaces, we've already seen two of the most powerful and handy ones, the TFormDesigner and TiToolServices interfaces. You'll see more examples of using these interfaces in the next chapter.

In the next two chapters, we'll also show you how to hook into the Delphi environment in unofficial ways: Delphi was written using Delphi itself, so you can use many well-known programming techniques to access or modify the environment without using any of the "official" interfaces. These "unofficial" techniques can also be applied to property and component editors, although we find them more useful for wizards.

CHAPTER

FOURTEEN

14

Wizards

- Wizard Basics

- Standard and Project Wizards

- Building Add-In Wizards

- A List Template Wizard

- A Component Wizard

- Writing Form Wizards

- Proxy-Based Form Wizards

- Using the Project Creator

- The PasToWeb Wizard

The most powerful way to customize the Delphi environment is to add wizards or experts to it. Wizards come in several varieties, and can provide different user interfaces, but there's a common theme for all wizards: they are tools used to generate or manipulate source code or attributes of your project.

> **NOTE**
>
> The terms *wizard* and *expert* should be considered synonymous. Borland used the term *expert* in the first editions of Delphi, then shifted to the term *wizard* with Delphi 3.0. Interestingly, Borland still uses the term *expert* to describe modules that interface with the ToolsAPI library. In other words, to add a new wizard to Delphi you have to write a new expert. Because this difference is very subtle and not very important, we'll use the two terms interchangeably.

Delphi comes with several predefined wizards: the Application Wizard, the Dialog Wizard, and the Database Form Wizard. Only the last of these tools does anything significant. The other two are very simple tools. Even simpler are the so-called "mini-wizards," such as the Component Wizard, the Automation Object Wizard, and few others. These simply prompt you for some key information and then produce some very simple source code.

Delphi provides two more wizards, but they're not accessible by default. The first is the Demo Explorer, which provides a cross-referenced database that describes the sample programs included in Delphi. This makes it easier to locate an example that addresses a specific component or feature.

> **WARNING**
>
> If you use this wizard, be sure to exit Delphi prior to using it again. The Demo Explorer contains a bug that causes Delphi to crash if you launch it a second time without exiting Delphi.

The second "hidden" wizard is the Project Explorer. This wizard allows you to view a tree list of your project's forms as well as a list of each form's components. From this list, you can activate a form (even if it's not yet open), view a component's properties in the Object Inspector, select a component in the form designer, rename a form or component, or delete a component.

These wizards are demonstration tools, and as such appear in the DEMOS\ EXPERT directory. To add either of these wizards (which reside in separate DLLs), you first open and compile the project, and then install the appropriate wizard by adding a corresponding entry to the Windows Registry. The new entry should appear in the

```
HKEY_CURRENT_USER\SOFTWARE\BORLAND\DELPHI\3.0\EXPERTS
```

section, as you can see in Figure 14.1, which shows how to use the Windows RegEdit application to update the Registry properly.

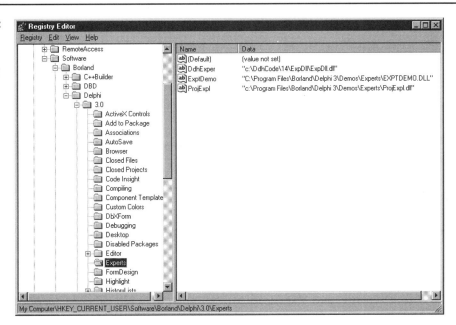

FIGURE 14.1:

Using the RegEdit Windows application to install one of the demo wizards

After you've updated the Registry you should exit and restart Delphi. When you do this, the new Project Explorer menu item will appear in the View menu. Once you've opened a project, you can explore its hierarchy, as shown in Figure 14.2.

NOTE The purpose of the Project Explorer wizard is to show how to build a DLL-based add-in wizard. In fact, Delphi includes the full source code of the wizard, which you can examine or extend. However, this code is very complex, and we suggest you study it only after working through the next few examples, which introduce the same techniques in simpler form.

FIGURE 14.2:

The output of the
Project Explorer, an
optional wizard
available in Delphi

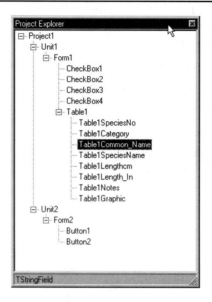

Before We Begin: Wizard Basics

Delphi allows you to build different kinds of wizards, which you can activate in different ways. For instance, some wizards appear in the Object Repository (activated with the File ➤ New command), while others are associated with menu items. You can even activate some of them both ways.

A wizard's *style* attribute (technically a value from the TExpertStyle enumeration) determines how it will be activated:

Standard wizards appear as a menu item in Delphi's Help menu (the value is esStandard). Standard wizards are easy to build, and are the most common form for third-party wizards.

Form wizards appear in either the Forms or Dialogs page of the Object Repository (the value is esForm). The Database Form Wizard and the Dialog Wizard are examples of form wizards.

Project wizards appear in the Projects page of the Object Repository (the value is esProject). The Application Wizard is an example of a project wizard.

Add-In wizards, which first appeared in Delphi 2, typically appear as menu items in a menu of your choosing (the value is *esAddIn*). The Component Wizard and the Database Form Wizard (again) are examples of add-in wizards. Third-party add-in wizards are actually quite rare. This is primarily because they are more complex to build, they don't work in Delphi 1, and very few articles or books deal with them.

Of course, you may want to activate a given wizard in different ways. While this makes sense in some cases, some styles are logically incompatible: a form wizard cannot also be a project wizard, and a standard wizard shouldn't also be an add-in wizard (unless you want to use two menu items to do the same thing). From a programming standpoint, each wizard must have a specific style. This means that you can build two *very similar* wizards, implementing two different styles, as we'll see in an example.

Another difference among various wizards is their executable format. This determines how you'll write the wizard and how it links to the Delphi environment. Along these lines, there are two categories of wizards:

DCU wizards are those you compile into a Pascal file, and then install into the VCL along with components and special-purpose editors. Since it's slightly easier to write a DCU wizard, you'll generally choose this type for simple wizards.

DLL wizards are those you compile as external DLLs (using a special interface), and then install by setting some entries in the system Registry. You'll typically want to put larger wizards in DLLs to avoid inflating the VCL library unnecessarily.

As we saw with the Project Explorer wizard, installing a DLL wizard is slightly more complex than installing a DCU wizard, but you can automate the process as part of a setup program. In contrast, installing DCU wizards is typically easier, since it's no more complicated than installing a component (and in fact, some components install their own wizards as part of the component installation process). You can incorporate the DCU wizard into a package, so that installing the package (possibly using a package collection) also installs the wizard. The package architecture makes it even easier to use DCU wizards as the standard alternative. As Table 14.1 shows, all of the wizards that ship with Delphi are DLL-based, except the Component Wizard.

TABLE 14.1: Categories and Styles of Delphi's Default Experts/Wizards

	esStandard	esForm	esProject	esAddln
DCU				Component Wizard
DLL	Demo Explorer	Dialog Wizard Database Form Wizard	Application Wizard	Database Form Wizard Project Explorer

We should mention one more thing before proceeding. The Object Repository window displays its various objects in a ListView control. As with any ListView control, you can choose among different views for this information: Large icons (the default), Small icons, List, and Details. To make this selection, just right-click on the ListView component in the Repository, select the appropriate view, and then select the appropriate sorting method. This feature is important because much of the information we'll generate for our own wizards (such as the author's name) will appear only if the user is using the Detailed view.

The TIExpert Interface

To create a wizard, whether it's DCU or DLL-based, you need to derive a new class from the TIExpert class. Here's the declaration of the class:

```
type
  TIExpert = class(TInterface)
  public
    { Expert UI strings }
    function GetName: string; virtual; stdcall; abstract;
    function GetAuthor: string; virtual; stdcall; abstract;
    function GetComment: string; virtual; stdcall; abstract;
    function GetPage: string; virtual; stdcall; abstract;
    function GetGlyph: HICON; virtual; stdcall; abstract;
    function GetStyle: TExpertStyle; virtual; stdcall; abstract;
    function GetState: TExpertState; virtual; stdcall; abstract;
    function GetIDString: string; virtual; stdcall; abstract;
    function GetMenuText: string; virtual; stdcall; abstract;

    { Launch the Expert }
    procedure Execute; virtual; stdcall; abstract;
  end;
```

This code appears in the ExptIntf.PAS file of the ToolsAPI source code directory. The base class, TInterface, is the parent class for every Delphi environment interface element. It's a very simple class (defined in the VitrIntf unit), which implements reference counting:

```
type
  TInterface = class
  private
    FRefCount: Longint;
  public
    constructor Create;
    procedure Free;
    function AddRef: Longint; virtual; stdcall;
    function Release: Longint; virtual; stdcall;
    function GetVersion: Integer; virtual; stdcall;
  end;
```

What's the behavior of a TInterface object? It's simply a reference-counted object. When you create a new TInterface object (by calling Create) the reference count is set to one. As you would expect, calling AddRef increments the reference count. Calling Free or Release decrements the reference count, and if it reaches zero, these methods will destroy the object. (The difference between the Release method and the Free method is that Free checks if the object is nil and then calls Release. If you are not sure whether an object is valid, you should call Free. Otherwise, you can call either of these methods without any real difference.) The last method, GetVersion, returns the version number of the interface, which in practice is the version of Delphi.

NOTE You may have noticed that this class looks suspiciously similar to a COM interface. Using interfaces to call functions implemented in DLLs isn't directly related to COM or to the interface keyword (discussed in the last chapter). In fact, it's similar to the way Delphi implements Windows API function calls (Pascal interface files and DLLs that contain the function implementations). In addition, these classes define several virtual abstract methods, which allow you to export the objects across the DLL boundary. As an added benefit, these class declarations make the objects language-independent—you can write them in C++ just as effectively as you can write them in Object Pascal.

Thanks to the design of this base class, you can derive new classes and place them in an external DLL. However, you must implement each and every one of the abstract methods, or you'll encounter run-time errors when you create these objects and call their methods. For this reason, every wizard class—even the simplest ones—must override several methods, even if it means providing do-nothing code. Here's a short description of each method:

GetStyle should return the style of the wizard we discussed before: esStandard, esForm, esProject, or esAddIn.

GetIDString should return a unique string to identify the wizard. The convention for this method is to return a company (or organization) name and the wizard name, separated by a period, as in DDH.FirstExpert.

GetName should return a *readable* name for the wizard that Delphi will display to users. This name should be short but descriptive. Surprisingly, you must return a name of some kind, even if Delphi never displays it for a standard wizard. If you don't return a name, you'll receive an error message.

GetAuthor should return the name of the author of the wizard. This name appears in the Object Repository (in the detailed view), and is necessary only for form or project wizards.

GetComment should return a description of the wizard. For form and project wizards, this name appears in the detailed view of the Object Repository wizard.

GetPage should return the name of the Object Repository page where you want the wizard to appear. This is necessary only for form and project wizards. It determines only the default page for the wizard; users can move the wizard to a different page.

GetGlyph should return the handle of an icon that will represent the wizard in the Object Repository (if it's a form or project wizard). Returning 0 indicates that Delphi should display the default icon. (If you've written wizards for Delphi 1.0, you'll remember that this function returned a handle to a bitmap. This is a subtle but important change.)

GetState should return the state of the wizard. The TExpertState return type declares a set of values, such as esChecked to place a check mark near a wizard's menu item, and esEnabled to activate the wizard.

GetMenuText should return the text that will appear as a menu item for standard wizards, including the "&" character used to identify the appropriate short-cut key. Delphi will call this function every time it's ready to display the Help menu, which means you can make the text context-sensitive.

Execute runs the actual code of the wizard, except for add-in wizards. For add-in wizards, you must install a handler for a menu item, as we'll see later.

Standard and Project Wizards

Using what we've learned so far, we're ready to build our first (very simple) Delphi wizards. We'll build a DCU-based standard wizard first, turn it into a project wizard (still DCU-based), and finally create a DLL-based standard wizard. Later in this chapter, we'll create more powerful and interesting wizards.

A DCU Standard Wizard

The first DCU-based Delphi wizard we're going to build is one that executes a very simple action. When you create a new project, Delphi typically adds an empty form to the project. Our first wizard is a Blank Project wizard that allows you to create a new project with no form. Furthermore, this wizard prompts the user immediately for the directory that will contain the project source code.

As we described earlier, to create a wizard you need to derive a new class from TIExpert, and override several methods:

```
type
  TBlankExpert = class (TIExpert)
  public
    function GetStyle: TExpertStyle; override;
    function GetName: string; override;
    function GetAuthor: string; override;
    function GetComment: string; override;
    function GetPage: string; override;
    function GetGlyph: HICON; override;
    function GetState: TExpertState; override;
    function GetIDString: string; override;
    function GetMenuText: string; override;
    procedure Execute; override;
  end;
```

Apart from Execute, the most important methods of this class are those returning the wizard's style and unique name:

```
function TBlankExpert.GetStyle: TExpertStyle;
begin
  Result := esStandard;
end;

function TBlankExpert.GetIDString: String;
begin
  Result := 'DDHandbook.BlankWizard'
end;
```

As the code implies, our first wizard is a standard wizard, and has a unique name constructed from a shortened version of the book title and the name of the wizard.

Most of the other methods provide simple or default values. Among these are the methods that return the wizard name, the menu item string, the comment, the state, the page, and the icon of the wizard:

```
function TBlankExpert.GetName: String;
begin
  Result := 'Blank Project Wizard'
end;

function TBlankExpert.GetAuthor: string;
begin
  Result := 'Marco and Tim';
end;

function TBlankExpert.GetComment: String;
begin
  Result := 'First DCU wizard';
end;

function TBlankExpert.GetPage: string;
begin
  Result := '';
end;

function TBlankExpert.GetGlyph: HICON;
begin
  Result := 0;
```

```
end;

function TBlankExpert.GetState: TExpertState;
begin
  // always enabled, never checked
  Result := [esEnabled];
end;

function TBlankExpert.GetMenuText: String;
begin
  // the text of the menu item
  Result := '&Blank Project Wizard'
end;
```

The principal element of this wizard is its Execute method, which closes the current project, asks the user for a directory, and then creates a new project in that directory. For consistency with the way Delphi creates new projects, this wizard creates a unique project name (which we obtain by trying to use *Project1*, *Project2*, *Project3*, and so on, until we find a file name that's unused in the project directory):

```
procedure TBlankExpert.Execute;
var
  DirName: string;
  I: Integer;
begin
  // try closing the project
  if ToolServices.CloseProject and
    // try selecting a directory
    SelectDirectory (DirName,
      [sdAllowCreate, sdPerformCreate, sdPrompt], 0) then
  begin
    // look for a unique project name in the directory
    I := 1;
    while FileExists (DirName + '\Project' +
        IntToStr (I) + '.dpr') do
      Inc (I);
    // open a project with that (unique) name
    ToolServices.OpenProject (DirName + '\Project' +
      IntToStr (I) + '.dpr');
  end;
end;
```

In this method, we use two methods of the ToolServices global object to close the current project and create the new one. As you'll recall from the last chapter, this global object belongs to the TIToolServices class and is available only within the Delphi environment. We'll use several of this class's methods while building wizards. Actually, this global variable is defined in the ExptIntf.PAS file. In the last chapter, we had to add this file to a uses clause so that we could access these system services from a component or property editor.

The remainder of this method is rather simple. However, notice that the wizard doesn't prompt the user for the project name since the user can change the default name by using the Save Project As command. If the user issues this command immediately after creating a project, Delphi won't create temporary files using the default name.

NOTE   As we'll see later in this chapter, a wizard for creating projects can ask the user to rename the file when it's first saved, as Delphi does with the default projects.

To install this DCU wizard, you must add a Register procedure to the unit that defines the wizard, write some registration code inside this procedure, and then add this file to the component library. As you can see, this is not significantly different from the procedure for installing components, property editors, or component editors. Here's the registration procedure:

```
procedure Register;
begin
  RegisterLibraryExpert(TBlankExpert.Create);
end;
```

Unlike the component or property editor registration procedures, the Register-LibraryExpert procedure expects an object as its only parameter, not a type name! Fortunately, this is not much more complex than calling the other procedures, since we can easily create the wizard object by calling the default constructor. After you install this unit, you'll find a new menu item in the Help menu, as you can see in Figure 14.3.

If you select the new wizard's menu item, Delphi will prompt you to save the current project (if it's been modified). At this point, you can use the Yes and No buttons to continue, or press Cancel to abort the wizard. If you select Cancel, the ToolServices.CloseProject method returns false. In response to this return

FIGURE 14.3:

The new item of Delphi's Help menu, which you can use to activate the Blank Project wizard

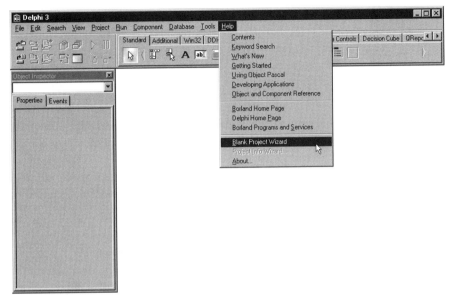

value, the wizard simply skips the rest of the code. (Of course, you must design this behavior into your own wizards—it doesn't happen automatically.)

Once the current project closes, the Blank Project wizard prompts the user for a project directory. As you can see in Figure 14.4, this dialog box doesn't present a state-of-the-art user interface, but it's good enough for this example. As before, the user can press the Cancel button, aborting the wizard.

FIGURE 14.4:

The dialog box shown by the SelectDirectory function, which we use to select the new blank project directory

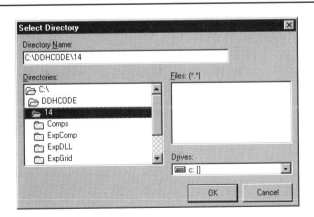

The reason this wizard searches for an existing project is that we've used the ToolServices.OpenProject method to create the new project. As the name suggests, this function opens the project named in the parameter. If the project does not exist, it creates a new one.

A DCU Project Wizard

Now that we've built our first standard wizard, let's implement it again, as a project wizard that has the same capability. Instead of copying and pasting the source code into a new class, we can simply derive a new class from the one we've just written, which makes the code much simpler; it's also easier to maintain, because we have only one copy of the source code of the Execute method. Here's the declaration of the new class:

```
type
  TBlankProjectExpert = class (TBlankExpert)
  public
    function GetStyle: TExpertStyle; override;
    function GetIDString: string; override;
    function GetGlyph: HICON; override;
    function GetPage: string; override;
  end;
```

In this class, we must override the GetStyle and GetIDString methods (since the ID string must be unique). We must also return actual data from the GetGlyph and GetPage methods, which returned dummy values in the TBlankExpert class. (We could have updated that class to return actual data instead of dummy values, and thereby avoided this duplication, but that would have added unnecessary complexity to the example.)

Another approach we could take in implementing this class is to write a base class that defines only the common methods, and then derive a subclass for each style of wizard. As you might guess, this approach requires more work, but it's more sound from an OOP perspective. Unfortunately, it seems that the benefits don't merit the extra effort, because most of the functions consist of terribly simple code.

Theoretical considerations aside, here's the code of the methods for the new class:

```
function TBlankProjectExpert.GetStyle: TExpertStyle;
begin
  // show up in the Object Repository
```

```
      Result := esProject;
  end;

  function TBlankProjectExpert.GetIDString: string;
  begin
    Result := 'DDHandbook.BlankProjectExpert'
  end;

  function TBlankProjectExpert.GetPage: string;
  begin
    Result := 'Projects';
  end;

  function TBlankProjectExpert.GetGlyph: HICON;
  begin
    Result := LoadIcon (HInstance, MakeIntResource ('BLANKPRJ'));
  end;
```

This code adds the wizard to the project page of the Object Repository, as you can see in Figure 14.5. By selecting the detailed view (simply right-click on the list), you'll be able to see the names of the authors, as well.

FIGURE 14.5:

The detailed view of the Object Repository shows some details of a project wizard.

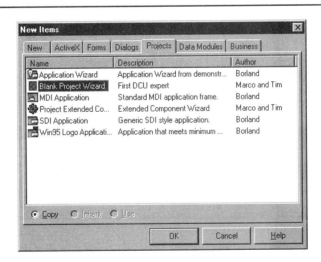

In both views, you'll see each wizard's icons as well. To create this icon you can use Delphi's Image Editor or any other resource editor. Next, create a RES file that includes an icon named *BLANKPRJ*. We'll link the resource file (which in our example happens to have the same name as the icon) to the wizard by adding the line

```
{$R BLANKPRJ.RES}
```

somewhere in the source code.

This code adds the icon to the wizard, and consequently, to the VCL. As a result, we can load the icon by calling the LoadIcon API function from within the Delphi environment—that is, within the VCL code. The LoadIcon function accepts either an icon number or a pointer to a string that contains the icon's name.

WARNING At this point, we've actually written these two wizards in a single source code file. This means that by simply installing the file as part of a package, we'll add both wizards to the component library. Naturally, you should remember to update the registration procedure so that it registers both wizards.

The First DLL Wizard

Now that we've built DCU-based wizards, let's create one that's DLL-based. While placing a wizard in a package is a convenient way to develop them, it loses its appeal when you try to deliver it to a broad user base. This is because package-based wizards must use unique names for all their units. For large-scale deployment, you'll want to place your wizard in a DLL, which doesn't suffer from the limitation of unique unit names.

Instead of building the same wizard again, we'll create something new, although it will still be a simple wizard. The first DLL-based wizard we're going to build is a standard wizard (one that appears as an item in the Help menu) that displays information about the current project.

Building a DLL wizard differs greatly from building a DCU wizard. One of the differences, of course, is that you have to create a DLL project to include the unit that defines the wizard class. Within that unit, you'll implement the registration process in a much different manner than you do for DCU-based wizards. Instead of exporting the Register procedure, as you might assume, the DLL must supply a special entry-point function.

When Delphi loads a DLL wizard, it passes several parameters to this entry-point function, which the wizard will in turn use to initialize various local data structures. For example, since a DLL resides in a separate executable file, it can't access system values such as the `ToolServices` object. As a result, Delphi passes several important values to the entry-point function, and from this function, you'll store the appropriate values. Specifically, the wizard initialization function must be compatible with the following type:

```
TExpertInitProc = function (
  ToolServices: TIToolServices;
  RegisterProc: TExpertRegisterProc;
  var Terminate: TExpertTerminateProc): Boolean; stdcall;
```

The first parameter of this function is the global `ToolServices` object, the second is the address of the wizard registration procedure, and the last is a parameter you can use to install a termination function. If this function returns `True`, it signals that the initialization was successful.

WARNING Writing a DLL has specific implications for the code you write. If you want to use Pascal strings, you'll need to add the ShareMem unit to the unit's uses clause. In addition, you can't use the `Application` global object unless you initialize it.

Now that we have a rough idea of what's involved in writing a DLL-based wizard, we can start building one (the source code files of this project are available in the ExpDLL subdirectory). As we mentioned before, this will be a simple wizard capable of showing project information.

In particular, this wizard will display a list of the project's forms and units, and allow a programmer to select any of those files—or activate it in the editor—by clicking on its name in the list. The user interface of this wizard is a simple form that contains a Label, a TreeView control, and a Panel with an *OK* button. The form's `UpdateTree` function copies the current project name to the Label and then fills the TreeView with the current list of units and forms, as you can see in Figure 14.6. Here's the code:

```
procedure TPrjInfoForm.UpdateTree;
var
  Node1: TTreeNode;
  I, nTot: Integer;
begin
```

```
    LabelProject.Caption := 'Project: ' +
      ToolServices.GetProjectName;
    with TreeView1.Items do
    begin
      Clear;
      // add units
      Node1 := AddChild (nil, 'Units');
      nTot := ToolServices.GetUnitCount;
      for I := 0 to nTot - 1 do
        AddChild (Node1,
          ToolServices.GetUnitName (I));

      // add forms
      Node1 := AddChild (nil, 'Forms');
      nTot := ToolServices.GetFormCount;
      for I := 0 to nTot - 1 do
        AddChild (Node1,
          ToolServices.GetFormName (I));
    end;
    TreeView1.FullExpand;
end;
```

FIGURE 14.6:

The form of the project information wizard, once it has been activated within the Delphi environment

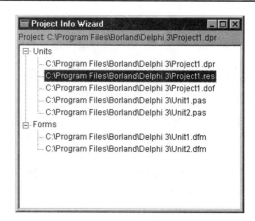

You'll notice that the UpdateTree function uses some of the ToolServices global object's methods to retrieve the appropriate project information. (You must initialize the reference to the ToolServices global object properly in the entry-point function, or you won't be able to call the object's methods. Similarly, you must initialize the `Application` object if you want to call any of its methods. Later, we'll examine the entry-point function in detail.)

The other user-interface method for this wizard is the TreeView component's `OnDblClick` event-handler:

```
procedure TPrjInfoForm.TreeView1DblClick(Sender: TObject);
begin
  if TreeView1.Selected.Level = 1 then
  begin
    ToolServices.OpenFile (TreeView1.Selected.Text);
    ModalResult := mrOK;
  end;
end;
```

Level numbering begins at zero; the first-level names indicate units and forms. If the current item in the TreeView isn't one of these level-zero names, but is on the second level, we'll open the corresponding file. Using the `OpenFile` method, we'll open Pascal files and project files in the source editor, and open form files as textual descriptions in the source editor. All other file types will appear in the source editor window as well, but although they can be opened as text, that is not terribly useful for DCU or EXE files.

Now that we have built the user-interface form for the wizard, we can create the wizard class. The declaration is actually quite simple:

```
type
  // standard wizard
  TPrjInfoExpert = class (TIExpert)
  public
    function GetStyle: TExpertStyle; override;
    function GetName: string; override;
    function GetAuthor: string; override;
    function GetComment: string; override;
    function GetPage: string; override;
    function GetGlyph: HICON; override;
    function GetState: TExpertState; override;
    function GetIDString: string; override;
    function GetMenuText: string; override;
    procedure Execute; override;
  end;
```

As you can see, this is almost identical to the declaration of a DCU-based wizard. Skipping the methods that return default values, here's the rest of the implementation of this class:

```
function TPrjInfoExpert.GetStyle: TExpertStyle;
begin
  Result := esStandard;
end;

function TPrjInfoExpert.GetName: string;
begin
  Result := 'Project Information Expert';
end;

function TPrjInfoExpert.GetIDString: string;
begin
  Result := 'DDHandbook.PrjInfo';
end;

function TPrjInfoExpert.GetMenuText: string;
begin
  Result := 'Project &Info...';
end;
```

The GetState function has a slightly different implementation than we've used before. We must change the implementation because we want to make this wizard available only if a project is currently open:

```
function TPrjInfoExpert.GetState: TExpertState;
begin
  if ToolServices.GetProjectName <> '' then
    Result := [esEnabled]
  else
    Result := [];
end;
```

Finally, here's the code for the Execute procedure. In this case, however, Execute creates the wizard form, calls the UpdateTree method to update the output (before displaying the form), and then activates the form modally:

```
procedure TPrjInfoExpert.Execute;
begin
  try
    PrjInfoForm := TPrjInfoForm.Create (Application);
    PrjInfoForm.UpdateTree;
```

```
    PrjInfoForm.ShowModal;
    PrjInfoForm.Free;
  except
    ToolServices.RaiseException(ReleaseException);
  end;
end;
```

In this method, we handle every exception raised by any of these method calls, extract the message of the exception object by calling the `ReleaseException` function (defined by the VirtIntf unit), and then pass the exception to the `ToolServices` object. (Since the `ToolServices` object is part of Delphi and not part of a DLL, it can raise exceptions that Delphi will handle properly.)

Now that we've written this wizard, we need to initialize it using the technique for DLL-based wizards. Here's the code of the `InitExpert` function (you can name this function as you like, but you must use these parameter types):

```
function InitExpert (ToolServices: TIToolServices;
  RegisterProc: TExpertRegisterProc;
  var Terminate: TExpertTerminateProc): Boolean;
begin
  Result := True;
  try
    ExptIntf.ToolServices := ToolServices;
    Application.Handle := ToolServices.GetParentHandle;
    RegisterProc (TPrjInfoExpert.Create);
  except
    ToolServices.RaiseException(ReleaseException);
  end;
end;
```

This function begins by setting the result value to `True` and then storing the `Tool-Services` parameter in the corresponding public variable of the ExptIntf unit (we added this unit to the project by placing it in the `interface` section's `uses` clause). You could instead define a new variable of the same type, but the code will probably be more confusing that way. By using the standard global variable you can more easily convert this DLL-based wizard into one that's DCU-based, and vice-versa.

Next, we copy the handle of Delphi's `Application` object (accessible as the parent handle of the `ToolServices` object) to the DLL's copy of the `Application` object. By default, the VCL initialization code sets the `Handle` property of the `Application` object for a DLL to `nil`. If you need to show a Delphi form from within the DLL wizard, you must initialize this variable with Delphi's `Application` object `Handle`.

Finally, we create the wizard object and pass it to the registration procedure. Since our wizard doesn't require resource clean-up when it exits, we don't need to set a value for the `Terminate` procedure.

To make the DLL export this initialization function properly, we must add a proper declaration in the project source (here's the full listing):

```
library DDHExper;

uses
  ShareMem, SysUtils, Classes, ExptIntf,
  DLLExper in 'DLLExper.pas',
  PrjForm in 'PrjForm.pas' {PrjInfoForm};

exports
  InitExpert name ExpertEntryPoint;
end.
```

You'll notice that the `exports` statement uses the ExpertEntryPoint name defined in the ExptIntf unit. For Delphi 3 it is:

```
const
  ExpertEntryPoint = 'INITEXPERT0017';
```

Delphi searches for this name when it loads any DLL that contains a wizard. However, to initiate this search, you must remember to add the DLL to the Delphi section in the Registry (using the RegEdit application, as we described earlier). By the way, keep in mind that different versions of Delphi (and Borland C++ Builder) use different names for the entry point. Your DLL should export all the different names if you want to make the DLL-based wizard compatible with different versions of Delphi.

NOTE Updating a wizard's code and recompiling it can be a problem. The DLL is in use by Delphi (even if the wizard isn't active), so you cannot update that file. In fact, Delphi won't be able to compile the new version unless you create a separate directory for storing the wizard DLL that's already in use. By keeping the installed copy of the DLL separate from the location where you're building the original, you can easily update the wizard by closing Delphi, copying the newer version over the older one, and then launching Delphi again to use the new version. Here's where some of the third-party tools, which allow you to load and remove DLL-based wizards while Delphi is running, come in very handy.

You can find the source code for this example in the ExpDLL directory on the companion CD. In fact, we use a single project for this and the next example, so that you'll need to hook only one wizard DLL to the Delphi environment to load both of them. You should move the DLL file from the CD to a directory on your hard disk, and then install it in Delphi by adding an entry in the Registry. The entry should look like this:

```
HKEY_CURRENT_USER\Software\Borland\Delphi\3.0\Experts\DdhExper
```

This entry should spell out the location of the wizard, which in our development system's directory structure was:

```
c:\DdhCode\14\ExpDll\ExpDll.dll
```

Building Add-In Wizards

Now that we've seen how to build some simple wizards, we can move on to something slightly more complex: add-in wizards. Add-in wizards are not more difficult to write than other types of wizards, but their development isn't documented nearly as well. This can be a problem because add-in wizards are structurally different from the other wizards: you must manually create an add-in wizard's menu items, and then respond to the user's selection of a menu item. This means that we need to learn how to use two more virtual interface classes, TIMainMenuIntf and TIMenuItemIntf, both of which are defined in the ToolIntf unit.

Our next wizard will expose a ToolServices method that doesn't show up as a standard Delphi menu item. This method performs a Reload (or revert) operation: reloading a file and discarding all the changes since the user last saved the file. This may not seem terribly useful, but it allows us to demonstrate how to add a new menu item to the File menu instead of the Help menu. Since a standard wizard automatically adds a menu item to the Help menu (and you can't change this), we need to write an add-in wizard. If you examine the class below, you'll find that the structure of this wizard is slightly different from the previous ones:

```
type
  TReloadExpert = class (TIExpert)
  public
    constructor Create;
    destructor Destroy; override;
    function GetStyle: TExpertStyle; override;
    function GetName: string; override;
```

```
      function GetAuthor: string; override;
      function GetComment: string; override;
      function GetPage: string; override;
      function GetGlyph: HICON; override;
      function GetState: TExpertState; override;
      function GetIDString: string; override;
      function GetMenuText: string; override;
      procedure Execute; override;
      procedure ReloadClick (Sender: TIMenuItemIntf);
    private
      NewMenuItem: TIMenuItemIntf;
    end;
```

The new elements are the constructor, the destructor, the ReloadClick method (of type TIMenuClickEvent), and the private NewMenuItem field.

The new methods do most of the work for this wizard. However, we'll need to implement a few of the familiar methods as well:

```
function TReloadExpert.GetStyle: TExpertStyle;
begin
  Result := esAddIn;
end;

function TReloadExpert.GetName: String;
begin
  Result := 'Reload Expert'
end;

function TReloadExpert.GetAuthor: string;
begin
  Result := 'Marco and Tim';
end;

function TReloadExpert.GetIDString: String;
begin
  // must be unique
  Result := 'DDHandbook.ReloadExpert'
end;
```

You can see that for this type of wizard the Execute procedure does nothing, because Delphi will never call it.

Accessing the Delphi Menu

The most complex code for an add-in wizard is typically in the constructor. This is because you must first retrieve the interface for the main menu. Fortunately, calling the ToolServices object's GetMainMenu method returns a TIMainMenuIntf object. Here's the definition of its class:

```
type
  TIMainMenuIntf = class(TInterface)
  public
    function GetMenuItems: TIMenuItemIntf;
      virtual; stdcall; abstract;
    function FindMenuItem (const Name: string):
      TIMenuItemIntf; virtual; stdcall; abstract;
  end;
```

The first method, GetMenuItem, returns the interface to the menu bar itself, while the FindMenuItem method locates a specific pull-down menu or menu item by name. However, to use FindMenuItem, you must provide an internal menu ID string—not the menu caption.

You can extract this information from the system simply by writing a Delphi wizard, as we'll do in a while. Let us first complete the description of the menu interfaces.

Instead of searching for a particular menu item by its ID string, in fact, you can navigate through the list of menus, and then scan them. To facilitate this, the TIMenuItemIntf class provides links to the submenus. For each menu, you can use the GetItemCount and GetItem methods to examine each of the submenus via a loop. Here's the definition of the TIMenuItemIntf class:

```
type
  TIMenuItemIntf = class(TInterface)
  public
    function DestroyMenuItem: Boolean; virtual;
      stdcall; abstract;
    function GetIndex: Integer; virtual; stdcall; abstract;
    function GetItemCount: Integer; virtual; stdcall; abstract;
    function GetItem(Index: Integer): TIMenuItemIntf; virtual;
      stdcall; abstract;
    function GetName: string; virtual; stdcall; abstract;
    function GetParent: TIMenuItemIntf; virtual;
      stdcall; abstract;
```

```
function GetCaption: string; virtual; stdcall; abstract;
function SetCaption(const Caption: string): Boolean; virtual;
  stdcall; abstract;
function GetShortCut: Integer; virtual; stdcall; abstract;
function SetShortCut(ShortCut: Integer): Boolean; virtual;
  stdcall; abstract;
function GetFlags: TIMenuFlags; virtual; stdcall; abstract;
function SetFlags(Mask, Flags: TIMenuFlags): Boolean; virtual;
  stdcall; abstract;
function GetGroupIndex: Integer; virtual; stdcall; abstract;
function SetGroupIndex(GroupIndex: Integer): Boolean; virtual;
  stdcall; abstract;
function GetHint: string; virtual; stdcall; abstract;
function SetHint(Hint: string): Boolean; virtual;
  stdcall; abstract;
function GetContext: Integer; virtual; stdcall; abstract;
function SetContext(Context: Integer): Boolean; virtual;
  stdcall; abstract;
function GetOnClick: TIMenuClickEvent; virtual;
  stdcall; abstract;
function SetOnClick(Click: TIMenuClickEvent): Boolean; virtual;
  stdcall; abstract;
function InsertItem(Index: Integer; Caption, Name, Hint: string;
  ShortCut, Context, GroupIndex: Integer; Flags: TIMenuFlags;
  EventHandler: TIMenuClickEvent): TIMenuItemIntf; virtual;
  stdcall; abstract;
end;
```

You can find descriptions of these methods in the source code comments of the ToolIntf unit.

The Delphi Menu Wizard

We can use the methods above to navigate through the Delphi menu and add a specific item or a new pull-down, but you can also create a list of the names of the menu items to be used by the FindMenuItem method of the TIMainMenuIntf class.

We've added this wizard to a separate package, because you'll need to run it only once for each new version of Delphi. The source code of the wizard, its package, and its output file (Delphi3.TXT) are all stored in the ExpMenu directory of the companion CD. The basic idea is that this wizard extracts the main menu, and then it loops through the menu items to reach each pull-down menu. We can skip the familiar usual code for a wizard, and focus on its Execute method:

```
procedure TExpMenu.Execute;
var
  MainMenu: TIMenuItemIntf;
  StrOut: TStrings;
  SaveDial: TSaveDialog;
begin
  MainMenu := ToolServices.GetMainMenu.GetMenuItems;
  StrOut := TStringList.Create;
  try
    AddSubItems (StrOut, MainMenu, 0);
    SaveDial := TSaveDialog.Create (nil);
    try
      SaveDial.DefaultExt := 'txt';
      SaveDial.Filter := 'Text file (*.txt)|*.txt';
      if SaveDial.Execute then
        StrOut.SaveToFile (SaveDial.FileName);
    finally
      SaveDial.Free;
    end;
  finally
    StrOut.Free;
  end;
end;
```

The code basically creates a string list to which it outputs the information, and then saves it to a text file. The core of the wizard is the AddSubItems call, which is executed on the main menu first, then on each pull-down, and then on any second-level menu items (such as those under File ➤ Reopen). Here's the code of the recursive procedure, which does all the formatting:

```
procedure TExpMenu.AddSubItems (StrOut: TStrings;
  Item: TIMenuItemIntf; Level: Integer);
var
  I: Integer;
  NewItem: TIMenuItemIntf;
begin
  for I := 0 to Item.GetItemCount - 1 do
  begin
    NewItem := Item.GetItem (I);
    // if there are subitems insert a blank line
    if NewItem.GetItemCount > 0 then
```

```
      StrOut.Add ('');
    StrOut.Add (Format ('%s%d'#9'%s'#9'%s',
      [StringOfChar (' ', Level * 2),
      NewItem.GetIndex,
      NewItem.GetCaption,
      NewItem.GetName]));
    AddSubItems (StrOut, NewItem, Level + 1);
  end;
end;
```

The wizard inserts a blank line before each item that has subitems, and it uses blank spaces to indent items according to their menu level. Each line of output consists of an items menu position, its caption, and its name (ID string). We've used tab characters (#9) instead of spaces to make it easy to format this text into a table.

The initial portion of the output file, after a little custom formatting, looks like this (the complete text is on the companion CD):

```
0     &File              FileMenu
  0     &New...            FileNewItem
  1     New Applica&tion   FileNewApplicationItem
  2     New &Form          FileNewFormItem
  3     New Data &Module   FileNewDataModuleItem
  4     &Open..            FileOpenItem
  5     &Reopen            FileClosedFilesItem
    0 &0                 C:\DDHCODE\14\ExpDLL\ExpDll.dpr
    1 &1                 C:\DDHCODE\14\Blank\Project1.dpr
```

The entire structure of the File menu (to which we're going to add a new item with the next wizard) is shown in Table 14.2.

TABLE 14.2:
Delphi's File Menu Items and Their Corresponding Menu ID Strings

Menu Item Caption	Menu Item Name (ID)String
&File	FileMenu
&New...	FileNewItem
New Applica&tion	FileNewApplicationItem
New &Form	FileNewFormItem
New Data &Module	FileNewDataModuleItem

TABLE 14.2 CONTINUED:
Delphi's File Menu Items and Their Corresponding Menu ID Strings

Menu Item Caption	Menu Item Name (ID)String
&Reopen	FileClosedFilesItem
&Open...	FileOpenItem
&Reopen	FileClosedFilesItem
&Save	FileSaveItem
Reloa&d	ReloadExpertItem
Save &As...	FileSaveAsItem
Sav&e Project As...	FileSaveProjectAs
Sa&ve All	FileSaveAllItem
&Close	FileCloseItem
C&lose All	FileCloseAllItem
– (blank)	N6
&Use Unit...	FileUseUnitItem
A&dd to Project...	FileAddItem
Remove from Pro&ject...	FileRemoveItem
– (blank)	N8
&Print...	FilePrintItem
– (blank)	
E&xit	FileExitItem

If you examine the Delphi3.TXT file on the companion disk you'll see the structure of the menu items of Delphi 3 at a given moment and for a given configuration. You'll see some extra items added by wizards we had installed, and the last files we've worked with (under the Reload menu). However, you'll notice that the list also includes hidden Delphi menu items (such as the CPU view menu item).

WARNING The list of menu items also includes the Help menu, but you cannot insert menu items for an add-in wizard into this menu. If you try to do so, Delphi will generate an access violation. Apparently, Delphi reserves the Help menu for standard wizards only (wizards that return the esStandard style).

Adding a New Menu Item (in the Add-in Wizard)

Now that you have a basic idea of how to access menus and menu items, here's the code for the add-in wizard's constructor. It retrieves first the interfaces to the main menu, then each of the menu items of the main menu, and then all of the items of the first menu (the contents of the File menu). Finally, it inserts the new menu item into the File menu.

```
constructor TReloadExpert.Create;
var
  MainMenu: TIMainMenuIntf;
  MainMenuItems, FileMenu: TIMenuItemIntf;
begin
  inherited Create;
  MainMenu := nil;
  MainMenuItems := nil;
  FileMenu := nil;
  NewMenuItem := nil;
  try try
    MainMenu := ToolServices.GetMainMenu;
    MainMenuItems := MainMenu.GetMenuItems;
    FileMenu := MainMenuItems.GetItem (0);
    NewMenuItem := FileMenu.InsertItem (7, 'Reloa&d',
      'ReloadExpertItem', '', 0, 0, 0,
      [mfVisible, mfEnabled], ReloadClick)
  finally
    FileMenu.Free;
    MainMenuItems.Free;
    MainMenu.Free;
  end;
  except
    ToolServices.RaiseException(ReleaseException);
  end;
end;
```

You'll notice that most of the processing takes place inside a `try` block. This is important because we might encounter problems creating some of these items. Instead of writing additional nested `try` blocks, we can simply initialize all the interfaces to `nil`. If there are problems creating one of the menu objects, calling `Free` will be harmless, even if the interfaces are not properly initialized.

The core of this method is the call to the `InsertItem` method of the File menu item interface. You can see its declaration in the `TIMenuItemIntf` class shown above. This method has many parameters, and it took some trial-and-error research (the documentation is very limited) to identify the purpose of each one:

Index indicates the item's position in the menu. If the value is zero or greater than the last menu item, Delphi will append the new item at the end of the menu. If you use a fixed value (as we've done) for this parameter, you may encounter problems if other add-in wizards attempt to use the same index value. Alternatively, you can scan the menu items, search for a particular caption, and then add the new item after it.

Caption represents the text of the menu item. Any letter preceded by an ampersand (&) will be assigned as the accelerator for the menu item.

Name is the internal ID string for the item, which must be unique. You can use this elsewhere to locate the interface of an item.

Hint is the hint text for the menu item. Delphi's user interface doesn't display menu hints, so you can safely set this to an empty string.

ShortCut is the character code of the shortcut key. Set this to zero if you don't provide a shortcut key.

Context is the help context identifier used to link to a custom help file page that the user has installed and integrated in the environment. It's not clear if this works correctly for add-in wizards.

GroupIndex is the group index, as found in regular `TMenuItem` components. This is useful if you want to create radio button menu items or to position new menus.

Flags holds the menu item flags that indicate if the item is visible, enabled, checked, and so on. Here's the declaration of this set:

```
type
  TIMenuFlag = (mfInvalid, mfEnabled, mfVisible,
    mfChecked, mfBreak, mfBarBreak, mfRadioItem);
  TIMenuFlags = set of TIMenuFlag;
```

EventHandler is a pointer to the method that will respond when the user selects the new menu item. You should use the name of an event-compatible method, such as the ReloadClick procedure of the TReloadExpert class. This method implements the functionality of an add-in wizard in a manner similar to the Execute method of other kinds of wizards.

Calling the InsertItem method as we've done adds a new menu item to Delphi's File menu, as you can see in Figure 14.7.

> **WARNING** Adding a single menu item is not the only thing an add-in wizard can do. It can add an entire menu, containing several menu items. Similarly, an add-in wizard can also replace an existing menu item with a new one. Since the menu interface classes give us complete access to the Delphi menu, we can do considerable damage if we're not careful. That's why we haven't demonstrated replacing an existing menu item.

Executing the Add-In Wizard

At the end of the constructor of the wizard class, you'll notice that we've commented out a call to the Windows API MessageBox function. Although we used this function for debugging purposes, it's common (and appropriate) to warn the user that you've installed a new wizard. Shareware wizards typically use this feature to remind you (every time you launch Delphi) that you're using an unregistered version of the wizard. If you decide to buy a shareware wizard, you'll typically get a new version that doesn't display the reminder.

Now let's look at the destructor of the wizard class, which executes when you exit Delphi:

```
destructor TReloadExpert.Destroy;
begin
  NewMenuItem.Free;
  inherited Destroy;
end;
```

Failing to destroy a menu item interface might actually be harmless, because Delphi is being completely released from memory. However, releasing items you've allocated is good programming practice, and may be important if future versions allow you to dynamically load and unload DLL wizards.

Finally, here's the very simple code we'll execute when the user selects the new Reload item of the File menu (this is the method we named as the event handler in the InsertItem method call):

```
procedure TReloadExpert.ReloadClick (Sender: TIMenuItemIntf);
begin
  try
    if MessageBox (ToolServices.GetParentHandle,
        'Are you sure you want to reload the file?',
        'Confirmation', mb_YesNo) = idYes then
      ToolServices.ReloadFile (
        ToolServices.GetCurrentFile);
  except
    ToolServices.RaiseException(ReleaseException);
  end;
end;
```

Again, you'll notice that we've protected the code from exceptions. Also notice that we use the MessageBox API function instead of displaying a form or using the message facilities of the Application object. The reason for this approach is that the resulting DLL won't contain the entire VCL, and we therefore won't be able to call many of the helper routines in the VCL. In the case of this wizard, we've included it in the same DLL as the previous one (which uses the VCL), so we haven't really saved anything. However, if you create a new DLL that contains just the Reload wizard, it won't contain the VCL code.

Since we've placed both of these wizards in the same DLL, we can install two wizards with one installation. In fact, we updated the `InitExpert` initialization function to install the Reload wizard by adding just one line of code:

```
RegisterProc (TReloadExpert.Create);
```

The List Template Wizard

The wizards we've written up to now offer simple capabilities, and demonstrate that you can use wizards to extend the Delphi environment in many different ways. Traditionally, however, a wizard is usually thought of as a code generator. In this section, we'll explore this concept by building a couple of wizards that generate Pascal code based on user input.

The first of these wizards is the List Template wizard, promised in Chapter 2 when we discussed type-safe lists. The second code generator will be an improved Component Wizard; Delphi's original is very limited. The third code-generating example will be more complex, because it will create both Pascal source code and the corresponding form. Adding further complexity, it will allow you to add the new form to an existing project.

In Chapter 2, we discussed different ways of building a type-safe list class, one that can host only objects of a specific data type. One of the problems we found is that although it's very simple to write similar classes, if you need several of them, you'll need to copy and paste the source code from one unit to another just to obtain a slightly different class. This is the kind of repetitive, boring task a computer can do for you!

In building the template list wizard, we have a bigger goal in mind, which is to create a sort of template wizard you can use with every data type. Generic programming (or templates, as the concept is known in the C++ language) provides a way of writing source code that uses undefined data types. The compiler will replace the occurrences of the generic type with the specific type supplied, and then will compile the code. It's important to keep in mind, in fact, that templates are a compile-time mechanism, which enforces compile-time type-checking (and doesn't skip them altogether, as a variant type does).

Another way of describing templates is that they are a clever form of macro substitution done by the compiler. Macros, which are not widely used in the Pascal programming culture, are a way to replace a string in a source code file with an equivalent string or even a parametric one. This lengthy introduction serves as background for our "poor man's Delphi template wizard," the List Wizard.

We'll look at the code of the wizard first, and then discuss the operation it performs. The TExpList wizard is a standard wizard with the usual class declaration plus an extra method:

```
type
  TExpList = class (TIExpert)
  public
    function GetStyle: TExpertStyle; override;
    function GetName: string; override;
    ...
    procedure Execute; override;
    procedure ApplyTemplate (SourceStr: TStrings;
      TypeName: string);
  end;
```

The Execute method does most of the work, except the ApplyTemplate method converts the source code file. The Execute method requests three items from the user: the input file (the template file marked by the .TTT extension), the replacement type, and the name of the output file. Next, the Execute method saves the file (after changing the unit name in the first line of its source code), and adds the file to the project. Here's the complete source code:

```
procedure TExpList.Execute;
var
  SourceStr: TStrings;
  OpenDial: TOpenDialog;
  SaveDial: TSaveDialog;
  TypeName: string;
begin
  // 1: choose template file
  OpenDial := TOpenDialog.Create (nil);
  SaveDial := TSaveDialog.Create (nil);
  SourceStr := TStringList.Create;
  try
    OpenDial.Filter := 'Template file (*.ttt)|*.ttt';
    TypeName := 'TObject';
    if OpenDial.Execute then
    begin
      SourceStr.LoadFromFile (OpenDial.FileName);
      // 2: ask for type name
      if InputQuery ('List Wizard', 'Template type:',
        TypeName) then
      begin
```

```
    ApplyTemplate (SourceStr, TypeName);
    // 3: save the file and add it to the project
    SaveDial.Filter := 'Pascal file (*.pas)|*.pas';
    SaveDial.DefaultExt := 'pas';
    if SaveDial.Execute then
    begin
      // fix unit name (removing path and filename)
      SourceStr.Strings [0] := 'unit ' +
        ChangeFileExt (ExtractFileName (
          SaveDial.FileName), '') + ';';
      SourceStr.SaveToFile (SaveDial.FileName);
      // add the file to the Delphi project
      ToolServices.CreateModuleEx (SaveDial.FileName,
        '', '', '', nil, nil,
        [cmAddToProject, cmExisting, cmShowSource]);
    end;
  end;
end;
finally
  OpenDial.Free;
  SaveDial.Free;
  SourceStr.Free;
end;
end;
```

From the perspective of a wizard writer, the most important call here is
`ToolServices.CreateModuleEx`. We'll see that it's possible to use this method
(and the similar `CreateModule` method) to add a new unit to a project, passing it a
virtual stream containing the source code of the unit and of the form. A simpler
approach to use, demonstrated here and available only for the `CreateModuleEx`
method, is to create a file first and then use the `cmExisting` flag. As you'll see in
the section about form wizards, the other alternative is much more complex.

Now that we've seen how the wizard interacts with the user (asking for input)
and with the system (adding a file to the current project), we can focus on the
transformations applied to the source file—that is, the template file. The basic
idea is that each time the sequence `'TTT'` appears in the source code file, it's
replaced with the type name supplied by the wizard's user. This operation is
done on each item of the string list, potentially more than once for each line:

```
procedure TExpList.ApplyTemplate (
  SourceStr: TStrings; TypeName: string);
var
```

```
    I, nPos, nDone: Integer;
begin
  nDone := 0;
  for I := 0 to SourceStr.Count - 1 do
  begin
    repeat
      nPos := Pos ('TTT', SourceStr [I]);
      if nPos > 0 then
      begin
        // replace template with type name
        SourceStr [I] :=
          Copy (SourceStr [I], 0, nPos - 1) +
          TypeName +
          Copy (SourceStr [I], nPos + 3, 10000);
        Inc (nDone);
      end;
    until nPos = 0;
  end;
  ShowMessage ('The List Wizard has inserted the ' +
    TypeName + ' type ' + IntToStr (nDone) + ' times');
end;
```

In the source code of the template list, you'll notice that we write 'TTT' instead of the actual type name, and we've also created a unique class name for the list. Here are some excerpts from List.TTT; the complete file is available in the ListTest directory on the companion CD:

```
type
  TTTList = class(TObject)
  private
    FList: TList;
    function Get(Index: Integer): TTT;
    procedure Put(Index: Integer; Item: TTT);
    function GetCount: Integer;
  public
    constructor Create;
    destructor Destroy; override;
    function Add(Item: TTT): Integer;
    function Equals(List: TTTList): Boolean;
    property Count: Integer
      read GetCount;
    property Items[Index: Integer]: TTT
      read Get write Put; default;
```

```
  end;

implementation

constructor TTTList.Create;
begin
  inherited Create;
  FList := TList.Create;
end;

function TTTList.Get(Index: Integer): TTT;
begin
  Result := FList[Index];
end;

procedure TTTList.Put(Index: Integer; Item: TTT);
begin
  FList[Index] := Item;
end;
```

For example, if we use TButton as the text for the replacement type, the generated code looks like this (it's available in the BtnList.PAS file of the ListTest directory):

```
type
  TButtonList = class(TObject)
  private
    FList: TList;
    function Get(Index: Integer): TButton;
    procedure Put(Index: Integer; Item: TButton);
    function GetCount: Integer;
  public
    constructor Create;
    destructor Destroy; override;
    function Add(Item: TButton): Integer;
    function Equals(List: TButtonList): Boolean;
    property Count: Integer
      read GetCount;
    property Items[Index: Integer]: TButton
      read Get write Put; default;
  end;

implementation
```

```
constructor TButtonList.Create;
begin
  inherited Create;
  FList := TList.Create;
end;

function TButtonList.Get(Index: Integer): TButton;
begin
  Result := FList[Index];
end;

procedure TButtonList.Put(Index: Integer; Item: TButton);
begin
  FList[Index] := Item;
end;
```

You'll only need to fix the initial uses statement to refer to the unit that defines the type you've used (in this case StdCtrls for TButton). This file is the result of using the List Wizard after creating a new application, ListDemo. This program simply keeps track of the buttons you've pressed by adding each one to a list of buttons, and showing the captions in a list box, as you can see in Figure 14.8.

FIGURE 14.8:

The caption and class type of the buttons stored in the template-based list are displayed in the ListTest example's list box.

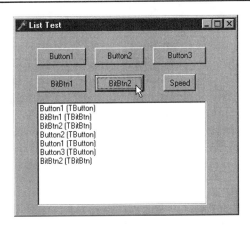

The details of the ListTest example are actually quite simple, as you'll see by looking at the source code on the CD. The only important thing to mention is that the code to add buttons to the list cannot be this:

```
procedure TForm1.AddToList(Sender: TObject);
begin
```

```
    List.Add (Sender);
    UpdateList (self);
  end;
```

because the list accepts TButton objects. The code above will be rejected by the compiler. You have to write it this way instead:

```
procedure TForm1.AddToList(Sender: TObject);
begin
  List.Add (Sender as TButton);
  UpdateList (self);
end;
```

This means that the list will invariably include only objects compatible with the TButton class; that is, instances of the TButton class or one of its subclasses. In the example, you can add to the list TBitBtn objects, but not TSpeedButton objects.

Again, the scope of this example is wider that its name implies. It's useful not only for lists, but any time you want to write code with a generic type and then (manually) create actual versions of the code, with given data types.

The Component Wizard

For our next code generator, we'll create another wizard that both generates Pascal source code and provides a useful tool at the same time: a component wizard. Actually, we'll build this tool in two steps. First, we'll build a program to generate components. Then, we'll turn it into a DCU-based wizard. (In reality, we'll build a pair of DCU-based wizards: a standard wizard and a project wizard.) The advantage of this two-step approach is that when you're finished, you can use either the stand-alone application or the Delphi-integrated wizard to build new components.

Keep in mind that this is not going to be a full-featured, professional component-building tool. For that purpose, you would need to extend this example in several ways, but (as mentioned in Chapter 5) if you need a professional component writing tool you should probably buy one. This wizard does provide a good starting point, and it illustrates many important Delphi programming tricks.

The Component Wizard Form

The main form of our new component wizard is based on the notebook metaphor. Instead of changing pages by pressing a Next button, the user can move (under some restrictions) from one page to another by selecting the corresponding tab. This design allows for flexibility and takes advantage of the PageControl component. The first page of the notebook is very similar to Delphi's component wizard, as you can see in Figure 14.9.

FIGURE 14.9:

The first page of the main form of the Extended Component Wizard is similar to Delphi's own component wizard.

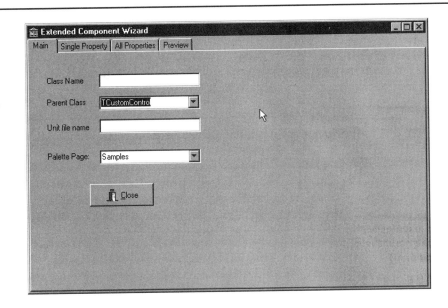

In the first Edit control, the user will enter the name of the component, which by convention should begin with the letter *T*. When the user shifts focus away from this component, we'll use the first eight characters (after the initial letter) as the unit name:

```
procedure TCompWizForm.EditClassNameExit(Sender: TObject);
begin
  if EditUnitName.Text = '' then
    EditUnitName.Text := Copy (EditClassName.Text, 2, 8);
end;
```

NOTE   Although Windows 95 and Windows NT can use long file names, we've decided to stick with short file names to make sure that components built with this wizard will be compatible (if possible) with Delphi 1.

Next, we provide two ComboBox components, in which the user will enter the parent class for the component and the name of the Component palette page where the component will appear. Initially, both combo boxes will be empty. When we convert this program into a wizard, we'll choose the base class and insert the appropriate name for the user. For the current version of the application, we'll just display the list of Component palette pages. To get this information, we need to access the Delphi configuration in the Windows Registry, using a TRegistryClass object that's part of the VCL. For more information about accessing the Windows Registry from Delphi, see *Mastering Delphi 3*.

NOTE   To access Delphi's current Registry entry, you can use the GetBase-RegistryKey method of the ToolServices global object. This function returns a string that contains the full path of Delphi's base Registry key, relative to the HKEY_CURRENT_USER section. We haven't used this technique in the example, because we want to be able to run the program alone; and in that case, the ToolServices object isn't available.

Delphi stores the current list of the palette pages under the *Software\Borland\Delphi\3.0\Palette* key. You can retrieve the list of values under this key by using the TRegistryClass class's GetValueNames method:

```
procedure TCompWizForm.FormCreate(Sender: TObject);
var
  Reg: TRegistry;
begin
  Reg := TRegistry.Create;
  try
    if Reg.OpenKey ('Software\Borland\Delphi\3.0\Palette',
        False) then
      Reg.GetValueNames (ComboPage.Items);
  finally
    Reg.Free;
  end
end;
```

When the user enters all the appropriate information on the first page, we'll let them proceed to the following one. We enforce this rule by responding to the PageControl component's OnChanging event:

```
procedure TCompWizForm.PageControl1Changing(
  Sender: TObject; var AllowChange: Boolean);
begin
  if PageControl1.ActivePage = SheetMain then
    if (EditClassName.Text = '')
      or (ComboParentClass.Text = '')
      or (ComboPage.Text = '') then
    begin
      AllowChange := False;
      MessageDlg (
        'You must fill the main form data first',
        mtError, [mbOK], 0);
    end;
end;
```

If any of these three text properties are empty, we display a warning message to the user and set the AllowChange parameter to False, which prevents the user from changing the page. (We don't check the text of the unit name edit box, because we set that value automatically.)

The second page is used to set values for the properties, one at a time. To see the complete list of properties you've defined, you can always jump to the third page (discussed shortly). The second page, labeled *Single Property*, has the layout you can see in Figure 14.10.

When the user selects this page, we copy the value of the current property (stored in the StringGrid component of the third page) to the various input controls:

```
procedure TCompWizForm.PageControl1Change(Sender: TObject);
begin
  if PageControl1.ActivePage = SheetSingle then
    UpdateSingle
  else
    UpdateGrid;
end;
```

We need to update the StringGrid for any change because it will hold the final values that we'll use to generate the code of the component. What are the effects of the UpdateSingle and UpdateGrid methods of the form? As their names imply, one copies the value of the current property to the controls on the third page, and the other updates the values for the current property in the StringGrid.

The second page of
the Extended Com-
ponent Wizard is used
to set the values of
each property.

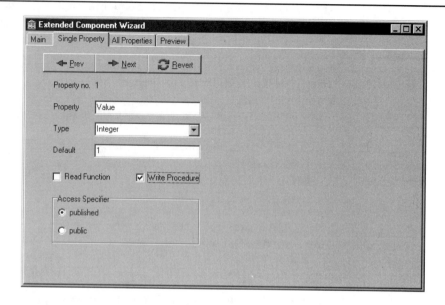

The `UpdateSingle` method uses several access methods that correspond to the
six attributes of the new component:

```
procedure TCompWizForm.UpdateSingle;
begin
  LabelPropNo.Caption := IntToStr (CurrProp);
  EditPropName.Text := GetProp (CurrProp);
  ComboTypeName.Text := GetType (CurrProp);
  EditDefault.Text := GetDefault (CurrProp);
  CheckRead.Checked := GetRead (CurrProp) <> '';
  CheckWrite.Checked := GetWrite (CurrProp) <> '';
  if GetAccess (CurrProp) <> '' then
    RadioAccess.ItemIndex :=
      RadioAccess.Items.IndexOf (GetAccess (CurrProp));
end;
```

You'll notice that the state of the check boxes depends on the existence of a name
for the *Get* and *Set* methods, while the RadioGroup component determines the
access specifier (public or published) for the current property.

The *Get* methods for this form simply make the code easier to read. Here are a
couple of them (the others have the same format):

```
function TCompWizForm.GetProp (Prop: Integer): string;
begin
```

```
      Result := StringGridProps.Cells [0, Prop];
  end;

  function TCompWizForm.GetType (Prop: Integer): string;
  begin
      Result := StringGridProps.Cells [1, Prop];
  end;
```

The reason we've written these methods is to make the code generation more understandable, as we'll see later on.

In contrast, the UpdateGrid method accesses the StringGrid cells directly:

```
  procedure TCompWizForm.UpdateGrid;
  begin
    with StringGridProps do
    begin
      Cells [0, CurrProp] := EditPropName.Text;
      Cells [1, CurrProp] := ComboTypeName.Text;
      if CheckRead.Checked then
        Cells [2, CurrProp] := 'Get' + EditPropName.Text
      else
        Cells [2, CurrProp] := '';
      if CheckWrite.Checked then
        Cells [3, CurrProp] := 'Set' + EditPropName.Text
      else
        Cells [3, CurrProp] := '';
      if RadioAccess.ItemIndex >= 0 then
        Cells [4, CurrProp] := RadioAccess.Items [
          RadioAccess.ItemIndex];
      Cells [5, CurrProp] := EditDefault.Text;
      Row := CurrProp;
    end;
  end;
```

As you can see, this code performs conversions that are complementary to those of the UpdateSingle method. In particular, you'll notice that we've built the names of the access methods according to the convention of prefixing the property name with *Get* or *Set*, depending on the method. The last statement in this method makes the row corresponding to the current property active.

When you begin editing the values of a property, you can move back and forth in the list of the properties using the *Next* and *Prev* buttons. These actions automatically update the value of the current property in the StringGrid (by calling

UpdateGrid), and then retrieve the values for the new property (by calling UpdateSingle):

```
procedure TCompWizForm.BtnPrevClick(Sender: TObject);
begin
  UpdateGrid;
  if CurrProp > 1 then
  begin
    Dec (CurrProp);
    UpdateSingle;
  end;
end;

procedure TCompWizForm.BtnNextClick(Sender: TObject);
begin
  UpdateGrid;
  if CurrProp < TotProps then
  begin
    Inc (CurrProp);
    UpdateSingle;
  end
  else
    if MessageDlg ('Do you want to add a new property?',
      mtConfirmation, [mbYes, mbNo], 0) = idYes then
    begin
      NewProperty1Click (self);
      Inc (CurrProp);
      UpdateSingle;
    end;
end;
```

The second method is slightly more complex; it prompts the user to confirm a new property when they advance past the last property. Whenever the user edits a new property or turns to a different page, we use the current values to update the value of the property. Accordingly, we've added a third button to the form to discard the changes and copy the original values of the property back to the input components:

```
procedure TCompWizForm.BtnRevertClick(Sender: TObject);
begin
  UpdateSingle;
end;
```

When you finish defining the new properties, you can advance to the third page, labeled *All Properties*, which contains a string grid that covers the page entirely. This is a summary page. You won't use it to input data, just to view a complete list of the properties for the new component. Initially, this page is empty, but we'll fill it with the name, data type, access functions, access specifier, and default value of each property you want to add to the new component.

In the OnCreate event handler for the form, we'll fill the top row of the StringGrid component with the description of the grid columns, which will serve as a header for the grid:

```
procedure TCompWizForm.FormCreate(Sender: TObject);
begin
  with StringGridProps do
  begin
    Cells [0, 0] := 'property';
    Cells [1, 0] := 'type';
    Cells [2, 0] := 'read';
    Cells [3, 0] := 'write';
    Cells [4, 0] := 'access';
    Cells [5, 0] := 'default';
  end;
  CurrProp := 1;
  TotProps := 1;
  PageControl1.ActivePage := SheetMain;
end;
```

Eventually, we'll need to merge this code with the code that retrieves the palette pages from the Registry, and with some additional code we'll see later on. Besides setting the StringGrid header text, the FormCreate method also sets the initial values of two fields: CurrProp, which stores the index number of the current property; and TotProps, which stores the total number of component properties. Initially, the first property is empty and undefined.

The string grid cannot be edited—the user should move to the previous page to edit each property—but it does provide a popup menu with two options: adding a new blank property or clearing the currently selected property.

```
procedure TCompWizForm.NewProperty1Click(Sender: TObject);
begin
  Inc (TotProps);
  StringGridProps.RowCount := TotProps + 1;
end;
```

```
procedure TCompWizForm.RemoveProperty1Click(Sender: TObject);
var
  I: Integer;
begin
  if MessageDlg ('Are you sure you want to delete the ' +
      StringGridProps.Cells [0, CurrProp] + ' property?',
      mtConfirmation, [mbYes, mbNo], 0) = idYes then
    // set the line to ''
    for I := 0 to 5 do
      StringGridProps.Cells [I, CurrProp] := '';
end;
```

To remove a property, we simply delete all of the strings that describe it. We don't need to delete the property's row in the StringGrid, since we might want to reuse it later. We can simply leave a row empty, since the code generator ignores blank properties.

To keep the value of the CurrProp field up-to-date, we need to handle the StringGrid component's OnSelectCell event:

```
procedure TCompWizForm.StringGridPropsSelectCell(
    Sender: TObject; Col, Row: Longint; var CanSelect: Boolean);
begin
  if (Row <> 0) then
    CurrProp := Row;
end;
```

Before setting the value, the code checks to see if the user has selected the first row, which displays the column headings. This takes place when the user moves to the last page, the *Preview* page, which contains a memo component. We've added one more statement to the PageControl1Change method to handle selecting this page:

```
if PageControl1.ActivePage = SheetPreview then
  FillMemo;
```

Now let's take a closer look at the FillMemo method.

Generating the Component Source Code

The FillMemo method is quite a long function, and performs the actual code generation. To make it easier to read, we've defined a helper method to generate the definition of each property.

```
function TCompWizForm.PropertyDefinition (I: Integer): string;
begin
  Result := 'property ' + GetProp (I) +
    ': ' + GetType (I);
  if GetRead (I) <> '' then
    Result := Result + ' read ' + GetRead (I)
  else
    Result := Result + ' read f' + GetProp (I);
  if GetWrite (I) <> '' then
    Result := Result + ' write ' + GetWrite (I)
  else
    Result := Result + ' write f' + GetProp (I);
  if GetDefault (I) <> '' then
    Result := Result + ' default ' + GetDefault (I);
  Result := Result + ';'
end;
```

As you'll recall, the format for a property definition is:

```
property <Name>: <Type> read <Method/Field>
  write <Method/Field> default <Value>;
```

To insert the access method names, we simply call the GetRead or GetWrite methods. However, if the property doesn't use access methods, we use the property name preceded by the letter *f*.

TIP

As you can see, this method doesn't allow the user to generate read-only or write-only properties. However, you can fix this quite easily by editing the source code of this project. We chose to focus on automatically generating the functions and a rough skeleton of their source code. Even without providing the less common types of properties, this will save the user time when they create new components.

Since the FillMemo method is quite long, we'll show you the listing in pieces, discussing each of them separately. At the beginning of this method, we use the information from the first page of the notebook to determine the unit name, the initial uses statement (a standard one), and the type declaration for the class:

```
procedure TCompWizForm.FillMemo;
var
  I: Integer;
begin
  with MemoPreview.Lines do
```

```
begin
  Clear;
  // intestation
  Add ('unit ' + EditUnitName.Text + ';');
  Add ('');
  Add ('interface');
  Add ('');
  Add ('uses');
  Add ('  Windows, Messages, SysUtils, Classes, Graphics,');
  Add ('  Controls, Forms, Dialogs, StdCtrls;');
  Add ('');
  Add ('type');
  Add ('  ' + EditClassName.Text +
    ' = class(' + ComboParentClass.Text + ')');
```

Next, we need to add a private field for each property. Although this step might not always be necessary, it's much easier to remove these lines later than to add them when you need them. Here's the property code:

```
Add ('  private');
// add a field for each property
Add ('    {data fields for properties}');
for I := 1 to TotProps do
  if GetProp (I) <> '' then
    Add ('    f' + GetProp (I) + ': ' +
      GetType (I) + ';');
```

Obviously, we'll only generate this code if the user supplies a name for this property.

The next step is to add the declaration of the property's access methods, which you should place in the class's protected section:

```
// add get functions and set procedures
Add ('  protected');
Add ('    {set and get methods}');
for I := 1 to TotProps do
begin
  if GetRead (I) <> '' then
    Add ('    function ' + GetRead (I) +
      ': ' + GetType (I) + ';');
  if GetWrite (I) <> '' then
    Add ('    procedure ' + GetWrite (I) +
      '(Value: ' + GetType (I) + ');');
end;
```

Again, you'll notice that we use the property type as the return type for the access function and as the parameter for the access procedure.

Next, we add the property definitions (built with the code above) either in the `public` or in the `published` section, depending on the value returned by the `GetAccess` method. We also add the declaration of the constructor to the `public` section:

```
// add public and published properties,
// plus the constructor
Add ('  public');
for I := 1 to TotProps do
  if (GetProp (I) <> '') and
    (GetAccess (I) = 'public') then
      Add ('    ' + PropertyDefinition (I));
Add ('    constructor Create (AOwner: TComponent); override;');
Add ('  published');
for I := 1 to TotProps do
  if (GetProp (I) <> '') and
    (GetAccess (I) = 'published') then
      Add ('    ' + PropertyDefinition (I));
```

With the property definitions in place, the class declaration for the new component is now complete. Unfortunately, we're not done yet. Now we need to provide skeletons of the class's methods. However, before we can do this, we need to add a few more lines to terminate the class declaration with an end statement, add the `Register` procedure, and indicate the beginning of the `implementation` section of the unit. We follow this code with the body of the constructor:

```
Add ('  end;');
Add ('');
Add ('procedure Register;');
Add ('');
Add ('implementation');
Add ('');

// constructor
Add ('constructor ' + EditClassName.Text +
  '.Create (AOwner: TComponent);');
Add ('begin');
Add ('  inherited Create (AOwner);');
Add ('  // set default values');
for I := 1 to TotProps do
```

```
if (GetProp (I) <> '') and (GetDefault (I) <> '') then
  Add ('  f' + GetProp (I) + ' := ' + GetDefault (I) + ';');
Add ('end;');
Add ('');
```

The constructor is necessary whenever we need to set default values for the properties; and in fact, we generate code to provide an assignment for each of them.
This is both an important reminder and a way to write less code. However, at
times you may find that the initialization code will require manual revisions.

Now we're ready to add the implementation of each property's access methods. Although you'll certainly need to customize these methods, having the
default code outline will certainly help. In addition, you'll notice that in the Set
procedures we check to see if the new value is different from the current one. This
is a convention for Set methods, but one that's easy to forget. The Set procedures
also provide a commented-out call to the Invalidate method as a side effect:

```
// rough code of the functions
Add ('{property access functions}');
Add ('');
for I := 1 to TotProps do
begin
  if GetRead (I) <> '' then
  begin
    Add ('function ' + EditClassName.Text + '.' +
      GetRead (I) + ': ' + GetType (I) + ';');
    Add ('begin');
    Add ('  Result := f' + GetProp (I) + ';');
    Add ('end;');
    Add ('');
  end;
  if GetWrite (I) <> '' then
  begin
    Add ('procedure ' + EditClassName.Text + '.' +
      GetWrite (I) + '(Value: ' + GetType (I) + ');');
    Add ('begin');
    Add ('  if Value <> f' + GetProp (I) + ' then');
    Add ('  begin');
    Add ('    f' + GetProp (I) + ' := Value;');
    Add ('    // to do: add side effect as: Invalidate;');
    Add ('  end;');
    Add ('end;');
    Add ('');
```

```
      end;
   end;
```

At the end, we register our component in the `Register` procedure, and end the unit properly:

```
      Add ('{registration procedure}');
      Add ('');
      Add ('procedure Register;');
      Add ('begin');
      Add ('  RegisterComponents (''' + ComboPage.Text +
         ''', [' + EditClassName.Text + ']);');
      Add ('end;');
      Add ('');
      Add ('end.');
   end;
end;
```

You can see an example of the generated code in the memo component in Figure 14.11. On the *Preview* page you'll notice that there's a *Generate* button. When you click this button, the program asks you to select a directory for the new file and then saves the file (as long as a file with that name isn't already there):

```
procedure TCompWizForm.BitBtnGenerateClick(Sender: TObject);
var
  Directory, Filename: string;
begin
  if SelectDirectory (Directory,
      [sdAllowCreate, sdPerformCreate, sdPrompt], 0) then
  begin
    Filename := Directory + '\' +
      EditUnitName.Text + '.pas'
    // check whether the file already exists
    if not FileExists (Filename) then
      // save the file
      MemoPreview.Lines.SaveToFile (Filename)
    else
      MessageDlg ('The file ' + Filename +
        ' already exists'#13#13 +
        'Choose a new unit name in the Main page'#13 +
        'or select a new directory for the file',
        mtError, [mbOK], 0);
  end;
end;
```

FIGURE 14.11:

An example of the code generated by the Extended Component Wizard in the *Preview* page of the wizard itself

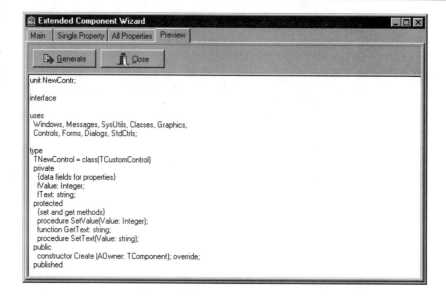

The result of this program is the generation of a new component source file. Once you've saved this file you can exit the program and return to Delphi. From there you can load the file, edit the source code, check the syntax, and then install the new component. Naturally, we could automate some of these steps with a wizard.

Converting the Stand-Alone Code Generator into a Wizard

As it turned out, writing our code generator as a stand-alone program made debugging it much easier. At any point in the long development process, we could simply run the program to see if everything was working correctly. Once we had the program working, we decided to keep the stand-alone version working instead of abandoning it to create the wizard version. The most common approach to building both a stand-alone program and a wizard from the same source code is to use conditional compilation (that is, use compiler variables to determine which version to build). However, in this case, we found a way to avoid that nuisance.

Although we might have been able to keep the wizard code separate from the stand-alone program code, we instead decided to add the wizard classes and the

`Register` procedure to the source code file that contains the new component wizard form. When you compile this as a stand-alone program, the compiler generates the classes and the procedure, but since the program doesn't use that code, it's harmless:

```
type
  // standard wizard
  TExtCompExp = class (TIExpert)
  public
    function GetStyle: TExpertStyle; override;
    function GetName: string; override;
    function GetAuthor: string; override;
    function GetComment: string; override;
    function GetPage: string; override;
    function GetGlyph: HICON; override;
    function GetState: TExpertState; override;
    function GetIDString: string; override;
    function GetMenuText: string; override;
    procedure Execute; override;
  end;

  // project wizard
  TPrjExtCompExp = class (TExtCompExp)
  public
    function GetStyle: TExpertStyle; override;
    function GetName: string; override;
    function GetIDString: string; override;
  end;

procedure Register;
```

The declarations look fairly normal, except for the fact that we've declared two classes—one to implement the wizard as a project wizard, and another to implement it as a standard wizard. The implementation of these methods is very simple, so we won't provide full listings. Just remember to give the two wizards different identifier strings, names, and the appropriate styles.

Following the standard approach, we decided to add the new wizard to the *Projects* page:

```
function TExtCompExp.GetPage: string;
begin
  Result := 'Projects';
end;
```

You can see the resulting effect (including the wizard's icon) in Figure 14.12. When you execute this wizard, it closes the current project (prompting the user to save any changes or to cancel), and then simply creates and shows the form:

```
procedure TExtCompExp.Execute;
begin
  // try closing the project
  if ToolServices.CloseProject then
  begin
    CompWizForm := TCompWizForm.Create (Application);
    try
      CompWizForm.ShowModal;
    finally
      CompWizForm.Free;
    end;
  end;
end;
```

FIGURE 14.12:

The icon of the Extended Component Wizard in the Object Repository

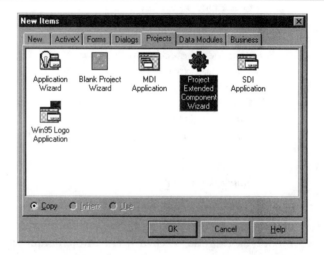

Since this is a modal form, we need to set the ModalResult property to close it. Here's the code of the OnClick event handler for the two Close buttons (one is on the first page, the other on the last):

```
procedure TCompWizForm.BitBtnCloseClick(Sender: TObject);
begin
  // alternative code (modal wizard form - main window)
  if MessageDlg ('Are you sure you want to quit the'#13 +
    'Extended Component Expert, losing your work?',
```

```
      mtConfirmation, [mbYes, mbNo], 0) = mrYes then
   begin
      ModalResult := mrCancel;
      Close;
   end;
end;
```

Since the user may be displaying this form either as the main form of a stand-alone program or as the modal form of a wizard, this method closes the form *and* sets the ModalResult property. As a result, the code will work for both cases.

We've already set the mrOK value for the Generate button's ModalResult property, even though the stand-alone program ignores this value. However, we need to update this method so that it opens the source file in Delphi as a new project after the wizard saves the file to disk. Here's the new code for the BitBtnGenerateClick method:

```
// special code for the wizard
if ToolServices <> nil then
   // open the component file as a project
   ToolServices.OpenProject (Filename);
```

By checking the value of the ToolServices global object, we can determine whether the form is running as part of a Delphi wizard or is part of a stand-alone program. It's good to perform this safety check in a wizard anyway (to make sure that the ToolServices object is available—as it should be), so the code is unnecessary only for the stand-alone program.

The only other change from the stand-alone version is in the FormCreate method. As you may know, a wizard can use the ToolServices global object to access the list of installed components. This means that we can use this capability to fill the combo box that displays the base classes. In addition to using the GetModuleCount, GetComponentCount, and GetComponentName methods (which are easy to understand once you know that there's a list of components for each installed module), the program iterates the base classes, using a while loop similar to the one we used in Chapter 2 to build the tree of the classes.

TIP
An important difference from the example in Chapter 2 is that we can now use the ToolServices object to retrieve the list of available classes without hard-coding them directly into our program. This is possible only because we're building a wizard. It might be interesting to integrate these two programs and create a VCL tree wizard.

Here's the new code for the FormCreate method of the Component Wizard form:

```
if ToolServices <> nil then
begin
  // get the list of installed components
  // plus their parent classes
  for nMod := 0 to
      ToolServices.GetModuleCount - 1 do
    for nComp := 0 to
        ToolServices.GetComponentCount (nMod) - 1 do
      begin
        ComboParentClass.Items.Add (
          ToolServices.GetComponentName (nMod, nComp));
        try
          CompClass := FindClass (ToolServices.
            GetComponentName (nMod, nComp)).ClassParent;
          while (CompClass <> TComponent) and
            (ComboParentClass.Items.IndexOf (
              CompClass.ClassName) = -1) do
          begin
            ComboParentClass.Items.Add (
              CompClass.ClassName);
            CompClass := CompClass.ClassParent;
          end;
        except on E: Exception do
          ShowMessage (E.Message);
        end;
      end;
end;
```

This ends our development of an extended Component Wizard. Although the program is far from perfect, it's already a handy tool that you can use when you're creating a new component. Unfortunately, you can't use this wizard to add properties to an existing component. In other words, if you've derived a TMyButton class from TButton, you won't be able to add new properties to that class without deriving yet another class from it. If you need to add several properties, you can create a new temporary component with those properties, and then copy the source code to the existing component's source file.

Writing Form Wizards

As we've just seen, generating a Pascal source file and opening it as a project is quite simple. What's not so easy is to add a new form to an existing project. In this section, we'll see how to accomplish that in two steps. First, we'll build a simple but useful program to create a custom form that contains a string grid. Afterwards, we'll turn the stand-alone program into a wizard. The rationale behind this program is that you cannot set the strings for the cells of a string grid at design-time (the Cells property is not published). Our wizard solves this problem by letting you edit the strings of the cells visually, and then generating the appropriate Pascal source code to initialize the cell strings during form creation.

The wizard also makes it simple to select bitmaps for the toolbar speed buttons. You can choose a new bitmap by simply clicking the button on the result form.

The Grid Form Wizard

The main form of this wizard is very simple. In fact, most of the editing operations take place on the temporary result form. As you can see in Figure 14.13, the main form contains just a few Edit components, three of which are connected to the corresponding UpDown components. (We've disabled the first Edit component since it displays the form's Name, an attribute that the user of this wizard is not supposed to change.)

NOTE   Refer to Chapter 2 for an in-depth discussion of the role of the Name property in the VCL.

FIGURE 14.13:

The main form of the
Grid Form Wizard

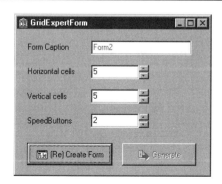

Once the user has selected the number of rows, columns, and speed buttons for the grid form, they can click the *(Re) Create Form* button to generate the form files. As its caption implies, this button will create the new grid form and delete the current form (if one exists). Since we need to reference this form from the main form's unit, we declared the ResultForm global variable in the main form's unit, and not in the unit that defines the TResultForm class, as usual.

The BtnCreateClick method frees the current form (if it exists), creates a new form, and then sets some properties of the StringGrid component and generates the speed buttons. Here's the code:

```
procedure TGridExpertForm.BtnCreateClick(Sender: TObject);
var
  I: Integer;
  SpeedButton: TSpeedButton;
begin
  if Assigned (ResultForm) then
  begin
    ResultForm.Free;
    ResultForm := nil;
  end;
  // create the new form...
  ResultForm := TResultForm.Create (Application);
  ResultForm.Caption := EditCaption.Text;
  for I := 1 to UpDownBtns.Position do
  begin
    SpeedButton := TSpeedButton.Create (ResultForm);
    SpeedButton.Parent := ResultForm.Panel1;
    SpeedButton.Name := 'SpeedButton' + IntToStr (I);
    SpeedButton.Left := 8 + (I - 1) * SpeedButton.Width;
    SpeedButton.Top := 8;
    SpeedButton.OnClick := ResultForm.SpeedClick;
  end;
  ResultForm.Show;
  BtnSave.Enabled := True;
end;
```

The rest of the properties for the components of the result form are static, as you can see in the following (abbreviated) form description:

```
object ResultForm: TResultForm
  OnCreate = FormCreate
  object StringGrid1: TStringGrid
```

```
        Align = alClient
        FixedCols = 0
        FixedRows = 0
        Options = [goFixedVertLine, goFixedHorzLine,
          goVertLine, goHorzLine, goRangeSelect,
          goColSizing, goEditing, goTabs,
          goAlwaysShowEditor]
    end
    object Panel1: TPanel
      Align = alTop
      BevelOuter = bvLowered
    end
  end
end
```

You can see an example of a generated form, after some editing operations, in Figure 14.14. This form has a dummy OnCreate event handler, with a comment used to prevent the Delphi environment from automatically removing the method:

```
procedure TResultForm.FormCreate(Sender: TObject);
begin
  // dummy code
end;
```

We've defined this event handler automatically (instead of waiting for the user to create it) because we'll need it to initialize the cells of the StringGrid. In addition, it's simpler to define this method when we're generating the form files than when the user starts interacting with them.

FIGURE 14.14:

An example of the form generated by the Grid Form Wizard while a user is editing it in the wizard itself

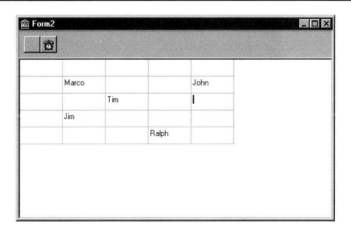

As you can see from the form description above, the StringGrid is fully editable from the wizard (since the wizard is executing the grid form in run-time fashion), and this allows the user to enter various strings in this preview of the resulting form. Similarly, the user can click on a SpeedButton to choose a bitmap for that button's Glyph property. When the user clicks on one of the SpeedButton components, the wizard will execute the following method, which we associate with the buttons as we create them (based on the number of SpeedButton components the user specified on the grid form). This method is a bit unusual in that we're defining the form class without knowing in advance how many SpeedButton components (if any) the user will place on the grid form. We'll assign the SpeedClick method to the SpeedButton component's OnClick event handler in the BtnCreateClick method we showed earlier. Here's the code we'll use to choose a bitmap from a file:

```
procedure TResultForm.SpeedClick(Sender: TObject);
var
  OpenDlg: TOpenDialog;
begin
  OpenDlg := TOpenDialog.Create (nil);
  try
    OpenDlg.Filter :=
      'Bitmap file (*.bmp)|*.bmp|Any file (*.*)|*.*';
    if OpenDlg.Execute then
      with (Sender as TSpeedButton) do
      begin
        Glyph.LoadFromFile (OpenDlg.Filename);
        if (Glyph.Width mod Glyph.Height) = 0 then
          NumGlyphs := Glyph.Width div Glyph.Height;
      end;
  finally
    OpenDlg.Free;
  end;
end;
```

In this method, you'll notice that after we load the button's bitmap we set the NumGlyphs property only if the width of the bitmap is an exact multiple of its height. If it is, we set the property to the ratio of the two values. The standard button bitmaps in the Images\Buttons subdirectory work perfectly with this code.

Generating the Grid Form and Source Code

When users finish editing the grid cell text and specifying bitmaps for the buttons, they can use the main form's Generate button to generate the form's code. As you might have guessed, this implies that we'll generate Pascal source code and a form description file.

The first decision we need to make is where to save the files we generate. We'll need to make these files available to the wizard (and therefore to the user's project), but in the meantime, we also needed to check these files in a debug project that tests the wizard forms. As we did with the previous wizard, we can make the two wizard forms part of a simple project (see the file ExpGridDebug.DPR in the ExpGrid directory on the companion disk). You can compile and run this project to experiment with this wizard prior to installing it.

During the debugging process, we added two Memo components to the main form as a means of previewing the output. As we'll see in a moment, these components also provide a convenient way to store the data we're generating. At design-time (or if you execute these forms as a wizard), the Memo components are invisible because we've set their height and width properties to zero. (Interestingly, you must set the WordWrap property to False for them to work at this size.) In contrast, if you execute these forms as part of the debugging project, we'll resize them (and the form) to make their text visible.

Another reason we decided to keep the Memo components on the main form (at zero size) is that we generate code in the BtnSaveClick method of the main form, but we'll still need to edit it later. Although we could have edited the text in memory (using memory streams) we found that it was much easier to use the Memo component to store the code text.

Here, then, is the first section of the BtnSaveClick method, which generates the Pascal source code. You'll notice that we've added calls to the Memo component's BeginUpdate and EndUpdate methods, to prevent the Memo component from updating its output until we finish adding the text. This technique yields good performance (and avoids flickering) when you need to add several lines of text to a Memo component.

```
procedure TGridExpertForm.BtnSaveClick(Sender: TObject);
var
  I, J: Integer;
begin
  {copy the unit source code in the first memo}
```

```
with MemoSource.Lines do
begin
  Clear;
  BeginUpdate;
  Add ('unit UnitName; // to be filled');
  Add ('');
  Add ('interface');
  Add ('');
  Add ('uses');
  Add ('  SysUtils, WinTypes, WinProcs, Messages, Classes,');
  Add ('  Graphics, Controls, Forms, Dialogs, ExtCtrls;');
  Add ('');
  Add ('type');
  Add ('  T' + ResultForm.Caption + ' = class (TForm)');

  // add each component
  for I := 0 to ResultForm.ComponentCount - 1 do
    Add ('    ' + ResultForm.Components[I].Name +
      ': ' + ResultForm.Components[I].ClassName + ';');
  Add ('    procedure FormCreate(Sender: TObject);');
  Add ('  private');
  Add ('    { Private declarations }');
  Add ('  public');
  Add ('    { Public declarations }');
  Add ('  end;');
  Add ('');
  Add ('var');
  Add ('  '+ ResultForm.Caption +
    ': T' + ResultForm.Caption + ';');
  Add ('');
  Add ('implementation');
  Add ('');
  Add ('{$R *.DFM}');
  Add ('');
  Add ('procedure T' + ResultForm.Caption +
    '.FormCreate(Sender: TObject);');
  Add ('begin');
  Add ('{initialize the string grid items}');
  Add ('  with StringGrid1 do');
  Add ('  begin');

  // add the initialization code
```

```
with ResultForm.StringGrid1 do
  for I := 0 to ColCount - 1 do
    for J := 0 to RowCount - 1 do
      if Cells [I, J] <> '' then
        Add (Format ('   Cells [%d, %d] := ''%s'';',
          [I, J, Cells [I, J]]));
  Add ('  end;');
  Add ('end;');
  Add ('');
  Add ('end.');
  EndUpdate;
end;
```

There are only two points of this method that do something unusual. The first is the loop we use to generate a corresponding field for each component of the form. In particular, you'll notice that we use the Name and ClassName properties to retrieve the appropriate information for the field declarations. The second new element is the set of nested loops that we use to add an assignment statement to the FormCreate method for each grid cell that's not empty.

The next section of the method generates the form description. As you can see in the code below, we copy the text of the form description to the MemoForm. In fact, we obtain this information by saving the form data to a memory stream (via the WriteComponentRes method) and then convert this stream into the textual description (via the global ObjectResourceToText procedure). Since this code is very similar to the StrComp example in Chapter 3, we won't explain it in detail.

```
var
  StrBin, StrTxt: TMemoryStream;
begin
  ...
  // remove the speed button events
  for I := 0 to ResultForm.ComponentCount - 1 do
    if ResultForm.Components [I] is TSpeedButton then
      TSpeedButton (ResultForm.Components [I]).
        OnClick := nil;

  {copy the form's textual description to the second memo}
  StrBin := TMemoryStream.Create;
  StrTxt := TMemoryStream.Create;
  try
    // write the form to a memory stream
```

```
StrBin.WriteComponentRes (
  ResultForm.Name, ResultForm);
// go back the beginning
StrBin.Position := 0;
// convert the form to text
ObjectResourceToText (StrBin, StrTxt);
// go back to the beginning
StrTxt.Position := 0;
// load the text
MemoForm.Lines.LoadFromStream (StrTxt);
```

Before we save the form to the stream, we must disable the SpeedButton events by setting them to nil. You'll recall that we use the OnClick event to set a button's Glyph property. Obviously, we don't want the old event handler to show up in the resulting code or properties, particularly since any event assignments will appear in the form description file. (Why do we need to save the form description file? We'll discuss that complex topic later in this chapter.)

After we generate the source and form description files, we can free the form and set its variable to nil. This will facilitate recreating the form properly the next time we perform the if Assigned(ResultForm) test. In fact, ResultForm is a global variable in the unit, and will become global to the VCL library once we install this wizard. For this reason, we have to preserve a correct value between different wizard sessions:

```
// delete the form
ResultForm.Free;
ResultForm := nil;
finally
  StrBin.Free;
  StrTxt.Free;
end;

// close the wizard form,
// skipping the confirmation message
OnClose := nil;
ModalResult := mrOk;
end;
```

The reason we set the OnClose event to nil is that we want to prevent the confirmation message the wizard displays (by default) when the user exits prematurely:

```
procedure TGridExpertForm.FormClose(Sender: TObject;
  var Action: TCloseAction);
```

```
begin
  if MessageDlg ('Do you want to quit the Grid Expert?',
    mtConfirmation, [mbYes, mbNo], 0) = idYes then
  begin
    ResultForm.Free;
    ResultForm := nil;
  end
  else
    Action := caNone;
end;
```

Debugging the Wizard

Unlike our last wizard, this wizard will reside in a different file than its main form. However, this form and the result form are also part of a project that you can use to debug the code and form-generation portion of the wizard.

The debug project includes the two forms, and also uses some special initialization code that makes the Memo components visible. To do this we need to resize the form (to allow some space for the Memo components), and then set the size and position of the Memo components. Since we don't want to affect the normal form operation with the code that resizes the Memo components (and we also want to avoid conditional compilation), we can place this code in the project source file. (Since the debugging project's source code isn't part of the wizard source, the resizing code has no effect on the wizard.) Here's the complete listing for the debugging project's source file:

```
program ExpGridDebug;

uses
  Forms,
  ExpGForm in 'ExpGForm.pas' {GridExpertForm},
  ExpGResF in 'ExpGResF.pas' {ResultForm};

{$R *.RES}

begin
  Application.Initialize;
  Application.CreateForm(TGridExpertForm, GridExpertForm);
  with GridExpertForm do
    Width := Width * 2;
  with GridExpertForm.MemoSource do
```

```
  begin
    Top := 0;
    Left := GridExpertForm.ClientWidth div 2;
    Width := GridExpertForm.ClientWidth div 2;
    Height := GridExpertForm.ClientHeight div 2;
  end;
  with GridExpertForm.MemoForm do
  begin
    Top := GridExpertForm.ClientHeight div 2;
    Left := GridExpertForm.ClientWidth div 2;
    Width := GridExpertForm.ClientWidth div 2;
    Height := GridExpertForm.ClientHeight div 2;
  end;
  Application.Run;
end.
```

It might seem strange to see this code in the project's source file, but there isn't a good reason to *not* do this. The advantage is that we won't have to change the source code of the debugging project's form to create the wizard.

If you run this debugging project, create a grid form, and then generate its code, you'll see the source code appear in the top Memo component, and the form description appear in the bottom one, as shown in Figure 14.15. By examining the contents of the two Memo components, we were able to fine-tune the code that we generated.

FIGURE 14.15:

Running the
GridExpDebug
example

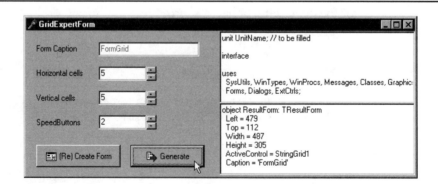

The Wizard Code

Now we can focus our attention on the wizard, which consists of two classes. As before, we want to create a standard wizard (which appears as a menu item under the Help menu), but we also want to make it available as a form wizard. Accordingly, we'll declare two classes (deriving the second from the first one and modifying some of the attributes). As usual, we've created a resource file that contains the icon and added it to the code using the $R directive. Here's the source code:

```
type
  TGridExpert = class (TIExpert)
  public
    function GetStyle: TExpertStyle; override;
    function GetName: string; override;
    function GetComment: string; override;
    function GetGlyph: HICON; override;
    function GetState: TExpertState; override;
    function GetIDString: string; override;
    function GetMenuText: string; override;
    function GetAuthor: string; override;
    function GetPage: string; override;
    procedure Execute; override;
  end;

  TGridFormExpert = class (TGridExpert)
  public
    function GetStyle: TExpertStyle; override;
    function GetName: string; override;
    function GetIDString: string; override;
  end;

{$R GRIDICON.RES}

function TGridExpert.GetStyle: TExpertStyle;
begin
  Result := esStandard;
end;
function TGridFormExpert.GetStyle: TExpertStyle;
begin
  Result := esForm;
end;

function TGridExpert.GetName: string;
begin
  Result := 'DDH Grid Wizard'
```

```
end;
function TGridFormExpert.GetName: string;
begin
  Result := 'DDH Grid Form Wizard'
end;

function TGridExpert.GetComment: string;
begin
  Result := 'String Grid Form Wizard';
end;

function TGridExpert.GetAuthor: string;
begin
  Result := 'Marco and Tim';
end;

function TGridExpert.GetGlyph: HICON;
begin
  Result := LoadIcon (HInstance,
    MakeIntResource ('GRIDFORM'));
end;

function TGridExpert.GetPage: string;
begin
  Result := 'Forms';
end;

function TGridExpert.GetState: TExpertState;
begin
  Result := [esEnabled];
end;

function TGridExpert.GetIDString: string;
begin
  Result := 'DDHandbook.GridStandardWizard'
end;
function TGridFormExpert.GetIDString: string;
begin
  Result := 'DDHandbook.GridFormWizard'
end;

function TGridExpert.GetMenuText: string;
```

```
begin
  Result := '&Grid Wizard...'
end;
```

As always with a Delphi wizard, the *important* element of the source code is the `Execute` method. Since this method is quite complex (and introduces some functions and classes we've not discussed yet), we need to explore two more topics before we examine it further.

ToolServices and the TIStream Classes

The ultimate purpose of our grid form wizard is to add a new form (and therefore its unit) to the current project. Fortunately, the `TIToolServices` class defines two methods that will simplify this task: `GetNewModuleName`, and `CreateModule`. The first method initializes two string parameters with the unit's unique unit identifier and its complete filename (including the path and the extension). In fact, Delphi uses this method to name new units (*Unit1*, *Unit2*, *Unit3*, and so on). Generally, you'll want to name forms according to the same pattern, so if the unit name is *Unit2*, the form name should be *Form2*. Alternatively, you can use the new `GetNewModuleAndFileName` method in `ToolsServices`. In this example we've decided to stick with the older, more portable method.

> **WARNING** Occasionally, the `GetNewModuleName` method may work improperly, generating names beginning with *Unit1*, even if this name is already in use in the project. In particular, this seems to happen if you work on a project, close it, and then reopen it later. We could have fixed this problem by checking the returned name against the existing modules of the project, but since this error is not common (and programmers should give more meaningful names to units anyway), we decided not to.

The first part of the `Execute` method extracts the unit and then builds the corresponding form name:

```
var
  FormName, UnitIdent, UnitFileName: string;
begin
  ToolServices.GetNewModuleName (
    UnitIdent, UnitFileName);
  FormName := 'Form' + Copy (UnitIdent, 5,
    Length (UnitIdent) - 4);
```

Unless you want to store the source file immediately (something you should generally avoid), the full path is unnecessary.

In contrast, the effect of the CreateModule method is to add a new unit (or module) to the current project, or create a new stand-alone module (a source file that's not part of a project) if no project is active. This method has many parameters, as you can see from its declaration (extracted from the ToolIntf unit):

```
function CreateModule(const ModuleName: string;
  Source, Form: TIStream;
  CreateFlags: TCreateModuleFlags): Boolean;
  virtual; stdcall; abstract;
```

The four parameters relate to a module name (such as the one we've obtained from GetNewModuleName), two streams (one for the unit and one for the form description), and several flags. We'll discuss the flags in a moment. First, we must focus on an important detail: the source and form parameters are not TStream objects, but TIStream objects.

Surprisingly, Borland didn't derive the TIStream classes from the plain TStream classes, and the two classes are completely incompatible. However, the TIStream class is part of a hierarchy that's very similar to that of the TStream classes. For instance, in this hierarchy, you'll find the TIStream, TIMemoryStream, TIFileStream, and TVirtualStream classes. By examining the source code in the VirtIntf and IStream units, you'll soon realize that these classes are merely wrappers over the existing stream classes. Within this hierarchy, TIStream is an abstract class, and the other three classes implement its various methods.

For example, the TIMemoryStream class (the class we'll actually use in the grid wizard) declares three fields and two related properties:

```
type
  TIMemoryStream = class(TIStream)
  private
    FMemoryStream: TMemoryStream;
    FOwnStream: Boolean;
    FModifyTime: Longint;
  public
    constructor Create(AMemoryStream: TMemoryStream);
    destructor Destroy; override;
    function Read(var Buffer; Count: Longint): Longint; override;
    function Write(const Buffer; Count: Longint): Longint; override;
    function Seek(Offset: Longint; Origin: Word): Longint; override;
```

```
function GetModifyTime: Longint; override;
procedure SetModifyTime(Time: Longint); override;
property OwnStream: Boolean
  read FOwnStream write FOwnStream;
property MemoryStream: TMemoryStream
  read FMemoryStream;
end;
```

You'll notice that the class's constructor accepts a TMemoryStream parameter, which we'll later use to manipulate the stream. The class can even own the stream (as the OwnStream property indicates), and destroy it accordingly:

```
destructor TIMemoryStream.Destroy;
begin
  if FOwnStream then FMemoryStream.Free;
  inherited Destroy;
end;
```

This is important because the constructor doesn't copy the stream but instead refers to it (unless it's nil), as you can see in its code:

```
constructor TIMemoryStream.Create(AMemoryStream: TMemoryStream);
begin
  inherited Create;
  if AMemoryStream = nil then
    FMemoryStream := TMemoryStream.Create
  else
    FMemoryStream := AMemoryStream;
  FOwnStream := AMemoryStream = nil;
  FModifyTime := DateTimeToFileDate(Now);
end;
```

Creating a New Module

Now we know the basic steps to create the new module: Ask Delphi for a new module name and name the unit and the form accordingly; save the form and unit to corresponding streams (most often memory streams); create two TIStream objects wrapping the two streams; and finally, call the CreateModule method of ToolServices.

There's only one step in this process that raises a problem. Although we can easily give a unit any name we want, the same can't be said for specifying the form name and the form class name, which belong in the form description file. As you might have noticed in the Memo component's form description, shown in Figure 14.15, the form name that the `WriteComponentRes` method generates is for the design form (`ResultForm`), and not the one the user specifies. The class name this method produces depends on the form class we used to create the design form. Although we know the class name we'll want to use before we create the form, there's no way to add new Delphi classes at run-time!

The solution is fairly obvious: just as we can edit the first line of the source code Memo component to set the unit name, we can edit the first line of the form description Memo component to set the form name (and its class name). This is actually the primary reason we decided to use the two Memo components in the wizard (and not just for debugging). It's also the reason we chose to convert the form file to its textual description prior to creating the final form file. We could find no easier way to change the class name without converting this file, although we could have modified the information in memory instead of using the Memo components. (We'll discuss a more complex but more professional way later on in this section.)

Now that you know why we designed the wizard this way, here's the complete listing of the Grid Form Wizard's `Execute` method:

```
procedure TGridExpert.Execute;
var
  FormName, UnitIdent, UnitFileName: string;
  FormStream, FormTextStream, UnitStream: TMemoryStream;
  FormIStream, UnitIStream: TIMemoryStream;
begin
  ToolServices.GetNewModuleName (
    UnitIdent, UnitFileName);
  FormName := 'Form' + Copy (UnitIdent, 5,
    Length (UnitIdent) - 4);
  // create and show the main form
  GridExpertForm :=
    TGridExpertForm.Create (Application);
  try
    // set the result form caption
    GridExpertForm.EditCaption.Text := FormName;
    if GridExpertForm.ShowModal = idOK then
    begin
      // create the three memory streams
      FormStream := TMemoryStream.Create;
      FormTextStream := TMemoryStream.Create;
```

```
        UnitStream := TMemoryStream.Create;
        // set some naming details
        GridExpertForm.MemoSource.Lines [0] :=
          'unit ' + UnitIdent + ';';
        GridExpertForm.MemoForm.Lines [0] :=
          'object ' + FormName + ': T' + FormName;
        // save the two memos to streams
        GridExpertForm.MemoForm.Lines.SaveToStream (FormTextStream);
        GridExpertForm.MemoSource.Lines.SaveToStream (UnitStream);
        // convert the form stream
        FormTextStream.Position := 0;
        ObjectTextToResource (FormTextStream, FormStream);
        // reset the two streams (just in case)
        FormStream.Position := 0;
        UnitStream.Position := 0;
        // create the two interface streams
        FormIStream := TIMemoryStream.Create (FormStream);
        UnitIStream := TIMemoryStream.Create (UnitStream);
        // let them own the actual streams
        FormIStream.OwnStream := True;
        UnitIStream.OwnStream := True;
        // create the new module
        ToolServices.CreateModule (
          UnitFileName, UnitIStream, FormIStream,
          [cmAddToProject, cmShowSource, cmShowForm,
          cmUnnamed, cmMarkModified]);
        // free the temporary stream
        FormTextStream.Free;
      end;
    finally
      // free the main form
      GridExpertForm.Free;
    end;
  end;
```

At this point, the only aspect of this method we haven't discussed is the CreateModule and CreateModuleEx methods' CreateFlags parameter. Here's a description of each flag value, taken from the source code of the ToolIntf unit:

cmAddToProject: This specifies that we want to add the new module to the currently open project, if one exists. If a project isn't open, the new form will be a stand-alone form. We use this flag in the Grid Form Wizard.

cmShowSource and cmShowForm: The cmShowSource flag specifices that the IDE should display the source file in the topmost editor window, and cmShowForm tells it to display the form above the editor (if we're creating a new form). In this wizard, we use both flags.

cmNewUnit and cmNewForm: These flags specify that we want to create either a new blank unit or a new blank form, and then add it to the current project. If you specify either of these flags, the CreateModule method will ignore all the other parameters.

cmMainForm: This flag makes the new form (if you use it in conjunction with the cmAddToProject flag) the main form of the project. For example, Delphi's Database Form Wizard allows you to enable this flag via a check box. We're not using this in our example.

cmMarkModified and cmUnNamed: These flags determine the behavior of the environment when saving or closing this module. If you specify cmMark-Modified, Delphi marks the file, and automatically tries to save it upon closing. If you use the cmUnNamed flag, Delphi will prompt the user with the Save As dialog box the first time they attempt to save the file. If you're creating a new module, as we are in this example, you should use both flags. We prefer this approach because users can still close the file without saving it, and this leaves no remnants of the file on their hard disk. Similarly, users should have a chance to give each module a more reasonable and readable name than Unit1 or Unit2 without having to save a file twice.

cmExisting: This flag specifies that you want to create a module from an existing disk file (and is available only for the CreateModuleEx version, as described in the List Wizard example).

NOTE

Beginning with Delphi 2, the ToolServices class has defined an alternate version of the CreateModule method, named CreateModuleEx. This method accepts an additional parameter that indicates the base class form. This method is key to implementing visual form inheritance, because the base form class may not be TForm.

There's not much left to do except to install the wizard and begin using it. In Figure 14.16, you can see an example of the form added to a project by this wizard. As before, we'll register this wizard with two calls, one for each class:

```
procedure Register;
begin
```

```
      RegisterLibraryExpert(TGridExpert.Create);
      RegisterLibraryExpert(TGridFormExpert.Create);
  end;
```

The first call adds an item to the Help menu and the second one adds a new element to the Forms page of the Object Repository.

FIGURE 14.16:

An example of a form added to a project by the Grid Form Wizard

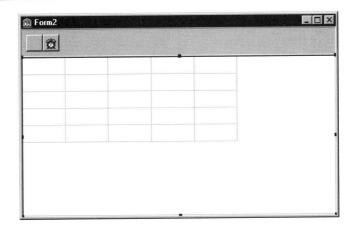

Proxy-Based Form Wizards

In the last example, we used a Memo component to store and edit a temporary version of the form's text description. We did this because we needed to create a form of a given class (TResultForm) and then change its class to a name determined by the wizard's user.

However, Delphi does this kind of thing frequently, and you can bet it doesn't patch a temporary file to do so. Instead, Delphi uses *proxies*, which allow you to dynamically modify the class information of an object. The only documentation you'll find in Delphi about this technique is the source code for the interface of the Proxies unit (available in the DOC directory):

```
procedure CreateSubClass(Instance: TObject;
  const ClassName: string; Ancestor: TClass);
procedure DestroySubClass(Instance: TObject);
procedure RenameSubClass(Instance: TObject;
```

```
    const ClassName: string);
  function GetSubClassInstance(Proxy: TClass): TObject;
  function CreateSubClassMethod(Instance: TObject;
    const MethodName: string): Pointer;
  procedure RenameSubClassMethod(Instance: TObject;
    Method: Pointer; const MethodName: string);
```

The two key routines (and the only two we'll use) are CreateSubClass and CreateSubClassMethod.

The first method transforms an object (the Instance) into an instance of the named class (ClassName), altering its base class (Ancestor) if necessary. It may not be apparent, but this technique allows you to create an object of a class you have not compiled!

CreateSubClassMethod allows you to go a step further and copy a method from a real class to a class that doesn't yet exist (and therefore to the transformed object), by simply supplying a method name. This allows you to assign event handlers to the object by associating nonexistent methods with an event (possibly of the nonexistent class). By *nonexistent* we're referring to the fact that classes and methods are not available yet, since we're working on an in-memory object that belongs to a class we haven't compiled.

As you might have assumed by now, this is exactly what Delphi does when you create a new form: Delphi copies the source code of class TForm1 to the editor, but you can already use an object of this "non-yet-compiled" class at design-time. When you compile the code and run the program, the form's class now exists, and the VCL will use it in place of the in-memory proxy object.

You can use the other routines in the Proxies unit to:

- Destroy the class information for the proxy object and restore the original class data (DestroySubClass).

- Change the class name of an existing proxy object (RenameSubClass) or method (RenameSubClassMethod).

- Get the address of the proxy object (GetSubClassInstance).

Delphi 1 defined a TProxy class that contains similar methods, but it's been replaced by this group of global procedures and functions.

> **TIP**
>
> The `TWinControl` class (in the Controls.PAS file) also defines a `CreateSubClass` method, which is completely unrelated. For this reason, you have to call the Proxies `CreateSubClass` method using the unit scope resolution format (listing the unit name and then the procedure or function reference) as in `Proxies.CreateSubClass`. If you don't do this, Delphi may attempt to call the `TWinControl` method instead of calling the proxy routine.

A Better Grid Form Wizard

As you've just seen, we can use a proxy class to manipulate the form before we save its resource description to a stream—and we can do this without using a Memo component to perform the class transformation. Since we don't need the form description Memo component at this point (we've already debugged the code that produces the form file), we decided to remove the Memo component that stores the Pascal source as well. However, this will be a problem because we used the Memo components to pass information from the grid form back to the wizard's `Execute` method.

In the revised ExpGridP example (the P stands for Proxy, and we've added it to every unit and class name), we resolve this by declaring two memory stream objects as part of the form class (in the public section). We then store the unit and form data in the streams, and then access the data from the wizard:

```
type
  TGridExpertPForm = class(TForm)
    ...
  public
    StrUnit, StrForm: TMemoryStream;
  end;
```

Besides adding the stream objects to the form class, we've also added another Edit component to the form to allow the user to name the unit. (Naturally, we've changed the attributes of the Edit components to allow the user to rename the form and the unit before they are generated.) Since this might produce strange errors if the user enters invalid names, we check the validity of these names (see the beginning of the next listing). This might not be foolproof, but it will probably catch most naming errors.

The BtnSaveClick method (executed in response to the Generate button's OnClick event) contains most of the changes for this version of the wizard. As you can see below, we prepare the source code using a new approach: we write the Pascal source into a single string, and then save the entire string to the StrUnit stream:

```pascal
procedure TGridExpertPForm.BtnSaveClick(Sender: TObject);
var
  I, J: Integer;
  S: String;
begin
  if not IsValidIdent (EditUnit.Text) or
    not IsValidIdent (ResultPForm.Caption) then
    raise Exception.Create ('Invalid form or unit name');

  StrUnit := TMemoryStream.Create;
  StrForm := TMemoryStream.Create;

  {copy the unit source code to a string, then to a stream}
  SetLength (S, 20000);
  S := 'unit ' + EditUnit.Text + ';'#13#13 +
    'interface'#13#13 +
    'uses'#13 +
    '  SysUtils, WinTypes, WinProcs, Messages, Classes,'#13 +
    '  Graphics, Controls, Forms, Dialogs, ExtCtrls;'#13#13 +
    'type'#13 +
    '  T' + ResultPForm.Caption + ' = class (TForm)'#13;

  // add each component
  for I := 0 to ResultPForm.ComponentCount - 1 do
    S := S + '    ' + ResultPForm.Components[I].Name +
      ': ' + ResultPForm.Components[I].ClassName + ';'#13;

  S := S +
    '    procedure FormCreate(Sender: TObject);'#13 +
    '  private'#13 +
    '    { Private declarations }'#13 +
    '  public'#13 +
    '    { Public declarations }'#13 +
    '  end;'#13#13 +
    'var'#13 +
    '  ' + ResultPForm.Caption + ': T' +
```

```
        ResultPForm.Caption + ';'#13#13 +
  'implementation'#13#13 +
  '{$R *.DFM}'#13#13 +
  'procedure T' + ResultPForm.Caption +
    '.FormCreate(Sender: TObject);'#13 +
  'begin'#13 +
  '{initialize the string grid items}'#13 +
  '  with StringGrid1 do'#13 +
  '  begin'#13;

  // add the initialization code
  with ResultForm.StringGrid1 do
    for I := 0 to ColCount - 1 do
      for J := 0 to RowCount - 1 do
        if Cells [I, J] <> '' then
          S := S + Format ('    Cells [%d, %d] := ''%s'';'#13,
            [I, J, Cells [I, J]]);

  S := S + '  end;'#13 +
  'end;'#13#13 +
  'end.'#13;

  // save the string to the stream
  StrUnit.WriteBuffer (Pointer(S)^, Length (S));
  StrUnit.Position := 0;
```

As we've mentioned before, we've used the proxy routines to modify the form's class and generate the form data. The code is not too complex, but this will force us to rebuild the FormCreate method in the proxy class.

Because the FormCreate method in the new proxy class doesn't exist, we have to create a new one. We'll copy the FormCreate method to the new class by setting the Data (the object the method is applied to) and the Code (the function address) fields of a TMethod record. One advantage to this approach is that we won't have to clear the SpeedButton components' event properties, since we'll lose the original event associations when we create the new proxy class. Here's the second part of the BtnSaveClick method:

```
var
  CreateMethod: TMethod;
begin
  ...
  {copy the form to the second stream}
```

```
// create a proxy
Proxies.CreateSubclass (ResultPForm,
  'T' + EditCaption.Text, TForm);
// change the name
ResultPForm.Name := EditCaption.Text;
// reinstall the event handler
CreateMethod.Code := CreateSubclassMethod (
  ResultPForm, 'FormCreate');
CreateMethod.Data := ResultPForm;
ResultPForm.OnCreate := TNotifyEvent (CreateMethod);
// write the form to a memory stream
StrForm.WriteComponentRes (
  EditCaption.Text, ResultPForm);
StrForm.Position := 0;

// delete the form
ResultPForm.Free;
ResultPForm := nil;

// close the wizard form,
// skipping the confirmation message
OnClose := nil;
ModalResult := mrOk;
end;
```

You'll notice that for both streams we must reset their position (by setting a value for the Position property or by calling the Seek method). If we don't do this, we won't be able to pass the streams to the ToolServices object's CreateModule method. Here's the new version of the Grid Form Expert's Execute method:

```
procedure TGridExpertP.Execute;
var
  FormName, UnitIdent, UnitFileName: string;
  FormIStream, UnitIStream: TIMemoryStream;
begin
  ToolServices.GetNewModuleName (
    UnitIdent, UnitFileName);
  FormName := 'Form' + Copy (UnitIdent, 5,
    Length (UnitIdent) - 4);
  // create and show the main form
  GridExpertPForm :=
    TGridExpertPForm.Create (Application);
  try
```

```
    // set the result form caption
    GridExpertPForm.EditCaption.Text := FormName;
    GridExpertPForm.EditUnit.Text := UnitIdent;
    if GridExpertPForm.ShowModal = idOK then
    begin
      // create the two interface streams
      FormIStream := TIMemoryStream.Create (
        GridExpertPForm.StrForm);
      UnitIStream := TIMemoryStream.Create (
        GridExpertPForm.StrUnit);
      // let them own the actual streams
      FormIStream.OwnStream := True;
      UnitIStream.OwnStream := True;
      // create the new module
      ToolServices.CreateModule (
        UnitFileName, UnitIStream, FormIStream,
        [cmAddToProject, cmShowSource, cmShowForm,
        cmUnnamed, cmMarkModified]);
    end;
  finally
    // free the main form
    GridExpertPForm.Free;
  end;
end;
```

Since we've modified all the unit names and class names (adding a *P* within each of them) you can install this wizard along with the previous version. The two wizards are actually both part of the package for this chapter. If you install the package and try using them, you'll see absolutely no difference at all. However, what happens behind the scenes is indeed different!

Using the Project Creator

Delphi 3 has added some new features related to wizards, in the form of project and module creators. Instead of simply opening a new project (as we did in the Blank Project Wizard, for example), you can use a project creator class to define many elements of the new project. Similarly, instead of using the CreateModule or CreateModuleEx methods you can use a module creator. Both of these new techniques are much more flexible than the older ones, and can be used to create very complex wizards (and other add-on tools). The documentation about the project and module creators is very limited, and these classes are not extensively commented in the source code files of the ToolsAPI directory.

To demonstrate these new techniques we've decided to adapt one of the existing examples. You may remember that the Blank Project Wizard had a problem we left unsolved: it defined a new file name for the project, and it did not create the file until a user saved it; but Delphi didn't ask for a new file name during the first save operation.

To solve this problem the wizard must indicate to Delphi that the project file doesn't really exist. This is something you cannot do with the plain OpenProject call of the ToolServices global object. Here's the updated source code of the blank wizard:

```
procedure TBlankExpert.Execute;
var
  DirName: string;
  I: Integer;
  BlankPrjCreator: TBlankPrjCreator;
begin
  // try closing the project
  if ToolServices.CloseProject and
    // try selecting a directory
    SelectDirectory (DirName,
      [sdAllowCreate, sdPerformCreate, sdPrompt], 0) then
  begin
    // look for a unique project name in the directory
    I := 1;
    while FileExists (DirName + '\Project' +
        IntToStr (I) + '.dpr') do
      Inc (I);
    // *** new code
    // open a project with that (unique) name
    BlankPrjCreator := TBlankPrjCreator.Create;
    try
      BlankPrjCreator.PrjName := 'Project' + IntToStr (I);
      BlankPrjCreator.FileName := DirName + '\Project' +
        IntToStr (I) + '.dpr';
      (ToolServices.ProjectCreate (
        BlankPrjCreator, [cpCanShowSource])).Free;
    finally
      BlankPrjCreator.Free;
```

```
        end;
      end;
    end;
```

The ProjectCreate method requires as parameters an instance of a project creator class (technically a subclass of TIProjectCreator), and it returns the interface of the new project module. Even if you don't want to use this module interface you should remember to free it, something the wizard does immediately by calling Free on the result of the ProjectCreate method.

> **NOTE** Module interfaces and other editor interfaces are introduced in the next chapter.

The TBlankPrjCreator class is a subclass of the TIProjectCreator, defined in the EditIntf unit of the ToolsAPI. This base class has several abstract methods you must override in the subclass:

```
type
  TBlankPrjCreator = class (TIProjectCreator)
  public
    FileName, PrjName: String;
    function Existing: Boolean; override;
    function GetFileName: string; override;
    function GetFileSystem: string; override;
    function NewProjectSource(
      const ProjectName: string): string; override;
    procedure NewDefaultModule; override;
    procedure NewProjectResource(
      Module: TIModuleInterface); override;
  end;
```

Here's a quick summary of the abstract methods:

Existing indicates whether the project already exists.

GetFileName returns the existing file name or the default one.

GetFileSystem allows you to use a virtual file system.

NewProjectSource allows you to define the complete source code of the new project in a string.

NewDefaultModule allows you to add new modules (forms or plain units) to the project.

NewProjectResource allows you to define custom resources for the project.

In our example, most of the methods either are empty or do something very simple. The only exception is the routine that creates the source code:

```
function TBlankPrjCreator.Existing: Boolean;
begin
  // the project file doesn't exist
  Result := False;
end;

function TBlankPrjCreator.GetFileName: string;
begin
  // the file name defined by the wizard
  Result := FileName;
end;

function TBlankPrjCreator.GetFileSystem: string;
begin
  // default
  Result := '';
end;

function TBlankPrjCreator.NewProjectSource(const ProjectName: string):
string;
begin
  // return the source code
  Result :=
    'program ' + PrjName + ';' + #13#10 +
    #13#10 +
    'uses' + #13#10 +
    '  Forms;' + #13#10 +
    #13#10 +
    '{$R *.RES}' + #13#10 +
    #13#10 +
    'begin' + #13#10 +
    '  Application.Initialize;' + #13#10 +
    '  Application.Run;' + #13#10 +
    'end.'+ #13#10;
end;
```

```
procedure TBlankPrjCreator.NewDefaultModule;
begin
  // no new modules
end;

procedure TBlankPrjCreator.NewProjectResource(
  Module: TIModuleInterface);
begin
  // must free the module passed as parameter
  Module.Free;
end;
```

This is only a very simple example of what you can do with a project creator. Module creators are even more powerful and complex to use, but we've found no real compelling reason to use this technique. What is important to note is that these creator classes are based on interfaces, and use the stdcall calling convention for the methods, which means you can implement them using a different programming language.

The PasToWeb Wizard

To finish this chapter we are going to show you a real-world wizard, something we've built for our own use in creating this book and its companion CD. Do you remember the PasToWeb example in Chapter 3? This program could convert a Pascal file into the corresponding HTML code, with full syntax highlighting. Of course, every Delphi project consists of several files. The advantage of using a wizard is that now we can gather from Delphi the information about the files for a given project and use them to create a single HTML file containing a short index and all the source code files.

The code of this wizard is not very different from all the others we've built in this chapter. What's new is the GetState method, which returns the enabled style if a project is currently open in the Delphi environment. The GetProjectName method of the ToolServices global object is used to make this test:

```
function TPrjToWebWizard.GetState: TExpertState;
begin
  if ToolServices.GetProjectName <> '' then
    Result := [esEnabled]
```

```
  else
    Result := [];
end;
```

As usual the core method is Execute, which simply asks for the copyright string, executes the CurrProjectToHTML function (which is a global function for the Convert unit), and then prompts the user to open the file in the default browser:

```
procedure TPrjToWebWizard.Execute;
var
  Copyr, ResFile: string;
begin
  Copyr := 'Source code copyright ...';
  if InputQuery ('PrjToWeb Wizard',
    'Enter Copyright notice:', Copyr) then
  begin
    ResFile := CurrProjectToHTML (Copyr);
    if MessageDlg ('HTML file generated.'#13 +
        'Do you want to open it in your browser?',
        mtConfirmation, [mbYes, mbNo], 0) = idYes then
      ShellExecute (ToolServices.GetParentHandle,
        'open', PChar (ResFile), '', '', sw_ShowNormal);
  end;
end;
```

At the heart of this wizard is the CurrProjectToHTML function, defined in the Convert unit. This function generates an HTML file using the project name and replacing its extension with the string _DPR.HTM (this file name is also returned by the function). After creating a generic HTML header, the function generates a list of the units and forms of the project. Each of the items of this list is actually a link to the name of the file, which is an internal name generated along with the file itself.

As a result, the HTML file of the project shows the list of the internal files (with the exclusion of a couple of special files), to be used as an index. You can see the effect in Figure 14.17.

The code of the CurrProjectToHTML function is quite long, but it's worth looking at two small excerpts: the code used to generate the list of units, and the code used to generate the portions of the HTML file for each unit. As usual, you can find the complete code on the companion CD:

```
// list of units...
for I := 0 to ToolServices.GetUnitCount - 1 do
```

FIGURE 14.17:

The HTML file generated by the PrjToWeb Wizard for a Delphi project

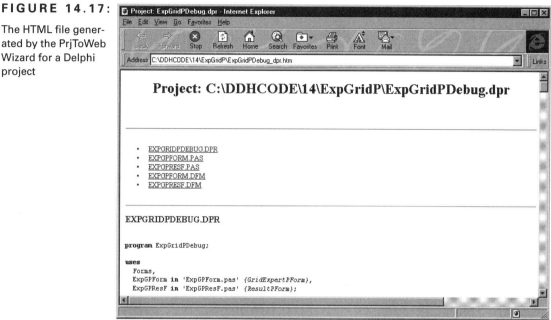

```
begin
  Ext := Uppercase (ExtractFileExt(
    ToolServices.GetUnitName(I)));
  FName := Uppercase (ExtractFilename (
    ToolServices.GetUnitName(I)));
  if (Ext <> '.RES') and (Ext <> '.DOF') then
    AppendStr (HTML, '<LI> <A HREF=#' + FName + '> ' +
      FName + '</A>'#13#10);
end;
// ...
// generate the HTML code for the units
for I := 0 to ToolServices.GetUnitCount - 1 do
begin
  Ext := Uppercase (ExtractFileExt(
    ToolServices.GetUnitName(I)));
  if (Ext <> '.RES') and (Ext <> '.DOF') then
  begin
    Source := TFileStream.Create (
      ToolServices.GetUnitName(I), fmOpenRead);
```

```
      Parser := THtmlParser.Create (Source, Dest);
      try
        Parser.Alone := False;
        Parser.Filename := ToolServices.GetUnitName(I);
        Parser.Convert;
      finally
        Parser.Free;
        Source.Free;
      end;
    end; // if
  end; // for
```

Along with the other examples in this chapter, the PrjToWeb Wizard is part of the DdhPk14 package on the companion CD. Of course you can easily move the three related source code files (PrjToWeb.PAS, Convert.PAS, and NewParse.PAS) to a different project to keep the wizard handy.

A slightly updated version of this wizard has been used to create the HTML version of the source code of this book, available in the each project's directory on the projects on the companion CD.

What's Next

Now that we've seen some complex examples of wizards, we're ready to move to a new topic—version control systems. In addition, we'll explore new capabilities that are available both for wizards and for normal Delphi applications, such as system notifications.

In fact, the next chapter also covers other techniques related to wizards, and shows how to modify the Delphi environment in unofficial ways. To obtain the necessary information, and to show some practical examples, we'll build a few more wizards.

We will also build some Delphi wizards related to database programming in Chapter 18. Keep in mind that every time you're doing a repetitive task in Delphi, you can write a wizard to do the work for you.

Other Delphi Extensions

- External Tools and Transfer Macros

- The Version Control System Interface

- Handling Delphi Notifications

- A Summary of the ToolsAPI

- Using Custom Design Modules

- "Hacking" the Delphi Environment

There are numerous ways to extend the Delphi environment. As we've seen in the previous three chapters, it's possible to extend Delphi's Object Inspector with custom property editors, extend the Form Designer with custom component editors, and extend the development environment with wizards. In addition to these three major techniques, there are many other ways to extend Delphi via the ToolsAPI, and by using other "unofficial" techniques.

In this chapter, we'll briefly explore the integration of generic external tools (a very simple but interesting technique), extend the Project Information Wizard we built in the last chapter, build a bare-bones Version Control System, create custom form designers, and finally explore some "unofficial" Delphi extensions.

External Tools and Transfer Macros

The easiest way to extend the Delphi environment is to add external applications to the Tools menu. There are several services available to external tools that, unfortunately, few Delphi programmers recognize and use.

When you install an external tool (by using the Tools ➤ Configure Tools menu command), you can use several *transfer macros* to specify the command-line parameters that Delphi will pass to that application, as you can see in Figure 15.1. Although these macros are not terribly powerful by themselves, you can use them in various combinations to automate many operations.

Specifically, the transfer macros allow you to supply the following types of command-line parameters to the tool you're activating:

- The name of the resulting executable file, provided you've already compiled the project (the $EXENAME macro).

- The name of the active file in the editor (the $EDNAME macro).

- The current text in the editor, or more precisely, the token closest to the cursor position (the $CURTOKEN macro).

- A parameter string to be entered by the user (the $PROMPT macro).

Other transfer macros allow you to extract the path, the filename, or the extension of a parameter (generally the editor or project file name, extracted using the above macros), or to save the current project's files before processing them with an external tool.

FIGURE 15.1:

Using transfer
macros in Delphi

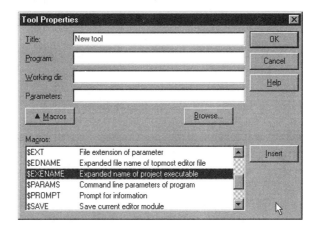

As a simple example, we can create a tool that displays the path of the current project. The external program is terribly simple: it displays in a dialog box the value passed as the command-line parameter. Below is the complete source code of the project (available in the PrjPath subdirectory on the companion disk):

```
program PrjPath;

uses
  Classes, Dialogs;

begin
  if ParamCount > 0 then
    ShowMessage (ParamStr (1))
  else
    ShowMessage ('No project active');
end.
```

We'll pass the path information to this external tool using a combination of two transfer macros. First, we need to create the new external tool. In the Tool Properties dialog box, enter the name of the compiled file in the Program field, and enter the following value for the Parameters field:

```
$PATH($EXENAME)
```

The effect of this tool is modest: when you select the new tool from the Tools menu, the message box shown here displays the current project's program path:

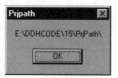

We built this example to emphasize a point about external tools: Programs that receive parameters from Delphi through transfer macros are easy to build, and yet they can be quite powerful. You could, for example, extend the PrjPath program to display a list of the files in the project directory, with detailed information about each source file.

The Version Control System Interface

A version control system (VCS for short) is a tool that can help several programmers work on a single project in an organized manner. Typically, such a tool keeps track of who changed a file and what changes occurred within each version, and it prevents two programmers from modifying a given file at the same time. The Client/Server Suite edition of Delphi ships with a limited version of Intersolv's PVCS source control software. Other tools are available, such as MKS's Source Integrity and the shareware ViCiouS originally developed by Bob Swart and now published by SureHand Software. (Evaluation versions of both are available on the companion CD.)

Professional version control systems are typically built upon the concept of storing the various files and revisions in a database. Some systems save just the changes to a file (such as added or deleted text), while others save the full content of the previous versions. This makes it possible to build several versions of a project with a given set of source files, but it also allows programmers to roll back changes to a more stable version in case of problems. More advanced systems can track different sets of changes and can integrate them.

Delphi's version control system interface is something of an alternative to the expert/wizard interface, but it works in a distinctive way, using the VCS Manager DLL. This results in two subtle differences between a Delphi VCS and a Delphi wizard. The first is that you can install only one VCS at a time, while you can install many wizards. Second, a Delphi VCS must reside in a DLL (you can't create a DCU-based VCS).

You can specify a preferred VCS by setting a Registry entry that identifies the filename of an appropriate DLL:

```
HKEY_CURRENT_USER\Software\Borland\Delphi\3.0\Version
Control\VCSManager
```

A more visible difference is that a VCS displays a pull-down menu, which can contain many items. This is much easier than adding menu items via one or more add-in wizards.

The TIVCSClient Interface

The ToolsAPI's VcsIntf unit defines the base class for Delphi's standard version control system interface. By default, this unit isn't part of the Delphi library, so you'll need to copy it into your project directory (and add it to the uses clause of the main form's source file). Here is the class declaration (which resembles the component editor interface class because of the GetVerbCount, GetVerb, and ExecuteVerb methods):

```
type
  TIVCSClient= class(TInterface)
    function GetIDString: string; virtual; stdcall; abstract;
    procedure ExecuteVerb(Index: Integer); virtual;
      stdcall; abstract;
    function GetMenuName: string; virtual; stdcall; abstract;
    function GetVerb(Index: Integer): string; virtual;
      stdcall; abstract;
    function GetVerbCount: Integer; virtual; stdcall; abstract;
    function GetVerbState(Index: Integer): Word; virtual;
      stdcall; abstract;
    procedure ProjectChange; virtual; stdcall; abstract;
  end;
```

This declares an abstract interface class, which is necessary whenever you implement a class in an external DLL. Accordingly, you simply build a DLL to create your own version control system. However, before we build a VCS, let's examine the TIVCSClient class's methods:

GetIDString: This method returns a unique identifier for the VCS client. We suggest using your company name followed by the VCS name.

GetMenuName: This method allows a VCS to specify its menu caption. This caption identifies a menu which will contain the Delphi VCS menu items. If there is no VCS menu, we simply return a new string. (If the menu name is empty, Delphi won't execute the three following methods).

GetVerbCount: This method returns the number of menu items in the VCS menu. If you return a blank string, Delphi creates a separator in the VCS menu.

GetVerbState: This method returns the state of a verb (menu item) as either vsEnabled or vsChecked. However, you'll notice that the data type is a word (not a specific set type), and that these two values are constants, not enumerated values. To return both flags at the same time you need to add their values.

ExecuteVerb: This method executes the action that corresponds to a given verb (determined by the Index parameter), when the user chooses a given menu item.

ProjectChange: Delphi calls this method whenever the state of the current project changes. This happens when the user opens or closes a project, and when the user adds a unit to the project or removes one from it. Creating a new project calls this method twice, since Delphi closes the current project before opening the new project. Delphi calls this method *after* changing the state of the project. For instance, if the user opens a project, Delphi calls this method when the project is active, but prior to opening any windows.

As with DLL wizards, to install a VCS you have to define a specific entry-point function in the DLL. Within this function you need to return a pointer to the newly created TIVCSClient object. This time, however, there is no need to call a registration function (since you can have only one VCS at a time). Here is the declaration of the entry-point function:

```
TVCSManagerInitProc = function (
    VCSInterface: TIToolServices): TIVCSClient stdcall;
```

When Delphi calls this function, it passes the global ToolServices object as the only parameter.

Project Information in a VCS

We can now start building our own VCS. Actually, we'll start using the VCS interface to build a tool that is not a true VCS. The code will be quite simple, but we'll still be able to create a program that does something meaningful.

In this last chapter, we built a project information wizard. The main form of our simple VCS tool is the same, and it displays the same information. However, here the form is modeless, so it can remain open while we work on the project. The VCS will receive notification for any change to the project, so we'll be able to update the window appropriately.

Here is the initial part of the DLL's source code. In the uses statement, you'll notice that we refer to the VcsIntf unit. However this unit isn't normally part of the VCL or standard libraries (and therefore isn't in the normal path), so you should add its path (C:\Program Files\Borland\Delphi 3\Source\ToolsAPI in the default installation) to the Search Path in the Project Options dialog box.

WARNING   The three VCS sample programs include the Delphi default path for the ToolsAPI source code directory. If you've installed the environment on a different drive or in a different directory (or if you are using a different version of Delphi), you should update the Search Path project option accordingly in order to recompile these programs.

```
library VcsPrj;

uses
  Sharemem, SysUtils, Classes, ExptIntf, Forms,
  ToolIntf, Dialogs, Windows, VcsIntf, VirtIntf,
  PrjForm in 'PrjForm.pas' {PrjInfoForm};

type
  TDdhProjectVcs = class (TIVCSClient)
  public
    function GetIDString: string; override;
    procedure ExecuteVerb(Index: Integer); override;
    function GetMenuName: string; override;
    function GetVerb(Index: Integer): string; override;
    function GetVerbCount: Integer; override;
    function GetVerbState(Index: Integer): Word; override;
    procedure ProjectChange; override;
    destructor Destroy; override;
  end;
```

Next comes the source code of the various methods. Most of these methods are quite simple and require no further explanation. The only moderately complex code is in the GetVerbState and ExecuteVerb methods. GetVerbState will enable the VCS menu items only if a project is active (except for the About menu item, which is always enabled). The ExecuteVerb method updates and displays the VCS form, which contains the project information.

```
function TDdhProjectVcs.GetIDString: string;
begin
  Result := 'DDHandbook.DDHProjectVCS';
end;

function TDdhProjectVcs.GetMenuName: string;
begin
  Result := 'DHH Project VCS';
end;

function TDdhProjectVcs.GetVerbCount: Integer;
begin
  Result := 3;
end;

function TDdhProjectVcs.GetVerb(Index: Integer): string;
begin
  case Index of
    0: Result := '&Project Information...';
    1: Result := ''; // separator
    2: Result := '&About DDH Project VCS...';
  end;
end;

function TDdhProjectVcs.GetVerbState(Index: Integer): Word;
begin
  // disable all but the last if no project is active
  if (ToolServices.GetProjectName <> '') or
     (Index = GetVerbCount - 1) then
    Result := vsEnabled
  else
    Result := 0;
end;

procedure TDdhProjectVcs.ExecuteVerb(Index: Integer);
begin
  case Index of
    0: try
         PrjInfoForm.UpdateTree;
```

```
      PrjInfoForm.Show;
   except
      ToolServices.RaiseException(ReleaseException);
   end;
  2: MessageDlg ('DDH Project Version Control System'#13#13 +
     'From the "Delphi Developer''s Handbook"'#13 +
     'by Marco Cantu and Tim Gooch',
     mtInformation, [mbOK], 0);
  end;
end;

procedure TDdhProjectVcs.ProjectChange;
begin
  PrjInfoForm.UpdateTree;
  {Application.MessageBox (PChar(
    'The project ' + ToolServices.GetProjectName +
    ' is changing'), 'DDH Project VCS', mb_OK);}
end;
```

The last method of the class, ProjectChange, simply calls the form's UpdateTree method to update the output of the project information form. To help you see when Delphi is calling this method, we also display a message box (we've disabled this code in the disk version). Unfortunately, this forces the user to close this message box fairly often (since the event occurs frequently).

Studying the code above, you might wonder when Delphi creates the project information form and when it destroys the form. We could have used a constructor and a destructor of the VCS class to illustrate this, but since we already have a VCS initialization function, we have used it to perform the form's creation. However, we've also created a destructor to perform the form's destruction. Here is the code of the destructor and of the initialization function:

```
destructor TDDHDemoVCS.Destroy;
begin
  PrjInfoForm.Free;
end;

function VCSInit (VCSInterface: TIToolServices): TIVCSClient; stdcall;
begin
  ToolServices := VCSInterface;
  Application.Handle := ToolServices.GetParentHandle;
  PrjInfoForm := TPrjInfoForm.Create (Application);
```

```
    Result := TDdhProjectVcs.Create;
end;

exports
  VCSInit name VCSManagerEntryPoint;
```

By the way, you'll notice that before returning the new VCS client object, the VCSInit function stores the ToolServices object and the handle of the Application object in the proper global variables, and then creates the output form.

> Be sure to notice the exports statement at the very end of the listing, which gives the entry function a specific, internal name. Delphi will use this name to locate and call the initialization function when you install this VCS DLL.

Now we're ready to install our new VCS into Delphi. To do so, simply launch RegEdit in Windows 95 or RegEdt32 in Windows NT, locate the Delphi 3.0 section, and edit or add the Version Control key, as specified earlier and shown in Figure 15.2. Then exit from Delphi (if it is open) and load it again to see the effect of the changes.

You'll see a new menu that contains a few items, as shown here:

If you want to test your VCS and modify it, we strongly suggest you copy and rename the DLL first (using a name such as VcsPrj1.DLL), and then reinstall the DLL under this new filename. Using this approach, you'll be able to compile the DLL. Windows won't let the Delphi compiler overwrite a DLL that's currently in use by Delphi itself! Using the same filename, you cannot simply update the VCS DLL without uninstalling and reinstalling it. (This is the same problem we have with DLL-based wizards.) By using a different filename, you can edit and recompile the DLL, exit from Delphi, delete the older DLL, rename the newly compiled one, and finally launch Delphi again.

FIGURE 15.2:

The information
added to the
Windows Registry
to activate the new
VCS DLL in the
Delphi environment

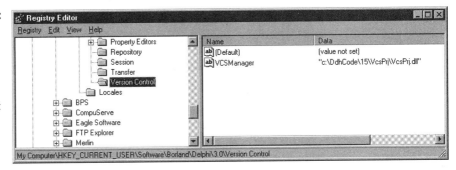

Handling Delphi Notifications

Our first VCS displayed the project information form we previously used in the
Project Wizard, with only a couple of minor changes. We updated this project
window each time the user changed the project, simply because the VCS interface
notifies us of a project change without telling us what happened.

To make the program more powerful—and to introduce another Delphi feature—
let's explore how we can handle Delphi file notifications via an *add-in notifier* object.
(This add-in notifier interface is available in any situation where you have access to
the global ToolServices object. Therefore, you can respond to Delphi notifications
in a VCS, a wizard, a component or property editor, and so on.)

To install an add-in notifier object in Delphi, you use the following
ToolServices method:

```
function AddNotifier(AddInNotifier: TIAddInNotifier):
  Boolean; virtual; stdcall; abstract;
```

The TIAddInNotifier class (the type of the first parameter) is quite simple, since
it declares only one method you should override:

```
type
  TIAddInNotifier = class(TInterface)
  public
    procedure FileNotification(NotifyCode: TFileNotification;
      const FileName: string; var Cancel: Boolean); virtual;
      stdcall; abstract;
    procedure EventNotification(NotifyCode: TEventNotification;
      var Cancel: Boolean); virtual; stdcall; abstract;
  end;
```

Whenever a file operation occurs, Delphi will call the `FileNotification` method. In the body of this method, you can access the filename and a notification code, as well as a Boolean reference parameter that you can use to cancel the operation causing the notification. By examining the list of notification codes, you'll immediately recognize when Delphi might send a notification to the object:

```
TFileNotification = (fnFileOpening, fnFileOpened,
  fnFileClosing, fnProjectOpening, fnProjectOpened,
  fnProjectClosing, fnAddedToProject,
  fnRemovedFromProject, fnDefaultDesktopLoad,
  fnDefaultDesktopSave, fnProjectDesktopLoad,
  fnprojectDesktopSave);
```

When you compile the project, Delphi will call the `EventNotification` method twice, once before the compilation and once when it's done, as indicated by the `TEventNotification` enumeration type:

```
TEventNotification = (enBeforeCompile, enAfterCompile);
```

Using the first of these methods, we'll improve our project view a little, and build the capabilities into our next example, named VcsPrj2. First, we want to add an ImageList component to the form to display icons that indicate the status of the project files. In particular, we want to indicate whether a file is open or closed. After preparing some bitmaps, we've assigned them using the ImageList component editor. The next step is to link the images in the ImageList component to the TreeView component's `StateImages` property. We've defined the following constants to make it easier to associate various states with the corresponding image in the list:

```
const
  stOpen = 1;
  stClosed = 2;
  stNode = 4;
```

These constants are part of the form unit's interface, so we'll be able to use them in other units of the program.

Using these constants and the methods we've discussed so far, we can now rewrite the form's `UpdateAll` method, set the open or closed images for the units and forms, and then display the node image for the first-level nodes:

```
procedure TPrjInfoForm.UpdateTree;
var
  I, nTot: Integer;
  ChildNode: TTreeNode;
```

```delphi
    FileName: string;
begin
  if ToolServices.GetProjectName = '' then
    Caption := 'Project VCS'
  else
  begin
    Caption := 'Project VCS - ' +
      ExtractFileName (ToolServices.GetProjectName);
    with TreeView1.Items do
    begin
      Clear;
      BeginUpdate;
      // add units
      UnitsNode := AddChild (nil, 'Units');
      UnitsNode.StateIndex := stNode;
      nTot := ToolServices.GetUnitCount;
      for I := 0 to nTot - 1 do
      begin
        FileName := ToolServices.GetUnitName (I);
        ChildNode := AddChild (UnitsNode, FileName);
        if ToolServices.IsFileOpen (FileName) then
          ChildNode.StateIndex := stOpen
        else
          ChildNode.StateIndex := stClosed;
      end;
      // add forms
      FormsNode := AddChild (nil, 'Forms');
      FormsNode.StateIndex := stNode;
      nTot := ToolServices.GetFormCount;
      for I := 0 to nTot - 1 do
      begin
        FileName := ToolServices.GetFormName (I);
        ChildNode := AddChild (FormsNode, FileName);
        if ToolServices.IsFileOpen (FileName) then
          ChildNode.StateIndex := stOpen
        else
          ChildNode.StateIndex := stClosed;
      end;
      EndUpdate;
    end;
    TreeView1.FullExpand;
  end;
end;
```

Instead of calling this method whenever the project changes (which is fairly often), we want Delphi to do so only when we need to update the project's status. To accomplish this we must declare a new add-in notification class (and a corresponding global variable):

```
type
  TDDHPrjNotifier = class(TIAddInNotifier)
  public
    procedure FileNotification(NotifyCode: TFileNotification;
      const FileName: string; var Cancel: Boolean); override;
    procedure EventNotification(NotifyCode: TEventNotification;
      var Cancel: Boolean); override;
  end;
```

```
var
  PrjNotif: TDDHPrjNotifier;
```

As you might guess, when Delphi creates and installs a version control system DLL, it then also creates and installs the PrjNotif object. The two new statements appear in the middle of the function:

```
function VCSInit (VCSInterface: TIToolServices): TIVCSClient; stdcall;
begin
  Result := nil;
  try
    ToolServices := VCSInterface;
    Application.Handle := ToolServices.GetParentHandle;
    PrjNotif := TDDHPrjNotifier.Create;
    ToolServices.AddNotifier (PrjNotif);
    PrjInfoForm := TPrjInfoForm.Create (Application);
    Result := TDdhProjectVcs.Create;
  except
    ToolServices.RaiseException(ReleaseException);
  end;
end;
```

Delphi later removes and destroys the form and the notification object along with the VCS object:

```
destructor TDdhProjectVcs.Destroy;
begin
  PrjInfoForm.Free;
  ToolServices.RemoveNotifier (PrjNotif);
  PrjNotif.Free;
end;
```

The most interesting part of this class is the method that responds to notification commands, the FileNotification method:

```
procedure TDDHPrjNotifier.FileNotification (
  NotifyCode: TFileNotification;
  const FileName: string; var Cancel: Boolean);
var
  Node: TTreeNode;
begin
  try
    case NotifyCode of
      fnFileOpened:
      begin
        // set the proper icon
        Node := PrjInfoForm.FindNode (FileName);
        if Node <> nil then
          Node.StateIndex := stOpen;
      end;
      fnFileClosing:
      begin
        // set the proper icon
        Node := PrjInfoForm.FindNode (FileName);
        if Node <> nil then
          Node.StateIndex := stClosed;
      end;
      fnProjectOpened:
        PrjInfoForm.UpdateTree;
      fnProjectClosing:
      begin
        // empty and repaint the tree
        PrjInfoForm.TreeView1.Items.Clear;
        PrjInfoForm.TreeView1.Repaint;
      end;
      fnAddedToProject:
        PrjInfoForm.UpdateTree;
      fnRemovedFromProject:
        PrjInfoForm.UpdateTree;
    end;
  except
    ToolServices.RaiseException(ReleaseException);
  end;
end;
```

The two events we handle in a specific way are opening files and closing them. However, it's important for us to see if the node is currently in the TreeView, since the user might be opening or closing a file unrelated to the project.

We accomplish this by calling the FindNode function we added to the form class. This function simply scans the TreeView component for the requested item:

```
function TPrjInfoForm.FindNode (Text: string): TTreeNode;
var
  I: Integer;
begin
  Result := nil;
  for I := 0 to TreeView1.Items.Count - 1 do
    if TreeView1.Items [I].Text = Text then
    begin
      Result := TreeView1.Items [I];
      Exit;
    end;
end;
```

To make this form work well as a VCS wizard, we've made one more change: When the user selects a file, we confirm that it exists (on disk) before we try to activate it.

WARNING   If the user selects a DPR file, the corresponding project is reopened, not simply redisplayed in the current editor window.

If the file doesn't exist, we display an error message. (We supply our own error message simply for backward compatibility with Delphi 2, which displayed a cryptic internal error message when OpenFile was called with a nonexistent file. If all users of the VCS have Delphi 3, however, you could simply let Delphi display its default dialog box prompting to create the file.) Here is the code as we've implemented it:

```
procedure TPrjInfoForm.TreeView1DblClick(Sender: TObject);
begin
  if (TreeView1.Selected.Level = 1) and (
    (TreeView1.Selected.Parent.Text = 'Units') or
    (TreeView1.Selected.Parent.Text = 'Forms')) then
  begin
    if FileExists (TreeView1.Selected.Text) then
      ToolServices.OpenFile (TreeView1.Selected.Text)
```

```
    else
      MessageDlg ('The physical file still doesn''t exist',
        mtError, [mbOK], 0);
  end;
end;
```

The effect of this code is that our demo version control system now displays different bitmaps to show the user whether a file is open or closed. You can see an example of the output in Figure 15.3.

FIGURE 15.3:

The form of the VcsDemo2 example shows bitmaps to indicate the status of the various files, and keeps track of the operations of the user.

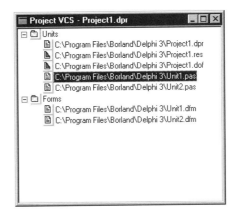

You'll notice that in this example you can simply double-click on a closed file (or close one that is open) to see its icon change, without having to refresh the whole tree. However, if you save a file with a new name, you'll have to close and reopen the window to refresh the status of the project, something we'll fix in the next (and last) version of the program.

Module Interfaces and Module Notifications

The file notifications we handled in the last example refer to the files of a project. Unfortunately, Delphi doesn't notify us for each and every action that takes place. For example, we don't know when the user has modified or saved a file. As you can imagine, this is something that might be helpful if you build a robust and powerful version control system, or if you create advanced Delphi wizards.

The ToolServices global object defines a couple of methods we haven't used yet: GetModuleInterface and GetFormModuleInterface. These two functions accept a filename parameter and return a TIModuleInterface object. This class is the interface to the Delphi editor and the form designer.

In the EditIntf unit of the ToolsAPI, you can find the following declaration of the TIModuleInterface class:

```
type
  TIModuleInterface = class(TInterface)
  public
    function GetEditorInterface: TIEditorInterface; virtual;
      stdcall; abstract;
    function GetFormInterface: TIFormInterface; virtual;
      stdcall; abstract;
    function GetAncestorModule: TIModuleInterface; virtual;
      stdcall; abstract;
    function GetProjectResource: TIResourceFile; virtual;
      stdcall; abstract;
    function IsProjectModule: Boolean; virtual; stdcall; abstract;
    function Close: Boolean; virtual; stdcall; abstract;
    function Save(ForceSave: Boolean): Boolean; virtual;
      stdcall; abstract;
    function Rename(const NewName: string): Boolean; virtual;
      stdcall; abstract;
    function GetFileSystem(var FileSystem: string): Boolean;
      virtual; stdcall; abstract;
    function SetFileSystem(const FileSystem: string): Boolean;
      virtual; stdcall; abstract;
    function ShowSource: Boolean; virtual; stdcall; abstract;
    function ShowForm: Boolean; virtual; stdcall; abstract;
    function AddNotifier(AModuleNotifier: TIModuleNotifier):
      Boolean; virtual; stdcall; abstract;
    function RemoveNotifier(AModuleNotifier: TIModuleNotifier):
      Boolean; virtual; stdcall; abstract;
  end;
```

You can find a complete description of each of these methods in the source code itself. In brief, the most useful functions give you the ability to interact with several elements of the IDE. For instance, you can access the edit buffer (GetEditorInterface) and then manipulate its contents. You can access the form designer (GetFormInterface) and then manipulate the form or its components and their properties. You can access the project's resource file (GetProjectResource) and then perform some action such as closing, saving, renaming, or displaying the file.

In each case above, the methods return an interface, which may return further interfaces such as a TIEditWriter (used to modify a source code file) or TICompo-nentInterface object. You can use the latter interface to interact with an existing component, examine its list of its properties and their values, and even change the property values by name.

Using the last two methods of the TIModuleInterface class, you can also install a specific notifier for the module. The TIModuleNotify interface declares a Notify method you should override, as well as a ComponentRenamed method. Here is a list of the notifications:

```
TNotifyCode = (ncModuleDeleted, ncModuleRenamed,
    ncEditorModified, ncFormModified, ncEditorSelected,
    ncFormSelected, ncBeforeSave, ncAfterSave,
    ncFormSaving, ncProjResModified);
```

Unfortunately, using these capabilities to their full extent would require very complex examples. (However, if you're interested in pursuing these topics, the Project Explorer demo wizard included in Delphi uses many of these techniques.)

Saving Author Information

We've decided to improve our VCS demo only slightly, but (we hope) enough to give you an idea of what you can do in a VCS. Our aim is to use the source code files to store some of the version control information. Our technique won't prevent programmers from editing this data, but it will demonstrate how closely an add-in tool can be integrated with Delphi. Along the way, we'll address a bug in the previous example that relates to the Save As operation.

To respond to file save notifications, we basically need to create a distinct module notifier object for every file the user opens. This is an important thing to understand, since the module notifications *don't* pass the associated filename as a parameter. Therefore, we'll need to store this information in each notifier object.

In addition, we need to install the module notifier into a module interface, and keep the interface object alive as long as the notifier object is active. More important, we need to destroy the module interface object when Delphi destroys the notifier.

To deal with these two issues, we can write a module notifier class that includes the filename of the current object and the module interface:

```
type
  TDDHModNotif = class (TIModuleNotifier)
```

```
private
  FileName: string;
  ModIntf: TIModuleInterface;
public
  constructor Create (FileN: string;
    ModInterface: TIModuleInterface);
  destructor Destroy; override;
  procedure Notify(NotifyCode: TNotifyCode); override;
  procedure ComponentRenamed(ComponentHandle: Pointer;
    const OldName, NewName: string); override;
end;
```

Before we examine the code of this function, we should discuss how the VCS manages these objects.

In fact, we need to make several changes to the VCS class in order to add a new menu item (to let the user choose whether to save the VCS data in the source code files). This VCS adds a couple of new fields and methods:

```
type
  TDdhProjectVcs = class (TIVCSClient)
  private
    // store the name in each file?
    StoreAuthor: Boolean;
    // list of installed module notifiers:
    NotifList: TStrings;
  public
    constructor Create;
    function GetIDString: string; override;
    procedure ExecuteVerb(Index: Integer); override;
    function GetMenuName: string; override;
    function GetVerb(Index: Integer): string; override;
    function GetVerbCount: Integer; override;
    function GetVerbState(Index: Integer): Word; override;
    procedure ProjectChange; override;
    destructor Destroy; override;
    // custom methods used to add/remove a module notifier
    procedure InstallNotifier (FileName: string);
    procedure RemoveNotifier (FileName: string);
  end;
```

As you would expect, the constructor initializes the new fields, and the destructor deletes the notifier list after confirming that it's empty (that is, after each module notifier has been deleted):

```
constructor TDdhProjectVcs.Create;
begin
  inherited Create;
  // default: don't store the name
  StoreAuthor := False;
  // create the list
  NotifList := TStringList.Create;
end;

destructor TDdhProjectVcs.Destroy;
begin
  try
    // destroy form and global notifier
    PrjInfoForm.Free;
    ToolServices.RemoveNotifier (PrjNotif);
    PrjNotif.Free;
    // check if the list is empty (it should
    // always be, at this time) and remove it
    if NotifList.Count > 0 then
      ShowMessage (Format (
        'Error: %d module notifiers have not been removed',
        [NotifList.Count]));
    NotifList.Free;
  except
    ToolServices.RaiseException(ReleaseException);
  end;
end;
```

If everything works correctly, you should never see the destructor's error message. However, in case of an error, some notifier objects might remain in memory when the destructor is called, and we prefer to leave this debug check in the code as a sort of warning tool. Failing to destroy a notifier causes a memory leak inside Delphi, but it shouldn't cause any other side effects.

The NotifList object manages notifiers using two methods, InstallNotifier and RemoveNotifier. To install a notifier, the program retrieves a module interface for the file, creates the notifier object (using the module interface filename and the module interface object as parameters), adds the notifier to the module interface, and then adds the object and the filename to the list:

```
procedure TDdhProjectVcs.InstallNotifier (FileName: string);
var
  ModIntf: TIModuleInterface;
  Notif: TDDHModNotif;
begin
  // get the module interface
  ModIntf := ToolServices.GetModuleInterface (FileName);
  if ModIntf <> nil then
  begin
    // create the module notifier
    Notif := TDDHModNotif.Create (FileName, ModIntf);
    // install the notifier
    ModIntf.AddNotifier (Notif);
    // add the notifier to the list
    NotifList.AddObject (FileName, Notif);
  end;
end;

procedure TDdhProjectVcs.RemoveNotifier (FileName: string);
var
  ItemNo: Integer;
begin
  // check if the notifier is in the list
  ItemNo := NotifList.IndexOf (FileName);
  if ItemNo >= 0 then
  begin
    // destroy the notifier
    TDDHModNotif (NotifList.Objects [ItemNo]).Free;
    // remove the corresponding list item
    NotifList.Delete (ItemNo);
  end;
end;
```

You'll notice that the method above removes the notifier but doesn't uninstall it. This is OK because the module notifier's destructor eliminates its connection to the module interface, and then releases the module interface as well. We'll see this code later on.

Now let's consider some of the changes to the VCS object that relate to the menu items. Here are the updated versions of the four verb methods that relate to counting, showing, and executing the code for the VCS menu items. These methods should be easy to understand without extensive discussion:

```
function TDdhProjectVcs.GetVerbCount: Integer;
begin
  Result := 4;
end;

function TDdhProjectVcs.GetVerb(Index: Integer): string;
begin
  case Index of
    0: Result := '&Project Information...';
    1: Result := '&Store Author on Save';
    2: Result := ''; // separator
    3: Result := '&About DDH Project VCS...';
  end;
end;

procedure TDdhProjectVcs.ExecuteVerb(Index: Integer);
begin
  case Index of
    0: try
         PrjInfoForm.UpdateTree;
         PrjInfoForm.Show;
       except
         ToolServices.RaiseException(ReleaseException);
       end;
    1: // toggle the flag
       StoreAuthor := not StoreAuthor;
    3: // about box
       MessageDlg ('DDH Project Version Control System'#13#13 +
         'From the "Delphi Developer''s Handbook"'#13 +
         'by Marco Cantu and Tim Gooch',
         mtInformation, [mbOK], 0);
  end;
end;

function TDdhProjectVcs.GetVerbState(Index: Integer): Word;
begin
  Result := vsEnabled; // default
  try
    case Index of
    0: // disable first item if no project is active
```

```
        if ToolServices.GetProjectName = '' then
          Result := 0;
      1: // check the second item when appropriate
        if StoreAuthor then
          Result := vsEnabled + vsChecked;
      //3: always enabled: nothing to do
      end;
    except
      ToolServices.RaiseException(ReleaseException);
    end;
  end;
```

In the GetVerbState method, notice how we handle the check mark for the Store Author menu item. As we mentioned before, the vsEnabled and vsChecked identifiers are integer constants—not enumerated values.

We had to make another set of changes in the TDDHPrjNotifier class's FileNotification method, because this class creates and removes the module notifiers when the user opens or closes a file. In reality, for the fnFileOpened notification we've added just few lines of code to register a notifier only if the file is a Pascal source file (that it, if it has a .PAS extension). In addition, we'll create the notifier when the user adds a new unit to the project. Here is the new code (not the complete listing) for these two branches of the FileNotification method's case statement:

```
fnFileOpened:
  if ExtractFileExt (FileName) = '.pas' then
    DdhPrjVcs.InstallNotifier (FileName);
fnAddedToProject:
  if ExtractFileExt (FileName) = '.pas' then
    DdhPrjVcs.InstallNotifier (FileName);
```

Of course, we'll remove the notifier when the user closes the file. The RemoveNotifier method checks whether the corresponding notifier actually existed:

```
fnFileClosing:
  if ExtractFileExt (FileName) = '.pas' then
    DdhPrjVcs.RemoveNotifier (FileName)
fnRemovedFromProject:
  if ExtractFileExt (FileName) = '.pas' then
    DdhPrjVcs.RemoveNotifier (FileName);
```

Now that we know how the rest of the program (the VCS object and the project notifier) interacts with the module notifier class, we can finally examine its methods. The constructor of the module notifier class is quite simple, since it simply stores its parameters:

```
constructor TDDHModNotif.Create (FileN: string;
  ModInterface: TIModuleInterface);
begin
  inherited Create;
  // store the parameters
  FileName := FileN;
  ModIntf := ModInterface;
  Modified := False;
end;
```

The destructor simply disconnects the notifier from the module interface, and then releases the module interface object:

```
destructor TDDHModNotif.Destroy;
begin
  // remove the module notifier
  ModIntf.RemoveNotifier (self);
  // release the interface
  ModIntf.Release;
  inherited Destroy;
end;
```

If you like, you can add a call to Beep (or SysUtils.Beep) inside this method to confirm that Delphi actually executes this code.

Of course, this class's key method is Notify. As we've already mentioned, this method receives only a notification code, but we know which file and module interface object the notification object refers to because we've stored them inside the object.

Since the code for this method is quite complex, we've divided it into smaller and more understandable pieces (dividing the local variable declarations, as well). The simplest code responds to the ncEditorModified notification:

```
procedure TDDHModNotif.Notify (NotifyCode: TNotifyCode);
begin
  case NotifyCode of
    ncEditorModified:
      // set the modified flag
      Modified := True;
```

By setting this flag, we avoid adding user information to a file when the user saves it without making any changes. This is one of the checks we do when the ncBeforeSave notification arrives:

```
var
  WriIntf: TIEditWriter;
  ReadIntf: TIEditReader;
  EditIntf: TIEditorInterface;
  FirstLine, UserName, NewFirstLine: string;
  NameSize, FirstLineLen: Integer;
begin
  ...
  ncBeforeSave:
    // if the file has changed
    // and the StoreAuthor flag is set
    if Modified and DdhPrjVcs.StoreAuthor then
    begin
      // get the module editor interface
      EditIntf := ModIntf.GetEditorInterface;
      if EditIntf <> nil then
      try
        // create a reader object
        ReadIntf := EditIntf.CreateReader;
        if ReadIntf <> nil then
        try
          SetLength (FirstLine, 100);
          ReadIntf.GetText (0, PChar(FirstLine),
            Length (FirstLine));
        finally
          // release the interface
          ReadIntf.Release;
        end;
        // define the output string
        // with username, date, and time
        NameSize := 100;
        SetLength (UserName, 100);
        GetUserName (PChar (UserName), NameSize);
        UserName := PChar (UserName); // length fix
        NewFirstLine := '// Updated by ' + UserName +
          ', ' + DateTimeToStr (Now) + #13;
        WriIntf := EditIntf.CreateWriter;
        if WriIntf <> nil then
        try
```

```
      // check if user and day have not changed
      if StrLComp (PChar(FirstLine),
        PChar(NewFirstLine), NameSize + 22) = 0 then
      begin
        // get the length of the first line
        FirstLineLen := Pos (#13, FirstLine) + 1;
        // remove the current first line
        WriIntf.DeleteTo (FirstLineLen);
      end;
      // insert the new string
      WriIntf.Insert (PChar (NewFirstLine));
      // release the interface
      WriIntf.Release;
      // reset the modified flag
      Modified := False;
    finally
      // release the interface
      WriIntf.Release;
    end;
  finally
    // release the interface
    EditIntf.Release;
  end;
end;
```

The core of this method is at the point where we create the reader and then the writer object by calling the editor interface's CreateReader and CreateWriter methods (we obtain the editor interface from the module interface). Once this is done, you can either access the current text or insert new text. These are the definitions of the reader and the writer interfaces:

```
type
  TIEditReader = class(TInterface)
  public
    function GetText(Position: Longint; Buffer: PChar;
      Count: Longint): Longint; virtual; stdcall; abstract;
  end;

  TIEditWriter = class(TInterface)
  public
    function CopyTo(Pos: Longint): Boolean; virtual;
      stdcall; abstract;
    function DeleteTo(Pos: Longint): Boolean; virtual;
```

```
      stdcall; abstract;
  function Insert(Text: PChar): Boolean; virtual;
      stdcall; abstract;
  function Position: Longint; virtual; stdcall; abstract;
  function GetCurrentPos: TCharPos; virtual; stdcall; abstract;
  property CurrentPos: TCharPos read GetCurrentPos;
end;
```

NOTE

To change the current position within a file (before writing to it), you'll need to use the TIEditView interface. Fortunately, we don't need this capability in our example (it would add a considerable amount of complexity).

The string we add at the beginning of the file is a comment (what else?) that we terminate with the newline character (#13) to avoid affecting the first line of the code. In this comment we store the user's name and the date and time. We'll retrieve the username from the system by calling the Windows API GetUserName function.

However, before writing the text, our VCS determines whether the first part of the string (holding the username and the date) has changed. If it hasn't changed, we remove the first line before inserting the new one, to avoid an output like the following:

```
// Updated by Marco, 11/11/97 5:52:54 PM
// Updated by Marco, 11/11/97 5:55:54 PM
// Updated by Marco, 11/11/97 5:58:54 PM
```

In other words, if the same user saves a file twice in a day, we'll record only the last operation. Of course, this is just a matter of how we wrote this program: since you have the source code, you can easily modify this rule to work the way you prefer.

As we've stated before, you need to remember to release all the interfaces you allocate. When you do this, it's important to call Release and not Free because (in theory) it's possible for two interface objects to refer to the same element. Release reduces the reference count, and it frees the object only when the reference count reaches zero. It's also better to release the interfaces inside a finally block, to avoid a memory leak should an exception occur.

The rest of the module notifier's Notify method is much simpler. When the user renames a module (by selecting the Save As menu command), we must first update the project view. Not handling the effect of renaming a unit was actually a bug of the previous versions of our VCS. The strange thing is that even if you handle Delphi project notifications, Delphi will completely ignore the Save As operation. This is only a file-level notification, not a project-level one.

Once we've refreshed the project view, we remove the current notifier (which now refers to a file that doesn't exist any more) and install a new notifier for the new file. However, since we don't know the new name of the file, the only technique we've found is to scan all the project files and install a notifier for each Pascal file that doesn't already have one:

```
var
  FileN: string;
  I: Integer;
begin
  ...
  ncModuleRenamed:
  begin
    // update the project view
    PrjInfoForm.UpdateTree;
    // remove the notifier for the old file
    DemoVCS.RemoveNotifier (FileName);
    // look for the new file name
    // and install a new notifier for it
    begin
      FileN := ToolServices.GetUnitName (I);
      if (ToolServices.IsFileOpen (FileN)) and
        (ExtractFileExt (FileName) = '.pas') and
        (DemoVCS.NotifList.IndexOf (FileN) < 0) then
          DemoVCS.InstallNotifier (FileN);
    end;
  end;
```

The last branch of the Notify method's case statement handles the module removal:

```
ncModuleDeleted:
  // unregister and remove the notifier
  DemoVCS.RemoveNotifier (FileName);
```

You'll recall that we also declared an implementation of the ComponentRenamed method in the notifier object class. We don't really need to implement this method, but we decided to do so anyway (just in case Delphi calls it). This is just a do-nothing method:

```
procedure TDDHModNotif.ComponentRenamed(
  ComponentHandle: Pointer; const OldName, NewName: string);
```

```
begin
  // do nothing
end;
```

As a result of all this effort, the Store Author option of the VCS (something you might turn on by default in the VCS constructor) adds the author's name to each source file (along with the date and time) whenever the user modifies or saves the file. You can see the result of this option in Figure 15.4. Of course, a real VCS should also store the changes to the file and not just the fact that something has changed. However, this example was meant to illustrate integration techniques, and not to build a professional version control tool.

FIGURE 15.4:

The new menu item of the Demo VCS adds the author and time of each edit in the source code itself.

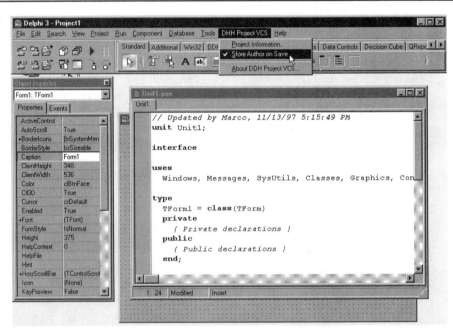

A Summary of the ToolsAPI

In this and the last few chapters, we've discussed a number of the ToolsAPI classes for extending the Delphi environment. However, other classes that relate to the Delphi environment (such as the run-time type information we'll discuss in the next chapter) appear in the VCL source code. What follows is a summary of the ToolsAPI, listing all of the classes in a single section. This is far from a complete reference: it is only a list of the classes defined by each unit, with short descriptions. You'll find additional details (primarily extended comments) in the source code files themselves, and there is no reason to duplicate that information here.

Below, you may notice that we've skipped a file of the ToolsAPI directory. In fact, we intentionally didn't include the DsgnIntf unit, since it doesn't define interfaces to the Delphi environment, but *internal* editor classes, such as component and property editors. We discussed these classes in detail in Chapters 12 and 13. Some more information on custom form designers will follow after this section.

The VirtIntf Unit

The classes in the VirtIntf unit are the base classes of the hierarchy of ToolsAPI interface classes. They are seldom used directly.

TInterface	A generic interface class, implementing a reference-counting mechanism. Most of the other interface classes derive from this one.
TIStream	The abstract base class of interfaces for the internal Delphi stream classes, described in the next section.

The IStreams Unit

The classes in the IStreams unit are the hierarchy of interface stream classes. Don't confuse these with the standard stream classes (discussed in Chapter 3). Each interface stream object encapsulates a corresponding stream object, used to perform the actual reading and writing operations.

TIVCLStreamAdapter and TIStreamAdapter	The base classes of the other interface streams, used to map a TIStream into a plain TStream object.
TIMemoryStream	Implements a wrapper for the TMemoryStream class and inherits from the TIStreamAdapter class. We used this class in the Form Wizard example from the previous chapter.

TIFileStream	Implements a wrapper for a TFileStream class and inherits from the TIVCLStreamAdapter class.
TVirtualStream	Implements a wrapper for a generic TIStream object and inherits from the TStream class.

The FileIntf Unit

The only class in the FileIntf unit is the base class for a virtual file system.

TIVirtualFileSystem	Implements the virtual file system for the Delphi environment. An add-in tool might implement and use a different file system.

NOTE   A *virtual file system* is a mechanism for mapping file operations onto data structures that are not file-based. For example, you have probably noticed that in Delphi you can open a string list into the editor. This is accomplished with a virtual file system: the editor thinks that the string list is a file and loads it. The read and write operations on this "fake" file are mapped by a virtual file system into operations on the string list object.

The ToolIntf Unit

The classes in the ToolIntf unit include the fundamental ToolServices class, the menu interfaces, and the notifier interfaces.

TIMenuItemIntf	The interface class for each menu item and pull-down menu of the Delphi environment. We used this class in the add-in wizard in the previous chapter.
TIMainMenuIntf	The interface for Delphi menu system. This is a light-weight class you'll use to access the menus.
TIAddInNotifier	Used by wizards and version control systems so that Delphi can notify them about some file or project action. We used this class in our VCS Demo.

`TIToolServices`	In practice, the interface to Delphi itself, including project information, actions you can perform, and many more features. We've used the global `ToolServices` object of this class in many examples in this chapter and the previous two. This is frequently the entry point for other interfaces.

The ExpIntf Unit

The only class in the ExptIntf unit is the base class of every custom wizard.

`TIExpert`	The class you should derive from to create custom wizards. We saw several examples in the previous chapter.

The VcsIntf Unit

The only class in the VcsIntf unit is the base class of every custom version control system.

`TIVCSClient`	The class from which you should derive to create a custom version control system. We've already seen examples of this class in this chapter.

The EditIntf Unit

The classes in the EditIntf unit include module interfaces (including resource files and others) and all the environment editors (including the source code editor, the form designer, and the components in the designer). In Delphi 3 this unit also includes the "creator" classes.

`TIModuleInterface`	The interface of a module: a form, a unit, a project file, a resource file, and so on. We've used this in the last version of the Project VCS example.
`TIModuleNotifier`	A notifier for the module, with more notifications than a generic project notifier. We've used this in the last version of the Project VCS example.
`TIResourceFile`	The interface to a resource file.

`TIResourceEntry`	The interface to an entry within a resource file.
`TIComponentInterface`	The interface for a component at design-time.
`TIFormInterface`	The interface for a form at design-time.
`TIEditorInterface`	The interface for a module loaded in the editor.
`TIEditReader`	The interface for reading text in the editor.
`TIEditWriter`	The interface for writing text in the editor. We've used this in the last version of the Project VCS example.
`TIEditView`	The interface for setting the reading or writing position within an editor file.
`TIProjectCreator`	The interface used by the `ToolServices.ProjectCreate` method to initialize a new project in a flexible way.
`TIModuleCreator`	The interface used by the `ToolServices.ModuleCreate` method to add a new unit to a project in a flexible way.

Using Custom Design Modules

In Delphi 1, you could only design forms based on classes derived directly from `TForm`. In Delphi 2, Borland added form inheritance and data modules as editable component containers. With Delphi 3, Borland has introduced different kinds of design-time forms, including ActiveForms, Web data modules, remote data modules, and many others. To make the design-time architecture flexible, Delphi 3 introduced the ability to specify a base class for a form designer, and also to customize the appearance of a form designer to display specific menu items for that base class.

By creating a custom form designer, you'll be able to extend the idea of a component editor to manipulating entire forms or modules. Unfortunately, we haven't found a way to customize the designer that Delphi uses for standard forms. Along the way to our custom form designer, we'll see many interesting examples, including how to publish and view your own form properties in the Object Inspector, which is a significant breakthrough. However, let's proceed step by step, and introduce the new VCL functions and some key ideas before we begin building the examples.

The TCustomModule Class and the RegisterCustomModule Procedure

The key step in creating your own form designer in Delphi is the RegisterCustomModule registration procedure:

```
procedure RegisterCustomModule(
  ComponentBaseClass: TComponentClass;
  CustomModuleClass: TCustomModuleClass);
```

The first parameter is the base class of the class you want to edit, such as TForm; the second parameter is the form editor's class (the class of the editor that the designer activates).

The first thing to notice is that the object you pass as the first parameter can be of a class derived from TCustomForm (including the TForm class), from TData-Module, from TWinControl, or from another component class. As documented in the source code of the DsgnIntf unit, the only compulsory element is that the base class must call the InitInheritedComponent in its constructor to load the proper form description from the associated DFM file. As you'd expect, the behavior of the designer depends on the ComponentBaseClass type:

- If your form is a TCustomForm descendant, you'll be able to edit it as usual, but you'll have access to all the published properties of the base class (which is now your class instead of TForm) in the Object Inspector.

- If the class derives from TWinControl instead of TCustomForm, Delphi places an instance of that control in a temporary design-time form. This is a good technique for creating compound components, like aggregate components based on a panel, as we'll see in the section "Creating a Compound Component."

- If the class derives from TComponent, Delphi will create a nonvisual container like that of a data module. You'll notice that the comments in the source code file imply that you must derive the class from TDataModule, which isn't true. Even using TComponent as the ComponentBaseClass type generates a valid designer.

The other important element of the module's registration is the custom designer. Delphi provides (in the DsgnIntf unit) a TCustomModule class. You can use this as a base class from which to derive new classes; but you can also use it directly, since it isn't an abstract class:

```
type
  TCustomModule = class
  private
    FRoot: TComponent;
  public
    constructor Create(ARoot: TComponent); virtual;
    procedure ExecuteVerb(Index: Integer); virtual;
    function GetAttributes: TCustomModuleAttributes; virtual;
    function GetVerb(Index: Integer): string; virtual;
    function GetVerbCount: Integer; virtual;
    procedure Saving; virtual;
    procedure ValidateComponent(Component: TComponent); virtual;
    property Root: TComponent read FRoot;
  end;
```

The constructor saves the form or data module we are working on as the Root property, so we'll have access to it. The GetVerbCount, GetVerb, and ExecuteVerb methods create the local menu and run the associated commands, using the approach first implemented by the VCS interface and the component editors.

The GetAttributes method is used only by editors of a TWinControl to determine the alignment of the control you are designing, relative to the temporary form containing it. Currently, there's only one attribute you can retrieve using this method, which suggests that it's there to support future extensions. Delphi calls the other two methods at specific times. It calls the Saving method every time you save a file (before saving the file) to allow you to perform specific processing; and it calls the ValidateComponent method every time you add a new component (passed as a parameter) to the designer, which allows you to interrupt the operation if the component is not a valid type. In fact, this is exactly what happens when you add a TWinControl-derived component to a data module.

Before we look at specific examples, let's reconsider the difference between the TForm class and its base class, TCustomForm. Borland added this new class to allow you to create a new designer based on a form that doesn't have the standard properties and methods of a TForm form. The relationship between these classes is the same as that between TEdit and TCustomEdit (as well as all the other

TCustom... classes of the VCL). To clarify this further, here's the definition of the TForm class (for Delphi 3, since the TCustomForm class wasn't available before):

```
type
  TForm = class(TCustomForm)
  public
    procedure ArrangeIcons;
    procedure Cascade;
    procedure Next;
    procedure Previous;
    procedure Tile;
    property ActiveMDIChild;
    property ClientHandle;
    property MDIChildCount;
    property MDIChildren;
    property TileMode;
  published
    property ActiveControl;
    property BorderIcons;
    property BorderStyle;
    property AutoScroll;
    property Caption;
    property ClientHeight;
    property ClientWidth;
    // and so on, including events...
  end;
```

Publishing the Custom Properties of a Form

Our first example of a custom designer will show you something users of earlier versions of Delphi have longed for. If you adhere to good OOP programming conventions, you should be frequently adding properties to your form classes. However, the properties you add to a form (even if they're published) won't appear in the Object Inspector. Although there's no "magic" way to add a property to a form and see it immediately in the Object Inspector, you can compile the form class, add it to a package, and then see the new properties in a further inherited class.

In the FormWVal unit (part of the Chapter 15 package and therefore included in the Comps directory for this chapter), we've declared the following form:

```
type
  TFormWithValue = class (TForm)
```

```
private
  fValue: Integer;
  fOnChangeValue: TNotifyEvent;
  procedure SetValue (Value: Integer);
published
  property Value: Integer
    read fValue write SetValue;
  property OnChangeValue: TNotifyEvent
    read fOnChangeValue write fOnChangeValue;
end;
```

This form class defines a new property that stores a value, and an event that is triggered when the value changes:

```
procedure TFormWithValue.SetValue (Value: Integer);
begin
  if Value <> fValue then
  begin
    fValue := Value;
    if Assigned (fOnChangeValue) then
      fOnChangeValue (self);
  end;
end;
```

In the Register procedure, we install this form as a new designer, but we associate it with the standard custom module:

```
RegisterCustomModule (TFormWithValue, TCustomModule);
```

How can we create a new module of this class at design-time? Simply registering a new form as a custom module (using the call above) adds it to the system, but Delphi doesn't automatically make it available in the File ➤ New dialog box. So we're on our own again, and we must create the new form by (as you might guess) writing a new wizard. In this case, we've written a new bare-bones standard wizard, which displays a *Form With Value Wizard* menu item that executes the following Execute method:

```
procedure TFormWithValueExpert.Execute;
var
  ModuleName, FormName, FileName: string;
  ModIntf: TIModuleInterface;
begin
  ToolServices.GetNewModuleAndClassName (
    'FormWithValue', ModuleName, FormName, FileName);
```

```
    ModIntf := ToolServices.CreateModuleEx (FileName, FormName,
      'FormWithValue', '', nil, nil,
      [cmNewForm, cmAddToProject, cmUnNamed]);
    ModIntf.ShowSource;
    ModIntf.ShowForm;
    ModIntf.Release;
  end;
```

The first call, GetNewModuleAndClassName, retrieves the unit and class name. You'll notice the use of the first parameter, which indicates a prefix for the class name: By default, Delphi adds a *T* in front of the class name, and a form number after it, such as TFormWithValue1. The second and more important call, CreateModuleEx, generates the new module and adds it to the current project. Again we have to specify the base class, but this time without the initial *T*, which is quite odd! This method returns a module interface we can use to open the source code file in the editor and display the form. The result is a new design-time form, derived from the given type and with the given properties, as you can see in Figure 15.5.

FIGURE 15.5:

You can install a new designer in Delphi, and add custom properties to a form within the environment, so that they'll appear in the Object Inspector.

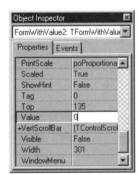 

Creating a Compound Component

Another interesting technique is to use a panel component as a designer that hosts other components. Using this approach, we can use Delphi to design compound components. Actually this is just a suggestion; the technique is flexible enough that you can use it to edit almost any component as if it were a form!

Here's the registration code of the new PanelEd unit (the source code of this new wizard is in the Comps directory, as usual):

```
procedure Register;
begin
  RegisterCustomModule (TPanel, TPanelModule);
  RegisterLibraryExpert(TPanelEditExpert.Create);
end;
```

Simple, isn't it? As in the last example, we've built a Panel Edit Wizard to create new modules based on this custom module. Here's the updated version of the Execute method:

```
procedure TPanelEditExpert.Execute;
var
  ModuleName, FormName, FileName: string;
  ModIntf: TIModuleInterface;
begin
  ToolServices.GetNewModuleAndClassName (
    'Panel', ModuleName, FormName, FileName);
  ModIntf := ToolServices.CreateModuleEx (FileName, FormName,
    'Panel', '', nil, nil,
    [cmNewForm, cmAddToProject, cmUnNamed]);
  ModIntf.ShowSource;
  ModIntf.ShowForm;
  ModIntf.Release;
end;
```

This time, however, we've also defined a new custom module class for the editor. This custom module allows users to place only Button controls in the panel at design-time, and it provides a popup menu as a shortcut to change the name of the component. Here's the declaration of the custom module class:

```
type
  TPanelModule = class (TCustomModule)
  public
    procedure ExecuteVerb(Index: Integer); override;
    function GetVerb(Index: Integer): string; override;
    function GetVerbCount: Integer; override;
    procedure ValidateComponent(Component: TComponent); override;
  end;
```

The code of its methods is actually quite simple, but we've included it here to show how easily you can define a custom module designer:

```
function TPanelModule.GetVerbCount: Integer;
begin
  Result := 1;
end;

function TPanelModule.GetVerb(Index: Integer): string;
begin
  if Index = 0 then
    Result:= 'Rename...';
end;

procedure TPanelModule.ExecuteVerb(Index: Integer);
var
  NewName: string;
begin
  if Index = 0 then
  begin
    NewName := Root.Name;
    if InputQuery ('Panel Module Editor',
        'New panel name:', NewName) then
      Root.Name := NewName;
  end;
end;

procedure TPanelModule.ValidateComponent(Component: TComponent);
begin
  if not (Component is TButton) and
      not (Component is TSpeedButton) then
    raise Exception.Create ('The panel can host only buttons');
end;
```

As soon as you add this unit to a package (it's part of the Chapter 15 package), and activate the Panel Edit Wizard, Delphi displays an editor for the panel, as you can see in Figure 15.6. Although there is a form surrounding the panel, it isn't really used, and it's not saved in the DFM or PAS files for this module. Here's the complete DFM file for a very simple example (notice that there is no form!):

```
object Panel2: TPanel2
  Left = 0
  Top = 0
```

```
      Width = 290
      Height = 173
      TabOrder = 0
      object Button1: TButton
        Left = 96
        Top = 72
        Width = 75
        Height = 25
        Caption = 'Button1'
        TabOrder = 0
      end
  end
```

And here is the complete PAS file generated by Delphi:

```
unit Unit2;

interface

uses
  Windows, Messages, SysUtils, Classes, Graphics, Controls,
  Forms, Dialogs, StdCtrls;

type
  TPanel2 = class(TPanel)
    Button1: TButton;
  private
    { Private declarations }
  public
    { Public declarations }
  end;

var
  Panel2: TPanel2;

implementation

{$R *.DFM}

end.
```

FIGURE 15.6:

In Delphi you can
install a designer for
a Panel, and edit it
in the environment
as usual.

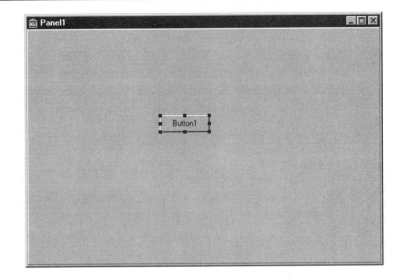

If you try to add a non-Button component to the panel, you'll see an error message (the exception raised by the designer); and if you right-click on the form
you'll see a new entry in the designer's local menu, as shown in Figure 15.7. The
extra menu items allow you to change the name of the derived panel class and
the name of the object.

FIGURE 15.7:

The extra menu of
our panel's custom
designer. We'll
install this panel as
a component.

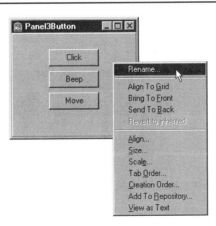

Now you might ask, "We can edit the panel, but what's this for?" We've used the panel of Figure 15.7 in two different ways: directly inside a program and as the basis of a new component. In both cases we have a problem: Delphi saves the status of the panel in a DFM file, but it can't reload the panel from the file. In fact, instead of using TPanel as a designer, we probably should have created a custom subclass to manage the initialization. However, for simplicity we've decided to add this code to the panel (something you might want to avoid if you need many such panels). Here's the custom constructor we add to the derived panel:

```
constructor TPanel3Button.Create (AOwner: TComponent);
begin
  inherited Create (AOwner);
  InitInheritedComponent (self, TPanel);
end;
```

In the CustPane directory on the companion CD you'll find this code, simple event handlers for the three buttons, and the PanelPrj project. This project has a main form plus the panel. You now have to remove the panel from the list of automatically created forms in the Project Options (after all, it isn't a form), so you can use the panel by writing code like this:

```
procedure TForm1.FormCreate(Sender: TObject);
begin
  Panel3Button := TPanel3Button.Create (Application);
  Panel3Button.Parent := self;
end;
```

This code will display the panel at run-time inside the main form, as you can see in Figure 15.8.

FIGURE 15.8:

You can use the custom panel directly inside a program, as demonstrated by the PanelPrj example (located in the CustPane directory).

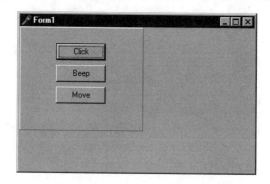

At the same time, you can add a `Register` procedure to the panel source code created by Delphi, and install the panel as a component:

```
procedure Register;
begin
  RegisterComponents ('DDHB', [TPanel3Button]);
end;
```

Now, simply adding this unit to a package will turn the panel we've built with the custom designer into a fully working component! As usual, we've installed this component in the PanelPack package (stored in the CustPane directory, as well). We've also built a very simple project based on this component. You can find it in the PaneDemo directory, and see it at design time in Figure 15.9. As you can see in the Object Inspector, there is only one component in the form, which means that the project considers the compound component to be a single component.

FIGURE 15.9:

The PaneDemo project uses the Panel component built with the panel designer we've just installed in Delphi.

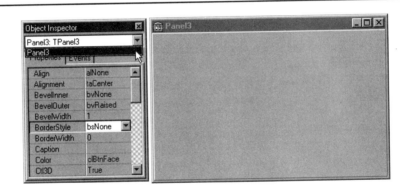

Besides designing special classes, such as the panel we just built, you can apply the same technique to many other uses. You can even create nonvisual compound components based on the TComponent class. Simply write

```
RegisterCustomModule (TComponent, TCustomModule);
```

and generate the module in a wizard exactly as before:

```
ToolServices.GetNewModuleAndClassName (
  'Component', ModuleName, FormName, FileName);
ModIntf := ToolServices.CreateModuleEx (FileName, FormName,
  'Component', '', nil, nil,
  [cmNewForm, cmAddToProject, cmUnNamed]);
ModIntf.ShowSource;
```

```
ModIntf.ShowForm;
ModIntf.Release;
```

Executing this code produces something similar to a data module, but the base class will be TComponent. Again, you'll need to add the code for the constructor to this component, and call the InitInheritedComponent method.

Since the practical use of a generic designer seems somewhat limited, we've decided not to build more examples. To pursue this further, you may want to consider creating a wizard that allows you to choose the base class for the designer and, if necessary, generates the proper constructor code automatically (you'll need to do this only if the base class is not TDataModule or TCustomForm, because we've already written similar code).

"Hacking" the Delphi Environment

All the techniques we've described so far in this part of the book, with very few exceptions, are "official" ways of customizing the Delphi development environment (even though some of them aren't properly documented). In this last section of the chapter, we'll explore a few "unofficial" techniques. To figure out how these techniques work, we had to do some hacking.

Here's the basic idea: When you write a property editor, component editor, or DCU-based wizard (but not a DLL -based wizard or a VCS DLL), you're actually adding classes and code to the Delphi environment itself. Since the Delphi environment is a Delphi application, you can apply all the Delphi programming techniques we've discussed to the environment itself. For example, consider what happens if you write the following within one of these extensions to the Delphi environment:

```
Application.Title := 'New Delphi';
```

The title of the Delphi main window and of the TaskBar icon will display the new string. You've basically changed the title of Delphi itself, and many message boxes displayed by the system will use this new title. However, this shouldn't surprise you, since Borland used Delphi to build Delphi itself.

In this section, we'll use similar techniques to build some useful tools. We'll first build a tool to explore the structure of Delphi's forms and components; then we'll create a Delphi customization tool that will allow a user to turn the Component palette into a multiline TabControl, to change the font of the Object Inspector, and to add new menu items to some windows. At the end we'll use a similar technique to call the internal event handlers for Delphi menu items directly, and even change them!

Delphi Exposed

Before we start examining the details of modifying the Delphi environment, we must know some of the implementation details, such as the names of the components and forms Borland uses. Fortunately, getting this information is quite simple; our Delphi Exposed Wizard creates a text file that outlines the relationships between the components Delphi uses internally. Of course, we can list only the components in use at a given moment, since some of the additional Delphi forms aren't always open.

The Delphi Exposed Wizard is part of a separate package (not the package for this chapter) stored in the DelphExp directory. The package includes this standard wizard, which defines a simple Execute method showing a separate form:

```
procedure TDelphiExposedWizard.Execute;
begin
  Application.Title := 'Delphi 3 (Exposed)';
  DelExForm := TDelExForm.Create (Application);
  try
    DelExForm.ShowModal;
  finally
    DelExForm.Free;
  end;
end;
```

You'll notice that, as a side effect, the wizard changes Delphi's own title! The secondary form, displayed by the wizard, contains a TreeView component and four buttons that do the following:

- Show the component hierarchy in two different ways.

- Save the contents of the TreeView to a text file.

- Close the form.

The first two buttons fill the TreeView with the structure of the Delphi environment, arranging components in either parent/child or owner/owned order. In
the first case, the wizard starts by adding the forms stored in the Screen object:

```
procedure TDelExForm.BtnParentClick(Sender: TObject);
var
  I: Integer;
  Node: TTreeNode;
begin
  TreeView.Items.BeginUpdate;
  Screen.Cursor := crHourGlass;
  try
    TreeView.Items.Clear;
    for I := 0 to Screen.FormCount - 1 do
    begin
      Node:= TreeView.Items.AddChild (nil,
        Format ('%s (%s)', [
          Screen.Forms[I].Name,
          Screen.Forms[I].ClassName]));
      AddChild (Node, Screen.Forms[I]);
    end;
  finally
    TreeView.Items.EndUpdate;
    Screen.Cursor := crDefault;
  end;
end;
```

You can see that for every form, the wizard calls the AddChild method, a custom method we've added to the form. This method simply lists all the controls of
the current form, and then recursively lists the controls for every TWinControl
descendant:

```
procedure TDelExForm.AddChild (
  Node: TTreeNode; Control: TWinControl);
var
  I: Integer;
  ChildNode: TTreeNode;
begin
  for I := 0 to Control.ControlCount - 1 do
  begin
    ChildNode := TreeView.Items.AddChild (Node,
      Format ('%s (%s)', [
        Control.Controls[I].Name,
        Control.Controls[I].ClassName]));
```

```
    if Control.Controls[I] is TWinControl then
      AddChild (ChildNode, TWinControl (
        Control.Controls[I]));
  end;
end;
```

Figure 15.10 shows the output of this wizard with the list of the Delphi main windows (for a given situation). You'll notice that this list doesn't display the names of the nonvisual components. By the way, in the directory of this project you'll find the file Parent.TXT, which we generated by saving this parent hierarchy to a text file (using the third button).

FIGURE 15.10:

The list of Delphi's own forms, along with all the controls they contain, produced by the Delphi Exposed Wizard

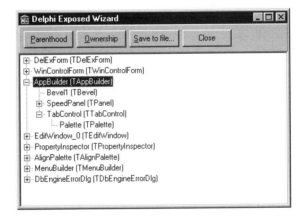

In contrast, when you click the Ownership button, the wizard begins with the Application object and navigates the object hierarchy, scanning each component's Components array, again using a recursive method:

```
procedure TDelExForm.BtnOwnerClick(Sender: TObject);
begin
  TreeView.Items.BeginUpdate;
  Screen.Cursor := crHourGlass;
  try
    TreeView.Items.Clear;
    AddOwned (nil, Application);
  finally
    TreeView.Items.EndUpdate;
    Screen.Cursor := crDefault;
  end;
end;
```

```
procedure TDelExForm.AddOwned (
  Node: TTreeNode; Component: TComponent);
var
  I: Integer;
  ChildNode: TTreeNode;
begin
  for I := 0 to Component.ComponentCount - 1 do
  begin
    ChildNode := TreeView.Items.AddChild (Node,
      Format ('%s (%s)', [
        Component.Components[I].Name,
        Component.Components[I].ClassName]));
    AddOwned (ChildNode, Component.Components[I]);
  end;
end;
```

The result of this operation is a much bigger tree, which includes (among other things), all of the Delphi main menu items. It also includes many strange and unnamed objects, used internally by Delphi but not visible in the development environment. Using this information, we can hook into the system again, change it, and thereby make it more flexible and configurable.

Customizing the Delphi Environment

What we really want to do is create a single wizard that we can use to customize the Delphi environment in many different ways. We haven't tried to add all the interesting customizations to this wizard, but once you understand the foundations, you'll be able to extend it as you see fit.

My Custom Delphi Wizard is another simple wizard; you'll find it in the Comps directory and as part of the Chapter 15 package. When you activate this wizard, it simply creates and displays a form, based on a PageControl component:

```
procedure TMyDelphiWizard.Execute;
begin
  MyDelphiForm := TMyDelphiForm.Create (Application);
  try
    MyDelphiForm.ShowModal;
  finally
    MyDelphiForm.Free;
  end;
end;
```

The various pages of this form allow the user to customize different areas of the Delphi environment.

The Font of the Object Inspector

If you've ever attended a conference presentation on Delphi programming, you'll know that the presenter can easily set the code editor font so that everyone, including people sitting far in the back, can read it. Unfortunately, there's no corresponding way to change the Object Inspector font, and people in the back of the room won't be able to see the names and the values of the properties you're setting.

Solving this problem is actually quite simple, because the Object Inspector form adapts itself very well to larger fonts. As a result, just a few lines of code will do the trick. By the way, the form defines a variable that refers to the Object Inspector form:

```
private
  Inspector: TForm;
```

We initialize this in the OnCreate event handler of the form:

```
procedure TMyDelphiForm.FormCreate(Sender: TObject);
var
  I: Integer;
begin
  Inspector := nil;
  for I := 0 to Screen.FormCount - 1 do
    if Screen.Forms[I].ClassName = 'TPropertyInspector' then
      Inspector := Screen.Forms[I];
  if not Assigned (Inspector) then
    raise Exception.Create ('Object Inspector not found');
end;
```

Now when the user presses the *Font* button of the Inspector page, the wizard simply changes the font (which you can see in Figure 15.11):

```
procedure TMyDelphiForm.BtnInspectorFontClick(Sender: TObject);
begin
  FontDialog1.Font := Inspector.Font;
  if FontDialog1.Execute then
    Inspector.Font := FontDialog1.Font;
end;
```

FIGURE 15.11:

The My Custom
Delphi Wizard allows
you to change the font
of the Object
Inspector.

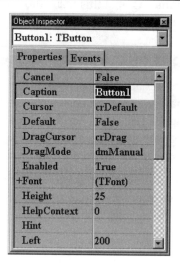

The Multiline Palette

An even more interesting trick is to toggle the value of the Multiline property of
the TabControl component, which hosts Delphi's Component palette:

```
private
   Palette: TTabControl;

procedure TMyDelphiForm.FormCreate(Sender: TObject);
begin
   Palette := Application.MainForm.
      FindComponent ('TabControl') as TTabControl;
```

Once we've retrieved a reference to the TabControl component, we can add a
check box to the wizard to perform this operation. The code is quite simple:

```
procedure TMyDelphiForm.CheckMultilineClick(Sender: TObject);
begin
   Palette.Multiline := CheckMultiline.Checked;
end;
```

A multiline Component palette is very handy when you have more palette pages
than your screen can host. The only problem with this code is that part of the palette
will be hidden from view when it changes from single-line to multiline mode. The
correct size for the palette depends on the number of lines it displays, the width of
your screen, and the font the palette uses. It's possible to write code for all this, but

we decided to keep the example simple, and let the user resize the Component palette using an UpDown component connected to a read-only edit box:

```
procedure TMyDelphiForm.UdHeightClick(Sender: TObject; Button:
TUDBtnType);
begin
  Palette.Height := UdHeight.Position;
  // force resize
  SendMessage (Application.MainForm.Handle,
    wm_Size, 0, 0);
end;
```

Simply setting the height of the Component palette isn't enough, though. The Delphi main Window has a fixed size, automatically computed based on the size of the components it hosts. For this reason, after we change the height of the palette, we just ask Delphi's main window (`Application.MainForm`) to resize itself. Delphi will ignore the size we ask for and simply reapply its own sizing rules. This does the trick.

Below you can see the multiline Component palette in Delphi, displayed at the proper size, and the wizard page that relates to its settings. There's also a Font button for the palette, but this doesn't work very well with bigger fonts. Finally, there's another button that refreshes the new Component palette popup menu.

Adding New Menu Items

The last addition we'll perform with this wizard is to change the Component palette's popup menu. Our wizard adds new items to this menu to let the user select a page of the palette. The code, executed when the wizard starts and when the user presses the *Refresh* button, simply removes any extra menu items we may have added before, and then adds a new menu item for each tab of the `Palette` TabControl component:

```
procedure TMyDelphiForm.BtnRefreshMenuClick(Sender: TObject);
var
  i: Integer;
  mi: TMenuItem;
```

```
begin
  // remove extra items
  with Palette.PopupMenu do
    if Items.Count > 5 then
      for i := Items.Count - 1 downto 5 do
        Items[i].Free;
  // add separator
  mi := TMenuItem.Create (Application);
  mi.Caption := '-';
  Palette.PopupMenu.Items.Add (mi);
  // add one item for every tab
  for i := 0 to Palette.Tabs.Count - 1 do
  begin
    mi := TMenuItem.Create (Application);
    mi.Caption := Palette.Tabs [i];
    mi.OnClick := ChangeTab;
    Palette.PopupMenu.Items.Add (mi);
  end;
end;
```

Once you've executed this code, the local menu of the palette will resemble
Figure 15.12. You'll notice that for every menu item we create, we associate a
common OnClick event handler. The event handler code changes the current tab
to the page that has the same text as the selected menu item (the Sender):

```
procedure TMyDelphiForm.ChangeTab (Sender: TObject);
begin
  Palette.TabIndex := Palette.Tabs.IndexOf (
    (Sender as TMenuItem).Caption);
  Palette.OnChange (self);
end;
```

After we've set the index of the new page, the wizard must explicitly call the
OnChange event handler (which doesn't execute automatically) to force Delphi to
update the current palette page properly.

Storing Default Values

The final improvement we want to make is that we'd like to set the multiline flag
and the palette height once, and then let the wizard restore those values when we
run Delphi in the future. In other words, we want to make these settings persistent. The best solution is to store the new values in the Windows Registry, using

FIGURE 15.12:

The extended popup
menu of the
Component palette
allows a user to move
to a new page faster.

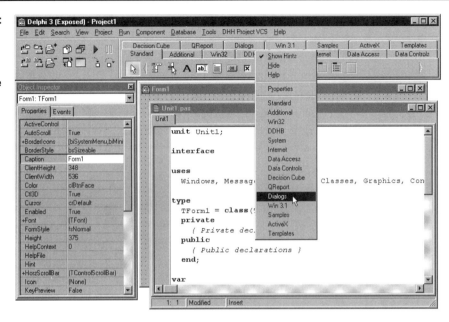

the standard Delphi entry. Here's the updated version of the wizard's `Execute`
method, showing the code we'll use to set the Registry values as you exit from
the form:

```
procedure TMyDelphiWizard.Execute;
var
  Reg: TRegistry;
  Palette: TTabControl;
begin
  MyDelphiForm := TMyDelphiForm.Create (Application);
  try
    MyDelphiForm.ShowModal;
  finally
    MyDelphiForm.Free;
  end;
  // save the status in the registry
  Reg := TRegistry.Create;
  Reg.OpenKey (ToolServices.GetBaseRegistryKey +
    '\MyDelphiWizard', True);
  Palette := Application.MainForm.
    FindComponent ('TabControl') as TTabControl;
```

```
    Reg.WriteBool ('Multiline', Palette.Multiline);
    Reg.WriteInteger ('PaletteHeight', Palette.Height);
    Reg.Free;
  end;
```

As we mentioned above, this method uses Delphi's own Registry key (retrieved by calling the ToolServices global object's GetBaseRegistryKey method), and then either creates or updates a custom key for the wizard, based on the Boolean OpenKey parameter. The values we add or update relate only to the multiline style and the height of the Component palette, but you can easily modify the method to store other options for the fonts and other settings.

If it makes sense to update these values after invoking the wizard, then it also makes sense to update the current setting without any user intervention. The only method in the wizard's unit called when Delphi loads the unit is the Register procedure. For this reason, we've updated this procedure as follows:

```
procedure Register;
var
  Palette: TTabControl;
  Reg: TRegistry;
begin
  RegisterLibraryExpert(TMyDelphiWizard.Create);
  // load the status from the registry
  Reg := TRegistry.Create;
  Reg.OpenKey (ToolServices.GetBaseRegistryKey +
    '\MyDelphiWizard', True);
  Palette := Application.MainForm.
    FindComponent ('TabControl') as TTabControl;
  if Reg.ValueExists ('Multiline') then
    Palette.Multiline := Reg.ReadBool ('Multiline');
  if Reg.ValueExists ('PaletteHeight') then
    Palette.Height := Reg.ReadInteger ('PaletteHeight');
  // force resize
  SendMessage (Application.MainForm.Handle,
    wm_Size, 0, 0);
  Reg.Free;
end;
```

Calling and Changing Delphi's Own Event Handlers

The last wizard we'll build in this chapter is a bit strange. We've called it the Rebuild Wizard, and it started out as a tool built by Marco to simplify the compilation of his *Mastering Delphi 3* book examples. Although it might not be terribly useful for other purposes, it demonstrates a few low-level and interesting tricks, as well as a couple of generic algorithms, so it should be worth studying the code.

The Form of the Rebuild Wizard

The purpose of this wizard is simple: We want to list all the Delphi project files in a given directory and its subdirectories, and then be able to issue a *Build All the Projects* command that will build each project, one by one. Creating the list of Delphi project files isn't too difficult. The wizard's main form displays an edit box to choose the initial directory, and a list box that will display the names of the projects we find. By the way, when you double-click on the edit box, the wizard calls the SelectDirectory VCL global procedure to let you choose a directory graphically:

```
procedure TRebWizForm.EditDirDblClick(Sender: TObject);
var
  Dir: string;
begin
  if SelectDirectory (Dir, [], 0) then
    EditDir.Text := Dir;
end;
```

Once we've set the starting directory, the user can press the *List* button to fill in the list box with the names of the available project files. The OnClick event handler of this button uses a hidden FileListBox component to list all the DPR files in the directory. Then we use the same component to select the subdirectories and repeat the process for each of them. Here's the complete code:

```
procedure TRebWizForm.BtnListClick(Sender: TObject);
begin
  ListBoxFiles.Items.Clear;
  FileListbox1.Directory := EditDir.Text;
  ExamineDir;
  // enable all buttons
  BtnOpen.Enabled := True;
  BtnCompOne.Enabled := True;
  BtnCompileAll.Enabled := True;
end;

procedure TRebWizForm.ExamineDir;
```

```
var
  FileList: TStrings;
  I: Integer;
  CurrDir: string;
begin
  // examine .dpr files
  FileListBox1.Mask := '*.dpr';
  FileListBox1.FileType := [ftNormal];
  FileList := TStringList.Create;
  try
    FileList.Assign(FileListBox1.Items);
    // for each file, add its path to the list
    for I := 0 to FileList.Count - 1 do
    begin
      ListBoxFiles.Items.Add (FileListbox1.Directory +
        '\' + FileList[I]);
    end;

    // examine subdirectories
    FileListBox1.Mask := '*.*';
    FileListBox1.FileType := [ftDirectory];
    FileList.Assign(FileListBox1.Items);
    CurrDir := FileListbox1.Directory;
    // for each dir re-examine...
    for I := 2 to FileList.Count - 1 do
    begin
      FileListbox1.Directory :=
        CurrDir + '\' + Copy (FileList[I], 2,
          Length (FileList [I]) - 2);
      ExamineDir;
    end;
    FileListbox1.Directory := CurrDir;
  finally
    FileList.Free;
  end;
end;
```

Once you have the project file list (shown in Figure 15.13) you can easily open any project in the Delphi environment:

```
procedure TRebWizForm.BtnOpenClick(Sender: TObject);
var
  CurrPrj: string;
```

FIGURE 15.13:

A list of projects selected in the Rebuild Wizard. You can compile them all with a single mouse click.

```
begin
  with ListBoxFiles do
    CurrPrj := Items [ItemIndex];
  ToolServices.OpenProject (CurrPrj);
end;
```

Activating a Delphi Menu Item

At this point, how do we compile the projects? We want to call the Rebuild All command, but there isn't a shortcut key for it, so we can't simply send the keystroke as we did for the Run menu command of the AddIn component editor built in Chapter 13. There are two alternatives: you can search for the necessary menu item and activate its OnClick event handler, or you can locate the appropriate event handler directly. We'll explore the first method soon, but for now let's look at the second and more complex one.

All the event handlers for a form are published methods, and so Delphi must export them as part of the class's RTTI information. Therefore, you can use the TObject class's MethodAddress method to return the address of the appropriate event handler. But how do you call this method once you have its address? You must pass the method address and the associated object to a TMethod record, and then cast it and call it as you would any other event handler. Sound complex? It is, but there isn't much code:

```
procedure TRebWizForm.DoCompile;
var
  ObjDelphi: TWinControl;
```

```
  Meth: TMethod;
  Evt: TNotifyEvent;
  P: Pointer;
begin
  ObjDelphi := Application.MainForm;
  P := ObjDelphi.MethodAddress ('ProjectBuild');
  Meth.Code := P;
  Meth.Data := ObjDelphi;
  Evt := TNotifyEvent (Meth);
  Evt (ObjDelphi);
end;
```

To write this code we simply had to know the name of the event handler, something we found by inspecting the Delphi system (although the Delphi Exposed tool we've shown you doesn't deliver this particular piece of information). Now you can compile a specific project, or all of them:

```
procedure TRebWizForm.BtnCompOneClick(Sender: TObject);
var
  CurrPrj: string;
begin
  with ListBoxFiles do
    CurrPrj := Items [ItemIndex];
  ToolServices.OpenProject (CurrPrj);
  DoCompile;
end;


procedure TRebWizForm.BtnCompileAllClick(Sender: TObject);
var
  CurrPrj: string;
  I: Integer;
begin
  with ListBoxFiles do
    for I := 0 to Items.Count - 1 do
    begin
      CurrPrj := Items [I];
      ToolServices.OpenProject (CurrPrj);
      DoCompile;
    end;
end;
```

If you have the Delphi environment option Show Compiler Progress active, you'll be asked to press the message box's *OK* button after compiling every project, but you'll also be able to keep track of any errors easily. If you disable this option, the wizard will compile all the projects without any manual intervention.

Now there are two remaining issues to resolve. The first is that the wizard should be a modeless form, because this allows us to determine when we create and destroy the form. The other issue is that it would be nice to open this wizard when the user selects the Build All command on the Delphi menu!

A Wizard with a Modeless Form

All the wizards we've built up to now have displayed modal forms. In this case, we need to display a modeless form, because we want to be able to open and work on several projects, and keep the wizard's form open. The Execute method creates the form only if it we haven't already done so:

```
procedure TRebuildWiz.Execute;
begin
  // the actual code
  if not Assigned (RebWizForm) then
    RebWizForm := TRebWizForm.Create (nil);
  RebWizForm.Show;
end;
```

We'll destroy the form later when the user closes it:

```
procedure TRebWizForm.FormClose(Sender: TObject; var Action:
TCloseAction);
begin
  Action := caFree;
  RebWizForm := nil;
end;
```

However, the user might happen to close Delphi or remove a package without closing the wizard first. In either case we can solve the problem by adding a finalization section to the wizard's unit:

```
initialization
  RebWizForm := nil;
```

```
finalization
  if Assigned (RebWizForm) then
    RebWizForm.Free;
```

Hooking to a Delphi Menu Item

The final step is to alter the Rebuild All menu item's event handler. The biggest problem here is to determine when we should perform this operation. Using the wizard unit's initialization and finalization sections might work, as well as using the Register procedure for the startup code as we did in the last wizard. There's a third alternative, which is probably more sound from an OOP perspective. We can add a constructor and a destructor to the wizard class:

```
type
  TRebuildWiz = class (TIExpert)
  private
    OriginalBuildClick: TNotifyEvent;
    BuildMenu: TMenuItem;
  public
    constructor Create;
    destructor Destroy; override;
    procedure BuildClick (Sender: TObject);
    // standard methods
    function GetStyle: TExpertStyle; override;
    function GetName: string; override;
    ...
```

NOTE   You'll notice that we haven't marked the constructor with the override keyword. This is because the TIExpert class's constructor isn't virtual. However, this isn't a problem, because the only instance of the wizard object that will exist is the one we create in the Register procedure.

The constructor simply searches for the appropriate menu item component, saves the original event handler, and then installs a new event handler, while the destructor restores the original event handler. (Having a Delphi menu with an event handler that refers to a method in a destroyed object would result in a very serious error!) Here's the code:

```
constructor TRebuildWiz.Create;
begin
  inherited;
```

```
    // change the event handler of the Build menu item
    BuildMenu := Application.MainForm.
      FindComponent ('ProjectBuildItem') as TMenuItem;
    OriginalBuildClick := BuildMenu.OnClick;
    BuildMenu.OnClick := BuildClick;
  end;

  destructor TRebuildWiz.Destroy;
  begin
    // restore the event handler
    BuildMenu.OnClick := OriginalBuildClick;
    inherited;
  end;
```

Now let's look at the code of the new event handler. It simply asks the user whether to execute the wizard or the standard Rebuild All functionality. If the user chooses the wizard, they have the option of rebuilding all the selected projects automatically:

```
  procedure TRebuildWiz.BuildClick (Sender: TObject);
  begin
    if MessageDlg ('Do you want to open the Rebuild Wizard',
      mtConfirmation, [mbYes, mbNo], 0) = idYes then
    begin
      Execute;
      if MessageDlg ('Do you want to Rebuild All the projects now?',
          mtConfirmation, [mbYes, mbNo], 0) = idYes then
        RebWizForm.BtnCompileAllClick (self);
    end
    else
      OriginalBuildClick (Sender);
  end;
```

Of course there's no guarantee that this code will work in a new version of Delphi (internal event handler names may change dramatically), but that is also the case for the other wizards in the final portion of this chapter. However, it's worth noticing that we've hooked into the Delphi menu item in a much simpler manner than by using the ToolsAPI menu-item interfaces. The only significant drawback is that this code is available only for DCU-based add-ins, and not for external DLLs (although it does work from within a package, which is not very different from a DLL).

What's Next

We began this chapter by looking at version control systems, and then we delved into some obscure Delphi topics, such as the module designers and the direct connection with the environment. You might think these topics are interesting to explore and discuss, but have little practical value for most Delphi programmers. On the contrary; writing wizards and other enhanced tools can significantly improve your workflow and productivity. This was one of our main reasons for writing the previous chapter and this one.

For the same reason, we'll show you more examples of wizards throughout the rest of the book. There's a final tool we're going to show you in the next chapter, but it's related more to the debugger than to the Delphi environment. It doesn't actually hook into the debugger; instead it's a stand-alone debug engine that allows you to inspect an application the same way you build it. In fact, the user interface of our Object Debugger closely mimics that of Delphi's Object Inspector.

CHAPTER

SIXTEEN

16

The Object Debugger

- The RTTI Helper Routines

- Viewing Run-Time Properties

- A Tree of Components

- Editing an Object's Properties at Run-Time

- Cloning the Object Inspector's User Interface

- Wrapping the Object Debugger in a Component

In the last four chapters, we've seen many ways to customize the Delphi programming environment. In this chapter we focus on customizing the debugging environment. To accomplish this we'll extensively use the run-time type information (RTTI) provided by Delphi (and explored in Chapter 4). In that chapter we saw how to access properties by name, and how to read and change their values. Now we want to apply this knowledge to build a powerful debugging tool.

When you build an application in Delphi, you can easily monitor the values of a component's properties by using the Object Inspector. It would be nice if we could also monitor the status of the components of a program when it's running. This is the aim of a tool built by Marco Cantù over the last year, called Object Debugger. It's a run-time clone of the Object Inspector, with similar capabilities. This chapter will give you all the details and source code of the first version of this freeware tool.

This tool was built in many steps, experimenting with different user interfaces, and the chapter documents real-world development of the tool. The Object Debugger still doesn't have all the features planned for it. Even so, it can indeed be a useful addition to your programming toolbox. Keep in mind, however, that the aim of the chapter, as usual, is to teach you a few programming techniques, such as practical applications of the RTTI functions, building forms dynamically (on the fly), and how to duplicate the Object Inspector's user interface.

The RTTI Helper Routines

Before we start exploring the Object Debugger's user interface, let's examine one of its foundations, the RttiHelp unit, which the different versions of the project will share. This unit is a collection of the routines built in various examples from Chapter 4, plus a few new ones:

```
// *** RTTI ***

// show RTTI info in a dialog box
procedure ShowRttiDetail (pti: PTypeInfo);
// show RTTI info (generic)
procedure ShowRTTI (pti: PTypeInfo; sList: TStrings);
// show RTTI information for method pointers (from Chapter 4)
procedure ShowMethod (pti: PTypeInfo; sList: TStrings);
```

```
// show RTTI information for class type (from Chapter 4)
procedure ShowClass (pti: PTypeInfo; sList: TStrings);
// show RTTI information for ordinal types (from Chapter 4)
procedure ShowOrdinal (pti: PTypeInfo; sList: TStrings);
// list enumerated values (from Chapter 4)
procedure ListEnum (pti: PTypeInfo;
  sList: TStrings; ShowIndex: Boolean);


// *** property values ***

// return the property value as a string
function GetPropValAsString (Obj: TObject;
  PropInfo: PPropInfo): string;
// turn the value of a set into a string
function SetToString (Value: Cardinal; pti: PTypeInfo): string;
// sort properties: extracted from TypInfo.PAS
procedure SortPropList(PropList: PPropList;
  PropCount: Integer); assembler;


// *** other ***

// test bit: extracted from Chapter 1 of DDH
function IsBitOn (Value: Integer; Bit: Byte): Boolean;
```

The first group includes many procedures discussed in Chapter 4, plus two more generic ones, ShowRtti and ShowRttiDetail. Then there are three routines related to properties (although one of them is simply an implementation routine, written in assembler, that we've copied from the TypInfo unit). The last function, IsBitOn, was discussed in Chapter 1 and is going to be useful for the example.

Showing Type Information in a Dialog Box

First let's examine the new routines in more detail. ShowRTTI is basically a wrapper for all the other RTTI routines, which add information for specific data types to the StringList object passed as a parameter:

```
procedure ShowRTTI (pti: PTypeInfo; sList: TStrings);
begin
  case pti^.Kind of
    tkInteger, tkChar, tkEnumeration, tkSet, tkWChar:
      ShowOrdinal (pti, sList);
    tkMethod:
```

```
        ShowMethod (pti, sList);
      tkClass:
        Showclass (pti, sList);
      tkString, tkLString:
      begin
        sList.Add ('Type Name: ' + pti^.Name);
        sList.Add ('Type Kind: ' + GetEnumName (
          TypeInfo (TTypeKind), Integer (pti^.Kind)));
      end
      else
        sList.Add ('Undefined type information');
    end;
  end;
```

This procedure adds all the type information to a string list. Most often, however, we'll need to show this data in a dialog box. We could have added an extra form to the program, but since we want to add this tool to existing programs with the least possible impact, we decided to create the form on the fly, without needing an extra unit and a DFM file. This is actually a general technique, which might come in handy in different circumstances:

```
procedure ShowRttiDetail (pti: PTypeInfo);
var
  Form: TForm;
begin
  Form := TForm.Create (Application);
  try
    Form.Width := 250;
    Form.Height := 300;
    // middle of the screen
    Form.Left := Screen.Width div 2 - 125;
    Form.Top := Screen.Height div 2 - 150;
    Form.Caption := 'RTTI Details for ' + pti.Name;
    Form.BorderStyle := bsDialog;
    with TMemo.Create (Form) do
    begin
      Parent := Form;
      Width := Form.ClientWidth;
      Height := Form.ClientHeight - 35;
      ReadOnly := True;
      Color := clBtnFace;
      ShowRTTI (pti, Lines);
    end;
```

```
  with TBitBtn.Create (Form) do
  begin
    Parent := Form;
    Left := Form.ClientWidth div 3;
    Width := Form.ClientWidth div 3;
    Top := Form.ClientHeight - 32;
    Height := 30;
    Kind := bkOK;
  end;
  Form.ShowModal;
finally
  Form.Free;
end;
end;
```

As you can see in the code above, the form has a memo component, which stores the text, and an *OK* button at the bottom. You can see the output of this form in Figure 16.1.

FIGURE 16.1:

The type information form displayed by many examples in this chapter isn't based on a DFM file, it is built on the fly.

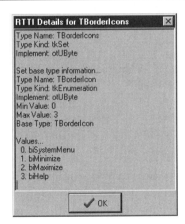

Getting Each Property as Text

The other two functions of the RttiHelp unit, GetPropValAsString and SetToString, are the core of this program. As its name suggests, the aim of the function GetPropValAsString is to return the value of a property as a string, whatever its original data type. As we'll see, we can use the function SetToString to implement one of the most complex cases, that of a set property. `GetPropVal-AsString` is based on a big `case` statement, with some simple cases and some exceptions:

```
function GetPropValAsString (Obj: TObject;
  PropInfo: PPropInfo): string;
var
  Pt: Pointer;
  Word: Cardinal;
begin
  case PropInfo.PropType^.Kind of
    tkUnknown:
      Result := 'Unknown type';
    tkChar:
    begin
      Word := GetOrdProp (Obj, PropInfo);
      if Word > 32 then
        Result := Char (Word)
      else
        Result := '#' + IntToStr (Word);
    end;
    tkWChar:
    begin
      Word := GetOrdProp (Obj, PropInfo);
      if Word > 32 then
        Result := WideChar (Word)
      else
        Result := '#' + IntToStr (Word);
    end;
```

These first three cases are quite simple. The first branch should never be reached (but it's better to use a conservative approach and return something, so that we acknowledge the error), while the second and the third have the kind of code we'll find in many other cases. We access the property value with the functions provided in the TypInfo unit; in this case, we use the function `GetOrdProp`, which is used for most of the types. Notice that when the value of the character is less than 32, the output is simply the # character followed by the character's decimal value.

```
// function GetPropValAsString continued
tkInteger:
  if PropInfo.PropType^.Name = 'TColor' then
    Result := ColorToString (GetOrdProp (Obj, PropInfo))
  else if PropInfo.PropType^.Name = 'TCursor' then
```

```
    Result := CursorToString (GetOrdProp (Obj, PropInfo))
  else
    Result := Format ('%d', [GetOrdProp (Obj, PropInfo)]);
```

If the property is an integer, we should consider two special cases, colors and cursors. We've already mentioned the VCL functions used here (ColorToString and CursorToString) in Chapter 4. The following branches are quite simple:

```
// function GetPropValAsString continued
tkEnumeration:
  Result := GetEnumName (PropInfo.PropType^,
    GetOrdProp (Obj, PropInfo));
tkFloat:
  Result := FloatToStr (GetFloatProp (Obj, PropInfo));
tkString, tkLString:
  Result := GetStrProp (Obj, PropInfo);
tkSet:
  Result := SetToString (GetOrdProp (Obj, PropInfo),
    PropInfo.PropType^);
```

In fact, this last branch only appears to be simple. It calls a special support function we have written, which extracts the names of the current values of the set, listing them in square brackets and separated by commas, as the Object Inspector does:

```
function SetToString (Value: Cardinal; pti: PTypeInfo): string;
var
  Res: String;  // result
  BaseType: PTypeInfo;
  I: Integer;
  Found: Boolean;
begin
  Found := False;
  // open the expression
  Res := '[';
  // get the type of the enumeration
  // the set is based onto
  BaseType := GetTypeData(pti).CompType^;
  // for each possible value
  for I := GetTypeData (BaseType).MinValue
      to GetTypeData (BaseType).MaxValue do
    // if the bit I (computed as 1 shl I) is set,
    // then the corresponding element is in the set
    // (the and is a bitwise and, not a Boolean operation)
    if IsBitOn (Value, I) then
```

```
    begin
      // add the name of the element
      Res := Res + GetEnumName (BaseType, I) + ', ';
      Found := True;
    end;
  if Found then
    // remove the final comma and space (2 chars)
    Res := Copy (Res, 1, Length (Res) - 2);
  // close the expression
  Result := Res + ']';
end;
```

The key element of this function is the if condition, which checks whether the bit I is present in the value of the property. To do this it calls the IsBitOn function (from the Bits1 example in Chapter 1). Figure 16.2 shows an example of the output, taken from the next example, ListView. Here's one more branch of the GetPropValAsString function's case statement:

```
// function GetPropValAsString continued
    tkClass:
    begin
      Pt := Pointer (GetOrdProp (Obj, PropInfo));
      if Pt = nil then
        Result := '(None)'
      else
        Result := Format ('(Object %p)', [Pt]);
    end;
```

The idea is to output the hexadecimal value of the memory address, if any. This is different from what the Object Inspector does; but knowing the object location in memory seems more useful for a debugging tool than simply knowing the data type. You'll notice that there's no special way to access an object, besides using GetOrdProp to retrieve its memory address, and then casting it to the proper type or inspecting its properties.

For events, instead, we can get very interesting output: the name of the associated method of the form, as you can see in Figure 16.3. Here's the code:

```
// function GetPropValAsString continued
    tkMethod:
    begin
      Pt := GetMethodProp (Obj, PropInfo).Code;
      if Pt <> nil then
        Result := GetOwnerForm (Obj as TComponent).
```

```
        MethodName (Pt)
    else
       Result := '';
    end;
```

FIGURE 16.2:

The textual descrip-
tion of a set prop-
erty, produced by
the SetToString
function, as dis-
played by the
ListView example

FIGURE 16.3:

The output of the
ListView example,
showing the name
of the method con-
nected to an event

After getting the method pointer, if it's not `nil`, we can use the `MethodName` function of class `TObject`, which returns the name of the published method that has the given memory address. With event handlers this function is very handy, because most often there are indeed published methods (this is the default behavior in Delphi, at least). This code uses the `GetOwnerForm` function to get the form owning the object (usually the direct owner for a component, or the same object for a form):

```
function GetOwnerForm (Comp: TComponent): TComponent;
begin
  while not (Comp is TForm) and
      not (Comp is TDataModule) do
    Comp := Comp.Owner;
  Result := Comp;
end;
```

The final branches of the `case` statement are quite simple (and almost never used). For this reason, we decided not to implement some of the new but rarely used Delphi 3 data types:

```
// function GetPropValAsString continued
tkVariant:
  Result := GetVariantProp (Obj, PropInfo);
tkArray, tkRecord, tkInterface:
  Result := 'Unsupported type';
else
  Result := 'Undefined type';
```

Well, that was a lot of work. Now we only have to build a nice user interface to output this information. There's actually one more step we have to do, get the list of the properties of a component.

Viewing Run-Time Properties

The first version of the Object Debugger is simply a run-time property viewer, which doesn't allow you to edit the properties. This viewer is part of a demo program (called ListView), but you can easily copy the unit that defines it (called ListVF.PAS, for ListViewForm) into a different program. For the final version, later in this chapter, we'll encapsulate the form in a component to make it easier to use.

As you saw in Figures 16.2 and 16.3 above, the form of the property viewer has a toolbar with two combo boxes and two speed buttons, a tab control taking up most of the area, and a tree view covering the tab control. The properties of these components have very simple values (mostly default ones). Here's their textual description (excluding the labels); it's useful mainly so you can see how methods are connected to events:

```
object ListViewForm: TListViewForm
  Caption = 'List Properties'
  Visible = True
  OnActivate = FormActivate
  object PanelToolbar: TPanel
    Align = alTop
    ShowHint = True
    object ButtRefresh: TSpeedButton
      Hint = 'Refresh'
      OnClick = ButtRefreshClick
    end
    object ButtonAbout: TSpeedButton
      Hint = 'About'
      OnClick = ButtonAboutClick
    end
    object ComboForms: TComboBox
      Style = csDropDownList
      Sorted = True
      OnChange = ComboFormsChange
    end
    object ComboComps: TComboBox
      Style = csDropDownList
      Sorted = True
      OnChange = ComboCompsChange
    end
  end
  object TabControl1: TTabControl
    Align = alClient
    Tabs.Strings = (
      'Properties'
      'Events')
    OnChange = ComboCompsChange
    object TreeProp: TTreeView
      ReadOnly = True
      Align = alClient
```

```
        OnDblClick = TreePropDblClick
      end
    end
  end
```

When the user activates the form (or clicks the *Refresh* speed button), we fill the first combo box with the names of the forms, excluding the form of the property viewer and that of a dialog box we'll add later on. The UpdateComboForms method performs this operation, and is called by the OnActivate event handler of the form and the OnClick event handler of the *Refresh* button:

```
procedure TListViewForm.UpdateComboForms;
var
  I: Integer;
begin
  // empty the combo
  ComboForms.Clear;
  // copy the current name of each form
  for I := 0 to Screen.FormCount - 1 do
    if (Screen.Forms [I] <> self) then
      ComboForms.Items.Add (
        Screen.Forms[I].Name);
  // select the main form
  ComboForms.ItemIndex := ComboForms.Items.IndexOf (
    Application.MainForm.Name);
  ComboFormsChange (ComboForms);
end;
```

The UpdateComboForms procedure ends by selecting the main form of the project in the list, simulating the selection, which fills the second combo box with the names of the components on that form (plus the form itself):

```
procedure TListViewForm.ComboFormsChange(Sender: TObject);
var
  I, nIndex: Integer;
  CurrentForm: TForm;
  CurFormName: string;
begin
  // update components combo
  ComboComps.Clear;
  // get the current form (if it still exists)
  CurrentForm := nil;
  CurFormName := ComboForms.Text;
  for I := 0 to Screen.FormCount - 1 do
```

```
    if Screen.Forms[I].Name = CurFormName then
      CurrentForm := Screen.Forms[I];
  // if the form has been destroyed
  if CurrentForm = nil then
    MessageDlg ('Form not found: Update the list',
      mtError, [mbYes], 0)
  else
  begin
    // list the components
    for I := 0 to CurrentForm.ComponentCount - 1 do
      ComboComps.Items.AddObject (
        CurrentForm.Components [I].Name,
        CurrentForm.Components [I]);
    // add the form itself
    nIndex := ComboComps.Items.AddObject (
      CurrentForm.Name, CurrentForm);
    // select the form
    ComboComps.ItemIndex := nIndex;
    ComboCompsChange (ComboComps);
  end;
end;
```

The code checks whether the form still exists before accessing it, simply because the user might have destroyed the form after the combo box with the list of forms was last updated. Notice that this method adds two items to the list in the second combo box: both the output string and the object we are referring to. This will make it easier to access the object (the component) when the user makes a new selection. Hopefully, the component itself won't be destroyed before a user selects it.

Again, the code at the end selects an item of the combo box (in this case the form added in the previous statement), and updates the tree view by calling the ComboCompsChange method. This code executes when the selection in the combo box changes and when the user selects a new tab:

```
procedure TListViewForm.ComboCompsChange(Sender: TObject);
var
  CurrComp: TComponent;
begin
  // get the current component
  CurrComp := ComboComps.Items.Objects [
    ComboComps.ItemIndex] as TComponent;
  TreeProp.Items.BeginUpdate;
  try
```

```
    TreeProp.Items.Clear;
    // update the list of properties
    ShowProperties (CurrComp, nil);
  finally
    // re-enable tree view
    TreeProp.Items.EndUpdate;
  end;
end;
```

This method disables the tree view by calling `BeginUpdate`. This makes the update much faster, because we'll update the control's user interface only after we call the `EndUpdate` method. It is very important to terminate the update operation, so we use a `try-finally` block.

The core of this method is the call to the `ShowProperties` procedure. We pass as parameters the component for which we want the properties listed and the parent node of the tree view. Since the properties of the component descend directly from the root of the tree view, we use `nil` as the parameter. To show subproperties, we'll pass the node of the main property as the parameter.

If you've read Chapter 4, the code of this method should already be familiar. The core of this method is the call to `GetPropInfos`, a system function that is part of the TypInfo unit, followed by the call to `SortPropList`. This function is also part of the same unit, but Borland didn't export it, so we had to copy it in the RttiHelp unit. These two procedure calls fill the `PropList` local variable with the sorted list of the component's properties.

There are also a few new aspects. One is the call to the `GetPropValAsString` function discussed in the last section. A second new element is that we filter either for method types or nonmethod types, depending on the current selection of the tab control. A third noteworthy aspect is that the effect of the method is to add new items to the tree view control, along with the pointer to the property information, used later on.

```
procedure TListViewForm.ShowProperties (
  Obj: TObject; BaseNode: TTreeNode);
var
  PropList: PPropList;
  CurrNode: TTreeNode;
  nTotProperties, nProp: Integer;
  fPropsPage: Boolean;
begin
  // get the number of properties
```

```
nTotProperties := GetTypeData(Obj.ClassInfo).PropCount;
if nTotProperties <> 0 then
begin
  fPropsPage := (TabControl1.TabIndex = 0);
  // get the list of properties (sorted)
  GetMem (PropList, sizeof (PPropInfo) * nTotProperties);
  try
    GetPropInfos (Obj.ClassInfo, PropList);
    SortPropList(PropList, nTotProperties);

    // show the name of each property or event
    for nProp := 0 to nTotProperties - 1 do
      // if we've asked for properties and it is not a method
      // or we've asked for methods and we find one...
      if (fPropsPage and
          (PropList[nProp].PropType^.Kind <> tkMethod)) or
        (not fPropsPage and
          (PropList[nProp].PropType^.Kind = tkMethod)) then
      begin
        // add the property to the tree
        CurrNode := TreeProp.Items.AddChildObject (
          BaseNode,
          Format ('%s: %s', [PropList[nProp].Name,
            GetPropValAsString (Obj, PropList[nProp])]),
            TObject (PropList[nProp]));
        // if the property is a class and the object exists
        // add its subproperties (with a recursive call)
        if (PropList[nProp].PropType^.Kind = tkClass) and
            (GetOrdProp (Obj, PropList[nProp]) <> 0) then
          ShowProperties (
            TObject (GetOrdProp (Obj, PropList[nProp])),
            CurrNode);
      end;
  finally
    FreeMem (PropList, sizeof (PPropInfo) * nTotProperties);
  end;
  end;
end;
```

When we find a class property, if the value of the object isn't nil (that is, if its ordinal value isn't zero) we call ShowProperties again, in a recursive way. This will add a plus sign on the side of the class property item in the tree, allowing a user to expand it, as you can see in Figure 16.4.

Last, when a user double-clicks on an item in the tree view, we want to be able to show RTTI information about the property, calling the helper routines seen before. To accomplish this we need to retrieve the information about the property, stored as Data of the node of the tree view:

```
procedure TListViewForm.TreePropDblClick(Sender: TObject);
var
  CurrProp: PPropInfo;
begin
  // show the RTTI details for the property type
  CurrProp := PPropInfo (TreeProp.Selected.Data);
  if CurrProp <> nil then
    ShowRttiDetail (CurrProp.PropType^);
end;
```

We've already seen the output of this function in Figure 16.1.

Version 2: A Tree of Components

Besides structuring the properties inside a tree, the second version of the Object Debugger also uses a tree to display the structure of the application, with forms and components. You can see an example in Figure 16.5. An interesting alternative to this approach would be to show the components using the parent/child relationship (as we did in the Delphi Exposed Wizard example in the last chapter).

FIGURE 16.5:

The TreeView version of the Object Debugger shows the forms and their components in a tree.

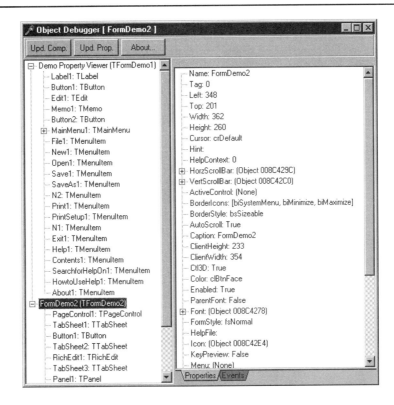

NOTE Only the last version of the Object Debugger will work with data modules, as well as forms and their components. If you like this user interface more than the final one, you can easily mix the code of the two examples.

The run-time property viewer form of the TreeView example has two tree view components, separated by a Splitter component. On the right, there's a panel that contains a label in the upper portion and the tree view. We'll use the label to display the selected property's data type.

The structure of the program is similar to that of the last version. The UpdateComp-Tree method updates the tree of components, and we call it when the user activates the form or presses the *Update* button. The only noteworthy aspect of its code is that we had to disable the tree view components' OnChange event handlers in order to avoid some useless operations that were slowing down the process:

```
procedure TTreeViewForm.UpdateCompTree;
var
  CurrNode: TTreeNode;
  CurrForm: TForm;
  nForm: Integer;
begin
  // show the hourglass cursor
  Screen.Cursor := crHourglass;
  // disable the output and the events
  TreeProp.Items.BeginUpdate;
  TreeComp.Items.BeginUpdate;
  TreeComp.OnChange := nil;
  TreeProp.OnChange := nil;
  try
    // empty the trees
    TreeProp.Items.Clear;
    TreeComp.Items.Clear;
    // for each form of the program
    for nForm := 0 to Screen.FormCount - 1 do
    begin
      CurrForm := Screen.Forms[nForm];
      if CurrForm <> self then
      begin
        // if the form is not the current one, show it
        CurrNode := TreeComp.Items.AddObject (
          nil, // no parent
          Format ('%s (%s)', [CurrForm.Caption, CurrForm.ClassName]),
          Pointer (CurrForm));
        // add the components of the form
        if CurrForm.ComponentCount > 0 then
          ListSubComponents (CurrForm, CurrNode);
      end;
    end;
  finally
    // remove the hourglass cursor
    Screen.Cursor := crDefault;
    // enable the output and the events
    TreeComp.OnChange := TreeCompChange;
    TreeProp.OnChange := TreePropChange;
    TreeComp.Items.EndUpdate;
    TreeProp.Items.EndUpdate;
```

```
    end;
  end;
```

The `ListSubComponents` method produces the same output for every subcomponent of the form (or other component) passed as its parameter. It's called recursively, even though very few components (apart from forms) own other components:

```
procedure TTreeViewForm.ListSubComponents (
    BaseComp: TComponent; BaseNode: TTreeNode);
var
  nComp: Integer;
  CurrNode: TTreeNode;
  CurrComp: TComponent;
begin
  // for each component owned by the current one
  // (possibly the form, but not always)
  for nComp := 0 to BaseComp.ComponentCount - 1 do
  begin
    CurrComp := BaseComp.Components [nComp];
    CurrNode := TreeComp.Items.AddChildObject (
      BaseNode,
      Format ('%s: %s', [CurrComp.Name, CurrComp.ClassName]),
      CurrComp);
    // recursively calls itself
    if CurrComp.ComponentCount > 0 then
      ListSubComponents (CurrComp, CurrNode);
  end;
end;
```

The next block of code fills the first tree and empties the second one. By selecting an item on the component tree you can activate its `OnChange` event handler; this updates the caption, stores the current component, and calls the `UpdateProperties` method. This updating happens automatically in some cases.

```
procedure TTreeViewForm.TreeCompChange(
    Sender: TObject; Node: TTreeNode);
begin
  // a new component has been selected
  Caption := Format ('%s [ %s ]',
    ['Object Debugger', TComponent (Node.Data).Name]);
  CurrentComponent := TComponent (Node.Data);
  // update the properties window or the events window
  UpdateProperties (CurrentComponent, TabSet1.TabIndex = 0);
end;
```

```
procedure TTreeViewForm.UpdateProperties (
  CurrComp: TComponent; Props: Boolean);
begin
  Screen.Cursor := crHourglass;
  TreeProp.Items.BeginUpdate;
  TreeProp.OnChange := nil;
  TreeProp.Items.Clear;
  try
    UpdateSubProperties (CurrComp, // component
      CurrComp.ClassType, // class type
      nil, // base tree node
      Props); // props or events
  finally
    // re-enable everything
    Screen.Cursor := crDefault;
    TreeProp.OnChange := TreePropChange;
    TreeProp.Items.EndUpdate;
  end;
end;
```

You can see that the UdpateProperties method is very similar to the previous example. The UpdateSubProperties method is also very similar, so we've decided not to list it in the text. Not surprisingly, the rest of the code is quite simple too. We update the value of CurrentComponent, one of the form's private fields, in the second tree view's OnChange event handler, which also updates the property type information in the label:

```
procedure TTreeViewForm.TreePropChange(
  Sender: TObject; Node: TTreeNode);
var
  TempProp: PPropInfo;
begin
  // get the active component in the first tree view
  // (it might have changed if we were accessing a subproperty)
  CurrentComponent := TComponent (TreeComp.Selected.Data);
  // get the selected property
  CurrentProperty := PPropInfo (Node.Data);
  // show the name of the data type in the label
  LabelType.Caption := CurrentProperty.PropType^.Name;
  // if it is a subproperty, select the "parent"
  // property as the current component
  if Node.Level > 0 then
```

```
begin
  TempProp := PPropInfo (Node.Parent.Data);
  CurrentComponent := TComponent (
    GetOrdProp (CurrentComponent, TempProp));
  end;
end;
```

We use the conditional section at the end of this method to extract the correct type information in case the property isn't part of the component itself, but is a subproperty, such as Font (as in Figure 16.6).

FIGURE 16.6:

The TreeView example must determine if the selected property is part of a subcomponent or subobject of the current component (like the Font subobject shown here).

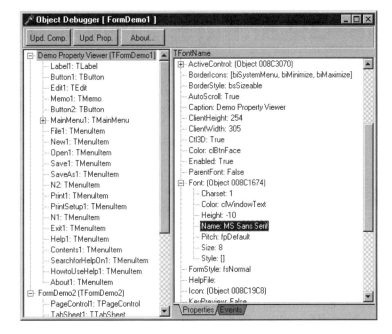

Finally, this form contains a new speed button that updates only the property values of the selected component (which might change as a result of interaction with the program you're monitoring). Here's the code:

```
procedure TTreeViewForm.SpeedToolUpdatePropClick(
  Sender: TObject);
var
  Node: TTreeNode;
begin
```

```
  // update the tree of properties, if a component is selected
  Node := TreeComp.Selected;
  if Node <> nil then
  begin
    CurrentComponent := TComponent (Node.Data);
    UpdateProperties (CurrentComponent, TabSet1.TabIndex = 0);
  end
  else
    ShowMessage ('No component selected');
end;
```

Version 3: Editing the Properties

The first two versions of the Object Debugger could only let you browse through the components and their properties. This third version and the next one also allow the user to change the values of most properties at run-time. Although doing so doesn't always make sense, and can even cause trouble (for example, if you change a component's Name property), by modifying properties at run-time you can sometimes determine the best solution for a programming problem. Yes, it's true that the edit/compile/execute cycle in Delphi is very fast, but testing different values with just a mouse click is even faster. After you've modified the property values of a component, you can easily get back to the development environment and apply those changes as well.

This new version of the Object Debugger, available as part of the TreeEdit example, is again based on two TreeView components, but has a small editing area hosted by a multipage notebook. Every page of the notebook has a different user interface (with edit boxes, combo boxes, confirmation buttons, and so on) and is appropriate for editing specific types of properties. You can see all the pages of the notebook listed in this excerpt from the form's textual description:

```
object NotebookEdit: TNotebook
  Align = alTop
  object TPage
    Caption = 'Default'
    object SpeedDefaultEll: TSpeedButton
      Caption = '...'
      Visible = False
      OnClick = SpeedDefaultEllClick
    end
  end
```

```
object TPage
  Caption = 'Edit'
  object SpeedEditOK: TSpeedButton
    Caption = 'v'
    OnClick = SpeedEditOKClick
  end
  object EditEdit: TEdit...
end
object TPage
  Caption = 'NumEdit'
  object SpeedEditNumOK: TSpeedButton
    Caption = 'v'
    OnClick = SpeedEditNumOKClick
  end
  object EditNum: TEdit
    Text = '0'
  end
end
object TPage
  Caption = 'Combo'
  object SpeedComboOK: TSpeedButton
    Caption = 'v'
    OnClick = SpeedComboOKClick
  end
  object SpeedComboEll: TSpeedButton
    Caption = '...'
    OnClick = SpeedComboEllClick
  end
  object ComboBox1: TComboBox...
end
  end
end
```

Now let us look at the new code. The notebook at startup shows the empty Default page; the other pages are activated when the user chooses a property. This takes place in the OnChange event handler of the second tree view component. This method has a case statement with branches for some but not all of the property types. Here's the initial portion and the first branch:

```
procedure TTreeEditForm.TreePropChange(
  Sender: TObject; Node: TTreeNode);
var
```

```
    TempProp: PPropInfo;
    I: Integer;
begin
  // display the type name in the label,
  // as in the TreeView example
  // ...

  // set up the proper editor in the mini notebook
  // this is the starting point of the editing code
  case CurrentProperty.PropType^.Kind of
    tkInteger:
    begin
      if CurrentProperty.PropType^.Name = 'TCursor' then
      begin
        ComboBox1.Items.Clear;
        GetCursorValues (AddToCombo);
        ComboBox1.ItemIndex := Combobox1.Items.IndexOf (
          GetPropValAsString (CurrentComponent, CurrentProperty));
        NotebookEdit.ActivePage := 'Combo';
      end
      else if CurrentProperty.PropType^.Name = 'TColor' then
      begin
        ComboBox1.Items.Clear;
        GetColorValues (AddToCombo);
        ComboBox1.ItemIndex := Combobox1.Items.IndexOf (
          GetPropValAsString (CurrentComponent, CurrentProperty));
        NotebookEdit.ActivePage := 'Combo';
        SpeedComboEll.Visible := True;
      end
      else
      begin
        EditNum.Text := GetPropValAsString (
          CurrentComponent, CurrentProperty);
        NotebookEdit.ActivePage := 'NumEdit';
      end;
    end;
```

If the property is a color or a cursor, the program activates the Combo page of the notebook and fills the combo box with the list of the colors or cursors available in the system. The two VCL global procedures, GetColorValues and

GetCursorValues, accept a call-back procedure as their only parameter (called for every possible value):

```
procedure TTreeEditForm.AddToCombo (const S: String);
begin
  Combobox1.Items.Add (S);
end;
```

Notice that if the type is a color, the program also activates an ellipsis speed button, connected to the standard color selection dialog box, as you can see in Figure 16.7.

FIGURE 16.7:

In the TreeEdit version of the Object Debugger, when the type of the property is TColor, a user can select a color in the drop-down combo box or press the ellipsis button for the standard dialog box.

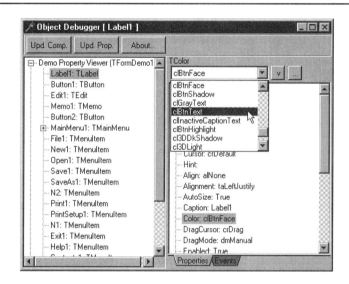

If the type is an enumeration, the program displays another combo box, containing all the possible enumeration values, which we extract from the run-time type information:

```
tkEnumeration:
begin
  ComboBox1.Clear;
  for I := 0 to GetTypeData(CurrentProperty.PropType^).MaxValue do
    AddToCombo (GetEnumName (CurrentProperty.PropType^, I));
  ComboBox1.ItemIndex := Combobox1.Items.IndexOf (
    GetPropValAsString (CurrentComponent, CurrentProperty));
  NotebookEdit.ActivePage := 'Combo';
end;
```

In case of a string, the code is much simpler, and the user can edit the string directly in an Edit box (as you can see in Figure 16.8):

```
tkString, tkLString:
    begin
      EditEdit.text := GetStrProp (
        CurrentComponent, CurrentProperty);
      NotebookEdit.ActivePage := 'Edit';
    end;
```

FIGURE 16.8:

The Edit page is the simplest of the TreeEdit example's property editors.

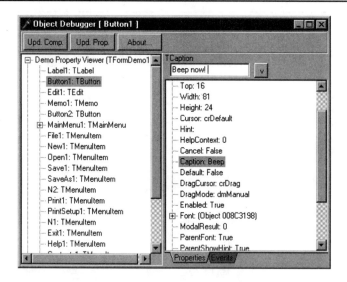

Finally, if the property refers to a class, the only case we handle is that of the TFont data type. This is an area we could extend to handle multiple data types, with specific editors:

```
tkClass:
begin
  if CurrentProperty.PropType^.Name = 'TFont' then
    SpeedDefaultEll.Visible := True;
  NotebookEdit.ActivePage := 'Default';
end;
```

There are several other data types (such as set or char) that we haven't considered in this version of the Object Debugger. Now, once we've displayed one of the notebook pages, the user can enter or select a new value. Usually, the user will press the check mark speed button that displays the simple caption. Here are the two simple event handlers for the Edit and NumEdit page *OK* buttons:

```
procedure TTreeEditForm.SpeedEditOKClick(Sender: TObject);
begin
  SetStrProp (CurrentComponent, CurrentProperty,
    EditEdit.Text);
end;

procedure TTreeEditForm.SpeedEditNumOKClick(Sender: TObject);
begin
  SetOrdProp (CurrentComponent, CurrentProperty,
    StrToInt (EditNum.Text));
end;
```

The code for the ComboBox page is more complex, since this page is used by different properties. Here the *OK* button should determine the type and convert the selected string properly:

```
procedure TTreeEditForm.SpeedComboOKClick(Sender: TObject);
var
  Col: LongInt;
begin
  if CurrentProperty.PropType^.Name = 'TCursor' then
    SetOrdProp (CurrentComponent, CurrentProperty,
      StringToCursor (ComboBox1.Text))
  else if CurrentProperty.PropType^.Name = 'TColor' then
  begin
    IdentToColor (ComboBox1.Text, Col);
    SetOrdProp (CurrentComponent, CurrentProperty, Col);
  end
  else // plain enumeration
    SetOrdProp (CurrentComponent, CurrentProperty,
      GetEnumValue (CurrentProperty.PropType^, ComboBox1.Text));
end;
```

We'll activate the ellipsis (. . .) button only for colors, but its code must convert the color from a string to the color value required by the standard dialog box, and vice versa:

```
procedure TTreeEditForm.SpeedComboEllClick(Sender: TObject);
var
  Col: LongInt;
  ColName: string;
```

```
begin
  if CurrentProperty.PropType^.Name = 'TColor' then
  begin
    IdentToColor (ComboBox1.Text, Col);
    ColorDialog1.Color := Col;
    if ColorDialog1.Execute then
    begin
      ColorToIdent (ColorDialog1.Color, ColName);
      ComboBox1.ItemIndex := ComboBox1.Items.IndexOf (ColName);
    end;
  end;
end;
```

Finally the *Default* page might have an ellipsis button connected to the standard font dialog box:

```
procedure TTreeEditForm.SpeedDefaultEllClick(Sender: TObject);
begin
  if CurrentProperty.PropType^.Name = 'TFont' then
  begin
    FontDialog1.Font := TFont (
      GetOrdProp (CurrentComponent, CurrentProperty));
    if FontDialog1.Execute then
      SetOrdProp (CurrentComponent, CurrentProperty,
        LongInt (FontDialog1.Font));
  end;
end;
```

This is all the code we've added to the TreeView example to turn it into the TreeEdit version. Although this property editor is still not complete, and the user interface isn't very usable, it already demonstrates how we can edit most of a Delphi application's component properties at run-time.

In the next version, we'll radically change the user interface and add support for a few extra data types. The code will be more complex, but we won't introduce new concepts.

Cloning the Object Inspector's User Interface

The last version of the Object Debugger has slightly improved capabilities, but the biggest change is in the user interface. Instead of finding better ways to display the editors used in the last version, we decided to clone a user interface familiar to every Delphi programmer, the Object Inspector.

The new form (part of the GridEdit example) contains a top-aligned panel and a PageControl component. The panel hosts two combo boxes, one for selecting a form and the other for selecting a component of that form. The PageControl has two pages, named Properties and Events, each of which contains a StringGrid component with two columns. You can see the form at design time in Figure 16.9 and the key elements of its textual description in the following listing:

```
object GridEditForm: TGridEditForm
  Caption = 'Object Debugger'
  Visible = True
  OnActivate = FormActivate
  OnCreate = FormCreate
  OnResize = FormResize
  object Panel1: TPanel
    Align = alTop
    object cbComps: TComboBox
      Style = csDropDownList
      Sorted = True
      OnChange = cbCompsChange
    end
    object cbForms: TComboBox
      Style = csDropDownList
      OnChange = cbFormsChange
    end
  end
  object PageControl1: TPageControl
    Align = alClient
    object TabSheet1: TTabSheet
      Caption = 'Properties'
      object sgProp: TStringGrid
        Align = alClient
        Color = clBtnFace
        ColCount = 2
```

```
                    DefaultColWidth = 120
                    DefaultRowHeight = 18
                    FixedCols = 0
                    RowCount = 12
                    Options = [goFixedVertLine, goFixedHorzLine,
                      goVertLine, goHorzLine]
                    ScrollBars = ssVertical
                    OnDblClick = sgPropDblClick
                    OnMouseDown = sgMouseDown
                    OnSelectCell = sgPropSelectCell
                  end
                  object ListSet: TListBox...
                  object EditCh: TEdit...
                  object EditStr: TEdit...
                  object EditNum: TEdit...
                  object ComboEnum: TComboBox...
                  object ComboCursor: TComboBox...
                  object ComboColor: TComboBox...
                end
                object TabSheet2: TTabSheet
                  Caption = 'Events'
                  object sgEvt: TStringGrid... // same as sgProp
                end
              end
              object ColorDialog1: TColorDialog...
              object FontDialog1: TFontDialog...
              object MainMenu1: TMainMenu...
            end
```

The first TabSheet of the PageControl hosts many controls used for editing the properties. As we'll see in a while, when you select a property, we place a corresponding editor over the grid, so the user appears to be editing the values in the grid.

Before we look at the editing code, however, there are a few other additions to the code worth exploring. One of the most important is the support for data modules, something we intentionally skipped in previous versions. The data modules of the current project are stored in a list of the global Screen object, in the same way the Screen object maintains a list of forms. Here's the code we use to fill the combo box that displays the list of forms and data modules:

```
procedure TGridEditForm.UpdateFormsCombo;
var
```

FIGURE 16.9:

The form displayed by the GridEdit version of the Object Debugger at design time

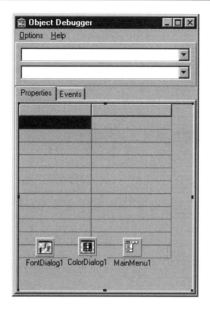

```
  I, nForm, Pos: Integer;
  Form: TForm;
begin
  Screen.Cursor := crHourglass;
  cbForms.Items.BeginUpdate;
  try
    cbForms.Items.Clear;
    // for each form of the program
    for nForm := 0 to Screen.FormCount - 1 do
    begin
      Form := Screen.Forms [nForm];
      // if the form is not the one of the ObjectDebugger, add it
      if Form <> self then
        cbForms.Items.AddObject (
          Format ('%s (%s)', [Form.Caption, Form.ClassName]),
          Form);
    end;
    // for each data module
    for I := 0 to Screen.DataModuleCount - 1 do
      cbForms.Items.AddObject (
        Format ('%s (%s)',
```

```
          [Screen.DataModules [I].Name,
          Screen.DataModules [I].ClassName]),
          Screen.DataModules [I]);
  // re-select the current form, if it exists
  if not Assigned (CurrForm) then
    CurrForm := Application.MainForm;
  Pos := cbForms.Items.IndexOfObject (CurrForm);
  if Pos < 0 then
  begin
    // was a destroyed form, retry...
    CurrForm := Application.MainForm;
    Pos := cbForms.Items.IndexOfObject (CurrForm);
  end;
  cbForms.ItemIndex := Pos;
  finally
    cbForms.Items.EndUpdate;
    Screen.Cursor := crDefault;
  end;
  UpdateCompsCombo;
end;
```

TIP   Notice that the CurrForm local field of the form was declared as type
TForm in previous versions, but is now declared as type TComponent to
accommodate data modules as well.

At the end, the UpdateFormsCombo calls UpdateCompsCombo, which fills the
combo box of the components of the current form of data module, with code very
similar to the last example. The code that fills the list of properties or events and
their values is similar to past versions, but this time the output it produces is different. The property and event names are added to the first column of the respective grid, along with the PProfInfo data.

Before reading the code, take a look at Figure 16.10, which shows the output of
the GridEdit example. Notice in particular that the first line (row zero) hosts the
information about the data type of the current property, so we will leave it blank for
the moment. Notice also that the UpdateProps procedure isn't recursive (as in past
versions of the Object Debugger) but simply expands the subproperties of objects
that aren't components, exactly as the Object Inspector does. The difference is that
the plus sign is fixed here, and you cannot expand or collapse subproperties.

FIGURE 16.10:

The output of the last version of the Object Debugger at run-time. Notice that the first line of the grid is reserved for type information about the current property.

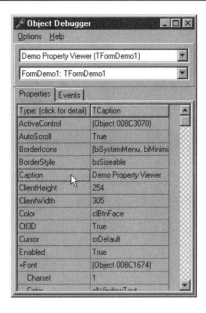

Here, then, is the complete listing of the UpdateProps method, which you should read carefully:

```
procedure TGridEditForm.UpdateProps;
var
  PropList, SubPropList: TPropList;
  NumberOfProps, NumberOfSubProps, // total number of properties
  nProp, nSubProp, // property loop counter
  nRowProp, nRowEvt: Integer; // items actually added
  SubObj: TPersistent;
begin
  // reset the type
  sgProp.Cells [1, 0] := '';
  sgEvt.Cells [1, 0] := '';

  // get the number of properties
  NumberOfProps := GetTypeData(CurrComp.ClassInfo).PropCount;
  // increase he size...
  sgProp.RowCount := NumberOfProps;
  sgEvt.RowCount := NumberOfProps;
```

```
// get the list of properties and sort it
GetPropInfos (CurrComp.ClassInfo, @PropList);
SortPropList(@PropList, NumberOfProps);

// show the name and value of each property
// adding it to the proper page
nRowProp := 1;
nRowEvt := 1;
for nProp := 0 to NumberOfProps - 1 do
begin
  // if it is a real property
  if PropList[nProp].PropType^.Kind <> tkMethod then
  begin
    // name
    sgProp.Cells [0, nRowProp] := PropList[nProp].Name;
    // value
    sgProp.Cells [1, nRowProp] := GetPropValAsString (
      CurrComp, PropList [nProp]);
    // data
    sgProp.Objects [0, nRowProp] := TObject (PropList[nProp]);
    sgProp.Objects [1, nRowProp] := nil;
    // move to the next line
    Inc (nRowProp);
    // if the property is a class
    if (PropList[nProp].PropType^.Kind = tkClass) then
    begin
      SubObj := TPersistent (GetOrdProp (
        CurrComp, PropList[nProp]));
      if (SubObj <> nil) and not (SubObj is TComponent) then
      begin
        NumberOfSubProps :=
          GetTypeData(SubObj.ClassInfo).PropCount;
        if NumberOfSubProps > 0 then
        begin
          // add plus sign
          sgProp.Cells [0, nRowProp - 1] := '+' +
            sgProp.Cells [0, nRowProp - 1];
          // add space for subproperties...
          sgProp.RowCount := sgProp.RowCount +
            NumberOfSubProps;
          // get the list of subproperties and sort it
          GetPropInfos (subObj.ClassInfo, @SubPropList);
          SortPropList(@SubPropList, NumberOfSubProps);
```

```
      // show the name of each subproperty
      for nSubProp := 0 to NumberOfSubProps - 1 do
      begin
        // if it is a real property
        if SubPropList[nSubProp].PropType^.Kind <>
          tkMethod then
        begin
          // name (indented)
          sgProp.Cells [0, nRowProp] :=
            '   ' + SubPropList[nSubProp].Name;
          // value
          sgProp.Cells [1, nRowProp] :=
            GetPropValAsString (SubObj,
              SubPropList [nSubProp]);
          // data
          sgProp.Objects [0, nRowProp] :=
            TObject (SubPropList[nSubProp]);
          sgProp.Objects [1, nRowProp] := SubObj;
          Inc (nRowProp);
        end; // if SubPropList...Kind <> thMethod
      end; // for nSubProp
    end; // if NumberOfSubProps > 0
  end; // if (SubObj <> nil)
  end; // adding subproperties
end // if Kind <> thMethod
else // it is an event
begin
  // name
  sgEvt.Cells [0, nRowEvt] := PropList[nProp].Name;
  // value
  sgEvt.Cells [1, nRowEvt] := GetPropValAsString (
    CurrComp, PropList [nProp]);
  // data
  sgEvt.Objects [0, nRowEvt] := TObject (PropList[nProp]);
  // next
  Inc (nRowEvt);
end;
end; // for nProp
// set the actual rows
sgProp.RowCount := nRowProp;
sgEvt.RowCount := nRowEvt;
end;
```

NOTE The data portion of the first cell of the grid stores the PPropInfo pointer for the property stored in the cell, while the data portion of the second cell is used to store the value of the main property if there is a subproperty. For this reason, this value is also used to distinguish plain properties from subproperties.

The Editing Code

If the code used by the GridView program to list the properties and their values in the grid is more complex than in past examples, the editing code is *much* more complex. For this reason, we won't list the entire code in the book. This section provides an overview and shows some of the code, but you'll need to study the source code for this form (almost 750 lines), available on the companion disk, to understand the details.

We execute the editing code when the user selects an element in the right column of the properties grid (in fact, there's no way to edit the component's events). The OnSelectCell event and its handler have a couple of peculiarities. First, the event handler uses a simple nested procedure, PlaceControl. Nested procedures were a common programming practice in Pascal, but aren't a typical object-oriented programming technique because there are other ways to enforce appropriate program scope. In this case, it's appropriate, so we've decided to retain this style. In fact, the procedure places one of the editing controls over the current grid cell, and makes no sense outside the context of this method.

Second, the sgPropSelectCell method uses conditional compilation to produce Delphi 2 and Delphi 3 versions of the same source code. The {$IFDEF VER100} expression is true only if we are compiling with Delphi 3, but a similar definition based on the compiler version (10.0 for Delphi 3) is available in each version of Delphi.

In Figure 16.11, you can see the effect of editing a string property.

Here's the code, which in functionality isn't very different from the last example.

```
procedure TGridEditForm.sgPropSelectCell(Sender: TObject;
  Col, Row: Longint; var CanSelect: Boolean);
var
  sg: TStringGrid;
  ppInfo: PPropInfo;
  I: Integer;
```

FIGURE 16.11:

In the GridEdit example, you can edit a string property *in-place* by working with a special edit box placed in front of the corresponding grid cell.

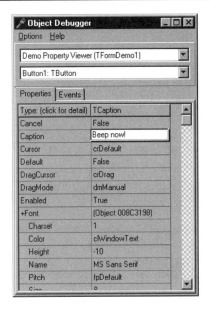

```
procedure PlaceControl (Ctrl: TWinControl);
begin
  Ctrl.BringToFront;
  Ctrl.Show;
  Ctrl.BoundsRect := sg.CellRect (Col, Row);
  Ctrl.SetFocus;
end;

begin
  sg := Sender as TStringGrid;
  // get the data and show it in the first line
  ppInfo := PPropInfo (sg.Objects [0, Row] );
  sg.Cells [1, 0] := ppInfo.PropType^.Name;
  {$IFDEF VER100}
  sg.Objects [1, 0] := Pointer (ppInfo.PropType^);
  {$ELSE} // Delphi 2
  sg.Objects [1, 0] := Pointer (ppInfo.PropType);
  {$ENDIF}
  // if second column activate the proper editor
  if Col = 1 then
```

```
begin
  CurrProp := ppInfo;
  CurrRow := Row;
  // if it is a subproperty, select the value of
  // the property as the current component
  if sg.Objects [1, Row] <> nil then
  begin
    RealComp := CurrComp;
    EditingSub := True;
    CurrComp := TComponent (sg.Objects [1, Row]);
  end;

  ////////// depending on the type, display an editor

  case ppInfo.PropType^.Kind of

    tkInteger: //////////////////////////////////
    begin
      if ppInfo.PropType^.Name = 'TCursor' then
      begin
        ComboCursor.Text := GetPropValAsString (CurrComp, ppInfo);
        PlaceControl (ComboCursor);
      end else if ppInfo.PropType^.Name = 'TColor' then
      begin
        ComboColor.Tag := GetOrdProp (CurrComp, ppInfo);
        ComboColor.Text := GetPropValAsString (CurrComp, ppInfo);
        PlaceControl (ComboColor)
      end else
      begin
        EditNum.Text := GetPropValAsString (CurrComp, ppInfo);
        PlaceControl (EditNum);
        EditModified := False;
      end;
    end;

    tkChar: /////////////////////////////////////////
    begin
      EditCh.Text := GetPropValAsString (CurrComp, ppInfo);
      PlaceControl (EditCh);
      EditModified := False;
    end;
```

```
  tkEnumeration: /////////////////////////////////////
  begin
    ComboEnum.Clear;
    {$IFDEF VER100}
    ListEnum (ppInfo.PropType^, ComboEnum.Items, False);
    {$ELSE} // Delphi 2
    ListEnum (ppInfo.PropType, ComboEnum.Items, False);
    {$ENDIF}
    ComboEnum.ItemIndex := ComboEnum.Items.IndexOf (
      GetPropValAsString (CurrComp, ppInfo));
    PlaceControl (ComboEnum);
  end;

  tkString, tkLString: //////////////////////////
  begin
    EditStr.Text := GetStrProp (
      CurrComp, ppInfo);
    PlaceControl (EditStr);
    EditModified := False;
  end;

  tkSet: /////////////////////////////////////////
  begin
    ListSet.Clear;
    ListEnum (
      {$IFDEF VER100}
      GetTypeData (ppInfo.PropType^).CompType^,
      {$ELSE} // Delphi 2
      GetTypeData (ppInfo.PropType).CompType,
      {$ENDIF}
      ListSet.Items, False);
    // select the "on" items
    for I := 0 to ListSet.Items.Count - 1 do
      ListSet.Selected [I] :=
        IsBitOn (GetOrdProp (CurrComp, ppINfo), I);
    PlaceControl (ListSet);
    ListSet.Height := ListSet.Height * 8;
  end;
  end;
  end;
end;
```

One of the more obvious new features of this version of the Object Debugger (besides the differences in the user interface) is its support for editing set properties. We copy all the possible values of the set into a multiple-selection list box (using the GetTypeData call), as you can see in Figure 16.12. Then we select all the list box entries that correspond to active values of the set. If the user selects one of the items, the program sets the corresponding value in the current property of the current component:

```
procedure TGridEditForm.ListSetClick(Sender: TObject);
var
  Value: Word;
  I: Integer;
begin
  Value := 0;
  // update the value, scanning the list
  for I := 0 to ListSet.Items.Count - 1 do
    if ListSet.Selected [I] then
      Value := Value + Round (Power (2, I));
  SetOrdProp (CurrComp, CurrProp, Value);
end;
```

FIGURE 16.12:

The set property editor is different than the one in the Object Inspector, but it's very easy to use.

For the other editors, we use similar methods to update the value upon completing the editing operation. The editors (based on edit boxes) keep track of whether the user actually made any change:

```
procedure TDdhGridEditForm.EditStrExit(Sender: TObject);
begin
  try
    if EditModified then
      SetStrProp (CurrComp, CurrProp, EditStr.Text);
  finally
    RefreshOnExit (Sender);
  end;
end;
```

We set the EditModified Boolean field to True in the OnChange event handler of every edit box. Here are the two combo box methods, one for cursors and the other for a generic enumeration:

```
procedure TGridEditForm.ComboCursorChange(Sender: TObject);
begin
  SetOrdProp (CurrComp, CurrProp,
    StringToCursor (ComboCursor.Text));
end;


procedure TGridEditForm.ComboEnumChange(Sender: TObject);
begin
  SetOrdProp (CurrComp, CurrProp,
    {$IFDEF VER100}
    GetEnumValue (CurrProp.PropType^, ComboEnum.Text));
    {$ELSE} // Delphi 2
    GetEnumValue (CurrProp.PropType, ComboEnum.Text));
    {$ENDIF}
end;
```

When the editing component loses the focus, we remove it from view. Here's the OnExit event handler for several of the editing controls:

```
procedure TGridEditForm.RefreshOnExit(Sender: TObject);
begin
  sgProp.Cells [1, CurrRow] :=
    GetPropValAsString (CurrComp, CurrProp);
  (Sender as TWinControl).Hide;
  if EditingSub then
    CurrComp := RealComp;
end;
```

Some of the editors require more complicated code than this. For example, here's the editor for characters, another feature we added to this version of the Object Debugger:

```
procedure TGridEditForm.EditChExit(Sender: TObject);
var
  Ch: Char;
begin
  try
    if EditModified then
    begin
      if Length (EditCh.Text) = 1 then
        Ch := EditCh.Text [1]
      else if EditCh.Text [1] = '#' then
        Ch := Char (StrToInt (Copy (
          EditCh.Text, 2, Length (EditCh.Text) - 1)))
      else
        raise EConvertError.Create ('Error');
      SetOrdProp (CurrComp, CurrProp, Word (Ch));
    end;
    RefreshOnExit (Sender);
  except
    on EConvertError do
    begin
      ShowMessage ('Not a valid character');
      EditCh.SetFocus;
    end;
  end;
end;
```

There are many other similar event handlers, but you should be able to understand them by reading the example's source code.

The only remaining features we want to describe are the direct editors. If you double-click on the value of a TStringList or TFont property, we'll display a specific editor for that property type:

```
procedure TGridEditForm.sgPropDblClick(Sender: TObject);
begin
  if CurrProp <> nil then
  begin
    if CurrProp.PropType^.Name = 'TFont' then
    begin
```

```
    FontDialog1.Font.Assign (
      TFont (GetOrdProp (CurrComp, CurrProp)));
    if FontDialog1.Execute then
    begin
      TFont (GetOrdProp (CurrComp, CurrProp)).
        Assign (FontDialog1.Font);
      UpdateProps;
    end;
  end;

  // string list editor...
  if CurrProp.PropType^.Name = 'TStrings' then
    EditStringList (TStrings (
      GetOrdProp (CurrComp, CurrProp)));
  end;
end;
```

To edit the font, the GridEdit version of the Object Debugger displays the standard font-selection dialog box. However, to edit the string list, you can't use Delphi's internal property editor. In fact, beginning with Delphi 3, property editors have become part of the design-time libraries, and we haven't found a way of using them at run-time. What we can do instead is clone these editors. In the case of the string list editor, we create a dialog box on the fly, just as we've done in the past for the RTTI information:

```
procedure TGridEditForm.EditStringList (Str: TStrings);
var
  F: TForm;
  I: Integer;
  Memo1: TMemo;
begin
  F := TForm.Create (Application);
  try
    F.Width := 250;
    F.Height := 300;
    // middle of the screen
    F.Left := Screen.Width div 2 - 125;
    F.Top := Screen.Height div 2 - 150;
    F.Caption := 'StringList Editor for ' + CurrProp.Name;
    F.BorderStyle := bsDialog;
    Memo1 := TMemo.Create (F);
    with Memo1 do
```

```
begin
  Parent := F;
  Width := F.ClientWidth;
  Height := F.ClientHeight - 30;
  for I := 0 to Str.Count - 1 do
    Lines.Add (Str [I]);
end;
with TBitBtn.Create (F) do
begin
  Parent := F;
  Width := F.ClientWidth div 2;
  Top := F.ClientHeight - 30;
  Height := 30;
  Kind := bkOK;
end;
with TBitBtn.Create (F) do
begin
  Parent := F;
  Width := F.ClientWidth div 2;
  Left := F.ClientWidth div 2;
  Top := F.ClientHeight - 30;
  Height := 30;
  Kind := bkCancel;
end;
if F.ShowModal = mrOk then
begin
  Str.Clear;
  for I := 0 to Memo1.Lines.Count - 1 do
    Str.Add (Memo1.Lines [I]);
end;
finally
  F.Free;
end;
end;
```

You can see the string list editor of the Object Debugger in Figure 16.13.

FIGURE 16.13:

The string list editor
of the Object
Debugger in action

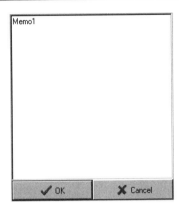

FIGURE 16.13:

The string list editor
of the Object
Debugger in action

Wrapping the Object Debugger
in a Component

We've built an interesting example here, but we can examine only the proper-ties of the current project's components. Of course you can copy the form and its unit and add it to any existing project to add this capability to it. However, it would be much faster if we could simply add a component with this capability to a Delphi program, and then remove the component to eliminate the extra debug-ging window.

The structure of the component is very simple. It has two simple properties, no events, and no visual elements. The component simply creates the component viewer form as we create the component itself. Here's the class definition:

```
type
  TDdhObjectDebugger = class(TComponent)
  private
    fOnTop: Boolean;
    fCopyright, fNull: string;
  public
    constructor Create (AOwner: TComponent); override;
  published
    property OnTop: Boolean
      read fOnTop write fOnTop;
```

```
    property Copyright: string
      read fCopyright write fNull;
  end;
```

As you can see in the code above, the Copyright property behaves unexpectedly. We want to display this information in the Object Inspector, so we can't make this property read-only—we must provide a write method. In fact, you can't publish read-only properties. However, we can't let the user update the value of this property; so if anything is entered, we'll write it into the fNull string and never use it.

A problem with this component is that all of the form's initialization code executes during the component's creation. We must delay the call to the UpdateComboForms method, so that Object Debugger will reflect the status of the program after the program creates all the initial forms. In practice, instead of writing this code:

```
constructor TDdhObjectDebugger.Create (AOwner: TComponent);
begin
  inherited Create (AOwner);
  if not (csDesigning in ComponentState) then
  begin
    DdhGridEditForm := TDdhGridEditForm.
      Create (Application);
    DdhGridEditForm.UpdateComboForms;
    DdhGridEditForm.Show;
  end;
end;
```

we could post a user-defined Windows message in the component constructor, and perform the actual update in the message's handler (declared in the form class with the message keyword). This works because posted messages are handled after the program executes the unit's initialization code.

Another alternative is to use a timer to delay the update slightly. In addition, we could use the same timer to refresh the list of forms, a feature we decided not to implement in this version. Here's the complete constructor code, which uses the two properties, and executes a slight delay using the OnTimer event handler:

```
constructor TDdhObjectDebugger.Create (AOwner: TComponent);
begin
  inherited Create (AOwner);
  fCopyright := 'Marco Cantƒ';
  if not (csDesigning in ComponentState) then
```

```
begin
  DdhGridEditForm := TDdhGridEditForm.
    Create (Application);
  if fOnTop then
  begin
    // set topmost style
    DdhGridEditForm.FormStyle := fsStayOnTop;
    DdhGridEditForm.TopMost1.Checked := True
  end;
  DdhGridEditForm.Timer1.Enabled := True;
  end;
end;

procedure TDdhGridEditForm.Timer1Timer(Sender: TObject);
begin
  Timer1.Enabled := False;
  Show;
  UpdateFormsCombo;
end;
```

Besides setting the Visible property to False (since we now show and update the form with the code above), the form has another new feature. When the user tries to close the form, we simply minimize it. We do that because there's no easy way to recreate the Object Debugger form, so we keep it open (although minimized) until the program exits.

In the ObjDebug directory on the companion CD you'll find a package that includes the final version of the Object Debugger. This package installs the component's unit, which is the same as that of its form. Using a single unit for a form and a very simple component means there's one less file to distribute. However, to include this component in a project, you'll need to add the RttiHelp unit to the project's path manually. In addition, we've renamed this unit with the usual *Ddh* prefix to reduce potential conflicts with other components (including other versions of this same tool).

A second directory, ObjDDemo, contains a complex example from *Mastering Delphi 3* (the TwoViews3 example from that book's Chapter 17) along with a copy of the Object Debugger. You can see this program in action in Figure 16.14.

FIGURE 16.14:

The ObjDDemo example is a complex database example, with three forms and a data module, used as a test bed for the Object Debugger.

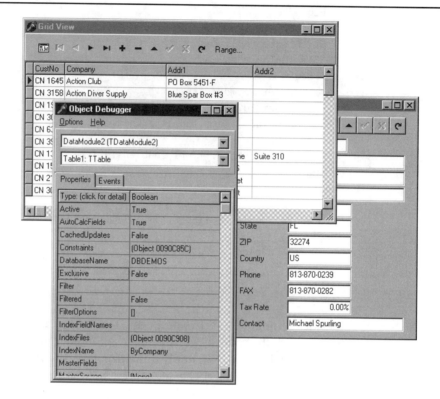

What's Next

This chapter examined the development of a complex debugging tool for Delphi programmers. As you saw, this real-world tool is still under development. You can find (free) updates of the Object Debugger on Marco's Web site, www.marcocantu.com.

This chapter ends Part III of the book, in which we extended Delphi's development environment, with properties and components editors, wizards, and many other design-time tools, as well as the run-time tool described in this chapter.

The next and final section of the book will cover advanced topics related to database programming in Delphi, including a chapter devoted to database publishing on the Web.

PART IV

Delphi Database Programming

Writing Data-Aware
Components

- ■ The Data Link

- ■ Writing Field-Oriented Data-Aware Controls

- ■ Creating Custom Data Links

- ■ Customizing the DBGrid Component

- ■ Replicatable Data-Aware Components

In the first part of this book, and particularly in Chapter 5, we explored the development of Delphi components in depth. Then, in Part II, we worked with Delphi components related to the Windows API. In this chapter we'll start exploring Delphi components related to databases.

Specifically, this chapter addresses *data presentation*, or data-aware components. We'll start by creating a component to view database data; then we'll build components to edit this data. In addition to simple field-oriented components, we'll look at record-oriented and table-oriented data-aware components. Finally, we'll customize the standard DBGrid control, and see how we can work with multiple data sources.

The Data Link

When you write a Delphi database program you generally connect some data-aware controls to a DataSource component, and then connect the DataSource component to a data set, usually a Table or a Query. The connection between the data-aware control to the DataSource is called a *data link*, and is represented by an object of class TDataLink. The data-aware control creates and manages this object, and represents its only connection to the data. From a more practical perspective, to make a component data-aware you need to add a data link to it, and surface some of its properties such as the DataSource and DataField properties.

NOTE	Since Object Pascal doesn't support multiple inheritance, the standard technique for adding a capability to a series of classes is to add to them an internal object, and then make some of the properties of the internal object available to the users of the component.

Together, Delphi uses the DataSource and DataLink objects for bidirectional communication: the data set uses the connection to notify the data-aware controls that new data is available (because the data set has been activated, or the current record has changed, and so on); the data-aware controls use the connection to ask for the current value of a field or to update it, notifying the data set of this event.

The relationships among all these components are complicated by the fact that some of the connections can be one-to-many. For example, you can connect multiple data sources to the same data set, and you generally have multiple data links to the same data source, simply because you need one link for every data-aware component, and in most cases you connect multiple data-aware controls to each data source. To make things even more complex, a single data-aware control can have multiple data links (and data sources), as in the case of the DBLookupList and DBLookupCombo components; and a data set can even refer to a data source to implement a master/detail relationship.

The TDataLink Class

We'll work for much of this chapter with TDataLink and its derived classes. Extracted from the db unit, here are the methods of the TDataLink protected virtual interface, its few public methods, and its properties:

```
type
  TDataLink = class(TPersistent)
  private
    // omitted
  protected
    procedure ActiveChanged; virtual;
    procedure CheckBrowseMode; virtual;
    procedure DataSetChanged; virtual;
    procedure DataSetScrolled(Distance: Integer); virtual;
    procedure FocusControl(Field: TFieldRef); virtual;
    procedure EditingChanged; virtual;
    procedure LayoutChanged; virtual;
    procedure RecordChanged(Field: TField); virtual;
    procedure UpdateData; virtual;
  public
    constructor Create;
    destructor Destroy; override;
    function Edit: Boolean;
    procedure UpdateRecord;
    property Active: Boolean
      read FActive;
    property ActiveRecord: Integer
      read GetActiveRecord write SetActiveRecord;
    property BufferCount: Integer
      read FBufferCount write SetBufferCount;
    property DataSet: TDataSet
      read GetDataSet;
    property DataSource: TDataSource
```

```
      read FDataSource write SetDataSource;
  property DataSourceFixed: Boolean
      read FDataSourceFixed write FDataSourceFixed;
  property Editing: Boolean
      read FEditing;
  property ReadOnly: Boolean
      read FReadOnly write SetReadOnly;
  property RecordCount: Integer
      read GetRecordCount;
end;
```

The virtual methods of this class (fully described in Delphi's help file) have a role similar to events. In fact, they are "almost-do-nothing" methods you can override in a specific subclass to intercept user operations and other data-source events. Actually, all of these virtual methods are called by the DataEvent private method of the TDataLink class:

```
procedure DataEvent(Event: TDataEvent; Info: Longint);
```

This method has a case statement based on the Event parameter, which can assume one of the following values, undocumented but easily understandable:

```
type
  TDataEvent = (deFieldChange, deRecordChange, deDataSetChange,
      deDataSetScroll, deLayoutChange, deUpdateRecord,
      deUpdateState, deCheckBrowseMode, dePropertyChange,
      deFieldListChange, deFocusControl);
```

These events originate in the data set, fields, or data source, and are generally applied to a data set. The DataEvent method of the data set component dispatches them to the connected data sources. The TDataSource class has a similar DataEvent private method, as well. It first calls the NotifyDataLinks method to forward the event to each data link connected to the data source, and then it triggers either the OnDataChange or the OnUpdateData event of the data source.

Derived DataLink Classes

The TDataLink class is not technically an abstract class, but you'll seldom use it directly. When you need to create data-aware controls you'll need to use one of its derived classes or derive a new one yourself.

The most important class derived from TDataLink is the TFieldDataLink class, which is used by data-aware controls that relate to single fields of the data set. Most of the data-aware controls fall into this category, and the TFieldDataLink class solves the most common problems of this type of component.

Although TFieldDataLink is the most important class derived from TDataLink, there are others. According to Delphi help file, the only class you'll use often is TMasterDataLink, which establishes the connection with a master data source in nonvisual relationships. The other data-link classes described in the help file are designed to connect to specific components, so you should use them only to connect to those components, or derived classes. Here's a short list of these specialized data links: TGridDataLink is a connection for a TCustomDbGrid-derived class, TDBCtrlGridLink for the DbCtrlGrid component, TNavDataLink for the DBNavigator, TDataSourceLink and TListSourceLink for the TDBLookupControl class, and THTTPDataLink for the DataSetTableProducer component.

Since we'll start using it in the next section, here's a summary description of the TFieldDataLink class, starting with its definition in the VCL source code:

```
type
  TFieldDataLink = class(TDataLink)
  private
    // omitted
  protected
    procedure ActiveChanged; override;
    procedure EditingChanged; override;
    procedure FocusControl(Field: TFieldRef); override;
    procedure LayoutChanged; override;
    procedure RecordChanged(Field: TField); override;
    procedure UpdateData; override;
  public
    function Edit: Boolean;
    procedure Modified;
    procedure Reset;
    property CanModify: Boolean
      read GetCanModify;
    property Control: TComponent
      read FControl write FControl;
    property Editing: Boolean
      read FEditing;
    property Field: TField
      read FField;
```

```
    property FieldName: string
      read FFieldName write SetFieldName;
    property OnDataChange: TNotifyEvent
      read FOnDataChange write FOnDataChange;
    property OnEditingChange: TNotifyEvent
      read FOnEditingChange write FOnEditingChange;
    property OnUpdateData: TNotifyEvent
      read FOnUpdateData write FOnUpdateData;
    property OnActiveChange: TNotifyEvent
      read FOnActiveChange write FOnActiveChange;
  end;
```

If you compare the list of the events of this class with the virtual methods of the base class it overrides, you'll immediately understand its key role: its overridden methods activate the corresponding event handlers, making this class easy to customize for different circumstances. To use this class you simply provide the proper handlers for the events you're interested in; you don't need to define a new derived class. Here's an example of an overridden method:

```
procedure TFieldDataLink.ActiveChanged;
begin
  UpdateField;
  if Assigned(FOnActiveChange)
    then FOnActiveChange(Self);
end;
```

Beyond this, the TFieldDataLink class contains some extra code and properties (Field, FieldName) that let you connect the data-aware control to a specific field of the data set. It also lets the data set know which is the current component, using the Control property. This information is necessary when the deFocusControl data event occurs, due to a request to move the focus away from the control (for example, when a data field validates input):

```
procedure TFieldDataLink.FocusControl(Field: TFieldRef);
begin
  if (Field^ <> nil) and (Field^ = FField) and
      (FControl is TWinControl) then
    if TWinControl(FControl).CanFocus then
    begin
      Field^ := nil;
      TWinControl(FControl).SetFocus;
    end;
end;
```

Writing Field-Oriented Data-Aware Controls

Now that you understand the theory of how the data link classes work, we can start building some data-aware controls. The first two examples we'll build are data-aware versions of the ProgressBar and TrackBar Windows 95 common controls. We can use the first to display a numeric value, such as a percentage, in a visual way. We can use the second to allow a user to change the numeric value as well. The source code of both components, along with few others of this chapter, is available in the Comps directory and is part of this chapter's package.

> **NOTE**
>
> We've placed the components of this chapter and the other Part IV chapters of the book on the DDHB DB page of the Component palette, instead of the DDHB page used by other components.

A Read-Only ProgressBar

For our first data-aware component, we've decided to go for a simple example, building a data-aware version of the Windows 95 ProgressBar control. This will be simple to implement because it is a read-only control, which means we'll have to implement only a minimal part of the data link interactions.

We've derived this component from the version that's not data-aware, and we've made public a few properties of the data link object it encapsulates:

```
type
  TDdhDbProgress = class(TProgressBar)
  private
    FDataLink: TFieldDataLink;
    function GetDataField: string;
    procedure SetDataField (Value: string);
    function GetDataSource: TDataSource;
    procedure SetDataSource (Value: TDataSource);
    function GetField: TField;
  protected
    // data link event handler
    procedure DataChange (Sender: TObject);
  public
```

```
  constructor Create (AOwner: TComponent); override;
  destructor Destroy; override;
  property Field: TField read GetField;
published
  property DataField: string
    read GetDataField write SetDataField;
  property DataSource: TDataSource
    read GetDataSource write SetDataSource;
end;
```

As with every data-aware component that connects to a single field, we make available the DataSource and DataField properties. There is very little code to write here; we simply export the properties from the internal data link object, as follows:

```
function TDdhDbProgress.GetDataField: string;
begin
  Result := FDataLink.FieldName;
end;

procedure TDdhDbProgress.SetDataField (Value: string);
begin
  FDataLink.FieldName := Value;
end;

function TDdhDbProgress.GetDataSource: TDataSource;
begin
  Result := FDataLink.DataSource;
end;

procedure TDdhDbProgress.SetDataSource (Value: TDataSource);
begin
  FDataLink.DataSource := Value;
end;

function TDdhDbProgress.GetField: TField;
begin
  Result := FDataLink.Field;
end;
```

Of course, to make this component work, you must create and destroy the data link when the component itself is created or destroyed:

```
constructor TDdhDbProgress.Create (AOwner: TComponent);
begin
  inherited Create (AOwner);
  FDataLink := TFieldDataLink.Create;
  FDataLink.Control := self;
  FDataLink.OnDataChange := DataChange;
end;

destructor TDdhDbProgress.Destroy;
begin
  FDataLink.Free;
  FDataLink := nil;
  inherited Destroy;
end;
```

In the constructor above, notice that the component installs one of its own methods as an event handler for the data link. This is where the most important code of the component resides. Every time the data changes we modify the output of the progress bar to reflect the values of the current field:

```
procedure TDdhDbProgress.DataChange (Sender: TObject);
begin
  if (FDataLink.Field <> nil) and
      (FDataLink.Field is TNumericField) then
    Position := FDataLink.Field.AsInteger
  else
    Position := Min;
end;
```

Following the convention of the VCL data-aware controls, if the field type is invalid, we don't display an error message—we simply disable the output. Alternatively, you might want to check the field type when SetDataField method assigns it to the control.

In Figure 17.1 you can see an example of the DbProgr application's output, which uses both a label and a progress bar to display an order's quantity information. Thanks to this visual clue, you can step through the records and easily spot orders for many items. One obvious benefit to this component is that the application contains almost no code, since all the important code is in the component itself.

FIGURE 17.1:

The data-aware
ProgressBar in
action in the
DbProgr example

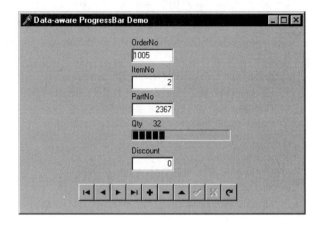

The DataSource Links and the Notification Method

One of the key elements of a data link is its connection with a data source. The data source holds a list of the data links connected to it, so the code that executes when you change the value of FDataLink.DataSource either adds the data link to the list of data source links, or removes it. This is the code the VCL uses to set the DataSource property of the TDataLink class:

```
procedure TDataLink.SetDataSource(ADataSource: TDataSource);
begin
  if FDataSource <> ADataSource then
  begin
    if FDataSourceFixed then
      DatabaseError(SDataSourceChange);
    if FDataSource <> nil then
      FDataSource.RemoveDataLink(Self);
    if ADataSource <> nil then
      ADataSource.AddDataLink(Self);
  end;
end;
```

For this reason, there's no need to call the AddDataLink and RemoveDataLink methods directly in the code of a data-aware component.

There is another important element, however. The VCL source code (like some books that discuss data-aware components) suggests adding a Notification method to the component, to track the destruction of the connected data source. In the VCL source, the method usually uses code like this:

```
procedure TDdhDbProgress.Notification (AComponent: TComponent;
  Operation: TOperation);
begin
  inherited Notification (AComponent, Operation);
  if (Operation = opRemove) and (FDataLink <> nil) and
      (AComponent = FDataLink.DataSource) then
    FDataLink.DataSource := nil;
end;
```

As we saw in Chapter 5, this method is called when a sibling component is destroyed. Similarly, you can call the FreeNotification method in case the data source is in a different form or data module:

```
procedure TDdhDbProgress.SetDataSource (Value: TDataSource);
begin
  FDataLink.DataSource := Value;
  if Value <> nil then
    Value.FreeNotification (Value);
end;
```

This is a standard Delphi programming pattern, and everyone seems to be using it. However, this code seems to be totally useless. The Borland manuals (and a few books) actually suggest that you *don't* use it. The fact is that when the data source component is destroyed, it destroys each of its data links, by calling RemoveDataLink, and only at the end calls the base class destructor; this triggers the Notification method:

```
destructor TDataSource.Destroy;
begin
  FOnStateChange := nil;
  SetDataSet(nil);
  while FDataLinks.Count > 0 do
    RemoveDataLink(FDataLinks.Last);
  FDataLinks.Free;
  inherited Destroy;
end;
```

The RemoveDataLink method doesn't really destroy the link (which is owned by the data-aware controls). Actually, this method sets the data link's DataSource property to `nil`, removes the link from the internal list, and then finally calls the `UpdateState` method of the data link:

```
procedure TDataSource.RemoveDataLink(DataLink: TDataLink);
begin
  DataLink.FDataSource := nil;
  FDataLinks.Remove(DataLink);
  DataLink.UpdateState;
  if DataSet <> nil then
    DataSet.UpdateBufferCount;
end;
```

This means that the `DataSource` property of the data link object inside our data-aware component will automatically be set to `nil`. As an experiment, you can write the following code (which we've included but commented out in the companion CD's source code):

```
procedure TDdhDbProgress.Notification (AComponent: TComponent;
  Operation: TOperation);
begin
  inherited Notification (AComponent, Operation);
  if (Operation = opRemove) and
     (FDataLink <> nil) and
     (AComponent = FDataLink.DataSource) then
  begin
    FDataLink.DataSource := nil;
    ShowMessage ('Data source set to nil');
  end
  else if (Operation = opRemove) and
     (FDataLink <> nil) and
     (FDataLink.DataSource = nil) then
    ShowMessage ('Data source was already nil');
end;
```

If you connect the control to a data source and then destroy the data source component, you'll see the second message, meaning that the destructor of the data source component already did its work properly.

A Read-Write TrackBar

The next step is to write a component that allows a user to modify the data in a database, not just browse it. The overall structure of this type of component isn't very different from the previous version, but there are a few extra elements. In particular, when the user starts interacting with the component, the code should put the data set into edit mode, and then notify the data set that the data has changed. The data set will then use an event handler of the FieldDataLink to ask for the updated value.

To demonstrate how you can create a data-aware component that modifies the data, we've decided to duplicate the Windows 95 TrackBar control. This probably isn't the simplest example, but it demonstrates several important techniques.

Here's the definition of the component's class:

```
type
  TDdhDbTrack = class(TTrackBar)
  private
    FDataLink: TFieldDataLink;
    function GetDataField: string;
    procedure SetDataField (Value: string);
    function GetDataSource: TDataSource;
    procedure SetDataSource (Value: TDataSource);
    function GetField: TField;
    procedure CNHScroll(var Message: TWMHScroll);
      message CN_HSCROLL;
    procedure CNVScroll(var Message: TWMVScroll);
      message CN_VSCROLL;
    procedure CMExit(var Message: TCMExit);
      message CM_EXIT;
  protected
    // data link event handlers
    procedure DataChange (Sender: TObject);
    procedure UpdateData (Sender: TObject);
    procedure ActiveChange (Sender: TObject);
  public
    constructor Create (AOwner: TComponent); override;
    destructor Destroy; override;
    property Field: TField
      read GetField;
  published
    property DataField: string
      read GetDataField write SetDataField;
    property DataSource: TDataSource
      read GetDataSource write SetDataSource;
  end;
```

Compared to the read-only data-aware control (TDdhDbProgress), this class is a bit more complex, because we've defined three message handlers, including component notification handlers, and two new event handlers for the data link. We install these event handlers in the constructor, which also disables the component:

```
constructor TDdhDbTrack.Create (AOwner: TComponent);
begin
  inherited Create (AOwner);
  FDataLink := TFieldDataLink.Create;
  FDataLink.Control := self;
  FDataLink.OnDataChange := DataChange;
  FDataLink.OnUpdateData := UpdateData;
  FDataLink.OnActiveChange := ActiveChange;
  Enabled := False;
end;
```

> **TIP**
>
> You'll notice how we force the value of the Enabled property to False. In theory, you should never override a base class property value in a constructor without also changing its default value with a new property declaration. In this case, however, we want the Enabled property always set to False, regardless of how a derived class sets the default value of this property. To accomplish this in general you should override the Loaded method, but with Boolean properties there is no need. In fact if the value of the property is False, this value will be applied again with no effect. If the value is True, it is not saved in the DFM file, so the new value we set won't be modified.

All of the property get and set methods, and the DataChange event handler, are very similar to those in the TDdhDbProgress component. The only difference is that whenever the data source or data field change, we check the status to see if we should enable the component:

```
procedure TDdhDbTrack.SetDataSource (Value: TDataSource);
begin
  FDataLink.DataSource := Value;
  Enabled := FDataLink.Active and
    (FDataLink.Field <> nil) and
    not FDataLink.Field.ReadOnly;
end;
```

We test for three conditions: the data link should be active, the link should refer to an actual field, and the field shouldn't be read-only. When the user changes the field, we should also consider that the field name might be invalid; to test for this condition we should write it in a `try-finally` block:

```
procedure TDdhDbTrack.SetDataField (Value: string);
begin
  try
    FDataLink.FieldName := Value;
  finally
    Enabled := FDataLink.Active and
      (FDataLink.Field <> nil) and
      not FDataLink.Field.ReadOnly;
  end;
end;
```

We execute the same test when the data set is enabled or disabled:

```
procedure TDdhDbTrack.ActiveChange (Sender: TObject);
begin
  Enabled := FDataLink.Active and
    (FDataLink.Field <> nil) and
    not FDataLink.Field.ReadOnly;
end;
```

The most interesting portion of this component's code is related to its user interface. When a user starts moving the scroll thumb, the component should do the following: put the data set into edit mode, let the base class update the thumb position, and alert the data link (and therefore the data source) that the data has changed. Here's the code:

```
procedure TDdhDbTrack.CNHScroll(var Message: TWMHScroll);
begin
  // edit mode
  FDataLink.Edit;
  // update data
  inherited;
  // let the system know
  FDataLink.Modified;
end;

procedure TDdhDbTrack.CNVScroll(var Message: TWMVScroll);
begin
  // enter edit mode
```

```
    FDataLink.Edit;
    // update data
    inherited;
    // let the system know
    FDataLink.Modified;
  end;
```

When the data set needs new data, for example to perform a Post operation, it simply requests it from the component via the TFieldDataLink class's OnUpdate-Data event:

```
procedure TDdhDbTrack.UpdateData (Sender: TObject);
begin
  if (FDataLink.Field <> nil) and
     (FDataLink.Field is TNumericField) then
    FDataLink.Field.AsInteger := Position;
end;
```

If the proper conditions are met, the component simply updates the data in the proper table field. Finally, if the component loses the input focus, it should force a data update (if the data has changed) so that any other data-aware components showing the value of that field will display the correct value as soon as the user moves to a different field. If the data hasn't changed, we won't bother updating the data in the table. This is the standard CmExit code for components used by the VCL and borrowed for our component as well:

```
procedure TDdhDbTrack.CmExit(var Message: TCmExit);
begin
  try
    FDataLink.UpdateRecord;
  except
    SetFocus;
    raise;
  end;
  inherited;
end;
```

Again there is a demo program for testing this component; you can see its output in Figure 17.2. The DbTrack program contains a check box to enable and disable the table, the visual components, and a couple of buttons you can use to detach the vertical TrackBar component from the field it relates to. Again, we placed these on the form to test enabling and disabling the track bar.

The DbTrack example has a couple of track bars you can use to enter data in a database table. The check box and buttons are used to test the enabled status of the components.

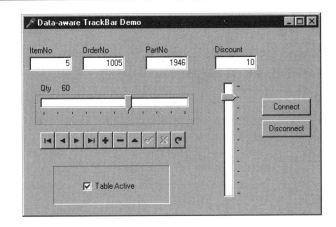

Creating Custom Data Links

The data-aware controls we've built up to this point all referred to specific fields of the data set, so we were able to use a TFieldDataLink object to establish the connection with a data source. Now we want to build a couple of data-aware components that work with a data set as a whole. The first will be a simple record viewer.

Delphi's database grid shows the value of several fields and several records simultaneously. In our record viewer component, we want to list all the fields of the current record, using a customized grid. This example will show you how to build a customized grid control, and a custom data link to go with it.

A second example will show you how to gather information from multiple records, and then display the status of the data set. This component will have a simpler user interface but a more complex data link.

A Record Viewer Component

In Delphi there are no data-aware components that manipulate a single record, without displaying other records. In fact, the only component that displays multiple fields from the same table is the DBGrid, which displays multiple fields, and multiple records.

The Record Viewer component we're going to describe in this section is based on a two-column grid; the first column displays the table's field names, while the second column displays the corresponding field values. The number of rows in the grid will correspond to the number of fields, with a vertical scroll bar in case they can't fit in the visible area.

NOTE   On the companion CD, you'll find the record viewer component in the DdhRView unit, which is part of this chapter's package. Keep in mind, however, that the component also implements the BLOB field viewer code described in the next section.

The data link we need in order to build this component is a simple class, connected only to the record viewer component, and declared directly in the implementation portion of its unit. This is the same approach used by the VCL for some specific data links. Here's the definition of the new class:

```
type
  TDdhRecordLink = class (TDataLink)
  private
    RView: TDdhRecordView;
  public
    constructor Create (View: TDdhRecordView);
    procedure ActiveChanged; override;
    procedure RecordChanged (Field: TField); override;
  end;
```

As you can see, the class overrides the methods related to the principal event, in this case simply the activation and data (or record) change. Alternatively, we could have exported some events, and then let the component handle them. That's what the TFieldDataLink does, but the approach we've taken makes more sense for a data link class, because you'll want to use it with different data-aware components.

The constructor requires the associated component as its only parameter:

```
constructor TDdhRecordLink.Create (View: TDdhRecordView);
begin
  inherited Create;
  RView := View;
end;
```

After storing a reference to the associated component, the other methods can operate on it directly:

```
procedure TDdhRecordLink.ActiveChanged;
var
  I: Integer;
begin
  // set number of rows
  RView.RowCount := DataSet.FieldCount;
  // repaint all...
  RView.Invalidate;
end;

procedure TDdhRecordLink.RecordChanged;
begin
  inherited;
  // repaint all...
  RView.Invalidate;
end;
```

As you've seen, the record link code is very simple. Most of the difficulties in building this example depend on our implementing a custom grid for the link. To avoid dealing with useless properties, we've derived our record viewer grid from the TCustomGrid class. This class incorporates much of the code for grids, but most of its properties, events, and methods are protected. For this reason, the class declaration is quite long, because we need to publish many existing properties:

```
type
  TDdhRecordView = class(TCustomGrid)
  private
    // data-aware support
    FDataLink: TDataLink;
    function GetDataSource: TDataSource;
    procedure SetDataSource (Value: TDataSource);
  protected
    // redefined TCustomGrid methods
    procedure DrawCell (ACol, ARow: Longint; ARect: TRect;
      AState: TGridDrawState); override;
    procedure ColWidthsChanged; override;
  public
    constructor Create (AOwner: TComponent); override;
    destructor Destroy; override;
    procedure SetBounds (ALeft, ATop, AWidth,
      AHeight: Integer); override;
```

```
      procedure DefineProperties (Filer: TFiler); override;
      // parent properties
      property Canvas;
      property Col;
      property ColWidths;
      property EditorMode;
      property GridHeight;
      property GridWidth;
      property LeftCol;
      property Selection;
      property Row;
      property RowHeights;
      property TabStops;
      property TopRow;
  published
      // data-aware properties
      property DataSource: TDataSource
        read GetDataSource write SetDataSource;
      // parent properties
      property Align;
      property BorderStyle;
      property Color;
      property Ctl3D;
      property DefaultColWidth;
      property DefaultRowHeight;
      property DragCursor;
      property DragMode;
      property Enabled;
      property FixedColor;
      property Font;
      property GridLineWidth;
      property ParentColor;
      property ParentCtl3D;
      property ParentFont;
      property ParentShowHint;
      property PopupMenu;
      property ShowHint;
      property TabOrder;
      property TabStop;
      property Visible;
      property VisibleColCount;
      property VisibleRowCount;
```

```
    property OnClick;
    property OnDblClick;
    property OnDragDrop;
    property OnDragOver;
    property OnEndDrag;
    property OnEnter;
    property OnExit;
    property OnKeyDown;
    property OnKeyPress;
    property OnKeyUp;
    property OnMouseDown;
    property OnMouseMove;
    property OnMouseUp;
    property OnStartDrag;
  end;
```

Besides redeclaring the properties to publish them, the component defines a data link object and the DataSource property. There's no DataField property for this component, because it refers to an entire record. The Get and Set methods for the DataSource property use the usual code:

```
function TDdhRecordView.GetDataSource: TDataSource;
begin
  Result := FDataLink.DataSource;
end;


procedure TDdhRecordView.SetDataSource (Value: TDataSource);
begin
  FDataLink.DataSource := Value;
end;
```

You'll notice that the DataSource property of the data link, like many of the others, is defined by the TDataLink base class, so we can use it in the TFieldDataLink examples.

The component's constructor is very important. It sets the values of many unpublished properties, including the grid options:

```
constructor TDdhRecordView.Create (AOwner: TComponent);
begin
  inherited Create (AOwner);
  FDataLink := TDdhRecordLink.Create (self);
  // set numbers of cells and fixed cells
  RowCount := 2; // default
```

```
    ColCount := 2;
    FixedCols := 1;
    FixedRows := 0;
    Options := [goFixedVertLine, goFixedHorzLine,
      goVertLine, goHorzLine, goRowSizing];
    DefaultDrawing := False;
    ScrollBars := ssVertical;
  end;
```

The grid has two columns, one of them fixed, and no fixed rows. The fixed column is used for resizing each row of the grid. Unfortunately, we can't add a fixed row to resize the columns, because you can't resize fixed elements, and the grid already has a fixed column.

We've used an alternative approach to resize the columns. The first column (holding the field names) can be resized either using programming code or visually at design-time, and the second column (holding the values of the fields) will be resized to use the remaining area of the component, leaving space for the borders, the lines, and the vertical scrollbar:

```
procedure TDdhRecordView.SetBounds (ALeft, ATop,
  AWidth, AHeight: Integer);
begin
  inherited;
  ColWidths [1] := Width - ColWidths [0] -
    GridLineWidth * 3 -
    GetSystemMetrics (sm_CXVScroll)
    - 2; // border
end;
```

This takes place when the component size changes. We should also do this when either of the columns change. With this code the DefaultColWidth property of the component becomes, in practice, the fixed width of the first column.

After everything has been set up, the key method of the component is the overridden DrawCell. This is where we display the information about the fields and their values. There are three things we need to draw. If the data link is not connected to a data source, the grid displays an "empty element" sign (*[]*); when drawing the first column, the record viewer shows the DisplayName of the field, which is the same value used by the DBGrid for the heading; and when drawing the second column, we access the textual representation of the field value, extracted with the DisplayText property. For nontextual fields this value will be the component type, such as Memo or Graphics.

```
procedure TDdhRecordView.DrawCell(ACol, ARow: Longint;
  ARect: TRect; AState: TGridDrawState);
var
  Text: string;
  CurrField: TField;
  Bmp: TBitmap;
begin
  Text := '[]'; // default
  // paint background
  if (ACol = 0) then
    Canvas.Brush.Color := FixedColor
  else
    Canvas.Brush.Color := Color;
  Canvas.FillRect (ARect);
  // leave small border
  InflateRect (ARect, -2, -2);
  if (FDataLink.DataSource <> nil) and
    FDataLink.Active then
  begin
    CurrField := FDataLink.DataSet.Fields[ARow];
    if ACol = 0 then
      Text := CurrField.DisplayName
    else
      Text := CurrField.DisplayText;
  end;
  // draw the text in the current cell
  DrawText (Canvas.Handle,
    PChar (Text), Length (Text), ARect,
    dt_vcenter or dt_SingleLine or dt_NoPrefix);
  if gdFocused in AState then
    Canvas.DrawFocusRect (ARect);
end;
```

Notice that we've set the DefaultDrawing property to False, so we're responsible for drawing the background and the focus rectangle ourselves. The component also calls the InflateRect API function to leave a small area between the cell border and the output text. We produce the actual output by calling another Windows API function, DrawText, which allows us to center the text vertically in its cell.

This drawing code works both at run-time and at design-time, as you can see in Figure 17.3. The output may not be perfect, but this component can certainly be very useful in many cases. If you want to display the data for a single record, instead of building a custom form with labels and data-aware controls, you can easily use this record viewer grid. Of course, it's important to remember that the record viewer is a read-only component: it's certainly possible to extend it to add editing capabilities (they're already part of the TCustomGrid class). However, instead of adding this support, we've decided to make the component more complete by adding support for displaying BLOB fields.

FIGURE 17.3:

The RecordView component at design time

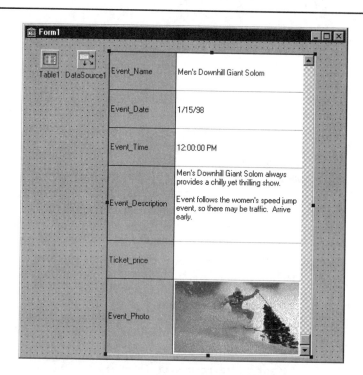

Viewing Memo and Graphic Fields

The record viewer component as described in the last section is useful, but we can't use it to view the contents of records with special fields, such as graphics or memo fields. In both of those cases, the value of the field's DisplayText property is simply a description of the field type.

Besides accessing the text or graphic data, we need to customize the output for these special fields. Before doing this, however, we should correctly resize the grid cells. We can do this when the data set connected to the data-aware control is activated; that is, when the ActiveChanged method of the data link is called:

```
procedure TDdhRecordLink.ActiveChanged;
var
  I: Integer;
begin
  // set number of rows
  RView.RowCount := DataSet.FieldCount;
  // double the height of memo and graphics
  for I := 0 to DataSet.FieldCount - 1 do
    if DataSet.Fields [I] is TBlobField then
      RView.RowHeights [I] := RView.DefaultRowHeight * 2;
  // repaint all...
  RView.Invalidate;
end;
```

However, at this point we stumble into a problem. In the DefineProperties method, the TCustomGrid class saves the values of the public RowHeights and ColHeights properties. This becomes a problem when we create the grid and set the number of Rows to 2—reading in a third value from RowHeights and applying it to the grid will generate an out-of-range error.

> **NOTE**   See Chapter 3 for a complete description of the DefineProperties method and related streaming mechanisms. By examining the TCustom-Grid.DefineProperties method in the VCL source code (in the Grids unit), you can fully understand the problem.

The solution is actually quite simple; since we compute the width and height of the cells at run-time, we can disable the streaming of these properties. Luckily, the base classes of TCustomGrid don't use this capability, so we can simply redefine this as a do-nothing method:

```
procedure TDdhRecordView.DefineProperties(Filer: TFiler);
begin
  // do nothing (skip base class code)
end;
```

Although we disabled the resizing the cells at design-time, keep in mind that a user can resize the rows at run-time. Unfortunately, there's no way to set the height of the rows at design-time and retain them when the program is running. What we could do instead is add some extra properties to the component—for example specifying the height of the rows for different data types.

Again, the core of the code relates to the drawing of the cells. The code of the first part of the DrawCell method is similar to the previous version, except that with a memo field we extract its entire text using the AsString property. The final portion of the method is where things change: if the field is a TMemoField the DrawText function call doesn't specify the dt_SingleLine flag, but uses dt_WordBreak flag to wrap the words when there's no more room.

For a graphic field, of course, the component uses a completely different approach. We assign the field image to a temporary bitmap, and then stretch the bitmap to fill the surface of the cell. Here's the complete listing of the method:

```
procedure TDdhRecordView.DrawCell(ACol, ARow: Longint;
  ARect: TRect; AState: TGridDrawState);
var
  Text: string;
  CurrField: TField;
  Bmp: TBitmap;
begin
  CurrField := nil;
  Text := '[]'; // default
  // paint background
  if (ACol = 0) then
    Canvas.Brush.Color := FixedColor
  else
    Canvas.Brush.Color := Color;
  Canvas.FillRect (ARect);
  // leave small border
  InflateRect (ARect, -2, -2);
  if (FDataLink.DataSource <> nil) and
    FDataLink.Active then
  begin
    CurrField := FDataLink.DataSet.Fields[ARow];
    if ACol = 0 then
      Text := CurrField.DisplayName
    else if CurrField is TMemoField then
      Text := TMemoField (CurrField).AsString
    else
      Text := CurrField.DisplayText;
  end;
```

```
    if (ACol = 1) and (CurrField is TGraphicField) then
    begin
      Bmp := TBitmap.Create;
      try
        Bmp.Assign (CurrField);
        Canvas.StretchDraw (ARect, Bmp);
      finally
        Bmp.Free;
      end;
    end
    else if (ACol = 1) and (CurrField is TMemoField) then
    begin
      DrawText (Canvas.Handle,
        PChar (Text), Length (Text),
        ARect, dt_WordBreak or dt_NoPrefix)
    end
    else // draw single line vertically centered
      DrawText (Canvas.Handle,
        PChar (Text), Length (Text), ARect,
        dt_vcenter or dt_SingleLine or dt_NoPrefix);
    if gdFocused in AState then
      Canvas.DrawFocusRect (ARect);
  end;
```

The result is certainly very nice, as you can see in Figure 17.4. This is the result of executing the ViewGrid example, which has a DbNavigator on top and a TDdhRecordView component aligned with its client area. At run-time, you can manually adjust the height of the rows that contain the memo and graphic.

A Table Status Bar

The second example of a record/table data-aware component is a simple status bar that displays information about the current database table. The component isn't terribly powerful as is, but you should be able to extend it easily to suit your needs.

We'll use the Windows 95 StatusBar control as the basis for our new control. As has been the case with the other examples, the control provides so many capabilities that our biggest problem is deciding how to make available only the features we need. Since there's no TCustomStatusBar class in the VCL (to provide common functionality without specific implementation), there are basically two ways for us to go: inherit from the TStatusBar class, and simply let users add or remove panels

FIGURE 17.4:

The ViewGrid example demonstrates the output of the RecordView component we've just built, using Borland's sample BioLife database table.

at design-time, using the Panels property, or rewrite the class from scratch, copying the source code from the VCL, and removing the properties we don't need.

After trying both approaches, we feel that the first is probably the best, even though we've implemented both. Since the second solution is inferior, we'll give you only a brief description of it. We've built the component using the first approach, called TDdhDbStatusBar and found in the DdhDbSt unit, and placed it in the package for this chapter. The other version, called TDdhDbStatus and found in the DdhDbStatus unit, is available in the same Comps directory but isn't installed in the package.

As usual for this type of component, the starting point of development (and the key element) is the custom data link. In this class we handle a few events by overriding the corresponding base-class methods:

```
type
  TDdhStatusLink = class (TDataLink)
  private
    FBar: TDdhDbStatusBar;
    FOnSummary: TGetStringEvent;
  public
    constructor Create (Bar: TDdhDbStatusBar);
    procedure ActiveChanged; override;
    procedure EditingChanged; override;
    procedure RecordChanged (Field: TField); override;
    function RecordSummary: String;
```

```
    property OnSummary: TGetStringEvent
      read FOnSummary write FOnSummary;
  end;
```

The final function, RecordSummary, builds a description of the current record, and then activates the OnSummary event to let the user customize the output further. As we'll see, this event is defined in the data link class, but we export it from the status bar class. By the way, the method pointer for this custom event is defined as follows:

```
type
  TGetStringEvent = procedure (Sender: TObject;
    var Text: string) of object;
```

However, let's focus on this class's methods first. The constructor simply establishes the connection with the component:

```
constructor TDdhStatusLink.Create (Bar: TDdhDbStatusBar);
begin
  inherited Create;
  FBar := Bar;
end;
```

This connection is critical, because the data link class displays its information directly to the panels of the status bar. The bar must have three panels (in a moment, we'll show how we enforce this), used as follows:

- The first panel displays the table name of the SQL query, or the word *Inactive* if the data set is not connected or not active.

- The second panel displays the status of the data set, either *Editing* or *Browsing*.

- The third panel displays a summary of the current record if the data set is active.

You can see an example of this component's design-time output in Figure 17.5. The ActiveChanged method is where most of the code resides, since we use it to set the initial text of the panels, with either current values or default strings:

```
procedure TDdhStatusLink.ActiveChanged;
begin
  if Active then
  begin
    if DataSet is TTable then
      FBar.Panels[0].Text := TTable(DataSet).TableName
```

```
    else if DataSet is TQuery then
      FBar.Panels[0].Text := TQuery (DataSet).SQL.Text
    else
      FBar.Panels[0].Text := DataSet.Name;
    FBar.Panels[1].Text := '[Browsing]';
    FBar.Panels [2].Text := RecordSummary;
  end
  else
  begin
    FBar.Panels[0].Text := '[Inactive]';
    FBar.Panels[1].Text := '[]';
  end;
end;
```

FIGURE 17.5:

The form displayed
by the Status pro-
gram at design-time,
with an example
of the data-aware
status bar

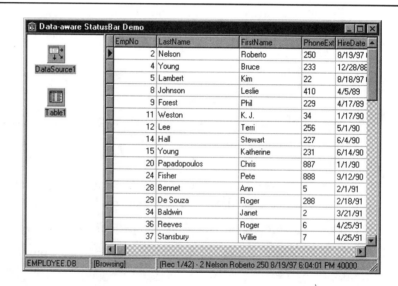

The text in the panels should change on two occasions (besides startup). One is
when the editing status changes. The EditingChanged method is called after such
a change, so its code is quite simple:

```
procedure TDdhStatusLink.EditingChanged;
begin
  if Editing then
    FBar.Panels[1].Text := '[Editing]'
  else
    FBar.Panels[1].Text := '[Browsing]';
end;
```

Finally, we want to update the output of the third panel to reflect the current record each time it changes. The RecordChanged method simply calls the same RecordSummary function called by the ActiveChanged method:

```
procedure TDdhStatusLink.RecordChanged (Field: TField);
begin
  FBar.Panels [2].Text := RecordSummary;
end;

function TDdhStatusLink.RecordSummary;
var
  I: Integer;
  Summary: string;
begin
  // add record count
  Summary := Format ('(Rec %d/%d)',
    [DataSet.RecNo, DataSet.RecordCount]);
  // add custom description of default one
  if Assigned (FOnSummary) then
    FOnSummary (FBar, Summary)
  else
  begin
    Summary := Summary + ' - ';
    for I := 0 to DataSet.FieldCount - 1 do
      Summary := Summary +
        DataSet.Fields[I].DisplayText + ' ';
  end;
  Result := Summary;
end;
```

As you can see, the RecordSummary function builds the output string using the record number (information that's useful only to local tables), and then calls the OnSummary event optionally installed by the user, which can modify this string by adding or deleting specific information (perhaps removing the record count). If no event handler has been installed, the function simply adds the DisplayText of each field in the data set.

TIP

You'll notice that when we call the event handler, we pass as its Sender parameter the status bar component, not the data link object (self). We need to do this because the user of this component has no access to the data link.

Here's an example of a handler for this event, which isn't part of any example (since the Status example can work on multiple database tables) but refers to the Employee table of the DBDEMOS sample database:

```
procedure TForm1.DdhDbStatusBar1Summary(
  Sender: TObject; var Text: String);
begin
  Text := Format ('%s – %s %s',
    [Text,
    Table1.FieldByName ('FirstName').DisplayText,
    Table1.FieldByName ('LastName').DisplayText]);
end;
```

Now we can move to the component class, looking at the version of the component inherited from TStatusBar. Its definition is quite simple. It has the usual DataSource property, plus the definition of the OnSummary event handler:

```
type
  TDdhDbStatusBar = class (TStatusBar)
  private
    FDataLink: TDdhStatusLink;
    function GetDataSource: TDataSource;
    procedure SetDataSource (Value: TDataSource);
    function GetSummary: TGetStringEvent;
    procedure SetSummary (Value: TGetStringEvent);
  public
    constructor Create (AOwner: TComponent); override;
    destructor Destroy; override;
    procedure Loaded; override;
  published
    property DataSource: TDataSource
      read GetDataSource write SetDataSource;
    property OnSummary: TGetStringEvent
      read GetSummary write SetSummary;
  end;
```

The values of the property and the event simply reflect the corresponding elements of the data link object. Since we've already seen the code of the GetData-Source and SetDataSource methods many times, here are the other two:

```
function TDdhDbStatusBar.GetSummary: TGetStringEvent;
begin
  Result := FDataLink.OnSummary;
end;
```

```
procedure TDdhDbStatusBar.SetSummary (Value: TGetStringEvent);
begin
  FDataLink.OnSummary := Value;
end;
```

The two crucial methods for defining the panels of the status bar are the constructor and the Loaded method. We use the constructor at design-time, to create the three panels when you create a new component:

```
constructor TDdhDbStatusBar.Create (AOwner: TComponent);
begin
  inherited Create (AOwner);
  FDataLink := TDdhStatusLink.Create (self);
  // status bar
  if csDesigning in ComponentState then
  begin
    // create three panels and initialize them
    Panels.Add.Text := '[Inactive]';
    Panels.Add.Text := '[]';
    Panels.Add.Text := 'Record';
  end;
end;
```

We use the second only at run-time; it makes sure there are at least three panels in the component:

```
procedure TDdhDbStatusBar.Loaded;
begin
  inherited;
  if not (csDesigning in ComponentState) and
      (Panels.Count < 3) then
    raise Exception.Create (
      'DdhDbStatusBar must have at least 3 panels');
end;
```

In fact, the component will still have its Panels property, which you can use to determine the size of each panel, but you should use this method to remove the existing panels (you'll get exceptions at design-time if you try to do so). Here is a sample of the textual description of this component (taken from the Status program):

```
object DdhDbStatusBar2: TDdhDbStatusBar
  Panels = <
    item
```

```
      Text = 'EMPLOYEE.DB'
      Width = 100
    end
    item
      Text = '[Browsing]'
      Width = 100
    end
    item
      Text = '(Rec 1/42) - 2 Nelson Roberto 250 8/19/87 40000 '
      Width = 50
    end>
  SimplePanel = False
  DataSource = DataSource1
end
```

Of course, we overwrite the text of the panels as soon as the program starts and we activate the data set.

Actually the example program is quite interesting. We fill its list box on the left with the names of the tables of the database referred to by the Table1 object:

```
procedure TForm1.FormCreate(Sender: TObject);
begin
  Session.GetTableNames (Table1.DatabaseName,
    '*.*', True, False, ListBox1.Items);
  ListBox1.ItemIndex :=
    ListBox1.Items.IndexOf (Table1.TableName);
end;
```

Clicking on this list box opens a different database table, as you can see in Figure 17.6:

```
procedure TForm1.ListBox1Click(Sender: TObject);
begin
  Table1.Close;
  Table1.TableName :=
    ListBox1.Items [ListBox1.ItemIndex];
  Table1.Open;
end;
```

NOTE   For a more detailed discussion of using the Session component to retrieve the BDE aliases and the tables of each database, you can refer to Chapter 16 of *Mastering Delphi 3*.

FIGURE 17.6:

The Status example, with the data-aware status bar, after opening a new database table

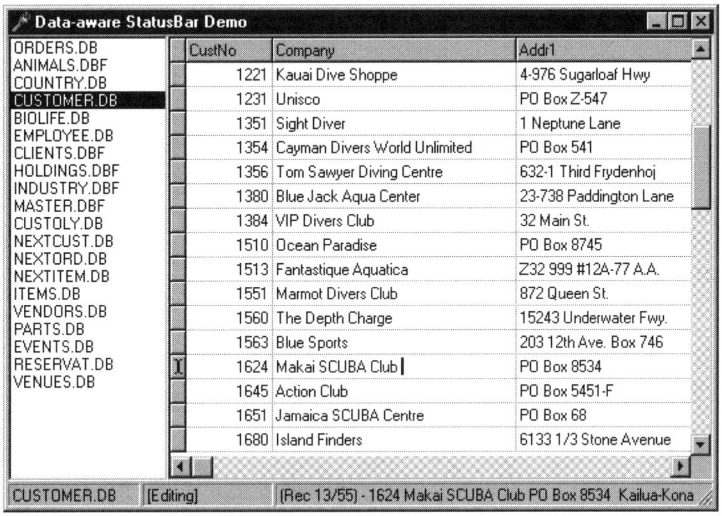

As we mentioned at the beginning of this section, there is a completely different approach we can use to write this component: instead of inheriting from the TStatusBar class, we can copy its code from the VCL source and then remove the features we don't want to make available, such as the Panels, SimplePanel, and SimpleText properties. The source code of this example is available in the DdhDbStatus unit (in the usual Comps directory). This unit isn't part of the package for this chapter, but you can install it along with the other data-aware status bar, because the class and unit names are different.

The data link class is very similar to the one we used in the previous example. The only missing piece is the OnSummary event. In contrast, the component class derives from TWinControl:

```
type
  TDdhStatusPanels = class;
  TDdhStatusPanel = class;

  TDdhDbStatus = class (TWinControl)
  private
    // data-aware support fields
    FDataLink: TDataLink;
    // status bar fields
    FPanels: TDdhStatusPanels;
    FCanvas: TCanvas;
```

```
      FSizeGrip: Boolean;
      // data-aware support methods
      function GetDataSource: TDataSource;
      procedure SetDataSource (Value: TDataSource);
      // status bar methods
      procedure SetSizeGrip(Value: Boolean);
      procedure UpdatePanel(Index: Integer);
      procedure UpdatePanels;
      procedure CNDrawItem(var Message: TWMDrawItem);
        message CN_DRAWITEM;
      procedure WMSize(var Message: TWMSize);
        message WM_SIZE;
    protected
      procedure CreateParams(var Params: TCreateParams); override;
      procedure CreateWnd; override;
      procedure DrawPanel(Panel: TDdhStatusPanel;
        const Rect: TRect); dynamic;
    public
      constructor Create (AOwner: TComponent); override;
      destructor Destroy; override;
      property Canvas: TCanvas read FCanvas;
    published
      property DataSource: TDataSource
        read GetDataSource write SetDataSource;
      property Align default alBottom;
      property DragCursor;
      property DragMode;
      property Enabled;
      property Font;
      property ParentFont;
      property ParentShowHint;
      property PopupMenu;
      property ShowHint;
      property SizeGrip: Boolean
        read FSizeGrip write SetSizeGrip default True;
      property Visible;
      property OnClick;
      property OnDblClick;
      property OnDragDrop;
      property OnDragOver;
      property OnEndDrag;
      property OnMouseDown;
```

```
    property OnMouseMove;
    property OnMouseUp;
    property OnStartDrag;
  end;
```

As we mentioned earlier, most of the code comes from the VCL source. Essentially, all we've done is remove the properties that don't apply to our version of the component, which has a fixed number of panels.

At the beginning of the listing, you can see that we also had to redefine the two classes for the panel collections, TDdhStatusPanels and TDdhStatusPanel. The problem is that the original classes refer to the TStatusBar component directly, and we had to change this reference to our new component class (which doesn't derive from the original one). Again, this was simply a matter of copying the source code and performing a search-and-replace on the class names.

The code for this class is complex, but because it's just a copy of the original VCL code we won't describe it. The only relevant changes are in two methods. First, the constructor creates the three panels in this class too, but at run-time as well as design time. Since we don't save the panels to the stream, we can't restore them from the DFM file at run-time, and so we must create them all once more:

```
constructor TDdhDbStatus.Create (AOwner: TComponent);
begin
  inherited Create (AOwner);
  // data link creation
  FDataLink := TDdhStatusLink.Create (self);
  // status bar
  ControlStyle := [csCaptureMouse, csClickEvents,
    csDoubleClicks, csOpaque];
  Color := clBtnFace;
  Height := 19;
  Align := alBottom;
  FPanels := TDdhStatusPanels.Create(Self);
  // new code
  // create three panels and initialize them
  FPanels.Add.Text := '[Inactive]';
  FPanels.Add.Text := '[]';
  FPanels.Add.Text := 'Record';
  UpdatePanels;
  // end of new code
  FCanvas := TControlCanvas.Create;
  TControlCanvas(FCanvas).Control := Self;
```

```
    FSizeGrip := True;
  end;
```

The other method we've customized (beyond just removing references to properties and events we've deleted) is the WMSize message-handling method. Since the user has no way of customizing the size of the panels at design-time, we automatically set the width of the first two panels to one-fourth of the total, leaving the third panel half of the area. You'll notice that we don't let the message reach the original component, which performs some custom resizing we don't want (the TStatusBar component intercepts this message, too). Here's the code:

```
procedure TDdhDbStatus.WMSize(var Message: TWMSize);
begin
  FPanels [0].Width := Width div 4;
  FPanels [1].Width := Width div 4;
  Repaint;
end;
```

Although this component is certainly a viable and robust alternative to the first version, it has disadvantages as well. For example, it's almost impossible to customize the alignment, bevel style, and width of the panels. With the previous approach, these elements were directly accessible in the Panels property editor, and a user could also add more custom panels to the component to display other information. In any case, the output of the two components is so similar that it's hard to tell one from the other at run-time.

Customizing the DBGrid Component

Besides writing brand custom data-aware components, it's common for Delphi programmers to customize the DBGrid control. In Delphi 1, this database grid was very limited, and many third-party database grids started to appear. Now the standard grid is much more powerful, but we can still improve it in various ways.

The goal for our next example is quite simple. We wanted to enhance the DBGrid with the same kind of custom output we've used for the RecordView component, directly displaying graphic and memo fields. To do this, we need to make the row height of the new grid class resizable, to allow space for a reasonable amount of text and big enough for graphics. You can see an example of this grid at design-time in Figure 17.7.

FIGURE 17.7:

An example of the DdhDbGrid component at design-time. Notice the output of the graphics and memo fields.

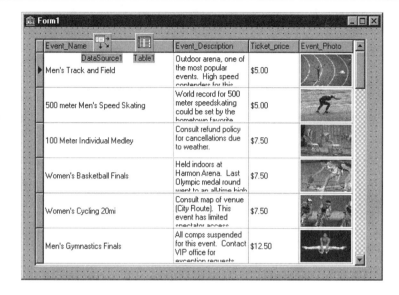

While creating the output was a simple matter of adapting the code used in our other example, setting the height of the grid cells ended up being a very difficult problem to solve. The lines of code you'll see for that operation may be few, but they cost us hours of work!

This time we don't have to create a custom data link, because we are deriving our new class from a component that already has a complex connection with the data. All we have to do in the new class is declare a new property to specify the number of lines of text for each row, and then override a few virtual methods:

```
type
  TDdhDbGrid = class(TDbGrid)
  private
    FLinesPerRow: Integer;
    procedure SetLinesPerRow (Value: Integer);
  protected
    procedure DrawColumnCell(const Rect: TRect; DataCol: Integer;
      Column: TColumn; State: TGridDrawState); override;
    procedure LayoutChanged; override;
  public
    constructor Create (AOwner: TComponent); override;
  published
    property LinesPerRow: Integer
```

```
      read FLinesPerRow write SetLinesPerRow
      default 1;
  end;
```

The constructor and the property set method are both very simple:

```
constructor TDdhDbGrid.Create(AOwner: TComponent);
begin
  inherited Create(AOwner);
  FLinesPerRow := 1;
end;

procedure TDdhDbGrid.SetLinesPerRow(Value: Integer);
begin
  if Value <> FLinesPerRow then
  begin
    FLinesPerRow := Value;
    LayoutChanged;
  end;
end;
```

The side effect of changing the number of lines is a call to the LayoutChanged virtual method. The system calls this method frequently when one of the many output parameters changes. In the code we first call the inherited version, and then set the height of each row. As a basis for this computation we use the same formula that we used in the TCustomDBGrid class: we compute text height using the sample word *Wg* in the current font (we chose this text because it includes both a full-height uppercase character and a lowercase letter with a descender). Here's the code:

```
procedure TDdhDbGrid.LayOutChanged;
var
  PixelsPerRow, PixelsTitle, I: Integer;
begin
  inherited LayOutChanged;

  Canvas.Font := Font;
  PixelsPerRow := Canvas.TextHeight('Wg') + 3;
  if dgRowLines in Options then
    Inc (PixelsPerRow, GridLineWidth);

  Canvas.Font := TitleFont;
  PixelsTitle := Canvas.TextHeight('Wg') + 4;
  if dgRowLines in Options then
```

```
    Inc (PixelsTitle, GridLineWidth);

  // set number of rows
  RowCount := 1 + (Height - PixelsTitle) div
    (PixelsPerRow * FLinesPerRow);

  // set the height of each row
  DefaultRowHeight := PixelsPerRow * FLinesPerRow;
  RowHeights [0] := PixelsTitle;
  for I := 1 to RowCount - 1 do
    RowHeights [I] := PixelsPerRow * FLinesPerRow;
end;
```

The difficult part here was to get the last four statements correct. You can simply set the DefaultRowHeight property, but in that case the title row will probably be too high. At first, we tried setting the DefaultRowHeight and then the height of the first row, but this complicated the code we use to compute the number of visible rows in the grid (the read-only VisibleRowCount property).

In fact, even if we specify the number of rows (which we need to do, in order to avoid having rows hidden beneath the lower edge of the grid), the base class keeps working against us by recomputing them. Although the code we finally arrived at (above) seems to work very well, the complexity of this code still concerns us.

Finally, here's the code we use to draw the data, which we ported from the RecordView component and adapted slightly for the grid:

```
procedure TDdhDbGrid.DrawColumnCell (const Rect: TRect;
  DataCol: Integer; Column: TColumn; State: TGridDrawState);
var
  Bmp: TBitmap;
  OutRect: TRect;
begin
  if FLinesPerRow = 1 then
    inherited DrawColumnCell(Rect, DataCol, Column, State)
  else
  begin
    // clear area
    Canvas.FillRect (Rect);
    // copy the rectangle
    OutRect := Rect;
    // restrict output
    InflateRect (OutRect, -2, -2);
```

```
// output field data
if Column.Field is TGraphicField then
begin
  Bmp := TBitmap.Create;
  try
    Bmp.Assign (Column.Field);
    Canvas.StretchDraw (OutRect, Bmp);
  finally
    Bmp.Free;
  end;
end
else if Column.Field is TMemoField then
begin
  DrawText (Canvas.Handle,
    PChar (Column.Field.AsString),
    Length (Column.Field.AsString),
    OutRect, dt_WordBreak or dt_NoPrefix)
end
else // draw single line vertically centered
  DrawText (Canvas.Handle,
    PChar (Column.Field.DisplayText),
    Length (Column.Field.DisplayText),
    OutRect, dt_vcenter or dt_SingleLine or dt_NoPrefix);
end;
end;
```

In the code above you can see that if the user displays just a single line, the grid uses the standard drawing technique with no output for memo and graphic fields. However, as soon as you increase the line count, you'll see the correct output.

To see this code in action, run the GridDemo example. This program has two buttons you can use to increase or decrease the row height of the grid, and two more buttons to change the font. This is an important test because the height in pixels of each cell is the height of the font multiplied by the number of lines. In Figure 17.8 you can see an example of this program's output; it has two fonts, one for the titles and the grid contents, again using Borland's BioLife database.

FIGURE 17.8:

In the GridDemo program you can set the height and the font of the grid, and see the familiar BioLife table in our new graphical grid.

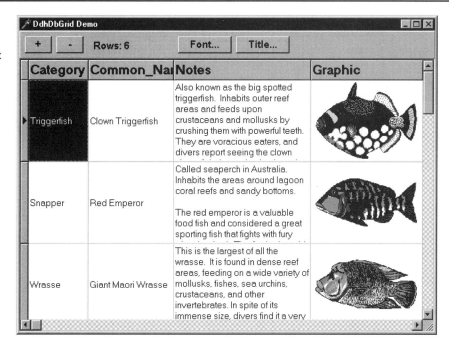

Replicatable Data-Aware Components

The last topic we want to cover in this chapter is the DbCtrlGrid component, or database control grid. This grid can host other data-aware components, and can duplicate them for the number of records visible on the screen. In Figure 17.9 we've used the DbCtrlGrid component to duplicate standard data-aware controls.

To appear in the DbCtrlGrid a component must have its `csReplicatable` control style set; otherwise you cannot use it. This flag is merely an indication that your component actually supports being hosted by a control grid, but you must add that support by yourself. Here's how the DbCtrlGrid component works: For each record we display in the grid, we'll display a panel and one or more field components like DbEdit or DbComboBox controls. However, we won't create field components for each record. Instead, we'll create one set of field components using the active record, and then reuse those components to display the output for the other records. We'll change the records and fields we're displaying by manipulating the data link for the active record.

An example of the DbCtrlGrid component, with some custom data-aware controls

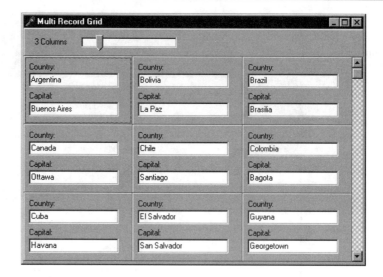

For this reason, the first thing a data-aware component must do is respond to the cm_GetDataLink Delphi control message and return a pointer to the data link, so that the control grid can use and change it. However, there's a further complication that's not widely documented: you can't just change the data link to point to the data of the other records and fields, because the component will display the output for those records and fields in the same grid cell. In fact, you have to customize the Paint method to draw the output in the appropriate cell as you change the manipulate the data link.

A Data-Aware LED for the DbCtrlGrid

As an example of a simple, replicatable, data-aware control, we've customized the DdhLed component from Chapter 5. The idea is to toggle on and off the status of this component depending on the value of a Boolean database field. Here's the new component class:

```
type
  TDdhDbLed = class(TDdhLed)
  private
    // data-aware support
    FDataLink: TFieldDataLink;
    function GetDataField: string;
    procedure SetDataField (Value: string);
```

```
    function GetDataSource: TDataSource;
    procedure SetDataSource (Value: TDataSource);
    function GetField: TField;
    // DbCtrlGrid support
    function GetStatus: TDdhLedStatus;
    procedure CmGetDataLink (var Msg: TMessage);
      message cm_GetDataLink;
  protected
    // data link event handler
    procedure DataChange (Sender: TObject);
  public
    constructor Create (AOwner: TComponent); override;
    destructor Destroy; override;
    procedure Loaded; override;
    procedure Paint; override;
    property Field: TField read GetField;
  published
    property DataField: string
      read GetDataField write SetDataField;
    property DataSource: TDataSource
      read GetDataSource write SetDataSource;
  end;
```

Besides all the usual code for data-aware support, this component has a few specific features. The first is the control style, which we set in the constructor:

```
constructor TDdhDbLed.Create (AOwner: TComponent);
begin
  inherited Create (AOwner);
  // enable use in DBCtrlGrid
  ControlStyle := ControlStyle + [csReplicatable];
  // data link
  FDataLink := TFieldDataLink.Create;
  FDataLink.Control := self;
  FDataLink.OnDataChange := DataChange;
end;
```

The DataChange event handler simply calls another method to compute the current status of the LED, depending on the value of the related data field:

```
procedure TDdhDbLed.DataChange (Sender: TObject);
begin
  Status := GetStatus;
```

```
end;

function TDdhDbLed.GetStatus: TDdhLedStatus;
begin
  if (FDataLink.Field <> nil) and
     (FDataLink.Field is TBooleanField) and
     FDataLink.Field.AsBoolean then
    Result := lsOn
  else
    Result := lsOff;
end;
```

However, what happens is that the DbCtrlGrid component can modify the data link after we return it from the cm_GetDataLink Delphi message (this special handler is required):

```
procedure TDdhDbLed.CmGetDataLink (var Msg: TMessage);
begin
  Msg.Result := Integer (fDataLink);
end;
```

Basically, the control grid component changes the data link for each of the copies it requires, and calls the Paint method each time (with the proper Canvas) to produce the output. However, when the control grid is calling the Paint method for a copy, the component shouldn't use the current status of the LED, but should obtain a new value from the data link, and then reset the older value:

```
procedure TDdhDbLed.Paint;
var
  OldStatus: TDdhLedStatus;
begin
  if csPaintCopy in ControlState then
  begin
    OldStatus := Status;
    Status := GetStatus;
  end;
  inherited Paint;
  if csPaintCopy in ControlState then
    Status := OldStatus;
end;
```

Actually this code is very inefficient because we change the status of the current LED component twice, causing a useless repaint operation. However, as you can see in Figure 17.10, the component works well enough.

FIGURE 17.10:

The LedDemo example shows the DdhDbLed control inside a DbCtrlGrid component.

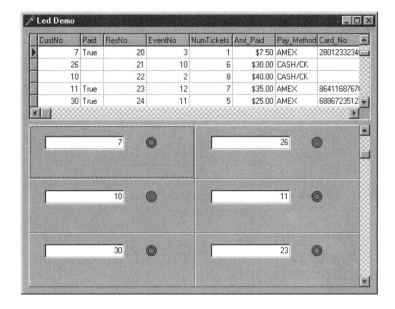

To make this work better, we should have defined the GetStatus method as a virtual function in the base class, and we should have written the original Paint method of the TDdhLed class using the value from the GetStatus function instead of using the field directly.

The modified source code would look like this (it's not available on the companion disk, because we decided not to modify the component written in the previous chapter):

```
// updated version - not on companion CD
procedure TDDHLed.Paint;
var
  Radius, XCenter, YCenter: Integer;
begin
  // same painting code
  if Height > Width then
    Radius := Width div 2 - 2
  else
    Radius := Height div 2 - 2;
  XCenter := Width div 2;
  YCenter := Height div 2;
  Canvas.Brush.Color := clDkGray;
```

```
      Canvas.Ellipse (
        XCenter - Radius, YCenter - Radius,
        XCenter + Radius, YCenter + Radius);
      // virtual function call
      if GetStatus = lsOn then
      begin
        Canvas.Brush.Color := fColor;
        Radius := Radius - 3;
        Canvas.Ellipse (
          XCenter - Radius, YCenter - Radius,
          XCenter + Radius, YCenter + Radius);
      end;
    end;


    // new virtual method for updated version
    procedure TDDHLed.GetStatus: TDdhLedStatus;
    begin
      Result := fStatus;
    end;
```

With the base class written this way, the new class could have had the following GetStatus overridden method and no Paint procedure:

```
    // updated version - not on companion CD
    function TDdhDbLed.GetStatus: TDdhLedStatus;
    begin
      if not (csPaintCopy in ControlState) then
        Result := Status
      else
        if (FDataLink.Field <> nil) and
           (FDataLink.Field is TBooleanField) and
           FDataLink.Field.AsBoolean then
          Result := lsOn
      else
        Result := lsOff;
    end;
```

While this code may look strange, it's exactly what you'll find in the VCL source code for the TDbText class. The class contains the following GetLabelText method, very similar to the one we've just seen:

```
    function TDBText.GetLabelText: string;
    begin
      if csPaintCopy in ControlState then
```

```
    Result := GetFieldText else
    Result := Caption;
end;
```

This method is called by the base class's drawing function, in the TCustomLabel class's DoDrawText method. Here's a simplified version of this method (we've also removed some special-case code that we added):

```
procedure TCustomLabel.DoDrawText(var Rect: TRect; Flags: Word);
var
  Text: string;
begin
  Text := GetLabelText;
  Canvas.Font := Font;
  if not Enabled then
    ...
  else
    DrawText(Canvas.Handle, PChar(Text),
      Length(Text), Rect, Flags);
end;
```

The situation here is actually quite simple, because we are working with a graphic (nonwindowed) control. To accomplish the same thing with a window control, particularly one defined by Windows and not in your code (since you don't have a paint method), is much more complex. The basic approach used by most of the data-aware controls in the VCL is to create a second control, set its status to match that of the main control, and then use it to paint on the canvas supplied by the DbCtrlGrid. The code is quite complex, but it's worth examining.

A ProgressBar for the DBCtrlGrid

We've applied this technique to a class derived from a Windows common control, the ProgressBar, improving on the first example of this chapter. The component class has a few new methods, and other minor changes:

```
type
  TDdhDbRepProgress = class(TProgressBar)
  private
    FDataLink: TFieldDataLink;
    FPaintControl: TPaintControl;
    function GetDataField: string;
    procedure SetDataField (Value: string);
    function GetDataSource: TDataSource;
```

```
    procedure SetDataSource (Value: TDataSource);
    function GetField: TField;
    // DbCtrlGrid support
    procedure CmGetDataLink (var Msg: TMessage);
      message cm_GetDataLink;
    procedure WmPaint (var Msg: TWmPaint);
      message wm_Paint;
    function GetPos: Integer;
  protected
    procedure WndProc(var Message: TMessage); override;
    // data link event handler
    procedure DataChange (Sender: TObject);
  public
    constructor Create (AOwner: TComponent); override;
    destructor Destroy; override;
    property Field: TField read GetField;
  published
    property DataField: string
      read GetDataField write SetDataField;
    property DataSource: TDataSource
      read GetDataSource write SetDataSource;
  end;
```

The constructor sets the csReplicatable flag, and the CmGetDataLink method returns the reference to the current data link, as in the previous component:

```
procedure TDdhDbRepProgress.CmGetDataLink (var Msg: TMessage);
begin
  Msg.Result := Integer (fDataLink);
end;
```

The really new feature is the use of a TPaintControl object. This class derives directly from TObject, and encapsulates a window of the same type as the current object. The idea is that when our component needs to paint one of the other panels of the DbCtrlGrid component, it assigns the value of the field in the data link to the window inside the TPaintControl object, and then paints the component inside the given device context.

Specifically, in the constructor we create the FPaintControl object, passing as parameters the connected control and the name of its window class:

```
constructor TDdhDbRepProgress.Create (AOwner: TComponent);
begin
```

```
  inherited Create (AOwner);
  FDataLink := TFieldDataLink.Create;
  FDataLink.Control := self;
  FDataLink.OnDataChange := DataChange;
  // enable use in DBCtrlGrid
  ControlStyle := ControlStyle + [csReplicatable];
  FPaintControl := TPaintControl.Create(
    self, PROGRESS_CLASS);
end;
```

The component has a new GetPos method, which retrieves the current value of
the data link and is used on a couple of different occasions:

```
function TDdhDbRepProgress.GetPos;
begin
  if (FDataLink.Field <> nil) and
     (FDataLink.Field is TNumericField) then
    Result := FDataLink.Field.AsInteger
  else
    Result := Min;
end;
```

The first use of GetPos is in the DataChange event handler. Before setting the
value, though, the component disables the redrawing operations, by sending the
wm_SetRedraw message. Afterwards, it reenables drawing, and actually forces a
redraw by calling the RedrawWindow API function:

```
procedure TDdhDbRepProgress.DataChange (Sender: TObject);
begin
  SendMessage(Handle, wm_SetRedraw, 0, 0);
  Position := GetPos;
  SendMessage(Handle, wm_SetRedraw, 1, 0);
  if HandleAllocated then
    RedrawWindow (Handle, nil, 0,
      RDW_INVALIDATE or RDW_ERASE or RDW_FRAME);
end;
```

The effect of all this code is to delay painting the component, which usually
takes place immediately after you change the position. Without this code, some
circumstances could cause us to repaint the component twice with different values and a very bad flickering effect.

The GetPos function is also called by the WmPaint method, to set the position of the replicated control in the FPaintControl object:

```
procedure TDdhDbRepProgress.WmPaint (var Msg: TWmPaint);
var
  Rect: TRect;
begin
  if not (csPaintCopy in ControlState) then
    inherited
  else
  begin
    SendMessage(FPaintControl.Handle, Wm_SetRedraw, 0, 0);
    SendMessage(FPaintControl.Handle, PBM_SETRANGE32, Min, Max);
    SendMessage(FPaintControl.Handle, PBM_SETPOS, GetPos, 0);
    SendMessage(FPaintControl.Handle, PBM_SETSTEP, Step, 0);
    SendMessage(FPaintControl.Handle, Wm_SetRedraw, 1, 0);
    SendMessage(FPaintControl.Handle,
      wm_Paint, Msg.DC, 0);
  end;
end;
```

This method sets the range, position, and increment of the replicated progress bar; then it paints the bar in the device context passed as a parameter (Msg.DC). This is the trick used to paint on a different area (since the cloned control is not visible on the screen). The only other new method is the new window procedure, used to remove the window connected to the paint control (and to create a new copy as soon as it's necessary):

```
procedure TDdhDbRepProgress.WndProc(var Message: TMessage);
begin
  with Message do
    if (Msg = WM_CREATE) or
        (Msg = WM_WINDOWPOSCHANGED) then
      FPaintControl.DestroyHandle;
  inherited;
end;
```

As you can see in Figure 17.11, the output is correct, although only the real progress bar displays a lowered border around the control.

The output of the
RepProgr example
shows the data-aware
Progress Bar inside
the DbCtrlGrid

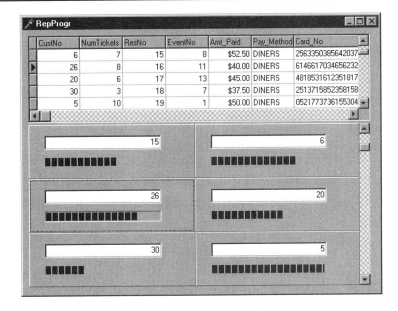

One of the key elements of this code is the TPaintControl class, which defines
two methods: Create (used only to store information related to the connected control) and GetHandle (which actually creates the replicates of the connected component). Here's the code for these methods, extracted from the VCL's DbCtrls unit:

```
constructor TPaintControl.Create(AOwner: TWinControl;
  const ClassName: string);
begin
  FOwner := AOwner;
  FClassName := ClassName;
end;

function TPaintControl.GetHandle: HWnd;
var
  Params: TCreateParams;
begin
  if FHandle = 0 then
  begin
    FObjectInstance := MakeObjectInstance(WndProc);
    TWinControlAccess(FOwner).CreateParams(Params);
    Params.Style := Params.Style and not (WS_HSCROLL or WS_VSCROLL);
```

```
   with Params do
     FHandle := CreateWindowEx(ExStyle, PChar(FClassName),
       PChar(TWinControlAccess(FOwner).Text), Style or WS_VISIBLE,
         X, Y, Width, Height, Application.Handle, 0, HInstance, nil);
   if FCtl3DButton and TWinControlAccess(FOwner).Ctl3D
     and not NewStyleControls then
     Subclass3DWnd(FHandle);
   FDefWindowProc := Pointer(GetWindowLong(FHandle, GWL_WNDPROC));
   SetWindowLong(FHandle, GWL_WNDPROC, Integer(FObjectInstance));
   SendMessage(FHandle, WM_SETFONT,
     TWinControlAccess(FOwner).Font.Handle, 1);
 end;
 Result := FHandle;
end;
```

The GetHandle method demonstrates a couple of techniques we've discussed in the book. We use the fake TWinControlAccess class to access some protected methods and properties of the connected control: CreateParams, Text, Ctl3D, and Font. This is the protected access technique described in Chapter 1. The other technique is the subclassing of the new control, obtained by calling SetWindowLong, as described in Chapters 7 and 8.

What's Next

In this chapter we've seen how you can make existing components data-aware, and how you can customize the database grid components. This isn't a simple topic, and for this reason we've devoted an entire chapter to it, and presented several data-aware controls.

In the next chapter, we'll move our attention to another aspect of database development in Delphi: data sets. We'll see how to write a custom data set, and how to extract information from it to generate an entire form automatically.

Extending Delphi Database Support

- An Enhanced Database Form Wizard

- Building Custom Data Sets

- Saving Database Data to a Stream

- Saving Components in a Custom Data Set

In the last chapter, we studied how you can create your own data-aware controls. In contrast, this chapter focuses on the data-set side of Delphi's database access. We'll cover two topics. In the first part of the chapter, we'll see how you can dynamically generate a form filled with data-aware controls that correspond to the structure of a database table. We'll also build an example that's actually a custom version of the Database Form Wizard provided by Borland.

> **NOTE** Marco developed an earlier version of this database form expert, along with Bob Swart, during a presentation for the Delphi UK User Group, and then extended and enhanced it into an article for *The Delphi Magazine*. We've updated the version we're presenting here, and we're using a different mechanism to generate the form at design-time, but it's based on the same foundations.

In the second part of the chapter, we'll create a custom data-set component. Beginning in Delphi 3, you can now derive a class from the abstract `TDataSet` class, and implement custom database access with no need for the BDE (Borland Database Engine) to be installed! This approach allows you to customize data access, but still use all the Delphi design tools, such as the Fields editor. Even more importantly, we'll be able to use all the standard Delphi data-aware components with our custom data set.

An Enhanced Database Form Wizard

How many times have you used Delphi's Database Form Wizard? It's really invaluable for starting the development of a data entry form, or of any form that displays data from one or more database tables. After a while, however, you might want to customize this wizard to place standard elements in your form by default, such as a company logo or some special combination of components. Of course, you could add those capabilities and change the way the data is presented after the form has been generated, but you might end up making the same changes over and over again. Similarly, you could create a new form template, but you'd lose the benefit of using the Database Form Wizard. It would be better if you could customize the Database Form Wizard to generate the forms as you want them in the first place. There's only one problem: Delphi includes the source code of other, less powerful experts, but no code for the Database Form Wizard. So to customize this tool—we need to write it from scratch!

Actually, there's a second reason for writing this tool. You might need a form-generation tool as part of a program. We're going to follow that approach in this chapter. We'll first build a dynamic form generator, and then turn it into a Delphi Form Wizard.

Building Database Forms Dynamically

We'll base this wizard on the standard notebook metaphor: a notebook component or a page control without tabs, and buttons labeled *Next* and *Previous* to navigate from page to page. The label of the caption will display the page number and its title, thanks to the following OnPageChanged event handler:

```
procedure TFormDbWiz.Notebook1PageChanged(Sender: TObject);
begin
  // copy the name of the page into the caption
  Caption := Format (
    'Ddh DB Form Wizard - Page %d/%d: ',
    [NoteBook1.PageIndex + 1,
    NoteBook1.Pages.Count,
    NoteBook1.ActivePage]);
end;
```

We'll replicate the two navigation buttons on each page because their OnClick event handlers contain most of the program code.

The first page of the DynaForm program (see Figure 18.1) prompts the user to choose a database, using its BDE alias. To accomplish this, we use the Session global object (which belongs to the TSession class) to retrieve a list of databases the application can use, to build a list of the tables in each database, and to configure the BDE connection in different ways.

We use the following code to fill the database list box on the first page of the wizard with the names of the available aliases:

```
procedure TFormDbWiz.FormCreate(Sender: TObject);
begin
  // fill the first list box with database names
  Session.GetDatabaseNames (
    ListDatabases.Items);
  // start in the first page
```

FIGURE 18.1:

The first page of the DynaForm example, where a user selects a database and a file filter for local tables

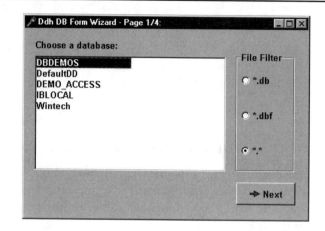

```
    Notebook1.PageIndex := 0;
    // default values (modified by the wizard)
    FormName := 'TResultForm';
    UnitName := 'ResultUnit';
  end;
```

As you can see, the FormCreate method sets two form fields for the program to their initial values, but the user will be able to change these via the wizard. In fact, we've already added the primary features of the DbForm Wizard to the main form of this application, so we'll be able to share the source code between the two projects.

Once the user selects an item in the database list box, we enable the *Next* button with this code:

```
procedure TFormDbWiz.ListDatabasesClick(Sender: TObject);
begin
  // database selected: enable the Next button
  BitBtnNext1.Enabled := True;
end;
```

On each page, we'll use the approach of enabling the Next button after the user has made a valid selection. We'll use the other component on this first page to select a filter for the database. We've prepared the available filters with local tables in mind, but you can adapt them to SQL server databases instead, or simply omit them. The filters are merely the strings of a list associated with a RadioGroup component, so you might want to let the user customize them.

As you'll see in a while, the only thing we'll need is the string corresponding to the selected filter, so we'll use this RadioGroup as if it were a list box.

When you click on the first page's *Next* button, now enabled, we retrieve the list of tables, again using the Session global object, and place them in a list box on the second page, as you can see in Figure 18.2:

```
procedure TFormDbWiz.BitBtnNext1Click(Sender: TObject);
var
  CurrentDB, CurrentFilter: string;
begin
  // get the database and filters
  CurrentDB := ListDatabases.Items [
    ListDatabases.ItemIndex];
  CurrentFilter := GroupFilter.Items [
    GroupFilter.ItemIndex];
  // retrieve the tables
  Session.GetTableNames (CurrentDB,
    CurrentFilter, True, False, ListTables.Items);
  // move to the next page
  NoteBook1.PageIndex := 1;
  BitBtnNext2.Enabled := False;
end;
```

FIGURE 18.2:

The second page of the DynaForm example, listing the tables available in the database we selected in the first page

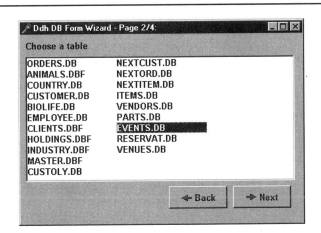

Using the Session component, we've been able to locate and display a specific database table. Now we need to determine the names of the fields in this table.

When you open a table, you can extract information about the structure of the table by using the Fields array property. However, we don't want to open the table, because that can take a considerable amount of time. Fortunately, the Table component has a little-known property, FieldDefs, that contains the definitions of the fields. This is an object of type TFieldDefs, which is an array of TFieldDef structures and has the following properties: FieldNo, Name, DataType, FieldClass, Required, and Size. The DataType property contains the field's original type definition in the database, and the FieldClass indicates the TFields descendant that we'll add to the Fields array when the table is opened. It's important to remember that you can access each field definition property even if the table isn't open, but you'll have to call the FieldDefs property's Update method.

To use this approach, we've added a Table component to the form, and we'll set its DatabaseName and TableName properties using the items selected from the list boxes on the first two pages of the notebook. Then we call the FieldDefs property's Update method, as you can see in the following listing:

```
procedure TFormDbWiz.BitBtnNext2Click(Sender: TObject);
var
  I: Integer;
begin
  // set the properties of the selected table
  with Table1 do
  begin
    DatabaseName := ListDatabases.Items[
      ListDatabases.ItemIndex];
    TableName := ListTables.Items[
      ListTables.ItemIndex];
    // load the field definitions
    FieldDefs.Update;
  end;
  // clear the list box, then fill it
  ListFields.Clear;
  for I := 0 to Table1.FieldDefs.Count - 1 do
    // add number, name, and class name of each field
    ListFields.Items.Add (Format (
      '%d) %s [%s]',
      [Table1.FieldDefs[I].FieldNo,
      Table1.FieldDefs[I].Name,
      Table1.FieldDefs[I].FieldClass.ClassName]));
  // move to the next page
  NoteBook1.PageIndex := 2;
```

```
    BitBtnNext3.Enabled := False;
  end;
```

The BitBtnNext2Click method scans the FieldDefs list, and fills a new list box with the field names and the corresponding class names for the associated TField object. As you can see in Figure 18.3, the third page of the notebook displays this field list and allows the user to select fields from the database table. We'll add components for the selected fields in the final form. We've set the list box's MultiSelect property to True and ExtendedSelect property to False, so clicking on an item will reverse its current selection status. We've also provided buttons to select all or none of the fields.

FIGURE 18.3:

The third page of the DynaForm example shows a list of the fields available in the database table selected by the user.

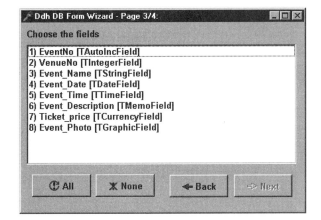

To map the data types of the database fields to the data types of the corresponding data-aware components, we've written the ConvertClass function, which accepts a field class reference and returns a control class reference.

NOTE   We discussed class references in detail in Chapter 1.

This conversion function simply scans a two-dimensional, constant array built by the program, and looks for a match in the field-class-reference column. When the function finds a match, it returns the corresponding control class. The function has to perform some casts between class references, but the rest of its operation should be clear enough. Here's the declaration code of the array and the implementation section of the function, both part of a separate DdhDynDb support unit:

```
const
  FieldTypeCount = 15;

type
  CVTable = array [1..FieldTypeCount, 1..2] of TClass;

// TBytesField and TVarBytesField are missing
const
  ConvertTable: CVTable = (
  (TAutoIncField, TDBEdit),
  (TStringField, TDBEdit),
  (TIntegerField, TDBEdit),
  (TSmallintField, TDBEdit),
  (TWordField, TDBEdit),
  (TFloatField, TDBEdit),
  (TCurrencyField, TDBEdit),
  (TBCDField, TDBEdit),
  (TBooleanField, TDBCheckBox),
  (TDateTimeField, TDBEdit),
  (TDateField, TDBEdit),
  (TTimeField, TDBEdit),
  (TMemoField, TDBMemo),
  (TBlobField, TDBImage),        {just a guess}
  (TGraphicField, TDBImage));

function ConvertClass(FieldClass: TFieldClass): TControlClass;
var
  I: Integer;
begin
  Result := nil;
  for I := 1 to FieldTypeCount do
    if ConvertTable [I, 1] = FieldClass then
    begin
      Result := TControlClass (
        ConvertTable [I, 2]);
      break; // jump out of for loop
    end;
  if Result = nil then
    raise Exception.Create ('ConvertClass failed');
end;
```

The associations we've defined in this array are far from perfect. In particular, our decision that BLOB fields should map to DBImage controls is a reasonable guess only for dBase tables.

The fourth page of the notebook, shown in Figure 18.4, uses this conversion function and the first column of a string grid to display the name of each selected field and of its corresponding control. By default, we're displaying the field name again in the second column, but you can edit it here to provide a more descriptive label that we'll place near the control. Here's the code used to fill the string grid:

```
procedure TFormDbWiz.BitBtnNext3Click(Sender: TObject);
var
  I, RowNum: Integer;
begin
  // reserve enough rows in the string grid
  StringGrid1.RowCount := ListFields.Items.Count;
  // empty the string grid
  for I := 0 to StringGrid1.RowCount - 1 do
  begin
    StringGrid1.Cells [0, I] := '';
    StringGrid1.Cells [1, I] := '';
  end;
  // for each field, if selected list it with the
  // corresponding data-aware component
  RowNum := 0;
  for I := 0 to ListFields.Items.Count - 1 do
    if ListFields.Selected [I] then
    begin
      StringGrid1.Cells [0, RowNum] := Format ('%d) %s [%s]',
        // field number, name, class name of data-aware control
        [Table1.FieldDefs[I].FieldNo,
        Table1.FieldDefs[I].Name,
        ConvertClass(Table1.FieldDefs[I].FieldClass).ClassName]);
      StringGrid1.Cells [1, RowNum] := Table1.FieldDefs[I].Name;
      Inc (RowNum);
    end;
  // set the real number of rows
  StringGrid1.RowCount := RowNum;
  NoteBook1.PageIndex := 3;
end;
```

FIGURE 18.4:

The fourth page of the DynaView example shows the class names of the data-aware controls the program is going to use, and it allows a user to customize the labels displayed in the second column.

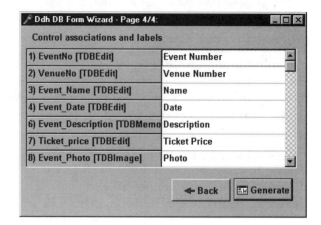

In the code above, the for loop increments the RowNum counter to keep track of the current row in the StringGrid. However, if the user selects some fields, the index of those fields won't match the rows of the grid. (We'll fix this later.) Notice also how we use the ClassName method with the result of the ConvertClass function to obtain a text description of the class. This is possible because ClassName is a class method, not a standard method.

Generating the Database Form

Now for the last page of the program. Clicking the *Generate* button builds and displays the new form using code in the support unit. The program simply prepares a string list that contains the labels and code for the related fields (the fields selected by the user), and then calls the GenerateForm method:

```
procedure TFormDbWiz.BitBtnNext4Click(Sender: TObject);
var
  StrList: TStringList;
  I, RowNum: Integer;
begin
  StrList := TStringList.Create;
  Screen.Cursor := crHourGlass;
  try
    RowNum := 0;
    for I := 0 to ListFields.Items.Count - 1 do
      if ListFields.Selected [I] then
```

```
      begin
        StrList.AddObject (
          StringGrid1.Cells [1, RowNum], TObject (I));
        // move to next row in string grid
        Inc (RowNum);
      end;
    ResultForm := GenerateForm (StrList, Table1);
    ResultForm.OnClose := GeneratedFormClose;
    ResultForm.Show;
  finally
    Screen.Cursor := crDefault;
    StrList.Free;
  end;
end;
```

What we want to generate is a form that contains a panel hosting a DBNavigator component and a scroll box covering the remainder of the client area (and aligned to it). We'll place the new components in the scroll box, so that if there are too many fields to map, the scrollbar will control the region of the form that contains the field components and labels, and the toolbar will remain in its place, because it's not in the scroll box. (This is the same approach used by Delphi's standard Database Form Wizard.) The form will also contain a Table component, connected to the database and table selected by the user, and a DataSource. You can see an example of the generated form in Figure 18.5.

TIP

The secondary forms this program creates are modeless, which allows the user to open many of them. As a result, closing the forms doesn't automatically free them. For this reason, we've mapped the GeneratedFormClose method as a main form OnClose event handler. This method simply sets the Action reference parameter to caFree, which indicates that the program should destroy the form object when the form window is closed.

In an earlier example, we used Delphi to display the resulting form. In this version, we've decided to create the form entirely at run-time, creating all the components we need and setting their properties via code. Here's the initial part of the listing:

```
function GenerateForm (StrList: TStringList;
  SourceTable: TTable): TForm;
```

FIGURE 18.5:

A database form
generated at
run-time by the
DynaForm example,
using Delphi's
Olympic Events
database table

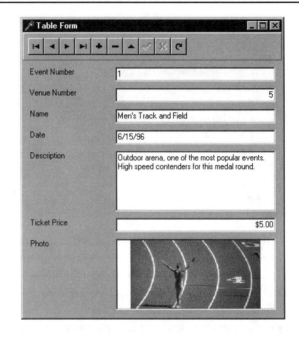

```
var
  ATable: TTable;
  I, NumField, YComp, HForm, Hmax: Integer;
  NewName: string;
  NewLabel: TLabel;
  NewDBComp: TControl;
  CtrlClass: TControlClass;
  ADataSource: TDataSource;
  APanel: TPanel;
  ANavigator: TDBNavigator;
  AScrollbox: TScrollBox;
begin
  // generate the form and connect the table
  Result := TForm.Create (Application);
  Result.Position := poScreenCenter;
  Result.Width := Screen.Width div 2;
  Result.Caption := 'Table Form';

  // create a Table component in the result form
  ATable := TTable.Create (Result);
```

```
ATable.DatabaseName := SourceTable.DatabaseName;
ATable.TableName := SourceTable.TableName;
ATable.Active := True;
ATable.Name := 'Table1';
// component position (at design time)
ATable.DesignInfo := MakeLong (20, 20);
```

This initial code creates the form and places the Table component on it. We then connect the table component with the database and table that correspond to the component passed as a parameter (SourceTable). Next, the program activates the table, so that in the rest of the function we can refer to the fields of this table directly.

TIP
We can place nonvisual components on a form at design-time, and save their positions in two fake properties, Left and Top. Delphi streams these properties via a call to DefineProperties. However, since the properties don't really exist, how to we modify them at design-time? Delphi stores the horizontal and vertical position of nonvisual components in the undocumented DesignInfo property. This is what we'll use to set the position of the table and data-source components of the dynamically built form. However, this will be useful only in the wizard version.

Next we take the following steps:

1. Create the DataSource component and connect it to the table.

2. Create a toolbar panel aligned to the top of the form.

3. Create a DBNavigator component (connected to the data source) within the panel.

4. Create a ScrollBox aligned with the client area on the form.

Here's the code for the ScrollBox component:

```
// create a scroll box
AScrollbox := TScrollBox.Create (Result);
AScrollbox.Parent := Result;
AScrollbox.Width := Result.ClientWidth;
AScrollbox.Align := alClient;
AScrollbox.BorderStyle := bsNone;
AScrollbox.Name := 'ScrollBox1';
```

You'll notice that the program assigns a name to each component, something that will be useful for the wizard version. After the `GenerateForm` function finishes building this fixed group of components, it moves on to building the series of labels and data-aware controls. By the way, the form is the owner of all these controls (as indicated in the parameter of the `Create` constructor), while the Parent of the controls is the ScrollBox:

```
// generate field editors
YComp := 10;
for I := 0 to StrList.Count - 1 do
begin
  NumField := Integer (StrList.Objects [I]);

  // create a label with the field name
  NewLabel := TLabel.Create (Result);
  NewLabel.Parent := AScrollBox;
  NewLabel.Name := 'Label' + IntToStr (I);
  NewLabel.Caption := StrList [I];
  NewLabel.Top := YComp;
  NewLabel.Left := 10;
  NewLabel.Width := 120;

  // create the data-aware control
  CtrlClass := ConvertClass (
    ATable.FieldDefs[NumField].FieldClass);
  NewDBComp := CtrlClass.Create (Result);
  NewDBComp.Parent := AScrollBox;
  NewName := CtrlClass.ClassName +
    ATable.FieldDefs[NumField].Name;
  NormalizeString (NewName);
  NewDBComp.Name := NewName;
  NewDBComp.Top := YComp;
  NewDBComp.Left := 140;
  NewDbComp.Width :=
    AScrollBox.Width - 150; // width of label plus border

  // connect the control to the data source
  // and field using RTTI support
  ConnectDataFields (NewDbComp,
    ADataSource,
    ATable.FieldDefs[NumField].Name);
```

```
// compute the position of the next component
Inc (YComp, NewDBComp.Height + 10);
end; // for each field
```

In this code, we're basing the name of the label on the loop counter, while its caption corresponds to the value the user inserted (this is also passed as a parameter to this procedure via the string list). The horizontal positions of the labels are fixed and their vertical positions increase each time. In the last statement of the listing above, we determine this increment by computing the height of the last control and leaving some blank space.

We set the name of the data-aware component using the control's class name plus the name of the field. Here, you'll notice that the code refers to the fields using the number stored in the Objects part of the string list that was passed as a parameter (temporarily moved in the NumField variable), and not the value of the for loop counter (I). As we pointed out earlier, the value of RowNum may not match the correct index in the string list.

The problem here is that the names of the fields might include spaces or other special characters that aren't valid for an identifier. To solve this problem, we've written a NormalizeString procedure, which replaces invalid characters with underscores. It also calls Delphi's IsValidIdent function, which checks whether a string is a valid Pascal identifier:

```
procedure NormalizeString (var S: string);
var
  N: Integer;
begin
  // remove the T
  Delete (S, 1, 1);
  {check if the string is a valid Pascal identifier:
  if not, replace spaces and other characters with underscores}
  if not IsValidIdent (S) then
    for N := 1 to Length (S) do
      if not ((S[N] in ['A'..'Z']) or (S[N] in ['a'..'z'])
          or ((S[N] in ['0'..'9']) and (N <> 1))) then
        S [N] := '_';
end;
```

Now we need to set the DataSource and DataField properties of the data-aware components. Unfortunately, each VCL class representing a data-aware component defines these properties directly and does not inherit them from a common ancestor class. This means we have no way to use inheritance or polymorphism to define these properties, but must use the direct property-access techniques introduced in Chapter 4.

Since this technique can be useful in different circumstances, we've pulled this portion of the code into a stand-alone procedure, which accepts the following parameters: the data-aware control, the data source to use, and the name of the field to connect:

```
procedure ConnectDataFields (DbComp: TControl;
  DataSource: TDataSource; FieldName: string);
var
  PropInfo: PPropInfo;
begin
  if not Assigned (DbComp) then
    raise Exception.Create (
      'ConnectDataFields failed: Invalid control');

  // set the DataSource property
  PropInfo := GetPropInfo (
    DbComp.ClassInfo, 'DataSource');
  if PropInfo = nil then
    raise Exception.Create (
      'ConnectDataFields failed: Missing DataSource property');
  SetOrdProp (DbComp, PropInfo,
    Integer (Pointer (DataSource)));

  // set the DataField property
  PropInfo := GetPropInfo (
    DbComp.ClassInfo, 'DataField');
  if PropInfo = nil then
    raise Exception.Create (
      'ConnectDataFields failed: Missing DataField property');
  SetStrProp (DbComp, PropInfo, FieldName);
end;
```

The final section of the GenerateForm function computes the height of the form, trying to accommodate all the controls if possible, or setting it almost to the height of the screen if this isn't possible. In contrast, we increase the width of the form only if the number of components forces us to add a scroll bar, in which case we add the width of the scroll bar (returned by the GetSystemMetrics API call):

```
// compute requested height for client area
HForm := YComp + APanel.Height;
```

```
    // max client area height = screen height - 40 - form border
    HMax := (Screen.Height - 40 -
      (Result.Height - Result.ClientHeight));
    // limit form height to HMax and reserve space for scrollbar
    if HForm > HMax then
    begin
      HForm := HMax;
      Result.Width := Result.Width +
        GetSystemMetrics (SM_CXVSCROLL);
    end;
    Result.ClientHeight := HForm;
```

Building the Wizard

The program we've just built, DynaForm, can create complex database forms on the fly. Now we can combine this program with the code of the Grid Wizard from Chapter 14. The wizard class (installed as part of the package for this chapter, and available in the Comps directory, as usual) follows the standard notation. However, we've actually built classes to install both a standard wizard (available via a help menu entry) and a form wizard (available in the Object Repository's Forms page).

Since we've discussed the DynaForm application thoroughly, the only relevant piece of wizard code left for us to examine is its Execute method. This method calls the ToolServices object's GetNewModuleAndClassName method to request a valid unit and form name, passes these names to a TFormDbWiz form (the main form of the previous example), and then shows this form modally. Here's the first part of this method:

```
procedure TDdhDbFormWizard.Execute;
var
  FormName, UnitIdent, FileName: string;
  FormIStream, UnitIStream: TIMemoryStream;
  StrForm, StrUnit: TMemoryStream;
begin
  // get new form and unit names
  ToolServices.GetNewModuleAndClassName(
    'Form', UnitIdent, FormName, FileName);
  // create and show the main form of the wizard
  FormDbWiz := TFormDbWiz.Create (Application);
  try
    FormDbWiz.FormName := FormName;
```

```
FormDbWiz.UnitName := UnitIdent;
if FormDbWiz.ShowModal = mrOK then...
```

When the user clicks the Generate button on the form, we generate both the form (without showing it) and its Pascal source code. Here's the updated version of the BitBtnNext4Click method of the form:

```
procedure TFormDbWiz.BitBtnNext4Click(Sender: TObject);
var
  StrList: TStringList;
  I, RowNum: Integer;
begin
  StrList := TStringList.Create;
  Screen.Cursor := crHourGlass;
  try
    RowNum := 0;
    for I := 0 to ListFields.Items.Count - 1 do
      if ListFields.Selected [I] then
      begin
        StrList.AddObject (
          StringGrid1.Cells [1, RowNum], TObject (I));
        // move to next row in string grid
        Inc (RowNum);
      end;
    ResultForm := GenerateForm (StrList, Table1);
    if not Assigned (ToolServices) then
    begin
      // stand-alone form
      ResultForm.OnClose := GeneratedFormClose;
      ResultForm.Show;
    end
    else
    begin
      // wizard
      SourceCode := GenerateSource (ResultForm,
        FormName, UnitName);
      ModalResult := mrOK;
    end;
  finally
    Screen.Cursor := crDefault;
    StrList.Free;
  end;
end;
```

> We wanted to use the same source code for the stand-alone and wizard versions of this form, but we needed to perform different operations at the end. To distinguish between the two, we use the `if not Assigned (ToolServices)` test. This works because the `ToolServices` global object is initialized only when the code executes inside the Delphi IDE. In the stand-alone program the object is not initialized and is `nil`.

The new code calls the `GenerateSource` function, which returns a string that contains the Pascal source code for the form. Basically, the source code is a form declaration, followed by the list of the component names and data types that are part of the form we just created. Interestingly, the code uses the newly created form as a source of information, so if we add new components in the `GenerateForm` function, the resulting code will adapt to the new components. Here's the code of the method, which you can easily adapt to work with other forms:

```
function GenerateSource (AForm: TForm;
  FormName, UnitName: string): string;
var
  I: Integer;
begin
  SetLength (Result, 20000);

  // generate the first part of the unit source
  Result :=
    'unit ' + UnitName + ';'#13#13 +
    'interface'#13#13 +
    'uses'#13 +
    '  SysUtils, WinTypes, WinProcs, Messages, Classes,'#13 +
    '  Forms, Graphics, Controls, Dialogs, DB, DBCtrls,'#13 +
    '  DBTables, ExtCtrls;'#13#13 +
    'type'#13 +
    '  T' + FormName + ' = class(TForm)'#13;

  // add each component to the form
  for I := 0 to AForm.ComponentCount - 1 do
    Result := Result +
      '    ' + AForm.Components[I].Name +
      ': ' + AForm.Components[I].ClassName + ';'#13;

  // generate the final part of the source code
```

```
      Result := Result +
        '  private'#13 +
        '    { Private declarations }'#13 +
        '  public'#13 +
        '    { Public declarations }'#13 +
        '  end;'#13#13 +
      'var'#13 +
        '  ' + FormName + ': T' + FormName + ';'#13#13 +
      'implementation'#13#13 +
      '{$R *.DFM}'#13#13 +
      'end.'#13;
  end;
```

Once it has generated the resulting form and the source code string, the Execute method of the wizard continues with some complex code, very similar to that used in Chapter 14 for the Grid Wizard:

```
// TDdhDbFormWizard.Execute continues...
if FormDbWiz.ShowModal = mrOK then
begin
  // create two streams
  StrUnit := TMemoryStream.Create;
  StrForm := TMemoryStream.Create;

  // save the string to the stream
  StrUnit.WriteBuffer (
    Pointer(FormDbWiz.SourceCode)^,
    Length (FormDbWiz.SourceCode));
  StrUnit.Position := 0;

  {copy the form to the second stream}
  // create a proxy
  Proxies.CreateSubclass (
    FormDbWiz.ResultForm, 'T' + FormName, TForm);
  // change the name
  FormDbWiz.ResultForm.Name := FormName;
  // write the form to a memory stream
  StrForm.WriteComponentRes (
    FormName, FormDbWiz.ResultForm);
  StrForm.Position := 0;
```

```
    // delete the form
    FormDbWiz.ResultForm.Free;
    FormDbWiz.ResultForm := nil;

    // create the two interface streams
    FormIStream := TIMemoryStream.Create (StrForm);
    UnitIStream := TIMemoryStream.Create (StrUnit);
    // let them own the actual streams
    FormIStream.OwnStream := True;
    UnitIStream.OwnStream := True;
    // create the new module
    ToolServices.CreateModule (
      FileName, UnitIStream, FormIStream,
      [cmAddToProject, cmShowSource, cmShowForm,
      cmUnnamed, cmMarkModified]);
  end;
finally
  // free the main form
  FormDbWiz.Free;
end;
end;
```

In short, the wizard creates two streams, saves the source code into the first, and then saves the form description (the DFM file) into the second (after changing the form class type using the Proxy technique described in Chapter 14). After this, the Execute method creates two interface streams, which own the two plain streams, and uses them to call the ToolServices global object's CreateModule method. This call adds the new unit and related form to the current project and displays them. The wizard then marks the new module as unnamed and modified, forcing Delphi to save it automatically and ask the user to replace the default name. You can see a form generated by this wizard at design time, along with its source code, in Figure 18.6.

Obviously, this wizard isn't terribly powerful. Even though it allows the user to customize the field labels, it provides no support for queries or master/detail relationships. However, you can easily extend the source code of this database form wizard to suit the needs of your own company, customizing the forms it generates, and adding appropriate pages to the wizard notebook.

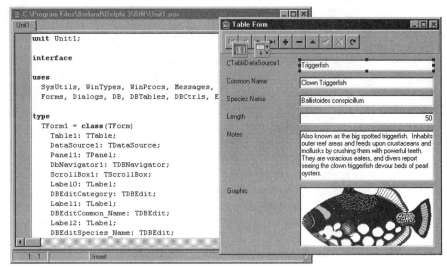

FIGURE 18.6:

The form and the source code generated by the DBForm Wizard, an enhanced version of the Database Form Wizard, using Delphi's Biolife sample table

Building Custom Data Sets

In Delphi 1 and Delphi 2 all the database-related components were designed around and strongly tied to the BDE. In Delphi 3 the situation has changed. Instead of defining a single TDataSet class that wraps the BDE connection, Delphi now offers an abstract TDataSet class; there is also a new TBdeDataSet class, which derives from TDataSet and is the base class for TDbDataSet, which is the base class for TTable and TQuery.

There are two important points to note about this change. First, the new TDataSet class is abstract, meaning that it declares several virtual abstract methods (virtual methods the class declares but doesn't implement, and marks as such with the abstract keyword). Every subclass of TDataSet must override those methods. The second point is that this abstract class, the unit that defines it, and all the data-aware components have no dependence on the BDE, and don't require you to install it on the client system. If you need only very simple database support, you can now deploy Delphi applications directly on the user's computer without installing the BDE too.

NOTE All these techniques are probably being introduced to support lightweight clients in the three-tier architecture, which we'll cover in the next chapter. Better support for the Web is probably a related issue.

As already mentioned, when you derive a component from TDataSet, you must override several virtual abstract methods, 23 to be precise. This makes the development of a custom data set quite complex. Moreover, Borland hasn't released documentation on writing custom data sets.

For this reason we'll proceed in steps. We'll begin by building a simple first data set, to demonstrate the methods you must write and to show when a Delphi application will call them. This component can actually serve as a tool that you can easily adapt to debug any data set, including those you write. Next, we'll describe in detail the various abstract methods of TDataSet, implementing a data set that stores its binary data in a stream. In a future version, we'll save Delphi components to a stream.

Debugging a Data Set

To understand when a Delphi application will call the various TDataSet abstract methods, we can build a custom data set that simply produces a string with the name of the method that the application called and some of its parameters. Since we don't want to implement the entire data set behavior yet, we must subclass an existing data-set class, such as the Table component. This component has a number of virtual methods, but we want to monitor only those that override TDataSet abstract methods, plus a few other methods.

The new component's class, which we won't install in Delphi but will simply use within an example, lists all these methods. In addition, it defines a custom event handler, which we use to produce the debug string:

```
type
  TDebugNotify = procedure (const DegubStr: string) of object;

  TDebugDataSet = class(TTable)
  private
    FDebugNotify: TDebugNotify;
  protected
    // TDataSet virtual abstract methods
```

```delphi
    function AllocRecordBuffer: PChar; override;
    procedure FreeRecordBuffer(var Buffer: PChar); override;
    procedure GetBookmarkData(Buffer: PChar;
      Data: Pointer); override;
    function GetBookmarkFlag(Buffer: PChar):
      TBookmarkFlag; override;
    function GetFieldData(Field: TField;
      Buffer: Pointer): Boolean; override;
    function GetRecord(Buffer: PChar; GetMode: TGetMode;
      DoCheck: Boolean): TGetResult; override;
    function GetRecordSize: Word; override;
    procedure InternalAddRecord(Buffer: Pointer;
      Append: Boolean); override;
    procedure InternalClose; override;
    procedure InternalDelete; override;
    procedure InternalFirst; override;
    procedure InternalGotoBookmark(
      Bookmark: Pointer); override;
    procedure InternalHandleException; override;
    procedure InternalInitFieldDefs; override;
    procedure InternalInitRecord(Buffer: PChar); override;
    procedure InternalLast; override;
    procedure InternalOpen; override;
    procedure InternalPost; override;
    procedure InternalSetToRecord(Buffer: PChar); override;
    function IsCursorOpen: Boolean; override;
    procedure SetBookmarkFlag(Buffer: PChar;
      Value: TBookmarkFlag); override;
    procedure SetBookmarkData(Buffer: PChar;
      Data: Pointer); override;
    procedure SetFieldData(Field: TField;
      Buffer: Pointer); override;
    // TDataSet virtual methods (optional)
    procedure InternalRefresh; override;
    function GetRecordCount: Integer; override;
    procedure SetRecNo(Value: Integer); override;
    function GetRecNo: Integer; override;
  public
    property OnDebugNotify: TDebugNotify
      read FDebugNotify write FDebugNotify;
  end;
```

The methods of this class simply call the inherited versions, and they pass a string to the FDebugNotify event if the field is assigned. Here are some of the methods:

```
procedure TDebugDataSet.InternalOpen;
begin
  if Assigned (FDebugNotify) then
    FDebugNotify ('InternalOpen');
  inherited;
end;

function TDebugDataSet.IsCursorOpen: Boolean;
begin
  Result := inherited IsCursorOpen;
  if Result then
    if Assigned (FDebugNotify) then
      FDebugNotify('IsCursorOpen: True')
  else
    if Assigned (FDebugNotify) then
      FDebugNotify('IsCursorOpen: False');
end;

function TDebugDataSet.GetRecordSize: Word;
begin
  Result := inherited GetRecordSize;
  if Assigned (FDebugNotify) then
    FDebugNotify('GetRecordSize: ' + IntToStr (Result));
end;

function TDebugDataSet.GetRecord(Buffer: PChar;
  GetMode: TGetMode; DoCheck: Boolean): TGetResult;
begin
  case GetMode of
    gmNext:
      if Assigned (FDebugNotify) then
        FDebugNotify('GetRecord: Next');
    gmPrior:
      if Assigned (FDebugNotify) then
        FDebugNotify('GetRecord: Prior');
    gmCurrent:
      if Assigned (FDebugNotify) then
        FDebugNotify('GetRecord: Current');
```

```
    end;
  Result := inherited GetRecord (Buffer, GetMode, DoCheck);
end;
```

As we mentioned, we use this component in a demo program, DebugDS. This example's form contains a table and a data source, a navigator, a DBGrid, a list box, three buttons, plus panels and splitter components to make the output flexible. The data-aware components and the data source are connected normally, and the table component should refer to a valid database and table.

When the user places this component, it creates a TDebugDataSet object with the same database connection as the Table1 component, and connects the data source to it:

```
procedure TForm1.FormCreate(Sender: TObject);
begin
  Table1.Close;
  TableClone := TDebugDataSet.Create (nil);
  TableClone.DatabaseName := Table1.DatabaseName;
  TableClone.TableName := Table1.TableName;
  TableClone.OnDebugNotify := LocalNotify;
  DataSource1.DataSet := TableClone;
end;
```

The most important element here is the assignment of the OnDebugNotify event to a form method that displays the string in the list box, and then selects the new item so that it remains in view:

```
procedure TForm1.LocalNotify (const DebugText: string);
var
  nItem: Integer;
begin
  if Assigned (ListBox1) then
  begin
    // add the text to the string
    nItem := ListBox1.Items.Add (DebugText);
    // select the new item
    ListBox1.ItemIndex := nItem;
  end;
end;
```

As soon as you press the button to open the custom database table, we start filling the list box with debug strings, as you can see in Figure 18.7. The three methods connected to the buttons are quite simple:

```
procedure TForm1.BtnOpenClick(Sender: TObject);
begin
  TableClone.Active := True;
end;


procedure TForm1.BtnCloseClick(Sender: TObject);
begin
  TableClone.Active := False;
end;


procedure TForm1.BtnClearClick(Sender: TObject);
begin
  ListBox1.Items.Clear;
end;
```

FIGURE 18.7:

The list box of the DebugDS example lists the calls to the abstract methods of the TDataSet class, plus a few extra virtual methods. Here you can see a series of edit, post, and insert operations.

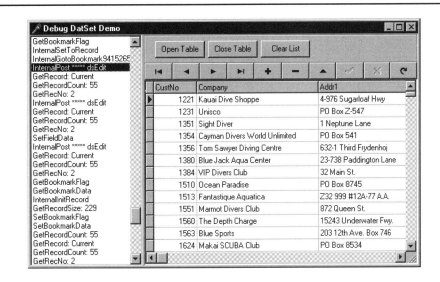

As you start using the DBGrid or DBNavigator components to operate on the table, you'll see many strings appear in the list box. This is due, in part, to the fact that we've connected a grid to the data set, and the grid frequently requires updates to all the records it's displaying.

In addition to using this example to see when a Delphi application calls the various data set functions, you can simply replace its base class with that of another data set component provided by Borland, or one you've built, to debug it.

Saving Database Data to a Stream

Now we're ready to look at the details of implementing a custom data set. As we mentioned earlier, this isn't simple, so you'll have to follow this section in detail. Our basic approach is to divide the methods into logical groups, explain what each of the methods is supposed to do, and then show some example code for each.

However, before we start, we need to discuss a few considerations about record buffering. The TDataSet class declares a list of buffers, which store the values of different records. These buffers store the actual data, but they also usually store further information for the data set to use when managing the records. In fact, these buffers don't have a predefined structure, and the data set allocates the buffers, fills them, saves them to a file, and destroys them. Delphi doesn't manage them. We must also copy the data from the record buffers to the various fields of the data set, and vice versa. Our data set is entirely responsible for handling these buffers.

In addition to managing the data buffers, we'll also be responsible for record navigation, for managing the bookmarks, for defining the structure of the data set, and for creating the proper data fields. The TDataSet class is nothing more than a framework, and we must fill it with the appropriate code. Fortunately, most of the code follows a standard structure, which the TDataSet-derived VCL classes use. Once you've grasped the key ideas, you'll be able to build custom data sets quite easily. We've intentionally tried to write our custom data-set class in a flexible way, to make it easier for you to derive other classes from it (as we'll do later in this chapter).

> **TIP**
>
> In the source code of this example on the CD, we've left in as comments some ShowMessage calls that we initially used to test the component. As an alternative to using the DebugDB class, and to help understand how the program works, you might want to enable some of these calls and rebuild the package. For convenience, we've removed all these commented-out calls from the listings published in the book. Because of this, there are some minor differences between the published listings and the source code, which we'll describe later on.

The Definition of the Class

The starting point, as usual, is the declaration of the component class. It contains a series of protected fields that we'll use to manage the buffers, track the current position and record count, and handle many other features. You should also notice another record declaration at the beginning, a record we'll use to store the extra data for every data record we place in a buffer. We'll place this information in the record buffer following the actual data, so we must also provide a local field that specifies the offset to access this memory location.

```
type
  EDataSetOneError = class (Exception);

  PRecInfo = ^TRecInfo;
  TRecInfo = record
    Bookmark: Longint;
    BookmarkFlag: TBookmarkFlag;
  end;

type
  TDdhDataSetOne = class(TDataSet)
  protected
    FStream: TStream; // the physical table
    FTableName: string; // table path and file name

    // record data
    FRecordCount, // current number of records
    FRecordSize, // the size of the actual data
    FRecordBufferSize, // data + housekeeping (TRecInfo)
    FRecordInfoOffset, // offset of RecInfo in record buffer
    FCurrentRecord, // current record (0 to FRecordCount - 1)
    BofCrack, // before the first record (crack)
    EofCrack: Integer; // after the last record (crack)

    // file header size (optionally used by subclasses)
    FDataFileHeaderSize: Integer;

    // status
    FIsTableOpen: Boolean;

    // field offsets in record
    FFieldOffset: TList;
```

```
protected
  // TDataSet virtual abstract method
  function AllocRecordBuffer: PChar; override;
  procedure FreeRecordBuffer(var Buffer: PChar); override;
  procedure GetBookmarkData(Buffer: PChar;
    Data: Pointer); override;
  function GetBookmarkFlag(Buffer: PChar):
    TBookmarkFlag; override;
  function GetFieldData(Field: TField;
    Buffer: Pointer): Boolean; override;
  function GetRecord(Buffer: PChar; GetMode: TGetMode;
    DoCheck: Boolean): TGetResult; override;
  function GetRecordSize: Word; override;
  procedure InternalAddRecord(Buffer: Pointer;
    Append: Boolean); override;
  procedure InternalClose; override;
  procedure InternalDelete; override;
  procedure InternalFirst; override;
  procedure InternalGotoBookmark(
    Bookmark: Pointer); override;
  procedure InternalHandleException; override;
  procedure InternalInitFieldDefs; override;
  procedure InternalInitRecord(Buffer: PChar); override;
  procedure InternalLast; override;
  procedure InternalOpen; override;
  procedure InternalPost; override;
  procedure InternalSetToRecord(Buffer: PChar); override;
  function IsCursorOpen: Boolean; override;
  procedure SetBookmarkFlag(Buffer: PChar;
    Value: TBookmarkFlag); override;
  procedure SetBookmarkData(Buffer: PChar;
    Data: Pointer); override;
  procedure SetFieldData(Field: TField;
    Buffer: Pointer); override;

  // TDataSet virtual method (optional)
  function GetRecordCount: Integer; override;
  procedure SetRecNo(Value: Integer); override;
  function GetRecNo: Integer; override;
public
  procedure CreateTable;
```

```
published
  property TableName: string
    read FTableName write FTableName;
  // redeclared data set properties
  property Active;
  property BeforeOpen;
  property AfterOpen;
  property BeforeClose;
  property AfterClose;
  property BeforeInsert;
  property AfterInsert;
  property BeforeEdit;
  property AfterEdit;
  property BeforePost;
  property AfterPost;
  property BeforeCancel;
  property AfterCancel;
  property BeforeDelete;
  property AfterDelete;
  property BeforeScroll;
  property AfterScroll;
  property OnCalcFields;
  property OnDeleteError;
  property OnEditError;
  property OnFilterRecord;
  property OnNewRecord;
  property OnPostError;
end;
```

In dividing the methods into sections (as you can see by looking at the source code files) we've marked each one with a roman number. You'll see those numbers in a comment describing the method, so that while browsing this long listing you'll immediately know which of the three sections you are in.

Section I: Initialization, Opening, and Closing

The first methods we'll examine are responsible for initializing the data set, and for opening and closing the file stream we'll use to store the data. In addition to initializing the component's internal data, these methods are responsible for initializing and connecting the proper TFields objects to the data set component. To make this work, all we need to do is to initialize the FieldsDef property with the definitions of the fields for our data set, and then call a few standard methods to generate and bind the TField objects.

Now we can start looking at the field definitions, initialized by the InternalInitFieldDefs method. For this example we've decided to base the field definitions on an external file. This is a simple INI file that provides a section for every field, and each section contains the name and data type of the field, as well as its size if it is string data.

Here's the Contrib.INI file that we'll use in the component's demo application (we invented the structure of the Contributors data set for testing various types of fields, not to implement a specific application):

```
[Fields]
Number = 6

[Field1]
Type = ftString
Name = Name
Size = 30

[Field2]
Type = ftInteger
Name = Level

[Field3]
Type = ftDate
Name = BirthDate

[Field4]
Type = ftCurrency
Name = Stipend

[Field5]
Type = ftString
Name = Email
Size = 50

[Field6]
Type = ftBoolean
Name = Editor
```

This file, or a similar one, must use the same name as the table file, and it must be in the same directory. The `InternalInitFieldDefs` method will read it from the beginning, using the values it finds to set up the field definitions. However, this method also has a second role. It initializes an internal `TList` object that stores the offset of every field inside the record, so we can easily access them when we need the related data. Here's the code:

```
// I: define the fields
procedure TDdhDataSetOne.InternalInitFieldDefs;
var
  IniFileName, FieldName: string;
  IniFile: TIniFile;
  nFields, I, TmpFieldOffset, nSize: Integer;
  FieldType: TFieldType;
begin
  FFieldOffset := TList.Create;
  FieldDefs.Clear;
  TmpFieldOffset := 0;
  IniFilename := ChangeFileExt(FTableName, '.ini');
  Inifile := TIniFile.Create (IniFilename);
  // protect INI file
  try
    nFields := IniFile.ReadInteger ('Fields', 'Number', 0);
    if nFields = 0 then
      raise EDataSetOneError.Create ('InitFieldsDefs: 0 fields?');
    for I := 1 to nFields do
    begin
      // create the field
      FieldType := TFieldType (GetEnumValue (
        TypeInfo (TFieldType),
        IniFile.ReadString (
          'Field' + IntToStr (I), 'Type', '')));
      FieldName := IniFile.ReadString (
        'Field' + IntToStr (I), 'Name', '');
      if FieldName = '' then
        raise EDataSetOneError.Create (
          'InitFieldsDefs: No name for field ' +
          IntToStr (I));
      nSize := IniFile.ReadInteger (
        'Field' + IntToStr (I), 'Size', 0);
      FieldDefs.Add (FieldName,
        FieldType, nSize, False);
```

```
      // save offset and compute size
      FFieldOffset.Add (Pointer (TmpFieldOffset));
      case FieldType of
        ftString:
          Inc (TmpFieldOffset, nSize + 1);
        ftBoolean, ftSmallInt, ftWord:
          Inc (TmpFieldOffset, 2);
        ftInteger, ftDate, ftTime:
          Inc (TmpFieldOffset, 4);
        ftFloat, ftCurrency, ftDateTime:
          Inc (TmpFieldOffset, 8);
      else
        raise EDataSetOneError.Create (
          'InitFieldsDefs: Unsupported field type');
      end;
    end; // for
  finally
    IniFile.Free;
  end;
  FRecordSize := TmpFieldOffset;
end;
```

The InternalOpen method is specifically responsible for calling the Internal-InitFieldDefs method to open the data set. Obviously, the most important action of this method is opening the file stream that represents the actual database file.

The remainder of the code initializes local component fields. For instance, the InternalInitFieldDefs method computes the size of each record from the structure of the fields, while the InternalOpen method computes the number of records we're storing (we calculate this by dividing the file size by the size of each record, and we—perhaps naively—check for errors by testing the modulus of this division), the size of the data structures, and the positions of the offsets.

TIP   In the next version of the data set, we'll add some header information to the file stream to store status and version information, making the persistent data set a bit more robust. In fact, some of the elements necessary to support this are already present in the class's source code, although they don't appear in the excerpted listings, and we'll describe them later on.

You'll notice that we must also set the parent `BookmarkSize` field, which determines the size of the bookmark data; the system then allocates and handles these bookmarks. We'll explain some of the other fields later, when we use them:

```
// I: open the table/file
procedure TDdhDataSetOne.InternalOpen;
begin
  // check whether the file exists
  if not FileExists (FTableName) then
    raise EDataSetOneError.Create ('Open: Table file not found');

  // create a stream for the file
  FStream := TFileStream.Create (FTableName,  fmOpenReadWrite);

  // initialize the field definitions
  // (another virtual abstract method of TDataSet)
  InternalInitFieldDefs;

  // if there are no persistent field objects,
  // create the fields dynamically
  if DefaultFields then
    CreateFields;
  // connect the TField objects with the actual fields
  BindFields (True);

  // get the number of records and check size
  FRecordCount := FStream.Size div FRecordSize;
  if (FStream.Size mod FRecordSize) <> 0 then
    raise EDataSetOneError.Create ('Open: Invalid table size');

  // sets cracks and record position
  BofCrack := -1;
  EofCrack := FRecordCount;
  FCurrentRecord := BofCrack;

  FRecordInfoOffset := FRecordSize;
  FRecordBufferSize := FRecordSize + sizeof (TRecInfo);

  // set the bookmark size
  BookmarkSize := sizeOf (Integer);

  // everything OK: table is now open
```

```
    FIsTableOpen := True;
  end;
```

Closing the table is simply a matter of disconnecting the fields (using some standard calls) and closing the stream by freeing the FStream object:

```
// I: close the table/file
procedure TDdhDataSetOne.InternalClose;
begin
  // free the internal list field offsets
  if Assigned (FFieldOffset) then
    FFieldOffset.Free;

  // disconnect field objects
  BindFields (False);
  // destroy field object (if not persistent)
  if DefaultFields then
    DestroyFields;

  // close the file
  FIsTableOpen := False;
  FStream.Free;
end;
```

Another function of the InternalOpen and InternalClose methods is to set the protected field, FIsTableOpen. This field stores the status of the data set:

```
// I: is table open
function TDdhDataSetOne.IsCursorOpen: Boolean;
begin
  Result := FIsTableOpen;
end;
```

These are the opening and closing methods we need to implement. However, most of the time, you'll add a method to your custom data set to create the table. In this example, the CreateTable method (which isn't overridden, so it can have the parameters you need) simply creates an empty file, after checking whether it already exists:

```
// I: Create a new table/file
procedure TDdhDataSetOne.CreateTable;
begin
  CheckInactive;
  InternalInitFieldDefs;
```

```
    // create the new file
    if FileExists (FTableName) and
      (MessageDlg ('File ' + FTableName +
        ' already exists. OK to overwrite?',
        mtConfirmation, [mbYes, mbNo], 0) = mrNo) then
      Exit;
    FStream := TFileStream.Create (FTableName, fmCreate);
    // close the file
    FStream.Free;
  end;
```

Section II: Movement and Bookmark Management

As mentioned earlier, one of the things we must implement is *bookmark management*, which is necessary for navigating through the data set. Logically, a bookmark is a reference to a specific record of the data set, something that uniquely identifies the record so that we can access it and compare it to other records. Technically, bookmarks are pointers. You can implement them as pointers to specific data structures that store record information, or you can implement them as simple record numbers. For simplicity, we'll use the latter approach.

Given a bookmark, you should be able to find the corresponding record, but given a record buffer, you should also be able to retrieve the corresponding bookmark. This is the reason for appending the TRecInfo structure to the record data in each record buffer. This data structure stores the bookmark for the record in the buffer, as well as some bookmark flags defined as:

```
type
  TBookmarkFlag = (bfCurrent, bfBOF, bfEOF, bfInserted);
```

The system will request us to store these flags in each record buffer, and will later ask us to retrieve the flags for a given record buffer.

To summarize, the structure of a record buffer stores the data of the record (saved and stored in the physical file, as we'll see in the next section), the bookmark, and the bookmark flags. To access the last two fields we can simply use the offset within the buffer for record information, cast the values to the PRecInfo pointer type, and then access the proper field of the TRecInfo structure via the pointer. The two methods used to set and get the bookmark flags demonstrate this technique:

```
// II: change the bookmark flags in the buffer
procedure TDdhDataSetOne.SetBookmarkFlag (Buffer: PChar;
```

```
    Value: TBookmarkFlag);
begin
  PRecInfo(Buffer + FRecordInfoOffset).BookmarkFlag := Value;
end;


// II: retrieve bookmark flags from buffer
function TDdhDataSetOne.GetBookmarkFlag (
  Buffer: PChar): TBookmarkFlag;
begin
  Result := PRecInfo(Buffer + FRecordInfoOffset).BookmarkFlag;
end;
```

The methods we use to set and get the current bookmark of a record are similar to the previous two, but they add some complexity because we receive a pointer to the bookmark in the Data parameter. Casting this pointer as an integer pointer (PInteger) and dereferencing it, we obtain the bookmark value:

```
// II: read the bookmark data from record buffer
procedure TDdhDataSetOne.GetBookmarkData (
  Buffer: PChar; Data: Pointer);
begin
  PInteger(Data)^ :=
    PRecInfo(Buffer + FRecordInfoOffset).Bookmark;
end;


// II: set the bookmark data in the buffer
procedure TDdhDataSetOne.SetBookmarkData (
  Buffer: PChar; Data: Pointer);
begin
  PRecInfo(Buffer + FRecordInfoOffset).Bookmark :=
    PInteger(Data)^;
end;
```

The key bookmark management method is InternalGotoBookmark, which your data set uses to make a given record the current one. You'll notice that this isn't the standard navigation technique, since it's much more common to move to the next or previous record (something we can accomplish using the GetRecord method presented in the next section), or to move to the first or last record (something we'll accomplish using the InternalFirst and InternalLast methods described shortly).

Oddly enough, the InternalGotoBookmark method doesn't expect a bookmark parameter, but a pointer to a bookmark, so we must dereference it to determine the bookmark value. The following method, `InternalSetToRecord`, is what you use to jump to a given bookmark, but it must extract the bookmark from the record buffer passed as a parameter. Then, `InternalSetToRecord` calls `Internal-GotoBookmark`. Here are the two methods:

```
// II: set the requested bookmark as current record
procedure TDdhDataSetOne.InternalGotoBookmark (Bookmark: Pointer);
var
  ReqBookmark: Integer;
begin
  ReqBookmark := PInteger (Bookmark)^;
  if (ReqBookmark >= 0) and (ReqBookmark < FRecordCount) then
    FCurrentRecord := ReqBookmark
  else
    raise EDataSetOneError.Create ('Bookmark ' +
      IntToStr (ReqBookmark) + ' not found');
end;

// II: same as above (but passes a buffer)
procedure TDdhDataSetOne.InternalSetToRecord (Buffer: PChar);
var
  ReqBookmark: Integer;
begin
  ReqBookmark := PRecInfo(Buffer + FRecordInfoOffset).Bookmark;
  InternalGotoBookmark (@ReqBookmark);
end;
```

In addition to the bookmark management methods we just described, there are several other navigation methods we use to move to specific positions within the data set, such as the first or last record. Actually, these two methods don't move the current record pointer to the first or last record, but move it to one of two special locations before the first record and after the last one. These are not actual records; Borland calls them *cracks*. The beginning-of-file crack, or `BofCrack`, has the value –1 (set in the `InternalOpen` method), since the position of the first record is zero. The end-of-file crack, or `EofCrack`, has the value of the number of records, since the last record has the position `FRecordCount - 1`. We've used two local fields, called `EofCrack` and `BofCrack`, to make this code easier to read:

```
// II: Go to a special position before the first record
procedure TDdhDataSetOne.InternalFirst;
begin
  FCurrentRecord := BofCrack;
end;
```

```
// II: Go to a special position after the last record
procedure TDdhDataSetOne.InternalLast;
begin
  EofCrack := FRecordCount;
  FCurrentRecord := EofCrack;
end;
```

Another group of optional methods is used to get the current record number (used in Delphi 3 by the DBGrid component to show a proper scroll bar, fixing a bug in Delphi 2), set the current record number, or determine the number of records. These methods are quite easy to understand, if you recall that the range of the internal FCurrentRecord field is from 0 to the number of records minus 1. In contrast, the record number reported to the system ranges from 1 to the number of records:

```
// II (optional): Record count
function TDdhDataSetOne.GetRecordCount: Longint;
begin
  CheckActive;
  Result := FRecordCount;
end;


// II (optional): Get the number of the current record
function TDdhDataSetOne.GetRecNo: Longint;
begin
  UpdateCursorPos;
  if FCurrentRecord < 0 then
    Result := 1
  else
    Result := FCurrentRecord + 1;
end;


// II (optional): Move to the given record number
procedure TDdhDataSetOne.SetRecNo(Value: Integer);
begin
  CheckBrowseMode;
  if (Value > 1) and (Value <= FRecordCount) then
  begin
    FCurrentRecord := Value - 1;
    Resync([]);
  end;
end;
```

Section III: Record Buffers and Field Management

Now that we've covered all the support methods, we can examine the core of a custom data set. Besides opening and creating records and moving around between them, we really need to move the data from the stream (the persistent file) to the record buffers, and from the record buffers to the TField objects that are connected to the data-aware controls. The management of record buffers is quite complex, because we also need to allocate and free the memory for the record buffers:

```
/// III: Allocate a buffer for the record
function TDdhDataSetOne.AllocRecordBuffer: PChar;
begin
  Result := StrAlloc(FRecordBufferSize);
end;

// III: Free the buffer
procedure TDdhDataSetOne.FreeRecordBuffer (var Buffer: PChar);
begin
  StrDispose(Buffer);
end;
```

The reason for allocating memory this way is that a data set generally adds more information to the record buffer, so the system has no way of knowing how much memory to allocate. You'll notice that in the AllocRecordBuffer method, the component allocates the memory for the record buffer, including both the database data and the record information. In fact, in the InternalOpen method we wrote

```
FRecordBufferSize := FRecordSize + sizeof (TRecInfo);
```

We also need to implement a function to reset the buffer, usually filling it with numeric zeros or spaces. Oddly enough, we must also implement a method that returns the size of each record, but only the data portion—not the entire record buffer. This method is necessary for implementing the read-only RecordSize property, used only in a couple of peculiar cases in the entire VCL source code. Here's our implementation of the GetRecordSize method:

```
/// III: Determine the size of each record buffer in memory
function TDdhDataSetOne.GetRecordSize: Word;
begin
  Result := FRecordSize; // data only
end;
```

There's one more method related to managing record buffers, one you use to initialize, or empty, the record buffer:

```
// III: Initialize the record (set to zero)
procedure TDdhDataSetOne.InternalInitRecord(Buffer: PChar);
begin
  FillChar(Buffer^, FRecordBufferSize, 0);
end;
```

Now we've actually reached the core of our data-set component. The methods of this group are GetRecord, which reads data from the file, InternalPost and InternalAddRecrd, which update or add new data to the file, and InternalDelete, which removes data.

The most complex method of this group is probably GetRecord, which serves multiple purposes. In fact, this method is used by the system to retrieve the data for the current record, fill a buffer passed as a parameter, and retrieve the data of the next or previous records. The GetMode parameter determines its action:

```
type
  TGetMode = (gmCurrent, gmNext, gmPrior);
```

Of course, a previous or next record might not exist. Even the current record might not exist; for example, when the table is empty (or in case of an internal error). In these cases we don't retrieve the data but return an error code. Therefore, this method's result can be one of the following values:

```
type
  TGetResult = (grOK, grBOF, grEOF, grError);
```

Checking to see if the requested record exists is slightly different than you might expect. We don't have to determine if the current record is in the proper range, only if the requested one is. For example, in the gmCurrent branch of the case statement, we use the standard expression FCurrentRecord >= FRecordCount, but in the gmNext branch the test becomes FCurrentRecord >= FRecordCount - 1.

To fully understand the various cases, you might want to read the code a couple of times. It took us some trial and error (and a number of system crashes caused by recursive calls) to get it straight. Also consider using the DebugDS application to see when it will call this method. In fact, if you use a DBGrid, the system will perform a series of GetRecord calls, until either the grid is full or

GetRecord returns grEOF. You can see an example of these calls in Figure 18.8. Here's the entire code of the GetRecord method:

```
// III: Retrieve data for current, previous, or next record
// (moving to it if necessary) and return the status
function TDdhDataSetOne.GetRecord(Buffer: PChar;
  GetMode: TGetMode; DoCheck: Boolean): TGetResult;
begin
  if FRecordCount < 1 then
    Result := grEOF
  else
  begin
    Result := grOK;
    case GetMode of
      gmNext:
      begin
        // if next record isn't out of range...
        if FCurrentRecord >= FRecordCount - 1 then
          Result := grEOF
        else
          Inc (FCurrentRecord);
      end;
      gmPrior:
      begin
        // if previous message isn't out of range
        if FCurrentRecord <= 0 then
          Result := grBOF
        else
          Dec (FCurrentRecord);
      end;
      gmCurrent:
      begin
        if (FCurrentRecord >= FRecordCount) or
            (FCurrentRecord < 0) then
          Result := grError;
      end;
    end;
    // load the data
    if Result = grOK then
    begin
      FStream.Position := FRecordSize * FCurrentRecord;
      FStream.ReadBuffer (Buffer^, FRecordSize);
```

```
    with PRecInfo(Buffer + FRecordInfoOffset)^ do
    begin
      BookmarkFlag := bfCurrent;
      Bookmark := FCurrentRecord;
    end;
  end
  else
    if (Result = grError) and DoCheck then
      raise EDataSetOneError.Create (
        'GetRecord: Invalid record');
  end;
end;
```

FIGURE 18.8:

The output of the
DebugDs example
shows that Delphi
calls the GetRecord
method many times
to fill a DBGrid
(during scrolling
operations).

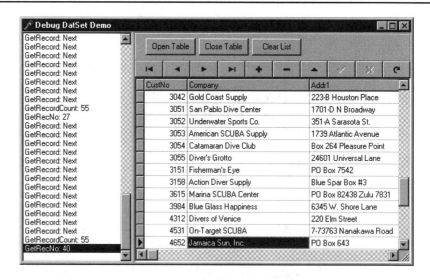

If everything goes fine during record selection, we actually load the data from the stream, moving to the position of the current record (given by the record size multiplied by the record number). In addition, we need to initialize the buffer with the proper bookmark flag and bookmark (or record number) value. Finally, if there's an error and the DoCheck parameter was True, we're supposed to raise an exception.

We move data to the file in two different cases: when you modify the current record (that is, a post after an edit) or when you add a new record (a post after an insert or append). We use the InternalPost method in both cases, but we can check the data set's State property to determine which type of post we're performing.

In both cases we don't receive a record buffer as a parameter, so we must use the ActiveRecord property of TDataSet, which points to the buffer for the current record:

```
// III: Write the current data to the file
procedure TDdhDataSetOne.InternalPost;
begin
  CheckActive;
  if State = dsEdit then
  begin
    // replace data with new data
    FStream.Position := FRecordSize * FCurrentRecord;
    FStream.WriteBuffer (ActiveBuffer^, FRecordSize);
  end
  else
  begin
    // always append
    InternalLast;
    FStream.Seek (0, soFromEnd);
    FStream.WriteBuffer (ActiveBuffer^, FRecordSize);
    Inc (FRecordCount);
  end;
end;
```

In addition, there's another related method, InternalAddRecord. This method is called by the AddRecord method, which in turn is called by InsertRecord and AppendRecord. These last two are public methods a user can call. This is an alternative to inserting or appending a new record to the data set, editing the values of the various fields, and then posting the data, since the InsertRecord and AppendRecord calls receive the values of the fields as parameters. All we must do at that point is replicate the code used to add a new record in the InternalPost method:

```
// III: Add the current data to the file
procedure TDdhDataSetOne.InternalAddRecord(
  Buffer: Pointer; Append: Boolean);
begin
  // always append at the end
  InternalLast;
  // add record at the end of the file
  FStream.Seek (0, soFromEnd);
  FStream.WriteBuffer (ActiveBuffer^, FRecordSize);
  Inc (FRecordCount);
end;
```

The last file operation we must implement is one that removes the current record. This operation is commonplace, but it is actually quite complex. If we take a simple approach, such as creating an empty spot in the file, then we'll need to keep track of that spot, and make the code for reading or writing a specific record work around that spot. An alternative solution is to make a copy of the entire file, without the given record, and then replace the original file with it. Given these choices, we felt that for this example we could forgo supporting record deletion:

```
// III: Delete the current record
procedure TDdhDataSetOne.InternalDelete;
begin
  // not supported in this version
  raise EDataSetOneError.Create (
    'Delete: Operation not supported');
end;
```

In the last few methods, we've seen how data sets move data from the data file to the memory buffer. However, there's little Delphi can do with this record buffer, because it doesn't yet know how to interpret the data in the buffer. We need to provide two more methods: GetData, which copies the data from the record buffer to the field objects of the data set, and SetData, which moves the data back from the fields to the record buffer. What Delphi will do automatically for us is move the data from the field objects to the data-aware controls, and back.

The code for these two methods isn't very complex, primarily because we saved the field offsets inside the record data in a TList object called FFieldOffset. By simply incrementing the pointer to the initial position in the record buffer of the current field's offset, we'll be able to get the specific data, which takes Field.DataSize bytes.

The only confusing element of these two methods is that they both accept a Field parameter and a Buffer parameter. At first, we thought that we were supposed to move the data from that buffer to the field. Actually, we found out that the Buffer passed as a parameter is a pointer to the field object's raw data. If you use one of the field object's methods to move that data, it will call the data set's GetData or SetData methods, probably causing an infinite recursion.

Instead, you should use the ActiveBuffer pointer to access the record buffer, use the proper offset to get to the data for the current field in the record buffer, and then use the provided `Buffer` to access the field data. The only difference between the two methods is the direction we're moving the data:

```
// III: Move data from record buffer to field
function TDdhDataSetOne.GetFieldData (
  Field: TField; Buffer: Pointer): Boolean;
var
  FieldOffset: Integer;
  Ptr: PChar;
begin
  Result := False;
  if not IsEmpty and (Field.FieldNo > 0) then
  begin
    FieldOffset := Integer (
      FFieldOffset [Field.FieldNo - 1]);
    Ptr := ActiveBuffer;
    Inc (Ptr, FieldOffset);
    Move (Ptr^, Buffer^, Field.DataSize);
    Result := True;
  end;
end;

// III: Move data from field to record buffer
procedure TDdhDataSetOne.SetFieldData(
  Field: TField; Buffer: Pointer);
var
  FieldOffset: Integer;
  Ptr: PChar;
begin
  if Field.FieldNo >= 0 then
  begin
    FieldOffset := Integer (
      FFieldOffset [Field.FieldNo - 1]);
    Ptr := ActiveBuffer;
    Inc (Ptr, FieldOffset);
    if Assigned (Buffer) then
      Move (Buffer^, Ptr^, Field.DataSize)
    else
      ShowMessage ('Very bad error in SetFieldData');
    DataEvent (deFieldChange, Longint(Field));
  end;
end;
```

WARNING The `GetField` method should return `True` or `False` to indicate whether the field contains data or is empty. However, unless you use a special marker for blank fields, it's very difficult to determine this, since we're storing values of different data types. For example, a test such as `Ptr^<>#0` makes sense only if you are using a string representation for all of the fields. If you use this test, zero integer values and empty strings will show as null values (the data-aware controls will be empty), which may be what you want. The problem is that Boolean `False` values won't show up. Even worse, floating-point values with no decimals and few digits won't be displayed, because the exponent portion of their representation will be zero!

There's one final method, which doesn't fall into any category: `Internal-HandleException`. Generally, this method uses the standard Delphi exception handling, but you can customize it by defining your own exceptions and reporting them to the user in a specific way, or logging them on a file:

```
procedure TDdhDataSetOne.InternalHandleException;
begin
  // standard exception handling
  Application.HandleException(Self);
end;
```

Testing Our First Custom Data Set

After all this work, we're finally ready to test our custom data-set component, installed in the standard package for this chapter, in an application example. The form displayed by the DOneDemo program is quite simple, as you can see in Figure 18.9. It has a panel with two buttons, a check box, and a navigator component, plus a DBGrid filling its client area.

Figure 18.9 shows the form of the example at design-time, but we've activated the custom data set so that its data is already visible. Of course we'd already prepared the INI file with the table definition (it's the file we already listed when discussing the data set initialization), and we executed the program to add some data to the file.

It's also possible to modify the form using Delphi's Fields editor (see Figure 18.10), and set the properties of the various field objects. Everything works as it does with one of the standard data-set controls! However, to make this work you'll

FIGURE 18.9:

The form of the DOneDemo example. The custom data set has been activated, so we can already see the data at design time.

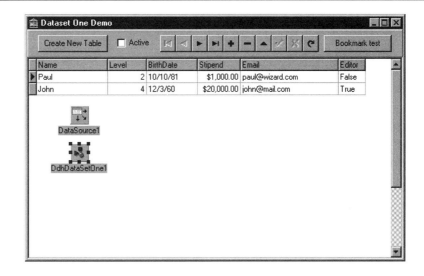

need to enter the name of the custom data set's file in the TableName property, using the complete path. You can set the key properties of the form components (including the field components) in the following listing:

```
object Form1: TForm1
  Caption = 'Dataset One Demo'
  OnCreate = FormCreate
  object DBGrid1: TDBGrid
    Align = alClient
    DataSource = DataSource1
  end
  object Panel1: TPanel
    Align = alTop
    object Button1: TButton
      Caption = 'Create New Table'
      OnClick = Button1Click
    end
    object CheckBox1: TCheckBox
      Caption = 'Active'
      OnClick = CheckBox1Click
    end
    object DBNavigator1: TDBNavigator
      DataSource = DataSource1
    end
```

```
      object Button2: TButton
        Caption = 'Bookmark test'
        OnClick = Button2Click
      end
    end
    object DataSource1: TDataSource
      DataSet = DdhDataSetOne1
    end
    object DdhDataSetOne1: TDdhDataSetOne
      TableName = 'c:\ddhcode\18\DOneDemo\contrib.dso'
      object DdhDataSetOne1Name: TStringField
        FieldName = 'Name'
        Size = 30
      end
      object DdhDataSetOne1Level: TIntegerField
        FieldName = 'Level'
      end
      object DdhDataSetOne1BirthDate: TDateField
        FieldName = 'BirthDate'
      end
      object DdhDataSetOne1Stipend: TCurrencyField
        FieldName = 'Stipend'
      end
      object DdhDataSetOne1Email: TStringField
        FieldName = 'Email'
        Size = 50
      end
      object DdhDataSetOne1Editor: TBooleanField
        FieldName = 'Editor'
      end
    end
  end
```

> **WARNING** We use the path of the table only at design-time, and you'll need to fix it if you copy the example to a different drive or directory.

The TableName property is required only to open the table at design-time. At run-time, the program looks for the table in the current directory:

```
procedure TForm1.FormCreate(Sender: TObject);
begin
```

```
DdhDataSetOne1.TableName :=
  ExtractFilePath (ParamStr (0)) +
  'Contrib.dso';
end;
```

FIGURE 18.10:

Delphi's field editor
can also be used with
a custom data set
component.

The rest of the code is even simpler. If the table doesn't exist yet, or if you want to create a new one, you can click the *Create* button:

```
procedure TForm1.Button1Click(Sender: TObject);
begin
  DdhDataSetOne1.CreateTable;
  DdhDataSetOne1.Open;
end;
```

You'll notice that we create the file first, open and close it, and then open the table. This is the same behavior as the TTable component (which accomplishes this using the CreateTable method). To simply open or close the table, you can click on the check box:

```
procedure TForm1.CheckBox1Click(Sender: TObject);
begin
  DdhDataSetOne1.Active := CheckBox1.Checked;
end;
```

Finally, we've created a method that will test the custom data set's bookmark management code, and we've connected it to the second button:

```
procedure TForm1.Button2Click(Sender: TObject);
var
  bm: TBookmark;
begin
  bm := DdhDataSetOne1.GetBookmark;
```

```
    DdhDataSetOne1.First;
    while not DdhDataSetOne1.EOF do
      DdhDataSetOne1.Next;
    DdhDataSetOne1.GotoBookmark (bm);
    DdhDataSetOne1.FreeBookmark (bm);
  end;
```

If you click the button, you'll see the record cursor on the side of the DBGrid move from the first to the last record, and then jump back to the original one.

Saving Components in a Custom Data Set

Now that we've completed this first simple data set, which we can easily use in a real-world application with a few simple changes (like adding support for a delete operation), let's move on to building a more interesting one. It won't implement more features, but it will have a different role. The idea is to build a persistence mechanism for objects and components, but one that behaves like a database. Usually, programmers try to accomplish this by saving the objects into a standard database. Using a completely different approach, we're going to build a specific data set for Delphi components.

The key element here is that instead of reading the field definitions from a file, as we did in the previous example, we want to read their published portions from a class's RTTI information. Using this information, we'll be able to move objects of that type into the data set and then create new objects from the existing records.

This will be the focus of the new example—storing and retrieving objects from a database using a custom data set. Since we've already implemented most of the housekeeping code, we don't need to write any more of those functions. Even better, we can derive the class for this new data set from the previous one we built, TDdhDataSetOne. Before we can do this, however, we must update the base class to make it a little more flexible.

Adding Header File Support to DataSetOne

For the new data set, and for most custom data sets in general, we want to be able to save some header information in the file with the data. To avoid making several minor changes in the new class's overridden methods, we've decided to add this support to the existing class. We didn't describe this in the previous section because we wanted to avoid adding complexity to the code.

Fortunately, the changes are quite simple. We need to add just one `protected` field (so that derived classes will be able to access its value) in order to store the size of the file header.

```
type
  TDdhDataSetOne = class(TDataSet)
  protected
    // file header size ((optionally used by subclasses)
    FDataFileHeaderSize: Integer;
    ...
```

We initialize this field in the TDdhDataSetOne class's InternalOpen method by setting it to zero (we don't need to provide this feature in the base class, we just need to support it in derived classes). Next, we must update two methods, GetRecord and InternalPost, which need to know the size of the header each time we access the physical stream:

```
function TDdhDataSetOne.GetRecord(Buffer: PChar;
  GetMode: TGetMode; DoCheck: Boolean): TGetResult;
begin
  ...
    // load the data
    if Result = grOK then
    begin
      FStream.Position := FDataFileHeaderSize +
        FRecordSize * FCurrentRecord;
      FStream.ReadBuffer (Buffer^, FRecordSize);
    ...

procedure TDdhDataSetOne.InternalPost;
begin
  ...
  if State = dsEdit then
  begin
    // replace data with new data
    FStream.Position := FDataFileHeaderSize +
      FRecordSize * FCurrentRecord;
    FStream.WriteBuffer (ActiveBuffer^, FRecordSize);
  end
  ...
```

With these minor changes in place, we can now derive a new data set from TDdhDataSetOne, overriding just a few methods.

The Class of the Object Data Set

As we've just mentioned, the new class inherits implementations for most of the virtual abstract methods of TDataSet from its immediate base class. The only code left to write relates to the structure of the data-set file, and all the methods we'll need to override are part of the first group of methods, which we described in the section "Initialization, Opening, and Closing." We'll precede the following data-set class declaration with the declarations of a new exception class and of the TDataFileHeader record (this code is extracted from the DdhObjDs unit):

```
type
  EObjDataSetError = class (EDataSetOneError);

  TDataFileHeader = record
    VersionNumber: Integer;
    RecordSize: Integer;
    RecordCount: Integer;
    ClassName: array [0..50] of Char;
  end;
```

```
type
  TDdhObjectDataSet = class(TDdhDataSetOne)
  protected
    // file header
    FDataFileHeader: TDataFileHeader;
    // data set definition class
    FDataClass: TPersistentClass;
  protected
    // TDataSet virtual abstract method
    procedure InternalOpen; override;
    procedure InternalClose; override;
    procedure InternalInitFieldDefs; override;
  public
    constructor Create (AOwner: TComponent); override;
    procedure CreateTable (CompClassType: TComponentClass);
    procedure AddObject (Comp: TComponent);
    function CreateObject (Owner: TComponent;
      Parent: TWinControl): TComponent;
  end;
```

The public methods at the end of the declaration are special methods that you'll use to copy components to the table and to create new components from the table data. However, before discussing them let's cover the class's file header support methods.

Adding a Header to the Data Set File

Three methods manipulate the file header information: `CreateTable`, `InternalOpen`, and `InternalClose`. However, we'll compute the size of the header when we create the component. This is because we don't know which method will be called first, `InternalOpen` or `CreateTable`, so instead of duplicating the code we execute it beforehand:

```
constructor TDdhObjectDataSet.Create (AOwner: TComponent);
begin
  inherited Create (AOwner);
  FDataFileHeaderSize := sizeOf (TDataFileHeader);
end;
```

We'll store the header information when we create the table. After it creates the new file, as the previous version did, the `CreateTable` method inserts the following information in the header: a fixed version number, a dummy record size (we don't know the size until we initialize the fields), the record count (which is zero to start), and the class name:

```
// I: Create a new table/file - modified
procedure TDdhObjectDataSet.CreateTable (
  CompClassType: TComponentClass);
begin
  CheckInactive;
  FDataClass := CompClassType;
  InternalInitFieldDefs;
  begin
    // create the new file
    if FileExists (FTableName) and
      (MessageDlg ('File ' + FTableName +
        ' already exists. OK to override?',
        mtConfirmation, [mbYes, mbNo], 0) = mrNo) then
      Exit;
    FStream := TFileStream.Create (FTableName, fmCreate);
    try
      // save the header
```

```
      FDataFileHeader.VersionNumber := 10;
      FDataFileHeader.RecordSize := 0; // used later
      FDataFileHeader.RecordCount := 0; // empty
      StrPCopy (FDataFileHeader.ClassName,
        FDataClass.ClassName);
      FStream.WriteBuffer (
        FDataFileHeader, FDataFileHeaderSize);
    finally
      // close the file
      FStream.Free;
    end;
  end;
end;
```

When a user opens the table file, the component reads the header, checks for the proper version number, stores the number of records, and extracts the class type from the class name. Then the InternalOpen method initializes the various record pointers and internal data, initializes and binds the field objects, and confirms that the record size for the type corresponds to the record size in the file (extracted from the header) and that the number of records is consistent with the file size:

```
// I: open the table/file - slightly modified
procedure TDdhObjectDataSet.InternalOpen;
var
  ClassName: string;
begin
  // check if the file exists
  if not FileExists (FTableName) then
    raise EObjDataSetError.Create ('Table file not found');

  // create a stream for the file
  FStream := TFileStream.Create (FTableName, fmOpenReadWrite);

  // initialize local data (loading header)
  FStream.ReadBuffer (FDataFileHeader, FDataFileHeaderSize);
  if FDataFileHeader.VersionNumber <> 10 then
    raise EObjDataSetError.Create ('File version not 10');
  FRecordCount := FDataFileHeader.RecordCount;
  ClassName := StrPas (FDataFileHeader.ClassName);
  FDataClass := FindClass (ClassName);

  // set cracks and record position
  BofCrack := -1;
```

```
      EofCrack := FRecordCount;
      FCurrentRecord := BofCrack;

      // initialize the field definitions
      // (another virtual abstract method of TDataSet)
      InternalInitFieldDefs;

      // if there are no persistent field objects,
      // create the fields dynamically
      if DefaultFields then
        CreateFields;
      // connect the TField objects with the actual fields
      BindFields (True);

      // check the record size (if this isn't the first time)
      if (FRecordCount > 0) and
          (FDataFileHeader.RecordSize <> FRecordSize) then
        raise EObjDataSetError.Create (
          'InternalOpen: File record size mismatch');
      // check the number of records against the file size
      if (FDataFileHeaderSize + FRecordCount * FRecordSize)
          <> FStream.Size then
        raise EObjDataSetError.Create (
          'InternalOpen: Invalid Record Size');

      FRecordInfoOffset := FRecordSize;
      FRecordBufferSize := FRecordSize + sizeof (TRecInfo);

      // set the bookmark size
      BookmarkSize := sizeOf (Integer);

      // everything OK: table is now open
      FIsTableOpen := True;
    end;
```

NOTE   As you'll recall from Chapter 3, for the FindClass function to work properly, you must remember to call RegisterClass for that class *in the program that uses the component.*

We update the file header every time we close the data set. In contrast, we save the data only if it has changed. In other words, if this is the first time we've saved (we should save the record size) or if the number of records has changed, we'll actually write the data out to the stream:

```
// I: close the table/file - modified
procedure TDdhObjectDataSet.InternalClose;
begin
  // if required, save updated header
  if (FDataFileHeader.RecordCount <> FRecordCount) or
      (FDataFileHeader.RecordSize = 0) then
  begin
    FDataFileHeader.RecordSize := FRecordSize;
    FDataFileHeader.RecordCount := FRecordCount;
    if Assigned (FStream) then
    begin
      FStream.Seek (0, soFromBeginning);
      FStream.WriteBuffer (
        FDataFileHeader, FDataFileHeaderSize);
    end;
  end;

  // disconnect field objects
  BindFields (False);
  // destroy field object (if not persistent)
  if DefaultFields then
    DestroyFields;

  // close the file
  FIsTableOpen := False;
  FStream.Free;
  FStream := nil;
end;
```

Database Fields and Component Properties

Although it's a little rudimentary as an object-oriented database, we want to create a data set with fields that match the class's properties passed as parameters to the CreateTable method, and then stored in the file header. Moreover, we want to be able to copy an object into the data set, and then re-create the object from that record's data.

We'll perform the first of these three operations, defining the fields, in the `InternalInitFieldDefs` method. The idea here is to scan the property list of the `FDataClass` field that indicates the object's class. As you can see, this code looks very similar to the code we wrote for the Object Debugger example in Chapter 16. Even so, there are a few things to notice:

- Before adding the other fields, we'll define one with the class name. This isn't a property, but it's vital information for re-creating the object. In fact, we can store objects not just of the given class, but also of derived classes (although we won't save their additional properties—just those of the base class).

- The data set supports properties of types `char`, `string`, and `integer` (including sets and enumerations), and floating-point numbers. It doesn't support class types, method types (that is, events), and a few other rarely used property types introduced in Delphi 3.

- We must handle the `Boolean` type in a specific way. In fact, within the Delphi type system, `Boolean` is simply a regular enumerated type. However, to obtain proper database support, we need to use this specific field type.

It's certainly possible to improve the support for other types, such as translating colors and cursors in strings, but this should be enough to demonstrate the concepts.

Keeping in mind the points above, we can now delve into the source code listing of this method:

```
const
  ClassNameString = 'ClassName';

// I: define the fields - totally different
procedure TDdhObjectDataSet.InternalInitFieldDefs;
var
  pti: PTypeInfo;
  ppi: PPropInfo;
  pPropertyList: PPropList;
  nProps, I, TmpFieldOffset: Integer;
begin
  // field offsets
  FFieldOffset := TList.Create;
  FieldDefs.Clear;
  TmpFieldOffset := 0;
```

```
// add the type name as the first field
FieldDefs.Add (ClassNameString, ftString, 50, False);
FFieldOffset.Add (Pointer (TmpFieldOffset));
Inc (TmpFieldOffset, 50);

// add a field for each property of the supported types
pti := FDataClass.ClassInfo;
nProps := GetTypeData(pti).PropCount;
if nProps > 0 then
begin
  // allocate the required memory
  GetMem (pPropertyList, sizeof (PPropInfo) * nProps);
  // protect the memory allocation
  try
    GetPropInfos(pti, pPropertyList);
    for I := 0 to nProps - 1 do
    begin
      ppi := pPropertyList [I];
      case ppi.PropType^.Kind of
        tkChar:
        begin
          FieldDefs.Add (ppi.Name,
            ftString, 1, False);
          FFieldOffset.Add (Pointer (TmpFieldOffset));
          Inc (TmpFieldOffset, 1);
        end;
        tkInteger, tkEnumeration, tkSet:
        begin
          if ppi.PropType^.Name = 'Boolean' then
          begin
            FieldDefs.Add (ppi.Name,
              ftBoolean, 0, False);
            FFieldOffset.Add (Pointer (TmpFieldOffset));
            Inc (TmpFieldOffset, 2);
          end
          else
          begin
            FieldDefs.Add (ppi.Name,
              ftInteger, 0, False);
            FFieldOffset.Add (Pointer (TmpFieldOffset));
            Inc (TmpFieldOffset, 4);
          end;
```

```
    end;
    tkFloat:
    begin
      FieldDefs.Add (ppi.Name,
        ftFloat, 0, False);
      FFieldOffset.Add (Pointer (TmpFieldOffset));
      Inc (TmpFieldOffset, 8);
    end;
    tkString, tkLString:
    begin
      FieldDefs.Add (ppi.Name,
        ftString, 50, False);
      FFieldOffset.Add (Pointer (TmpFieldOffset));
      Inc (TmpFieldOffset, 50);
    end;
    // types ignored (not saved)
    {tkClass, tkVariant, tkArray, tkRecord,
    tkInterface, tkUnknown, tkWChar, tkMethod}
  end; // case
 end; // for
    finally
  // free the allocated memory
  FreeMem (pPropertyList, sizeof (PPropInfo) * nProps);
    end;
    FRecordSize := TmpFieldOffset;
  end;
end;
```

This code is now capable of obtaining the proper list of fields. Figure 18.11 shows the fields for an object data set based on the TButton type, displayed in Delphi's Fields editor.

However, you'll notice in the listing above that to open the Fields editor, you must open the data set at design-time first. In fact, if you haven't executed the InternalOpen method, the class type we want to work with won't be available. To address this problem, we've added the following code at the beginning of the InternalInitFieldDefs method:

```
procedure TDdhObjectDataSet.InternalInitFieldDefs;
var
  ...
  ClassName: string;
begin
```

```
    // if the stream is unassigned, read the data from it...
    if not Assigned (FStream) then
    begin
      // check if the file exists
      if not FileExists (FTableName) then
        raise EObjDataSetError.Create ('Table file not found');

      // create a stream for the file
      FStream := TFileStream.Create (FTableName, fmOpenReadWrite);
      try
        // initialize local data (loading header)
        FStream.ReadBuffer (FDataFileHeader, FDataFileHeaderSize);
        if FDataFileHeader.VersionNumber <> 10 then
          raise EObjDataSetError.Create ('File version not 10');
        ClassName := StrPas (FDataFileHeader.ClassName);
        FDataClass := FindClass (ClassName);
      finally
        FStream.Free;
        FStream := nil;
      end;
    end;
    ...
```

FIGURE 18.11:

The list of the fields used to save the properties of a TButton object, as shown by the Fields editor

Now we can examine the code we use to add an object to the data set, which creates a new record and initializes its fields. The idea is actually quite simple: For every field, we'll retrieve the type information (TPropInfo) of the property that has the same name as a field definition (not the same name as a field object). Once we have this type information, we'll retrieve the data using the appropriate direct property-access method. Since we want to add a new record, we can call the data set's Insert method at the beginning, and we'll call the Post method near the end.

There are a few other elements of this method worth describing. First, we perform a type compatibility check between the object types we store in the data set and the new component type. (We use the InheritsFrom method instead of the is operator to perform this test, because the is operator doesn't support class references.) Next, we've added some special code to handle the *ClassName* field; this isn't always the first field object, because fields can be arranged in a different order by the user. Finally, we've added some special support for Boolean values. Here's the complete listing:

```
procedure TDdhObjectDataSet.AddObject (Comp: TComponent);
var
  PropInfo: PPropInfo;
  I: Integer;
begin
  // add a new record to the table
  Insert;
  // check the class type
  if not Comp.InheritsFrom (FDataClass) then
    raise EObjDataSetError.Create (
      'AddObject: Invalid class type');
  // add the data to each field
  for I := 0 to FieldCount - 1 do
  begin
    if Fields[I].FieldName = ClassNameString then
      Fields[I].AsString := Comp.ClassName
    else
    begin
      PropInfo := GetPropInfo (Comp.ClassInfo,
        Fields[I].FieldName);
      if PropInfo = nil then
        raise EObjDataSetError.Create (
          'AddObject: Invalid Property');
      case PropInfo.PropType^.Kind of
        tkChar, tkInteger, tkEnumeration, tkSet:
```

```
      if Fields[I] is TBooleanField then
        Fields[I].AsBoolean := Boolean (GetOrdProp (Comp, PropInfo))
      else
        Fields[I].AsInteger := GetOrdProp (Comp, PropInfo);
    tkFloat:
      Fields[I].AsFloat := GetFloatProp (Comp, PropInfo);
    tkString, tkLString:
      Fields[I].AsString := GetStrProp (Comp, PropInfo);
    // types ignored (not saved)
    {tkClass, tkVariant, tkArray, tkRecord,
    tkInterface, tkUnknown, tkWChar, tkMethod}
    end; // case
  end; // if
  end; // for
  // post the data
  Post;
end;
```

Just as we can add objects to the data set, we can also extract them. In fact, what we do is create a brand-new object of the type stored in the ClassName field of the current record, and then restore the property values by reading the other fields. To be more precise, we initialize the object using the class property values stored in the data set, which can be a base class of the object.

The code isn't exactly the reverse of the previous method, but it's very similar. The primary difference is that at the beginning of the method, we extract the class name (which should be registered with RegisterClass in the examples), create the component using the first parameter of the function as Owner, and if the object is a control, set its Parent using the second parameter. Once again, we've added special code to test the data types, to handle Boolean types, and to exclude the ClassName field we already used at the beginning:

```
function TDdhObjectDataSet.CreateObject (Owner: TComponent;
  Parent: TWinControl): TComponent;
var
  PropInfo: PPropInfo;
  I: Integer;
  ClassType: TComponentClass;
  Comp: TComponent;
begin
  // create the component and set its parent
  ClassType := TComponentClass (FindClass (
```

```
      FieldByName (ClassNameString).AsString));
  if not ClassType.InheritsFrom (FDataClass) then
    raise EObjDataSetError.Create (
      'CreateObject: Invalid class type');
  Comp := ClassType.Create (Owner);
  try
    if Comp is TControl then
      TControl (Comp).Parent := Parent;
    // retrieve the values of the fields
    for I := 0 to FieldCount - 1 do
    begin
      if Fields[I].FieldName <> ClassNameString then
      begin
        PropInfo := GetPropInfo (Comp.ClassInfo,
          Fields[I].FieldName);
        if PropInfo = nil then
          raise EObjDataSetError.Create (
            'AddObject: Invalid Property');
        case PropInfo.PropType^.Kind of
          tkChar, tkInteger, tkEnumeration, tkSet:
            if Fields[I] is TBooleanField then
              SetOrdProp (Comp, PropInfo, Integer (Fields[I].AsBoolean))
            else
              SetOrdProp (Comp, PropInfo, Fields[I].AsInteger);
          tkFloat:
            SetFloatProp (Comp, PropInfo, Fields[I].AsFloat);
          tkString, tkLString:
            SetStrProp (Comp, PropInfo, Fields[I].AsString);
          // types ignored (not saved)
          {tkClass, tkVariant, tkArray, tkRecord,
          tkInterface, tkUnknown, tkWChar, tkMethod}
        end; // case
      end; // if
    end; // for
    Result := Comp;
  except
    Comp.Free;
    raise;
  end;
end;
```

You'll notice that if anything goes wrong, the `CreateObject` method deletes the component, and then allows the exception to follow its normal flow. The most common reason for this method to fail is that a component with the same name already exists in the program and has the same owner.

Using the Object Data Set

Now that we've completed our description of this component, we're ready to see an example of its use. The OdsDemo example's main form contains a toolbar with a few buttons, a check box to toggle the `Active` property of the data set, and a DBGrid and a ScrollBox component sharing the client area (separated by a horizontal splitter).

> **WARNING**
>
> In this example you can set the `Active` property of the custom data to `True` at design-time, even if you only provide the table file name and not the full path. However, if the file is open at design time, when you run it, the component won't find the file because of a sharing violation (the file is opened both by the design-time component and by the running program). You can fix this problem by adding the `fmShareDenyNone` flag to the `Create` call of the `TFileStream` object in the `InternalOpen` method of the component. However, this exposes you to much worse problems if you run two instances of the program that read and write the same file.

The `CreateButton` method creates a table, and again uses a fixed table name set up in the `OnCreate` event handler, so that the program will work even if you place it in a different directory. (You'll still have to include a valid path in the `TableName` if you want to work on the table at design-time.) Here's the code of the two methods:

```
procedure TForm1.FormCreate(Sender: TObject);
begin
  DdhDataSetOne1.TableName :=
    ExtractFilePath (ParamStr (0)) +
    'Buttons.otl';
end;

procedure TForm1.BtnCreateClick(Sender: TObject);
begin
  DdhObjectDataSet1.CreateTable (TButton);
  DdhObjectDataSet1.Open;
end;
```

As you can see, the data set is simply a table of TButton objects. This means we can add a button to the data set, as demonstrated by the BtnAddClick button, which we've connected to the OnClick event handler of both a button and a bitmap button on the tool bar panel:

```
procedure TForm1.BtnAddClick(Sender: TObject);
begin
  if DdhObjectDataSet1.Active then
  begin
    DdhObjectDataSet1.AddObject (Sender as TComponent);
    // edit the name field of the new record randomly
    DdhObjectDataSet1.Edit;
    DdhObjectDataSet1.FieldByName('Name').AsString :=
      (Sender as TComponent).Name + IntToStr (Random (10000));
    DdhObjectDataSet1.Post;
  end;
end;
```

After we add the new object, we change the Name field's value from the record, so that it will be possible to create a component using this data without a Name property conflict with the other components the form owns. Figure 18.12 shows an example of adding the two components to the data set several times.

FIGURE 18.12:

The records added to the Object data set after pressing the two *Add* buttons of the toolbar panel a few times

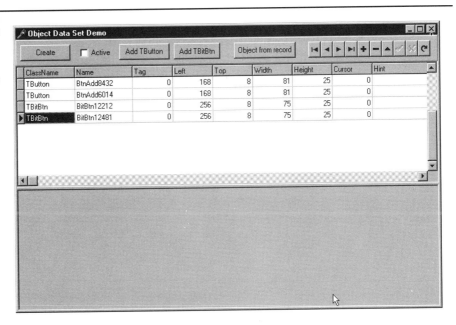

Now that we've built this support for the Name property into the save operation, re-creating the component (inside the scroll box) becomes very simple. The only extra tasks we'll need to manage are placing it in an appropriately random position, using its Name as a new caption, and connecting the BtnAddClick event to its OnClick event handler (so that you can add further records in the data set). These last two statements use two different techniques to access the Caption and OnClick properties (we used different techniques simply to demonstrate alternatives for accessing the data):

```
procedure TForm1.BtnGetClick(Sender: TObject);
var
  NewControl: TControl;
begin
  // owner is the form, parent is the ScrollBox
  NewControl := DdhObjectDataSet1.CreateObject (
    self, ScrollBox1) as TControl;
  NewControl.Left := Random (ScrollBox1.ClientWidth);
  NewControl.Top := Random (ScrollBox1.ClientHeight);
  NewControl.SetTextBuf (PChar (NewControl.Name));
  if NewControl is TButton then
    TButton(NewControl).OnClick := BtnAddClick;
end;
```

In Figure 18.13 we've created several buttons, used to update the data set.

Finally, remember that in the initialization section, you must call the RegisterClass method for classes you want to store in the database. Here, you can also add a call to the Randomize procedure to make the names and positions really random:

```
initialization
  Randomize;
  RegisterClass (TButton);
  RegisterClass (TBitBtn);
end.
```

FIGURE 18.13:

The OdsDemo exam-
ple can be used to
store many records in
the object data set,
and to create buttons
in a scroll box using
the information stored
in the data set.

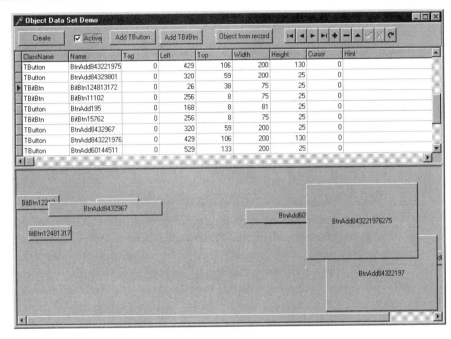

What's Next

In the first part of this chapter, we discussed creating data-aware components for
a database table dynamically, both at run-time and inside a Delphi wizard. In the
second part of the chapter, we explored how you can define and build your own
custom data-set components, which allow you to access data in a standard Delphi
way but without requiring the BDE.

We'll discuss custom data sets further in the next chapter. In fact, while we're
focusing on Delphi's three-tier architecture, we'll review the TClientDataSet
component, the only non-BDE data set of the VCL. However, there will be much
more than that in the next chapter, and from there we'll move on to publishing
database tables on the Web.

These last two chapters will use a more tutorial style, and won't go quite as
deep as most of the other chapters of the book, because they cover more complex
and extensive topics, many of which are also quite new for Delphi programmers.
Finally, keep in mind that some of the topics we'll be covering in these last two
chapters are available only to owners of the Delphi Client/Server edition.

CHAPTER
NINETEEN

Remote Data Modules
and Thin Clients

- One, Two, Three Levels

- Building a Sample Application

- Adding Constraints to the Server

- Adding Features to the Client

Among many other new features, Delphi 3 introduced support for a physical three-tier database architecture. This, along with support for AS/400, SAP, and other server-side technologies, is probably one of the most important directions of future Delphi extensions.

This chapter will introduce the key ideas and the fundamental programming elements of Delphi's three-tier architecture, with coverage of MIDAS, remote data sets and the IProvider interface, and the Provider, RemoteServer, and ClientData-Set components. We'll build examples on both the client and server sides, but in each case, we'll concentrate more on the programming aspects of this architecture than on installation and configuration (these aspects are subject to change in future versions of Delphi and across different operating systems).

Before we continue, we should emphasize two important elements. First, the tools to support this kind of development are available only in the Client/Server Suite version of Delphi 3, and second, you'll have to pay royalties to Borland in order to install the necessary server-side software. This second requirement makes this architecture cost-effective mainly for large systems (that is, servers connected to dozens, if not hundreds, of clients).

One, Two, Three Levels

Initially, database PC applications were client-only solutions: The program and the database files were on the same computer. From there, adventuresome programmers moved the database files onto a network file server. The client computers still hosted the application software and the entire database engine, but the database files were now accessible to several users at the same time. You can still use this type of configuration with a Delphi application and Paradox files (or, of course, Paradox itself), but the approach was much more widespread just few years ago.

The next big transition was to client/server development, embraced by Delphi since its first version. In the client/server world, the client computer requests the data from a server computer, which hosts both the database files and a database engine to access them. This architecture downplays the role of the client, but it also reduces its requirements for processing power. Depending on how the programmers implement client/server, the server can do most (if not all) of the data processing. In this way, a powerful server can provide data services to several less powerful clients.

Naturally, there are many other reasons for using centralized database servers, such as the concern for data security and integrity, simpler backup strategies, central management of data constraints, and so on. The database server is often called a SQL server, because this is the language most commonly used for making queries into the data, but it may also be called a DBMS (DataBase Management System) reflecting the fact that the server provides tools for managing the data, such as support for backup and replication.

Of course, some applications you build might not need the benefits of a full DBMS, so a simple client-only solution might be sufficient. On the other hand, you might need some of the robustness of a DBMS system, but on a single, isolated computer. In this case, you can use a *local* version of an SQL server, such as Local InterBase (included with both the Professional and Client/Server Suite editions of Delphi). For example, military and financial institutions have built applications that use copies of Local InterBase on laptop computers, instead of simple database files, because they contain very sensitive data and they must be able to connect with a central server to synchronize the data only from time to time.

Traditional client/server development is done with a two-tier architecture. However, if the DBMS is primarily performing data storage instead of data and number crunching, the client might contain both user interface code (formatting the output and input with customized reports, data-entry forms, query screens, and so on) as well as code related to managing the data (also known as *business rules*). In this case, it's generally a good idea to try to separate these two sections of the program, and build a logical three-tier architecture. The term *logical* here means that there are still just two computers (that is, two physical tiers), but we've now partitioned the application into three distinct elements.

Delphi 2 introduced support for a logical three-tier architecture with data modules. As you'll recall, a data module is a nonvisual container for the data access components of an application, but it often includes several handlers for database-related events. You can share a single data module among several different forms, and provide different user interfaces for the same data: There might be one or more data-input forms, reports, master/detail forms, and various charting or dynamic output forms.

The logical three-tier approach solves many problems, but it also has a few drawbacks. First, you must replicate the data-management portion of the program on different client computers, which might hamper performance, but more of an issue is the complexity it adds to code maintenance. Second, when multiple clients modify the same data, there's no simple way to handle the resulting update conflicts. Finally, for logical three-tier Delphi applications, you must install and configure the BDE on every client computer.

The next logical step up from client/server is to move the data-module portion of the application to a separate server computer, and design all the client programs to interact with it. This is exactly the purpose of remote data modules, introduced in Delphi 3. Remote data modules run on a server computer—generally called the application server. The application server in turn communicates with the DBMS (which can run on the application server or on another computer). Therefore, the client machines don't connect to the SQL server directly, but indirectly via the application server.

At this point there is a fundamental question: Do we still need to install the BDE? The traditional Delphi client/server architecture (even with the logical three tiers) requires you to install the BDE on each client, something quite troublesome when you must configure and maintain hundreds of machines. In the new physical three-tier architecture, you need to install and configure the BDE only on the application server, not on the client computers. This generally means installing the BDE and configuring the drivers and the aliases only on one computer! Since the client programs have only user interface code, and are extremely simple to install, they now fall into the category of so-called *thin clients*. To use marketing-speak, we might even call this a *zero-configuration thin-client architecture*. But let us focus on technical issues instead of marketing terminology.

The Technical Foundation: DCOM and MIDAS

Delphi's physical three-tier architecture has two foundations. The operating system foundation is based on Distributed COM (or DCOM), introduced by Microsoft in Windows NT 4.0 and available as a free add-on for Windows 95. DCOM is basically an extension of COM technology (discussed in Chapters 10 and 11) allowing a client application to use server objects that exist and execute on a separate computer. Through low-level network connections, the two applications communicate as if they were on the same computer. DCOM is a solid foundation, but it lacks some advanced features necessary for a multiple-tier architecture.

To address these limitations, Borland developed MIDAS (Middle-tier Distributed Application Services Suite), a collection of distinct technologies that work together to make it easier to build multiple-tier, DCOM-based, distributed applications with Delphi. There are three key elements of MIDAS:

- The Remote Data Broker, which provides the data connection between the client and the application server.

- The Business Object Broker and the OLEnterprise technology, which allow you to put the application server on multiple servers, providing crash protection and load balancing.

- The Constraint Broker, which provides a simple method of distributing constraints, or integrity rules, along with the data. Besides improving data validation, this can potentially reduce network traffic (you don't have to perform validation at the client).

As you would expect, the client side of MIDAS is extremely thin, and it's easy to deploy. The only file you need is DBCLient.DLL, a small (140K) DLL that implements the `ClientDataSet` and `RemoteServer` components and provides the connection to the application server. This DLL is basically a small, stand-alone database engine, which caches data from a remote data module and enforces the rules requested by the Constraint Broker.

The application server uses the same DLL to handle the data sets (called *deltas*) returned from the clients when they post updated or new records. However, the server also requires several other libraries, all of which are installed by MIDAS. The two sides of the application communicate though a protocol or interface called `IProvider`.

NOTE   Delphi Client/Server Suite ships with the developer's license for MIDAS, but you should buy additional licenses to deploy it, with the license for each server costing almost as much as a single copy of Delphi Client/Server. You should check the Borland web site (www.borland.com/midas/) or your local Borland office for updated information about MIDAS distribution royalties.

Providing Data Packets

The entire Delphi multiple-tier data access architecture centers around the idea of *data packets*. In this context, a data packet is a block of data that moves from the application server to the client or from the client back to the server. Technically, a data packet is a sort of subset of a data set. It describes the data it contains (usually a few records of data), and it lists the names and types of the data fields. Even more importantly, data packets include the constraints—that is, the rules to be applied to the data set. You'll typically set these constraints in the application server, and the server sends them to the client applications along with the data.

All communication between the client and the server occurs by exchanging data packets, and is governed by the IProvider interface:

```
type
  IProvider = interface(IDispatch)
    ['{6E644935-51F7-11D0-8D41-00A0248E4B9A}']
    function Get_Data: OleVariant; safecall;
    function ApplyUpdates(Delta: OleVariant; MaxErrors: Integer;
      out ErrorCount: Integer): OleVariant; safecall;
    function GetMetaData: OleVariant; safecall;
    function GetRecords(Count: Integer;
      out RecsOut: Integer): OleVariant; safecall;
    function DataRequest(Input: OleVariant): OleVariant; safecall;
    function Get_Constraints: WordBool; safecall;
    procedure Set_Constraints(Value: WordBool); safecall;
    procedure Reset(MetaData: WordBool); safecall;
    procedure SetParams(Values: OleVariant); safecall;
    property Data: OleVariant read Get_Data;
    property Constraints: WordBool
      read Get_Constraints write Set_Constraints;
  end;
```

The provider manages the transmission of several data packets within a big data set, with the goal of responding faster to the user. As the client receives a data packet, the user can edit the records it contains. As we mentioned earlier, during this process the client also receives and checks the constraints. When the client has updated the records and sends a data packet back, that packet is known as a *delta*. The delta packet tracks the difference between the original records and the updated ones, recording all the changes the client requested from the server. When the client asks to apply the updates to the server, it sends the delta to the server, and the server tries to apply each of the changes. We say *tries* because if a server is connected to several clients, the data might have changed already.

Since the delta packet includes the original data, the server can quickly determine if another client has already changed it. If so, the server fires an OnReconcileError event, which is one of the vital elements for the thin-client applications.

In other words, the three-tier architecture uses an update mechanism similar to the one Delphi uses for cached updates. The ClientDataSet manages data in memory, in a sort of data cache, and typically reads only a subset of the records available on the server side, loading more elements only as they're needed. When the client updates the records, or insert new ones, it stores these pending changes in another local cache on the client, the delta cache.

The client can also save the data packets to disk, which means users can work off-line. Even error information and other data move using the data packet protocol, so it is truly one of the foundation elements of this architecture.

NOTE It's important to remember that data packets and the IProvider interface are protocol-independent. A data packet is merely a sequence of bytes, so anywhere you can move a series of bytes, you can move a data packet. This means the architecture is suitable not only for DCOM, but also for TCP/IP and other transport protocols.

Delphi Support Components

Now that we've examined the general foundations of the new three-tier architecture, we can focus on the Delphi 3 components that support it. For developing client applications, Delphi provides the ClientDataSet component, which provides all the standard data-set capabilities (it derives from TDataSet) but doesn't requires the BDE, just like the custom data-set components we built in the last chapter. Instead, the server application provides access to the data. This connection is made via another component, RemoteServer, which you'll also need in the client application.

On the server side, you'll need to use a remote data module, a special version of the TDataModule class. To maintain the data packet communications, you'll need to add the stand-alone Provider component, or the version of this component that's embedded in the TBdeDataSet subclasses, TTable and TQuery. In either case, the server application becomes an (OLE) Automation server that exports the proper provider interfaces to the client applications. In fact, a single server can export several IProvider interfaces, one for each data set (table, query, or stored procedure) it wants to make available to the clients. The client applications will then use a separate ClientDataSet component for every exported data set (or provider) they want to use.

The New MidasConnection and SocketDispatcher Components

As this book was going to press, Borland shipped an update of Delphi 3 Client/Server Suite, with two new MIDAS-specific classes, available in the new MIDASCon unit. These components have been added to let the client application use TCP/IP sockets or Borland's own OLEnterprise transport layer instead of DCOM to connect the client and the server side of a multiple-tier application.

The TMIDASConnection component (which inherits from the TRemoteConnection component) is used on the client side. It has a special ConnectType property you can use to indicate the type of connection; this property can assume three values:

```
TConnectType = (ctDCOM, ctSockets, ctOLEnterprise);
```

When you use the ctSockets connection type, the client application uses a TCP/IP socket to connect to a socket dispatcher component on the application server. This server-side socket dispatcher can be provided by adding a TSocketDispatcher object to a separate form or data module of the server application (not the remote data module).

As an alternative, you can keep the server-side project as it is, and simply run the ScktSrvr.EXE application (available in Delphi's BIN directory) on the application server computer. If you use TCP/IP, the ServerPort property of the MIDAS-Connection component should match the Port property of the socket dispatcher.

When you use the ctOLEnterprise connection type, the component establishes the connection using Borland's OLEnterprise, which must be installed on the client machine. If you set the UseBroker property of the MIDASConnection component to True, the ComputerName property will indicate the name of the OLEnterprise Business Object Broker, instead of the name of the server machine.

You don't need to use this new component if you want to use DCOM. In fact, to use the MIDASConnection component you must also distribute the INET30.DPL package (which is not required if you simply use the RemoteServer component), even if you don't use the TCP/IP service.

To learn more about these components, you can refer to two examples available in the Delphi 3 update, EmpEdit and MstrDtl.

Building a Sample Application

Now we're ready to build a sample program. This will allow us to see some of what we've described, but will also allow us to focus on some other problems, shedding some light on other pieces of the Delphi three-tier puzzle. We'll build the client and application server portions of our three-tier application in two steps. The first step will simply test the technology using a bare minimum of elements. These programs will be very simple.

From that point, we'll add more power to the client and the application server. In each of the examples, we'll display data from local Paradox tables, and we'll set up everything to allow you to test the programs on a stand-alone computer.

The First Application Server

The server side of our basic example is very easy to build. Simply create a new application, and add a remote data module to it using the corresponding icon in the New page of the Object Repository. The simple Remote Dataset Wizard will ask you for a class name and the instancing style. As you enter a class name, such as TDdhFirstRM, and click the OK button, Delphi will add a data module to the program. This data module will have the usual two properties and two events, but its class will have the following (surprising) Pascal declaration:

```
type
  TTDdhFirstRM = class(TDataModule, ITDdhFirstRM)
  private
    { Private declarations }
  public
    { Public declarations }
  end;
```

In addition to inheriting from the TDataModule base class, this class implements a new interface, ITDdhFirstRM, which derives from a default Borland interface (IDataBroker). At the end of the unit, you'll find the class factory declaration:

```
initialization
  TComponentFactory.Create(ComServer, TTDdhFirstRM,
    Class_TDdhFirstRM, ciMultiInstance);
end.
```

Now you can add a Table component to the data module, connect it to a database and a table, activate it, and obtain a simple DFM file like this:

```
object TDdhFirstRM: TTDdhFirstRM
  object Table1: TTable
    DatabaseName = 'DBDEMOS'
    TableName = 'CUSTOMER.DB'
  end
end
```

At this point, if you right-click on the Table component, you'll see an extra menu item, *Export Table1 from data module*, as shown in Figure 19.1. Notice that this menu item is available only once—after you execute this command, Delphi removes it from the menu (something we find a little odd; it should appear disabled).

FIGURE 19.1:

The extra menu item added to the Table component in a remote data module

When you select this menu command, the remote data module exports the IProvider interface built into the Provider object of the Table component, making the interface available to a client application. In fact, this operation modifies the ITDdhFirstRM interface, and therefore the type library it embeds in the server application.

NOTE   For more information about type libraries and OLE Automation servers, refer to Chapters 10 and 11.

What happens to our server application as it exports the IProvider interface for the table? The interface of our remote data module changes as follows:

```
type
  ITDdhFirstRM = interface(IDataBroker)
```

```
['{AE857761-2114-11D1-98D0-444553540000}']
function Get_Table1: IProvider; safecall;
property Table1: IProvider read Get_Table1;
end;

ITDdhFirstRMDisp = dispinterface
['{AE857761-2114-11D1-98D0-444553540000}']
function GetProviderNames: OleVariant; dispid 22929905;
property Table1: IProvider readonly;
end;
```

This updates the data module class, too, since the new method exports the Provider property of the table:

```
function TTDdhFirstRM.Get_Table1: IProvider;
begin
  Result := Table1.Provider;
end;
```

What about the main form of this program? Well, it's almost useless, so we can simply add a label to it indicating that it's the form of the server application. When you've built the server, you should compile it and run it once. This operation will automatically register it as an Automation server on your system, making it available to client applications.

This application server is unrealistically simple, but, as we'll see later on, you can customize the remote data module's interface in various ways. Doing so is as simple as executing the Add To Interface command from the remote data module's local menu.

The First Thin Client

Now that we have a working server, we can build a client that will connect to it. We'll again start with a standard Delphi application, but this time, we'll add a RemoteServer component to it. This component defines a ComputerName property that you'll use to specify the computer that hosts the application server. If you want to test the client and application server from the same computer, you can leave this blank.

Once you've selected an application server computer, you can simply display the ServerName property's combo-box list to view the available servers. As shown in Figure 19.2, you'll see a list of the servers' registered names (by default the name of the executable file of the server followed by the name of the remote data module class). Alternatively, you can type the GUID of the server object in the ServerGUID property. Delphi will automatically enter this property as you set the ServerName property if it can determine the GUID.

FIGURE 19.2:

The property editor for the ServerName property automatically lists all the registered servers on the selected computer that export an IProvider interface.

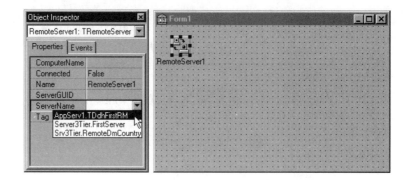

At this point, if you set the RemoteServer component's Connected property to True, the server form will appear, indicating that the client has activated the server. You don't usually need to perform this operation, because the ClientDataSet component typically activates the RemoteServer component for you. We've done this simply to emphasize what's happening behind the scenes.

As you might expect, the next step is to add a ClientDataSet component to the form. You must connect the ClientDataSet to the RemoteServer1 component via the RemoteServer property, and thereby to one of the providers it exports. You can see the list of available providers in the ProviderName property, via the usual combo box. In this example, you'll be able to select only Table1. This operation connects the data set in the client's memory with the file-based data set on the server. If you activate the client data set and add a few data-aware controls, you'll immediately see the server data appear in them, as illustrated in Figure 19.3.

Here is the DFM file for our minimal client application, ThinCli1:

```
object Form1: TForm1
  Caption = 'ThinClient1'
  object DBGrid1: TDBGrid
    Align = alClient
    DataSource = DataSource1
  end
  object RemoteServer1: TRemoteServer
    Connected = True
```

```
      ServerGUID = '{AE857762-2114-11D1-98D0-444553540000}'
    end
    object ClientDataSet1: TClientDataSet
      Active = True
      ProviderName = 'Table1'
      RemoteServer = RemoteServer1
    end
    object DataSource1: TDataSource
      DataSet = ClientDataSet1
    end
  end
```

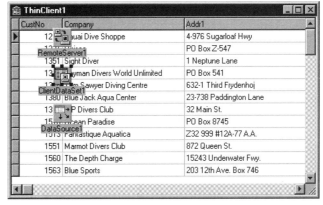

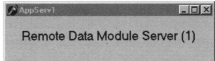

Obviously, our first client and server applications are very simple, but they demonstrate how easy it is to create a data set viewer that splits the work between two executable files. At this point, our client is only a viewer. If you edit the data on the client, it won't update the server files with those changes. To accomplish this you'll need to add some more code to the client. However, before we do that, let's add some features to the server.

Adding Constraints to the Server

When you write a traditional data module in Delphi, you can easily add some of the application logic, or business rules, by writing handler methods for the dataset events, and by setting field object properties and handling their events. When you first start working with remote data modules, you might consider the same approach. Unfortunately, it isn't possible.

The provider interface creates data packets to send to the client based on the Table component's properties, but not its events. At the same time, the provider creates and uses field objects, but not in the same way as in a traditional Delphi program. In fact, you can manually add field objects to your three-tier Delphi application, but you must add them to the client side. The only thing you can do to customize the middle tier and build distributed application logic is to create SQL-based constraints—you can't do so by writing Pascal code.

> **NOTE** It's not clear whether the limited use of Pascal in the middle tier is a temporary limitation or is intrinsically part of the architecture. This will probably become clearer as Borland releases new versions of Delphi.

The constraints you create using SQL expressions can be assigned to an entire table or to specific fields. The provider sends the constraints to the client along with the data, and the client applies them before sending updates back to the server. This reduces network traffic, compared to having the client send updates back to the application server and eventually up to the SQL server only to find that the data is invalid. Another advantage of coding the constraints on the server side is that if the business rules change, you need to update only the server application, and not the clients. The Constraint Broker provides the basic infrastructure for this logic.

But how do you write constraints? There are several properties you can use:

- The Table component has a `Constraints` property, which has a custom property editor. Similarly, the `Constraints` property of the BDEDataSet components is a collection of `TCheckConstraint` objects, as you can see in Figure 19.4. Every object has a few properties, including the expression and the error message.

- The Query component defines the same `Constraints` property, plus a `Constrained` Boolean property.

- The Field objects define the `CustomConstraint`, `ImportedConstraint`, and `ConstraintErroMessage` properties, which are functionally equivalent to the `TCheckConstraint` object's properties.

FIGURE 19.4:

The editor of the Constraints property of the Table component, and the properties of one of the TCheckConstraint objects selected in the Object Inspector using this editor

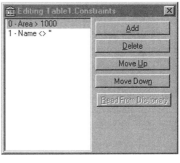

TIP

An important thing to consider is that if you are using a data dictionary, you can extract constraints directly from it.

For our next example, we've added a few constraints to a remote data module connected to the DBDEMOS database's Country.DB table. After connecting the table to the database and creating the field objects for it, you can set the following special properties (listed here in the textual description of the remote data module):

```
object RdmCount: TRdmCount
  object Table1: TTable
    Active = True
    DatabaseName = 'DBDEMOS'
    Constraints = <
      item
        CustomConstraint = 'Area > 1000'
        ErrorMessage = 'Area too small'
        FromDictionary = False
      end
      item
        CustomConstraint = 'Name <> '#39#39
```

```
          ErrorMessage = 'Must provide a name'
          FromDictionary = False
        end>
      TableName = 'COUNTRY.DB'
      Left = 16
      Top = 16
      object Table1Name: TStringField
        FieldName = 'Name'
        Size = 24
      end
      object Table1Capital: TStringField
        FieldName = 'Capital'
        Size = 24
      end
      object Table1Continent: TStringField
        DefaultExpression = #39'Europe'#39
        FieldName = 'Continent'
        Size = 24
      end
      object Table1Area: TFloatField
        FieldName = 'Area'
      end
      object Table1Population: TFloatField
        CustomConstraint = 'Value > 10000'
        ConstraintErrorMessage = 'Population out of range'
        FieldName = 'Population'
      end
    end
  end
end
```

There are a couple of table-wide constraints, one field-specific constraint, and a field that uses the `DefaultExpression` property to define a constraint propagated to the client application.

The AppServ2 example also has another feature. We've placed the `DDhAppExt` component from Chapter 8 on its main form, activated some of its properties to make the application show up in the tray icon area, and created a custom pop-up menu:

```
object Form1: TForm1
  Caption = 'AppServ2'
  object DdhAppExt1: TDdhAppExt
    TrayIconActive = True
```

```
      TrayHint = 'AppServ2 (DDH)'
      TrayPopup = PopupMenu1
    end
    object PopupMenu1: TPopupMenu
      object Close1: TMenuItem
        Caption = 'Close'
        OnClick = Close1Click
      end
      object About1: TMenuItem
        Caption = 'About...'
        Default = True
        OnClick = About1Click
      end
    end
  end
end
```

Finally, to force the program to display only the tray icon (and not the main form), we've edited the application's project source code to add a statement that sets the ShowMainForm property to False, as follows:

```
begin
  Application.Initialize;
  Application.ShowMainForm := False;
  Application.CreateForm(TForm1, Form1);
  Application.Run;
end.
```

This way, the server won't show up as a regular application with a main window; it will be visible only in the tray icon area. That's enough to let us know it's running.

WARNING   Of course, to load this program in the Delphi environment, you must first install the package for Chapter 8.

Adding Features to the Client

After adding constraints and tray icon support to the server, it's now time to return our attention to the client application. The first version was very simple, but now there are a number of features we must add to make it work well.

We'll start by demonstrating how the client works, by checking the record status and by receiving the Delta information (the updates to be sent back to the server). Then we'll add features to the program that handle updates, reconcile errors, and support the briefcase model.

Keep in mind that while you're using this client to edit the data locally, you'll be reminded of a failure to match the business rules of the application, set up on the server side using constraints. The server will also provide us with a default value for the Continent field of a new record. In Figure 19.5 you can see one of the error messages this client application can display, which it receives from the server. This message is displayed while editing the data locally, not when you send it back to the server.

FIGURE 19.5:

The error message displayed by the ThinCli2 example when the value of the Area field is too small

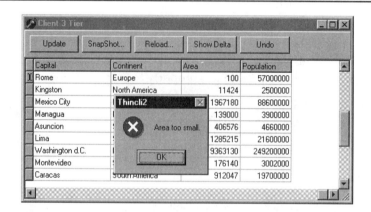

The Status of the Records

The ClientDataSet component has a feature that lets us monitor what's going on within the client/server data packets; this is the UpdateStatus method, which returns one of the following indicators for the current record:

```
type
  TUpdateStatus = (usUnmodified, usModified,
    usInserted, usDeleted);
```

What's odd is that the usUnmodified state should indicate that the record hasn't changed, when in fact it denotes records that were extracted from the first data packet. Similarly, records requested from the server after the first group indicate the usInserted state, which is supposed to mark new records.

To check the status of every record in the client data set easily, we can add a string-type calculated field to the table, and compute its value with the following method:

```
procedure TForm1.ClientDataSet1CalcFields(
  DataSet: TDataSet);
begin
  ClientDataSet1Status.AsString :=
    GetEnumName (TypeInfo(TUpdateStatus),
      Integer (ClientDataSet1.UpdateStatus));
end;
```

This method converts the current value of the TUpdateStatus enumeration to a string. You can see an example of this conversion inside a DBGrid in the output of the ThinCli2 example (illustrated in Figure 19.6).

FIGURE 19.6:

The ThinCli2 example shows the status of the records in the ClientDataSet (in this case a new and a modified record).

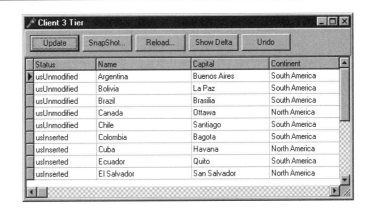

As we mentioned earlier, the first five records in a data packet are marked as usUnmodified in order to force the client to download the first packet from the server. The number of records per packet is determined by the value of the ClientDataSet component's PacketRecords property. The default value is 5, which means that the provider will put five records in a packet. Alternatively, you can set this value to zero to request only for the field descriptors, and no actual data. At the other end of the spectrum, using -1 transfers all the records at once (something that's reasonable only for a small data set).

Accessing the Delta

Beyond examining the status of each record, the best way to understand which changes have occurred in a given ClientDataSet (but haven't been uploaded to the server) is to look at the delta, the list of changes waiting to be applied to the server. We've defined this property as follows:

```
property Delta: OleVariant;
```

The format used by the Delta property is the same as that used to transmit the data from the client to the server. What we can do, then, is add another ClientDataSet component to the application, and connect it to the data in the Delta property of the first client data set:

```
procedure TForm1.ButtonDeltaClick(Sender: TObject);
begin
  if ClientDataSet1.ChangeCount > 0 then
  begin
    ClientDataSet2.Data := ClientDataSet1.Delta;
    ClientDataSet2.Open;
    FormDelta.DataSource1.DataSet := ClientDataSet2;
    FormDelta.Show;
  end
  else
    FormDelta.Hide;
end;
```

FormDelta is a very simple form that contains a DataSource and a DBGrid component, as you can see in Figure 19.7. You'll notice that the Delta data set has two entries for each modified record, the original values and the modified fields.

This code displays the current records in the Delta, but it won't automatically refresh them when the user makes other changes unless the program copies the new Delta to the second ClientDataSet component every time the data changes.

You can accomplish this in the ClientDataSet component's AfterPost event handler, executed when the data changes in memory, but not when it's sent to the server:

```
procedure TForm1.ClientDataSet1AfterPost(DataSet: TDataSet);
begin
  if FormDelta.Visible and
    (ClientDataSet1.ChangeCount > 0) then
  begin
```

```
        ClientDataSet2.Data := ClientDataSet1.Delta;
    end;
end;
```

FIGURE 19.7:

The ThinCli2 example allows you to see the temporary update requests stored in the Delta property of the ClientDataSet.

Updating the Data

Now that we have a better understanding of what goes on during local updates, we can try to make this program work by sending the local update (stored in the Delta) back to the application server. To apply all the updates from a data set at once, you pass -1 to the ApplyUpdates method:

```
procedure TForm1.ButtonUpdateClick(Sender: TObject);
begin
  ClientDataSet1.ApplyUpdates (-1);
  FormDelta.Hide;
end;
```

The update operation might trigger the OnReconcileError event, which allows us to modify the Action parameter (passed by reference); this value in turn determines how the server behaves in case of an update collision:

```
procedure TForm1.ClientDataSet1ReconcileError(
  DataSet: TClientDataSet; E: EReconcileError;
  UpdateKind: TUpdateKind; var Action: TReconcileAction);
begin

end;
```

This method has three parameters: the client data set component (in case more than one client application is interacting with the application server), the exception that caused the error (with the error message), and the kind of operation that failed (ukModify, ukInsert, or ukDelete). The return value, which you'll store in the Action parameter, can be any one of the following:

```
type
  TReconcileAction = (raSkip, raAbort, raMerge,
    raCorrect, raCancel, raRefresh);
```

- The raSkip value specifies that the server should skip the conflicting record, leaving it in the delta (this is the default value).

- The raAbort value tells the server to abort the entire update operation, and not even try to apply the remaining delta operations.

- The raMerge value tells the server to merge the data of the client with the data on the server, applying only the new client values.

- The raCorrect value tells the server to replace its data with the current client data, ignoring changes from other clients.

- You use the raCancel value to cancel the update request and remove the entry from the delta.

- The caRefresh value tells the server to dump the current client delta, and you can replace it with the data of the server.

WARNING   The Delphi online help for these values is a bit cryptic, so we hope these descriptions help. We've tested their behavior, and it's consistent with these descriptions.

If you want to test collisions on a stand-alone computer, you can simply launch two copies of the client application, change the same record in both clients, and then post the updates from both. We'll do this later to generate an error, but let's first see how to handle the OnReconcileError event.

This is actually a simple thing to accomplish, but only because we'll receive a little help. Since building a specific form to handle an OnReconcileError event is very common, Delphi already provides such a form in the Object Repository. Simply go to the Dialogs page and select the *Reconcile Error Dialog* item. As the source code of this unit indicates, it exports a function you can directly use to initialize and display the dialog box:

```
procedure TForm1.ClientDataSet1ReconcileError(DataSet: TClientDataSet;
  E: EReconcileError; UpdateKind: TUpdateKind;
  var Action: TReconcileAction);
begin
  Action := HandleReconcileError (DataSet, UpdateKind, E);
end;
```

WARNING   As the source code of the *Reconcile Error Dialog* unit suggests, you should use the Project Options dialog to remove this form from the list of automatically created forms (if you don't, an error will occur when you compile the project).

The HandleReconcileError function simply creates the form of the dialog box and shows it:

```
function HandleReconcileError(DataSet: TDataSet;
  UpdateKind: TUpdateKind; ReconcileError: EReconcileError):
  TReconcileAction;
var
  UpdateForm: TReconcileErrorForm;
begin
  UpdateForm := TReconcileErrorForm.CreateForm(DataSet,
    UpdateKind, ReconcileError);
  with UpdateForm do
  try
    if ShowModal = mrOK then
    begin
      Result := TReconcileAction(ActionGroup.Items.Objects[
        ActionGroup.ItemIndex]);
```

```
        if Result = raCorrect then
          SetFieldValues(DataSet);
      end
      else
        Result := raAbort;
    finally
      Free;
    end;
  end;
```

The Reconc unit, which hosts the Reconcile Error dialog, contains over 350 lines of code, so we can't describe it in detail. However, you should be able to understand the source code by studying it carefully. Alternatively, you can simply use it without caring about how everything works.

The dialog box will appear in case of an error, reporting the requested change that caused the conflict, and allowing the user to choose one of the possible TReconcileAction values. You can see an example in Figure 19.8.

FIGURE 19.8:

The Reconcile Error dialog provided by Delphi in the Object Repository, and used by the ThinCli2 example

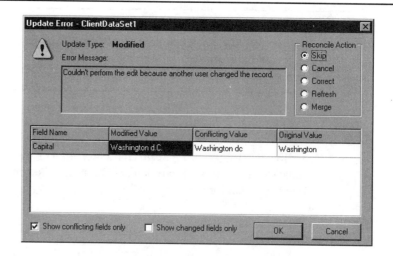

Adding an Undo Feature

Since the update data is stored in the local memory (in the delta), besides applying the updates sending them to the application server, we can reject them, removing entries from the delta. The ClientDataSet component has a specific UndoLastChange method to accomplish this. The parameter of this method allows you to *follow* the undo operation (the name of this parameter is FollowChange). This means the client data set will move to the record that has been restored by the undo operation.

Here is the code connected to the *Undo* button of the example:

```
procedure TForm1.ButtonUndoClick(Sender: TObject);
begin
  ClientDataSet1.UndoLastChange (True);
end;
```

We suggest you try using this feature yourself, to fully understand how it works.

Supporting the Briefcase Model

The last capability we'll add to the client application is support for the "briefcase" model. The idea here is that you might need use the client program even when you're not physically connected to the application server. In this case, you can save all the data you expect to need in a local file, for travel with a laptop (perhaps visiting client sites). You'll use the client program to access the local version of the data, edit the data normally, and when you reconnect, apply all the updates you've performed while disconnected.

The ThinCli2 example's main form has two buttons: one to save a snapshot of the data to a local file, and one to restore it. The OnClick event handlers for these buttons use the standard OpenDialog and SaveDialog components to connect to the database file:

```
procedure TForm1.ButtonSnapClick(Sender: TObject);
begin
  if SaveDialog1.Execute then
    ClientDataSet1.SaveToFile (SaveDialog1.FileName);
end;

procedure TForm1.ButtonReloadClick(Sender: TObject);
begin
  if OpenDialog1.Execute then
    ClientDataSet1.LoadFromFile (OpenDialog1.FileName);
end;
```

After working off-line and modifying the local file, you can reload it and apply the updates to the server.

When you use the briefcase model, it's best to download the whole data set before saving it locally; as you'll recall, you can do that by setting the Packet-Records property of the ClientDataSet to -1. If you don't do this, you'll simply save the records that happened to be in the memory table, and the client application won't know about the other records still on the server.

Moving Multiple Data Packets at Once

In the examples we've built so far, we've simply placed one table in the server application and connected one ClientDataSet component to it in the client application. However, in many instances you might want access to multiple tables from the same client application, such as when the tables have a logical master/detail relationship.

As an example, we've built the MdServer application, which contains a remote data set that exports the Customer.DB and Order.DB tables from the DBDEMOS local database. This server wasn't built to demonstrate a specific feature, and the two tables aren't connected on the server side. We'll connect them on the client side.

To connect these tables on the client side, we can add to the remote data module's interface a custom function that returns data packets from both tables at once. This allows the client program to perform a single network operation, and simultaneously get data for both the master and detail tables. This is an advantage here, but it's even more important if you're working with a dozen tables instead of two. The practical effect is to reduce network traffic, but the aim of this example is also to show you how easy it is to customize the connection between the client and the server applications.

To add this new method to the remote data module's interface, simply select the source code of the data module in the editor, right-click on it, and select Add to Interface from the pop-up menu. In the dialog box that appears, type the following function:

```
procedure GetBoth (out Customer, Order: variant);
```

Delphi will now add the procedure to the interface in the type library, and will then open the data module's source code so you can add the code:

```
procedure TMdDataModule.GetBoth(out Customer, Order: OleVariant);
begin
  Customer := TableCustomers.Provider.Data;
  Order := TableOrders.Provider.Data;
end;
```

On the client side you'll have two different ways to retrieve the data: independently use the IProvider interfaces exported by the two tables, or use the new GetBoth procedure. We've added two DBGrid controls to the client and connected them via two DataSource components, which are in turn connected to two Client-DataSet components. Of course, the client application's main form also contains a RemoteServer component set to connect to the server we just built.

It's important to note that what we've done is set up a master/detail relationship between the two ClientDataSet components, as you can see in the following textual description of the form:

```
object Form1: TForm1
  Caption = 'Master-Detail Client'
  object Panel1: TPanel
    Align = alTop
    object Button1: TButton
      Caption = 'Get Both'
      OnClick = Button1Click
    end
  end
  object DBGrid1: TDBGrid
    Align = alTop
    DataSource = DataSource1
  end
  object Splitter1: TSplitter
    Cursor = crVSplit
    Align = alTop
    Beveled = False
  end
  object DBGrid2: TDBGrid
    Align = alClient
    DataSource = DataSource2
  end
  object ClientDataSet1: TClientDataSet
  end
  object ClientDataSet2: TClientDataSet
    IndexFieldNames = 'CustNo'
    FetchOnDemand = False
    MasterFields = 'CustNo'
    MasterSource = DataSource1
    PacketRecords = 0
  end
```

```
  object DataSource1: TDataSource
    DataSet = ClientDataSet1
  end
  object DataSource2: TDataSource
    DataSet = ClientDataSet2
  end
  object RemoteServer1: TRemoteServer
    ServerGUID = '{C5DDE906-2214-11D1-98D0-444553540000}
  end
end
```

By default, when you set up the master/detail relationship, Delphi sets the FetchOnDemand property of the detail ClientDataSet to False, and its Packet-Records property to zero. The reason for this is that we initially want to retrieve only the detail table's definition (or metadata), and then we'll let Delphi call the detail ClientDataSet component's AppendData method to fetch the actual records, based on the current record in the master ClientDataSet.

Notice in the listing above that we haven't set the provider's connection to the ClientDataSet component at design-time. Instead, we initialize the connection using the GetBoth procedure we've added to the server to fetch the data for both data sets. Here is the code:

```
procedure TForm1.Button1Click(Sender: TObject);
var
  Customers, Orders: Variant;
begin
  RemoteServer1.Connected := True;
  RemoteServer1.AppServer.GetBoth (
    Customers, Orders);
  ClientDataSet1.Data := Customers;
  ClientDataSet2.Data := Orders;
  ClientDataSet1.Open;
  ClientDataSet2.Open;
end;
```

You can see the MdClient example in action in Figure 19.9. The only minor problem with establishing the connection using code instead of a direct design-time connection is that when the master record has no detail record, you'll see an error message complaining that the provider or the data packet is missing.

FIGURE 19.9:

The MdServer and MdClient programs demonstrate how you can build a three-tier master/detail application.

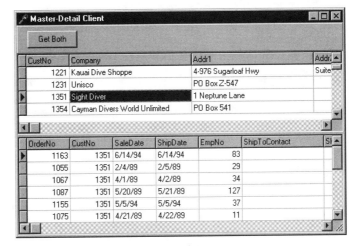

What's Next

Borland introduced support for a true three-tier architecture for the first time in Delphi 3. As we've suggested, you should expect Borland to extend this architecture to play a fundamental role in the future of client/server computing. For example, it's reasonable to expect that we'll be able to write client and server applications in different development environments (based on different languages)—not just in Delphi and C++Builder, but also in JBuilder.

Now that we've explored Delphi's new three-tier architecture, we're ready for our last step, an introduction to the techniques you can use to publish live databases on the Web. This will be the last chapter of the book.

Publishing a Database on the Web

- Static and Dynamic Web Pages

- Introducing CGI Programming

- CGI Database Programming

- Using Plain ISAPI

- Delphi 3 ISAPI Support

- The HTML Producer Components

- ActiveForms as Database Front-Ends

With the advent of the Internet era, writing programs for the World Wide Web has become commonplace. Since this is a dynamic area, the tools and techniques for Web programming change frequently, and it would be difficult to write about them comprehensively. Even if that were possible, this book is about Delphi programming, not Web programming. Of course, any Delphi developer planning to tackle Web projects needs a thorough grounding in HTML, HTTP, and related technologies.

Accordingly, we won't try to discuss the various approaches to Web programming, but will focus on a simple fact: You can write Web programs to run on the server computer or on the client computer. Programs that run on the server generally use the Common Gateway Interface (CGI) or one of the Web server extension APIs (such as NSAPI from Netscape or ISAPI from Microsoft). Programs that run on the client side are generally written in Java or based on the ActiveX technology. Delphi is capable of producing all of these types of programs except Java client-side programs. (And tools are starting to appear that will convert simple Delphi programs to equivalent Java programs.)

Here we'll focus on database publishing on the Web, and we'll leverage the specific components and tools provided in Delphi 3 Client/Server.

We'll begin by examining the Web server extensions, and then we'll move on to data-aware ActiveForm development. As usual, we'll build many examples. Keep in mind that while we'll discuss the available technologies in general, you can apply them to both Internet and intranet programming. (An *intranet* is an internal, private network that uses the same protocols and technologies as the Internet. As we'll see later on, it is in intranets that ActiveX and three-tier technologies will probably have a wider role.)

WARNING   To test most of this chapter's examples, you'll need access to a Web server. If you don't have one, you can download Microsoft's Personal Web Server for free (at www.microsoft.com), or you can acquire one of the personal servers from other vendors. Some of the sample programs are also available on Marco's Web site (www.marcocantu.com), so you can test them by simply pointing your Web browser to that site.

Static and Dynamic Web Pages

When you browse a Web site, you generally download static pages—HTML-format text files—from the Web server to your client computer. As a Web developer, you can create these pages manually, but for most businesses it makes more sense to build the static pages from information in a database. Using this approach, you're basically generating a snapshot of the data, which is quite reasonable if the data isn't subject to frequent changes (for example, a catalog that's updated only monthly).

NOTE
For an example of generating static HTML pages from database data, you can refer to the DbToHtml and the TableH examples in Chapter 24 of *Mastering Delphi 3*. The source code for those applications is available on this book's CD-ROM, in the folder for this chapter.

As an alternative to static HTML pages, you can build dynamic ones. To do this, you extract information directly from a database in response to the browser's request, so that the HTML sent by your application displays current data, not an old snapshot of the data. This approach makes sense if the data changes frequently. (A good example of this is the schedule for an airport, where departure and arrival information changes every minute.)

As we mentioned earlier, there are a couple of ways you can program custom behavior at the Web server, and these are ideal ways for you to generate HTML pages dynamically. The two most common protocols for programming Web servers are CGI (the Common Gateway Interface) and the Web server APIs.

An Overview of CGI

CGI is a standard protocol for communication between the client browser and the Web server. It's not a particularly efficient protocol, but it is widely used and is not platform-specific. This protocol allows the browser to both ask for and send data, and is based on the standard command-line input and output of an application (usually a console application). When the server detects a page request for the CGI application, it launches the application, passes command-line data from the page request to the application, and then sends the standard-output results from the application back to the client computer.

There are many tools and languages you can use to write CGI applications, and Delphi is only one of them. Given the obvious limitation that your Web server must be an Intel-based Windows NT or Windows 95 system, you can build some fairly sophisticated CGI programs in Delphi. As we'll see later on, Delphi 3 Client/Server also offers some specific support for creating CGI applications, which makes this even easier.

Despite the fact that it's called a standard, there are actually different flavors of CGI. Besides plain CGI, which uses the standard command-line input and output, along with environment variables, there is something called WinCGI. This newer incarnation of CGI uses an INI file passed as a command-line parameter to the application (instead of environment variables), and specific input and output files (instead of using command-line input/output). Server vendors developed WinCGI primarily for Visual Basic programmers, who cannot access environment variables. Another new variation, called FastCGI, is supposed to make the entire process of calling a CGI application much faster, but it's not widely supported yet.

The plain CGI protocol was modeled after Unix techniques, while WinCGI is more tailored to the Windows world. However, you can use both quite easily, and we'll focus mainly on plain CGI.

An Overview of ISAPI/NSAPI

A completely different approach is the use of the Web server APIs, ISAPI (Internet Server API) and NSAPI (Netscape Server API). These proprietary APIs allow you to write a DLL that the server loads into its own address space, and usually keeps in memory for some time. Once it loads the DLL, the server can execute individual requests via threads within the main process, instead of launching a new EXE, as you must do in CGI applications.

A page request comes into the server, the server loads the DLL if necessary and executes the appropriate code (which may launch a new thread to process the page request), and then that code sends back the appropriate data to the client that requested the page. Since this communication generally occurs in memory, this type of application is much faster, and a given system will be able to support more simultaneous page requests this way. However, a buggy DLL can crash the server, which is very unusual for a CGI application.

Another problem is that every server has its own API. NSAPI and ISAPI are similar, but there are important differences because NSAPI is designed to support both Intel and non-Intel processors. For Intel-based systems, ISAPI is rapidly becoming a de-facto standard.

<table>
<tr><td>TIP</td><td>Keep in mind that Delphi 3 Client/Server flattens the differences between CGI, WinCGI, and ISAPI by providing a common class framework. This way, you can easily turn a CGI application into a WinCGI one, or upgrade it to use the ISAPI model.</td></tr>
</table>

Introducing CGI Programming

Of course, there is much more to say in comparing these two server programming techniques as well as other available solutions. Instead of covering the theory behind these two techniques in detail, we'll show you some examples of plain CGI before moving to database-related, server-side applications. As we build an increasingly complex example, we can introduce some theory along the way.

What's the Time?

We'll begin our exploration of server-side programming techniques by building a very simple CGI application. Suppose you want to show the users of your Web site the local time. Of course, there's no way to hard-code the time information in a fixed HTML page, since time is dynamic by nature.

This example will be simple, because we don't need to process any data from the user; we just need to return an HTML file built on the fly. We'll start with a brand-new Delphi application and turn it into a console application using the appropriate linker option, or by adding the {$APPTYPE CONSOLE} compiler directive to the source code. The next step is to eliminate the main form (a console application produces output in a terminal window and doesn't use a normal window or form). Finally, we'll remove most of the project source code and replace it with the following statements:

```
program CgiDate;

{$APPTYPE CONSOLE}

uses
  SysUtils;
```

```
begin
  writeln ('CONTENT-TYPE: TEXT/HTML');
  writeln;
  writeln ('<HTML><HEAD>');
  writeln ('<TITLE>Time at this site</TITLE>');
  writeln ('</HEAD><BODY>');
  writeln ('<H1>Time at this site</H1>');
  writeln ('<HR>');
  writeln ('<H3>');
  writeln (FormatDateTime(
    '"Today is " dddd, mmmm d, yyyy,' +
      '"<p> and the time is" hh:mm:ss AM/PM',
    Now));
  writeln ('</H3>');
  writeln ('<HR>');
  writeln ('<I>Page generated by CgiDate.exe</I>');
  writeln ('</BODY></HTML>');
end.
```

This is the complete source code of our simple CGI application. As you can see
by examining the code, all we do is generate some lines of HTML text, using the
standard output device. If you execute this program directly, you'll see the text in
a terminal window. If you instead run it in a Web browser, the formatted HTML
text will appear in the browser window, as shown in Figure 20.1.

The format of the program's output is very simple. The first line generates a
description (CONTENT-TYPE), which you must follow with a blank line. The rest of
the code simply generates the HTML file. To activate this CGI program, create an
HTML file that links to it, as this fragment does:

```
<a href="/scripts/cgidate.exe"> Today </a>
```

> **NOTE**　The HTML file that contains the code above and the links to all the
> server-side applications of this chapter is available in the Scripts direc-
> tory of the companion CD, as Ch20Serv.HTM. In this same directory,
> you'll find all the files you must move to the *scripts* or *cgi-bin* directory
> in order to use the links. Also, keep in mind that you might have to
> update any configuration file that identifies the *scripts* directory to your
> Web server.

FIGURE 20.1:

The output of the CgiDate application, as seen in Microsoft's Internet Explorer

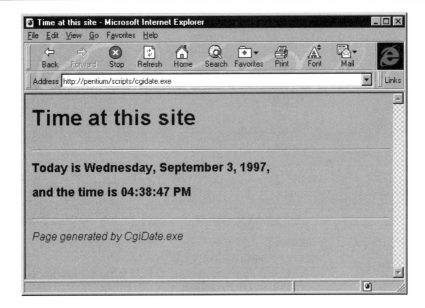

Processing the Command Line

This example works, but it's really too simple, since the output is invariably fixed and doesn't depend on the user input in any way. If we want to build database applications, we'll need a little more power.

A CGI application receives input in two ways:

- Its command-line parameters identify the URL of the page that activated it, and the URL usually includes extra parameters after the application name.

- The system uses a series of environment variables to pass further information to the CGI application. (In WinCGI the same information is passed via an INI file, instead of using environment variables.)

To demonstrate simple parameter passing, we'll extend the CgiDate example by letting the user pass different requests. Specifically, we'll let them request the time, the date, or both. Here is how you write a series of requests as HTML links:

```
<a href="/scripts/cgidate2.exe?date"> Date </a> <p>
<a href="/scripts/cgidate2.exe?time"> Time </a> <p>
<a href="/scripts/cgidate2.exe?both"> Both </a> <p>
<a href="/scripts/cgidate2.exe?wrong"> Wrong </a> <p>
<a href="/scripts/cgidate2.exe"> Missing </a> <p>
```

In the CGI application, you can easily retrieve the parameter by checking to see if there's any parameter (using the ParamCount function), and then extracting the value of ParamStr(1). If there's a parameter, the program compares it with one of the valid values, and produces an error message if it's invalid or missing. Here is the updated code:

```pascal
program CgiDate2;

{$APPTYPE CONSOLE}

uses
  SysUtils;

begin
  writeln ('CONTENT-TYPE: TEXT/HTML');
  writeln;
  writeln ('<HTML><HEAD>');
  writeln ('<TITLE>Time at this site</TITLE>');
  writeln ('</HEAD><BODY>');
  writeln ('<H1>Time at this site</H1>');
  writeln ('<HR>');
  writeln ('<H3>');
  if ParamCount > 0 then
  begin
    if ParamStr (1) = 'date' then
      writeln (FormatDateTime(
        '"Today is " dddd, mmmm d, yyyy',
        Now))
    else if ParamStr (1) = 'time' then
      writeln (FormatDateTime(
        '"The time is" hh:mm:ss AM/PM',
        Now))
    else if ParamStr (1) = 'both' then
      writeln (FormatDateTime(
        '"Today is " dddd, mmmm d, yyyy,' +
          '"<p> and the time is" hh:mm:ss AM/PM',
        Now))
    else
      writeln ('Error. Invalid parameter: ' +
        ParamStr (1) + '.')
  end
  else
```

```
        writeln ('Error. Missing parameter.');
    writeln ('</H3>');
    writeln ('<HR>');
    writeln ('<I>Page generated by CgiDate.exe </I>');
    writeln ('</BODY></HTML>');
end.
```

You can see the output of this example in Figure 20.2. Obviously, this program isn't too difficult to write. Unfortunately, you'll usually need to pass many complex parameters to your CGI applications. The parameters you pass are usually separated by the plus sign (+), which means they'll show up in the CGI application as a single parameter that contains embedded plus signs. This is necessary because a URL cannot include spaces.

FIGURE 20.2:

The output of the CgiDate2 example, when the input parameter is date

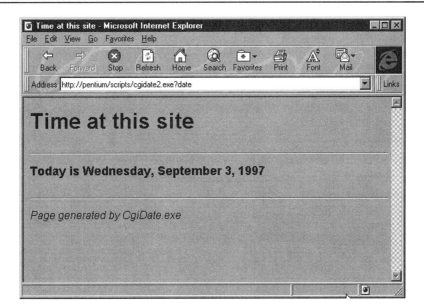

CGI Environment Variables

A second problem with URL-passed parameters is that URLs cannot exceed a given size. This means that if you need to pass several parameters to a CGI application, you'll need to use environment variables. Interestingly, you can use these same variables to retrieve system information. Table 20.1 lists the most important CGI system variables, along with a short description (we've omitted a few rarely used variables).

TABLE 20.1: The Most Important CGI Environment Variables

Environment variable	Description
SERVER_NAME	Host name (or IP address) of the Web server
SERVER_PROTOCOL	Protocol of the HTTP request
SERVER_SOFTWARE	Name and version of the Web server software
GATEWAY_INTERFACE	Version of CGI supported
REQUEST_METHOD	Method used by the request (can be GET or POST)
DOCUMENT_ROOT	Directory hosting documents or the Web server
PATH_TRANSLATED	Physical path relative to the server
HTTP_REFERER	URL of the document which has activated the CGI application
SCRIPT_NAME	Relative path of the CGI application being executed (based on the server's address)
PATH_INFO	Path passed to the CGI application, located between the name of the application and the query string
QUERY_STRING	Query passed to the program; when the request method is GET, this string is appended to the URL with a question mark
CONTENT_TYPE	MIME type of the data, when the request method is POST
HTTP_ACCEPT	MIME types the remote browser can accept
CONTENT_LENGTH	Length in bytes of the data passed via standard input, when the request method is POST
REMOTE_HOST	Name of the host of the remote user (if it can be identified)
REMOTE_USER	Name of the remote user (if available)
REMOTE_IDENT	IP address of the remote user
HTTP_FROM	E-mail address of the remote user (available depending on the browser's security features)
HTTP_USER_AGENT	Name and version of the browser of the remote user
HTTP_COOKIE	List of cookies sent by the browser of the remote user

You'll notice that the PATH_INFO and QUERY_STRING parameters are separate portions of the command line parameter that we pass to the CGI application. For example, in the command-line parameter

```
href="/scripts/cgidate2.exe/pathname?date"
```

the path is pathname and the query is date.

To demonstrate how you can fetch environment variables, we've built a simple CGI application that displays some of them. The code is actually quite simple, and the only unusual element of this example (GetVars) is the call to the GetEnvironmentVariable Windows API function:

```pascal
program CgiVars;

{$APPTYPE CONSOLE}

uses
  Windows;

const
  VarList: array [1..17] of string [30] =
    ('SERVER_NAME', 'SERVER_PROTOCOL',
     'SERVER_PORT', 'SERVER_SOFTWARE',
     'GATEWAY_INTERFACE', 'REQUEST_METHOD',
     'PATH_TRANSLATED', 'HTTP_REFERER',
     'SCRIPT_NAME', 'PATH_INFO',
     'QUERY_STRING', 'HTTP_ACCEPT',
     'REMOTE_HOST', 'REMOTE_USER',
     'REMOTE_ADDR', 'REMOTE_IDENT',
     'HTTP_USER_AGENT');

var
  I: Integer;
  ReqVar: string;
  VarValue: array [0..200] of Char;

begin
  writeln('Content type: text/html');
  writeln;
  writeln('<HTML><HEAD>');
  writeln('<TITLE>CGI Variables</TITLE>');
  writeln('</HEAD><BODY>');
```

```
      writeln('<H1>CGI Variables</H1>');
      writeln('<HR><PRE>');

      // show the variables listed in the array
      for I := Low (VarList) to High (VarList) do
      begin
        ReqVar := VarList[I];
        if (GetEnvironmentVariable (PChar(ReqVar),
            VarValue, 200) > 0) then
        else
          VarValue := '';
        writeln (VarList[I] + ' = ' + VarValue);
      end;
      writeln('</PRE></BODY></HTML>');
    end.
```

You can see the output of this program in Figure 20.3. By combining the techniques of the last two examples (parameter passing via the command line and via environment variables), we can now move on and build a more powerful CGI application, one that connects with a database.

CGI Database Programming

After these preliminary examples, we're now ready to build a database CGI application. This will be the last CGI example that we'll build without using the specific support provided by Delphi 3. Later, we'll duplicate this example using those tools.

Our CGI database application will allow users to browse an entire table (in this case the Employee.DB table in DBDemos) or look for specific records. The program is quite complex, so we'll discuss it in sections.

Listing the Records of a Table

First, let's examine the core source code of a procedure that lists all the records of this database table. Of course, before we can execute this code, we'll have to declare and open a Table component, and then connect it to the proper database table:

```
var
  Table1: TTable;
```

```
begin
  ShowHeader;
  // create and connect the table
  Table1 := TTable.Create (nil);
  try
    Table1.DatabaseName := 'DBDEMOS';
    Table1.TableName := 'Employee.db';
    Table1.IndexName := 'ByName';
    Table1.Open;
    ShowTableIndex
  finally
    Table1.Close;
    Table1.Free;
  end;
  // show footer
  writeln('</BODY></HTML>');
end.
```

FIGURE 20.3:

The output of the CgiVars example as seen in Internet Explorer

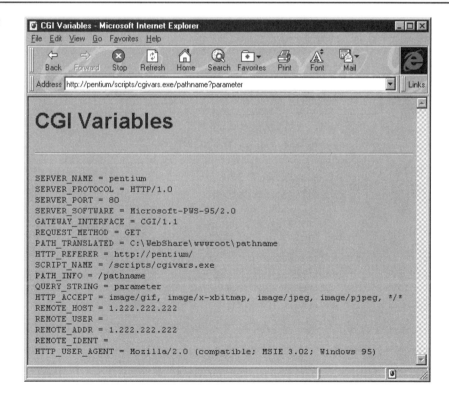

The ShowHeader procedure simply creates the initial section of the HTML file, as usual:

```
procedure ShowHeader;
begin
  writeln('Content type: text/html');
  writeln;
  writeln('<HTML><HEAD>');
  writeln('<TITLE>CgiEmpl</TITLE>');
  writeln('</HEAD><BODY>');
  writeln('<H2>CGI Employee Demo</H2>');
  writeln('<H3>from Delphi Developers Handbook</H3>');
  writeln('<HR>');
end;
```

Here is a first version of the code, which we use to produce a list of employees:

```
procedure ShowTableIndex;
begin
  // show a summary of the entire table
  Table1.First;
  // show a list
  writeln ('<ul>');
  while not Table1.EOF do
  begin
    // show each name
    writeln (Format (
      '<li> %s %s',
      [Table1.FieldByName ('FirstName').AsString,
      Table1.FieldByName ('LastName').AsString]));
    Table1.Next;
  end;
  // end of the list
  writeln ('</ul>');
end;
```

This code is certainly interesting, but we want to allow the user to select a specific employee and see the details about him or her. In fact, the program allows you to use the following syntax:

```
<a href="/scripts/cgiempl.exe?Johnson">Look for "Johnson"</a>
```

to search for a specific person in the list. You can also provide a second parameter for the name (since some of the employees in the database have the same last name):

```
<a href="/scripts/cgiempl.exe?Johnson+Leslie">
  Look for "Leslie Johnson"</a>
```

Of course you don't want to write HTML code that references the various records, so you can let the CGI application do so. To accomplish this, we first must determine the script's URL name:

```
var
  ScriptName: array [0..100] of Char;
begin
  GetEnvironmentVariable ('SCRIPT_NAME',
    ScriptName, sizeof (ScriptName));
```

Now we can update the code of the ShowTableIndex procedure, and let it generate the links. Here's the core of the procedure:

```
while not Table1.EOF do
begin
  // show names with a link to the CGI application
  writeln (Format (
    '<li> <a HREF="%s?%s+%s">%s %s</a>',
    [ScriptName,
    Table1.FieldByName ('LastName').AsString,
    Table1.FieldByName ('FirstName').AsString,
    Table1.FieldByName ('FirstName').AsString,
    Table1.FieldByName ('LastName').AsString]));
  Table1.Next;
end;
```

This writeln statement generates HTML code such as:

```
<li> <a HREF="/scripts/cgiempl.exe?Baldwin+Janet">
  Janet Baldwin</a>
<li> <a HREF="/scripts/cgiempl.exe?Bender+Oliver H.">
  Oliver H. Bender</a>
```

Now that we're displaying a list of live links, as shown in Figure 20.4, we can consider how we'll display each record.

FIGURE 20.4:

The list of live links displayed by the CgiEmpl application when it is activated with no parameters

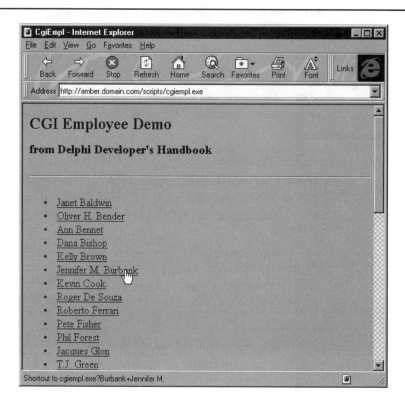

Showing a Specific Record

When a user clicks on one of the links generated by the ShowTableIndex procedure, or one of the links we manually inserted in the HTML file, the CGI application can process this information normally by examining the parameters on the
command line. To do so, we'll replace the call to ShowTableIndex in the first listing above with the following code:

```
if ParamCount <= 0 then
  ShowTableIndex
else
begin
  // select the record
  if ParamCount = 1 then
    Table1.FindNearest ([ParamStr (1)])
  else
```

```
    Table1.FindNearest ([ParamStr (1), ParamStr (2)]);
  // show a single record
  ShowRecord;
end;
```

Here we use the FindNearest method to locate the current record, passing it one of two parameters. Then we call ShowRecord to display the names of the fields and their values, all inside an HTML table:

```
procedure ShowRecord;
var
  I: Integer;
begin
  writeln ('<table border>');
  for I := 1 to Table1.FieldCount - 1 do
    writeln ('<tr><td>' + Table1.Fields [I].FieldName +
      '</td><td>' + Table1.Fields [I].AsString +
      '</td></tr>');
  writeln ('</table><hr>');
end;
```

NOTE   HTML tables are marked by the <table> and </table> tags. Each row of the table is marked by the <tr> and </tr> tags, and each data cell of each row is indicated by the <td> and </td> tags. You can also use the <th> and </th> flags to indicate header cells and define a header row for the table.

This code is quite simple. What's more complex is that we want to add another small navigational table below the table that displays the record data, as you can see in Figure 20.5. To accomplish this, we need to extract the first and last names of the employees from the preceding and following records (if they are available), and then add a corresponding link. When the current record is at the beginning or end of the file, the program displays the same caption (*Next* or *Prior*), but there's no link and the text appears in italics. Finally, we've provided a fixed link to retrieve the index, and therefore the list of records:

```
writeln ('<table border><tr>');
  // add pointer to the index
  writeln ('<td><a HREF="' +
    ScriptName + '"> Index </a></td>');
  // add pointer to the prior record
  Table1.Prior;
```

```
if not Table1.BOF then
begin
  writeln (Format (
    '<td><a HREF="%s?%s+%s"> Prior </a></td>',
    [ScriptName,
    Table1.FieldByName ('LastName').AsString,
    Table1.FieldByName ('FirstName').AsString]));
  // get back
  Table1.Next;
end
else
  // empty spot
  writeln ('<td><i>Prior</i></td>');
// add pointer to the next record
Table1.Next;
if not Table1.EOF then
  write (Format (
    '<td><a HREF="%s?%s+%s"> Next </a></td>',
    [ScriptName,
    Table1.FieldByName ('LastName').AsString,
    Table1.FieldByName ('FirstName').AsString]))
else
  // empty spot
  writeln ('<td><i>Next</i></td>');
// end of the line and table
writeln ('</tr></table>');
```

A better alternative to displaying the words *Next* or *Prior* might be to copy Delphi's DBNavigator component bitmaps, and then create navigational buttons using these images.

An HTML Search Form

Finally, we want to let users search for a specific record in a CGI-accessed table. They might want to search using an incomplete portion of the last name, search by first name, or do something similar. In either case, we'll need to use a different CGI technique, POST, and then read the information from the standard input device with our CGI application.

Besides formatting text in various ways, you can also use HTML to prepare forms. As in Delphi, a form is a series of controls (typically, things like input

FIGURE 20.5:

A record's detailed information, generated by the CgiEmpl application. Notice the table of links below the data table. In this case, the *Prior* link is disabled because we are on the first record.

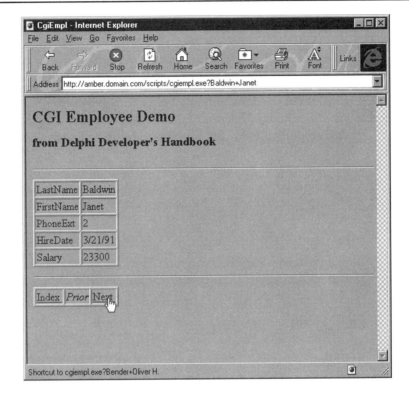

fields), but HTML forms appear within a browser window. There are visual tools to help you design these forms, or you can manually enter the proper HTML code. The available controls include buttons, input text (or edit boxes), selections (or combo boxes), and radio buttons (or input buttons). You can define buttons as specific types, such as Submit or Reset, which imply a standard behavior. In Table 20.2 you can see a summary of the various input types.

TABLE 20.2: HTML Form Components and Their Tags

Name	Tag	Description
Text field	type= text	An edit box where a user can enter text. You can specify the width of the field and the maximum number of input characters.

TABLE 20.2 CONTINUED: HTML Form Components and Their Tags

Name	Tag	Description
Masked text field	type=password	Just like an edit box, but asterisks appear when you enter text.
Radio button	type=radio	An exclusive selection radio button, marked as checked if the user selects it.
Check box	type=checkbox	A nonexclusive selection check box, marked as checked if the user selects it.
Submit push button	type=submit	A button that automatically sends the contents of the form to the server application, using the program name that appears in the action parameter of the form.
Reset push button	type=reset	A button that automatically clears the contents of other fields in the form.
Custom push button	type=image	A custom push button, which displays a specified image file, and sends the coordinates of the mouse click to the Web server application.
Multiple choice lists	<option>	A combo box or a plain list (depending on the value of the size attribute). You define the list items using the <select> and </select> tags.
Multiline text fields	<textarea>	While a text field is limited to one line, these allow multiples lines of text entry (similar to a memo component in Delphi).

As an example, the following code generated the HTML form illustrated in Figure 20.6:

```
<h4>CgiEmp Search form</h4>

<form action="/scripts/cgiempl.exe" method="POST">
Last Name: <input type="text" name="LastName">
<p>
First Name: <input type="text" name="FirstName">
<p>
<input type="Submit">
</form>
```

FIGURE 20.6:

The simple HTML form used to search the Employee database table, using the CgiEmpl application

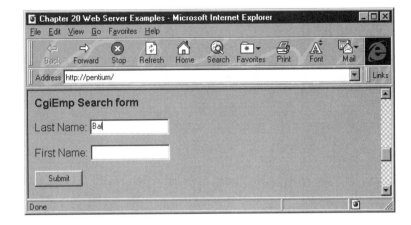

TIP

To obtain more attractive output, you can place the HTML form's controls inside a table, as we'll do in a later example.

The form displays two edit boxes and a *Submit* button. The browser will execute the action parameter of the form when the user clicks the button. Since the method parameter is POST, the browser won't pass the data via environment variables, but will do so through the standard input. See the sidebar "GET and POST CGI Request Methods" for more information on these two techniques for passing data to a CGI application.

First, the CGI application should determine which request method the form uses. We do this in the main program, shown here in its final version:

```
var
  ScriptName: array [0..100] of Char;
  MethodName: array [0..5] of Char;
  Table1: TTable;
begin
  ShowHeader;
  // get the name of the CGI script and the method
  GetEnvironmentVariable ('SCRIPT_NAME',
    ScriptName, sizeof (ScriptName));
  GetEnvironmentVariable ('REQUEST_METHOD',
    MethodName, sizeof (MethodName));
```

GET and POST CGI Request Methods

There are two ways, called *request methods*, by which a CGI application can receive input. The POST method passes data via standard input (accessed by the CGI application using a read call).

When you use the GET method, the browser passes user input via the QUERY_STRING environment variable, which reduces the number of input/output operations slightly. However, with this approach, the amount of data you can transfer is limited by the size of the environment variables; using the standard input you can pass much more information.

Another difference is that when you use the POST method, the data is appended to the URL, which can become very long and look quite strange. In a program, we can easily determine which technique the form uses by reading the REQUEST_METHOD environment variable.

```
// create and connect the table
Table1 := TTable.Create (nil);
try
  Table1.DatabaseName := 'DBDEMOS';
  Table1.TableName := 'Employee.db';
  Table1.IndexName := 'ByName';
  Table1.Open;
  // if the method is POST, then read in the data
  if StrComp (MethodName, 'POST') = 0 then
  begin
    GetToRecordPost;
    ShowRecord;
  end
  else if ParamCount <= 0 then
    ShowTableIndex
  else
  begin
    // select the record
    if ParamCount = 1 then
      Table1.FindNearest ([ParamStr (1)])
    else
      Table1.FindNearest ([ParamStr (1),
        ParamStr (2)]);
```

```
    // show a single record
      ShowRecord;
    end;
  finally
    Table1.Close;
    Table1.Free;
  end;
  // show footer
  writeln('</BODY></HTML>');
end.
```

The core of this section of the application is the GetToRecordPost procedure. This procedure sets the length of a string (DataStr) according to the value of the CONTENT_LENGTH CGI environment variable, and then reads the input data into that string. The program then extracts the data from the First Name and Last Name input boxes (using the ExtractFromData function), and determines the appropriate search method, either using the index (FindNearest) or not (Locate):

```
procedure GetToRecordPost;
var
  DataStr, First, Last: string;
  ContentLength: array [0..10] of Char;
begin
  GetEnvironmentVariable ('CONTENT_LENGTH',
    ContentLength, sizeof (ContentLength));
  SetLength (DataStr, StrToIntDef (ContentLength, 100));
  readln (DataStr);
  First := ExtractFromData (DataStr, 'FirstName');
  Last := ExtractFromData (DataStr, 'LastName');
  writeln ('<i>Request: Last Name = "' + Last +
    '", First Name = "' + First + '"</i><p>');
  if Last <> '' then
    Table1.FindNearest ([Last, First])
  else
    // look for the first name only
    Table1.Locate('FirstName', First,
      [loPartialKey, loCaseInsensitive]);
end;
```

An important element of this approach is the function we use to extract the data from the input string, ExtractFromData. To understand this function, let's examine the format of the request:

```
LastName=johnson&FirstName=leslie
```

The first part of each section is the input text field's name, and the second is the actual value. The sections for each input field are separated by the & character. To view this information you can add the following line to the GetRecordPost procedure:

```
writeln ('<i>Debug: DataStr = ' + DataStr + '</i><p>');
```

(This statement is actually in the source code of this example on the companion CD, but we've commented it out. To enable it you'll simply need to remove the comment marker.)

The ExtractFromData function searches for the requested field name followed by the = character. Then it scans for the & character, which will determine the end of the Result string. Here's the code:

```
function ExtractFromData (
  DataStr: string; SearchTag: string): string;
var
  nPos: Integer;
begin
  nPos := Pos (SearchTag + '=', DataStr);
  if nPos > 0 then
  begin
    Result := Copy (DataStr, nPos + 1 + Length (SearchTag),
      Length (DataStr) - nPos);
    nPos := Pos ('&', Result);
    if nPos > 0 then
      Result := Copy (Result, 1, nPos - 1);
  end
  else
    Result := '';
end;
```

The output of the application here is similar to the plain record output, although this time you can also view the request, as you can see by comparing Figure 20.7 with Figure 20.5.

This is the final version of the CgiEmpl example, a rather complete example of a CGI database application written in Delphi. We'll now start focusing on writing ISAPI applications, first by writing all the code, and then by using the support provided by Delphi 3. After we review the basics of this type of application, we'll return to building database applications, and we'll rewrite this program using Delphi 3 support for ISAPI.

FIGURE 20.7:

After a search, the record information generated by the CgiEmpl application is prefixed with the request.

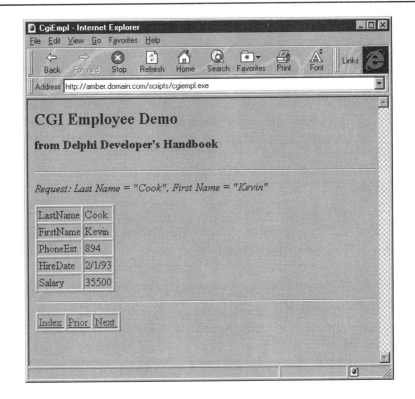

NOTE   The CgiEmpl example we've just built is a CGI application that accesses a Paradox table via the Borland Database Engine. Since this CGI application executes once for every request, it will actually load and unload the BDE each time it runs. This is a good reason to use ISAPI, as discussed next, but it's also a reason to consider accessing the data from a plain file, or by using the custom data set component we built in Chapter 18. This will undoubtedly speed up the CGI application, and make the Web site seem more responsive.

Using Plain ISAPI

As we mentioned at the beginning of the chapter, there are a few good reasons for using a Web server extension based on a server API, instead of using CGI. The most obvious reason is efficiency: A CGI program executes once for each call (loading and unloading all its resources each time), and uses files to pass information. In contrast, the server can load a server API DLL and keep it in memory, and can pass information to the DLL directly via memory buffers.

The main drawback to server API DLLs is that their tight integration with the server is an Achilles' heel: if the DLL crashes or produces memory leaks, the entire Web server can crash. Another problem is complexity; server extensions should generate and maintain a separate thread for each request, to avoid conflicts and optimize performance. Finally, you must shut down the Web server to replace or remove an existing DLL.

> **NOTE**
>
> We'll actually focus on just one of the server APIs, ISAPI, promoted by Microsoft for its Web Server product. However, this one is supported by most of the other servers running on the Windows NT platform (the only Web server platform we can target with Delphi applications).

ISAPI DLLs are not very different from plain Windows DLLs. However, ISAPI DLLs export a couple of specific functions that the Web server will call when the browser issues a special type of request. How do you write an ISAPI DLL? That's actually quite simple. The DLL must export the first two of the following three functions:

```
function GetExtensionVersion(var Ver:
  THSE_VERSION_INFO): BOOL; stdcall;
function HttpExtensionProc(var ECB:
  TEXTENSION_CONTROL_BLOCK): DWORD; stdcall;
function TerminateExtension(dwFlags: DWORD): BOOL; stdcall;
```

The server calls the first function when it loads the DLL for the first time, and the last function (which is optional) when it's ready to unload the DLL. The GetExtensionVersion function accepts a single parameter, which is a record with the following structure:

```
type
  THSE_VERSION_INFO = packed record
    dwExtensionVersion: DWORD; // should be $00010000
    // description of the ISAPI DLL
    lpszExtensionDesc: array [0..HSE_MAX_EXT_DLL_NAME_LEN-1]
      of Char;
  end;
```

The function should return True to indicate success, or the server will immediately terminate the DLL and unload it. The primary function is HttpExtensionProc, which the server calls for every request sent to the DLL. The function accepts one parameter, defined as follows (in the Isapi2 unit, part of Delphi's Windows API support):

```
type
  TEXTENSION_CONTROL_BLOCK = packed record
    cbSize: DWORD;                  // size of this struct
    dwVersion: DWORD;               // version info of this spec
    ConnID: HCONN;                  // Context number not to be modified!
    dwHttpStatusCode: DWORD;        // HTTP Status code
    // null-terminated log info specific to this Extension DLL
    lpszLogData: array [0..HSE_LOG_BUFFER_LEN-1] of Char;
    lpszMethod: PChar;              // REQUEST_METHOD
    lpszQueryString: PChar;         // QUERY_STRING
    lpszPathInfo: PChar;            // PATH_INFO
    lpszPathTranslated: PChar;      // PATH_TRANSLATED
    cbTotalBytes: DWORD;            // Total bytes indicated from client
    cbAvailable: DWORD;             // Available number of bytes
    lpbData: Pointer;               // pointer to cbAvailable bytes
    lpszContentType: PChar;         // Content type of client data

    GetServerVariable: TGetServerVariableProc;
    WriteClient: TWriteClientProc;
    ReadClient: TReadClientProc;
    ServerSupportFunction: TServerSupportFunctionProc;
  end;
```

While the purpose of most fields in the first section is easy to understand, the last four fields probably seem quite strange. They are function pointers you can use as follows:

GetServerVariable provides access to the server variables not available inside the extension control block. This gives you access to all the CGI variables we discussed previously.

WriteClient writes data for the client to a buffer, using HTML or some other format.

ReadClient reads data from the client, but is useful only in the rare cases in which the data exceeds 48KB, the maximum size of the memory block referenced by the lpbData field.

ServerSupportFunction provides the ISAPI application with some additional general-purpose functions, as well as server-specific functions.

To understand these function pointers better, it's worth examining their parameters (again, these aren't listed in the help file):

```
type
  TGetServerVariableProc = function (hConn: HCONN;
    VariableName: PChar; Buffer: Pointer; var Size: DWORD):
    BOOL stdcall;
  TWriteClientProc = function (ConnID: HCONN; Buffer: Pointer;
    var Bytes: DWORD; dwReserved: DWORD): BOOL stdcall;
  TReadClientProc  = function (ConnID: HCONN; Buffer: Pointer;
    var Size: DWORD): BOOL stdcall;
  TServerSupportFunctionProc = function (hConn: HCONN;
    HSERRequest: DWORD; Buffer: Pointer; Size: LPDWORD;
    DataType: LPDWORD ): BOOL stdcall;
```

You'll notice that all these functions require the handle of the connection, known as the connection ID, as their first parameter. The server passes this value to the DLL in the ConnID field of the extension control block, and the client passes it back to identify itself. The server might generate multiple simultaneous requests, and uses this ID to track the various connections.

A Simple ISAPI DLL

We'll write most of the ISAPI examples of this chapter using the specific Delphi 3 approach. However, it's important to give you an idea of what bare-bones ISAPI development is like. This example simply displays some fixed text, the value of the ISAPI DLL's pathname (removing the initial /), and the current date and time. With what you've learned about ISAPI DLLs in the last section, the source should be quite easy to understand:

```
library IsapiDem;

uses
  SysUtils, Classes, Windows, Isapi2;

function GetExtensionVersion (
  var Ver: THSE_VERSION_INFO): BOOL; stdcall;
begin
  with Ver do
```

```
begin
  dwExtensionVersion := $00010000;
  StrCopy (lpszExtensionDesc, 'First DDH Isapi Demo');
end;
Result := True;
end;

function HttpExtensionProc (
  var ECB: TEXTENSION_CONTROL_BLOCK): DWORD; stdcall;
var
  OutStr: string;
  StrLength: Integer;
begin
  with ECB do
  begin
    OutStr :=
      '<HTML><HEAD><TITLE>First DDH Isapi Demo</TITLE></HEAD><BODY>' +
      '<H2><CENTER>First DDH Isapi Demo</CENTER></H2>' +
      'Hello DDH Readers...<p><hr>' +
      '<b>Activated by ' + PChar (@lpszPathInfo[1]) + '</b><p>' +
      '<i>From IsapiDLL on ' + DateToStr (Now) +
      ' at ' + TimeToStr (Now) + '</i>' +
      '</body></html>';
    StrLength := Length (OutStr);
    WriteClient(ConnID, PChar (OutStr), StrLength, 0);

  end;
  Result := HSE_STATUS_SUCCESS;
end;

exports
  GetExtensionVersion,
  HttpExtensionProc;

end.
```

You can see the output of this simple ISAPI DLL in Figure 20.8, where we've activated the DLL using the following link:

```
<li> <a href="/scripts/IsapiDem.dll/marco">First Isapi Demo</a>
```

FIGURE 20.8:

The output of the simple IsapiDem DLL

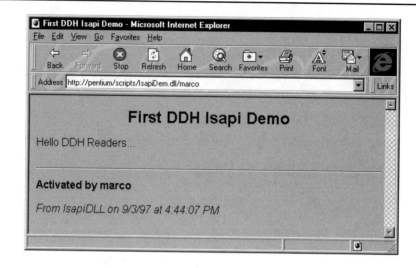

Delphi 3 ISAPI Support

All the CGI and ISAPI examples we've built up to now have used a plain and direct approach to the protocol and API, and haven't taken advantage of any specific Delphi components or features. We did this for two reasons: first, to introduce and focus on the foundations of these two technologies, and second, to let every Delphi programmer try the examples.

Along the way, you've probably noticed that we haven't used good object-oriented techniques and built a component to encapsulate CGI or ISAPI. The reason for this is simple: Client/Server Delphi already includes a framework that provides this support. The fact that this support is available only in the Client/Server Suite edition of Delphi is one reason we didn't introduce it up front. Using the information that we've just reviewed, everyone should be able to understand Delphi's CGI/ISAPI framework and appreciate its helpfulness. Readers who don't own the Client/Server version will be able to adapt the examples using the direct API approach we've just taken.

In addition to Borland's components, there are several third-party companies which offer their own Internet component frameworks for Delphi. The two best-known are probably WebHub (from HREF) and Web Solution Builder (from Shoreline Software), but there are many others. Evaluation copies of both WebHub and Web Solution Builder can be found on the companion CD.

The Building Blocks

In Delphi 3 Client/Server, you can begin developing an ISAPI application very easily. On the first page (*New*) of the Object Repository, select the Web Server Application icon. The subsequent dialog box will offer you three alternatives, ISAPI, CGI, and WinCGI, as you can see in Figure 20.9. If you select the first option, Delphi will generate the basic structure of an ISAPI application for you.

FIGURE 20.9:

The alternative options for building a Web server application in Delphi 3 Client/Server Suite

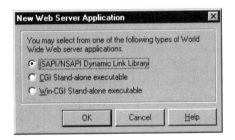

The application that Delphi generates (no matter which type you choose) is based on the TWebModule class, a container very similar to a data module, but with specific properties and editors to support CGI, WinCGI, and ISAPI applications.

NOTE   Instead of basing your application on a WebModule, you can use a plain data module and add a WebDispatcher component to it. This is a good approach if you want to turn an existing Delphi application into a Web server extension. The WebModule incorporates the WebDispatcher, and doesn't require it as a separate component.

The WebModule code is similar to that of a form or data module, as we'll see in a moment, but the code of the library is worth looking at:

```
library Project1;

uses
  HTTPApp, ISAPIApp,
  Unit1 in 'Unit1.pas' {WebModule1: TWebModule};

{$R *.RES}

exports
  GetExtensionVersion,
  HttpExtensionProc,
  TerminateExtension;

begin
  Application.Initialize;
  Application.CreateForm(TWebModule1, WebModule1);
  Application.Run;
end.
```

Although this is a library that exports the ISAPI functions, the code looks similar to that of an application. However, it uses a trick—the Application object used by this program is not the typical global object of class TApplication, but an object of a new class. This new Application object is of class TISAPIApplication (or TCGIApplication if you've built that type of application), which derives from TWebApplication. You'll find these class definitions (along with many others) in the HTTPApp, ISAPIApp, and CGIApp units.

Although these application classes provide the foundations, you won't generally use them very often (just as you don't use the Application object very often in a form-based Delphi application). The most important operations take place in the WebModule. This component derives from TCustomWebDispatcher, which provides support for all the input and output of our programs.

In fact, the TCustomWebDispatcher class defines Request and Response properties, which store the client request and the response we're going to send back to the client. Each of these properties is defined using a base class (TWebRequest and TWebResponse), but an application initializes them using a specific object (such as the TISAPIRequest and TISAPIResponse subclasses). These classes make available all the information passed to the server, and so you have a single, simple approach to accessing all the information. The same is true of a response, which is very easy to manipulate. One advantage to this approach is that an ISAPI DLL written with this framework is very similar to a CGI application; in fact, they are frequently identical in the custom source code you write.

TWebRequest is an abstract class, which defines a generic HTTP client request. A list of the abstract methods (extracted from the HttpApp unit, part of Delphi's Internet support) should give you a better understanding of the operations available in either an ISAPI or a CGI server:

```
type
  TWebRequest = class(TObject)
  public
    // Read count bytes from client
    function ReadClient(var Buffer; Count: Integer): Integer;
      virtual; abstract;
    // Read count characters as a string from client
    function ReadString(Count: Integer): string; virtual; abstract;
    // Translate a relative URI to a local absolute path
    function TranslateURI(const URI: string): string; virtual; abstract;
    // Write count bytes back to client
    function WriteClient(var Buffer; Count: Integer): Integer;
      virtual; abstract;
    // Write string contents back to client
    function WriteString(const AString: string): Boolean;
      virtual; abstract;
    // Utility to extract fields from a given string buffer
    procedure ExtractFields(Separators, WhiteSpace: TCharSet;
      Content: PChar; Strings: TStrings);
    // Fill the given string list with the content fields
    // as the result of a POST method
    procedure ExtractContentFields(Strings: TStrings);
    // Fill the given string list with values from the
    // cookie header field
    procedure ExtractCookieFields(Strings: TStrings);
    // Fill the given TStrings with the values from the Query data
    // (data following the "?" in the URL)
    procedure ExtractQueryFields(Strings: TStrings);
    // Read an arbitrary HTTP/Server Field not listed here
    function GetFieldByName(const Name: string): string;
      virtual; abstract;
    // The request method as an enumeration
```

```
property MethodType: TMethodType
  read FMethodType;
...
```

In addition to this list of methods (implemented by the subclasses), TWebRequest has several properties. You can use a few of these properties (ContentFields, CookieFields, and QueryFields) to access some of the data provided, and you can use several others to access the environment variables. All of these properties are indexed, which means they map to a single function, and pass a numeric index to it. The definition

```
property Method: string
  index 0 read GetStringVariable;
```

corresponds to writing

```
GetStringVariable (1)
```

The list of the available environment variables is quite long; here are their names (the types are string or Integer):

Method	ProtocolVersion	URL
Query	PathInfo	PathTranslated
Authorization	CacheControl	Cookie
Date	Accept	From
Host	IfModifiedSince	Referer
UserAgent	ContentEncoding	ContentType
ContentLength	ContentVersion	Content
Connection	DerivedFrom	Expires
Title	RemoteAddr	RemoteHost
ScriptName	ServerPort	

Similarly, the TWebResponse class encapsulates a generic HTTP response and defines virtual abstract methods that are implemented by the subclasses:

```
type
  TWebResponse = class(TObject)
  public
    function GetCustomHeader(const Name: string): String;
    procedure SendResponse; virtual; abstract;
```

```
  procedure SendRedirect(const URI: string); virtual; abstract;
  procedure SendStream(AStream: TStream); virtual; abstract;
  procedure SetCookieField(Values: TStrings;
    const ADomain, APath: string; AExpires: TDateTime;
    ASecure: Boolean);
  procedure SetCustomHeader(const Name, Value: string);
  ...
```

In addition to many other properties (some of which also access the environment variables), there are a few you can use to return data of different types:

```
  property StatusCode: Integer...
  property Content: string...
  property ContentStream: TStream...
```

If this is the structure of Borland's framework, how do you write the application code? Well, in the WebModule, you can use the Actions editor (shown in Figure 20.10) to define a series of actions (stored in the Actions array property) depending on the pathname of the request. This way, your application can easily respond to requests with different pathnames, and you can then let the WebModule call a different OnAction event handler for every possible pathname. Of course, you can omit the pathname to handle a generic request.

FIGURE 20.10:

The Actions property editor of the Web-Module, along with the properties of one of the actions in the Object Inspector

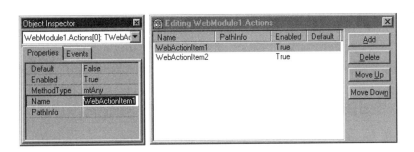

The end result is that you will define pathnames (that is, the last section of the URL) that correspond to the actions you want the WebModule to take, and then you'll define OnAction event handlers that map to those pathnames. When you define the accompanying HTML pages that launch the application, the links will make page requests to the URLs for each of those paths.

NOTE   Having one single ISAPI DLL that can perform different operations depending on a parameter (in this case the pathname) allows the server to keep a copy of this DLL in memory and respond much faster to user requests. The same is true for a CGI application: the server has to run several instances, but can cache the file and make it available faster.

The OnAction event is where you put the code to specify the *response* to a given *request*, the two main parameters passed to the event handler:

```
procedure TWebModule1.WebModule1WebActionItem1Action(
    Sender: TObject; Request: TWebRequest;
    Response: TWebResponse; var Handled: Boolean);
begin

end;
```

To let other actions handle this request, you'll set the last parameter, Handled, to False. Otherwise, the default value is True, and once you've handled the request with your action, the WebModule assumes you're finished.

Most of an ISAPI application's code will be in the OnAction event handlers for the actions defined in the WebModule container. These actions receive a request from the client and return a response using the TWebRequest and TWebResponse abstract types. The definitions of the actual types for the request and the response depend on the type of server application we're building. To make sure you understand this process, let's build an example step by step.

Building a Multipurpose WebModule

To demonstrate how easily you can build a feature-rich ISAPI application using Delphi's support, we'll create an ISAPI DLL, called IsaMulti, which implements almost all the features of the entire set of CGI applications we built in the first part of the chapter, including database support. A key element is the list of actions we're going to support with this application, which you can see in the Actions editor in Figure 20.11.

FIGURE 20.11:

The actions of the IsaMulti example, as shown by the Actions editor. Notice that we've renamed each action object.

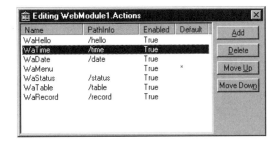

If you examine the figure or the example code, you'll notice that we've given a specific name to every action, instead of using the default names, such as `WebActionItem1`. We've also given meaningful names to the OnAction event handlers; for instance, `HelloAction` as a method name should be much more understandable than the `WebModule1WebActionItem1Action` name automatically generated by Delphi. The list of actions and event handlers is present in the WebModule's form description, which also references a database table we'll use later on:

```
object WebModule1: TWebModule1
  Actions = <
    item
      Name = 'WaHello'
      PathInfo = '/hello'
      OnAction = HelloAction
    end
    item
      Name = 'WaTime'
      PathInfo = '/time'
      OnAction = TimeAction
    end
    item
      Name = 'WaDate'
      PathInfo = '/date'
      OnAction = DateAction
    end
    item
      Default = True
      Name = 'WaMenu'
      OnAction = MenuAction
    end
```

```
    item
      Name = 'WaStatus'
      PathInfo = '/status'
      OnAction = StatusAction
    end
    item
      Name = 'WaTable'
      PathInfo = '/table'
      OnAction = TableAction
    end
    item
      Name = 'WaRecord'
      PathInfo = '/record'
      OnAction = RecordAction
    end>
  object Table1: TTable
    DatabaseName = 'DBDEMOS'
    IndexName = 'ByName'
    TableName = 'EMPLOYEE.DB'
    object Table1EmpNo: TIntegerField
      FieldName = 'EmpNo'
    end
    object Table1LastName: TStringField...
    object Table1FirstName: TStringField...
    object Table1PhoneExt: TStringField...
    object Table1HireDate: TDateTimeField...
    object Table1Salary: TFloatField...
  end
end
```

If you look carefully, you'll notice that almost every action has a different path-name; the exception is one that has no pathname, and is used when a pathname is invalid. This action is indicated by its Default property being set to True (marked by an asterisk in the Actions editor). The simplest action event handler is that of the Hello pathname, which returns some fixed text:

```
procedure TWebModule1.HelloAction(Sender: TObject;
  Request: TWebRequest; Response: TWebResponse;
  var Handled: Boolean);
begin
  Response.Content :=
    '<HTML><HEAD><TITLE>Hello Page</TITLE></HEAD><BODY>' +
    '<H1>Hello</H1>' +
```

```
      'Hello. Ciao. Salut. Hallo. Hi.<p>' +
      '<hr><I>Page generated by IsaMulti</I>' +
      '</BODY></HTML>';
  end;
```

The `Content` property of the `Response` parameter is where we'll enter the HTML code that we want the user to see. The only drawback of this technique is that the HTML source code this method produces will appear on a single line. To split it up onto multiple lines, you'll need to insert the #13 new-line character, as we've done in most of the other event handlers.

Here's a more dynamic and properly formatted output, the action event handler that displays the current time:

```
procedure TWebModule1.TimeAction(Sender: TObject;
  Request: TWebRequest; Response: TWebResponse;
  var Handled: Boolean);
begin
  Response.Content :=
    '<HTML><HEAD><TITLE>Time</TITLE></HEAD><BODY>'#13 +
    '<H1>Time</H1>'#13 +
    FormatDateTime(
      '"The time is" hh:mm:ss AM/PM "<p>"'#13, Now) +
    '<hr><I>Page generated by IsaMulti</I>'#13 +
    '</BODY></HTML>'#13;
end;
```

The really interesting code begins with the Menu, which is the default action. In its `OnAction` event handler, the ISAPI application simply builds a list of the available actions (as you can see in Figure 20.12), providing a link to each of them in a for loop:

```
procedure TWebModule1.MenuAction(Sender: TObject;
  Request: TWebRequest; Response: TWebResponse;
  var Handled: Boolean);
var
  I: Integer;
begin
  Response.Content :=
    '<HTML><HEAD><TITLE>Multi Menu</TITLE></HEAD><BODY>'#13 +
    '<H1>Multi Menu</H1>'#13 +
    '<ul>'#13;
  for I := 0 to Actions.Count - 1 do
    Response.Content := Response.Content +
```

```
      '<li> <a href="' + Request.ScriptName +
      Action[I].PathInfo + '"> ' + Action[I].Name + '</a>'#13;
  Response.Content := Response.Content +
    '</ul><hr>'#13 +
    '<I>Page generated by IsaMulti</I>'#13 +
    '</BODY></HTML>'#13;
end;
```

FIGURE 20.12:

The default action of the IsaMulti application creates a list of links to all the available actions.

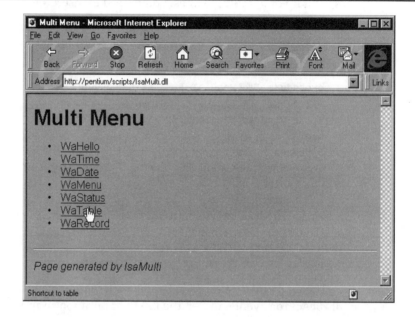

Another action of the IsaMulti example provides users with a list of the environment variables, something that is quite useful for debugging purposes. This event handler simply looks for the value of each property of the TWebRequest class, in a very naive way. The properties aren't published, so there isn't a list of properties available; similarly, the GetStringVariable method that implements most properties is protected, so you can't call it directly. The result is a somewhat boring method, here listed only in part, producing the display shown in Figure 20.13:

```
procedure TWebModule1.StatusAction(Sender: TObject;
  Request: TWebRequest; Response: TWebResponse; var Handled: Boolean);
var
  I: Integer;
begin
  Response.Content :=
```

```
    // header
    '<HTML><HEAD><TITLE>Status</TITLE></HEAD><BODY>'#13 +
    '<H1>Status</H1>'#13 +
    // status information
    'Method: ' + Request.Method + '<br>'#13 +
    'ProtocolVersion: ' + Request.ProtocolVersion + '<br>'#13 +
    'URL: ' + Request.URL + '<br>'#13 +
    'Query: ' + Request.Query + '<br>'#13 +
    'PathInfo: ' + Request.PathInfo + '<br>'#13 +
    'PathTranslated: ' + Request.PathTranslated + '<br>'#13 +
    'Authorization: ' + Request.Authorization + '<br>'#13 +
    'CacheControl: ' + Request.CacheControl + '<br>'#13 +
    'Cookie: ' + Request.Cookie + '<br>'#13 +
    'Date: ' + DateTimeToStr (Request.Date) + '<br>'#13 +
    ... // and so on for the other properties
  // list of strings
  Response.Content := Response.Content +
    'ContentFields:<ul>'#13;
  for I := 0 to Request.ContentFields.Count - 1 do
    Response.Content := Response.Content +
      '<li>' + Request.ContentFields [I]+ #13;
  ... // and so on for the other string lists
```

Simple ISAPI Database Reporting

IsaMulti defines two more actions, indicated by the /table and /record path-names. For these two last actions, our ISAPI DLL produces output very similar to the CgiEmpl example. Specifically, it produces a main list of names, and then displays the details of each record with a small navigational table.

The ISAPI DLL version of the code is simpler for several reasons:

- We simply place the Table component on the WebModule, and set its properties at design-time using the Object Inspector. Naturally, we can generate the field objects at design-time (as you would in a traditional Delphi database application), and then use them to access the values in specific fields.

- The framework provides us with a correlation of pathnames to event handlers, which simplifies writing the HTML that requests a certain behavior.

- If we use the & sign instead of the + sign to separate the parameters, we'll automatically have access to the parameters in multiple strings of the QueryFields list.

FIGURE 20.13:

The initial portion of
the IsaMulti example's
page showing the
environment variables

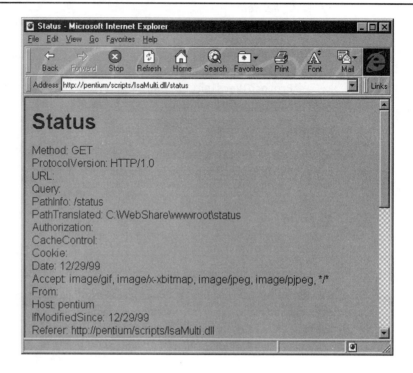

- Accessing the environment variables such as the ScriptName is now straightforward.

A minor difference in the new version of the program is how we display the complete table using an HTML table:

```
procedure TWebModule1.TableAction(Sender: TObject;
  Request: TWebRequest; Response: TWebResponse; var Handled: Boolean);
begin
  Response.Content :=
    '<HTML><HEAD><TITLE>Employee Table</TITLE></HEAD><BODY>'#13 +
    '<H1>Employee Table</H1>'#13 +
    '<table border>'#13;
  // show a summary of the entire table
  Table1.Open;
  Table1.First;
  while not Table1.EOF do
  begin
    // show names with a link
```

```
      Response.Content := Response.Content + Format (
        '<tr><td><a HREF="%s/record?%s&%s">%s %s</a></td></tr>'#13,
        [Request.ScriptName,
        Table1LastName.AsString,
        Table1FirstName.AsString,
        Table1FirstName.AsString,
        Table1LastName.AsString]);
      Table1.Next;
    end;
    // end of the table and footer
    Response.Content := Response.Content +
      '</table>'#13 +
      '<hr><I>Page generated by IsaMulti</I>'#13 +
      '</BODY></HTML>'#13;
  end;
```

The structure of this code is actually very similar to the original CGI version. The same holds true for the second method, which we use to create the record output and the navigational table:

```
procedure TWebModule1.RecordAction(Sender: TObject;
  Request: TWebRequest; Response: TWebResponse; var Handled: Boolean);
var
  I: Integer;
begin
  if Request.QueryFields.Count = 0 then
    TableAction (Sender, Request, Response, Handled)
  else
  begin
    if Request.QueryFields.Count = 1 then
      Table1.FindNearest ([Request.QueryFields[0]])
    else
      Table1.FindNearest ([Request.QueryFields[0],
        Request.QueryFields[1]]);
    Response.Content :=
      '<HTML><HEAD><TITLE>Employee Record</TITLE></HEAD><BODY>'#13 +
      '<H1>Employee Record: ' + Request.QueryFields[0] +
      '</H1>'#13 +
      '<table border>'#13;
    for I := 1 to Table1.FieldCount - 1 do
      Response.Content := Response.Content +
        '<tr><td>' + Table1.Fields [I].FieldName +
        '</td>'#13'<td>' + Table1.Fields [I].AsString +
```

```
          '</td></tr>'#13;
      Response.Content := Response.Content +
        '</table><hr>'#13 +
        '<table border><tr>'#13 +
        // pointer to the table index
        '<td><a HREF="' + Request.ScriptName + '/table">' +
        ' Index </a></td>'#13;
      // pointer to the prior record, if any
      Table1.Prior;
      if not Table1.BOF then
      begin
        Response.Content := Response.Content + Format (
          '<td><a HREF="%s/record?%s&%s"> Prior </a></td>#13',
          [Request.ScriptName,
          Table1LastName.AsString,
          Table1FirstName.AsString]);
        // get back to the current record
        Table1.Next;
      end
      else
        // empty spot
        Response.Content := Response.Content +
          '<td><i>Prior</i></td>#13';
      // pointer to the next record, if any
      Table1.Next;
      if not Table1.EOF then
        Response.Content := Response.Content + Format (
          '<td><a HREF="%s/record?%s&%s"> Next </a></td>#13',
          [Request.ScriptName,
          Table1LastName.AsString,
          Table1FirstName.AsString])
      else
        // empty spot
        Response.Content := Response.Content +
          '<td><i>Next</i></td>'#13;
      // end of the line and table + footer
      Response.Content := Response.Content +
        '</tr></table>'#13 +
        '<hr><I>Page generated by IsaMulti</I>'#13 +
        '</BODY></HTML>'#13;
  end;
end;
```

Notice in particular the code at the beginning of the method, which determines the number of items and the actual items of the `QueryFields` string list. There is also a check here to ensure that the request has at least one parameter. If this isn't true, the `RecordAction` method calls the handler of a different event, `TableAction`.

The HTML Producer Components

In addition to the HTTP framework consisting of the WebModule, the application, and the request and response objects, Delphi includes a family of components that generate and customize HTML files. These components are also called HTML producers, because they share a common base class called `TCustomContentProducer`.

There are three ready-to-use components in this group, PageProducer, DateSetTableProducer, and QueryTableProducer, which we'll discuss in the next three sections.

Producing HTML Pages

The simplest of the HTML producer components is the PageProducer, which manipulates an HTML file in which you've embedded special tags. (You can generate such a file using any HTML editor you prefer.) At run-time, the PageProducer converts the special tags to actual HTML code, giving you a straightforward method for modifying sections of an HTML document. The special tags have the basic format `<#tagname>`, but you can also supply named parameters within the tag. You'll process the tags in the `OnTag` event handler of the PageProducer.

A very simple example of using tags is creating an HTML file that displays fields with the current date or a date computed relative to the current date, such as an expiration date. If you examine the PageProd example (a new ISAPI DLL), you'll find the following component in the WebModule:

```
object PageProducer1: TPageProducer
  HTMLDoc.Strings = (...)
  OnHTMLTag = PageProducer1HTMLTag
  Left = 40
  Top = 24
end
```

The HTML code in the HTMLDoc property is a plain HTML file that contains a few of the special tags:

```
<HTML><HEAD>
<TITLE>Producer Demo</TITLE>
</HEAD><BODY>

<H1>Producer Demo</H1>

This is a demo of the page produced by the <b><#appname></b>
application on <b><#date></b>.<p>

<hr>
The prices in this catalog are valid until <b><#expiration
days=21></b>.<p>

<hr><I>Page generated by PageProd</I>

</BODY></HTML>
```

The WebModule's only action contains very simple code; it copies the PageProducer component's output to the response's output:

```
procedure TWebModule1.WebModule1WebActionItem1Action(
  Sender: TObject; Request: TWebRequest;
  Response: TWebResponse; var Handled: Boolean);
begin
  Response.Content := PageProducer1.Content;
end;
```

The important code for this application (beyond the HTML file the PageProducer starts with initially) is in the OnTag event handler of this component. In this method we determine the value of the TagString, returning different HTML text and producing the output shown in Figure 20.14.

The PageProducer will actually begin scanning the HTML document, and will call the OnTag event-handler when it locates one of the special tags:

```
procedure TWebModule1.PageProducer1HTMLTag(Sender: TObject; Tag: TTag;
  const TagString: String; TagParams: TStrings; var ReplaceText: String);
var
  nDays: Integer;
begin
  if TagString = 'date' then
```

```
      ReplaceText := DateToStr (Now)
    else if TagString = 'appname' then
      ReplaceText := Request.ScriptName
    else if TagString = 'expiration' then
    begin
      nDays := StrToIntDef (TagParams.Values['days'], 0);
      if nDays <> 0 then
        ReplaceText := DateToStr (Now + nDays)
      else
        ReplaceText := '{expiration tag error}'
    end;
  end;
```

FIGURE 20.14:

The output of the Page-Prod ISAPI example, a simple demonstration of the PageProducer component

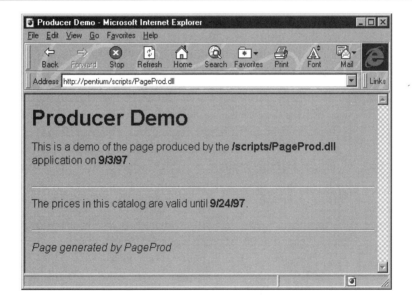

Notice in particular the code we've written to convert the last tag, expiration, which requires a parameter. The PageProducer places the entire text of the tag parameter (in this case, days=21) in a string that's part of the TagParams list. To extract the value portion of this string (the portion after the equal sign), you can use the Values property of the TagParams string list, and search for the proper entry at the same time. If it can't locate the parameter, or if its value isn't an integer, the DLL displays an error message.

NOTE   The PageProducer component supports user-defined tags, which can be any string you like, but you should first review the tags defined by the TTags enumeration. The possible values include tgLink (for the LINK tag), tgImage (for the IMAGE tag), tgTable (for the TABLE tag), and a few others. If you create a custom tag, as in the PageProd example, the value of the Tags parameter will be tgCustom.

Producing HTML Tables

In addition to the simple PageProducer component, Delphi's Client/Server Suite provides two HTML producer components specifically designed for creating ISAPI DLL database applications, DataSetTableProducer and QueryTableProducer. The DataSetTableProducer component is generally useful for displaying the contents of a table (although it works for queries or other data sets too); and QueryTableProducer is specifically tailored for parametric queries, as we'll see in the next section.

Before building a complex database application with these components, let's introduce the DataSetTableProducer with a simple example. This component produces a table, including a header and a footer (if necessary), but it doesn't include support for generating complete HTML pages. For this reason, you'll generally use the DataSetTableProducer together with a PageProducer component. In the EmplProd example, which displays data from the Employee.DB table, we define just one action, which contains the usual code (but opens the table first):

```
procedure TWebModule1.WebModule1WebActionItem1Action(
  Sender: TObject; Request: TWebRequest;
  Response: TWebResponse; var Handled: Boolean);
begin
  Table1.Open;
  Table1.First;
  Response.Content := PageProducer1.Content;
end;
```

TIP   The call to the Table's First method initially seemed useless, so we didn't add it. The ISAPI DLL works fine without it, at first. However, as soon as you refresh the data, you'll see no records in the output. We're not sure why this happens, but it's probably because the DataSetTableProducer component starts from the current record rather than from the first one. Adding the call to the First method fixed the bug.

As in the previous example, we've defined the HTML code in the `HtmlDoc` property of the PageProducer component:

```
<html><head>
<title>Employee Producer</title>
</head><body>
<h1>Employee Producer</h1>
<#table>
<hr><i>Produced by EmplProd on <#date></i>
```

This HTML code contains two special tags, one to show the date, and the other to display the information generated by the DataSetTableProducer component:

```
procedure TWebModule1.PageProducer1HTMLTag(
  Sender: TObject;  Tag: TTag; const TagString:
  String; TagParams: TStrings; var ReplaceText: String);
begin
  if TagString = 'table' then
    ReplaceText := DataSetTableProducer1.Content
  else if TagString = 'date' then
    ReplaceText := DateToStr (Now);
end;
```

This new DataSetTableProducer component is connected to the database table, and it has a title, an extra header, and a few other special properties. In addition to the general properties for the table, you can set up properties for the specific columns. You should use the Table component's Field Editor to generate the field objects; then you can open the `Columns` property editor of the DataSetTableProducer (see Figure 20.15). Next, you'll click the *Add All Fields* button to get an initial view of the output. If you activate the database table at this point, you'll see the values for the records; otherwise you'll see only the heading. You can then customize the properties of each column, changing the alignment and the background color.

Here is the summary of the DataSetTableProducer component's properties (from this example):

```
object DataSetTableProducer1: TDataSetTableProducer
  Caption = '<h3>Employee Table</h3><p>'
  Columns = <
    item
      FieldName = 'EmpNo'
      Title.Caption = 'Code'
    end
    item
```

FIGURE 20.15:

The editor of the Columns property of the DataSetTable-Producer component provides you with a preview of the final HTML table, particularly if the database table is active.

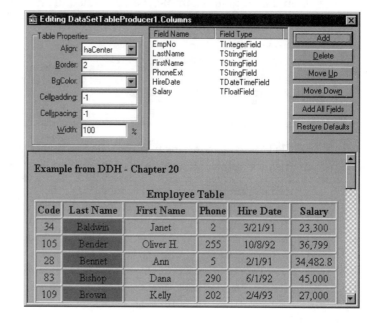

```
      BgColor = 'Gray'
      FieldName = 'LastName'
      Title.Caption = 'Last Name'
    end
    item
      FieldName = 'FirstName'
      Title.Caption = 'First Name'
    end
    item
      FieldName = 'PhoneExt'
      Title.Caption = 'Phone'
    end
    item
      FieldName = 'HireDate'
      Title.Caption = 'Hire Date'
    end
    item
      FieldName = 'Salary'
    end>
  Header.Strings = (
    '<b>Example from DDH - Chapter 20<p></b>')
```

```
  MaxRows = 50
  DataSet = Table1
  RowAttributes.Align = haCenter
  RowAttributes.VAlign = haMiddle
  TableAttributes.Align = haCenter
  TableAttributes.Border = 2
  OnFormatCell = DataSetTableProducer1FormatCell
end
```

There are three techniques you can use to customize the output of this program, and it's worth exploring each of them:

- You can use the table producer component's `Column` property to set properties such as the text and color of the title, or the color and the alignment for the cells in the rest of the column. You can see the values for the example in the listing above.

- You can use the field objects' properties, particularly those related to output. In the example, we've set the `DisplayFormat` property of the `Table1Salary` field object to ###,###.##. This is the correct approach to use to determine the actual output of each field. You might go even further and embed HTML tags in the output of a field.

- You can handle the DataSetTableProducer component's `OnFormatCell` event to customize the output further. In this event, you can set the various column attributes uniquely for a given cell, but you can also customize the output string (stored in the `CellData` parameter) and embed HTML tags. This is something you can't do using the `Columns` property. In the example, we've used a handler for this event to turn the text of the LastName column to bold. Here is the code:

```
procedure TWebModule1.DataSetTableProducer1FormatCell(
  Sender: TObject; CellRow, CellColumn: Integer;
  var BgColor: THTMLBgColor; var Align: THTMLAlign;
  var VAlign: THTMLVAlign; var CustomAttrs, CellData: String);
begin
  if CellColumn = 1 then
    CellData := '<b>' + CellData + '</b>';
end;
```

You can see the output of this program in Figure 20.16. We've also listed an excerpt of the HTML file (the initial part of the table) the program generates so that you can see the richness of its output, and therefore the advantage of using this component. You'll also see how the component property settings affect the output we produce:

```
<Table Width="100%" Align="Center" Border=2>
  <Caption><h3>Employee Table</h3><p></Caption>
<TR Align="Center" VAlign="Middle">
  <TH>Code</TH>
  <TH><b>Last Name</b></TH>
  <TH>First Name</TH>
  <TH>Phone</TH>
  <TH>Hire Date</TH>
  <TH>Salary</TH>
</TR>
<TR Align="Center" VAlign="Middle">
  <TD>34</TD>
  <TD BgColor="Gray"><b>Baldwin</b></TD>
  <TD>Janet</TD>
  <TD>2</TD>
  <TD>3/21/91</TD>
  <TD>23,300</TD>
</TR>
<TR Align="Center" VAlign="Middle">
  <TD>105</TD>
  <TD BgColor="Gray"><b>Bender</b></TD>
  <TD>Oliver H.</TD>
  <TD>255</TD>
  <TD>10/8/92</TD>
  <TD>36,799</TD>
</TR>
  ...
</Table>
```

Of Queries and Forms

The last of the three producer components we're going to examine is the QueryTableProducer. This component is very similar to the previous one, but it's specifically tailored for building parametric queries based on input from an HTML search form. As we'll see in a moment, this makes building even complex database programs a breeze. This is also an area in which Delphi's ISAPI and HTTP support helps us dramatically.

FIGURE 20.16:

The output of the EmplProd example, based on the Data-SetTableProducer component

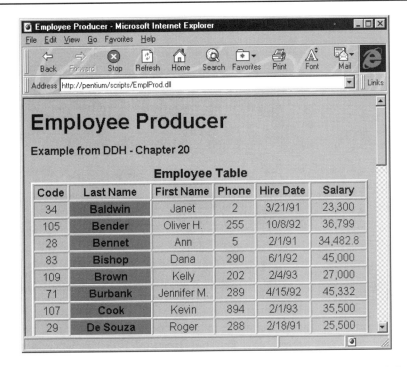

Suppose you want to search for some customers in a database. You might construct the following HTML form (embedded in an HTML table for better formatting):

```
<h4>Customer QueryProducer Search Form</h4>
<form action="/scripts/CustQueP.dll/search" method="POST">
<table>
<tr><td>State:</td>
  <td><input type="text" name="State"></td></tr>
<tr><td>Country:</td>
  <td><input type="text" name="Country"></td></tr>
<tr><td></td>
  <td><center><input type="Submit"></center></td></tr>
</form>
```

You can see the output of this form in Figure 20.17. There is another important element to notice: the names of the input components (*State* and *Country*), which should match the parameters of a Query component:

```
select
    Company, State, Country
```

```
from
    CUSTOMER.DB
where
    State = :State or Country = :Country
```

FIGURE 20.17:

The HTML form used by the CustQueP example has been formatted by placing the controls in an HTML table.

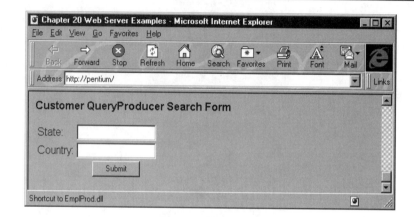

We've placed a Query component inside the WebModule of the CustQueP (Customer Query Producer) example, and we've generated the field objects for it. The same WebModule also contains a QueryTableProducer component, which publishes some very simple properties. As before, we'll write the code for one action (the /search action):

```
procedure TWebModule1.SearchAction(
    Sender: TObject; Request: TWebRequest;
    Response: TWebResponse; var Handled: Boolean);
begin
    Response.Content := QueryTableProducer1.Content;
end;
```

The ISAPI DLL will generate the proper response, as you can see in Figure 20.18.

How does this work? When we activate the QueryTableProducer component by calling its Content function, it initializes the Query component by obtaining the parameters from the HTTP request. The component can automatically examine the request method, and then use either the QueryFields property (if the request is a GET) or the ContentFields property (if the request is a POST).

FIGURE 20.18:

The output of the
QueryTableProducer
component gathers
information automati-
cally from an HTTP
request, filtering the
table using the proper
parameters.

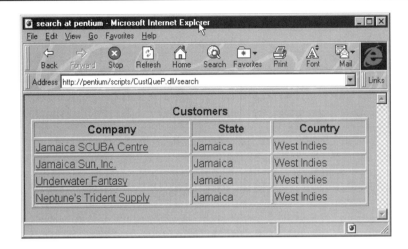

One problem with using a static HTML form as we did before is that it doesn't tell us which states and countries we can search for. To address this, we can use a selection control instead of an edit control in the HTML form. However, if the user adds new records to the database table, we'll need to automatically update the element list. As a final solution, we can design the ISAPI DLL to produce a form on the fly, and we can fill the selection controls with the available elements.

We'll generate the HTML for this page in the CustQueP example inside the /form action, which we've naturally connected to a PageProducer component:

```
procedure TWebModule1.FormAction(Sender: TObject;
  Request: TWebRequest; Response: TWebResponse;
  var Handled: Boolean);
begin
  Response.Content := PageProducer1.Content;
end;
```

The PageProducer contains the following HTML text, which embeds two special tags:

```
<h4>Customer QueryProducer Search Form</h4>
<form action="/scripts/CustQueP.dll/search" method="POST">
<table>
<tr><td>State:</td><td><select name="State">
<#State>
</select>
```

```
</td></tr>
<tr><td>Country:</td><td><select name="Country">
<option> </option>
<#Country>
</select>
</td></tr>
<tr><td></td><td><center><input type="Submit"></center></td></tr>
</form>
```

You'll notice that the tags have the same name as some of the table's fields. When the PageProducer encounters one of these tags, it adds an <option> HTML tag for every distinct value of the corresponding field. Here's the OnTag event-handler's code, which is quite generic and reusable:

```
procedure TWebModule1.PageProducer1HTMLTag(Sender: TObject;
  Tag: TTag; const TagString: String; TagParams: TStrings;
  var ReplaceText: String);
begin
  ReplaceText := '';
  Query2.SQL.Clear;
  Query2.SQL.Add ('select distinct ' +
    TagString + ' from customer');
  try
    Query2.Open;
    try
      Query2.First;
      while not Query2.EOF do
      begin
        ReplaceText := ReplaceText +
          '<option>' + Query2.Fields[0].AsString +
          '</option>'#13;
        Query2.Next;
      end;
    finally
      Query2.Close;
    end;
  except
    ReplaceText := '{wrong field: ' + TagString + '}';
  end;
end;
```

This method used a second Query component, which we placed on the form and connected to the DBDemos database, and it produces the output shown in Figure 20.19.

FIGURE 20.19:

The *form* action of the CustQueP example produces an HTML form with a selection component dynamically updated to reflect the current status of the database.

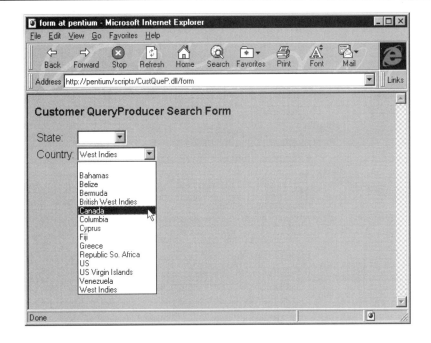

Finally, this Web server extension, like many others we've built, allows the user to view the details of a specific record. As you'll notice by glancing back at Figure 20.18, the search result table contains links to specific records. We accomplish this by customizing the output of the first column (column zero), which is generated by the QueryTableProducer component:

```
procedure TWebModule1.QueryTableProducer1FormatCell(
  Sender: TObject; CellRow, CellColumn: Integer;
  var BgColor: THTMLBgColor; var Align: THTMLAlign;
  var VAlign: THTMLVAlign; var CustomAttrs, CellData: String);
begin
  if (CellColumn = 0) and (CellRow <> 0) then
    CellData := '<a HREF="' + Request.ScriptName +
      '/record?' + CellData + '">' + CellData + '</a>'#13;
end;
```

The action for this link is /record, and we'll pass a specific element after the ? parameter. The code we use to produce the HTML tables for the records doesn't use the producer components as we've been doing, but is very similar to the code of an early ISAPI example. Unfortunately, we can't provide links to the previous or next record because the Query2 component can retrieve only one record:

```
procedure TWebModule1.RecordAction(
  Sender: TObject; Request: TWebRequest;
  Response: TWebResponse; var Handled: Boolean);
var
  I: Integer;
begin
  if Request.QueryFields.Count = 0 then
    Response.Content := 'Record not found'
  else
  begin
    Query2.SQL.Clear;
    Query2.SQL.Add ('select * from customer ' +
      'where Company="' + Request.QueryFields[0] + '"');
    Query2.Open;
    Response.Content :=
      '<HTML><HEAD><TITLE>Customer Record</TITLE></HEAD><BODY>'#13 +
      '<H1>Customer Record: ' + Request.QueryFields[0] +
      '</H1>'#13 +
      '<table border>'#13;
    for I := 1 to Query2.FieldCount - 1 do
      Response.Content := Response.Content +
        '<tr><td>' + Query2.Fields [I].FieldName +
        '</td>'#13'<td>' + Query2.Fields [I].AsString +
        '</td></tr>'#13;
    Response.Content := Response.Content +
      '</table><hr>'#13 +
      // pointer to the query form
      '<a HREF="' + Request.ScriptName + '/form">' +
      ' Next Query </a>'#13 +
      '</BODY></HTML>'#13;
  end;
end;
```

This example concludes our exploration of Delphi Web server extensions. We've examined simple CGI applications, database CGI applications, simple ISAPI applications, complex ISAPI applications built with the Delphi ISAPI framework, and finally, the producer components. Now it's time to take a quick look at client-side Web applications that we deliver dynamically from the server.

ActiveForms as Database Front-Ends

All the programs we have built so far execute on the server, as either stand-alone CGI applications or as Web server extension DLLs. However, there's a completely different approach you can use to build active and responsive database-driven Web sites: let the server upload a program to the client computer, and have the client computer execute it.

Usually the execution of client-side programs takes place directly within a browser. There are two major technologies you can use to build these client-side applications:

- Java byte-code, an intermediate language interpreted by a Java Virtual Machine (JVM) embedded in the Web browser. The main advantage of this approach is that the byte-code is platform- and CPU-independent, and that the code can be considered safe (since the JVM restricts the program's access to the computer's resources). The drawback to Java is that because of the safety mechanisms, we'll have limited access to the computer's resources!

- ActiveX components, which are binary files compiled for the Win32/Intel 80x86 platform and use an extension of OLE control technology. The main advantage to ActiveX is that the application can call any Win32 API function and perform any file operation, and it can be very fast. The drawback to ActiveX is the flip side of its advantage—an ActiveX component can do everything you might imagine to destroy data on your computer or steal information from it. Another drawback to ActiveX controls is that they are binary-specific to the platform you've compiled them for. If the technology moves to other processor architectures, you'll need to create new binaries to deploy on those platforms.

So many magazine articles and conferences have been devoted to debating the advantages and disadvantages of these two approaches, pushed by the respective proponents (Java is promoted by Sun and several other companies, and ActiveX is promoted by Microsoft), that we've decided to provide only the limited summary above. Java is clearly outside the scope of this Delphi book. On the other hand, we don't want to discuss ActiveX security, which is a major problem, but also a source of fierce debates.

Instead, we take the position that ActiveX technology is very interesting and powerful for intranets on which most of the computers are Intel Win32-platform systems. In this environment, you can use ActiveX technology to distribute the latest version of your programs automatically, delivering them via a Web browser, and thereby give users access to a remote server with no need for them to install the BDE to access to the data. This is something we mentioned in the last chapter, but we'll return to it here with a specific example.

Delphi 3 provides two ways to build ActiveX controls. The first is called One-Step ActiveX, and allows you to transform a standard TWinControl-based VCL component into an ActiveX control with very little effort (literally, it's one step). The second is called ActiveForm, and allows you to build ActiveX controls from a Delphi form. In the final portion of this chapter, we'll focus on this second approach. (The first is useful primarily as a way to distribute custom TWinControl-based components.)

> **NOTE**
>
> For an introduction to both techniques available for generating ActiveX controls, you can refer to *Mastering Delphi 3*.

Actually, we won't cover all the aspects of the ActiveForm development, but will focus only on a specific perspective: making database data available within a user's Web browser. In doing so, we'll see two totally different approaches. In the first example, we'll demonstrate delivering the program along with the data to the client. In the second we'll show how you can connect a client to live data on the server.

Distributing ActiveForms and Database Tables

Here's a simple (and fairly common) scenario, which is worth exploring. Suppose that a table's data doesn't change often, and you want the users to browse but not edit the data. In this case, you can use a very simple approach to delivering the data to the user: you can pack an ActiveForm along with the database table, compress everything, and upload both to the user at once. This requires you to install the BDE on the user's computers (unless you use a custom data set which doesn't need the BDE), and it's useful only if the table isn't too large.

> **TIP**
>
> In the following example we've also made the assumption that the standard Delphi packages are available on the client computer. This makes the ActiveForm file much smaller.

Building an example that fits this scenario should be quite simple. First, create a new ActiveForm by selecting the corresponding icon in the ActiveX page of the Object Repository. Delphi will automatically create the ActiveLibrary project for you. Now we can build the ActiveForm just as we would build a plain database form.

This is the form description of the AfLocal example:

```
object ActiveLocalData: TActiveLocalData
  Caption = 'ActiveLocalData'
  object Panel1: TPanel
    Align = alTop
  end
  object DBGrid1: TDBGrid
    Align = alClient
    DataSource = DataSource1
  end
  object Table1: TTable
    ReadOnly = True
    TableName = 'COUNTRY.DB'
  end
  object DataSource1: TDataSource
    AutoEdit = False
    DataSet = Table1
  end
end
```

Now we must take two more steps. First, we need to distribute the table along with the active form. To do this, we can simply go to the Web Deployment options dialog box (using the Project ➤ Web Deployment Options menu item) and select the *Use CAB file compression* and *Deploy additional files* check boxes in the Project page. Then, move to the Additional Files page, add the table and the index files, and select the *Compress in project CAB* radio button, as shown in Figure 20.20.

The second step is to connect the active form to the local copy of the table. This file resides in the same directory as the active form. To determine the full file and pathname, we can extract the name of the DLL file, using the Windows API function `GetModuleFileName`, extract the pathname with the `ExtractPathFromFile` function, and then use the file and pathname for the table component's `Database-Name` property. We show this name in the panel at the top of the form, as you can see in Figure 20.21.

FIGURE 20.20:

The options used to add the table files to the compressed CAB hosting the ActiveX form of the AfLocal example

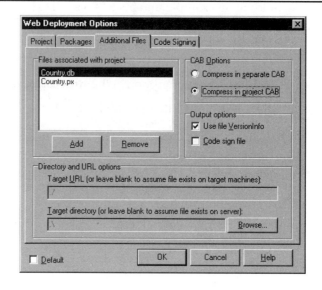

```
procedure TActiveLocalData.ActivateEvent(Sender: TObject);
var
  ModuleName: string;
begin
  if FEvents <> nil then
    FEvents.OnActivate;
  // specific code
  SetLength (ModuleName, 1000);
  GetModuleFileName (HInstance, pChar (ModuleName), 1000);
  Table1.DatabaseName := ExtractFilePath (PChar (ModuleName));
  Panel1.Caption := Table1.DatabaseName + '/' + Table1.TableName;
  Table1.Open;
end;
```

You'll notice that the program doesn't use the OnActivate event handler. That's because when a container application creates the form, most of the form's event handlers will be connected to external OLE interface events. This allows the programmer to use the active form inside a program, and place event handlers in the container application. If you want to provide some specific code for an event, you just change the active form method that calls the OLE event, if any. In this case, the method is called ActivateEvent. We've left the original code at the beginning, and appended our specific initialization to the end.

FIGURE 20.21:

The AfLocal active form allows a user to browse the database data from a table automatically down-loaded on the client computer, as you can see from the table file name in the upper panel.

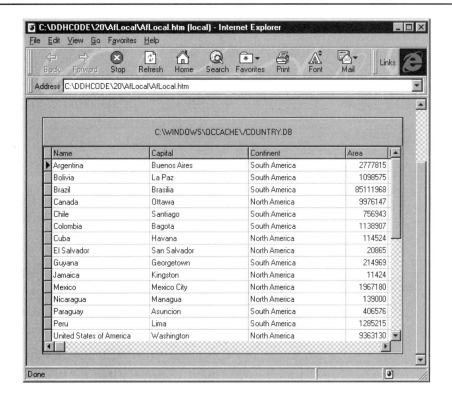

This behavior is shared by most of the form's event handlers, as you can see by reviewing the Initialize method, so you shouldn't create normal event handlers for any of them. Here's the code of the Initialize method:

```
procedure TActiveLocalData.Initialize;
begin
  OnActivate := ActivateEvent;
  OnClick := ClickEvent;
  OnCreate := CreateEvent;
  OnDblClick := DblClickEvent;
  OnDeactivate := DeactivateEvent;
  OnDestroy := DestroyEvent;
  OnKeyPress := KeyPressEvent;
  OnPaint := PaintEvent;
end;
```

WARNING The ActiveX control we built in this last example isn't a *signed control*—a control that has an accompanying certificate that identifies who created it (for determining its trustworthiness). Therefore, to execute it inside Internet Explorer you'll need to set the security level to medium and answer Yes to the browser's request to download this "potentially dangerous" program.

Three-Tier Intranet Applications

The approach used in the last example is interesting, but it has several limitations. These limitations are mainly related to the fact that we're browsing a local copy of the data, that the amount of data you can deliver is limited, and that there's no way of editing it. A better alternative, in most cases, is to use the three-tier architecture discussed in the last chapter to overcome most of these limitations.

In fact, if we build an active form that connects to an application server, the server will deliver live SQL data to us as necessary, we'll be able to send back updates, and we won't need to install the BDE on the client computer.

The active form of this example, called AfRemote, is almost as simple as the previous one, but this time we'll connect to one the application servers we built in the last chapter (specifically, AppServ2). If you haven't already done so, you'll need to build and run this server application to register it and make it available to this client ActiveX control.

If you've read the last chapter, then configuring this form's components will be obvious to you (if you haven't read that chapter, we suggest you do so to fully understand this example):

```
object ActiveRemote: TActiveRemote
  object Panel1: TPanel
    Align = alTop
    object CheckActive: TCheckBox
      Caption = 'Active'
      OnClick = CheckActiveClick
    end
    object BtnApply: TButton
      Caption = 'Apply Updates'
      OnClick = BtnApplyClick
    end
  end
end
```

```
  object DBGrid1: TDBGrid
    Align = alClient
    DataSource = DataSource1
  end
  object RemoteServer1: TRemoteServer
    Connected = True
    ServerGUID = '{C5DDE903-2214-11D1-98D0-444553540000}'
  end
  object ClientDataSet1: TClientDataSet
    ProviderName = 'Table1'
    RemoteServer = RemoteServer1
    OnReconcileError = ClientDataSet1ReconcileError
  end
  object DataSource1: TDataSource
    DataSet = ClientDataSet1
  end
end
```

In our test case, the remote computer is the same as the local computer. However, in most situations, you'll need to set the RemoteServer component's Remote-Computer property to connect to a specific server on your network. Also, keep in mind that you'll need a MIDAS-compatible transmission protocol on the client system, and that you must install MIDAS itself on the server.

The code of the AfRemote example's three methods is very straightforward and requires almost no comment:

```
procedure TActiveRemote.BtnApplyClick(Sender: TObject);
begin
  if ClientDataSet1.Active then
    ClientDataSet1.ApplyUpdates (-1);
end;

procedure TActiveRemote.CheckActiveClick(Sender: TObject);
begin
  ClientDataSet1.Active := CheckActive.Checked;
end;

procedure TActiveRemote.ClientDataSet1ReconcileError(
  DataSet: TClientDataSet; E: EReconcileError;
  UpdateKind: TUpdateKind; var Action: TReconcileAction);
begin
  Action := HandleReconcileError (DataSet, UpdateKind, E);
end;
```

As we did in the last chapter, on an update error we display the standard Reconcile dialog box (found in the Object Repository and added to the example). The output of this active form in Microsoft's Internet Explorer appears in Figure 20.22.

FIGURE 20.22:

The Active Form of the AfRemote example uses the live data provided from an application server, following Delphi's three-tier architecture.

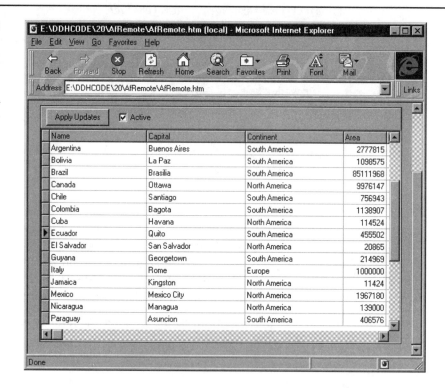

FIGURE 20.22:

The Active Form of the AfRemote example uses the live data provided from an application server, following Delphi's three-tier architecture.

What's Next

In this, the last chapter of the book, we've focused on different techniques you can use to publish databases on the Web or an Intranet. Specifically, we've discussed CGI and ISAPI server-side technologies, and ActiveX client-side controls. We've covered the foundations of these technologies, explored how Delphi supports them, and built many examples, as usual.

Since this is the last chapter of the book, the next step for you is to apply the information from this book to your work with Delphi. We would appreciate suggestions that arise from your experience and feedback on any errors or omissions.

As we mentioned in the introduction, you'll find updates to this book, such as changes required by future versions of Delphi, on either the Sybex Web site (www.sybex.com), or Marco's Web site (www.marcocantu.com).

INDEX

Note: Page numbers in *italics* refer to figures or tables; page numbers in **bold** refer to significant discussions of the topic.

A

abstract functions, error from calling, 77

accelerator characters, messages related to, 327

`ActivateEvent` method, 1076

activation interface, 462, 525

activation messages, 325

`ActiveBuffer` pointer, 960

`ActiveChange` procedure, 873

`ActiveChanged` procedure, 877, 883, 887–888, 889

ActiveForms, **1073–1080**

creating, 1075

distributing, **1074–1078**

ActiveX components, 1073

ActiveX controls, and COM components, **446–447**

ActiveX Data Objects, 447

ActiveX Document Object technologies, 447

ActiveX servers, registration, 491

ActiveX technology, 1016

add-in notifier object, 751

add-in wizards, 653, **671–682**

adding menu item, **678–680**

constructor for, 683

executing, **680–682**

`AddChild` method, 788

`AddClass` method, 23–24

`AddFileHeader` method, 139

`AddObject` procedure, 23, 977–978

`AddRef` function, 464–465, 477, 655

`AddSubItems` procedure, for menu wizard, 675–676

`AddType` procedure, 154, 159

AfLocal example

active form, *1077*

form description, 1075

AfRemote example, 1078–1079, *1080*

`AllEqual` method, 585

`AllocRecordBuffer` function, 955

and operator, 11

AnsiString objects. *See* long strings

Apartment threading model, 492, 540, 541

COM components labeled for, 542

components for run-time resizing operations, 389

round, **379–385**, *385*

Byte property, editor for, 561

(

C++, name mangling conventions for, 450

callback function, converting TWndMethod procedure to, 534

Caption property, updating, 586

casts, 8

CD-ROM

xxxi, 4

commented ShowMessage calls, 942

record viewer component, 876

centering, buttons, 299–300

CGI (Common Gateway Interface), 1016

application to give local time, **1019–1020**, *1021*

code to show specific record, **1030–1032**

database programming, **1026–1039**

environment variables, **1023–1026**

HTML link for, 1020

HTML search form, **1032–1038**, *1035*

input to application, **1021–1022**

main program, 1035–1037

overview, **1017–1018**

request methods in, 1036

URL of script, 1029

CgiDate2 program, 1022–1023, *1023*

CgiEmpl example, 1035–1039, *1039*

CgiVars program, 1025–1026, *1027*

ChangeOwner example program, *47*, 47–48

Char property, editor for, 561

characters, Object Debugger editor for, 848

check box

on HTML form, *1034*

Tag property, 13

CheckSpecialToken function, 135

child components, messages sent to, 325

child window, buttons as, 299

class factory

declaration, 506

implementation, **488–489**

to initialize object, 525

mapping calls from COM libraries to, 490

class function, 507

class identifiers (CLSID), 457

class instance, displaying size, 164

class keyword, 480, 486

class references, **15–35**

to access class information, **16–18**

declaring data type for, 16

as pointers, 23

classes

creating object of uncompiled, 726

D

E

H

J

K

L

N

O

P

Q

S

U

V

X

Z

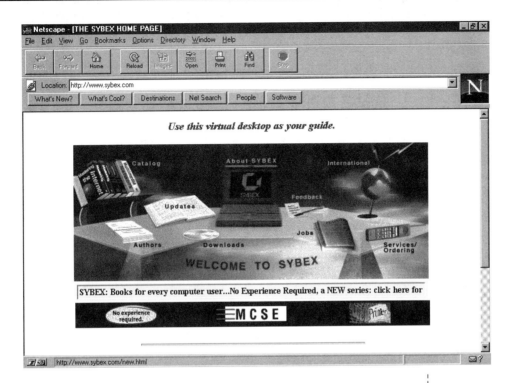

Delphi Developer's Handbook Companion CD-ROM

All the Program Examples The DDHCODE directory includes executable files and source code for all the examples in the book, including Pascal files, form description files, project files, and all the files you need to build the examples, in ASCII and syntax-highlighted HTML formats.

A Selection of the Best Third-Party Delphi Software In the ADDONS directory you can try out evaluation versions of Delphi tools provided for this CD by some of todays's most important software publishers:

- **DrBob:** Dr. Bob's Collection of multipurpose wizards.
- **Eagle:** Raptor (a Delphi IDE enhancement add-in), ReAct (a component testing tool), CDK Help (a description of the Component Developer Kit).
- **HREF:** WebHub, a tool for building dynamic Internet sites with Delphi.
- **Luxent:** Apollo (a database engine) and LightLib (graphic and multimedia components).
- **Microgold:** WithClass, a CASE tool for Delphi.
- **MKS:** SourceIntegrity Test Drive, a version control system.
- **NuMega:** BoundsChecker, a Windows debugging tool.
- **Shoreline:** Web Solution Builder, a tool for building dynamic Internet sites with Delphi.
- **SureHand:** ViCiouS Pro, a Delphi-based version control system.
- **TurboPower:** Orpheus, SysTools, Async Professional, OnGuard, Abbrevia, Essentials, MemSleuth. Tools ranging from serial port communication to memory testing and debugging, from shareware distribution support to data-aware controls.
- **WhiteAnts:** White Ants Model Maker, a CASE tool for Delphi.
- **Woll2Woll:** InfoPower, a collection of data-aware controls.

Magazines So that you can explore Delphi further, we've collected electronic issues of *Delphi Developer's Journal*, *Delphi Informant*, *Delphi Magazine*, and the *Unofficial Newsletter of Delphi Users*.

Installation and Usage You can use the source code from the CD directly, so there's no installation program. (Most of the third-party tools have their own Setup programs). You can:

- Copy the source code to your hard disk (removing the read-only attribute from the files).
- With your favorite browser, use the CROSSREF.HTM file in the DDHCODE directory to look up Delphi identifiers and jump to example programs that use them.
- Browse the HTML version of the source code files to see them with Delphi's default syntax highlighting.
- Set up and run the third-party add-ons directly from the CD, or copy them to your hard drive first. Be sure to read and comply with each program's license agreement, and see the readme files for other important information.

Where specified in files on the CD, owners retain copyright to their respective contents. Where not otherwise noted, all contents copyright © 1998 Sybex, Inc.